WORLD HISTORY IN BRIEF

Major Patterns of Change and Continuity

FIFTH EDITION

VOLUME II SINCE 1450

PETER N. STEARNS

George Mason University

PEARSON

Longman

New York   San Francisco   Boston
London   Toronto   Sydney   Tokyo   Singapore   Madrid
Mexico City   Munich   Paris   Cape Town   Hong Kong   Montreal

Vice President and Publisher: Priscilla McGeehon
Acquisitions Editor: Erika Gutierrez
Supplements Editor: Kristi Olson
Media Editor: Patrick McCarthy
Executive Marketing Manager: Sue Westmoreland
Production Manager: Eric Jorgensen
Project Coordination, Text Design, and Electronic Page Makeup: Electronic Publishing
    Services Inc., NYC
Cover Designer/Manager: Wendy Ann Fredericks
Cover Art: Anonymous © The Newark Museum/Art Resource, NY. Man's Kente cloth.
    Ewe people, Ghana. 1990's. Cotton, 125 1/4″ x 92″. Collection of the Newark
    Museum. Inv.: 97.25.6. Location: The Newark Museum, Newark, New Jersey
Manufacturing Buyer: Roy L. Pickering, Jr.
Printer and Binder: Hamilton Printing Co.
Cover Printer: Phoenix Color Corp.

For permission to use copyrighted material, grateful acknowledgment is made to the
copyright holders on pp. 679–680, which are hereby made part of this copyright page.

Library of Congress Cataloging-in-Publication Data

Stearns, Peter N.
  World history in brief : major patterns of change and continuity / Peter N. Stearns.--
5th ed.
      p. cm.
  Includes bibliographical references and index.
  ISBN 0-321-19672-4
  1. World history. I. Title.
D21.3.S768 2004
909--dc22

                                                    2004005537

Visit us at http://www.ablongman.com

ISBN
0-321-19672-4 (SVE version)
0-321-19673-2 (Volume 1)
0-321-19674-0 (Volume 2)

1 2 3 4 5 6 7 8 9 10—HT—07 06 05 04

Detailed Contents

PART VI **The Contemporary World   493**

List of Maps and Features

Maps

Features

Preface

World history courses are steadily gaining ground at the college level for several reasons. Global issues dominate our newspapers, television screens, and computer monitors daily. Americans must gain a perspective on the dynamics of these issues and understand the diverse societies around the globe that help shape them and our future. History—even history that might seem rather remote—explains how the world became what it is now, including why global influences loom larger than ever before. Global issues are at work even within the United States, since it is increasingly a nation of people of different heritages from around the world. Finally, world history raises some classic issues of historical interpretation, allowing its students to sharpen their understanding of how to interpret change and historical causation and providing a rich field for comparative analysis. Some educators still prefer to concentrate on Western civilization, arguing that it lies at our origins and, sometimes, that it is measurably superior. Although Western heritage must be included in any study of world history, it is increasingly clear that a purely Western interpretation cannot describe the world as we need to know it.

APPROACH

World History in Brief, now entering its fifth edition, has always had two goals. The first is to present a truly global approach to world history. This is accomplished through the focus on forces that cut across individual societies, through a balanced treatment of major societies themselves, and through invitations to comparisons on a global scale. The second goal is brevity and manageability. It is no secret that many world history texts

are large and demand a major commitment from instructors and students. *World History in Brief* offers an alternative. Its length is compatible with a serious treatment of the major issues in world history, but it is concise enough to set aside time for careful analysis and to use with other types of materials beyond the textbook. The purpose here is allowing instructors and students to have some cake while eating it: to have the advantages of a coherent textbook overview, but the opportunity also to spend serious time with documents and with other kinds of historical scholarship.

World history demands a commitment to a global rather than a Western-centered approach. *World History in Brief* shows how different civilizations have encountered the various forces of life—for example, population growth, economic changes, and international currents in diplomacy and art—over the centuries. Western civilization is included as one of the major world societies, but east Asian, Indian, Middle Eastern, east European, African, and Latin American civilizations are all subjects of study in order to achieve a genuine worldwide perspective. World history also demands a balance between the examination of individual societies, within which the lives of most people are played out, and attention to the larger interactions across regional boundaries. These global interactions include trade, cultural contact, migrations, and disease. *World History in Brief* presents the major civilizations through a narrative overview combined with emphasis on regional and global political, cultural, social, and economic characteristics and trends. A grasp of these characteristics, in turn, facilitates comparisons and assessments of change.

World History in Brief is also designed to inspire additional readings and analytical exercises. World history teaching must follow the precedent of other survey history courses in reducing the emphasis on coverage and sheer memorization in favor of materials that provide facts that can be used to build larger understandings. Overwhelming detail, therefore, is not the chief goal of this book. Instead, *World History in Brief* presents enough data to facilitate comparison and assessment of changes and to highlight major developments in the world's history. Students can readily refer to large reference works if they wish to follow up on themes of special interest with greater factual detail. For this purpose, a list of suggested readings and Web sites follows each chapter.

PERIODIZATION

Chronological divisions—the basic periods of world history—reflect successive stages of international contact, from relative isolation to regional integration to the formation of global systems. This periodization is not conveniently tidy for the whole of world history, but it captures the leading dynamics of change at the global level. *World History in Brief* focuses on six major periods. The first involves the early features of human development, particularly the emergence of agriculture and civilization as a form of organization. The second examines the great classical societies from 1000 B.C.E. to 500 C.E. and their relationships with surrounding regions. The third, the postclassical period, from 500 to 1450 C.E., highlights the emergence of new contacts in trade and culture, the spread of world religions, and the development of civilizations in new as well as established centers. The fourth, the early modern period, from 1450–1750 C.E., treats the new world role of Europe, but also the diverse and often quite independent developments in many other societies. The fifth period emphasizes the age of European industrialization and imperialism in the "long" 19th century and again the opportunity for varied reactions. The emergence

of a new period in world history in the twentieth century draws the text to a close. In all these periods, major themes are carefully defined, as a springboard for assessing the interactions of individual societies with more global forces and as a basis for both comparison and discussions of change and continuity over time.

THEMES

Using the global focus plus international periodization, students can follow the themes of change and continuity across time and comparative analysis. For example, we can track and compare the juxtaposition of the traditions and novel forces that have shaped the modern world; the response of China or Latin America to the issues of the modern state; or the conditions of women in developing and industrial economies. How different societies respond to common issues and contacts, and how these issues and contacts change over time—this is the framework for examining world history. By focusing on these problems of comparison and assessment of change, the text uses the leading patterns of world history to provide experience in analysis that will apply to other historical studies beyond a survey.

FEATURES

World History in Brief is the most accessible world history text available in the market. Its brevity allows instructors and students flexibility about what additional readings will be included in their study of world history. The text focuses only on substantive topics, so students understand major themes and developments in world history rather than memorizing an array of unconnected facts. The text is organized chronologically by civilizations, allowing for easy and orderly understanding by students. A number of features distinguish *World History in Brief*, and they have been carefully constructed over five editions.

■ *History Debates*, now included in every chapter, offer students a brief synopsis (usually two paragraphs long) of some topic over which historical debate currently rages. Among the many topics explored are the causes of the abolition of slavery; women in patriarchal societies; the contributions of nomads; the political implications of Islam; how Western is Latin America; and consumerism and industrialization. Students are given an opportunity to see that the discipline of world history is focused on actively debating the past.

■ An increased number of *World Profiles* (formerly *Biographical Portraits*) provide additional emphasis on the human component of world history through biographies. These profiles explore the history of an individual and how his or her story illuminates aspects of his or her society or a particular cultural interaction.

■ The *Understanding Cultures* sections have been augmented, to help students explore specific cultural issues in world history, such as the role of cultures in causing historical changes, the nature of cultural contact, the unique cultural features of particular societies, and the interaction of social and economic forces.

NEW TO THIS EDITION

■ *Key Questions*, appearing after each chapter's introduction, provide students guidance, helping them to focus on the major issues they will grapple with as they read the chapter.

■ *Issues and Connections*, at the end of each chapter, help return the focus to interpretive questions students may find both challenging and fundamental. The "issues" segments cast a glance back over the chapter in terms of what problems need to be thought through, with the goal of expanding active learning beyond memorization. The "connections" part goes further, in calling attention to ways developments covered in the chapter link to current patterns in world history—for history does shape the present, and it is important to deal with the connections recurrently, not just at the end of the course. In the final time period (20th–21st centuries), the connections are reversed, pointing to features from the past that still show up in the present.

■ *Contacts and Identities*, at the end of each chronological part, deal with the main contacts and shared forces among major societies during the period discussed in the part and how the identities of these individual societies were shaped and maintained in the face of these contacts and larger influences. Here is an ongoing tension in world history, the specifics of which evolve over time. The contacts focus provides historical context for discussions of globalization, now a key part of the book's chronological section.

The third basis for revision involves better reflecting gains in world historical understanding. New chapters (1–3) on "Human Prehistory to the Rise of Agriculture," "Early Civilizations," and "Nomadic Societies," provide students with a better framework for understanding the key early developments in world history, the nature of early civilizations, and nomadic societies. The chapter order in the early modern period has been altered to emphasize the world economy. Discussions of Asia, particularly, have been modified to recognize the continent's complex role in a world economy too often seen in terms of purely Western domination. Chapter order has also been rationalized concerning the long 19th century. Throughout, additional attention is given to social history, including issues of gender but also developments, such as consumerism, where knowledge is advancing steadily.

SUPPLEMENTS

The following supplements are available to qualified college adopters for use in conjunction with *World History in Brief.*

Instructor's Manual/Test Bank   Written by Peter Stearns, this tool provides guidance in using the textbook, and suggestions for structuring the syllabus for a world history course complete with assignment ideas; chapter summaries; multiple-choice, short-answer, and essay questions; and map exercises.

TestGen-EQ Computerized Testing System
An easy-to-customize test-generation software package that presents a wealth of multiple-choice, true-false, short-answer, and essay questions. Allows users to add, delete, and print test items.

CourseCompass/BlackBoard/WebCT
Longman's extensive World History Content is available for CourseCompass, BlackBoard, and WebCT. All quickly and easily customizable for use with *World History in Brief*, the content includes primary sources, maps, and map exercises. Book-specific testing is simply loaded. Ask your Longman representative for details.

Longman World History–Primary Sources and Case Studies (longmanworldhistory.com)
The core of this Web site is its large database of thought-provoking primary sources, case studies, maps, and images—all carefully chosen and edited by scholars and teachers of world history. The contents and organization of the site encourage students to analyze the themes, issues, and complexities of world history in a meaningful, exciting, and informative way. Bundled at a deep discount to qualified college adopters. Professors can visit the site for a free three-day trial.

The Historical Digital Media Archive CD-ROM
This new CD-ROM contains hundreds of images,
maps, interactive maps, and audio/video clips ready for classroom presentation, or downloading into PowerPoint™, or any other presentation software. **Free to qualified college adopters.**

Discovering World History Through Maps and Views   Updated Second Edition, by Gerald A. Danzer, University of Illinois, Chicago, winner of the AHA's James Harvey Robinson Award for his work in developing map transparencies. This set of over 100 four-color transparency acetates is an unparalleled supplement that contains four-color historical reference maps, source maps, views and photos, urban plans, building diagrams, and works of art. The Update has been repackaged and comes in an easy-to-carry envelope rather than a bulky binder. The pedagogical material that currently appears on tabs throughout the binder will now be available **only** on Supplements Central. Instructions as to how to download these are located in the front of the transparency package. **Free to qualified college adopters.**

Longman-Penguin Putnam Inc. Value Packages
Students and professors alike will love the value and quality of the Penguin books offered at a deep discount when bundled with *World History in Brief, Fifth Edition.*

NEW Longman Atlas of World History
Featuring 52 carefully selected historical maps, this atlas provides comprehensive global coverage for the major historical periods, ranging from the earliest of civilizations to the present and including such maps as The Conflict in Afghanistan 2001, Palestine and Israel from Biblical Times to Present, and World Religions. Each map has been designed to be colorful, easy-to-read, and informative, without sacrificing detail or accuracy. In our global era, understanding geography is more important than ever. This atlas makes history—and geography—more comprehensible. Offered at a tremendous discount when packaged with *World History in Brief, Fifth Edition.*

For the Student

World History Map Workbook   Volume I (to 1600) and Volume II (from 1600), both prepared by Glee Wilson of Kent State University. Each volume includes over 40 maps accompanied by more than 120 pages of exercises. Each volume is designed to teach the location of various countries and their relationship to one another. Also included are numerous exercises aimed at enhancing students' critical thinking capabilities.

Documents in World History   Volume I (The Great Traditions: From Ancient Times to 1500) and Volume II (The Modern Centuries: From 1500 to the Present), both edited by Peter N. Stearns of George Mason University. A collection of primary source documents that illustrate the human characteristics of key civilizations during major stages of world history.

Mapping Civilizations: Student Activities   A free student workbook compiled by Gerald Danzer, University of Illinois, Chicago. Features numerous map skill exercises written to enhance students' basic geographical literacy. The exercises provide ample opportunities for interpreting maps and analyzing cartographic materials as historical documents. Free when bundled.

Longman World History: Primary Sources and Case Studies (www.longmanworldhistory.com)   A fully functional online source "book" to be used in a world history survey course. The core of the Web site is its large database of thought-provoking primary sources, case studies, maps and images carefully chosen and edited by scholars and teachers of world history. The contents and organization of the site encourage students to analyze the themes, issues, and complexities of world history in a meaningful, exciting, *and* informative way.

Full-Color Longman Comparative World History Timeline   Free to qualified college adopters when packaged with the text, this fold-out, illustrated timeline provides a thorough and accessible chronological reference guide for world history. The timeline notes key events and trends in political and diplomatic, social and economic, and cultural and technological history.

Research Navigator and Research Navigator Guide   Research Navigator is a comprehensive Web site comprising three exclusive databases of credible and reliable source material for research and for student assignments: (1) EBSCO's ContentSelect Academic Journal Database, (2) the *New York Times* Search by Subject Archive, and (3) "Best of the Web" Link Library. The site also includes an extensive help section. The Research Navigator Guide provides your students with access to the Research Navigator Web site and includes reference material and hints about conducting online research. **Free to qualified college customers when packaged.**

NEW Longman Atlas of World History   The 52 four-color maps of this atlas from Longman and Maps.com provide comprehensive global coverage for the major historical periods, ranging from the earliest of civilizations to the present. Each map has been designed to be colorful, easy-to-read, and informative, making history and geography more comprehensible.

Mapping World History   This workbook was created for use in conjunction with *Discovering World History Through Maps and Views*. Designed to teach students to interpret and analyze cartographic materials as historical documents.

ACKNOWLEDGMENTS

Many people helped shape this book. I am grateful to Barry Beyer, Donald Schwartz, William McNeill, Andrew Barnes, Donald Sutton, Erick Langer, Jayashiri Rangan, Paul Adams, Merry

Wiesner-Hanks, and Michael Adas, who aided my understanding of world history in various ways. Comments by Steven Gosch and Donald Sutton, and editorial assistance by Clio Stearns, greatly aided in the preparation of this revised edition. Other colleagues who have furthered my education in world history include Ross Dunn, Judith Zinsser, Richard Bulliet, Jerry Bentley, and Stuart Schwartz. I also thank the various readers of earlier drafts of this manuscript, whose comments and encouragement improved the end result: Jay P. Anglin; Richard D. Lewis; Kirk Willis; Arden Bucholz; Richard Gere; Robert Roeder; Stephen Englehart; Marc Gilbert; John Voll; Erwin Grieshaber; Yong-ho Choe; V. Dixon Morris; Elton L. Daniel; Thomas Knapp; Edward Homze; Albert Mann; J. Malcom Thompson; Peter Freeman; Patrick Smith; David McComb; Charles Evans; Jerry Bentley; John Powell; B. B. Wellmon; Penelope Ann Adair; Linda Alkana; Samuel Brunk; Alexander S. Dawson; Lydia Garner; Surendra Gupta; Craig Hendricks; Susan Hult; Christina Michelmore; Lynn Moore; Joseph Norton; Elsa Nystrom; Diane Pearson; Louis Roper; Thomas O'Toole; John D. Boswell; Connie Brand; Robert Cassanello; John K. Hayden; Ben Lowe; Kenneth Wilburn; Dennis A. Frey Jr.; Matthew Maher; Kenneth J. Orosz; Warren Rosenblum; Brian Williams; and Robert H. Welborn. J. Michael Farmer's assistance has been invaluable.

My gratitude extends also to Erika Gutierrez and Doug Tebay, whose editorial assistance has been vital. Sincere thanks to Debbie Williams for help with the manuscript. I have been taught and stimulated as well by my students in world history courses at George Mason University. And thanks, finally, to my family, who have put up with my excited babble about distant places for some time now.

PETER N. STEARNS

PART IV

A New World Economy, 1450–1750

INTRODUCTION: THE NEW THEMES IN WORLD HISTORY

Between 1450 and 1750, world history developed a new framework. The centerpiece was a huge transformation of the world network that had developed during the postclassical period. It should be no surprise that the most active society in the new global economy now was western Europe, rather than the Middle East or China. The rise of the West rested on several factors, but the new naval technology ranked high among them. A second change involved the incorporation of the Americas in international exchange. This had immense impact on the Americas but also, particularly through the spread of American foodstuffs like corn and potatoes, on the rest of the world. A third change involved, quite simply, the increasing importance of global commerce and the growth of internal trade. Several societies saw their basic political and social structures altered by their place in world trade, whereas commercial relationships affected life in an even broader range of civilizations.

This new global age saw many other changes besides a redefinition of the world economy. A host of new empires formed, not just those that evolved from western Europe's new colonial outreach. Individual civilizations experienced significant innovations, like the new cultural influences in India or the expansion of Confucianism in Japan. Changes of this sort left their mark even later on, defining varied opportunities in both the 19th and 20th centuries.

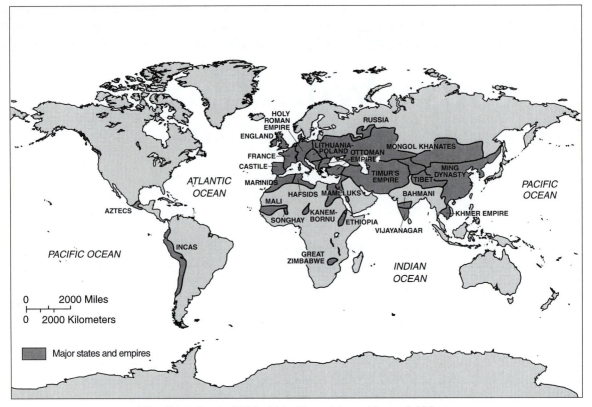

The Postclassical World in Transition, About 1400 C.E.

This new period in world history is usually called *early modern* because of the importance of many of the new features, including the world economy, in establishing a framework for developments in the past 200 years. The early modern period began with the rise of the West, the opening of the Americas to international contact, and the surge of several new Asian empires along with Russia—all occurring soon after 1450. It ended around 1750, when the West began to experience a further transformation—known as the Industrial Revolution—that would alter world relationships yet again.

THE RISE OF THE WEST

Between 1450 and 1750, the West, led initially by Spain and Portugal, then by Britain, France, and Holland, gained control of the key global trade routes. It established colonies in the Americas and, on a much more limited basis, in Africa and parts of Asia.

At the same time, partly because of its new global position and the growing impact of commerce, the West itself changed rapidly, becoming an unusual kind of agricultural civilization. Commerce began to alter the social structure and also affected basic attitudes toward family life and the natural environment. A host of new ideas, some of them advocated by religious reformers, created a novel cultural climate in which scientific principles became increasingly more important; the Scientific Revolution gradually reshaped Western culture as a whole. More effective political structures emerged by the 17th century, as Western monarchs began to introduce bureaucratic principles similar to those pioneered long before in China.

A vital facet of the early modern period, then, consisted of the West's expansion as a global force and its simultaneous internal transformation. Like the previous world-class civilization, Arab Islam, the West developed a diverse and dynamic culture and society, which were both the results and causes of its ascending international position.

THE WORLD ECONOMY AND GLOBAL CONTACTS

The world network established during the previous period of history intensified and took on new dimensions. This change involved more than the fact that the Europeans, not the Muslims, dominated world trade. It involved an expansion of the world network to literally global proportions, well beyond the geographical scope of previous connections. Far more of Africa, and above all the Americas, were brought into contact with other cultures and included in global exchanges for the first time. At the end of the period, in the 18th century, Polynesian and Australian societies began to undergo the same painful experience of integration.

Effectively, by 1750 there were no more fully isolated societies of any great size. The new globalism of human contacts had a variety of impor-

tant consequences that permeated early modern centuries. The human disease pool became fully global for the first time, and peoples who had previously been isolated from the rest of the world suffered immensely from their exposure to diseases for which they had developed no immunities. The global network also permitted a massive exchange of plants and animals. Cows and horses were introduced in the Americas, prompting significant changes in the American Indian economy and fighting techniques. American food crops were exported around the world, bringing sweet potatoes, corn, and manioc (a plant grown for its root) to China, corn to Africa, potatoes and tobacco to Europe—innovations that in many places initiated great changes in agricultural production. This set of biological transfers is called the *Columbian exchange*.

One result of the Columbian exchange, through most of the world including Asia and western Europe, was rapid population growth. World population had declined in the late classical period and then bounced back as people gained new resistance to contagious disease. Population growth in the postclassical period, in places such as Europe, was significant. However, rates of increase during the early modern centuries, except in Latin America and Africa, reached unprecedented levels.

Even globalization, although its impact was vast, did not exhaust the changes wrought in the world network during the three centuries after 1450. Far more than in the postclassical era, the period between 1450 and 1750 saw a set of definite and highly unequal relationships established among a number of civilizations. During the postclassical millennium, 450–1450 C.E., a few areas had contributed relatively inexpensive raw materials and slaves to more advanced societies, notably China and the Islamic world; this was true for the West and parts of Africa and southeast Asia. These unequal economic relationships did not constrain the "raw-materials-producing" societies too severely, because international trade was simply not of overriding importance yet. After 1450 or 1500, as Western commerce expanded internationally, the West began to establish relationships with a number of areas that produced pronounced dependence and subordination within the international economy. Areas such as Latin America depended heavily on sales to export merchants, on imports of processed goods, and on Western ships and merchants to conduct international trade. Dependence of this sort had political ramifications in creating weak governments open to foreign intervention. It encouraged the commercial exploitation of slaves and serfs. It even corresponded to several full-scale attempts to impose Western religion on some dependent nations. Much of the world, particularly in the great Asian civilizations, remained outside this set of relationships, but there was a growing tendency to draw closer toward it, as occurred in India and Indonesia by the 18th century when the level of Western overseas expansion increased further.

THE GUNPOWDER EMPIRES

The centuries after 1450 could also be designated "the age of the gunpowder empires." The development of cannons and muskets in the 14th and 15th centuries, through the combination of Western technology with previous Chinese invention, obviously spurred the West's expansion. Ship-based artillery was fundamental to the West's mastery of world sea-lanes and journeys to many ports and islands. Nonetheless, gunnery was developed by other societies as well. The Ottoman Turks used Hungarian-built cannons in their successful siege of Constantinople in 1453. They also used cannon to finish off the remnants of the Byzantine Empire around the Black Sea. The subsequent Ottoman Empire relied heavily on land-based guns to supplement trained cavalry. The rise of a new Russian Empire after 1480 also built on the growing use of guns, and the Russian economy was subsequently reshaped to provide the manufacturing base for new military hardware. Three other key empires—the Mughal in India, the Safavid in Persia, and the 17th-century Manchu dynasty in China—relied on the strength of the new gun-supported land armies. Guns also played a role in Japanese and African history during the same period.

Clearly, guns supported important military changes that, in turn, supported new political organization—colonial empires in the case of the West and new land agglomerations through much of Asia and eastern Europe and, to an extent, in Africa. New Asian empires counterbalanced the growth of Western power to a considerable degree. The rise of the Russian Empire ran the course of the entire period. Although not as important as the rise of the West, it was certainly a predominant theme, involving among other things the progressive elimination of an independent central Asia. For the first time since the development of agriculture, nomadic herding peoples ceased to be a major force in world history. The rise of the Ottomans and Mughals was a bit shorter lived, but it echoed through the first two centuries of the period and, in the case of the Ottomans, created one of the most durable empires known in world history. The new land-based empires affected a massive number of people and long overshadowed, at least in the eyes of most Asian leaders, the surge in the West.

COMMERCE AND ITS OUTREACH

This was also an age of world commercialization. Market exchange played an increasing role in shaping economic activity. The world remained predominantly agricultural, but agriculture was now modified more than ever by specializations that depended on market transactions, as well as by the activities of merchants and the lure of money. Heightened commercial activity was one of the means by which rising populations could be sustained in advance of major technological change in the means of production. Commerce not only spread knowledge of new foodstuffs but also allowed increased specialization in production that could heighten output, as some regions concentrated on goods they were best suited to grow or manufacture, relying on trade for other materials.

The intensification of global trade, under the sponsorship of Western traders but also involving merchants in other societies, played an important part in the general expansion of commerce. Not only did many Latin Americans produce precious metals and agricultural products for sale to the West, but many other Latin Americans produced foods and clothes to sell to workers in the export sectors. Internal trade increased within Latin America, particularly by the 18th century. Similar patterns emerged in west Africa. Earlier interregional trade routes, oriented toward north Africa, were diverted to a new Atlantic commerce organized by European merchants. African kings and merchants organized goods to sell in this trade, particularly slaves, and received manufactured prod-

ucts, including guns, in exchange. Again, the West was encouraged in its own commercial expansion, as considerable profits could be realized in the slave trade; the Americas were transformed through the introduction of new African populations and a new kind of slavery; and Africa itself was diversely affected by the new exchange.

The spread of commerce went beyond these Western-dominated transactions, however. Both China and Japan witnessed the rapid growth of market exchanges within their own boundaries, as the production and sale of foodstuffs, beverages, and the like expanded. Chinese commerce gained also from the American silver it amassed through trade with western Europe. A general trend—the Western-dominated world economy and its growth—was thus supplemented by some parallelisms in other parts of the world, where internal trade often combined with international exchange. This meant not only surprisingly widespread commercial and urban growth, but also some broader social effects. In most cases without toppling the land-based aristocracy, merchants in a number of societies, not just the West, gained new influence. Growing trade also played a role in some societies (in the West but also, for instance, in Japan) in encouraging some groups to reduce their commitment to religion and otherworldly goals in favor of a focus on secular pursuits. The expansion of commerce thus had wider reverberations in many parts of the world.

MAJOR CIVILIZATIONS

The redefining of the world economy—the intensification of commerce, the inclusion of the Americas, and the rise of the West with its new naval technology—affected each major civilization

TIMELINE: The Early Modern World

East Asia	Middle East (Ottoman Empire)	India and Southeast Asia	Latin America
1336–1573 Return of Japan to feudalism.	**1453** Capture of Contantinople.	**1498** Vasco da Gama (Portugal) to India.	**1501** Introduction of African slaves.
1368–1644 Ming dynasty.	**1520–1566** Suleiman the Magnificent.	**16th century** Portugal's acquisition of trading rights, some trading stations in Siam, Burma, Indonesia.	**1500–1519** Spanish conquest of West Indies, including Puerto Rico, Cuba.
1405–1433 Great Chinese fleets.		**16th century and later** Formation of Sikh religion.	**16th century** Church organization of Spanish colonies established; Jesuit and other missions.
	1526 Capture of Hungary.	**1510** Portuguese acquisition of Goa.	**1519 ff.** Cortés expedition to Mexico.
		1526–1529 Babur invasion from Afghanistan.	**1521** Capture and destruction of Tenochtitlán; building of Mexico City.
		1526–1761 (officially 1857) Mughal empire.	**1531** Pizarro conquest of Inca Empire.
1542 Portuguese traders to Japan.			**1527–1542** Viceroyalties established for Central and South America.
1557 Macao taken by Portugal.			**1532 ff.** Spanish explorations of California and Pacific coast of North America.
1577–1598 Hideyoshi general in Japan; centralization.			**1536** Spanish settlement in Buenos Aires.
1597 Ban on foreign missions.			**1542** Enactment of new laws forbidding Indian slavery.
			1549 First Portuguese government in Brazil.

Western Civilization	Russia and Eastern Europe	Sub-Saharan Africa
1300 ff. Italian Renaissance: i.e., Giotto (1276–1337); Petrarch (1304–1374); Leonardo da Vinci (1452–1519); Machiavelli (1469–1527); Michelangelo (1475–1514). **1450 ff.** Northern Renaissance. Erasmus (1466–1536). **1455** First European printing press, Mainz, Germany. **1494 ff.** French and Spanish expeditions in Italy. **1517** Luther's 95 theses; beginning of Protestant Reformation. **1534** Beginning of Church of England. **1541–1564** Calvin in Geneva. **1519–1521** Magellan expedition around world. **1550–1649** Religious wars in France, Germany, Britain. **1588** Defeat of Spanish Armada by English. **1618–1648** Thirty Years' War. **1642–1649** English Civil War.	**1462** Much of Russia freed by Ivan III (Ivan the Great) from Tatars. **1480** Moscow region free. **1533–1584** Ivan the Terrible, first to be called tsar; boyar power reduced. **1552–1556** Russian expansion in central Asia, western Siberia.	**16th century** Spanish, Portuguese, and Dutch ports on West African Coast. **1562** Beginning of British slave trade. **1591** Fall of Songhai Empire.

East Asia	Middle East (Ottoman Empire)	India and Southeast Asia	Latin America
			1565 Rio de Janeiro founded by Portuguese.
	1571 Loss of Lepanto naval battle.		**1569** Catholic Inquisition established for Spanish America; limitation of intellectual freedom.
1600–1868 Tokugawa shogunate.		**1608** First trade concessions from regional princes granted to England.	**1612** Wider colonization of Brazil begun by Portugal.
1635 Japanese travel abroad forbidden; policy of isolation.		**1627–1668** Jehan emperor; tolerance for Hindus reduced.	
1644 Suicide of Ming emperor.		**1632–1653** Taj Mahal built.	
1644–1912 Qing Dynasty.		**1641** Capture by Dutch of major spice trade center in Indonesia; beginning of control of island of Java.	
1662–1722 Emperor Kang Hsi.	**1683** Failure of assault on Vienna.		
1727 Chinese-Russian frontier treaty.		**17th century** British and French forts on east coast of India.	
1774 ff. White Lotus society risings.		**1658–1707** Aurangzeb emperor; high taxes, intolerance against Hindus; rise of Hindu resistance.	
1784 Chinese persecution of Jesuits.	**1710–1711, 1736–1739, 1768–1774** Wars with Russia and Austria; loss of Balkan and central Asian territory.	**18th century** Mughal decline; rise of Sikh state (1708 ff) and states of southern India.	
			1717 ff. Spanish colonies established new provincial capitals.
	1729 First Muslim Arabic printing press.	**1744, 1756–1763** French-British wars in India.	**1720** Occupation of Texas by Spain.
			18th century Several popular rebellions in Spanish colonies and by Creoles.
	1798 Brief capture of Egypt by Napoleon.	**1756** "Black hole" of Calcutta.	**1794** Haitian uprising against France led by Toussaint L'Ouverture; independence and end of slavery there.
		1764 ff. British control of Bengal.	

Western Civilization	Russia and Eastern Europe	Sub-Saharan Africa
17th century Scientific revolution. Galileo (1564–1642); Newton (1642–1727).		
	1604–1613 Time of Troubles.	**1626 ff.** French coastal settlements.
1643–1715 Louis XIV in France; absolute monarchy; wars (1667–1668; 1672–1678; 1688–1697; 1701–1713).	**1613–1917** Romanov dynasty.	**1650 ff.** Intensification of slave trade.
	1637 Russian pioneers to Pacific.	**1652** Dutch colony on Cape of Good Hope.
1688–1690 Glorious Revolution in Britain; parliamentary regime; some religious toleration; political writing of John Locke.	**1649** Law enacted making serfdom hereditary.	
	1689–1725 Peter the Great.	
18th century Enlightenment. Voltaire (1694–1778).	**1700–1721** Wars with Sweden.	
1712–1786 Frederick the Great of Prussia; "enlightened despotism."	**1703** Founding of St. Petersburg.	
1756–1763 Seven Years' War: France, Britain, Prussia, Austria.		
1775–1783 American Revolution.		**1713** Right granted to Britain to import slaves to Spanish colonies.
		18th century Regulation of regional slave trade by West African kingdom of Fon.
		1760 ff. Fanning out of Dutch in South Africa.
	1762–1786 Catherine the Great.	**1770 ff.** Encounter with Bantu farmers; conflict for land.
	1773–1775 Pugachev revolt.	**Late 18th century** Increase in Muslim conversions in Sudan region.
	1772, 1793, 1795 Partition of Poland.	**1754–1818** Founding of Islamic kingdom (in present-day Nigeria) by Usman dan Fodio.
	1785 Laws enacted tightening landlord power over serfs.	

to some degree. Even more than during the post-classical period, it becomes important to ask the following: how was each civilization affected by the new global developments? How were relationships with the West defined? How were new foodstuffs utilized? How was commerce handled? These questions follow the new framework of world history during the early modern period, but the answers still vary. Because of prior traditions and new, separate developments, each civilization related to the global framework in distinctive ways. Western Europe by no means exercised uniform authority around the world; in many places its explicit influence, during the early modern period, remained negligible.

Furthermore, developments within each civilization, independent of the global framework, also caused important changes. Some societies displayed great dynamism during the 15th and 16th centuries, only to trail off later; their new problems affected their regions' history during this period and subsequently as well. However, other societies developed important new political and cultural resources during the period, which would have an impact later.

The global framework intensified within the early modern period. By 1700, the West's activities were looming larger not just in key areas such as the Americas, the Asian island groups, and the coast of west Africa, but in Asia and eastern Europe as well. A new Russian urge to selectively copy certain aspects of Western culture and the establishment of growing British control in parts of India were two indicators of this shift. Even Japan, which had responded to the new world economy by effective isolation, began to show new, albeit modest, openness, rescinding a ban on translating Western books.

By 1750, it is fair (with all the advantages historians have of knowing how the story turns out) to note that civilizations which were not in a position to react effectively to the West's new world role were verging on decline—whereas a mere century before, this would have been a considerable distortion of a more complex international balance. After 1750, in large part because of another major transformation within the West—the emergence of a revolutionary industrial economy—the theme of Western predominance took on new meaning, which is why the period of world history changes at this point once again.

The chapters in this section begin with the emergence of the world economy and the West's new colonial empires, with their particular impacts on the Americas but also on Africa and south Asia. We then turn to changes within western Europe, which interacted with shifts in its world role. The special case of Russian expansion and partial westernization comes next. Gunpowder empires affected the Islamic world, and a chapter deals with the Middle East and India. East Asia was another key region, with a complex relationship to the global developments of the early modern era.

The West and the World: Discovery, Colonization, and Trade

Why does a civilization begin to ascend within the ranks of the various cultures of the world, gaining new power and importance? The question is hardly less complex than the issue of why civilizations decline. In the case of the West, in its rise to world prominence after 1450, the problem was enhanced by some of the civilization's overall drawbacks: here was a society still politically divided, often locked in internal wars and intense social unrest, with a relatively small total population. How could it, in the space of a few centuries, seize control of the world's oceans and some of its richest lands?

The answer to this question involves two kinds of factors: those that are measurable and material, and those deriving from culture and outlook. On the material side, the West, even as it launched its systematic explorations of the Atlantic in the 15th century, was gaining in technological sophistication. It was not yet the world's most advanced society in overall technology, but it was fast moving in that direction. It certainly had superiority over sub-Saharan African and American Indian cultures in manufacturing and agricultural know-how. More specifically, Western skills in shipbuilding and navigation, aided by refinements in the compass and other directional devices, were at a high level and would improve steadily to the point that, by the 16th century, they surpassed those of east Asia. More specifically, west Europeans had been quickest to develop high-quality gunnery, using the knowledge they gained of Chinese explosive powder to forge weaponry that was awesome by the standards of the time (and more than a bit terrifying to many Europeans, who had reason to fear the new destructive power of their own armies and navies). The West would maintain its weapons advantage over all other civilizations in the world into the 20th century, and even today its arms technology remains among the most highly developed. A crude but possibly accurate explanation of the West's rise, then, would focus simply on its technological edge in the art of war and intimidation.

However, sophisticated weaponry and other technological superiority may not have been the whole story. We have seen that Europe's problems, including an unfavorable balance of trade with Asia and the fear of Muslim power, created some special motives for Western leaders. East Asia had some comparable technological leads, surpassing the West not in weaponry but in navigation during the 15th century, but it chose not to exploit these advantages in a quest for new power in the wider world. Outlook, as well as material means, had to play an important role in the West's rise. Earlier civilizations that had influenced wide sectors of the world beyond their borders, notably classical India and then Islam, had usually possessed an active merchant spirit, and certainly the West had this in abundance from its medieval heritage. In Christianity, the West also had a religion eager to spread the truth to nonbelievers, even by force. Trade and Christianity would typically go hand in hand in the West's new rise. The specific culture of the Renaissance may have contributed as well. We will see in the next chapter that a new set of beliefs developed in Europe. This change, called the Renaissance, brought new interest in worldly affairs and a new sense of confidence and individualism to key leaders. Certainly, it was no accident that the first discoveries in the Atlantic occurred during the Renaissance, when some Europeans were experiencing a new thirst for achievement and knowledge. The zeal of a Henry the Navigator to penetrate the unknown and the sheer adventurism of a Christopher Columbus related closely to other Renaissance enthusiasms. Finally, even the divisions within Europe pushed all the many vying civilizations toward a new world role. National monarchies soon competed for discoveries and colonies, as part of their overall rivalry.

The period of discovery and early colonization was an exciting example of Western power and daring. It also changed some key patterns of world history, which means that it must be assessed not only from the standpoint of European efforts but also in terms of impact on the cultures it affected. Here, several zones developed, ranging from the Americas—where the European arrival began quickly to change basic cultural patterns toward creation of new civilizations or outright assimilation with the West—to east Asia, where European activities made little difference to the historical patterns of the next several centuries. Between these two extremes were several societies: Africa, where European contact caused important alterations in some regions but had little impact on others; India and the Middle East, where Western pressure grew but without undermining earlier traditions; and Russia, whose own new quest for power was colored by knowledge that the West had forged ahead.

KEY QUESTIONS   *Try to decide what caused the West's rise, and then figure out its differential impact on the rest of the world. How did the West and the world economy it engendered affect Africa compared to Latin America, or Asia compared to either of these? How were superiority and inferiority in the world economy defined? How did the world economy affect political and labor systems? What were the characteristics of the new civilization that began to emerge in Latin America?*

PATTERNS OF EXPLORATION AND TRADE

When west Europeans began to venture forward into the wider world, their knowledge of where they were going was surprisingly scanty. To be sure, Viking adventurers from Scandinavia had crossed the Atlantic in the 10th century, reaching Greenland and then North America, which they named "Vinland." But they quickly lost interest, in part because they encountered Indian warriors whose weaponry was good enough to vanquish the intruders.

As we have seen, scattered expeditions from Spain and Italy into the Atlantic dotted the later Middle Ages, but they had no specific results. It

History Debate

THE WEST AS WORLD LEADER

The view of the West's new role in the world has undergone some striking transformations in recent decades. Old history textbooks—in the West, of course—used to picture Columbus as a clear hero, opening the New World to progress. But in an age of anticolonialism, new views of Western ascendancy have shifted the picture. Columbus brought disease and dominance to the Americas, and European exploitation would gradually worsen the environment as well. What is the most accurate historical evaluation?

Historians have also compared Westerners with another previous world power, the Arabs. Both world powers seized slaves and interfered with local cultures; both could look down on other peoples; both encouraged economic imbalances in world trade to their own profit. Other comparisons are even more unflattering. Christians were often less tolerant than Muslims had been. The West seized more territory by force and was more likely to seek complete surrender in war than the Arabs. In some quarters, West-bashing has become a popular intellectual pastime. Even aside from these negative interpretations of Western conquests, questions about Western motives and culture remain important. At the same time, of course, new technology gave the West greater powers than the Arabs had enjoyed, and some results may have reflected this new imbalance rather than simple greed. Finally, at various points and in some areas, growing Western influence (even when resented) may have had some beneficial effects, aside from the growing profits in Western coffers.

took new technical knowledge, particularly the navigational devices imported from Asia, and growing problems, in the form of new needs to reach Asia directly and to seek gold as payment for the desired Asian products, to permit a more systematic effort in the 15th century.

The initiative began in the small kingdom of Portugal. The rulers of this country had just finished driving out the Muslims, who still threatened from north Africa. This threat, and the surge of energy that sometimes accompanies the expulsion of an occupation force, prompted the Portuguese during the 15th century to look for conquests in Africa. Portugal's rulers were drawn by the excitement of discovery, the harm they might cause to the Muslim world, and a thirst for wealth—for European legends of gold in Africa and elsewhere were abundant. This was not a matter of mere greed; Europe's lack of gold for its trade with Asia

was becoming a serious problem. A Portuguese prince, Henry the Navigator, directed a series of expeditions down the African coast and outward to islands such as the Azores. Beginning in 1434, the Portuguese began to journey down the African coast, each expedition going a little farther than its predecessor. They brought back some slaves and perpetuated the tales of gold that they had not yet been able to find.

Later in the 15th century, Portuguese sailors ventured around the Cape of Good Hope, planning to find India and also the African east coast, which was thought to be the source of gold. They rounded the Cape in 1488, but weary sailors forced the expedition back before it could reach India. Then, after news of Columbus's discovery of America for Spain in 1492, Portugal redoubled its efforts, hoping to stave off the new Spanish competition. In 1497, Vasco da Gama's

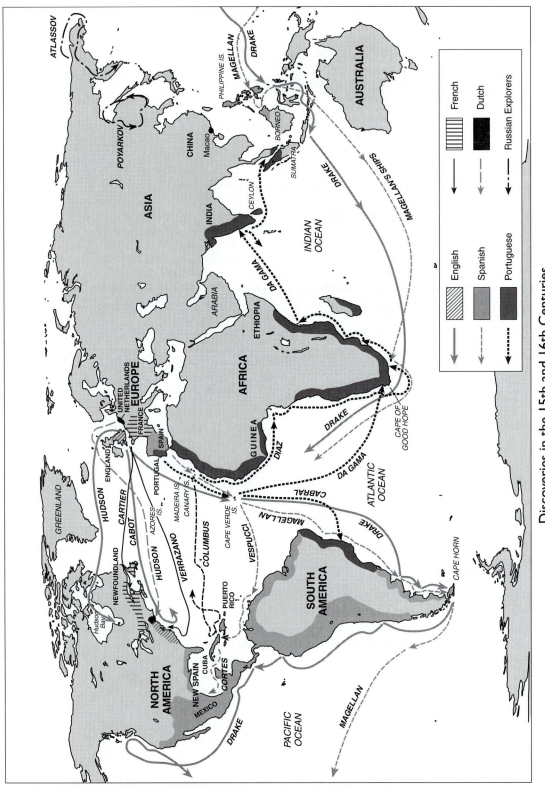

Discoveries in the 15th and 16th Centuries

Legend:

English
Spanish
Portuguese
French
Dutch
Russian Explorers

Labels on map:

AUSTRALIA

ASIA

CHINA

Macao

INDIA

CEYLON

PHILIPPINE IS.

BORNEO

SUMATRA

INDIAN OCEAN

ARABIA

ETHIOPIA

AFRICA

GUINEA

CAPE OF GOOD HOPE

DA GAMA

DRAKE

DIAZ

CABRAL

MAGELLAN

ATLANTIC OCEAN

MAGELLAN'S SHIPS

POYARKOV

ATLASSOV

EUROPE

UNITED NETHERLANDS

FRANCE

SPAIN

PORTUGAL

MADEIRA IS.

CANARY IS.

CAPE VERDE IS.

AZORES

GREENLAND

NORTH AMERICA

NEWFOUNDLAND

HUDSON

CABOT

CARTIER

VERRAZANO

COLUMBUS

VESPUCCI

PUERTO RICO

CUBA

NEW SPAIN

CORTES

MEXICO

ENGLAND

Hudson Bay

SOUTH AMERICA

CAPE HORN

PACIFIC OCEAN

DRAKE

MAGELLAN

Ship technology in the expanding West. This is the *Vittoria*, the only one of Magellan's five ships that completed the first circumnavigation of the globe in 1522. (Granger Collection)

fleet of four ships reached India, with the aid of a Muslim pilot picked up in east Africa. The Portuguese mistakenly believed that the Indians were Christians, for they assumed the Hindu temples they encountered to be churches. Although they faced the hostility of Muslim merchants, who had long dominated trade in this part of the world, the Portuguese nonetheless managed to return home with a small load of spices.

This success set in motion an annual series of Portuguese voyages to the Indian Ocean. Da Gama went back to India, this time heavily armed. He killed a number of Indians, eager to intimidate the region into greater trade. Another expedition, blown off course, reached Brazil, where it proclaimed Portuguese sovereignty. With growing experience, both Portuguese and Spanish expeditions became increasingly comfortable with voyages in the South Atlantic and the Indian Ocean. Portugal began to establish forts on the African

coast and also in India—the forerunners of such Portuguese colonies as Mozambique, in east Africa, and Goa, in India. By 1514, the Portuguese had reached the islands of Indonesia, the center of spice production, and also China. By 1542, a Portuguese expedition also arrived in Japan, where a Christian missionary effort was launched that met with some success for several decades.

Meanwhile, only a short time after the Portuguese quest began, the Spanish reached out with even greater force. Here, too, was a country only recently freed from Muslim rule, full of missionary zeal and a desire for riches. The Spanish had traveled into the Atlantic during the 14th century. Then in 1492, in the same year that the final Muslim fortress was captured in Spain, the Italian navigator Christopher Columbus, sailing in the name of the new Spanish monarchy and its rulers, Ferdinand and Isabella, set off on a westward route to India, convinced that the round earth would make

World Profiles

AMERIGO VESPUCCI (1451–1512)

Amerigo Vespucci is the only person in world history to give his name to not just one continent, but two. Vespucci, a talented Italian navigator in the service of Spain and then Portugal, crossed the Atlantic on the heels of Christopher Columbus and charted some of the coast of North America. Like Columbus, he was a tireless self-publicist who reached out to Europe's educated readership with information about the New World and his country's accomplishments. Vespucci's first name was applied to the continents of the Western Hemisphere because his charts showed that whole continents, not just strings of islands, were involved. Vespucci is here portrayed in association with the new scientific and technical devices beginning to capture European imagination, important to the voyages of discovery. He holds an astrolabe that, by measuring the altitudes of stars, allowed calculations of latitudes and times. What other symbols helped promote the new European surge and Vespucci's own exaggerated reputation?

Vespucci Studying the Stars, by Stradanus

---

his quest possible. As is well known, he failed, reaching the Americas instead and mistakenly naming their inhabitants "Indians." Although Columbus believed to his death that he had sailed to India, later Spanish expeditions indicated that he had voyaged to a region to which Europeans and Asians had not traveled before. One expedition, led again by an Italian initially in Spanish service, Amerigo Vespucci, gave the New World its name. Spain, eager to claim this American land, won papal approval for Spanish dominion over most of what is now Latin America, although a later treaty awarded Brazil to Portugal.

Finally, a Spanish expedition under Ferdinand Magellan set sail westward in 1519, passing the southern tip of South America and sailing across the Pacific, reaching the Indonesian islands in 1521 after incredible hardships. It was on the basis of this voyage, ultimately the first trip around the world, that Spain claimed the Philippines, which remained Spanish territory until 1898.

Portugal emerged from this first round of exploration with coastal holdings in various parts of Africa and the Indian port of Goa; a lease on a Chinese port, Macao; short-lived interests in trade with Japan; and, finally, the claim on Brazil. Spain asserted its hold on the Philippines and various Pacific islands, and on the bulk of the Americas. (The Pope helped to rule which Catholic power held which American territory.) During the 16th century, the Spanish attempted to assert its American claims through military expeditions to Mexico and South America. The Spanish also held Florida in North America, and they ultimately launched expeditions northward from Mexico into California and other parts of what later became the southwestern United States.

Later in the 16th century, the lead in further exploration passed to northern Europe. In part, this resulted because Spain and Portugal were now busy ruling their new territories; in part, it was because northern Europeans, particularly the Dutch and the British, improved the design of oceanic vessels, producing lighter, faster ships than those of their Catholic adversaries. Britain won a historic sea battle with Spain in 1588, in which the British navy and adverse weather routed a massive Spanish armada. From this point onward, the British and Dutch, and to an extent the French, vied for dominance on the seas.

French explorers first crossed the Atlantic in 1534, reaching Canada, which was claimed in France's name. French voyages increased during the 17th century, as various expeditions pressed down from Canada into the Great Lakes region and the Mississippi valley.

The British also turned their attention particularly to North America, starting with a brief expedition as early as 1497. The English hoped, in vain, to discover a northwest passage to India, but in fact they accomplished little beyond an exploration of the Hudson's Bay area of Canada during the 16th century. England's serious expeditions commenced in the 17th century, with the colonization of the east coast of North America.

The Dutch entered the picture after winning independence from Spain and quickly became a major competitor with Portugal in southeast Asia. The Dutch sent a significant number of sailors and ships to the region, ousting the Portuguese from the Indonesian islands by the early 17th century. Voyagers from the Netherlands explored the coast of Australia, although without much immediate result. Finally, toward the middle of the 17th century, Holland established a settlement on the southern tip of Africa, mainly to provide a relay station for its ships bound for the East Indies.

Dutch and British exploration and trade were government sponsored, but unlike the Spanish and Portuguese expeditions, and to some extent the French, they owed much to the private initiative of merchant groups. The Netherlands, Britain, and France all chartered great trading companies, such as the Dutch East India Company or the British firm of similar name. These companies were given government monopolies of trade in the regions designated, but they were not rigorously supervised by their own states. Thus, semiprivate companies, formed by pooling merchant capital and amassing great fortunes in commerce, long acted almost like independent governments in the regions they claimed. For some time, a Dutch trading company virtually ruled the island of Taiwan, off the coast of China; the British East India Company played a similar role in parts of India during much of the 18th century.

TOWARD A WORLD ECONOMY

By the 16th century, west Europeans had gained control of most of the world's seas. They were moving freely across the Atlantic Ocean and with some regularity across the vast Pacific as well—the first time in world history that an endeavor of this magnitude had ever occurred. The Europeans did not displace all Asian shipping from the coastal waters of China and Japan, nor did they completely monopolize the Indian Ocean; in east Africa, Muslim merchants remained active. But Muslim and Hindu traders were now confined to regional specialties; they did not command the chief routes. In the Mediterranean, finally, where European power had been growing even earlier, the Spaniards inflicted a decisive defeat on the navy of the Ottoman Empire, in the battle of Lepanto in 1571. Although Ottoman forces won some later battles, they could not systematically rival European naval power. By this time, the greatest competitors Europeans faced were other European states, and their battles would pepper world history from this point until the mid-20th century. By the 16th century, European traders even shipped products from one part of Asia to another, making profits by handling goods with which Europe had no direct involvement at all. World trade and its expansion lay largely in Western hands.

Into the 18th century, however, the Europeans' power, although astonishing by their own or anyone else's previous standards, was a sea power, and sea power had limits. Only in rare special circumstances were the Europeans able to penetrate inland, far from the protection of their ever-improving ship's cannon. The major exception, of course, was in the Americas, where the Spanish gained continental control and the English and Portuguese important regional centers. Elsewhere, the European grasp extended mainly to islands—with the control of major parts of the Indonesian islands the most significant achievement—and scattered port cities. Even in Africa, where the Europeans had greater influence than they did in most parts of Asia, European control was mainly coastal until after 1800. In the Middle East and eastern Europe, Westerners seized no territory at all, although their trading influence was actively felt; in east Asia, even their commercial efforts were kept to a minimum after a brief initial flurry.

Hence, outside the Americas, the Europeans affected but did not dominate major civilizations. We will examine their influence and its limitations in subsequent chapters. Even in India, until the 18th century, European presence and the seizure of a few coastal cities were fairly minor incidents, hardly rivaling the ongoing presence of a Muslim government in a largely Hindu population.

It is important, then, not to exaggerate the significance for world history of what the Europeans liked to call their age of exploration. There was no question of their new strength, but until about 1800, when the situation changed, they were not yet directing the world stage.

Nonetheless, western Europe was beginning to shape new global economic contracts, which brought them great advantage and affected economic activity in many other parts of the world. Europe's wealth increased rapidly because of profits drawn from the Americas, Africa, and even Asia. The Europeans never uncovered the golden treasures they had hoped for, but they did gain access to vast supplies of silver in the New World. Spain was the chief initial beneficiary of this wealth within Europe, but bankers and merchants in northern Europe soon profited even more substantially. With the new supply of precious metals and resulting control of shipping, the Europeans were able to improve the balance of world trade for the first time. Spice and tea plantations in southern Asia began to produce for the growing European market on terms of trade that were no longer set by the rarity of their products but by the buying power of the West—expressed particularly through its use of New World silver.

Awareness and use of silver spread rapidly in the 16th century. Europeans utilized silver in the Americas, particularly in the great mines of Potosi in the Andes, and they quickly learned how to increase production. They traded silver for the goods they sought in Asia, leading to new accumulations in places such as China. Huge amounts of silver went through the Western-controlled port in Macao; by the end of the century, the Ming dynasty could require that taxes be paid in silver. For a time, Japan also participated actively in silver production, which linked the nation to world trade until greater isolation was imposed after about 1600. The extent of the silver trade and its results showed the dimensions of the world economy, and how quickly it could promote change.

By the 17th century, as Europeans used some of their wealth to improve their own manufacturing base, they increasingly offered manufactured products to the world market—guns, cloth, and metal wares—instead of precious metals alone. The division was deliberately fostered by the policies of the Europeans, whether as governments or as giant trading companies. The reigning theories of mercantilism urged 17th- and

18th-century Europe to monopolize as much manufacturing as possible, leaving other parts of the world to specialize in agricultural production or mining. By the 18th century, several parts of the world were producing raw materials or food-stuffs for a Western market and receiving more sophisticated and expensive manufactured goods in return. Russia and Poland sold grain; Africa, slaves; the Americas, sugar, silver, and tobacco. These goods, because they involved less process-ing, tended to command lower prices than did Europe's own products. So a global economy was being shaped in which much of the world sold goods (generated by cheap labor) to the West, which sold more expensive items and in whose ships the goods were exchanged. Here was the beginning of a division in the world economy between have's and have-nots, which echoes to the present day.

The impact of this division could run deep. Basic labor systems increasingly responded to eco-nomic position. Western Europe required labor flexible enough to participate in growing manu-facturing; hence, it increasingly developed a wage-labor force, often ill-paid. Areas dependent on producing raw materials, particularly where work-ers were in short supply because of disease, relied on compulsory labor systems, such as slavery or extensive serfdom, that could keep costs down for unskilled work. Gender was affected. In many areas, men were responsible for an increasing amount of production for sale, relegating women to domestic tasks. New slave traders preferred men: two-thirds of all African slaves sent to the Americas were male, and this extended systems of polygamy in Africa as a means of dealing with an overpopulation of females.

However, this was only the beginning of an international economy dominated by the West. Most people were not deeply affected by the new patterns of trade. The Chinese were far more heavily influenced by new foodstuffs brought by European traders, by the seeds and tubers they introduced from the Americas, than by Europe's economic position within the world community. Indeed, as we will see, China still did very well in the world economy. Most Asians, Russians, Africans, and even many American Indians were not drawn into produc-tion for the world market as yet, although it is true that Europe's financial influence reached farther than their ships. Here is another factor, along with outright European contacts, to be considered in contemplating the development of major civilizations between 1450 and 1800.

In three major cases, however, European influ-ence did penetrate farther, even in the early mod-ern centuries, so that major alterations in historical patterns resulted. Developments in sub-Saharan Africa, Spanish or Latin America, and North America revealed the extent of Western penetra-tion and an emerging New World economy to reshape politics, culture, and individual lives.

AFRICA

It was long assumed, by prideful Westerners, that African history did not really begin until the coming of the Europeans. This, of course, is non-sense; African culture had evolved to a significant extent before Europeans journeyed down the Atlantic, and more to the point, it continued into the 19th century to develop apart from European influence. However, Europeans did have pro-found effects on a number of regions, and this new factor must be linked with other trends to describe African diversity after about 1500.

European exploration of Africa was limited by several factors. Transportation barriers were as great for them as for Africans; it was hard to move inland from the coast, particularly in the thickly forested areas. Moreover, the main rivers were not navigable for any distance. Disease also hit the Europeans hard, for they lacked the immunity to tropical diseases that Africans had developed over time. Most importantly, the political powers of most African kingdoms were sufficient to block European entry until the 19th century. To be sure, the great African empires ended with the fall of Songhai late in the 16th century; in the south, there was nothing to match the earlier Zimbabwe. But regional kingdoms flourished, some old, some rising for the first time. This meant that in most instances, Europeans had to negotiate carefully with African leaders, offering real value in exchange for value received; with a few exceptions, they could not seize territory.

Here, for example, is how a Dutch representative described the king of the west African kingdom of Benin (where the Dutch traded actively during the 17th century, replacing the Portuguese as principal European contacts):

> I saw and spoke to the king of Benin, in the presence of his great counselors. He was seated on an ivory throne under a canopy of Indian silk. He was about forty years old and of lively expression. According to custom I stood about thirty feet away from him. So as to see him better I asked permission to draw closer. He laughingly agreed.

The representative was also awed by the splendor of the palace, as big as the stock exchange in Amsterdam, supported by "wooden pillars encased in copper, where the victories of the kingdom are recorded."

European activity, however, did make a difference in Africa. The Portuguese and then other Europeans, particularly the French, established forts and urban settlements along the western coast, usually leased or made available by other arrangement with local rulers. With this base, the Europeans altered west African trading patterns. They encountered many valuable goods in Africa—cloth and iron items—but their main interests lay in gold, ivory, and slaves. They found African merchants as well as political rulers to be demanding negotiators, but they did have goods to offer in return: cloth, iron tools, and above all muskets. European imports reduced African craft production, which disrupted the economy severely. Dependence on weapons imports also brought change. Not infrequently, Europeans participated as allies in wars among African kingdoms, where

their firepower could spell the difference in outcome. These trading activities brought new contacts to west Africa, drawing the region into a European-dominated world economic network and away from traditional trade routes across the Sahara to north Africa. The presence of Western trading stations on the coast also had an effect on some urban Africans, leading to a limited number of conversions to Christianity.

West Africa was more specifically and deeply affected by the growing Atlantic slave trade, which began in the 16th century but intensified greatly after about 1650. West African slaves were purchased by sea captains from Holland, Britain, and particularly France, to be sold in the North and South American colonies and the West Indies. Slavery was not new to this region of Africa, as many states had held troops captured in battle as slaves. But the European demand transformed a traditional practice beyond recognition. Between 1500 and the end of the slave trade in the 19th century, as many as 12 million Africans may have been taken away as slaves. This exodus, one of the greatest and most terrible forced movements of peoples in human history, devastated some regions of west Africa, which lost population rapidly and found it difficult, in the absence of sufficient younger workers, to maintain traditional economic levels. Nonetheless, some west African states profited from the slave trade, at least in the short run. The actual capture and sale of slaves to European merchant sailors was almost always handled by African agents, who traded slaves for guns, gold, and other goods. One new, unusually centralized state, the Fon kingdom of the 18th century, organized all its dealings with Europeans in a single location, to minimize contact between Europeans and inland Africans. The state carefully regulated and taxed the slave trade, controlling the import of firearms and ammunition.

Thus, the impact of the massive slave trade on west Africa was mixed and not simply the result of unchallenged European profiteering (although there were huge profits to be made from the exchange, even after the African agents

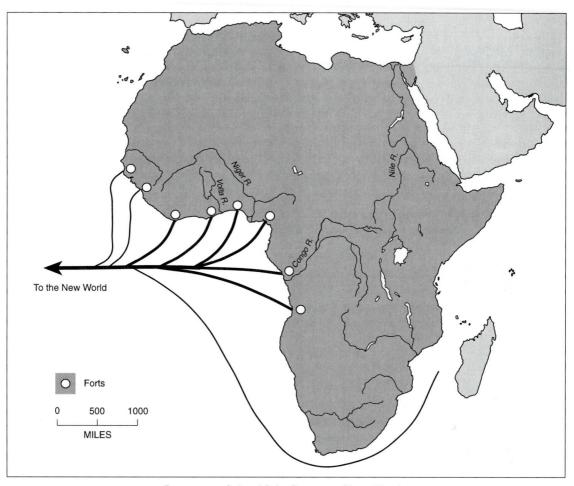

Patterns of the 18th-Century Slave Trade

were paid; this was one source of rising merchant wealth in western Europe). Many parts of west Africa came to depend on the slave trade for their own economies. However, the long-term damage overshadowed any gains. African birth rates grew more slowly than those of most other societies throughout the 19th century, in part as a result of sheer population loss. Economic development was surely slowed down, although it is hard to say exactly how much change would have resulted had the slave trade not interfered. In addition, relations among west

African kingdoms grew more warlike and chaotic, as various states clashed to gain slaves, and others armed to prevent raids. Destabilization was not complete, and again there was variety, depending on how a given kingdom handled negotiations. Indeed, some west African kingdoms deliberately stayed out of the slave trade altogether. But there is no question about the serious impact this practice had on west African history for more than two centuries.

There was also no question about the harsh life slaves were soon forced to endure, and the

World Profiles

OLANDAH EQUIANO

Olandah Equiano was one of the few enslaved Africans able to later write about his experiences. He was born in a Nigerian village, Isseke, in 1745, to a wealthy, slaveholding family. He was kidnapped by slave traders and in 1756 taken to Barbados and then Virginia. Finally able to buy his freedom from a Quaker master, he went to England in 1767. By this point, he was both literate and well read. He became active in the antislavery movement, publishing his memoirs in 1788 as a protest against the entire institution of slavery. Equiano poignantly described his desperate feelings when he and his sister were tied up and put in sacks, and then separated from each other. He detailed the greater brutality of European slave shippers, compared to his initial African captors, and the ordeal of imprisonment among strangers and the frightening voyage to an unknown land with little hope of return. This account was one of the first in a wave of memoirs by former slaves and part of a growing movement against the system on both sides of the Atlantic. What kind of antislavery arguments would work best in the context of 18th-century Europe?

Olandah Equiano

inhuman circumstances to which they were often subjected upon capture:

> As the slaves come down . . . from the inland country, they are put into a booth or prison, built for that purpose near the beach, all of them together; and when the Europeans are to receive them, they are brought out into a large plain, where the ships' surgeons examine every part of every one of them. . . . Such as are allowed good and sound are set on one side, and the others by themselves; these rejected slaves are called Makrons, being above 35 years of age, or defective in their lips, eyes or teeth, or grown grey. . . . Each of the others passed as good is marked on the breast with a red-hot iron, imprinting the mark of the French, English, or Dutch companies so that each nation may distinguish their own property.

Typically, a week after capture, the voyage across the Atlantic began, a terrifying, foul experience in which as many as half the slaves would die. For the survivors, a life of servitude in a strange land was the reward.

Slave trading also disrupted another part of the west Africa coast, in the territory of Angola, which came under increasing Portuguese control. The Portuguese, initially interested in precious metals, soon concentrated on capturing slaves for trade with Brazil. Ruling Angola outright, through corrupt local officials, they produced growing chaos in this region for centuries. Here, in contrast to the picture farther north in present-day countries such as Nigeria, there was no question of some compensatory benefits from the European quest for slaves; Angola simply suffered.

The southern end of Africa was affected greatly by European exploration. Holland established a small colony on the Cape of Good Hope in 1652, to help supply its ships bound for Asia. This community of *Boers* (the Dutch word for farmers) soon escaped Dutch control, fanning out on large farms in a region still lightly populated by Africans. The Boers clashed with local hunting groups, enslaving some of them. Later, after 1770, they came into increasing contact with Bantu farmers, initiating a long struggle for control of the region that still affects the nation of South Africa today.

European influence on African history between 1450 and 1800 was thus intense but, for the most part, regional. It set new forces in motion in southern Africa and Angola, and strongly affected the economic and political life of west Africa without, however, overturning all previous patterns.

Other parts of Africa were scarcely affected by the West during these centuries. Ethiopia, although Christian and in some contact with Portuguese missionaries, remained aloof. East Africa had little to do with Europeans; here, trading patterns were still oriented toward the Middle East, and both Africans and Arab traders pushed into the eastern interior in search of agricultural products and slaves. The slave trade to the Middle East and north Africa also expanded in the early modern period; totaling perhaps three million people, it remained more modest than its Atlantic counterpart.

Overall, the patterns of African culture remained much as before. Politically, most of the continent was organized in regional kingdoms, with rulers who allied with local leaders and operated as divine monarchies. Most Africans remained polytheistic, although Islam was a potent force in the Sudan region. Late in the 18th century, conversions to Islam began to increase in this area, as the religion became a popular force and not simply an elitist movement. Scholars like Usuman dan Fodio (1754–1818) argued against the traditional policy of living tolerantly alongside nonbelievers. Usuman and his followers, active in Muslim scholarship and law, conducted several holy wars in the western Sudan, winning over many ordinary people and producing a number of well-organized new states.

In another continuing trend, Bantu migration southward persisted. This movement, as noted, would bring Bantus into conflict with Dutch settlers. The severe crowding it produced in Bantu lands by around 1800 prompted Bantus to begin organizing into more coherent political units.

Finally, although African economic life was deeply affected by European trade at least in some key regions, there was no massive change in economic forms or technologies on the continent overall. Europeans did import corn seeds from the New World, which were adopted by many African farmers and thereafter used as a food staple. But because of the slave trade and the loss of so many men of childbearing age, the crop did not result in a significant population increase at this point; indeed, relative to world population growth, the African share actually decreased.

In sum, major changes occurred in Africa between 1450 and 1800. Some of these changes were of European origin or represented African reaction to European contacts, but others were quite distinct, resulting from Islam or Bantu migration. No single force mobilized more than individual regions of the continent; beneath the surface, important traditional patterns of politics, art, belief, and social organization largely persisted.

COLONIZATION IN LATIN AMERICA: THE BIRTH OF A NEW CIVILIZATION

European impact in the Americas was far more significant than that in Africa: here, the Europeans began to alter basic patterns as early as the 16th and 17th centuries, creating a new civilization in Latin America and extending Western civilization to the eastern seaboard colonies of North America. The natives' lack of iron weapons and their vulnerability to disease, often with devastating consequences, created a context far different from that in Africa.

Latin America by the 18th Century

African independence long contrasted with the growing European colonies in the Americas. The colonization process, of course, also brought the Americas into mainstream world history and linked the two continents to the emerging world economy on conditions set mainly by the Europeans.

In Central and South America and the West Indies, Spanish efforts to follow exploration with outright conquests began early in the 16th century. The chief goals were God and gold. The Spanish hoped to tap what they believed was the vast wealth of the new lands—their appetites having been whetted by the rich ornaments they encountered among groups such as the Aztecs and by a taste for myth. And, as the most powerful Catholic state, soon heavily influenced by the active Jesuit order, Spain planned to win new converts to Christianity. Expeditions led to the occupation of leading West Indian islands, including Cuba, starting in 1512. Soon after this, a small army under Hernán Cortés conquered Mexico from the Aztecs. Although pockets of American Indian resistance remained in parts of Central America until the later 17th century, Spanish control was essentially complete by 1550. By this point, the empire extended loosely into parts of what are now the southern and southwestern United States.

From their colony in Panama, the Spanish moved into South America. They took over the northern part of the continent fairly easily, conquering loosely organized American Indian cultures. In 1531, an expedition attacked the Inca empire, inspired by tales of its many treasures. Intense combat was necessary to seize Peru, but the Spanish commander, Pizarro, ultimately prevailed. From this base, other missions extended along the Andes mountain chain, finding the Amazon River and seeking the silver mines of Bolivia. Spanish expeditions also moved into Argentina, founding a settlement in Buenos Aires in 1536. Only at the end of the 16th century, however, did the Spanish really begin to colonize Argentina, introducing cattle raising and other forms of agriculture once the thirst for quick riches had somewhat diminished. Finally, early in the 17th century, the Portuguese began to journey inward from small coastal settlements in Brazil, taking effective hold of much of the vast interior territory.

The conquest of Latin America, complete in outline during the 17th century, was amazingly swift. This was no well-coordinated, carefully planned venture. Many expeditions, such as Pizarro's against Peru, were essentially mounted by groups of adventurers or private merchants. All the campaigns, even those sponsored by the Spanish government, were small. How did they conquer such a vast territory so easily?

Superior technology was, of course, a key. The American Indians lacked not only guns and cannons but also horses and metal weapons of any sort. The Europeans also profited from civil wars and dissent within American Indian ranks. Hostility to the Aztecs provided Cortés with many American Indian allies at first. The Inca empire was weakened by internal warfare shortly before Pizarro's arrival. Trickery played a role: many Spanish commanders initially negotiated treaties with Inca, Aztec, and other leaders, only to violate the agreements at the earliest opportunity, often putting their erstwhile allies to death. But the hold of the Europeans was not at first thorough. Many villages were untouched by a Spanish or Portuguese presence for decades; many local American Indian leaders were given considerable autonomy so long as they pledged loyalty to the new colonial government.

However, in scarcely more than a century, the Spanish had leveled the leading American Indian civilizations, destroying their political structures and obliterating their formal cultures. Their task was aided not only by their desire to impose "civilization" on non-Christian peoples, but also by the diseases, particularly smallpox, that they brought with them. American Indians, so long isolated, had no resistance to these scourges. The result was plagues that resembled those at the end of the classical and postclassical periods in Eurasia, but even worse. Within less than a century, 90 percent of the Mexican population had been wiped out; entire populations on the West Indian islands vanished. Overall, as has been noted, 80 percent of the previous American Indian population of North and South America would die as a result of disease. Here was a vacuum Europeans increasingly tried to fill.

Franciscan mission cloister in Brazil

LATIN AMERICAN CIVILIZATION

After the conquest period, the Spanish and Portuguese settled down to the construction of new political and religious institutions and a new economic framework for their vast colonies. The result, during the 17th and 18th centuries, was essentially a formative period for a new, Latin American civilization, closely tied to Europe but also distinct in significant ways.

Politically, this new civilization was characterized by the rule imposed from the outside by the monarchies of Spain and Portugal. European-born men held virtually all of the administrative positions, in what became significant bureaucracies. Two main provinces were created, called *viceroyalties*—one administered from Mexico, the other from Peru. Later, the huge South American holding was further divided, with new centers in Argentina and Colombia. In theory, this governmental system was highly centralized. In fact, the territories were much too vast for effective central control, which meant that church leaders, estate owners, and villagers had considerable latitude. Latin America would long be characterized by a gap between seemingly strong political authority and the actual weakness of the state in relation to local regions and to institutions such as the village and hacienda.

One result of the gap between government claims and the reality of very lax state control was a sense that government power ought to be increased, that this was the chief problem in Latin American society. Even in the 18th century, Spanish colonial administration tried to expand its authority, and the quest would continue into the 19th and 20th centuries as well. A second result was that the centralized system, however superficial in reality, prevented much participation in the new society, as most colonials were firmly barred from governmental activity. Spain further tightened the monopoly of Spanish-born appointees in the later 18th century, resulting in new grievances among the native-born Creoles.

Culturally, the leading feature of the new society was a fervent and pervasive Catholicism. Far more than the Spanish and Portuguese governments, the Jesuits and other missionaries moved actively among the common people, working hard to undermine the influence of indigenous religions and replace them with Christianity. Many American Indian groups long remained isolated from this effort, but there was steady change. Mission schools, an extensive network of local churches, and the destruction of American Indian culture soon produced measurable results. The power and success of the new conquerors helped make the missionaries persuasive. But they also offered a gentler religion with greater compassion for ordinary people than any of the religions the American Indian civilizations of South and Central America had developed.

The Portuguese baroque style of architecture was used frequently in South America: San Francisco Church in Salvador de Bahia, Brazil.

Although American Indians resented the abolition of many ceremonies and even maintained some in secret, the elimination of human sacrifice and the power of the earlier priestly castes may have been welcomed by many. And there were numerous opportunities for syncretism. Many American Indians combined the notions of certain earlier gods or goddesses with Catholic saints, thus helping to transition change while producing a lively and distinctive religious art.

The Europeans also sought to introduce some features of their own wider culture. Major cathedrals were built in the Spanish baroque style, and public buildings also followed European architectural models. Cities were established as islands of European order, building on the traditional belief in urban life that the Spanish inherited from the

Romans and Arabs. Grid-like streets radiated from a central plaza, which was graced by a major church and a government building and jail. However, westernized artistic culture was not yet advanced. Spanish-style religious paintings were attempted, but they did not match the vigor of Christianized Indian or mestizo designs. Literature was virtually nonexistent, as the Spanish authorities discouraged printing save in a few centers. Furthermore, American Indian artistic forms continued to survive, in pottery and textile design. This was not high art, but it was responsible for an important diversity in Latin American culture that would have more important effects in the future. Outside of the extension of Catholicism, then, Latin American culture was clearly in a formative stage but showed signs of some differentiation from purely European models.

Two kinds of economic activity coexisted in this early period of Latin American history. First, many American Indians and mestizos—people of mixed Spanish and Indian ancestry—operated in a village or small-town economy, producing corn and other foods for largely local needs. The economic life of many American Indian villages, even their communal ownership of the land, was left virtually undisturbed—although the Spanish eliminated the leading institutions of American Indian society, they did not eliminate all traces of this culture.

Along with this local village structure was an economy geared for export, and specifically for the profit of the Spanish and Portuguese. This economy involved mining operations, particularly in the Andes region, where 16,000 tons of silver were produced for Europe by the year 1650.

The market economy also promoted large landed estates established by the Spaniards or Creoles—Europeans born in the new land. The Spanish did not attempt to enslave many American Indians, partly because of fierce resistance and partly because Catholic leaders, eager to protect their new converts, opposed such a policy. But they did set up a network of large estates. As American Indians died of European diseases, land

was left vacant and often seized by mestizos or Spaniards, who benefited from the government authorization of such ownership. At first, it seemed that the original Spanish conquerors might become a feudal nobility, but the Spanish government, aware of the importance of more central control, resisted this pattern save in a few areas. Nevertheless, many large estates resulted from land grants and seizures, particularly when a brief effort at the direct governmental distribution of American Indian labor failed. Estate owners worked hard to command labor resources, increasingly scarce as the Indian population shrank. An early form of labor control, not necessarily corresponding to a single estate, was the *encomienda*, where the Spanish or Creole grantee was given rights over a certain percentage of American Indian labor. This was one source of the labor used in silver and mercury mines in the Andes region; at its height, labor drafts generated 13,000 workers a year for the leading mine. More common still was the *hacienda*, a large estate on which a number of American Indian villages were granted to a Spaniard, often one of the initial conquerors. Village inhabitants on the hacienda were required to pay tribute in goods (food and textiles) plus providing labor service. This system, which after a generation or two turned into effective ownership of the village lands, closely resembled the harsher forms of earlier European serfdom; the landlord provided some protection and a court system for his villagers, in return for payments in kind and almost absolute control over the farmers. In a few cases, estate owners hired low-paid American Indian or mestizo laborers, who were encouraged to go into debt and officially forbidden to leave until often impossible sums were paid off—again, a means of attempting to reduce rural freedom in order to address the twin realities of labor shortage and market opportunity.

Haciendas and the other estate forms did not, for the most part, produce for the export trade directly. But they did yield grains and meats that were sold to mining centers and the growing

Indians in South America work gold and silver for the Spaniards: 16th century woodcuts.

populations of port cities and administrative capitals like Mexico City. Thus, a vigorous Latin American market agriculture developed, but on the basis of low-paid or servile labor under effective landlord control.

A somewhat different version of estate agriculture arose in the West Indies and some parts of the South American continent, particularly Brazil. Here the crops produced—tobacco and especially sugar—were intended for sale in Europe. These estates used hundreds of thousands of black slaves imported from Africa, initially in part because local labor was so scarce as a result of disease. Three times as many Africans were brought to Latin America and the Caribbean as to North America. Not only Spanish and Portuguese holdings, but also British, French, and

Dutch West Indian islands, developed this slave-holding system. This was a slave-based economy on a scale never before known, the result of the commercial opportunities and appetites of the new global economy.

Latin America thus quickly developed an economy dependent on a world market, for which it produced agricultural and mining products; additional specialized commercial farming led to the development of mining and governmental centers. Relatively little manufacturing was undertaken, save for local needs; sophisticated manufactured products and craft items were imported from Europe. Here was the most acute case of a European intrusion producing a dependent economy. Latin American landowners could reap tidy profits from their market sales, but for

World Profiles

SOR JUANA INÉS DE LA CRUZ (1651–1695)

Sor Juana Inés de la Cruz was one woman in pre-
modern times who rose to public prominence
on the basis of her intellectual qualities and piety.
An author, poet, musician, and social thinker, she
was welcome at the viceroy's court in Mexico City.
She represented the growing attempt to produce a
European-style and predominantly Catholic culture
in the new Latin American civilization. Like many
Christian thinkers before her, she ultimately abandoned her wider interests, at the urging of her religious superiors, to concentrate on purely spiritual
matters. Why did religion give some women a
chance to rise in early modern world history? Were
colonial conditions in the Americas more or less
favorable to women in public life than were conditions in most established societies?

Sor Juana Inés de la Cruz

their success they relied on a low-paid, fully or
partially enslaved, labor force.

Clear social divisions followed from this economic pattern, and they were enhanced by racial
divisions. Spanish and Portuguese settlers were
much less firmly racist than their English counterparts to the north. However, Latin American
society was rather firmly split between a minority of political officials, mine owners, and landlords, and the majority of impoverished workers.
The privileged classes were European-born or
Creole; the masses were American Indian, black,
and—the largest group overall—mestizo. There
were, of course, some local merchants and shopkeepers, but the size of this middling group was
small. Almost all European trade was conducted
by Europeans themselves.

Colonization and economic change
inevitably affected gender relations. Although
European officials tried to discourage intermarriage, the fact that most colonists and imported
slaves were male inevitably encouraged sexual
unions with American Indian women. American
Indian family arrangements were often disrupted,
and the growth of the mestizo population accelerated. Marriage among African slaves was often
forbidden—for example, in Brazil—which led to
an additional set of sexual patterns.

As agriculture spread, based on local crops and
also crops and animals introduced from Europe
(cattle, sheep, rice, wheat), the Latin American
population began to grow, despite the staggering
effects of disease among the American Indians.
Prosperity increased also, during the 18th century,

and many Creole owners became wealthy. However, resentment grew as well. Spanish and Portuguese policies were designed to keep Latin America subservient, and in the 18th century, would-be enlightened despots in both countries tightened controls over the colonies. The colonial administrations imposed heavy taxes on Latin American trade and limited it to a few ports and a handful of privileged companies. Contact with the more advanced economies of northern Europe was banned, although in fact some illegal trade developed, particularly with Britain, which was allowed to import slaves. Latin Americans grew increasingly restless under these limitations and also because of their exclusion from political rule. Many Creoles traveled in Europe and learned of the new political theories of the Enlightenment. In Colombia and other centers, new kinds of intellectual activity arose, as scientific discoveries and reform ideas were discussed. This intellectual ferment was modest, confined mainly to cities and Creoles, but combined with the other, more widespread grievances, it was the basis for a series of wars of independence that produced the first massive slave revolt in Haiti, in 1798, and then swept across virtually the entire society between 1808 and 1820.

By the 18th century, a Latin American civilization was taking shape on the basis of ongoing popular traditions among many American Indian peoples; new political, cultural, and technological influences from Europe; and the special conditions of the colonial economy and government. The civilization depended heavily on European models, but it was not identical to Europe. Racial diversity, slavery and the estate systems, the nature of the export economy, and a popular culture combined with Catholicism set it apart; so did the combination of wide governmental claims with limited actual authority over local conditions. Latin American civilization, still new, was also capable of important change. New cultural products, a more vigorous internal economy, and Creole contacts with the European Enlightenment all exhibited the spirit of innovation characteristic of the 18th century itself. In a different sense, a series of Amer-

ican Indian risings in the Andes region, toward the end of the century, performed a similar function, with leaders combining novel political demands with references to Inca heritage.

WESTERN CIVILIZATION IN NORTH AMERICA

French colonial holdings in Canada and along the Mississippi River, although vast on paper, were only lightly administered. Important French settlements were established only in parts of Canada. The French were far more interested in their West Indian islands, which produced so profitably for the European market. From North America, they gained only some fur trade and some leverage against Britain's growing empire.

The British colonies along the eastern seaboard, however, were another matter. By the 18th century, three million Europeans had settled in these colonies, and a large number of African slaves had been imported as well. In the southern colonies, a slaveholding estate system developed— producing rice, sugar, tobacco, and dyes—that in many ways resembled that of the West Indies and Brazil. Britain imposed some of the same limitations on all the colonies that Spain established for its Latin American holdings. Governors were appointed from Britain; taxes were high; manufacturing was discouraged as the British sought to protect their markets in the colonies and procure cheap raw materials and foodstuffs.

Nonetheless, the society that developed in the British colonies was far closer to western European forms than was that of Latin America. The colonies operated their own assemblies, which provided considerable political experience; local town governments were also active. Despite British regulations, a substantial manufacturing economy developed, and the North Americans ran extensive trading companies and merchant shipping. North American products were less interesting to western Europe than were those of Latin America and the West

Indies. The southern colonies, to be sure, produced tobacco and later cotton, using slave labor, which served as the leading exports. And southern planters imported expensive craft products from Europe. Here was a dependent economy quite similar to that of Latin America. But in New England and the Middle Atlantic colonies, aside from some furs and woods, there were no natural resources of great interest in the early modern world economy. These colonies were therefore left free to develop their own localized agriculture and also their own trading patterns, including merchant shipping and local manufacturing based on family businesses and wage labor. Britain did try to impose more characteristic dependency with new regulations and taxes in the 1760s, but by this point such attempts to control the colonies were too late. The colonial economy was not as advanced as that of western Europe, but it demonstrated a somewhat similar range of activities, including growing merchant zeal.

The North American colonists' intellectual contacts with Europe were also vigorous. North America was closer to Europe than Latin America was. The tie with Britain gave North Americans access to one of the most dynamic centers of political theory and scientific inquiry in the Western world. Hundreds of North Americans during the 18th century contributed scientific findings to the British Royal Society, and discussion groups among American intellectuals were active as well. North American literacy rates were quite high, which encouraged participation in a European-derived intellectual life. In contrast, Latin America's ties to Spain, where Enlightenment activity was more modest, limited its access to the new intellectual currents of Western civilization.

British, and to an extent French, North America thus evolved less as a separate culture than as part of Western civilization. There were vital differences, of course. The North American colonies did not produce a full aristocracy, of the sort that still dominated west European society; this fact gave the values of merchant groups and

free farmers freer rein. Colonial governments were also weak, by European standards, with few functions beyond defense and a rudimentary system of law courts. In addition, North American family patterns were somewhat distinctive. Blessed with more abundant land, North Americans had higher birth rates than their European counterparts during the 17th and 18th centuries. They treated children with greater care; thus, the practice of swaddling children was less common in British North America. Americans also placed somewhat greater emphasis on the family as the center of emotional stability, perhaps because of the strangeness of their surroundings. Most importantly of all, the North American colonies did establish a slaveholding system that, although concentrated particularly in the South, would strongly affect the history of the whole region—even after slavery was finally abolished.

North Americans were conscious of their distinctiveness. They lacked Europe's elaborate art and great cities, although by the 18th century, the imitation of European artistic forms was well underway. Americans felt somewhat inferior to Europe but rejoiced in what they perceived as their greater freedom (slavery aside) and a more youthful vigor. But the habit of imitating Europe remained strong as well. In fact, the British colonies were so similar to Europe that the course of their history would closely resemble that of the rest of the expanded Western world. Even when the colonies rebelled, in 1776, they did so in the name of Western political ideals and proceeded to establish a government that, although it maintained certain distinctive features, remained clearly within the range of Western political values.

NORTH AND SOUTH AMERICA: REASONS FOR THE DIFFERENCES

Western penetration of the Americas from 1450 to 1800 had two leading results. It created an important although distinctive version of West-

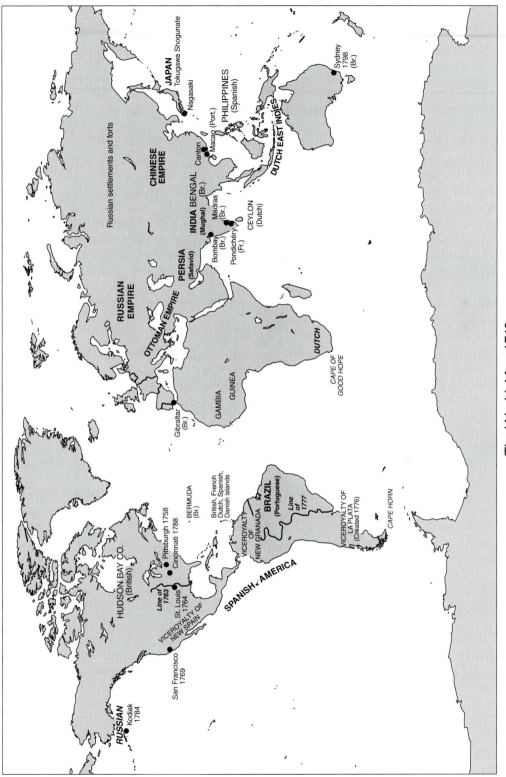

RUSSIAN
Kodiak
1784

San Francisco
1769

HUDSON BAY CO.
(British)

Pittsburgh 1758
Cincinnati 1788

*Line of
1763*

St. Louis
1764

VICEROYALTY OF
NEW SPAIN

BERMUDA
(Br.)

British, French,
Dutch, Spanish,
Danish islands

SPANISH AMERICA

VICEROYALTY
OF
NEW GRANADA

BRAZIL
(Portuguese)

*Line
of
1777*

VICEROYALTY OF
LA PLATA
(Created 1776)

CAPE HORN

Gibraltar
(Br.)

GAMBIA

GUINEA

DUTCH

*CAPE OF
GOOD HOPE*

RUSSIAN
EMPIRE

OTTOMAN EMPIRE

PERSIA
(Safavid)

CHINESE
EMPIRE

Russian settlements and forts

INDIA
(Mughal)

BENGAL
(Br.)

Bombay
(Br.)

Pondichéry
(Fr.)

Madras
(Br.)

CEYLON
(Dutch)

Canton

Macao (Port.)

JAPAN
Tokugawa Shogunate

Nagasaki

PHILIPPINES
(Spanish)

DUTCH EAST INDIES

Sydney
1798
(Br.)

The World After 1763

ern civilization in North America. It created an essentially new civilization, albeit one with unusually close ties to Western patterns, in South and Central America and Mexico. Because of its size and economic role, Latin American civilization was by far the more important in world history during the early modern period.

How and why did these two outcomes differ? Part of the distinction rests with differences between Spain and Portugal on the one hand, and Britain and northern Europe on the other. Spain was an intensely Catholic country, with a fervent missionary movement, but it was somewhat removed, particularly after 1600, from the mainstream of European intellectual life. Spain lacked a substantial merchant class of its own, which contributed to the Latin American emphasis on landed estates rather than elaborate commerce. Spain's tendency toward centralized control discouraged extensive political life in the new colonies. Latin American civilization, although still not fully formed, thus emerged with a political tradition, an economy, and a social structure quite different from what came to characterize its northern neighbor.

Latin America also developed a different racial balance from that of the English colonies. Disease decimated the American Indian population everywhere, but because of its prior size, substantial concentrations persisted in Latin America. North American Indians were also less fully organized into agricultural societies, and they were more easily forced to move. The American Indian role in the ultimate culture and social structure of North America was not great. In Latin America, in contrast, particularly in Central America and the Andes region, the values and labor contributions of a sizable American Indian population played an ongoing role. The rise of a large mestizo population, virtually unknown in the more racially conscious English colonies, added to the differentiation. Latin American civilization resulted, in part, from a fusion of Western and American Indian peoples and social forms; it also had a much larger African slave contingent. North America saw a much more straightforward extension of Western values over small, often badly treated and segregated, American Indian and African minorities.

From these early differentiations, Latin America and what became the United States and Canada were to follow largely different historical rhythms. To be sure, struggles for independence occurred almost simultaneously. The North American colonies (apart from Canada) rose first, and most of Latin America, inspired in part by this very example, soon followed. But from these wars came quite different results, in the political features of the new nations and in their economic base, as the new United States quickly joined western Europe in industrialization, whereas Latin America remained in a more dependent position in the world economy.

THE WORLD ECONOMY REVISITED

Like all major developments in human history, the rise of the Western-dominated world economy resulted in both gains and losses. It tended to increase economic inequalities among civilizations. Latin America and major parts of Africa, drawn into the world economy as producers of largely unprocessed goods that depended on cheap labor or slaves, had scant reason for rejoicing, although individuals in these societies profited along with the Europeans. Furthermore, the inequalities of the world economy tended to be self-perpetuating. In some basic respects, Africa and Latin America remain dependent economies to this day, unable to control their own economic destinies; in many respects, the West continues to benefit from this sort of relationship. Only the English colonies of North America, on the fringe of dependency into the 18th century, later managed to break free and become part of the dominant economy of the West.

The world economy also unleashed a new profit motive, through the spread of commercial capitalism. This motive, although capable of generating large-scale exploitation, also supported technological innovation as another means of increasing production at low cost. Before long this thirst, backed by the capital already earned in world trade, would produce vast changes in manufacturing methods, which in turn yielded measurable benefits even beyond Western society.

Before this occurred, however, other civilizations in the world, not fully caught up in the world economy but nonetheless affected by it, had to define their own relationship to the West and new patterns of trade. Some, like China and the Middle East, were not strangers to commercial capitalism, although they had not before encountered it on such a scale. Because of previous economic and technological strength, and strong political structures and distinctive values, most of Asia and eastern Europe remained partly aloof to the world economy well into the 18th century, participating to a degree but not engulfed by it. However, such civilizations, too, faced the prospect of change, even if they resolved otherwise.

The world economy, with its inclusion of the Americas, also had significant environmental impact. Europeans were eager to introduce plants native to one region to as many other areas as possible, to increase production and profit. American forests began to be cut back in favor of crops such as sugar. The importance of new animals such as horses challenged the American environment as well. The Spanish actively experimented with American crops like corn and the potato in the Philippines, from where they spread to other parts of Asia.

ISSUES AND CONNECTIONS

Figuring out how Europeans, Africans, and American Indians reacted to each other helps put a human face on the new contacts of the period. It is important not to overgeneralize.

European missionaries, planters, and slave traders all reacted to American Indians in different ways. Many African kings and merchants reacted differently to European merchants than did ordinary west Africans (those who had contacts with Europeans or the world economy at all).

Another way to deal with impact is to analyze why positions in the world economy tended to endure. Superior positions were hard to lose. Why? Dependent positions were hard to escape as well, and the reasons should be fairly clear.

Connections to the present leap out. Slavery is gone, at least officially, and colonies have mostly been freed. But memories of slavery and colonization still burn bright, affecting global relationships. The two American presidents who visited Africa in the past decade both spent time in buildings used in the slave trade, where they said appropriate things about how awful the trade was; here's a sign of the need still to deal with memory. Western superiority, though different from its early modern form, still operates, in terms of power and assumptions. Most importantly, an identifiable world economy, with dominant and dependent players, still operates, building quite directly on the system created between 1500 and 1750.

SUGGESTED WEB SITES

On the lives of early European explorers, see http://www.win.tue.nl/cs/fm/engels/discovery/index.html. On the interactions between Spanish conquerors and North American Indians, see http://www.FloridaHistory.com.

SUGGESTED READINGS

Recent work includes Sanjay Sumbrahmanyam, *The Career and Legend of Vasco da Gama* (1997); Merry Wiesner Hanks, *Christianity and Sexuality in the Early Modern World* (2000); Kenneth Pomeranz, *The Great Divergence: China, Europe and the Making of the Modern World Economy* (2000)—a very important world history study.

Excellent discussions of Western exploration and expansion are C. M. Cippolla, *Guns, Sails and Empires* (1985), and J. H. Parry, *The Discovery of South America* (1979). Important recent work includes Alan K. Smith, *Creating a World Economy: Merchant Capital Colonization and World Trade, 1400–1825* (1991); Michael Pearson, *Port Cities and Intruders: The Swahili Coast, India, and Portugal in the Early Modern Era* (1998); and James Tracy, ed., *The Rise of Merchant Empires* (1990), and *The Political Economy of Merchant Empires* (1991). See also C. R. Boxer, *Four Centuries of Portuguese Expansion* (1969); W. Dorn, *The Competition for Empire* (1963); Alfred Crosby, *The Columbian Exchange: Biological and Cultural Consequences of 1492* (1972); C. A. Bayh, *Indian Society and the Making of the British Empire* (1988); and D. K. Fieldhouse, *The Colonial Empires* (1971). See also J. H. Elliott, *The Old World and the New, 1492–1650* (1970), and J. K. Thornton, *Africa and the Africans in the Making of the Atlantic World, 1400–1800* (1997).

On Latin America, consult James Lockhart and Stuart B. Schwartz, *Early Latin America* (1982); Lyle N. Macalister, *Spain and Portugal in the New World* (1984); Eric Williams, *Capitalism and Slavery* (1964); J. Fagg, *Latin America* (1969); S. J. Stein and B. H. Stein, *The Colonial Heritage of Latin America* (1970); and A. Lavin, ed., *Sexuality and Marriage in Colonial Latin America* (1989).

Useful on the slave system are Robert Blackburn, *The Making of New World Slavery* (1997); O. Patterson, *Slavery and Social Death: A Comparative Study* (1982); and D. B. Davis, *Slavery and Human Progress* (1984). On other key topics, consult Nancy Farriss, *Maya Society under Colonial Rule* (1984); Louisa Schell Hoberman and Susan Migden Socolow, eds., *Cities and Society in Colonial Latin America* (1986); and Stuart Schwartz, *Sugar Plantations and the Formation of Brazilian Society* (1985). On the slave trade, see James Rawley, *The Transatlantic Slave Trade* (1981); Roger Anstey, *The Atlantic Slave Trade and British Abolition* (1975); Paul Lovejoy, *Transformations in Slavery: A History of Slavery in Africa* (1983); Patrick Manning, *Slavery and African Life* (1990); and Joseph Miller, *Way of Death* (1989).

Readable texts on the West and Asia and Africa include Paul Bohannan and Philip Curtin, *Africa and Africans*, 3rd ed., (1988); Martin Hall, *The Changing Past: Farmers, Kings, and Traders in Southern Africa* (1987); Leonard Thompson, *A History of South Africa* (1990); A. Hyma, *The Dutch in the Far East: A History of the Dutch Commercial and Colonial Empire* (1942); and S. D. Pen, *The French in India* (1958). See also K. N. N. Chaudori, *Trade and Civilization in the Indian Ocean* (1985). A provocative although controversial overview of the development of a new global economy is Immanuel Wallerstein's *The Modern World System*, 2 vols. (1980). For source reading, see P. Curtin, ed., *Africa Remembered: Narratives by West Africans from the Era of the Slave Trade* (1967). On colonial North America, see Jack Greene and J. R. Pole, eds., *Colonial British America: Essays on the New History of the Early Modern Era* (1984). See also, Paul Ahluwalia, *White and Deadly: Sugar and Colonialism* (1999).

Western Civilization Changes Shape in the Early Modern Centuries

17

Developments in early modern western Europe reflected the region's gains in the world economy, adding up to new revenue and power. Europe's world role encouraged dynamic internal patterns, which in turn affected its global activities. Western Europe changed in many ways during the early modern period: compare a summary of the year 1750 with that for 1450. Europe's world position, its political structures, its social structures, and its culture had all shifted profoundly. Big changes in this period include the replacement of feudalism with national monarchies; greatly increased commercialization and the shift away from serfdom to wage labor; and a decline of traditional popular beliefs plus the rise of science.

Between 1450 and 1750, west European society went through a series of profound transformations. Each century produced at least one major new current. The 15th century featured the Renaissance, which began indeed a bit earlier in Italy and then spread to northern Europe. In the 16th century, the Protestant Reformation upstaged the continuing impact of the Renaissance, breaking the unity of Western Christendom; the Catholic Reformation, in turn, responded. Political turmoil dominated the first half of the 17th century, but still more profound change resulted from the Scientific Revolution, which was one of the most basic reorientations of intellectual life in the history of any civilization. Finally, during the first half of the 18th century, the Enlightenment extended the principles of the Scientific Revolution to generate new views of politics and society, indeed new views of human nature itself.

Thinkers during the Enlightenment professed embarrassment at the very existence of the medieval period, which seemed to them remote and backward in contrast to their own sophisticated world. Such a view was, in fact, too extreme, as well as unfairly demeaning to the achievements of medieval society: the heritage of the Middle Ages was still visible in political, intellectual, and economic life. There was no question, however, that Western civilization showed a marked ability to change its focus.

So much seemed to be changing that it is sometimes difficult to identify coherent directions in the period as a whole. Transformation was not neat and tidy: different movements overlapped, such as the Renaissance and the Reformation. Some events represented a resurgence of earlier values. The Reformation, for example, stemmed in part from a very medieval piety, although it had quite nonmedieval results. Although it is important to gain a sense of specific developments, it is also possible to observe general trends. Various movements tended to strengthen the central state in European monarchies, but for different reasons. Historical processes led, even more clearly, to a significant transformation of Western intellectual and artistic life. This ultimately resulted in a decline in the religious approach to understanding the world in favor of a rational, scientific framework. Trends of this sort were gradual, often complex, and usually incomplete. But they gave shape to a vibrant period in Western history.

This was also a time of fundamental change in Western economic and social life. Developments in these areas were just as important as the overall intellectual revolution and, indeed, more important than political change. The Western economy became commercialized in an unprecedented way, and technologically—for the first time—the most advanced in the world. The European family took on unusual dimensions, and its importance in certain aspects of Western life grew.

Between 1450 and 1750, political, cultural, and economic shifts involved Western civilization increasingly in the larger world. Traders and explorers in overseas colonies brought back new techniques and cultural values. Even more obviously, from 1500 onward, Western society drew increasing wealth from its global contacts. In turn, based on its new internal dynamism, Western Europe began to influence other civilizations in a variety of ways.

KEY QUESTIONS   *How did specific events, such as the Reformation, relate to the big changes of the early modern period as a whole in the West? It is important to capture the specific currents, each with its own character, but not lose sight of the big picture. Why did western Europe change so much in these centuries? Finally, what continuities accompanied change? In what ways were earlier features of Western civilization still present by 1750?*

PATTERNS OF EARLY MODERN WESTERN HISTORY

The Renaissance

The spotlight in Western history, around 1400, was on Italy. This region had never fully embraced medieval customs, especially feudalism. The peninsula was largely organized in terms of city-states, some ruled by kings, others by aristocratic or merchant councils, still others by military tyrants. Many city-states had extensive trade and cultural contacts with other parts of the Mediterranean. From these exchanges, especially with Byzantium, Italian scholars gained a new appreciation of Greek and Latin literature. At the same time, growing commercial wealth encouraged cities like Florence and Venice to create new artistic styles to celebrate their exciting achievements.

From Italy's mixture of trade and scholarly and artistic endeavor arose the movement known as the Renaissance, which took shape in the 1300s. It started most clearly as a literary and artistic movement. Writers such as Dante, Petrarch, and Boccacio—all three writing in Italian as well as the traditional Latin—began to address more strictly secular subjects than had been popular in the Middle Ages. Petrarch wrote love sonnets to his Laura; other poems praised his own valor in climbing mountains—a new sign of individualism and pride in human achievement. Boccacio wrote earthy stories of love and lust,

World Profiles

MARIA PORTINARI

Maria Portinari (b. 1456) was the wife of a Florentine banker (Tommaso, c. 1432–1501) who made a fortune as a representative of the Medici banking family in Bruges, Flanders (now Belgium). The image here shows her richly but somberly dressed. Her slightly melancholy expression may have seemed appropriate in terms of religious piety, for the Renaissance in northern Europe set a strong spiritual tone for laypeople. Historians have also realized that the Renaissance, striking as it was in terms of cultural innovation, may have led to a deterioration in the position of upper-class women, treated increasingly as ornaments and kept apart from most of the new sources of learning. How might a woman like Maria Portinari have reacted to the changes sweeping through western Europe during the 15th century?

This portrait of Maria Portinari is by the Flemish master Hans Memling. (Metropolitan Museum of Art, Bequest of Benjamin Altman, 1913, 14.40.627)

and although he later recanted, professing his devotion to religious faith, his earlier writings won a wide audience. In art, Giotto developed a new sense of perspective, allowing three-dimensional portrayals of nature. Both writers and artists began to copy classical styles, writing of and painting gods and goddesses and human scenes, rather than strictly Christian motifs; their work thus reflected increasing realism.

Seldom has an age produced as many cultural greats as did the Renaissance in Italy. A host of architects designed churches and public buildings in classical styles, renouncing the Gothic aesthetic. Leonardo da Vinci advanced the realistic portrayal of the human body in art, even painting pictures of medical dissections. Michelangelo's statues offered graphic displays of human musculature. Overall, Italian Renaissance art, developed from the 14th through the early 16th centuries, stressed themes of humanism—a focus on humankind as the center of intellectual and artistic endeavor. The humanistic concerns spread also to music, where elegant choruses sang of love, drink, and the beauties of nature. A new interest in human history also

Classical themes and styles in the Italian Renaissance: *Birth of Venus* by Botticelli.

emerged, and several Renaissance historians, using a newly critical approach to past documents, challenged traditional church claims in such areas as the origins of the papacy.

The new spirit extended also to political theory. Writing around 1500, the Florentine Niccolò Machiavelli described what a ruler must do to gain and maintain power: how to use cruelty, how to sway public opinion. Machiavelli combined a detailed knowledge of Italian politics of his time with the use of Greek and Roman examples—a characteristic Renaissance mixture.

The Italian Renaissance had flourished in part because Italy was free from the medieval political forms that continued to influence much of the rest of Europe. During a good deal of the Italian Renaissance, France and England were locked in their Hundred Years' War. Then, late in the 15th century, the larger monarchies started to gain strength. France and Spain looked greedily upon the weak Italian city-states and embarked on wars of conquest in the 1490s. Italian trade also began to decline as interest shifted away from the Mediterranean to the Atlantic trade routes that France, Spain, and England soon dominated.

However, as Renaissance creativity faded in its Italian birthplace, it passed northward. Northern artists directly copied the new themes and styles of the Italians. Palaces in the classical style became the rage among northern rulers such as Francis I of France, who increasingly fancied themselves patrons of the arts. Northern humanists gained growing knowledge of Latin and Greek literary and philosophical sources; soon they turned to writing in their own languages. Typical northern humanists, like Erasmus in the Netherlands, were more religious than some of their Italian counterparts but shared their interest in human affairs and a pure style. The Renaissance spirit also prevailed in such 16th-century writers as England's Shakespeare and France's Rabelais; they addressed a wide variety of earthly subjects, with an emphasis on human passions and drama. Their works, and those of Spain's Cervantes, developed new literary traditions in their respective nations.

The northern Renaissance had political implications as well. Renaissance kings increased the pomp and ceremony within their courts and tried to expand their power. Francis I claimed new authority over the operations of the Catholic church in France. Leading monarchs from the Tudor dynasty in England, particularly Henry VIII and Elizabeth I, ruled with firm hands. They encouraged trading companies and colonial enterprises, and they even passed laws on how to deal with the poor. During the Renaissance, monarchs also cultivated a more open interest in wars of conquest than their medieval predecessors. England engaged in a lengthy effort to conquer Ireland; France invaded Italy and tried to construct alliance systems to counter the power of Spain and the Holy Roman Empire, both ruled for a time by a single royal family, the Habsburgs. Francis I even allied briefly with the sultan of the Ottoman Empire; the alliance meant little in practical terms but showed that political interests had gained ascendancy over traditional Christian hostility to Islam.

The Religious Upheaval

Political and economic patterns in Renaissance Europe were soon embroiled in the currents of the next major change—the Reformation. In 1517, a German monk named Martin Luther nailed a document containing 95 theses to the door of a church in Wittenberg. He was specifically protesting claims made by a papal representative that the buying of indulgences for money would advance salvation. For Luther, the idea of indulgences became an utter perversity; according to his reading of the Bible, salvation could come only through faith, not through works and certainly not through the money that the Renaissance popes sought for the upkeep of their own expensive court. Luther's protest, rebuffed by the papacy, soon led him to challenge most of the traditional Catholic sacraments and the authority of the pope himself.

The stand taken by the German monk gained wide support. Many Christians believed that the Catholic church had become too corrupt and many of its practices meaningless. Some Renaissance intellectuals welcomed Luther's use of original documents, such as the Bible, and also his nationalistic defiance, as a German, against religious rule from Rome. A number of individual rulers liked Lutheranism because it broadened their authority; they could direct Lutheran churches without the interference of still powerful popes. Some ordinary people, finally, saw in Lutheranism an opportunity to speak out against their poverty and the landlords who dominated their lives, although Luther did renounce the idea of popular protest. As Luther firmly rejected Catholic attempts to undermine his influence, Lutheranism spread widely in Germany and also Scandinavia.

Once Christian unity was breached, other Protestant groups evolved. In England, Henry VIII established the Anglican church, initially to challenge papal attempts to enforce his first marriage, which had failed to produce a male heir. (Henry would ultimately have six wives in sequence; he had two of them executed.) Henry was also attracted to some Lutheran doctrines. His son and his daughter, who later became Queen Elizabeth I, were Protestants outright, so the Anglican church became increasingly Protestant in doctrine as well as a separate form of church government. Still more important were the churches inspired by Jean Calvin, a Frenchman who established his base in the city of Geneva. Calvinism insisted on God's predestination, or prior determination, of those who would be saved; nothing humans did, and certainly no sacraments, could win God's favor. At the same time, those elected to God's grace had the obligation to encourage others to behave morally and seek knowledge of the Bible. Calvinist ministers became moral guardians and preachers of God's word, not special sacramental representatives of the deity. Like other Protestant ministers, they could marry. Calvinism sought the participation of other believers in local church government; it also promoted wider popular education, so that more people could have direct access to the Bible (which various Protestant groups now translated

The Northern Renaissance emphasized greater introspection and spirituality: *Melancholia* by the German painter Albrecht Dürer. (Metropolitan Museum of Art, Fletcher Fund, 19.73.85)

into the vernacular languages). Calvinism was accepted not only in parts of Switzerland but also in Germany and France, where it produced strong minority groups, and in the Netherlands, England, and Scotland.

Beginning about 1550, the Catholic church, although unable to restore religious unity, reacted to Protestantism. Church councils not only condemned Protestant doctrine; they also communicated a message of greater religious concern to the pope. A new order of monks, the Jesuits, became active in politics, education, and missionary work, helping to strengthen the faith of most Catholics in Italy and Spain and to regain some territories initially open to Protestantism, such as Hungary. The result was a revivified Catholic church.

The rise of the Protestant churches triggered a long period of religious war in Europe. During the second half of the 16th century, France was the scene of major battles between Protestant and Catholic groups. The conflict ended only with

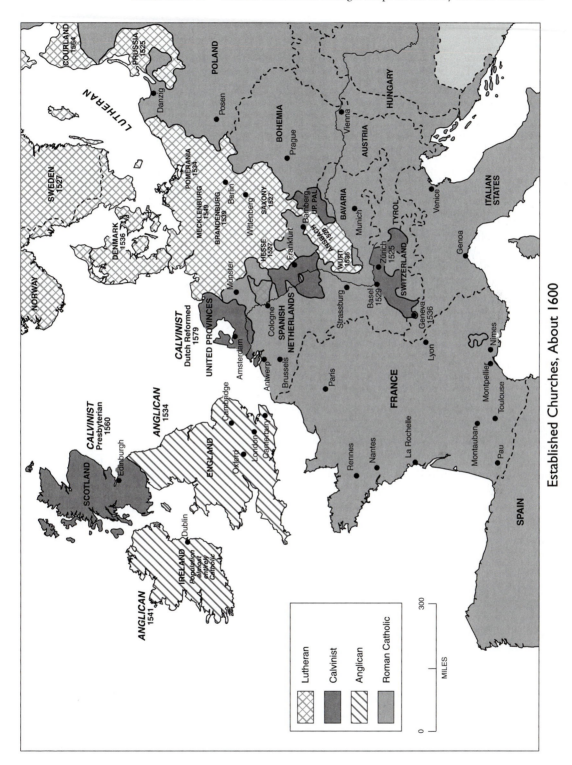

Established Churches, About 1600

COURLAND 1564

PRUSSIA 1525

POLAND

SWEDEN 1527

NORWAY

DENMARK 1536

LUTHERAN

Danzig

Posen

POMERANIA 1534

MECKLENBURG 1549

BRANDENBURG 1539

Berlin

SAXONY 1527

Wittenberg

HESSE 1527

Frankfurt

BOHEMIA

Prague

HUNGARY

Vienna

AUSTRIA

BAMBERG UP. PAL

ANSBACH 1528

BAVARIA

Munich

TYROL

ITALIAN STATES

Venice

WÜRT 1536

Zürich 1525

SWITZERLAND

Basel 1529

Genoa

Münster

CALVINIST Dutch Reformed 1579

UNITED PROVINCES

Cologne

SPANISH NETHERLANDS

Amsterdam

Antwerp

Brussels

Strasbourg

Geneva 1536

Lyon

Nîmes

CALVINIST Presbyterian 1560

SCOTLAND

Edinburgh

ANGLICAN 1534

Cambridge

ENGLAND

Oxford

London

Canterbury

Paris

FRANCE

Montpellier

Toulouse

Rennes

Nantes

La Rochelle

Montauban

Pau

SPAIN

ANGLICAN 1541

IRELAND Population almost entirely Catholic

Dublin

Lutheran

Calvinist

Anglican

Roman Catholic

300

MILES

0

the granting of tolerance to Protestants in 1598. Catholics and Protestants waged war recurrently in Germany, although several negotiations were held in the hope of dividing Germany among Catholic and Protestant states. In 1618, the Thirty Years' War broke out, in which foreign powers as well as Germans fought over their religious beliefs. The Spanish monarchy, self-appointed chief defender of the Catholic faith, tried to aid its co-religionists, whereas Swedish armies assisted the Protestant cause in a war so bloody that it reduced Germany's economic activity and its population level for many decades. The war ended with Spain's power reduced and a reluctant agreement to permit religious division among the German states. Religious passions helped fuel a war between the Netherlands and Spain, in which the former ultimately won its independence. Religious strife simmered in England during parts of the 16th century, until Queen Elizabeth I imposed a peace under a rather tolerant Anglican church; strife erupted again in the 1640s, contributing to a civil war in which Calvinists fought Catholic sympathizers. Eventually, the Anglican church was restored, but with tolerance for other Protestant groups. The English Civil War ended formally in 1660, but the full settlement, including limited religious toleration, was reached only in 1688–1689.

For the most part, the Reformation, which had dominated Western political as well as religious history during the greater part of the 16th century, was assimilated in Europe by the first half of the 17th century. Even the Thirty Years' War in Germany was as much a battle among national monarchies as it was a religious dispute. Thus, France during that war sided with Protestant forces in order to weaken its enemy Spain. Although Protestantism and revived Catholicism had a lasting impact on not only the religious map but also social and economic life, the battles among Christian groups no longer set the agenda for events in Europe itself. By 1650, it was becoming clear that Western Christianity was permanently divided, and unintentional reper-

cussions of the Reformation began surfacing in business and family life.

In this context, during most of the 1600s, attention shifted to culture and politics. In culture, the leading development was the spate of new scientific discoveries, culminating in the great physical laws as advanced by Isaac Newton. Scientists learned how gravity works; they determined that the Earth was not the center of the universe but, rather, rotated around the sun; they discovered how blood circulates in the human body. Perhaps most importantly, they developed a coherent understanding of how the scientific method functions, through a combination of rational hypothesis, empirical testing through observation or experiment, and final generalization in theory or law. Far more than the Renaissance, the Scientific Revolution of the 17th century produced a fundamental reorientation of Western intellectual life.

The Rise of the Monarchies

During the same period, leading Western monarchies gained new organizational power. With Spain in growing eclipse, after a century of glory in defense of the church and as Europe's major colonizer in the New World, France emerged as the bellwether nation. The French monarchy decisively defeated the remnants of feudal political forces during the 17th century. After 1614, the kings stopped summoning the national parliament. The greatest French monarch of this period, Louis XIV, also rescinded the toleration of Protestants. No group was allowed officially to limit the monarch's power. This political system, perfected under Louis XIV, was called, appropriately enough, *absolute monarchy*. Louis, dubbing himself the Sun King, extended his patronage of the arts. He built sumptuous palaces, where the nobles competed for royal favor instead of cultivating their independent power base in the provinces. Military administration improved, as Louis's advisors built better forts and established ways to supply provisions to troops in the field.

Louis set up military hospitals and even a military pension plan. Absolute monarchy also meant increasing attention to economic controls, mainly in the interest of securing greater tax revenue. The state tried to encourage exports and regulated manufacturing within France.

Absolutism was copied in a number of other countries. Particularly noteworthy was the rise of monarchies in central Europe along absolutist lines. Prussia, long a backward regional state in eastern Germany, began to strengthen its administration and expand its armies, gaining new power among the various German states. The Habsburg monarchs, although still claiming to be Holy Roman Emperors, worked to develop a solid monarchy in Austria. After Habsburg forces managed to repel the armies of the Ottoman Empire, by 1700 their rule extended to Hungary as well.

One of the clear purposes of the new absolute monarchs was to wage war. Louis XIV conducted several major wars, extending France's boundaries in the north and east. It took a coalition of other powers, including England, Holland, and some of the German states, to keep his ambitions in check. In the 18th century, France and England fought several times, although mainly in their colonies in North America and India. Prussia and Austria also fought, with Prussia winning important new territory. The idea of recurrent battle among the national monarchies and alliance systems designed to prevent any one European power from becoming dominant gained increasing ground.

The pattern of absolute monarchy continued into the 18th century. The French monarchy, exhausted by the wars and ruinous taxation of Louis XIV, was weaker than before. But despite numerous reform movements, no new political system emerged. Prussian administration became more efficient. The Prussian kings, led by the able Frederick the Great, tried to improve agricultural production and extend education while maintaining absolute political power and emphasizing military strength. Rulers like Frederick, because of their reform interests and their fascination with

new political ideas, liked to call themselves *enlightened despots* rather than absolute monarchs, but the difference was not substantial.

Absolutism, enlightened or otherwise, was not the only political form to surface in Europe during the 17th and 18th centuries. In Britain and the Netherlands, parliamentary monarchies developed that built more clearly on older postclassical traditions through which kings would be checked by some kind of assembly. In England, the power of Parliament had been curbed during the reign of the strong Tudor kings of the 16th century, but the institution had not disappeared. Then, when less able monarchs in the 17th century tried to introduce taxes without parliamentary consent, supporters of Parliament joined religious dissidents in attacking royal power. One king, Charles I, was executed during the English civil wars of the 1640s, and for a time England was ruled by a military dictatorship. The monarchy, restored in 1660, again tried to defy Parliament while flirting with Catholicism. It was this combination that resulted in a final settlement, the so-called Glorious Revolution of 1688–1689. A new king was crowned, under parliamentary authority, establishing the principle that Parliament, not the king, had supreme power in the realm, although royal power remained considerable through the 18th century. The crown could not suspend laws, levy taxes without parliamentary consent, or maintain a standing army in times of peace. The assembly was to meet regularly rather than depending on the king's summons. Parliament itself remained a largely medieval body, with a hereditary House of Lords and a House of Commons, whose members were elected by small numbers of voters. Campaigns for parliamentary office after the Glorious Revolution involved few questions of principle and a great deal of bribery. But Parliament had unquestioned authority, and no English king's power could be considered absolute, although it remained extensive throughout the century.

Thus, Western civilization, now divided by religion, was for a time divided by political systems as well. Absolute monarchs not only ruled without parliaments but also created governments with larger bureaucracies and greater functions than the government of England (united with Scotland in 1700 to form Great Britain). At the same time, absolute monarchies were in some ways less flexible than the parliamentary states. They depended on efficient rulers, not always produced by heredity, and they tended to provoke discontent if their wars were unsuccessful or their taxes too high. Popular dissatisfaction mounted particularly in France during the 18th century and would result in massive revolution in 1789. Ultimately, through this revolutionary current, a greater degree of political unity would return to Western society. Until then, the absolutist and parliamentary impulses were largely separate, and both were important in expressing significant aspects of the evolving Western political tradition.

After the turmoil of the religious wars, it was the development of the new political systems and the recurrent military conflicts that gave the clearest superficial shape to Western history from the early 1600s until the 1750s. Ironically, the new divisions within Europe only spurred Western influence in other parts of the world. Catholics and Protestants, not content with their internal rivalry, spilled over into rival missionary efforts in Asia and the Americas. National monarchies battled overseas as well. Prussia and the Habsburg monarchy fought in Europe alone, but by the 18th century, Britain and France were prepared to wage war on virtually a worldwide basis. Thus, the last of the strictly monarchical wars in Western history, called the Seven Years' War in Europe for the good reason that it lasted from 1756 to 1763, saw Prussia defeat an effort by Austria to restrict its growing power, while Britain and France battled on three continents. Even earlier, English-Dutch, English-Spanish, and French-Spanish conflicts over territory and control of the seas had encouraged the formation of new European colonies in various parts of the world. Seemingly endemic tensions in Western society were now affecting the wider course of world history.

POLITICAL INSTITUTIONS AND IDEAS

The growth of the power and efficiency of the national state was the key political trend in early modern Europe. The Renaissance encouraged the greater splendor and ceremony, including artistic patronage, of the ruler's court. Renaissance interests also tended to weaken religious restraints on political power; even the Renaissance papacy acted more like a secular government, concerned with amassing wealth and acquiring art objects, than like a religious institution. Except in the Italian city-states, new government structures were not developed during the Renaissance, but there was a change in tone and motivation.

The Reformation enhanced the power of the state quite simply by weakening that of the church. Even Catholic monarchies, such as those of France or Spain, gained because the Catholic papacy during the Reformation depended on them for support. Jesuit advisors, although devoted to the Catholic cause, also helped secular rulers increase their power base. In the Protestant camp, Lutheran kings and princes and the English monarch as head of the Anglican church took over control of church government directly.

Still, before 1600, important medieval patterns persisted in politics. In particular, the aristocracy retained considerable power. Many church disputes, like the religious wars in France, found some aristocrats using the Protestant cause to support their claims against the monarchy. Revolts by nobles occurred again in France in the 1660s, when Louis XIV was a child, but this was a last gasp. The English civil wars featured landowning gentry backing the parliamentary cause against the king—whose main defenders were also landowning aristocrats. But the political power of the nobility finally declined. Many landowners could not keep pace with economic change, and they depended for their livelihood on securing government jobs. Improvements in the quality of guns and cannons weakened aristocratic military power,

Louis XIV's palace at Versailles. Built as a lavish tribute to the absolute monarchy, Versailles demonstrates the symmetrical, classical style predominant in 17th- and 18th-century western Europe.

although for the most part leading army commanders were appointed from the ranks of the nobles. The aristocracy was by no means dead as a political force, even aside from the parliamentary system in England, which gave landowners great power. However, in most monarchies, the balance had shifted decisively to the kings.

As stronger monarchies emerged, culminating in absolutism and enlightened despotism, bureaucracies became more sophisticated. French kings began to appoint regular administrators of provincial districts, who could manage the court system, supervise roads and other public works, and oversee the collection of taxes. Many bureaucrats were drawn from middle-class ranks, which helped check aristocratic power. The steady improvement in military organization gave kings larger and more reliable armies than ever before in Western history. These forces were used not only to fight wars but also to repress popular protest at home. New measures like the provision of regular uniforms for troops, introduced widely by 17th century kings, symbolized the increasing professionalism of military forces.

New state functions developed. During most of the 17th and 18th centuries, the reigning economic theory, called *mercantilism*, held that states should provide the basic framework for the economy, to promote tax revenue and make sure that other nations did not gain an advantage. England and Holland, as well as the absolute monarchies, practiced a mercantilist system. They levied tariffs on imported goods, tried to encourage the growth and activity of their merchant fleets, and sought colonies to provide raw materials and a guaranteed market for manufactured goods. Some governments even built factories to foster national industry and discourage imports from foreign producers. In the 18th century, enlightened kings such as Frederick the Great also tried to introduce new crops and farming methods and to stimulate population growth, held to be a vital source of military strength. Many governments broke down local internal barriers to trade, again for the sake of the national economy. State-sponsored road building increased. Here were important extensions of Western ideas of what the state should be responsible for. While economic activities were valued mainly for their impact on military capability and international competition, some rulers were starting to believe that one of the duties of government was the promotion of national prosperity.

During the early modern period, the growth of state powers and functions propelled the leading west European governments toward the front rank of all governments in the world, in terms of the resources they commanded and the ways in which they could control relatively large territories. Some of the Western measures, of course, duplicated earlier advances in administration introduced in places such as China. It was also true that Western governments could not rival the territorial size of the great empires of the day. But they did have more effective contact with their national units than many of the Asian empires maintained with their more diverse holdings. Popular loyalty to kings, and some hints of national identity, especially where the formation of national churches was concerned, supplemented the institutions of the monarchy. This period was, in sum, an important stage of state-building and organizational efficiency in a number of Western nations. The state still did not have regular contacts with ordinary people, but popular protests began to suggest the expectation that government should help the disenfranchised in times of need.

The practical limits on the power of the expanding states of early modern Europe were buttressed by increasing ideological attacks, for political theory grew in importance as an expression of Western culture. A few theorists, to be sure, supported the absolute monarchs. In addition to Machiavelli's frank appraisal of how to use

raw power, there emerged a "divine right" school of thought, which held that kings derived their power directly from God and were accountable only to Him. This theory differed from traditions in some other civilizations, which claimed that the king or emperor was himself divine, but such a distinction meant little in practice.

Nonetheless, divine right theory was not the dominant approach in Western political theory of this time. Machiavelli himself, in his longer works, wrote of the importance of councils to balance a ruler's power. From the Renaissance onward, classical examples were cited, from Athens and republican Rome, to show the importance of representative institutions to express some popular sentiment and curb the excesses of kings. Calvinist writers, building on the experience of self-government in local churches and eager to protect their "true" faith against hostile governments, also developed theories about the limited powers of kings and states. The most significant theoretical statements arose in England in the aftermath of the civil wars. John Locke believed that basic political power lay with the people, who could withdraw their approval, even through revolution, if a ruler behaved arbitrarily. According to Locke, peoples' rights to life, liberty, and property should be protected against the state. These ideas were embraced, during the 18th century, by Enlightenment writers in France and elsewhere, many of whom advocated the founding of parliaments on the English model and even the drafting of formal constitutions to ensure individual rights and provide additional constraints on royal power.

In other words, as some of the traditional limits on kings declined and royal power expanded notably in many countries, some new restraints were being suggested. The fact that England provided an alternative model of government structure was vital in this ideological movement. But the theories themselves were even more important. Many people in France came to believe that absolute monarchy was an inappropriate political form. Some ideas, not just of upper-class parliaments but also of genuine popular political rights, were advanced, and ordinary people began to share similar beliefs. During the English civil wars, and again in the 1760s, popular movements arose in Britain to demand direct political representation for the common folk.

Along with growing government power, then, came a new statement of ideas that governments should be controlled and limited—a significant restatement, in other words, of a recognizable Western political tradition.

THE FERMENT IN WESTERN CULTURE

Renaissance humanism added important new elements to Western culture, in part, of course, by reviving classical styles and values in literature and art. The aesthetic value of the arts, rather than their service to religious goals, gained new attention. The Reformation and the Catholic response to it represented a distraction, to some extent, from this movement. Protestant churches were characteristically sparse and unadorned compared to the great Catholic cathedrals, the idea being that artistic images should not detract from a focus on God's great power. Church music assumed a vital role, and Luther himself wrote some well-known, stirring hymns. In fact, Renaissance-inspired artistic themes continued even as religious conflict spread. Shakespeare's plays, for example, showed little interest in religious subjects in their evocation of political drama and human comedy and tragedy. Then, in the 17th century, classically inspired art and literature gained a new lease on life. In France, a series of powerful dramatic writers, led by the playwright Racine, used classical themes to directly express human emotions. Architecture and painting similarly borrowed classical motifs and scenes—although with some new decorative embellishments, in what is called the *baroque* style.

More fundamentally, the Renaissance and Reformation, although very different in specific focus, promoted important new cultural values.

Individualism was one such value. Renaissance writers emphasized the power of the individual. The concept of the "Renaissance man" expressed the conviction that talented human beings could excel in many fields and take legitimate pride in their own accomplishments. Reformation theology, to be sure, carefully placed God's power above human capability. But Reformation writers also talked of the importance of a direct relationship between the individual and God, without the mediation of priests and sacraments. Although Protestant churches exercised significant control over the moral and religious behavior of their flocks, individuals were encouraged to think on their own about their relationship to God.

Writers of both the Renaissance and Reformation spoke of the importance of the past, the source of stylistic inspiration or religious guidance. Scholars from both periods turned to a critical examination of historical documents as a key source of truth. Particularly during the Renaissance, the idea of human progress also began to surface. Renaissance writers believed in their superiority over medieval authors, and some wondered whether a more general advance in human knowledge and aesthetic sensibility was not underway.

Finally, secular interests gained ground. Renaissance writers incorporated humanistic themes in their works, although most continued to accept the importance of religious values as well. Reformation theologians were adamant in their hostility to purely secular concerns. However, by undoing Christian unity and producing a series of religious wars, the Reformation led many people to question whether the church was as important as medieval thinkers, or Reformation leaders, had claimed. Even by the late 16th century, some writers, like Michel de Montaigne in France, emphasized that tolerance and peace were far more vital than any effort to establish a single religious truth. Western Christianity had long depended on the idea of religious uniformity. This is not an essential belief in a religious society; most Asian civilizations

This shop in Italy shows the early printing press in the West and Renaissance technology at work.

had long generated more religious diversity or promoted tolerance. In the West, however, Christianity since the Roman Empire had produced a passionate commitment to a single truth, with alternatives seen not just as wrong but also as dangerous. Early Protestant leaders maintained this view; Calvin even had heretics executed. But the fact was that religious unity no longer existed, and given this challenge to the particular Western religious tradition, it was probably inevitable that secular values would become prominent.

The Renaissance and Reformation also drew more people than ever before into contact with formal ideas. Renaissance intellectuals were very interested in promoting education, although primarily for the elites. They wanted the upper classes to gain a new appreciation of classical literary styles and philosophies, and they set standards for upper-class education that have lasted, in Western society, into our own century. It was

also during the Renaissance that Western society developed the printing press, a technique well advanced in Asia but new to the West and now improved by the use of movable block type. (Paper also became common in the West at this point, although the first papermaking factory, copied from the Arabs, had been established in the 13th century.) Printing was first used by its German inventor, Gutenberg, to produce Bibles, but by the end of the 15th century, printing presses were publishing a variety of Renaissance materials. Then, with the Reformation, printing presses spread to the literate public the theological disputes that consumed Western religious leaders. Most people still could not read, but the rate of literacy began to rise, particularly in Protestant areas, and those who could read now had a variety of styles and viewpoints to consider.

It was during the 17th century, however, that the real break in Western culture occurred, thanks in large part to the Scientific Revolution. Impor-

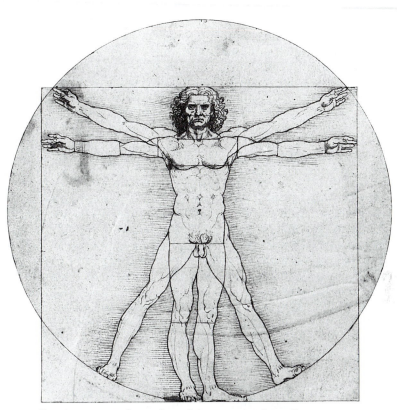

Renaissance art often reflected the emerging Scientific
Revolution: anatomical sketches by Leonardo da Vinci.

tant artistic work continued. So did significant endeavors in theology, both Protestant and Catholic. The most widely published works were sermons and other religious tracts. Western culture, in other words, remained vigorously diverse, even contradictory. However, it was the rise of science that provided the most significant single theme.

The Scientific Revolution consisted of new knowledge, particularly about physics and astronomy but also about biology and chemistry. It consisted of new instrumentation to measure the heavens and examine microscopically the creatures of the earth. The movement became increasingly defiant of past wisdom. Scientists who proved that old ideas about an Earth-centered universe were wrong were also showing up

the glaring inadequacies of ancient knowledge. Many people found these claims shocking, precisely because a belief in ancient wisdom was so deeply ingrained. Galileo, who insisted on the heliocentric universe, was forced to recant his claims by the Catholic church. Nonetheless, the idea of progress in knowledge through experiment and critical thinking steadily gained ground. In France, René Descartes boldly set out to reexamine all past wisdom, his theory being that nothing should be assumed correct simply because of tradition. Skepticism was the order of the day among vanguard intellectuals; by the 1680s, this approach was being directly applied to religion, as writers sought to disprove beliefs in miracles and other Christian claims.

The European Scientific Revolution built on the current of direct observation and experiment that had begun in the later Middle Ages, with work on optics and other subjects. In the 16th century, this current began to swell. It was then that a Polish monk, Copernicus, used astronomical observation and mathematical calculation to prove that the Hellenistic belief in the Earth as the center of the universe was wrong; rather, the Earth moved around the sun. His finding was taken up shortly before 1600, when a great deal of astronomical observation began, from Italy to Scandinavia. Scientists developed a new understanding of the principles of planetary motion. Again using a combination of observation and experiment, Galileo and others began to generate theories about the impact of gravity, proving experimentally that Aristotle was incorrect in claiming that heavy bodies fell more quickly than light ones. Here was another blow to the dominance of traditional wisdom. Scientists shifted to an emphasis on what new truths they could discover.

Although work of this sort greatly advanced the knowledge of physics, biology also gained ground. Better instrumentation and observation led to a more accurate understanding of the human anatomy. The Englishman William Harvey showed how blood circulates through the body. Other scientists studied the behavior of gases. Thus, by the mid-17th century, the Western world was responsible for a veritable explosion of knowledge about the physical universe. As part of this process, many intellectuals came to challenge the idea that learning was best approached through a reverence for tradition, for experiment was seen as an alternative, and sometimes more accurate, path to truth.

The Scientific Revolution also applied to science much of the rationalism that had informed Greek and then medieval scholastic thinking. Here was a crucial link in Western intellectual life, even amid great change. Most scientists believed that they could do more than disprove old theories and discover new data. They believed that they could formulate general laws of natural behavior—that there was a correlation between human reason and the orderliness of the universe. Here, the physics of Isaac Newton late in the 17th century seemed to culminate a long quest. In three basic laws, Newton established how physical motion operated, on Earth and throughout the universe: a physical body preserves its momentum in a straight line unless forced by outside pressure to deviate; change of motion is proportional to the impressed force and takes place in the direction to which the force is applied; and to every action there is always an equal reaction. Additional work on the law of gravity showed why the planets remain in orbit and explained why objects fall at the same speed. Laws of this sort could be mathematically expressed, and Newton and others added to not only scientific theory but also mathematical knowledge, particularly in the area of calculus.

What had occurred, by 1700, was a real intellectual revolution in the West, and the establishment of a central scientific approach that no civilization had ever before ventured. The importance of a scientific outlook in Western history after the late 16th century therefore raises the obvious comparative question: why the West? Several other civilizations had produced significant scientific achievement. Byzantium preserved Hellenistic science, although it did not advance it and encourage scientific work elsewhere in eastern Europe. Important science in India and the Middle East was ultimately limited by the rise of narrower religious concerns and, at key points, by political instability. China poses a more interesting case still, for the Chinese preserved a long tradition of elaborate empirical work. Unlike the West, of course, China had little contact with scientific discoveries outside its borders; its intellectual pursuits lacked the exciting challenge of mastering Greek and Arab learning. Chinese thought also tended to stress ethical knowledge over elaborate inquiry. Zhu Xi's emphasis on knowledge might have encouraged scientific inquiry, but it was modified by traditional Confucian stress on the individual's values. Chinese science itself differed from the Western approach in its more complete empiricism—its lack of large-scale, rationalistic attempts to fathom general laws of nature. Thus, despite extensive biological and physical data, the Chinese did not promote an overall belief that science was key to a basic understanding of the universe. Finally, we will see that at the time Western science began to surge, Chinese intellectual life was becoming more stagnant, a fact that would, ironically, encourage Chinese scholars to ignore Western scientific achievements for some time.

Western science involved popularization as well as basic discoveries. Information about the new science spread widely among the educated public. Scientific societies were founded to promote research. Many business and professional people began to dabble in science, finding new species of plants and animals and participating, however humbly, in this exciting expansion of knowledge. Popularized tracts explained scientific laws and advanced the idea that knowledge was progressing and reason, not faith, was the key to understanding how the physical world works.

Through scientific ferment, which simply grew as time passed, religion declined in importance in providing a basic intellectual framework. Rationalistic science became more vital in shaping habits of thought than ever before, in any civilization. Without necessarily eroding the importance of art, it did supersede creative expression as the foremost cultural influence; as one result, the late 17th and 18th centuries were not particularly significant in terms of stylistic developments, except in music. Scientific thought was heralded as the way to knowledge. And rationalism would generate steady progress in the development of such knowledge, as intellectual leaders gradually turned away from a belief that classical learning was the basic path to truth. It was thought that rationalism might have other beneficial effects as well. Scientific writers such as Francis Bacon, in England, argued that further discoveries would lead to technological improvements, making life easier and more rewarding.

These ideas gained ground during the 18th century. Scientific work continued. Chemists discovered much about the functions of oxygen. Biologists acquired increasing knowledge of a variety of animal and plant species. The science of psychology began to take shape, as scholars studied the workings of the human mind.

More important still was the effort to apply the principles of the Scientific Revolution to discussions of human nature and human affairs. Enlightenment thinkers, centered in France but operating in many countries, continued to popularize science and to attack errors of faith and superstition. They also developed a number of social sciences by writing of political and economic systems. The basic idea was that rational laws could be applied to social as well as physical behavior, producing an understanding of how humankind throughout the world operates. The Scottish philosopher Adam Smith, in his *Wealth of Nations*, thus posited a number of clear principles of economic behavior, based on the notion that people act according to self-interest and, through competition, would work to promote economic advancement if they are not distracted by government interference. This was a compelling statement of the doctrine of laissez-faire, that private initiative rather than state intervention promotes economic progress. Smith's work was also a ground-breaking treatise on social science, as it suggested that general models of human behavior could be rationally derived.

In addition, Enlightenment thinkers believed in the inherent goodness and rationality of human beings. Progress in knowledge convinced them that more general human progress was also possible. Children can improve through education; old-fashioned methods of discipline were ridiculed. Criminals can become useful members of society if treated humanely; traditional methods of punishment were replaced or outlawed. Political life can improve if people are free, and the state does not try to force religious conformity and pays some attention to popular demands. The Enlightenment did not, in fact,

Understanding Cultures

A REVOLUTION IN POPULAR CULTURE

The big cultural developments of the early modern period may seem abstract. The rise of Protestantism and Catholic reaction, the printing press, the Scientific Revolution are easy to list, but what did they mean? And particularly, what did they mean beneath the level of a formal intellectual life?

Historians have increasingly realized that between about 1600 and 1750, some huge changes occurred in the ways most ordinary people thought about quite basic aspects of life. Here are some examples:

- In 1600, many peasants did not bother naming children until age 2, because so many died. When parents did name infants, they often reused the names of children who had died. In 1750, naming occurred soon after birth, names were not reused, and many parents chose unusual, more distinctive names. This is a concrete example of the new individualism.

- In 1600, young people when they kissed often bit each other hard. In some regions, young men claimed possession of a woman by urinating on her dress. By 1750, kissing became a more private and gentler experience, and biting declined. Here are some concrete examples of changing attitudes about love and emotion, and about the family.

- In 1600, when a valued object was lost, ordinary Europeans turned to cunning men, who used magic sticks and incantations to find the misplaced object. By 1750, cunning men no longer existed—part of the growing (although still not complete) trend against magic. Instead, people visited official lost-and-found offices, at least in cities, or advertised in local newspapers. Attitudes toward the natural world and social environments were changing.

These examples are just a few. Under the impetus of new commercial levels, new family forms, growing literacy (thanks in part to printing), and religious and scientific change, people were thinking differently. There was no organized movement, such as a major religion, behind this great cultural change, although the Enlightenment may be viewed as somewhat missionary in its attempts to undermine what it termed common superstition. The work of historians also results from change, for example, in providing cultural bases for later developments in politics and industry. The transformation of culture raises basic questions about cause, result, and participation (who still believed in the old ways). It also raises questions about how Europeans, armed with some of these new ideas, would view the rest of the world.

produce a single political theory. Many writers were attracted to the idea of enlightened despotism, believing that a reform-minded ruler could produce social progress. Others talked of the importance of constitutions and parliaments. But they all agreed that political life, like other aspects of life, could be reformed, through rational calculations and a belief in the essential goodness of human nature. Late in the Enlightenment, during the 1780s and 1790s, this kind of thinking even produced statements of socialism, arguing

that property laws should be reformed in the name of equality, and of feminism, asserting that women as well as men should participate in political life and benefit from legal reforms.

The Enlightenment, then, served as the intellectual origin of a number of modern impulses in Western society. It set the stage for modern political movements, from liberalism through socialism. In emphasizing secular rather than religious thinking, it outlined a rationalistic approach rooted in social science that continues to describe this part of the Western intellectual world even today. It promoted a host of humanitarian reform movements. Most basically, by extending and translating the results of the Scientific Revolution, it established the framework for modern Western intellectual life. There were changes to come, to be sure. Most Westerners no longer think in precisely the same terms as those of the Enlightenment. However, many of the issues and fundamental approaches of the Enlightenment remain current. Simply put, the modern way of thinking, in Western society, took shape between about 1680 and 1750.

The Enlightenment hardly resulted in unanimous approval of its basic beliefs. A broader dissemination of some of the basic ideas was still to come. Numerous Christian writers objected vigorously to Enlightenment thinking, and they had many followers. Nonetheless, the Enlightenment was a popularizing movement. Leading writers, such as the Frenchman Voltaire, who argued for human freedom and against church domination, became wealthy through the widespread sale of their works. From the aristocracy to the urban artisanry, many people were aware of at least some of the Enlightenment claims. Huge publishing ventures, like the *Encyclopédie* in France and later the *Encyclopaedia Britannica* in England, tried to summarize all relevant human knowledge in Enlightenment terms, with an emphasis on science and social science and a pronounced interest in technological improvements. Furthermore, the Enlightenment was essentially a Western-wide movement, striking chords in France and Britain but also Italy, Germany, Scandinavia, and the British colonies of North America. In this sense, it rivaled the earlier spread of Christianity in providing a common cultural framework for Western civilization.

TRANSFORMATIONS IN ECONOMIC AND SOCIAL LIFE

The Role of Commerce

During the early modern period, a steady expansion of commerce, along with significant changes

in culture, helped transform Western life. Renaissance leaders were proud of the commercial bustle in their cities. Reformation thinkers also tended to favor trade. Luther and Calvin actually influenced the public to discard the traditional belief that merchants might be pursuing false values. Since ordinary people could have direct links with God, the duties and tasks of everyday life were not seen as contradicting religious purposes. Of course, God came first, but commercial success could be construed as proof that God's favor had been won. Not all Protestants became fervent entrepreneurs, however, and Catholic business activities grew as well. But there was some relationship between the spread of Protestantism and the increasing interest in commerce. Finally, the expanding monarchies encouraged merchants to form powerful trading alliances. State backing helped organize great merchant companies to trade with Russia, India and southeast Asia, and the Americas.

Commerce was also stimulated by the new supplies of gold and silver brought back from the New World, particularly from Spain's American colonies. During the 16th century, these precious metals produced a price revolution in Europe. As the supply of money rose on its traditional gold-and-silver base, the production of foods and manufactured goods could not keep pace, and the result was rapid inflation. Rising prices encouraged merchants to take greater risks, because they could borrow money with the understanding that it would be worth less when they had to pay it back. Capitalists also saw the profits to be made in trade with far-flung parts of the world. Asian spices commanded handsome prices. From the late 16th century onward, grain from Poland and Russia and furs, sugar, and tobacco from the Americas were imported at increasingly rapid rates, all through trade organized by European merchants.

Commercial expansion began to focus greater attention on Europe's manufacturing base. Growing wealth at home produced new markets for goods, and there was also a need to produce goods to sell to foreign markets. Although most production remained in artisan hands, a significant expansion of domestic manufacturing took place under capitalist auspices. Merchants in this system provided raw materials, particularly textile fibers, to workers scattered in rural settings, who spun and wove the fibers into cloth on simple machines; their products were then collected and paid for, and sold by the merchants on a wide market. Even in the artisan system, commercial expansion created a growing gap between guild masters and their journeymen; as masters pressured their workers to produce more, many journeymen became a permanent paid labor force, manufacturing items such as books, guns, and metal tools for wide market sales.

European technology steadily improved in this climate of economic expansion. Better mining techniques allowed the increased production of iron and coal. Better mill wheels facilitated the processing of grains. Textile equipment, although still manually guided, was also becoming more sophisticated. By the 17th century, European technology had no peer in the world in most branches of production, and the pace of change continued to be high. Early in the 18th century, the first steam engine was devised in England to pump water out of deep mine shafts. In 1733, the Englishman James Kay invented the flying shuttle, which automatically interwove fibers to make cloth; with this new system, one weaver could now complete the work of two, although the looms were still powered by hand.

Improvements in agriculture were somewhat slower in coming, but the expansion of commerce and the growth of cities encouraged increasing numbers of farmers to produce for the market. Late in the 17th century, Dutch farmers began to experiment with new crops that would replenish the fertility of the soil without necessitating periods of fallow, in which nothing could be grown. The Dutch, hard-pressed to support a large population in a small land, also developed new methods of draining swamps and constructing dikes to keep out ocean tides. Interest in agricultural improvement spread further in the 18th century, and many societies were organized to

disseminate knowledge of new crops and fertilizers and new machines to sow seeds.

The tide of economic change must not be exaggerated, however. Most people continued to use rather traditional methods, in both agriculture and manufacturing. Most people still did not depend heavily on market sales for their livelihood. The merchant class expanded, but it did not yet command the highest social levels. Many, indeed, still aspired to become aristocrats in their own right, for moneymaking alone did not provide adequate prestige. Nonetheless, Western Europe became more substantially commercialized than ever before. Enlightenment thinkers, generally hostile to the aristocracy, which they saw as an idle class, praised hard work and profitmaking, a sign that social values were changing even before the social structure had been revolutionized.

One clear effect of commercial expansion was that Europe's wealth increased. An Englishman, writing in the late 1580s about village life, noted "three things to be marvelously altered in England within his own sound remembrance." First, farmers' cottages had more chimneys, which meant they were bigger and better heated. Second, beds and pillows had replaced straw mats for sleeping. And third, pewterware, instead of wooden utensils, was used for eating. With time, the list of advances in the standard of living continued to expand. By the early 1600s, French peasants began to consume wine fairly regularly with their meals. This was a sign of greater wealth, and also of the growing market production of wines, which could not be effected in every area of France. A frenzy of tulip buying occurred in the Netherlands in the early 17th century, one of Europe's first great consumer fads. People invested in tulip bulbs, tried to be the first to have a new flower, even bought pictures of tulips. By 1700, ordinary people in western Europe were consuming coffee, tea, and sugar— all imported goods that they had to buy on the market and that they therefore had to have enough money to afford. By this time, European farmers and artisans had far more objects in their possession—tools, furnishings, and the like—than any other people in the world. Consumerism advanced still further in the 18th century.

However, new wealth was by no means evenly distributed. Some parts of the Western world were richer than others. Material standards lagged in Germany, in part because of the devastation of the Thirty Years' War. They also lagged in Spain, where merchant activity remained rather low despite the influx of wealth from the colonies; most Spanish gold passed to the vigorous merchants and banks of northern Europe. Social disparities also intensified. As a core group of farmers or peasants increased in size—the people who could sell to urban markets and whose standard of living thus rose—the poverty of those without property also grew. Western Europe by the 17th century faced significant problems of poor relief. Almshouses and other institutions designed to aid the poor, but also to isolate them, were one common result. The existence of growing pockets of poverty amid rising wealth represented another important theme for European society; it is a social contradiction with which Westerners are still grappling today.

Social and economic change also produced recurrent unrest. Many journeymen resented the growing power of guild masters and formed associations to promote their own interests. The first strikes in Western history occurred during the Renaissance. Riots were even more common, continuing a theme from the later Middle Ages. Peasants periodically rebelled against ever steeper exactions from landlords. Both rural and urban riots commonly arose when grain and bread were in short supply. Considerable popular unrest accompanied the tensions of the Reformation. French peasants rose in many regions during the 1590s, in the aftermath of the religious wars. They attacked their landlords, who "had reduced them to starvation, violated their wives and daughters, stolen their cattle and wasted their land," while urban merchants with whom they had to trade sought "only the ruin of the poor people, for our ruin is their wealth." Popular unrest also surfaced during the English civil wars, with farmers and urban workers organizing to demand political rights and economic reforms. These uprisings produced an amazing series of revolts around 1648, in not only England but also southern Italy and elsewhere. Protest declined somewhat during the next decades, partly because population growth, which had been substantial during the 16th century, leveled off. But the early modern period was not a peaceful time in Western society, even aside from the recurrent wars.

The Role of the Family

Social change also involved the Western family. During the 15th and 16th centuries, the characteristic structure of the family began to shift, producing a "European-style" family that was quite different from the patterns of most other agricultural societies. The contributing factors were simple. First, common people began to marry at a rather late age—about 27 or 28 (members of the aristocracy, in contrast, married much earlier). A rather sizable minority of ordinary people never married at all. The reason for these developments was a desire to protect family property against the demands of too many children. Late marriages led to reduced birth rates, so that a given family would not have more than three or four children living to adulthood. While understandable, such a system required considerable self-control and family supervision, for it meant that young people passed many years between puberty and the point at which heterosexual activity was generally permissible—in marriage. Tensions increased between young adults and older parents, for economic independence and marriage normally depended on the death or retirement of the elderly. Suspicion and fear led many older people to prepare careful contracts to spell out what support they would receive from their children if they turned over their land. The new family pattern also promoted greater interaction between men and women. Men remained officially and legally the heads of their families. But with the emphasis now on rather small units, a husband

and wife and their children, economic cooperation between men and women increased. Generally, the new family structure shielded Europeans from the population density that had long been a fact of life in east Asian and Indian society.

During the 17th century and beyond, changes in the quality of family life contributed to earlier structural shifts. Europeans began to spend more leisure time within the family environment. Meals at home became more elaborate than before. This was partly the result of growing wealth, but it also involved some explicit choices. Women became the family agents who regulated its social life, preparing more intricate dishes and presiding over mealtime ceremonies and conversation. Here was a new aspect of Western family life that continued to gain in importance until very recently.

Family affection was also increasingly encouraged. Seventeenth-century Protestant writers stressed the importance of love as an ingredient of family life. As one English minister put it, "Keep up your Conjugal Love in a constant heat and vigor." This growing emphasis on the family as a center of emotional pleasure, which spread to Catholic areas by the 18th century, resulted in significant transformation. Fostered by religious developments, it may also have been a reaction to rapid social and economic change in the wider environment; families were seen as a comfortable and reliable refuge. Here, too, themes were set in motion that perpetuated to recent times. There were implications, finally, for the treatment of children within this new family environment. By the late 17th century, many writers were advocating love, rather than harsh physical discipline, as the means of raising children. They developed the revolutionary idea that parents owed children certain rights and protections, rather than espousing the traditional belief that children were obliged to accept whatever their parents might impose. The implications of all this change where women were concerned was not so clear. Their role in the family other than as bearers of children improved, but opportunities narrowed; in Protestant areas, the abolition of religious orders made marriage even more important for women.

Overall, changes for women pointed in conflicting directions. Their family status improved, but they were more tied to it. Skilled urban jobs became harder to get, as male guilds pushed women out. The interdependence of men and women in Europe's nuclear families might encourage joint decision-making, but it could promote dispute. Some women gained new education, but the Reformation stressed the father as the family's Bible-reader and moral guide. During times of ferment, such as the English civil wars, women petitioned for political attention, but they were turned away. Even the freedom-loving Enlightenment mainly ignored women or ridiculed their intellectual powers. But some upper-class women gained prestige by sponsoring *salons*—receptions—for male artists and philosophers. Finally, the emergence of greater consumerism emphasized attractive clothing for women, as if the gender had a particular obligation to be pretty.

Changes in family life, along with the shifts in broader economic and social structure, reveal a society that was beginning to alter some very basic patterns. Fundamental features of daily existence, even human emotion or at least its recommended expression, were taking new forms. Here was a potential source of further change as well. As an example, if parents began to change the way they treated their children, spanking them less often, drawing them more actively into an orbit of parental affection, these children might mature into somewhat different kinds of adults. During the 18th century, child-rearing practices changed still further. Widespread Western practices of swaddling young children—wrapping them tightly so that parents could work without worrying about their coming to harm—began to disappear. Children grew up a bit freer, receiving more active adult care in place of physical restraints. These changes, widely urged by Enlightenment writers, who believed that children would improve through better treatment, had significant implications for Western adults. If child-rearing became freer, might adults not also seek greater liberty?

HOW EARLY MODERN TRENDS IN THE WEST INTERRELATED

The various trends of early modern Western society did not neatly mesh. There was overlap, to be sure. Commercial development and economic expansion were encouraged by some of the ideas of the Renaissance and Reformation, although not always intentionally; economic change also was the catalyst for some of the key values of the Enlightenment. Increased interest in carefully planned organization showed in business ventures, publishing, and government bureaucracy. Even more amorphous values, such as greater individualism, related cultural and religious movements to capitalism and possibly to family organization—the family was seen less as an economic institution, more as an emotional bond among individuals.

On the other hand, different currents had varied results, and many key shifts were slow and uneven. Changes in beliefs and the economy, however, added up to a major strain on people at various levels. One key symptom was a wave of witchcraft trials that occurred in many parts of western Europe, and ultimately New England, from the late 15th century until the middle of the 17th century. Europeans had long believed in witches and magical powers, but they had never considered these forces to be such ominous threats as they did during these decades, when witchcraft trials sent hundreds of accused people to death and involved many thousands in mounting hysteria. Many factors were behind this sweeping fear. New anxieties about the poor were one cause, since many of the accused were among those bypassed by the growing prosperity. Protestant–Catholic divisions, shaking convictions about where religious truth lay, contributed to the fear. So did uncertainties about the changing roles of women and the elderly in the family (most accused witches were female, said to be "used by the devil," and a disproportionate number were elderly). There were also new confusions about how to respond to sickness (whether through doctors or by superstitious remedies). A new belief system was taking shape in Western society, but its early stages left many people insecure and fearful.

Just as the witchcraft hysteria stemmed from a variety of intense concerns generated by change, so the end of the witchcraft trials signified the continuing spread of new ideas about how to understand the world. Growing numbers of officials and ordinary people simply stopped believing that witchcraft was a real phenomenon, capable of disrupting the laws of nature. Although beliefs in witchcraft persisted and a few trials continued into the 18th century, the craze ended in most places by the 1680s. The spread of Enlightenment ideas in later decades, although again not universal in a society in which most people still could not read, was a further sign that the Western outlook was shifting in some common directions.

For all its tensions and confusions, the fact remained that by the 18th century, western Europe had created a distinctive kind of agricultural society, compared to the traditions of the other great civilizations of the world. Its unusual qualities stemmed primarily from the changes that had been occurring since the late 15th century at almost all levels of social activity. The West was unusually commercial, unusually scientific, and shaped by family structures that encouraged property control and considerable individualism. Not accidentally, Western society was simultaneously extending its influence to the rest of the world, despite political organizations that were in many ways inferior to the world's great empires of the time.

ISSUES AND CONNECTIONS

Early modern western Europe did not change in a clear, straight direction. The Reformation stressed religious values after the more worldly Italian Renaissance. New religions, such as Methodism, were still cropping up in the 18th century, even though the larger trend was toward a more secular culture. Different groups and regions changed at different paces. There were traditional subsistence villages quite close to villages actively participating in a market economy for money. As respectable people turned against the witchcraft concept by 1700, many ordinary people still saw witches behind every misfortune. The key point is to see the major themes of change while not ignoring complexity. In politics, given the split between the parliamentary monarchies and absolutism, there was outright disunity in the West quite apart from military rivalries.

Despite complexity, it is easy to see the arrival, in early modern western Europe, of many patterns that persist today, though all have changed a lot since 1750. Scientific culture, more commercial capitalism, signs of consumerism, new tensions over poverty, new questions about women's roles—the list is considerable. Some historians have argued that the modern West had emerged, particularly in culture, by the 1680s.

SUGGESTED WEB SITES

For Renaissance art and daily life, refer to http://history.evansville.net/renaissa.html. On the life of Martin Luther, see http://luther.de/legenden.html in German, or the English version http://www.luther.de/e/legenden.html.

SUGGESTED READINGS

For an overview of developments in Western society during this period, including extensive bibliographies, see Sheldon Watt, *A Social History of Western Europe, 1450–1720* (1984), and John Merriman, *History of Modern European Civilization*, Vol. 1 (1996). Charles Tilly, *Big Structures, Large Processes, Huge Comparisons* (1985), offers an analytical framework based on major change; see

also Tilly's edited volume, *The Formation of National States in Western Europe* (1975), and Fernand Braudel, *Civilization and Capitalization*, 3 vols. (1952). Coverage of the Renaissance and the religious transformations can be found in J. F. New, *The Renaissance and Reformation: A Short History* (1977); K. H. Kannenfeldt, ed., *The Renaissance: Medieval or Modern* (1959); J. Atkinson, *Martin Luther and the Birth of Protestantism* (1981); D. Knowles, *Bare Ruined Choirs* (1976); J. H. Plumb, *The Italian Renaissance* (1986); O. Chadwick, *The Reformation* (1983); Steven Ozment, *The Age of Reform, 1520–1550* (1980); and Hubert Jedin and John Dolan, eds., *Reformation and Counter Reformation* (1980). On the important changes in science, consult H. Butterfield, *Origins of Modern Science* (1965), and A. R. Hall, *From Galileo to Newton, 1630–1720* (1982). Crucial political changes are addressed in G. Clark, *Early Modern Europe from about 1450 to about 1750* (1960). Europe's economic development is treated in R. L. Reynolds, *Europe Emerges: Transition Toward an Industrial World Wide Society 1600–1750* (1972), and R. Ehrenberg, *Capital and Finance in the Age of the Renaissance* (1948). On important transformations in popular life and behavior during the period, see Peter Burke, *Popular Culture in Early Modern Europe* (1978); P. Ariès, *Centuries of Childhood: A Social History of Family Life* (1965); P. Stearns, ed., *The Other Side of Western Civilization*, Vol. 2, 6th ed. (1999); and Merry Wiesner Hanks, *Women and Gender in Early Modern Europe* (1993). See also Robert Duplessis, *Transitions to Capitalism in Early Modern Europe* (1997).

For additional recent work, see Samuel Cohn, *The Black Death Transformed* (2002); Andrew Zega, *Palaces of the Sun King: Versailles, Trianon, Marly* (2002); Elizabeth Cohen, *Daily Life in Renaissance Italy* (2001); and Alina Payne, *Antiquity and its Interpreters* (2000).

The Rise of
Eastern Europe

Along with Africa and the Americas, Russia and eastern Europe were dramatically affected by the rise of the West during the early modern period. By the 18th century, some smaller regions, such as Poland, produced cheap grains for export to the West, using serf labor in a fashion not unlike the estate systems in Latin America. The Russian story was different, however. In contrast to the Americas, where local populations had little choice, Russian leaders deliberately chose to imitate certain Western ways. This pattern began haltingly in the 16th century and then accelerated during the 18th century. Explicit choice did not preclude important tensions as the Russian economy experienced still more Western influence and cultural reactions formed against too much imitation. Nonetheless, Russia's relation to the West remained unique.

One reason for the distinctiveness lay in the new trend toward expansion, initiated in the 15th century, that to begin with had nothing to do with the West. Russia's dynamism increased long before it had significant contacts with the West. The West was later courted, although very selectively, to help maintain the surge of expansion.

What causes a civilization to rise? The question, now a familiar one, remains complex. Western civilization expanded on the basis of a diverse but distinctive culture, which produced an aggressive, conquering spirit, plus, a rapidly improving technology. Russia's case, coincident in time, was different. Shaking off Mongol domination, the Russians embarked on a policy of conquest without a major technological impetus.

Russia shared some expansionist thinking with the West. Both could look back to the precedent of the Roman Empire as an example of what societies could do when they were truly great. Both were Christian, and although the Russian missionary spirit was perhaps less active than that of the West, Christianity may help explain a common desire to achieve new victories. However, Russia long lagged behind the West technologically; it remained backward by

Western standards into the 20th century. It lacked the merchant tradition or commercial expertise of the West; indeed, Russia during the early modern period depended considerably on Western-directed trade patterns. In these respects, Russian differences from the West increased in the early modern period.

Russia did have a large and gradually growing population. It occupied a strategic geographical location, hovering between Europe and Asia, surrounded, except in the north, by few natural barriers. This position made it vulnerable to invasion, as the Mongols had proved, but it also facilitated expansion when the Russians decided to follow the Mongol example. Russia also had the advantage of excellent natural resources, although its climate placed certain limits on agriculture. Russia's iron ore spurred manufacturing and weaponry. Furs and timber could be traded not only with the West but also with Asia, which helped fuel expansion.

The early modern period saw an elaboration of characteristic Russian social and political institutions. Earlier, Russian civilization had been barely defined. Now, building on many precedents, it was more fully formed. It became increasingly important as the Russians constructed one of the world's great empires.

KEY QUESTIONS   *Russia proved to be the most successful of the land-based "gunpowder empires" formed in the early modern period. How does it compare to the other empires, like the Ottoman or Mughal? How, also, did it change, when its characteristics of 1750 are compared with those of 1450? Russia's contacts with the West set the final main questions: what did Russia westernize, and why, and what did it shelter from westernization?*

PATTERNS OF EARLY MODERN RUSSIAN HISTORY

Russia's emergence as a new power, first in eastern Europe and western Asia and ultimately on a still larger scale, depended initially on its winning freedom from Mongol (Tatar) control. Mongol influence had not reshaped Russian institutions significantly, although many Russians had adopted Mongol styles of dress and social habits. Most Russians remained Orthodox Christians; most maintained a separate identity from that of the Mongols. Moreover, local Russian princes had continued to rule, although paying tribute to their Mongol military overlords. It was the duchy of Moscow that served as the center for the Russian liberation effort, beginning in the 14th century. Under Ivan III, or Ivan the Great, who claimed succession from the Rurik dynasty, a large part of Russia was finally freed after 1462. Ivan organized a strong army—giving the new government a military emphasis it would long retain. He also capitalized on Russian and Orthodox loyalties—that is, a kind of nationalism along with religion—to win support for his campaigns. By 1480, Moscow had been freed from Mongol control and acquired a vast territory running from the borders of Poland, in the west, to the Ural Mountains.

It was under Ivan that Russian beliefs in an imperial mission took on a new shape. Ivan's marriage to the niece of the last Byzantine emperor prompted him to proclaim himself the protector of all Orthodox churches and also to insist that Russia had succeeded Byzantium as the "third Rome." Accordingly, Ivan entitled himself *tsar*, or Caesar—the "autocrat of all the Russians." The next important tsar, Ivan IV, or Ivan the Terrible, attacked the Russian nobles whom he suspected of conspiracy; many were killed. But Russian expansion continued nevertheless. Ivan III and Ivan IV encouraged some peasants to migrate to the lands seized from the Mongols and other groups, particularly in the south, along the Caspian Sea, and in the Urals. These peasant-adventurers, called *cossacks*, were true Russian pioneers, combining agricultural skills with impressive military prowess on horseback. During the 16th century, the cossacks not only completed their conquest of the Caspian Sea area but also, early in the century, moved across the Ural Mountains into Siberia, beginning the gradual takeover and settlement of these vast plains.

Russian expansion occurred despite the setbacks the Russian economy and culture had suffered under Mongol rule. Russia had become almost entirely agricultural, its earlier urban and merchant past largely forgotten. There was little trade and only localized manufacturing; although some commerce developed with central Asia, creating regional economic ties, subsistence agriculture predominated. Not only peasants but also many landlords lived under poor material conditions. Rates of illiteracy were unusually high for an agricultural society, and artistic and literary production had almost ceased. In this situation, Russia was open to new influences from western Europe, with its expanding commercial powers. Ivan III had been eager to launch diplomatic missions to leading Western states as a symbol of Russia's renewed independence and a sign that it wanted contact with the Western network of international relations. During the reign of Ivan IV, British merchants established trading relations with Russia, selling manufactured products in exchange for furs and raw materials. Soon, outposts of Western merchants were established in Moscow and other centers.

Ivan IV's death without an heir set off the Time of Troubles, early in the 17th century, in which Russian nobles, the boyars, attacked tsarist power; several neighboring states, including Sweden and Poland, captured Russian territory. However, in 1613, a noble assembly chose a member of the Romanov family as tsar; this family would rule Russia until the great revolution of 1917. Michael Romanov drove out foreign invaders and restored order, although the power of the nobles limited the tsarist government until late in the 17th century. Even amid some confusion, however, Russian military efforts continued; successful wars against Poland resulted in the annexation of the Ukraine, including Kiev, and extended Russian boundaries in southeastern Europe to the Ottoman Empire. Russian settlers

moved into some of these areas, forming new minorities, and use of the Russian language gradually spread.

A second Romanov, Alexis, restored tsarist autocracy by abolishing the assemblies of nobles and claiming new authority over the Russian church. Alexis was eager not only to gain power, but also to purge the Orthodox church of many of the superstitions that had developed during Mongol rule. His reform movement, however, antagonized some Russians, who were known as "Old Believers"; their resistance to church reforms caused thousands of them to be exiled to Siberia or southern Russia, where they extended Russia's colonizing activities. Alexis also developed cultural as well as economic contacts with Western nations.

Alexis's son, Peter I, or Peter the Great (1689–1725), greatly expanded his father's work. He was an energetic leader of exceptional intelligence. A giant himself, standing 6 feet, 8 inches tall, he was eager to reform his giant nation still further. He traveled widely in the West, incognito, seeking Western allies for a crusade against Turkish power in Europe. He even worked as a ship's carpenter in Holland, gaining an interest in Western science and technology and bringing back scores of Western artisans with him to Russia. Politically, Peter defended tsarist autocracy firmly, vanquishing revolts with great cruelty. In foreign policy, Peter attacked the Ottoman Empire without significant results, then warred with Sweden, winning extensive Russian territory on the eastern coast of the Baltic Sea and reducing Sweden to the status of a second-rate power. Russia now had a "window on the Baltic," including an ice-free port, and from this time onward became a major player in European diplomatic and military conflict. Peter the Great, in accordance with his desire to reform Russia in some Western directions, commemorated Russia's emergence into the European diplomatic orbit by moving his capital from Moscow to a new Baltic city that he named St. Petersburg.

РАСКОЛЬНІКЪ ГОВОРИТЪ
СЛУШАИ ЦЫРЮЛЬНИКЬ
Я БОРОДЫ СТРИЗЬ НЕ
ХОЧУ ВОТЪ ПЕД НЯ НА
ТЕБЯ СКОРО КАРАУЛЬ ЗАКРУ

ЦЫРЮЛ НІИКЪ ХО
ЗТЪ РАСКОЛЬНІКУ
БОРОДУ СТРИЗЬ •

Tsar Peter the Great cutting off the beard of an
Orthodox Old Believer. This 18th-century cartoon
shows the westernization of hair styles.

Internally, Peter's reforms concentrated mainly on streamlining Russia's bureaucratic and military apparatus and increasing central control under the tsar. He improved the organization and weaponry of the army and, with help from Western advisors, created the first Russian navy. New munitions factories and shipyards facilitated this effort, and a substantial iron industry developed: Russia would not come to depend on the West for weapons production. Peter eliminated former noble councils, establishing a set of advisors under his control and a specialized set of ministries in their stead. The central government appointed provincial governors, and although town councils were elected, here too a tsar-appointed magistrate served as the final authority. The church was placed still more firmly under state control, with the tsar as head of the church and a committee of bishops, under his direction, responsi-

ble for running religious affairs. Peter's regime rationalized law codes and extended them throughout the empire. The tax system was reformed, and taxes on ordinary Russian peasants steadily increased. Finally, the bureaucrats who ran the government were given special training, and Peter relied on non-nobles as well as nobles in his search for the best possible talents.

Peter the Great thus sought to create a state and military force that could compete with those of his rivals and peers in western Europe. He also introduced some additional reforms designed to make Russian manners—particularly those of the aristocracy—more westernized. Edicts were issued requiring nobles to shave off their beards and wear Western dress; in symbolic ceremonies, Peter removed the Mongol features, for instance, long sleeves, of nobles' garments. Women in the upper classes were encouraged to become less isolated. Upper-class women could attend theater and ballet, as in the West. Peter abolished a wedding tradition whereby the bride's father handed a whip to the groom, symbolizing the transfer of male power. Russia even imported the custom of Christmas trees, from Germany. These reforms were more than cosmetic. They were designed to enhance Russia in Western eyes and to jolt the noble class out of their established routine.

This was, however, a very selective process of westernization. Although the education and culture of the aristocracy were profoundly altered (enhancing the tsar's control along with westernizing much of the ruling class), the conditions of the masses were not significantly changed. Peter had no desire to initiate wage labor, as opposed to serfdom, in western Europe. Nor was he interested in the parliamentary monarchies of the West. Nor, finally, did he wish to fully imitate the Western economy. His technological borrowing focused on heavy industry and munitions. He did not encourage a massive merchant class or a major role in the world economy. Westernization increased Russia's economic contacts with the West, as not only technology but artistic items had to be imported, paid for by growing raw

World Profiles

CATHERINE THE GREAT (1762–1796)

Catherine the Great was one of the most important rulers in Russian history and the only woman in their number. A German-born princess, she married Peter III, who was mentally impaired, and soon took over effective control of the government. She continued to rule as tsarina after Peter III's death. True to her own origins and the legacy of Peter the Great, Catherine continued a program of westernization. In the 1762 portrait shown here, she appears dressed in Western fashion—although with a military emphasis that was no accident. Catherine also maintained more distinctive Russian traditions and was not willing to allow Western influences to weaken her autocratic power. Many of her reform moves, as a result, were mere facades. Catherine was also responsible for laws that gave nobles more power over their serfs and, at the end of her life, for banning Western contacts and Western-inspired writings during the French Revolution. In addition to her impact on Russian history, which included successful expansion, Catherine was one of the liveliest personalities of world history, her person inspiring numerous stories and myths of great and varied sexual appetites. Even with the advantages of noble birth and marriage, what qualities would a woman need to make this kind of mark in history?

Catherine the Great, woman of uncommon power.

materials and grain exports. Russia was an unequal partner in this trade, which was handled for the most part by Western trading companies. But the bulk of the Russian economy remained outside this orbit, focusing on agriculture and limited trade with central Asia; it remained far different from its counterpart in the West.

Peter's death in 1724 was followed by several decades of weak rule, dominated by various power plays among army officers who guided the selection of several ineffective emperors and empresses. Peter III, the nephew of Peter the Great's youngest daughter, reached the throne in 1762. He himself was retarded, but his wife, a German-born princess who changed her name to Catherine, soon took matters in hand and continued to rule as empress after Peter III's death. Catherine—later, Catherine the Great—flirted with the ideas of the French Enlightenment, summoning various reform commissions that did

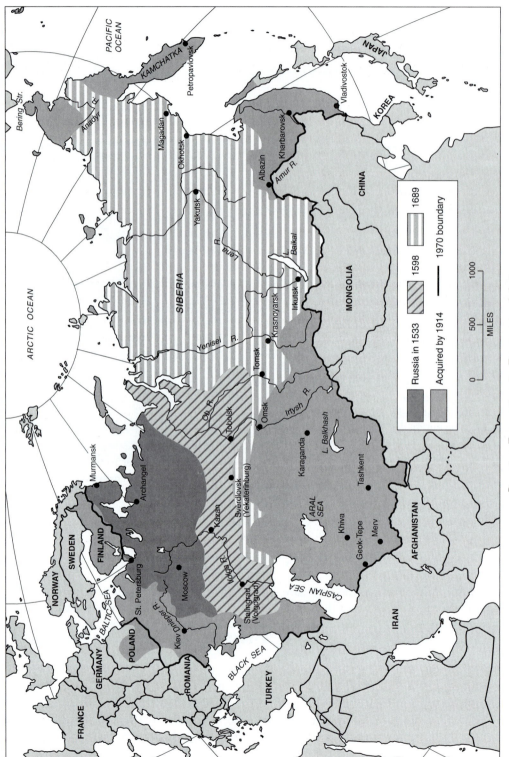

Russian Expansion in Europe and Asia

History Debate

A RUSSIAN CIVILIZATION?

Historians continue to wonder how best to fit Russia into the larger patterns of world history. A traditional impulse among Western historians was to include Russia as part of overall European history from the 15th century onward. In the 1970s, even at the height of the cold war, a French leader said that Russia was at least as European as England was. However, Russia has never been fully Western (although, of course, it may become so in the future, as many Russians currently hope and as others fear). In the 15th and 16th centuries, even as Italian artists and technical advisors were brought in, Moscow's high culture remained Byzantine; libraries, although still small, were filled with Byzantine books, mainly religious. Social structures remained dramatically different from those in the West. Russia was also heavily influenced by central Asia. The tsar called himself the khan of the north, to impress central Asian peoples, and individuals from this region took oaths of loyalty on the Qur'an. Central Asian models long guided the bureaucracy. Clearly, Russia emerged as a civilization under mixed influences, which it would continue to blend when more extensive, although selective, westernization began. The issue of how European Russia was, aside from geography, depends on what factors we use to determine the basic nature of a society.

very little. In fact, her goals continued to be those of her illustrious predecessors: to centralize power under the crown and enlarge Russia's territory. She put down a vigorous peasant uprising, led by Emelian Pugachev, who was subsequently executed. She used the Pugachev rebellion as an excuse to extend the powers of the central government in regional affairs, while confirming the nobles' control over most of the land. Catherine resumed Peter the Great's campaigns against the Ottoman Empire, with much greater success; she won new territories, including the Crimea, bordering the Black Sea. Catherine also accelerated Russian interference in Polish affairs, finally agreeing with Austria and Prussia to divide, or partition, this once vigorous state. Three partitions of Poland, in 1772, 1793, and 1795, finally eliminated Poland as an independent state, giving Russia the lion's share of the spoils. Finally, Catherine speeded the colonization of Russia's holdings in Siberia and encouraged further exploration, claiming the territory of Alaska.

Russian explorers even moved down the Pacific coast of North America into what is now northern California, while tens of thousands of pioneers spread over Siberia.

By the time of Catherine's death, in 1796, Russia had passed through slightly over three centuries of extraordinary development. It had freed itself from all traces of foreign rule, had constructed a strong central state, and perhaps most importantly of all, had extended its control over the largest land empire in the world at that point.

Russia's expansion had followed three basic directions. First, it had moved eastward, into the vast stretches of Siberia, most of which had previously been inhabited by hunting-and-gathering peoples. This expansion had brought Russia to China's borders, which were regulated by the 18th-century Amur River agreement. Russia's thrust into east Asia was bolstered by vigorous, sometimes forced, colonization; being "sent to Siberia" was no 20th-century invention, as thousands of Old Believers and other dissidents could attest. Siberia also offered new lands for agriculture; colonization not only added to Russian resources but also benefited some of the colonizers.

The second direction of Russia's expansion was toward the south, into central Asia. This expansion brought Russia to the borders of the Ottoman Empire, and Russia's increasingly successful rivalry with this empire was a key factor in Ottoman decline. Russia's central Asian holdings resulted in Russian control over a number of diverse ethnic groups, mostly Muslim. This control was again enhanced by vigorous colonization by the cossacks, bringing not only Russian rule but also a strong ethnic Russian presence into this region. Russian occupation of central Asia eliminated once and for all this region's long-standing role as a center of periodic invasions directed at other parts of Europe and Asia.

Finally, Russia moved westward along the Baltic and into Poland. By 1796, Russian borders met those of Prussia and Habsburg Austria; most of the smaller nations of eastern Europe had been eliminated. Here, too, Russia assumed control over the government of many minority peoples, including various Slavic groups, some Germans, and many Jews. The Russian empire propelled itself into the mainstream of European diplomacy, winning alliances at various points with a number of Scandinavian and central European nations and increasing both naval and overland access further into Europe.

Russian expansion was by no means complete by 1800. Further efforts to expand extended in all three directions. The Russian government had established a clear and successful tradition of careful military aggrandizement. Segments of the Russian people had demonstrated a vigorous pioneering spirit, which took them into new, sometimes hostile lands, quite like the settlers of North America during the same period. Not too long after 1800, a French aristocrat, Alexis de Tocqueville, commenting on the dynamism of the new United States, compared American growth to that of the world's "sleeping giant"—Russia. He predicted that these two pioneering nations

would someday emerge even more strongly in world affairs, and that they resembled each other, in their exuberant growth, more than anyone yet realized. His foresight was impressive.

RUSSIAN POLITICAL INSTITUTIONS

Russia's political structure was firmly autocratic, a centralized government under the tsar. This structure had been suggested in earlier Russian history, through Byzantine example and the Orthodox tradition of church-state unity; it was further enhanced by the military government's need to expel the Mongols and by the example of the khans. Russia's steady territorial expansion was aided by such a strong central government and, in turn, served to bolster the regime.

Russian tsars did not, to be sure, develop extensive direct contacts with ordinary Russian subjects, although they claimed to be "fathers" to their people. Newly acquired territories were often run for a time rather separately from tsarist control, by freedom-minded cossacks. Only gradually did the tsarist government regularize all their holdings. Most peasants were ruled by noble landlords, particularly during the 17th and 18th centuries. They had scant access to tsarist courts but, rather, were confined to a judicial system directed by their own landlords. Peasants on a given estate regulated their own mutual relations through village governments, which tried to settle land disputes and other matters on the basis of communal tradition. Because of the power of landlords and the importance of village, or *mir*, governments, Russia was in some ways quite decentralized, as Latin America was becoming, although without the colonial overlay. At this point, the Russian empire could not compare to its Chinese counterpart in size or the varied functions of its bureaucracy.

However, the tsars did wield great power, and by the 18th century there was no formal institution to check their power. Like China, for example, but unlike the Western monarchies, the tsars established a secret police to prevent dissent and to supervise the bureaucracy. The Chancery of Secret Police was initially established by Peter the Great and survived, although under different names and with changing functions, until the late 20th century.

One key to the tsars' great power rested in their special relationship with the nobility—the Russian boyars. At the end of the period of Mongol rule, the boyars possessed extensive landholdings and hereditary titles. There was potential here for significant aristocratic defiance of the tsar's wishes. Periodically, as during the Time of Troubles, this kind of opposition did develop; it had some institutional base, for a time, in the councils of nobles called to determine tsarist succession. But Russians had no tradition of feudalism to compare with that of the West. Furthermore, Russia's rapid expansion allowed tsars to grant additional lands to new nobles, whose loyalties were more firmly tied to the crown. Here was a key way in which military expansion strengthened tsarist rule and encouraged the tsars to continue seeking more territory. From Ivan III onward, tsars steadily pressed both new and old nobles to serve the state as military commanders and bureaucrats; they were not allowed to develop separate political loyalties. Thus, Russia's aristocracy differed crucially from its counterpart in the West, since it viewed itself as an extension of the state rather than as a force of partial opposition. Later tsars, such as Peter the Great, in promoting new bureaucrats to aristocratic ranks, reinforced this state-service orientation. They could not tamper with social structure, lest they offend their aristocratic allies.

In many ways, the expansion of the tsarist state resembled the rise of the absolute monarchy in western Europe. Indeed, Peter the Great deliberately copied some of the organizational and military structures of states like Prussia. In the West, as in Russia, aristocratic power declined in relation to that of the central state. The collapse of the nobles' councils in Russia was reminiscent of the long period in which the French Parliament was not convened. The seeming resemblance between their government and that of much of the West encouraged rulers like Catherine the Great to dabble in the Western theories of enlightened despotism. Nonetheless, similarity was not identity. Russia lacked the church-state division and the feudal and parliamentary traditions that still flourished in the West. It did not generate the constitutional political theories that developed in the West during this period, and indeed Russian rulers were at pains to censor literature incorporating this kind of Western thought. It was not astonishing, then, that when political revolution rekindled the idea of limiting monarchical power in the West, from 1789 onward, Russia stayed resolutely apart.

Russia's efforts at partial westernization, not surprisingly, confirmed the empire's autocratic tradition. Under Peter the Great and Catherine the Great, change came from the top down. It increased the hold of the tsar over the nobles, while genuinely seeking to retrain them. No Western monarch treated the aristocracy in such a superior manner, as Peter did in patronizingly and publicly ridiculing the traditional costumes of his boyars. None tried to impose education on them, as Peter did in requiring that all nobles and other bureaucrats learn mathematics. Russian bureaucratic procedures and culture may indeed have benefited from this forced dose of westernization, in the form of better schools, increased literacy, and more science. But it was clear that this kind of reform movement reflected and enhanced the special place of an autocratic central government in Russian political life.

RUSSIAN CULTURE

For most Russian people, culture during the early modern period meant the Orthodox religion and traditional forms of oral expression—the heroic epics, the rich musical life, the often witty proverbs designed to explain life's vagaries. The carefully

Russian religious art: icon of the Annunciation, Moscow school.

Miracle of St. George and the Dragon, early 16th century.

structured rituals of the Orthodox church and the worship of many saints allowed ordinary Russians to pray for victories or for protection from disease and famine. They represented the focal point of an elaborate system of festivals, more numerous in Russia than in the West, in which feasting and celebration contrasted with the ordinary, often harsh, routine of work. Early modern Russia did not experience the change in popular culture that was occurring in the West.

Russian cultural traditions revived in many ways after the Mongol period. From the 15th to the 17th centuries, icon painting became increasingly distinctive as a Russian art form. From individual heads of saints and the Holy Family, Russian painters moved to more abstract and complex religious scenes. In literature, the tradition of narrative histories and chronicles written by monks resumed. Church building picked up

again, not only in Moscow but also in regional centers like Kiev.

During the early modern period as a whole, however, Russian culture was marked by important tensions—between popular tradition and elite tastes, and between westernizing tendencies and a desire to define special Russian characteristics. Under Ivan the Great and Ivan the Terrible, Italian architects were summoned to design church buildings and the magnificent tsarist palace in the Kremlin in Moscow. These architects did not introduce Western styles without modification. They generated some fusion between Renaissance classicism and Russian building traditions, producing the ornate, onion-shaped domes that became characteristic of Russian (and other east European) churches.

With Peter the Great and Catherine the Great, the desire to westernize went even further. The

Steeple of the Preobrazhenskaya Church, showing wooden carving of characteristic Russian domes. (Granger Collection)

leading aristocrats almost entirely embraced Western cultural influences. Many nobles during the 18th century spoke only French, and some did not know Russian at all. European artistic styles began to displace the icon-painting tradition; cultural forms such as the ballet were embraced so fervently that they became part of Russia's own heritage. Western-style schools encouraged a new interest in science and secular philosophy. The public buildings of St. Petersburg were carefully constructed in Western classical styles. Russia was at this juncture still absorbing Western culture; later, in the 19th century, Russians would make power-ful contributions to the Western pool of literature, science, and music. At this point, before 1800, elite culture was largely imitative.

Furthermore, Western influence was by no means uniformly welcomed. Ordinary Russian peasants, even the provincial nobility, were largely unaffected by these developments. A growing cultural gap between the upper class and the masses developed that would be resolved only through revolution in the 20th century. Some literate priests and nobles protested westernization in the name of an often vaguely defined Russian soul. One wrote to the tsar Alexis: "You feed the foreigners too well, instead of bidding your folk to cling to the old customs." A number of cultural leaders tried to articulate traditional or "patriotic" forms opposed to the new influences.

Russian culture during the early modern period thus saw important improvements represented by revitalized art forms and some fruitful mergers with Western styles. Literacy and schooling advanced, although only a minority of Russians benefited; few Russians entered an essentially Western intellectual orbit. But this was not yet an integrated culture. While a revived interest in science and new forms of painting and architecture were significant influences in Russian intellectual life, the most enduring single legacy was a heritage of ambivalence about Russia's relationship to the West. Collectively, after a period of stagnation in their own nation's artistic development, Russia's cultural representatives were torn between a desire to imitate the West and a desire to define Russian values as different from and superior to those of the West. In one form or another, this ambivalence continues to characterize Russian cultural development.

ECONOMY AND SOCIETY IN RUSSIA

As Russia moved partially into a Western diplomatic orbit and appropriated a number of Western cultural forms, the empire's economy and society pushed in rather different directions. Here was one of the key signs that Russia remained a separate civilization, although with special ties to the West.

As the Western economy became increasingly commercial, Russia continued to be resolutely agricultural, save for the iron-manufacturing sector and the continuation of active trade in central Asia. Its economic growth, although considerable, rested on the extension of its agricultural lands as the empire expanded, as well as on the increasingly effective use of vast mineral resources. Russia developed only a small merchant class. Indeed, aristocrats deliberately discouraged local merchants, who were seen as potential rivals. Growing trade with the West was handled by the communities of British, Dutch, and other Western traders from their enclaves in Moscow and St. Petersburg, although Russian merchants were more active in the overland commerce with Asia. Russian cities, as a result, were small, less than 5 percent of the total population.

Most Russian agriculture was designed for local consumption; few peasants were engaged in a market economy, and few handled much money. Village artisans supplied most of the manufactured goods that the masses required and could not make themselves. Luxury items and more complex equipment were largely imported from the West. Village-level technology did not change rapidly.

Russia did, however, enter the world economy, and on somewhat better terms than areas such as Latin America or even sub-Saharan Africa, despite the empire's rather backward economic condition after the period of Mongol rule. In exchange for Western goods and commercial services, including merchant shipping, Russia initially offered furs, along with timber supplies from its vast northern forests. Then, in the 18th century, the empire began to sell grain to the West, from the rich lands of the Ukraine and, later, Poland. Furthermore, Peter the Great used government officials to help organize a growing mining industry, so that Russia sold considerable quantities of iron ore to the West as well. Government-sponsored improvements in Russia's network of rivers and the development of St. Petersburg as a major Baltic port facilitated this process.

The government in Russia essentially took the place of merchant capitalists in organizing mining exports, just as it assumed the lead in sponsoring munitions factories and related iron-processing works. Here was an important extension of government functions under the tsars, from Peter the Great on, that helped Russia maintain some balance with the more commercially developed West. Russia used government regulation and unusually rich natural resources to avoid falling hopelessly behind in the world economy.

However, the key to Russia's economic advances lay in its reliance on unfree labor. Some slaves were used, into the 18th century, as war brought many captives. More important, however, was the pervasive and rigorous system of serfdom. As serfdom increasingly unraveled in the West, it became more rigid in Russia and other parts of eastern Europe. By using cheap servile labor, eastern Europe sought to participate in the world market, taking advantage of the West's growing demand for grains and minerals. Serfs worked most of the land, and the government also assigned serfs to the iron mines and metallurgical factories.

Ironically, prior to the Mongol conquest, Russian peasants had been mainly free farmers, with their legal position superior to that of their Western counterparts. But after the expulsion of the Tatars, increasing numbers of Russian peasants fell into debt and had to accept servile status under the noble landowners when they could not repay their debt. From the 16th century onward, the Russian government actively encouraged this process. Essentially, the government offered the support of serfdom to the aristocracy, in exchange for loyalty. As new territories were added to the empire, this system of serfdom extended to areas where it had not been known before. By 1800, half of Russia's peasantry was enserfed to the landlords, and much of the other half owed comparable obligations to the state. Various laws passed during the 17th century tied serfs to the land; a 1649 act proclaimed the status of serfs to be hereditary, so that people born to this station could not legally escape it.

On landed estates, serfs were taxed and policed through their landlords and even bought and sold like ordinary property. Although the earnings of peasants varied somewhat and they sometimes used village governments for community regulation, most remained impoverished and ill educated. And the legal servitude of most peasants only increased with time. Although Catherine the Great sponsored a few model villages to exhibit an enlightened form of serfdom, she, in fact, turned over the rule

of serfs to the landlords more completely than ever before. A law of 1785 allowed landlords to administer harsh penalties to any of their serfs convicted of major crimes or rebellion. Serfdom spread to new regions, with nobles granted other new rights. Here was proof positive of the vital political basis of serfdom, as Catherine garnered the loyalty of the nobles by giving them, in effect, rule over half of the Russian masses.

In Russian serfdom, not only on the landed estates but also in the mines, the key obligation was not payment in cash or payment in kind, although taxes were high and rising as the government needs for revenue increased. Labor service was the obligation that made economic sense of this system. Peasants owed up to a tenth of their yearly labor to their landlords or the state. This was the labor that produced the grain available for export and serviced the mines and factories.

Russia's distinctive social and economic system worked well in many respects. It produced enough revenue to support an expanding state and empire. It underwrote a wealthy upper aristocracy and its glittering, westernized culture. It supported a far larger number of gentry, who lived more modestly and often resented the Western ways of the imperial court but who were nonetheless secure in their position and loyalty to the tsar. The system also promoted considerable population growth. Population nearly doubled in the 18th century, to 36 million people, and although some of this growth was the result of territorial expansion, most was due to a natural increase. For an empire that contained few regions of great fertility and where the climate was harsh, this was no small achievement, although periodic famines and epidemics continued to plague Russia into the 20th century, for this was a poor land in many ways. But there could be no question that the economy had advanced.

However, the Russian system suffered from important limitations. There was little incentive for agricultural improvements; most methods remained rather primitive. Peasants certainly lacked the motivation, for whatever surplus they produced was not theirs. Landlords, inspired by

Western advances in the 18th century, did form associations to exchange information on new crops and methods, but little was done to improve production on a large scale. Given the secure base in servile labor, there seemed little need for change. Indeed, pressure from landlords caused the government to enact measures against a growing system of peasant-run domestic manufacturing and trade in the 18th century, for the aristocracy feared that growing peasant wealth might challenge its rule. Thus, Russia did not experience a significant increase in internal commerce or consumer-directed production comparable to that occurring in the West.

Most importantly, the system generated recurring peasant unrest. Russian peasants, although mainly loyal to the tsar, harbored bitter resentments against their landlords, who were seen as having taken lands that rightfully belonged to the peasants. Periodic rebellions attacked manorial records, seized land directly, and sometimes resulted in the deaths of landlords and their officials. The Pugachev uprising was the leading 18th-century example of this kind of outburst. But there were others, and popular unrest would continue to swell into the 19th century. Peasants had more than a sense of grievance; they also had tight links to each other through village governments and traditions of communal support. They maintained strong family ties, extending among many relatives; the network of the Russian family was thus larger than that of the West, with less stress on a purely nuclear unit. Community and family bonds provided a political basis for action, and although the peasants were never successful against the power of the landlords or the military strength of the state, they could not be permanently repressed.

Not surprisingly, by the early 1800s, it was clear that Russia had a major "peasant problem." Not only by Western standards, but also in terms of economic advance and political order, it seemed increasingly clear that something had to be done about Russia's unfree masses. Also not surprisingly, it was very difficult for those in a position of authority or oppression to decide what to do.

THE WORLD'S FIRST EFFORT AT WESTERNIZATION

Russia, particularly during Peter the Great's rule and onward, was the first non–Western civilization to attempt a partial "westernization." The country was geographically close to the West and shared some of the same religious traditions. It had emerged from the Mongol period aware of its backwardness and eager to employ Western models as a partial remedy. What Russian leaders had attempted, in westernization from the top down, would be tried to some extent in other societies and is still being tested today. The Russians sought to adapt key Western forms, not to make their society entirely Western but to modify it in such a way that it could compete with the West militarily. Thus, the emphasis was on bureaucratic training and military organization and armament. However, there was some sense within Russia that yet more should be done, that cultural styles and even personal manners should move in Western directions; hence, the changes, among the upper classes, in styles of dress as well as art.

Nonetheless, westernization represented a limited effort. It served to enhance the distinctive Russian autocracy, not to import the full, complex political culture of the contemporary West, and certainly not to change the beliefs of the masses. Russia's leaders—like many later cultures in their attempts to westernize—did not want to reproduce Western civilization wholesale. Small wonder that by the late 18th century, some intellectual dissidents, attracted by the West, pressed for further change—although other writers continued to urge the sanctity of Russian traditions.

Rather, the current of westernization fed into the more general growth of the Russian state and empire. Limited changes were sufficient, in combination with Russia's vast size, population, and resources, to maintain the country's growing role in world diplomacy, challenging smaller nations in eastern and central Europe plus China and the Ottoman Empire in Asia. In strictly economic terms, Russia's relationship to the Western-dominated world economy was not vastly superior to that of Latin America; in both cases, the terms of trade were not advantageous, and any success depended on an unfree labor force. But in the military and political sphere, the story was quite different. Russia carved out one of the great landed empires in world history.

ISSUES AND CONNECTIONS

Key issues in studying early modern Russia involve grasping Russia's complicated relationship with western Europe, the mixture of attraction, separation, and outright rejection. Russia became part of European history in this period, but not as part of Western civilization. Russia must also be seen as part of Asian and Middle Eastern history.

Russia has changed greatly since the early modern period. But three vital connections stand out. First is the huge size of what is still a multiethnic, though Russian-dominated, state. Russia stretches over 11 time zones, and this is the fruit of early modern expansionist achievements and ambitions. Second is a tendency toward authoritarian politics, though since 1985 this has been under new debate. Third is the love-hate relationship with the West, which changes with new

contexts but never seems to be fully resolved—a final gift from Russia's dynamic innovations of the early modern centuries.

SUGGESTED WEB SITE

For a Web site on key individuals in early modern Russian history, go to http://www.departments.bucknell.edu/russian.

SUGGESTED READINGS

Two important source collections for this period of Russian history are T. Riha, ed., *Readings in Russian Civilization*, Vol. 2: *Imperial Russia 1700–1917* (1969), and Basil Dmytryshyn, *Imperial Russia: A Sourcebook, 1700–1917* (1967). Excellent general coverage is provided in N. Riasanovsky, *A History of Russia*, 4th ed. (1993); see also Otto Hoetzsch, *The Evolution of Russia* (1966). On more specialized topics, consult H. Kohn, *The Mind of Modern Russia* (1955); M. Raeff, *Peter the Great, Reformer or Revolutionary?* (1963); H. Rogger, *National Consciousness in Eighteenth Century Russia* (1963); and A. Kahan, *The Knout and the Plowshare: Economic History of Russia in the 18th Century* (1985). Peter Kolchin, *Unfree Labor: American Slavery and Russian Serfdom* (1987), is an important comparative study.

For additional recent work, see Lindsey Hughes, *Peter the Great and the West: New Perspectives* (2001); Michael Khodarkovsky, *Russia's Steppe Frontier: The Making of a Colonial Empire, 1500–1800* (2002); Alexander Chubarov, *The Fragile Empire: A History of Imperial Russia* (1999); and Geoffrey Hosking, *Russia: People and Empire* (1997).

19

The Ottoman and Mughal Empires

Two great Islamic states were created during the early modern period, one covering much of the Middle East and the Balkans, the other much of India. Both the Ottomans and Mughals brought new influences to these regions, including great political and military strength. The two empires resembled Russia in establishing large landed holdings with new boundaries during the early modern period. They also, like Russia, included a host of different linguistic, ethnic, and religious groups. Neither empire, however, attempted westernization during this period, even selectively. Early Mughal emperors had a tolerant interest in Western culture, including its religion, but there were few real attempts to imitate it; the Western intrusion into India later on was a matter of conquest and economic exploitation. Ottoman rulers, with minor exceptions, explicitly avoided borrowing from the West.

Both Islamic empires followed their own paths during most of the early modern period, introducing important changes that had little to do with the West or the world economy. Contacts with the West did increase with time, so that in contrast to east Asia, a more substantial Western presence began to affect internal developments by the late 17th to early 18th centuries. Here again are distinctive cases, unlike either east Asia's greater isolation or Russia's partial westernization. Trends during the early modern period created important new patterns, ultimately shaping the relationship of these key regions to the larger global framework.

The evolution of the Middle East and India after 1450 revolved around the rise of the two new empires, one brought by the Turks to the Middle East, the other by Turkish-Mongol conquerors who ruled over the Hindu majority in India. (A third Islamic empire, the Safavids, developed for a time in Persia.) The Muslim empires provided new political and military solidity to their Asian territories. Under the Ottomans, the previous political decline of the Arab caliphs was reversed. Under the early

Mughals, India achieved a degree of political unity rarely before attained.

The Ottoman and particularly the Mughal empires were not, however, as solidly based as those of China and Russia. The Mughals represented a minority religion as well as a foreign political force. The Ottomans, though sharing religion with the Arab majority of their empire, were also outsiders who looked down on the Arab population for their political and military weakness. Both empires were partially drawn into the European-dominated world economy on decidedly disadvantageous terms. Finally, both empires began to decline well before 1800. In India, this resulted in direct European penetration during the 18th century. The Ottoman Empire remained intact, but by 1800, it was becoming a weaker force in regional and world affairs.

KEY QUESTIONS *What did the Mughals add to the characteristics of India? What did the Ottomans add to the Middle East? Beyond some general similarities, how did the two empires differ?*

THE EXPANDING FORCE OF THE OTTOMAN EMPIRE

The Ottoman Empire had taken shape during the several centuries before the early modern period, although its complete development followed the Turkish conquest of Constantinople in 1453. Turkish groups had been moving into the Middle East, from their original lands in central Asia, for some time. They served in the armies of the caliphs and as advisors. This interaction spread Islamic belief and knowledge of urban cultural styles and government even to those Turks still in central Asia.

The Osmanli group of Turks, or Ottomans as Europeans knew them, were not one of the original Turkish peoples involved in Middle Eastern affairs. Their movement into the region came later, stimulated in part by the rise of the Mongol empire in Asia during the 13th and 14th cen-

turies. Large numbers of migrants took over lands at the northern rim of the Middle East, in the country that is now Turkey—the only part of the Middle East that was heavily populated by Turks—where they became an agricultural people. Regional Osmanli leaders, exhibiting their military abilities, began to challenge both the Arabs and Byzantines. The Ottomans were fervent warriors, spurred by intense Islamic beliefs and a tightly knit military. By the 14th century, their leaders began to call themselves sultans, as they settled in the plains of Anatolia, the heartland of present-day Turkey. The first sultan, Orkhan, established a new army of soldiers called *janissaries* in order to fight remnants of the Byzantine Empire in southeastern Europe. He had already conquered some European territory by 1400. The Ottomans viewed this conquest of Christian lands as a virtual crusade, and during the 1390s they captured Serbia, Bulgaria, and Greece. Already, the Ottoman Empire was the strongest state in the Middle East in the wake of the collapse of the Abbasid caliphate.

Nonetheless, the chief prize was Constantinople, the capital city of eastern Christendom. Several Turkish sieges failed before Sultan Mehmet II, known as "the Conqueror," finally succeeded in 1453, aided by the use of a huge cannon and the strict discipline he imposed on his troops. The Turks set up their imperial capital in what was now a Muslim city, renamed Istanbul. Soon after this, the Turks conquered Arab Syria and also took control of the Greek islands and the last Byzantine settlements around the Black Sea. By 1517, Egypt was vanquished, the last of the regional Arab kingdoms that had survived the fall of the caliphate. The Ottoman Empire was thus heir to both Arab and Byzantine lands, establishing one of the largest empires the Middle East had ever known; it was the last great attempt at unification in the region, to the present day.

During the 16th century, Ottoman conquests continued. The sultans conquered part of Persia and much of the southern Arabian peninsula. They pursued territories in Europe,

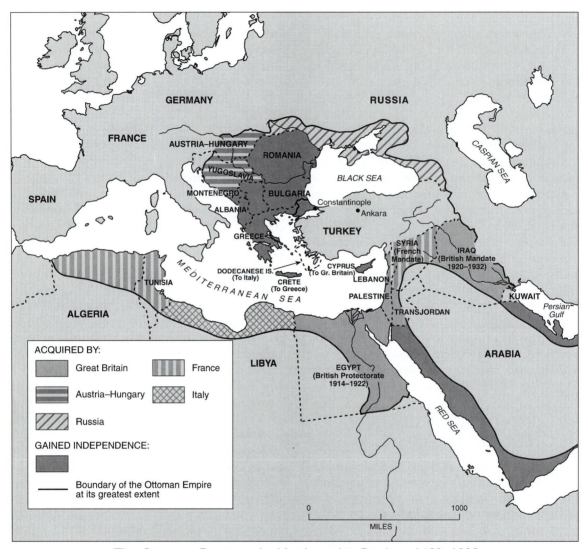

The Ottoman Empire at Its Height and in Decline, 1683–1923

attacking several Italian cities and conquering Hungary after a victory in 1526. In 1529, they besieged the Habsburg capital city of Vienna, in Austria, although this effort failed. They also captured islands in the Mediterranean. The conquest of the island of Cyprus in 1571 led to the establishment of a Turkish settlement that coexisted uneasily with the Greek majority, a tense situation that persists to this day. Minor

conquests continued until 1715, although in most respects the high-water mark of the empire as a conquering force was reached in the late 16th and early 17th centuries.

By this point, the Ottoman Empire embraced the whole of southeastern Europe to the Danube River. It included a protectorate over Tatar provinces in the Crimea as the Ottoman Empire stretched around virtually the entire circumference of the Black Sea. It encompassed most of the Middle East, with some Arab settlements in desert regions and the smaller Safavid empire in Persia alone escaping its grasp; it also controlled most of north Africa. Ottoman rule over the holy cities of Mecca and Medina gave the empire new religious force, and the sultans assumed the title of caliph of Islam, implying a direct link to the Muslim faith. As caliphs, the sultans required that their names be used in the prayers of the faithful in the mosques.

The Ottoman Empire, although of greatest importance in the Islamic world, played a crucial role in European history as well. In its hold over the Balkan lands of southeastern Europe, the Ottomans preserved this region from direct Western control; a minority of Balkan people converted to Islam.

The Ottoman Empire's success rested on two leading factors. The first, visible from the early Osmanlis onward, involved strong military organization and conquest. The Ottomans, like many other imperial conquerors, depended heavily on a fairly steady course of expansion, which gave military leaders rewards in the form of new territories, plus slaves to serve as troops. When conquests largely ceased, the empire became increasingly troubled.

The second factor was Ottoman leaders' considerable tolerance for the various peoples in their vast realms, like that of Arab conquerors before them. Mehmet II did not attack the Greek Orthodox church; indeed, he appointed a new patriarch to provide separate religious government for this people. Christians were taxed more heavily than Muslims, and in the provinces of southeastern Europe, they were forced to perform labor duties and allow the conscription of some of their youth as soldiers. For the most part, Christianity remained strong in southeastern Europe and, as a minority religion, in parts of the Middle East, and individual Christians rose high in the Ottoman government. Jews were also widely tolerated, as the Turks again demonstrated their willingness to accept a multiracial and multireligious society. The Turks did harbor some

disdain for their fellow Arab Muslims and decidedly favored Sunni beliefs over the Shi'a minority. But on the whole, Arab Muslims, from ulema scholars to the ordinary faithful, were not disturbed in their religious practices. Many Ottoman sultans were personally pious, interested in religion and culture as well as military affairs.

The greatest of the Ottoman sultans, near the height of the empire's power, was Suleiman, who ruled from 1520 to 1566. Known as "the Magnificent" to European traders, who marveled at the wealth of his court, he was called "the Legislator" by the Turks themselves because of his interest in just and disciplined rule. Although not a joyful warrior—indeed, his portraits reveal a rather gloomy man burdened by the cares of his state—Suleiman did pursue a policy of conquest. It was under his rule that the kingdom of Hungary was conquered and new portions of the Middle East, particularly present-day Iraq, were won from the Persians. Suleiman also constructed a major Mediterranean fleet, hoping in this way to extend his challenge of the Christian West. He strengthened Ottoman control of north Africa, especially Algeria, and frequently raided Italian and Spanish ports. In his later years, Suleiman grew less interested in battle and concentrated on the building of new mosques. However, his life remained troubled, as he had to put to death one son to please his favorite wife, leaving her incompetent son as his heir.

Under Suleiman, the institutions of the Ottoman Empire assumed their fullest shape, forming a successful political system long capable of administering vast and diverse territories. In theory, this was an absolute state, claiming control over all wealth and property in the empire. Annual tax revenue was massive by the standards of Western kingdoms. Although all power officially rested in the sultan, he, in fact, delegated much authority to his chief minister, the grand wazir. The wazir and other leading ministers were able to accumulate their own considerable fortunes through bribery and graft, although they had to struggle against rivals and the sultan's power to retire—and often execute—them at any given moment.

The provinces of the empire were ruled by governors called *pashas*, who paid for their office with an annual fee. A pasha of Cairo was said to have bribed the grand wazir with a large yearly payment in order to preserve his lucrative position. Under the pashas, most land outside the cities was parceled out in fiefs to Turkish and other Muslim landlords, who collected revenues and enforced the laws on a local basis. Under a levy, or conscription, system, each landlord was obligated to furnish soldiers to the sultan. Under this decentralized system, regional rulers and landlords were encouraged to milk their holdings for as much revenue as they could. There was no hereditary nobility, since in theory the sultan owned all the land. This fact initially gave sultans control over regional officials who owed their position to the central court, but it also promoted short-term exploitation of the provinces by officials eager to turn a profit while they could still enjoy it. Suleiman did prepare a centralized law code, which served as a unifying legal force throughout the empire until the 19th century.

The Ottomans expanded the earlier Arab use of slaves in the army and administration. Using slaves of Christian origin in the central bureaucracy, from the wazirs on down, bypassed the Qur'an's prohibition on enslaving Muslims and also integrated non-Muslims, who formed a majority in the empire for its first 200 years. Government slaves were carefully educated, alongside the sultans' own sons, and promoted according to merit and seniority. Here was another solution to the government of an agricultural society, different from both Chinese bureaucracy and feudalism. It made the Ottoman Empire the best-governed state in the world well into the 16th century.

The army was the main unifying element throughout the empire. In addition to the landlord levies, sultans like Suleiman directly controlled the force of janissaries, who were recruited from the families of Christians, particularly in southeastern Europe, in what amounted to an annual slave tax. These young men were taken from their homes at an early age, converted to Islam, and trained to become fierce and able soldiers. They seldom numbered more than 15,000, because the sultans feared that they might otherwise grow too powerful; indeed, janissary revolts troubled the empire periodically even so. Forbidden to marry, the janissaries were expected to remain loyal to the sultan alone, from whom they received good pay and many other benefits. Until the 18th century, when their fighting spirit declined and their interference in internal politics increased, they did indeed serve the empire well. The janissaries were normally well disciplined and remained an excellent fighting force, particularly in battles with European Christians, which were still seen to an extent as holy wars.

The Ottoman navy, on the other hand, was rather limited. Although it operated in the eastern Mediterranean, it could not wrest control of the Mediterranean from Italian and Spanish forces. The empire lacked a large merchant marine, a fact that weakened its efforts on the seas. It used slaves as oarsmen; they had little interest in battle save as a chance to escape. Although the navy gained brief prominence under Suleiman, it soon declined and then was further weakened by the defeat at European hands in the battle of Lepanto in 1571. After this point, Turkish naval activities were confined to the eastern coast of the Mediterranean, where they protected existing Ottoman provinces.

Even at its height, the Ottoman Empire displayed some important weaknesses. It ruled over the oldest commercial economy in the world, but it did not sponsor significant economic advance. As the focus of world trade moved away from the Mediterranean, the empire was obviously at a disadvantage. Great efforts were exerted to sustain the magnificent city of Istanbul. Most farming was done by serfs, who were routinely exploited by greedy landlords and regional governors. This system did not encourage agricultural productivity. The Turks were not greatly interested in commerce. Most regional trade was conducted by

This Turkish artifact of the 16th century maintained earlier Islamic styles of art. (Granger Collection)

Arabs, Greeks, and Jews, who maintained an active urban economy. The empire's role in the larger world economy declined. Once Europeans learned to sail around Africa directly to Asia, the position of the Middle East as an intermediary between Asia and Europe became less important. Trade between the Middle East and Europe lay largely in Western hands, and a growing colony of Western traders emerged in Istanbul.

The empire embraced and encouraged a lively religious life, although the most renowned Islamic scholars were more often Arab than Turk. The building of mosques and palaces stimulated architecture and crafts, which maintained earlier Arabic styles for the most part, although to some extent Persian influences were also evident. Decorative arts, including rich carpets and fine metalwork, flourished. But there was little new literature, particularly in Turkish; Arab poetry continued, but as in the later days of the caliphate, mainly in a religious vein. Arab schools and universities concentrated primarily on religious instruction and the complicated scholarship of Islamic law. Egypt served as the cultural center for Arab intellectual life, but most Egyptian writers devoted their efforts to compiling older works and commenting on them, or preparing biographies of ancient Muslim holy men. The rich and diverse cultural traditions of the earlier Arab civilization at its height were not revived. In the 16th century, Turkish literature began to develop, as sultans encouraged the writing of state histories highly favorable to those in power and as Turkish poets and songwriters copied Persian and Arabic verse. Much Turkish writing was devoted to accounts of the life of the prophet Muhammad and leading dervishes, confirming the heavily religious orientation of Middle Eastern culture.

Conditions for Ottoman women maintained Middle Eastern patterns. Many urban women were veiled and secluded. Leaders maintained several wives and, often, additional concubines. But an active social life could develop among women in extended households, including opportunities for private enjoyment of consumer goods. Since upper-class boys were raised in the harems for their first seven years, the informal influence of mothers could be considerable. Women could also own property, a key source of bargaining power within families.

Major innovations in popular culture, however, favored men. The most important was the development of coffee consumption. Coffee had first been cultivated in southern Arabia in the 14th century, from wild plants brought in from Ethiopia. It was popularized for Sufi religious ceremonies, because it encouraged wakefulness for nighttime rituals. But by the 16th century, coffee's social functions were spreading, and coffeehouses began to spring up in Egypt and in

Istanbul. Arab and Turkish men now used coffeehouses for social purposes, and all sorts of serving equipment developed. By 1560, there were over 600 coffeehouses in Istanbul, some with elaborate gardens, others very simple. Arab merchants and growers in Africa and southern Arabia controlled the coffee trade.

The Ottoman Empire remained, in part, a military movement. Turkish leaders continued to esteem military virtues above all, although they often tempered their commitment to warfare by pursuing religious concerns and the enjoyment of art. The Turks had little interest in the dull work of the bureaucracy. Most administrative posts under the sultans were held not by Turks, but by east Europeans—mainly Slavs and Greeks—and by Jews. Only a minority of the wazirs was Turkish. Most of the literate bureaucrats were Europeans, Christian Armenians, and Jews. Decentralized rule combined with strong military power held this empire together, although high taxes, forced labor, and military recruitment caused discontent, particularly in southeastern Europe, where the Turks became cordially detested.

Despite its weaknesses, however, the Ottoman Empire enjoyed over three centuries of power, from its dynamic beginnings in the 14th century until well after the defeat at Lepanto. This is hardly a record of failure, for it compares favorably with the glory days of other military empires such as that of Rome.

THE OTTOMAN EMPIRE IN DECLINE

A certain degree of Ottoman decline began late in the 17th century. The quality of individual sultans deteriorated after Suleiman. Many ruled for only brief periods; a few were mentally incapacitated. Many devoted themselves to sensual pleasures, surrounded by large harems of concubines. Palace intrigues and military interference increasingly dominated the Ottoman state, which perhaps helps account for the poor political performance of those who became sultans. Periodic reform efforts, to tighten central control and reduce the corruption of regional governors, had no permanent effects, although they helped sustain the regime. Religious and local institutions supplemented the government by providing courts, charity, education, and public works—another reason the system survived. The government also tried to defend against unrest by limiting certain innovations. Printing, for example, was fully banned until the 18th century.

During most of the 17th century, the empire held onto its territory. Its control over north Africa (aside from Egypt) weakened, in part because of the declining navy. North African states became small principalities and were the source of considerable piracy until the 19th century. However, Western powers, caught up in their own colonial expansion, had no interest in a direct attack on Ottoman lands.

The Ottoman Empire made one last attempt at conquest in 1683, in a new assault on Vienna. For three months, a huge Turkish army laid siege to this city, until a mixed German and Polish force drove them back. Soon after this, the Austrian Habsburg emperor, in a loose alliance with the Russian tsar Peter the Great, attacked the Ottomans. Austrian troops drove the Turks from Hungary, inflicting the worst defeat the Turks had suffered since the early days of the Osmanlis. From this point onward, the Ottomans were on the defensive in southeastern Europe and central Asia. In the 18th century, Russian attacks pushed them from the northern coast of the Black Sea, while Austria also gained some territory in Serbia.

During the 18th century, the quality of internal government deteriorated further. Control over provincial governors declined; a few governors even rebelled against Constantinople. Many governors became increasingly corrupt, using their rule as a means of acquiring vast personal fortunes. Taxation, earlier restrained by some central regulations, grew heavier. Popular discontent increased, although there were no vast uprisings.

History Debate

GUNS AND THEIR IMPACT

It is easy to write early modern world history as if guns were European. Without question, Europe's advance in world trade and colonialism owed much to European advances in gunnery, particularly on ships. Guns also had massive effects within early modern Europe, making feudal warfare and strongholds like castles less effective. Siege cannon could reduce noble castles to ruin; this forced the nobility into new behaviors and clearly weakened feudal politics and the feudal ethic.

Increasingly, however, historians examine the use of guns in other cultures. Obviously, explosive powder was Chinese in origin. But nomadic peoples quickly picked up the implications. Siege cannon did not cause the rise of the Mongols, which was based on cavalry, but they were added to the Mongol arsenal as the armies began to attack cities in China, Russia, and Islamic areas. The Ottomans used janissaries as their artillery corps, and this became a driving force behind Ottoman expansion. Babur, in forming the Mughal empire in India, used cannon as well. There is no question that guns played a major role in the formation of Asian as well as European empires. One key result was the decline of nomadic attacks. Even though Mongols and other nomads were initially adept with cannon, in the long run developing an armament industry and improving weaponry depended on a large tax base, that is, on established governments. Here was a key component in the nomadic decline in the early modern period.

Guns also complicated the later development of many of the land-based gunpowder empires as well. Guns allowed expansion of territory in advance of effective communication or government. In both the Ottoman and Mughal empires, a key result of such expansion was weak central control and great power in the hands of regional military leaders. This in turn weakened the empires still further. Western European states, smaller, managed a more effective bureaucratic and taxation system, which Russia was able to copy to some extent. This increased the Western or Russian competitive edge against the Islamic empires. Ultimately, the story of guns tips the global balance of power in favor of Europe—which brings the story back to more familiar contours. But there is important complexity in the middle of the process—the 14th to 17th century transition period in the relationship of guns and empires—that needs attention as well.

Arab involvement with intense Muslim piety, under the leadership of Sufi mystics, helped limit the impact of protest, expressing hostility to the existing order but through attention to religious rather than political goals. On the southern borders of the empire, however, a puritanical version of Islam developed in the Wahabi movement. This formed partly in protest against the secular tone of Ottoman rulers. The Wahabis developed military forces and later in the 18th century, for a time, seized Mecca from the Ottomans.

As the power of the empire faltered, Europe's economic penetration of the Middle East began to intensify. Even before, Western traders, led by the French, had won special privileges from the sultans, establishing merchant colonies that were exempt from Ottoman law. French, British, and Dutch groups thrived in not only Constantinople but Syria and Egypt as well. The West also had some cultural impact, as Middle Eastern Christians, particularly those in Lebanon, sought new ties with the Catholic church. Christian printing presses were set up in Arabic, although presses were banned by the Turks for Muslims until 1729.

For the most part, Turkish political leaders and Arab cultural leaders remained uncertain in reacting to the declining strength of their civilization, although officials were aware of the specific problems this decline posed. There was no successful effort at political reform until after 1800. Muslim cultural figures were convinced of their superiority over their European neighbors. No attempts were made, again until after 1800, to translate European scientific or technological works, for this intellectual current seemed irrelevant in Muslim eyes. A few Western doctors were imported by the sultans—which was ironic, because medicine was one area where Muslim science was just as good as its Western counterpart—but the larger disparities with western Europe were simply ignored. Many Ottoman merchants were quite familiar with the West, but they had little impact back home. The cultural blanket of Islamic legalism and faith, plus the army and bureaucracy, continued to protect this important civilization, even as both Western and Russian interests in the region increased.

THE MUGHAL EMPIRE: INVASION, CONSOLIDATION, AND DECLINE

India during the 15th century was locked in its recurrent pattern of regional states. The Delhi sultanate, which earlier had provided Muslim rule for much of northern India, was now merely one among many principalities, most of them headed by Hindu princes.

This situation changed as a result of another invasion early in the 16th century, the last echo, in a way, of the great period of Mongol conquests. Babur, a regional chieftain in Afghanistan and a Muslim, was of mixed Turkish and Mongol ancestry. Beginning in 1526, he used the familiar passes through the mountains of northwestern India to mount a war of conquest, within four years bringing a large part of the northern plains under his control.

Babur's conquests benefited obviously from India's political division, as regional states could not join forces effectively. But Babur was no ordinary raider. His vision was a new empire, for himself and his descendants, not plunder. He was a bold, often cruel general, but a lover of gardening and poetry who wrote a long memoir that showed real sensitivity for the rest of humankind. He cherished books and liked to select prize volumes from the libraries that came under his dominion. The dynasty he established was called *Mughal*, from the Persian word for "Mongol"; from the wealth of Babur and his successors came the English word *mogul*. At the outset, however, this was a regime with serious political purposes, not simply a luxury-loving enterprise. To solidify his new dynasty, Babur carefully avoided acts of intolerance against Hindus, whose customs he studied closely.

Babur's chief heir, after a brief period of confusion under a weak son, was his grandson Akbar, who took charge in 1555. Initially winning only a portion of Babur's empire, Akbar soon conquered one of the largest empires ever established in India, recalling the former days of the Maurya dynasty. Akbar's awe-inspiring achievements gained him the respect of many Europeans, who named him the "Great Mughal." Akbar was brave almost to the point of foolhardiness. As a boy, he liked to ride his own fighting elephants; he reveled in the hunt, once killing a tiger with his sword in single combat. He was also an excellent marksman—and guns spread to India initially through Muslim influence. But Akbar was also a cultivated man, a book collector and patron of painting and architecture. Mughal culture reached its peak under his rule. Furthermore, Akbar carried the tolerance of Hinduism to an unusual extreme, marrying a Hindu princess and allowing Hindu women in his court to practice their religion openly, an unprecedented act for a Muslim ruler. He even listened to Portuguese Jesuit missionaries who reached the west coast

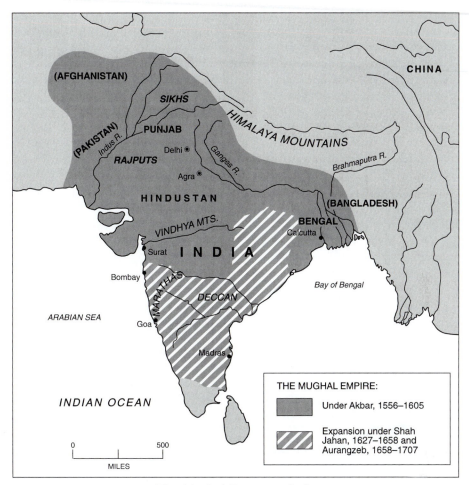

The Mughal Empire in India

under his regime, although he himself never converted. Akbar seems to have had a vague notion of sponsoring a new religion that would blend Hinduism and Islam, although it never had much of a significant following.

Akbar's empire built on a combination of great military force and careful administration. His army numbered 140,000 troops at its height, a massive number for the age, far greater than the forces of the leading European powers. At the same time, he established a clearly defined bureaucracy, divided into specialized ministries to

deal with finance, law, and military affairs. Akbar's administrative reform drew on practices in Afghanistan that were refined by his Hindu chief minister. Eighteen provincial governors, called *subahdars*, administered the major regions of his empire. Akbar united virtually the whole of northern India and began the conquest of the Deccan region in the south. His legal system sought to moderate what he saw as some excesses in Hindu customs; thus, he attempted to ban sati, the practice of suicide by widows, and he forbade child marriage by insisting on a marriage age of

Mughal book painting: late 16th-century hunting scenes. (Granger Collection)

Mughal art: Jahangir embracing Nur Jahan. Compare this to the earlier Indian styles shown in Chapters 5 and 9.

16 for boys, 13 for girls. Akbar also endeavored to create a common language for his empire, enabling his scholars to produce the synthetic mixture called *Urdu*, or Hindustani, which provided a vehicle of communication for his bureaucrats and ultimately spread to a large minority of his subjects, particularly Muslims. The language combined Persian with elements of Turkish and Hindi. Urdu forms one of three major languages, along with English, on the subcontinent today, and it is the official language of Pakistan. Above

all, Akbar and his subordinates developed an efficient system of military recruitment and taxation, the latter based on landed property. Even with the huge demands of his government for revenue, prosperity increased in northern India. Muslim rule provided India with not only stable government but also new products such as paper. India continued an active regional trade with southeast Asia in spices and other products, even as Western shipping spread.

Akbar's reign was the high point of Mughal rule in India, yet the empire survived until the 19th century. Akbar's immediate successors, although less able than he, maintained the policy of conquest; during the first half of the 17th century, the empire reached its greatest size through gains in the south. Patronage of the arts contin-

Understanding Cultures

REACTIONS TO WESTERN VALUES

By the 18th century and certainly since that time, the ways individuals and groups have reacted to what they perceived as Western culture form an important part of world history. The basic subject of reactions to other cultures was not, of course, new. But extensive contact with the West was, and it was occurring at a time when, given the rise of science and the Enlightenment, Western culture was changing rapidly. It may be tempting to assume that, once exposed to modern Western values, peoples in Asia and Africa would enthusiastically embrace them, but not surprisingly, that is not what usually happened. Many people not only preferred their established cultures but also found specific Western beliefs particularly objectionable.

If you were a not-very-religious Muslim in the 18th century who had the unusual opportunity to visit England, what criticisms would you emphasize? Abu Taleb Khan was an Indian Muslim, born in 1752, who visited London late in the 18th century, hoping (in vain) to find work in the colonial administration. He was not a strict Muslim—the chance to drink wine in England pleased him—and he was not at all typical of the time. He liked many aspects of England, including the women, whom he found quite beautiful and, although unveiled, more strictly disciplined than the women back home. But he

also had several serious criticisms of English culture, which he carefully listed in a travel account he wrote, in Persian, when he returned home.

Point one, the English whom Abu Taleb met were not religious enough, and they indeed were "positively inclined" to atheism. Abu Taleb found this particularly true of the lower classes, who were dishonest and stole a lot.

Point two, the English were too proud and blindly confident, and they also, point three, had a "contempt for the customs of other nations," greatly preferring their own. Abu Taleb found that the English ridiculed his clothing as well as his religion, and he was deeply offended.

Point four, the English displayed an undue "passion for acquiring money," again a sign of the lack of proper balance in values. Some not only lusted after worldly riches but also were not generous, another obvious fault.

Few Muslims at this time had the chance to meet the English firsthand. Abu Taleb's comments are interesting in expressing Muslim values compared to some genuine trends in late Enlightenment England. Were Abu Taleb's criticisms those you anticipated in thinking about a non-Westerner's possible objections to Western culture?

---

ued. Mughal portrait painters flourished, and some influences from Western art crept into their works—as in the halos painted around the heads of the emperors. Mughal art had a distinctive style, different from Middle Eastern tradition, as the use of portraits demonstrates. In architecture, the Muslim heritage, including the use of decorative motifs, loomed larger. Under the emperor Shah Jehan I, who ruled from 1627 to 1658, the great tomb called the *Taj Mahal* was built. Designed by a Turkish architect, it required 14

years to construct. Initially intended for Jehan's favorite wife, it also served as a shrine for Jehan himself and is still rated one of the two or three most beautiful buildings in the world. Thus, in painting and architecture, as in the development of Urdu, the Mughals contributed greatly to India's artistic and cultural legacy. European Catholic missionaries to India encountered a solid culture. Except in Portuguese Goa, they effected few conversions. Several missionaries, in fact, picked up Hindu values and styles.

The political structure of the Mughal empire, however, began to unravel during the mid-17th century. Jehan departed from the tradition of toleration for Hindus. Hindu officials still served in his bureaucracy, and the emperor patronized Hindu poets and musicians, but many Hindu temples were demolished. Jehan also attacked Portuguese settlements in the east (near present-day Calcutta), although his huge army had great difficulty subduing a force of merely 1000 troops, whose superior weaponry foreshadowed later Western power on the subcontinent. Many Christian churches were destroyed, and thousands of Christian converts were killed. Taxes were increased to cover the growing expenses of the luxurious court. Many peasants were forced off the land because of escalating taxes, and rural crime became a growing problem.

Tensions increased under Jehan's son Aurangzeb, the last important Mughal ruler (1658–1707). Aurangzeb, who seized power by imprisoning his father, did manage to reduce taxation. But he intensified the attacks on the Hindu majority in the name of Islamic law. More temples were destroyed, and taxes on Hindus were raised. Hindus who sought bureaucratic service normally had to convert to the Muslim faith. Hindu resistance, not a major factor in most of the empire previously, now increased. This helped to rally regional princes in the south, who prevented the further conquest of the Deccan region. A new Hindu leader in the south, Shivaji, generated something akin to Hindu nationalism in forming a new Deccan state against which Aurangzeb battled in vain until his death.

Another important center of resistance arose in the northwest. Here, a new religion had evolved in the 16th century, in part as a reaction to earlier Muslim influence. This Sikh religion was closely related to Hinduism, although it was held by its leaders to be inspired directly by God. The Sikh faith combined Hindu practices and beliefs with a more activist approach. Sikhs abolished the caste system in

their religion, creating a military brotherhood dedicated to a vigorous role in the affairs of this world, including something like a holy war. The contemplative side of Hinduism was played down, although Sikh temples maintained many Hindu rituals, and a belief in reincarnation persisted. As the Mughal empire weakened, Sikhs established a regional realm of their own that lasted until 1849. Not only fierce fighters, the turbaned Sikhs were active in business and agricultural improvements. They formed an important religious minority in India from the 17th century onward, along with the larger Muslim group.

By the time of Aurangzeb's death, India was divided into essentially three major states: the Mughal empire (the largest), the new Deccan state, and the Sikh empire. Several smaller states survived in the south, while European settlements—Portuguese Goa, but also British and French ports—dotted both the east and west coasts. Within the Mughal empire, Hindus and Muslims were increasingly in conflict. Many Hindus withdrew into their own communities, fervently embracing their religious rituals in order to preserve their identity in a state they could no longer actively accept. Under Aurangzeb's 18th-century successors, Mughal administration became increasingly conservative and inefficient. Not only did political control become more lax, but India's educational system also declined as a result of Hindu isolation and Mughal inattention, and the economy deteriorated. Merchants suffered under the taxation of the later Mughals, who had no love for commerce. Indian technology—like that of much of Asia by the 17th and 18th centuries—stagnated.

In sum, an empire that had commenced with great brilliance and promise declined with extraordinary rapidity. Intolerance seems to have been a key to the downfall, along with the continued ability of most Hindus to retain their faith. In this situation, Mughal rulers became increasingly beleaguered and ineffective.

WESTERN INTRUSION INTO THE MUGHAL EMPIRE

Growing weakness and division in 18th-century India provided an unintended invitation to more active European intervention. Western merchant companies were drawn increasingly into Indian political affairs, to provide what they saw as necessary stability for their commercial operations. This was the most important impact of the new world economy on Asia in the early modern period. This motive for intervention was enhanced by conflicts among the European groups for influence on the subcontinent and particularly by the recurrent battles between England and France. Although European forces were small, their superiority in weapons gave them centralizing power in a divided region.

By the 18th century, Portugal's role in India was minor; the colony at Goa remained, but Portugal was too weak to reestablish other centers after the Mughal attacks. Dutch power was also declining, as the Dutch were preoccupied with administering their important holdings in the Indonesian islands. France and Britain had both established toeholds on the subcontinent during the 17th century, winning port rights by bargaining with local princes. The British East India Company operated a station at Calcutta, which gave them some access to the great wealth of the Ganges valley. The company had enormous influence over the British government and, through Britain's superior navy, excellent communication on the ocean routes. Their French rivals, in contrast, had less political clout at home, where the government was often distracted by purely European wars. The French were also more interested in missionary work than the British, who were long content to leave Hindu customs alone and devote themselves to commercial profits.

French-British rivalry raged bitterly through the middle decades of the 18th century. Each side recruited Indian princes as allies. Outright war-

fare erupted in 1744, and then again during the Seven Years' War. British officials had become alarmed at growing French influence with local princes. They were also roused in 1756 by the capture of Calcutta, by an Indian official, who imprisoned British captives in a "Black Hole"— an underground chamber originally used as a jail by the British themselves; many British officials suffocated. The East India Company's army recaptured Calcutta and then seized additional French and Indian territory, aided by generous bribes distributed to many regional princes. French power in India was decimated, and Britain was committed, without plan or clear intent, to the administration of Bengal, which stretched inland from Calcutta. Soon after this, the British also gained the island of Sri Lanka (Ceylon) from the Dutch. Although the British military force remained small, its superior weaponry, including field artillery, proved decisive in battles with Indian rulers. At the same time, more sophisticated naval power allowed Britain to outdistance its European rivals. Thus, from 1764 onward, a British empire in India was truly launched. Along with Indonesia and the Americas, India became one of the great territorial acquisitions of the West prior to 1800.

The complete history of British India did not begin until late in the 18th century, when the British government took a more active hand in Indian administration, supplementing the quasi-government of the East India Company. Indeed, before 1800, British control of the subcontinent was incomplete. The Mughal empire survived, although it was increasingly powerless, as did other regional kingdoms, including the Sikh state. Britain gained some new territories by force of arms but was also content to ally with local princes without disturbing their internal administration, again until after 1800.

However, British, and to an extent French and Dutch, commercial activities in India had an important effect even before the full implications of India's new colonial status were clear. Throughout the 18th century, much of India was increasingly drawn into the world trading patterns dominated by the West. Like Indonesia, but unlike the Americas, India offered a well-developed manufacturing economy along with a vast population and solid agricultural base. European merchants were eager to exploit India's wealth but were concerned that India not compete with their own manufacturing capabilities. Early in the 18th century, Britain began to levy high tariffs on the import of cotton cloth. This was one of India's chief industries, but it was just getting started in Britain. By limiting Indian access to a British market, London effectively reduced India's opportunities in world trade. British-made goods, including textiles, were widely sold on the subcontinent, while hundreds of thousands of Indian textile workers began to lose their jobs. In turn, the Indians exported gold and also agricultural products, such as tea, which were grown on commercial estates staffed by low-paid wage laborers. British agents also assumed growing command over Indian textile production, dictating wages and conditions to the workers, while the British East India Company claimed Indian gold as payment for their costs of administration.

These exploitative economic policies were not Britain's final statement on Indian affairs. As the British Empire matured after 1800—and particularly after 1830—economic relations with India became less one sided. In this early period, however, India was clearly added to the list of world territories that helped feed European wealth. An 18th-century Indian account described the climate of exploitation:

> But such is the little regard which they [the British] show to the people of this kingdom, and such their apathy and indifference for their welfare, that the people under their dominion groan everywhere, and are reduced to poverty and distress.

To be sure, some Indians welcomed British rule as an alternative to intolerant Muslim control. And many, particularly those in the independent kingdoms that still, in 1800, governed over half of the subcontinent in loose alliance with British administration, were scarcely aware of the British presence as yet. But the initial impact of European, especially British, operations deepened India's decline from the high point of Mughal rule. The Hindu religion, still the fundamental cultural resource for the majority, had ceased to spark vigorous philosophical and artistic statements. India's schools and universities were inactive. Manufacturing stagnated, and the level of prosperity reached under Akbar was not regained.

Basic structures—the family, the village, and the caste system—still organized daily life effectively. However, the subcontinent had suffered yet another foreign-imposed regime, the Mughals, whose ultimate political legacy involved the embittered relations between Hindus and Muslims and its own decline. As the 18th century drew to a close, India experienced yet another administration imposed from the outside. British rule relied on superior military technology rather than the sheer numbers of its forces, as earlier Muslims had. The British concentrated more on commercial purposes, in contrast to the Muslim tendency, at least ultimately, to focus on religious gain. But in many ways, the British occupation confirmed what was now a well-established Indian tradition of long-suffering subjugation and control by outside forces, secure in the belief that basic local and religious structures could be preserved and were unable, in any event, to offer an effective political or military alternative. It could not be predicted, in 1800, whether British rule would finally overturn this aspect of the Indian tradition.

THE RISE AND DECLINE OF ASIAN EMPIRES

The rise of the great early modern empires in India and the Middle East, dazzling though they were, had not prevented the relative decline of both regions in the face of the rapid change and expansion of Western civilization. Partly because of the persistence of cultural and political traditions, partly because of the institutions of foreign military rule, neither Indian nor Middle Eastern civilization remained actively innovative, in their technology or intellectual life, between 1700 and 1800. The conditions of most ordinary people, the bulk of them peasants, changed little. Taxes rose, especially under rapacious Ottoman governors, and economic conditions deteriorated somewhat—most obviously in India—but the basic framework remained the same.

This pattern was not totally different from that of China during the same period. Here, too, we will discuss a growing stagnation, even as the West continued to develop rapidly. Here, too, there was relative decline as a result. But in the Middle East and particularly India, the outcome of relative decline was more quickly visible. Neither civilization was able to mount a policy of strict isolation. In both cases, European merchants dominated in growing numbers. Also unlike the Chinese, the Ottomans were unable to establish any durable agreement with expanding Russian forces, in part because the Russian heartland was closer, and in part because Russian appetites for warm-water ports and contact with Middle Eastern Orthodox Christians were more vigorous than vaguer interests concerning expansion against China. Despite outside pressures and the example of imaginative individual leaders like Suleiman and Akbar, the Ottoman and Mughal empires were no more eager than the Chinese to undertake significant internal reform. For Muslims, a reluctance to copy the West, so long viewed as culturally barbarian, was at least as great as a similar sentiment in China.

The results of first relative, then absolute, decline began to emerge after 1700. The growing British hold over much of India was the most dramatic sign that internal weakness plus

Western ambition was a powerful combination. But the Middle East was vulnerable as well. In 1798, a small naval expedition under a discontented French revolutionary general, Napoleon Bonaparte, sailed to Egypt and conquered the province after brief fighting. This was a minor episode in the European history of the time, and the French were indeed soon routed by British naval forces as Napoleon returned to France to pursue grander scenarios. But to Muslims, the shock waves were profound; they came to realize that even a minor European excursion could now topple a proud Ottoman province. The question of a Western threat for the Turks and Arabs and of Western domination for the Indians was becoming paramount by 1800, despite the important political strengths that had surfaced in the 16th and 17th centuries. Indian and Middle Eastern responses, after 1800, would differ widely. However, for a moment, both civilizations seemed caught in a similar midposition among the ancient civilizations, between the expansive rise of the West and Russia and the proud isolation of east Asia.

ISSUES AND CONNECTIONS

Two issues regarding the Ottoman and Mughal empires deserve particular attention. First, although decline occurred before the early modern period ended, particularly with the Mughals, it is important to understand achievements as well. Second, the two different societies must not be homogenized. Two Islamic gunpowder empires, imposed in part by outside nomadic invaders, constitute real similarities. But key features differed, and so did the fate of the regimes by 1750.

Both empires have now perished. Continuities from Mughal India are particularly cultural, in art and in cooking for example. But the firmer position of the Muslim minority on the subcontinent, the use of Urdu as Pakistan's official language, and some additional tensions between Muslims and Hindus owe something to the Mughals as well.

The hold of Turks in the northern Middle East, and their interest in Europe as well as Asia, is an ongoing Ottoman heritage. So are some of the achievements of Ottoman art and architecture, plus the great contribution to global popular culture through the coffeehouses. Movements born within Islam in the period also persist. The Middle East today cannot be understood without grasping the Ottoman contributions—and the impact of the empire's later collapse without to date any real replacement.

SUGGESTED WEB SITES

For virtual visits to Ottoman palaces, see http://www.ee.bilkent.edu.tr/~history/topkapi.html. For a simulated interview with Akbar, on his methods of rule, go to http://itihaas.com/medieval/akbar2.html.

SUGGESTED READINGS

Recent work includes Donald Quataert, *Consumption Studies and the History of the Ottoman Empire* (2000); Daniel Goffman, *Britons on the Ottoman Empire* (1998); Asli Curakman, *From the "Terror of the Word" to the "Sick Man of Europe": European Images of Ottoman Empire and Society from the Sixteenth Century to the Nineteenth* (2002); and Lynda Carroll, ed., *Historical Archaeology of the Ottoman Empire: Breaking New Ground* (2000).

On the Middle East generally, L. S. Stavrianos, *The Ottoman Empire: Was It the Sick Man of Europe?* (1957), offers some cohesive interpretations of key issues. For comprehensive surveys, see Stanford Shaw, *History of the Ottoman Empire and Modern Turkey*, Vol. 1, 1280–1808 (1976), and Peter F. Sugar, *Southeastern Europe Under Ottoman Rule, 1354–1804* (1977). For India, see M. Prawdin, *The Builders of the Mogul Empire* (1963); P. Spear, *Twilight of the Mughals* (1951), provides additional insight. On Mughal cultural development, consult Gavin Hambly, *Mughal Cities* (1968). For an excellent overview, see Ira Lapidus, *A History of Islamic Societies* (1988).

East Asia: Degrees of Isolation

The response of east Asia to the West and the new world economy differed greatly from the reactions that developed in Russia during the early modern period. At the same time, the east Asian situation differed from that of the Muslim empires as well. China, Japan, and Korea made absolutely no attempt at westernization, although Japan briefly flirted with the idea. But there was little intrusion from the West, in contrast to India. Geographically most distant from the West, operating in a culture much more accustomed to proud isolation, east Asia stood apart from the rest of the continent. Nonetheless, this was an important period in the region's history, as different sets of trends took root in China and Japan.

Both China and Japan adopted new policies in response to the growing level of global contacts under Western auspices after the 15th century. Japan decided on isolation quite explicitly, after over a half-century of intense interaction with Western influence and participation in the silver trade. China's decisions were more complex. The active commercial outreach of the Song and early Ming dynasties was not resumed. Chinese merchants remained active in the Philippines and southeast Asia, but not beyond. World trade came to China, not the other way around. But it did come, with significant profits for China because of its unrivaled manufacturing of silks and other luxury products. Westerners were not entirely banned, but they were treated as an insignificant and decidedly inferior group. These policies succeeded during the early modern period itself. But the policy of relative isolation raised problems for the more distant future, for by the 18th century, east Asian civilization no longer possessed sufficient dynamism to maintain on its own the pace set by other areas of the world, particularly the West. By standing apart, it fell behind.

Japanese and Chinese patterns during the early modern period were not identical. Here, the importance of purely regional developments must be recognized, along with the larger relationship to the world economy. Japan changed more than China did, in part through the belated utilization of its Confucian heritage. As a result, by the 18th century, Japanese government and society were more vigorous internally than their Chinese counterparts.

KEY QUESTIONS   *What was China's position in the world economy? How did Chinese and Japanese responses to the West and the world economy compare? What were the most important changes in Japan during the early modern period?*

CHINA: THE RESUMPTION OF THE DYNASTIES

Mongol rule in China turned out to be no more than a painful but passing episode, lasting from the later part of the 13th century until 1368. Chinese resentment of the Mongols as barbarians confirmed their suspicions of the world outside their boundaries. In fact, the Mongol episode paid tribute once again to the historic assimilating power of Chinese culture. The Mongol rulers used the bureaucracy, rather than destroying it, for the simple reason that they, like earlier invaders, could think of no better administrative system. Kubilai Khan, himself a Buddhist, supported Confucian scholarship, although Confucianists did not return his affection. Trade actually increased, as contacts with Islamic merchants expanded. Chinese culture continued to experiment with new forms, particularly new dramatic and musical styles for urban audiences.

Although Chinese vitality seemed unaffected by Mongol rule, resentment increased, especially when serious flooding pushed the peasantry to revolt. Revolutionary forces drove out the Mongols, to the northern plains of Mongolia, in 1368. A rebel leader, born of peasant stock, seized the Mongol capital of Beijing and proclaimed a new *Ming*, meaning "brilliant," dynasty, which was to last until 1644.

The Ming dynasty early on experimented with great trading expeditions through the Indian Ocean and then, in 1433, suspended these voyages, on the grounds that the effort was too costly for what it yielded to China. The initiative was noteworthy, but the decision to establish greater isolation was in many ways more important to China's course during the early modern period. Other expenses, for a dynasty bent on building a splendid capital while protecting China from any Mongol resurgence, helped prompt the decision. However, the withdrawal reflected other, more important factors, beginning with a preference for traditional expenditures rather than distant foreign involvements. Chinese merchant activity continued to be extensive in southeast Asia. Chinese trading groups established permanent settlements in the Philippines, Malaysia, and Indonesia, where they contributed to the cultural diversity of the area and maintained a disproportionate role in local and regional trading activities into the 20th century. But China's chance to become a dominant world trading power was lost, at least for some centuries, with a decision that in essence confirmed the relatively low status of commerce within the official Chinese worldview.

To Western eyes, accustomed to judging a society's dynamism by its ability to reach out and acquire new territories or trading advantages, China's decision may seem hard to understand, the precursor to some inevitable decline. In Chinese terms, of course, it was the brief trading flurry that was unusual, not its cessation. And China did not obviously suffer from its decision to pull back. The government carefully regulated contacts with the West, permitting trade only through the Portuguese-controlled port of Macao. Ming emperors consolidated their rule over the empire's vast territory, although there was more factional fighting in the imperial court than had been true in earlier dynasties. The bureaucracy functioned well, as the Ming sent out representatives to guard against corruption by local officials. Internal economic development continued as well. Industry expanded, with growth in the production of textiles and porcelain. Ongoing trade with southeast Asia enriched the port cities. Agricultural production and the general population both increased. There was one striking economic change. Because Chinese goods were so widely sought abroad—Europeans began calling porcelain tableware *china* in the 17th century—the country gained new profits in world trade. In particular, it imported more New World silver (brought in Western ships either to China directly or to the Philippines) than any other country in the world. (India was second, and for similar reasons in terms of balance of trade.) Silver provided new tax resources for the state.

Historians of China have characterized the Ming period in terms of the importance of "change within tradition." The phrase aptly summed up developments under Ming rule, after the trading expeditions ceased. Chinese society evolved within frameworks previously established. There were no intellectual breakthroughs, no basic alterations in social structure, with the continued preeminence of the educated gentry-bureaucrat group. The expansion of trade, and the rise of a group of "overseas Chinese" merchants in southeast Asian cities with close ties to the homeland, did not shake the earlier social priorities. Cultural activity focused on summarizing expanding knowledge in medicine, agriculture, and technology; on maintaining the interest in drama and poetry; and on pursuing philosophical training in Confucianism. Family structure remained similarly stable, with an emphasis on patriarchal control, reverence for elders and ancestors, and the provision of male heirs.

The Ming dynasty began to decline early in the 1600s. Emperors grew weaker, the bureaucracy more corrupt, while peasant unrest increased under the impact of population pressure. Rebellions and roving gangs of bandits became widespread. A popular rebellion caused the last Ming emperor to hang himself. This internal disorder attracted invaders from southern Manchuria, who in 1644 established a new dynasty, the Qing (sometimes called *Manchu*), which lasted until 1912—the last royal house to rule China.

Again traditionally, the Qing (or Pure) dynasty started out with a flourish. The Manchurian emperors were foreigners in the eyes of most Chinese, and they maintained a separate military establishment to support their regime. But on the whole, their rule quickly took on familiar patterns, with a substantial reliance on the bureaucracy, which remained in Chinese hands, dominated by the educated scholar-gentry. The emperors also encouraged Confucianism. Like most early dynasties, the Qing initially expanded the empire's territory. They pushed the Mongols still farther north and extended the empire into Muslim central Asia; they also took over the supervision of Tibet. Finally, they conquered the offshore island of Taiwan, which had previously been ruled by trading officials from the Dutch East India Company. This expansion, directed by the able emperor Kang Hsi from 1662–1722, revealed the successful merger of Manchurian military skill and Chinese administrative expertise. Kang Hsi himself mastered the Confucian classics and sponsored important cultural competitions, endearing him to the Chinese scholar-gentry class.

Kang Hsi and his 18th-century successors also worked on increasing government centralization—another common impulse of vigorous early dynasties in the Chinese tradition. Central schools for training would-be bureaucrats expanded, and a Grand Council was established to direct the bureaucracy and process the mountain of paperwork resulting from the regular reports of local and provincial administrators. Carefully formulated regulations specified the punishments for local rebellions. Village leaders were held responsible for individuals within their community who committed crimes or tried to evade legitimate debts. Chinese society remained the most closely regulated and the most centralized in the world. Local and central administrations intertwined, and there was no real separation, as in the Western tradition, between public and private concerns.

During this vigorous period, the Qing dynasty continued to regulate European contacts

Christian missionary (a Bajan Jesuit) in China, 17th century. Jesuits proceeded cautiously, respecting Chinese culture.

Portuguese community set up on Macao. Although some officials wanted to force the Portuguese out, the dominant view was that it was safe to leave them there because they could be so closely supervised. Indeed, it would be easier to control them in this single center than to try to monitor their activities on the high seas. As one viceroy put it:

> Our military forces can watch over the foreigners by just guarding the surrounding sea. We shall know how to put them at death's door as soon as they cherish any disloyal design. Now if we move them to the open sea, by what means could we punish the foreign evildoers and how could we keep them in submission and defend ourselves against them?

Cultural contacts with the West, or indeed with any other civilizations outside the traditional Chinese orbit, thus reached only modest levels by 1800. Some conscious policies of regulating foreign merchants and missionaries combined with great confidence in the superiority of Chinese ways to produce this result. Efforts by Britain and other Western countries to open further trading contacts were consistently rebuffed. An English representative in 1793 was treated as if he brought tribute from an inferior state. He was forced to kowtow (to bow by kneeling and knocking one's head on the floor), as the subject-state envoys from countries like Korea or Vietnam were required to do. Then the emperor, rejecting the representative's request for more trade, wrote a long, patronizing letter to King George III explaining that China had no need of English goods.

with China. Kang Hsi negotiated an agreement with the expanding Russian empire, setting their mutual border along the Amur River, that was to last until 1850. This checked Russian expansion into Chinese territory, although the Russians continued to move eastward into Siberia. Small numbers of Jesuit missionaries had been allowed into China since the 16th century, from western Europe, mainly because they brought useful scientific and technical knowledge, including superior clocks. For their part, the missionaries were careful to adopt many Chinese ways, approving ancestor worship and wearing Confucian clothing. In the 18th century, the government, growing less secure, began to persecute the small number of Christians in China.

The Chinese outlook toward limited Western contacts was symbolized by its reaction to the

CULTURAL AND SOCIAL TRENDS: SOME NEW PROBLEMS

There was no reason to suspect in 1800 that China was on the eve of some unprecedented difficulties going beyond the usual decline of a dynasty. However, significant problems in the

Scholar and crane returning home, 15th century. Note the similarities to earlier Chinese styles (illustrated in Chapter 8).

empire occurred under the Qing even before this point. These problems were not initially political; the institutions of government remained secure. But they raised important issues nevertheless.

In the first place, Chinese culture even under the early Qing seemed to stagnate. The Qing, as foreign rulers, favored traditional expressions as a means of proving their sympathy with Chinese ways; thus, the emphasis on the classics of Chinese literature and philosophy, already extensive, increased. By the 18th century, most educated Chinese turned to collecting older examples of art and expounding literary criticisms of ancient works, rather than seeking to create new styles. The amount of cultural effort was great; many bureaucrats and other educated people painted nature scenes or dabbled in calligraphy and poetry writing. But the goal was decidedly uninspired, with trivial themes emphasized and traditional styles rigidly defended. Similarly in philosophy, attention focused on expounding past principles and offering extended commentary on what had

been written in earlier periods. Thus, the earlier Chinese ability to blend a reverence for tradition with an interest in promoting new styles and stimulating new thinking seemed somewhat stultified.

The Chinese economy, for its part, did not break fundamental new ground either. Revealingly, after the early Ming advances in navigational devices, the Chinese produced no significant technologies during the Ming and Qing dynasties. It was not a matter of decline. As in the arts, Chinese levels of achievement remained high, and Chinese craft products, such as porcelain (now known simply as *china* to the Europeans), were greatly valued. However, an earlier ability to build on past accomplishments seemed to have been lost.

One key symptom of the new outlook toward technology showed in the Chinese reaction to European superiority in weapons. The Chinese were perfectly capable, in the 16th and 17th centuries, of building cannons as good as the Europeans had, even though they had not pioneered their design. But, in fact, they did not care to; the subject did not interest them greatly, and they were content to assemble inferior muskets and small guns, confident that their strength on the land was sufficient to keep any European threat at bay. To be sure, the Chinese had never been as interested in military advances as in manufacturing technology, but their earlier creativity in the whole area was demonstrably slipping.

The interruption of China's tradition of innovation in basic technology did not, indeed, prevent continued internal economic development, supported by both the government and private business interests. During the late Ming and early Qing dynasties, manufacturing, city growth, and internal trade surpassed all previous levels. China's strong production base and extensive market activities help explain why, well into the 19th century, the nation could largely ignore Western goods, leaving Western merchants casting about for items to trade for sought-after Chinese products such as silk and porcelain. However, China's economic surge did not bring fundamental economic transformation of the sort that might have generated new manufacturing technology. Much production lay in the hands of rural cottage artisans whose low wages discouraged more elaborate capitalist arrangements. And by the mid-18th century, the economy began to stagnate, bringing renewed poverty and distress. Why did China not make a fuller turn to new economic forms?

The Chinese upper class had, of course, always esteemed traditionalism and looked rather scornfully at purely economic activity; such a viewpoint, nonetheless, had not prevented earlier technological or commercial advance. The increasing centralization of the government under Qing rulers, who were more cautious than their Han or Tang forebears, may have been a cause as well.

The influx of New World silver had both exhilarating and disruptive effects on Chinese society. As early as 1600, officials worried about growing income inequality. One wrote, "One man in a hundred is rich, while nine out of ten

are impoverished. The poor cannot stand up to the rich who, though few in number, are able to control the majority. The lord of silver rules heaven and the god of copper cash reigns over the earth." Even Europeans noted price inflation in China, thanks to the silver influx. In China itself, Confucian traditionalists were troubled by flashy new wealth along with new signs of dire poverty.

A more fundamental problem was a rapid increase in population levels, from the late Ming dynasty onward. Between 1600 and 1800, the Chinese population more than doubled, from 150 million to over 300 million people. China's well-organized agriculture and the strong cultural emphasis on high birth rates, in order to produce male heirs in the family, had long encouraged population growth. Many dynasties had previously declined when such growth outstripped available resources, creating greater poverty. Usually, however, population levels would then level off, but this did not happen during the late Ming and early Qing periods. Agricultural techniques were advanced enough to maintain a large but impoverished population. Cultivation of some crops brought in from the Americas by European traders and missionaries, particularly corn and the sweet potato, added to the agricultural production that could support high population levels. New strains of rice, which grew more rapidly than older varieties, achieved the same end. As a result of these crop changes, China began to shift from a society in which population sometimes outstripped resources to a society chronically challenged by its population levels.

Population pressure, in turn, had two clear effects, quite apart from the great poverty of many Chinese peasants and urban workers. First, it made political unrest a greater threat than had usually been the case except when dynasties were losing their grip. Second, it diverted resources that might have been used to encourage further manufacturing or trade to a desperate effort to sustain the vast population. The empire's economic flexibility was reduced by the need to devote so much labor and land to agricultural

History Debate

CHINESE AND WESTERN ECONOMIES

By 1750, western Europe's economy was on the verge of a major transformation, the Industrial Revolution. China's was not. Most historians acknowledge China's great prowess in manufacturing, its skilled workers, and important natural resources. Some, eager to expand this recognition and to avoid overvaluing the West, argue that the difference between China and the West was trivial. Britain, faced with shrinking forests, had to develop a more coal-based economy to compensate, and by chance, it had well-located coal deposits; Spain had discovered the Americas by accident. But there were no deep gaps involved, no huge Western plus or Chinese minus.

Other historians stress the importance of key Western values in promoting technological change, such as a desire to dominate nature. They note greater Chinese conservatism, including the suspicion of merchant values. Europeans, by the 17th century, commented on how the Chinese tended to prefer old ways and scorn technological change, in contrast to eager European interest. (By this point, Europeans were prone to judge other societies by their technological prowess, which usually left Europeans feeling good about themselves.)

This debate has contemporary implications. China is now growing fast industrially. Some historians see this as a big change, others as a resumption of more traditional manufacturing prowess, though with new machines.

Which point of view—China and the West running neck and neck, or traditional China as flawed in industrial potential compared to the West—makes most sense?

subsistence. This may be the clearest cause of the lack of innovation in the economy and possibly even in the culture.

By the late 18th century, massive poverty and slow economic growth began to surface as clear political problems. The Qing government found it increasingly difficult to collect adequate taxes. Collection efforts, along with grinding misery, also began to produce a new series of popular revolts. Peasants in many regions formed secret societies. An uprising by one such society in the 1790s, the White Lotus, was vanquished only with great difficulty. At the same time, the Qing dynasty was showing signs of internal decay: military virtues waned among the Manchu generals, who preferred more luxurious living, and court officials became more corrupt, siphoning off money from the state. This kind of decline normally prefaced a

period of growing instability and, ultimately, the rise of a new dynasty. Greater disorder came, without question, in the 19th century, but for once in China's long history a new regime, not a new dynasty, was the ultimate result.

Stagnation and political problems were not the only feature of Chinese society under the Qing. Some interesting changes occurred in popular culture, as Confucian leaders managed to persuade more and more peasants to abandon older beliefs in magic and superstition, and to use doctors instead of shamans in cases of illness. This shift in outlook, somewhat similar to changes occurring in the West during the same period, differentiated China from most agricultural societies, where popular religion had yet to be disturbed. The scholar-bureaucrats also pressed peasants and city dwellers to standardize the worship of local gods and goddesses. The practice of celebrating various deities and building temples to them had persisted from the classical period or before, along with other belief systems, and the government long tried to bend this popular faith toward loyalty to the state. Certainly, in 1800, the Chinese government remained easily able to regulate China's contacts with other cultures. European influence, most notably, remained no greater than it had been two centuries before, and European traders were powerless to escape government supervision. Only developments after 1800 would break this stalemate, to China's disadvantage.

Japanese garden style: Sanbro-In Temple, Kyoto, laid out under Hideyoshi at the end of the 16th century. The pond, waterfall, and bridge show the move toward a disciplined nature.

JAPAN AND THE ORIGINS OF ISOLATION

Japanese social forms were less firmly set around 1450 than those of China, so it is not surprising that Japanese history shows more movement, more basic changes, than the evolution of its giant neighbor. However, the Japanese did come to share one basic concept with the Chinese: the outside world was a risky and inferior place, best kept at bay.

Japan was touched only indirectly by the Mongol invasions. The failure of the two great Mongol attacks bolstered Japanese confidence in the god-protected superiority of their own society even over that of China, which now lay under foreign thrall. But the defense effort was very costly to the ruling government of the shogun; it contributed to the fall of this essentially feudal monarchy in 1338. Japan returned to a stage of regional feudal governments, of the warlike daimyos and their samurai supporters. A central government remained in form only. In fact, disorder and warfare, punctuated by some peasant rebellions, continued until 1573. A host of classic campaigns, celebrated in legend and more recently in Japanese films, dotted this period, in which samurai fighting techniques and codes of honor were perfected.

Despite disorder, the Japanese economy continued to progress. Because the daimyos were well aware of the importance of prosperous agriculture for their own tax revenues, they promoted irrigation efforts and improved methods of farming. Trade also grew, and the use of banking and money expanded. Daimyo supervision of trade established a pattern of government-business collaboration that in many ways has remained to the present day.

Japanese culture continued to develop as well, again creating durable new forms. The Zen strain of Buddhism, stressing calm meditation and a love of nature, predominated in religion, although there were many Buddhist sects, and Shintoism still guided family ceremonies as well. Zen Buddhism encouraged an interest in rituals, as demonstrations of the simplicity of true beauty and as signs of self-control. Tea ceremonies and flower arrangements were important parts of family and social life. The Zen spirit also influenced art, leading to a focus on simple but dramatic representations of nature.

In literature, adventure stories and poetry continued to dominate. Soon after 1600, a new poetic form, the *haiku*, a 17-syllable verse in a 5–7–5 pattern, became popular. Although this

The Portuguese come to Japan, 16th century.

was a new style, it maintained the east Asian tradition of carefully enunciated rules of poetry and an interest in the clever play on words. Composing haiku became a favored pastime among all social classes.

By the mid–1500s, however, the Japanese combination of feudal warfare and economic and cultural creativity was eroding. Feudalism could no longer contain the forces at work in Japanese society. A rising merchant class complicated the feudal pattern. Armies of peasant soldiers were sometimes able to beat samurai swordsmen—just as common bowmen in Europe had ultimately dislodged the feudal cavalry. Furthermore, Portuguese traders reached Japanese shores in 1542 and, although they were initially welcomed by a people who had once before learned from others, their presence encouraged a desire among more conservative cultural and political leaders to develop a stronger government that could regulate foreign intrusion. And the guns and cannons the Portuguese brought obviously threatened the fighting traditions of the samurai. Many regional daimyos tried to ally with the foreigners to gain a weapons advantage; the result, for a time, was simply further disorder. In the long run, however, the advent of gunpowder increased the possibility of greater governmental centralization.

As the Japanese quickly learned to manufacture their own muskets, the fate of the undiluted feudal system was sealed.

The end of pure feudalism came in the form of several brutal wars at the conclusion of the 16th century in which a successful general, Hideyoshi, emerged victorious. Hideyoshi was able to reestablish centralized rule by using the allegiance of the daimyos. Thus, the feudal classes remained in Japan but were once again overseen by a national administration. After Hideyoshi's death, a general from the Tokugawa family took over the office of shogun and completed the process of centralization. A "great peace" settled on Japan, after more than two centuries of internal warfare.

This new centralization caused a reassessment of Japan's contacts with the outside world. Hideyoshi contemplated a policy of foreign conquest to keep the warlike samurai busy—a policy later renewed by Japan after 1890. However, an attempt to invade Korea failed, as Chinese armies supported their vassal government there, and this convinced the new Japanese government to concentrate instead on its own unique territories.

Hideyoshi and the early Tokugawa shoguns thus turned to what they saw as the problem of Western influence. Initial Western contacts had

World Profiles

TOYOTOMI HIDEYOSHI (1536–1548)

Toyotomi Hideyoshi was an outstanding military leader who extended earlier 16th-century efforts to tame the power struggles among the daimyos in favor of more centralized, orderly rule. The son of a peasant, Hideyoshi used his military acumen to rise to power in Japan; he then parlayed even greater diplomatic talents into the creation of a string of alliances with the daimyos that resulted in a central state by 1590. Hideyoshi, unlike most Japanese leaders before or after, dreamed of wider achievements as he contemplated ruling China and even India (despite, or perhaps because of, knowing little about either place). He did launch two abortive attacks on Korea, the last still in progress when he died. More importantly, Hideyoshi also launched the campaign to limit European and Christian influence in Japan. Hideyoshi's hopes to pass power to his son were dashed as the Tokugawa family seized control and his plans of overseas expansion were dropped. Nevertheless, he had contributed greatly to changing the course of Japanese history. How does Hideyoshi compare, in achievements and goals, to other great military leaders in world history who rose from the ranks?

This portrait reflects the military might and confidence that spurred Toyotomi Hideyoshi's achievements. (Granger Collection)

been welcomed not only for the guns and navigation technology the Westerners brought but also, among some Japanese, for the religious message of Christianity. Interested in learning from foreign example and impressed by a religion that seemed to accompany military and trading success, several thousand Japanese converted to Catholicism in the port cities where Europeans clustered, during the late 16th century. But Japan's new rulers looked harshly on this development. They feared European power and thought that where Western religion went, political control might not be far behind. When the Spanish government established military outposts in the Philippines, to enhance the missionary effort there, Hideyoshi's fears deepened. In 1597, he banned all foreign missionaries, crucifying nine of them and seventeen of their Japanese followers.

Western weapons seemed at least as great a threat as Christianity. The new central rulers feared the results of independent daimyo access to

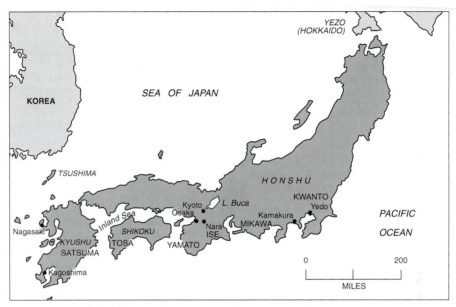

Feudal Japan Under the Shogunate, 16th Century

Western firearms. Rather, they sought state control over guns, while also protecting samurai warrior values. To do this, they needed to restrict foreign trade.

The Tokugawa shogunate completed the destruction of Christianity in Japan. It severely curtailed Western trade as well. Only merchants from the Netherlands were allowed in Japan—Holland was feared less than Spain or Portugal because, being Protestant, it was not linked to what seemed to the Japanese an ambitious and powerful papacy. Dutch traders were confined to one isolated, carefully controlled port (Nagasaki). Even Chinese merchants were supervised. In 1635, the Japanese themselves were forbidden to travel abroad, and those already overseas were not allowed to return home. Finally, the government prohibited the construction of large, seagoing ships; only vessels for coastal trade were permitted. Japan, far more than China, was ostensibly cut off from the outside world. A nation that had once eagerly imitated foreign example, and would do so again in the 19th century, pulled

back on this occasion. European ways seemed too foreign, and too inferior, to be allowed free play, and attacking outside influence was a useful way of cementing new national loyalties after the long period of disunity.

The policy of isolation combined with the regulation of military technology, now that foreign items could not be imported. The shogunate deliberately turned against guns, preferring to preserve the Japanese social structure. Only a few could be manufactured each year—sometimes no more than nine for the whole country. Even more than in the Ottoman Empire, where printing was long shunned, Japan decisively rejected the idea that new technology is always good technology.

In isolation, Japan proceeded to construct effective political forms and completed the development of a national culture, sponsoring considerable social change while seeming to maintain older values. Unlike the earlier Kamakura shogunate, the Tokugawa rulers depended less on personal ties with feudal lords and more on an efficient bureaucracy imbued with Confucian values. The warrior aristocracy was given great social prestige, including special privileges in law, and special costumes, although in fact there was no fighting to be done. Although warrior values and military training continued to describe the samurai ethic, upper-class bureaucrats learned the importance of administrative efficiency and training—Confucian principles that gained ground during the 17th and 18th centuries. This was an important period of cultural change in Japan, as Confucianism, and therefore secular interests, increasingly dominated intellectual life. The rapid spread of Confucian education and literacy disseminated the new cultural interests by the 19th century. The Japanese interpretation of Confucianism involved far wider access to schools than in China, and Buddhist schools contributed as well. Thanks to extensive schooling, literacy (at 25 percent among adult men) was far higher than in any society outside Western Europe and North America.

Although confined to internal trading, merchant activity flourished during the Tokugawa period. The government favored commerce but was somewhat scornful of the merchant class. Great trading houses emerged, selling rice, textile goods, metals, and liquor all over Japan; some of these big family firms still operate in Japan today. This was a key period for the development of banking and merchant experience in Japan. Japanese agriculture advanced as well, becoming more technologically sophisticated than any other system in Asia. Japanese farmers learned about crop specialization and the better use of fertilization; they also became increasingly accustomed to producing for sale on the market. Although economic growth slowed somewhat after 1700, Japan had the most advanced commercial economy in the world after that of Western society. In another important development, population size was controlled in the 18th century, in contrast to the situation in China. Many peasants practiced infanticide of unwanted—and particularly female—children.

Japanese literature and art remained vigorous under the Tokugawa, who supervised cultural life to prevent disorder. Enthusiasm for haiku poetry and the stylized *No* theater continued. Literacy and book publishing spread. As in China, the growth of cities—particularly the capital city, Edo, which had a million inhabitants by 1700—encouraged a flourishing entertainment industry. Professional women entertainers, called *geisha*, or "accomplished persons," specialized in singing and dancing for male clientele. A new form of drama, Kabuki, developed in the 18th century, more popular in its portrayals than the No forms; Kabuki theater remains active in Japan today. Not surprisingly, the varied artistic endeavors and continuing isolation of Japan produced a heavy emphasis on the nation's uniqueness and superiority, the forerunner of a cultural nationalism that still runs strong in Japan.

Japan thus emerged, by the 18th century, as an unusually diverse society, tolerating more internal tensions than China. Feudal and Confucian elements coexisted. An official lack of interest in commerce belied rapid commercial expansion; Buddhist spiritual fervor could survive in the face of a national emphasis on controlled expression and secular education. These tensions contributed to the dynamism of Japanese society, which had unquestionably advanced under the policy of isolation.

Indeed, by the 18th century, the policy of isolation was slightly relaxed. Some Japanese were allowed greater contact with Dutch traders in the port of Nagasaki; a few scholars learned Dutch and became familiar with Western advances in military technology and medicine. These early exchanges helped prepare the way for the fuller adaptation of Western ways in the 19th century. At the same time, they whetted the appetites of those few Japanese aware of the gap between their society and the West; Japanese backwardness in scientific and medical knowledge seemed particularly galling.

There were problems by 1800. Japan did not experience the kind of population pressure that burdened China, although its islands were severely crowded. But Japan's commercial agriculture resulted in a division between landowning peasants and landless paid laborers, whose discontent produced periodic revolts. On the whole, however, Japan's strengths, generated by the important developments of the early modern period, would help explain the nation's extraordinary reaction to challenges in the 19th century, when isolation finally had to be abandoned completely. The contrast with the looming crisis in China was marked, but there were some new concerns, and these too help explain why Japan became more open to the possibility of more radical transformations.

VITALITY AND TENSION IN EAST ASIA

East Asian history between 1400 and 1800 was no mere record of isolation. Although during this period the civilization was set apart from some of the wider currents of world history, these were centuries of considerable internal change. Change meant new political dynasties but also new cultural and economic forms, particularly in Japan. It also meant some new problems, such as the overpopulation that surged in China. The role of tradition was strong as well, in Japanese culture and its sense of national identity, in Chinese politics and society more generally.

East Asia's lag behind Western levels of technology and military organization during these centuries would leave the civilization vulnerable after 1800. It might have been preferable if the society had assimilated or reacted to European styles more gradually, to the extent necessary to keep pace with European power. This was the sentiment that inspired China's communist leader in 1984 to claim that the Ming-Qing period of isolation—as well as a more recent, brief attempt to insulate China from foreign contact—was a mistake. However, in our own day, it seems clear that east Asian civilization, or at least significant portions of it, has

been most successful in developing competitive alternatives to Western ways. In this sense, the period of isolation, as a time for solidifying traditions apart from the distraction of foreign influences, may not have been totally ill conceived. Certainly, the decisions to limit ties with the West allowed east Asian societies to continue to follow their own complex dynamic for a final few centuries, before confronting some of the larger currents of modern world history.

ISSUES AND CONNECTIONS

A major challenge in the study of east Asian history involves judging Japanese and, even more, Chinese developments by relevant standards. Many have noted that Chinese policies contributed to a relative lag with Europe, particularly in technology. But China prospered in the world economy and avoided significant invasions or disruptions. There was little reason for dissatisfaction with major policies at the time. Similarly, a few symptoms of decline by the later 18th century, relative to China's own past standards, need to be handled carefully. The symptoms were subtle compared, say, to Mughal India.

Japan, making a decision toward much greater isolation, managed significant internal change even so. In the process, Japan opened some new differences with China, even in the implementation of Confucianism.

Because Japan introduced more innovations in the early modern period than China did, it is not surprising that there are more direct links between early modern and present-day Japan. The new commitment to education is the most important point here, even though the nature of Japanese education differed from its present form. China added to its intellectual and political heritage without generating major new features except for the drumbeat of population growth.

SUGGESTED WEB SITES

On palaces and cities under the Ming, see http://chinavista.com/beijing/gugong/!start.html. On the Tokugawa capital, Edo, see http://www.us-japan.org/edomatsu/Start/frame.html. On the Tokugawa, see http://www.namos.co.jp/aichi-hatsu/english/ittop.htm.

SUGGESTED READINGS

An excellent collection of sources is W. T. de Bary, ed., *Sources of Chinese Tradition* (1966); close to source reading, offering fascinating insight into Chinese provincial life, is Jonathan Spence, *The Death of Woman Wang* (1979). Larger studies of China in the early modern period include J. D. Spence and J. E. Wills Jr., eds., *From Ming to Qing: Conquest, Religion and Continuity in Seventeenth Century China* (1979); Albert Chan, *The Glory and Fall of the Ming Dynasty* (1982); Roy

Huang, *1587: A Year of No Significance; The Ming Dynasty in Decline* (1981); Jonathan Spence, *The Memory Palace of Matteo Ricci* (1984) and *The Search for Modern China* (1990); and J. K. Fairbank, ed., *The Chinese World Order: Traditional Chinese Foreign Relations* (1968). On Japan, consult Peter Duus, *Feudalism in Japan* (1976); H. D. Harootunian, *Toward Restoration: The Growth of Political Consciousness in Tokugawa Japan* (1970); and E. O. Reischauer, *Japan: The Study of a Nation*, 3rd ed. (1981). Noel Perrin, *Giving up the Gun* (1979), is a fascinating account of shogun policies on weapons and trade. On the much debated, important topic of peasant conditions in the Tokugawa shogunate, see H. Bix, *Peasant Protest in Japan, 1590–1884* (1986).

Recent work includes Anthony Reid, *Sojourners and Settlers: Histories of Southeast Asia and the Chinese* (*2001*); Paul Varley, *Japanese Culture* (2001); and Kenneth Pomeranz, *The Great Divergence: China, Europe and the Making of the Modern World Economy* (2000).

CONTACTS AND IDENTITIES

Part IV A New World Economy, 1450–1750

The early modern centuries featured contacts. The inclusion of the Americas and, by the later 1700s, Polynesia; the Columbian exchange; the formation of the world economy; the West's new outreach; Russian arrival in central Asia—all these overlapping trends highlighted contacts. Thanks to contacts, people had access to new foods, to new technologies, even to new entertainments (as in the spread of coffeehouses from the Middle East).

Yet, with some important exceptions, the early modern period did not see massive challenges to established identities. The contacts were not extensive enough, and they involved few efforts at cultural imposition. Notably, there were no massive conversions away from one of the world religions to another. The African slave trade did not jeopardize African culture. Silver imports into China plus a small amount of Christian missionary effort left Chinese values intact; when a threat seemed to arise, in the early 18th century, new attacks on Christians turned the tide. Japanese isolation even more clearly protected identity, amid significant internal change. European penetration in India brought little cultural baggage before 1800, because of the fierce concentration on economic gain and military power.

There were exceptions to the prevalence of existing regional cultures. Native Americans in South and Central America, encountering Europeans insistent on changing their religion as well as intruding in so many other ways, inevitably faced massive identity questions. By the 18th century, through syncretic combinations, some had forged a new Latin American identity shared with mestizos; others tried to remain separate.

Africans transported to the Americas, mixing with Africans from different regions, also faced the painful task of creating partially new identities, amid conditions they did not control. Their ability to maintain African memories and cultural features was impressive, but there was confusion even so. Some Russians also faced identity questions as they wondered about degrees of westernization.

For most people, pressing identity issues were more regional than global, because there simply were not many global-level cultural movements in this period. Hindus had to work out relationships with a Muslim state. Some Arabs worried about their identity amid Ottoman control. The Wahabi movement in Arabia was one response. Russian expansion raised questions, some of which hover still today: were Ukrainians, brought into Russia in the mid-17th century, Ukrainians or Russians with a slightly different language? Were the Manchurian rulers of China Chinese or foreign? The expansion of land-based empires raised the most acute new identity issues for much of the world in a period when most cultural forces remained regional.

PART V

The World's First Industrial Period, 1750–1914

INTRODUCTION: THE INTERNATIONAL IMPACT OF INDUSTRIALIZATION

This section covers about 160 years, in what is often called the extended or "long" 19th century. The period started with new economic and political developments in the West that soon had global impact. It ended with a fierce war among the West's major powers that had global impact as well.

Toward the end of the 18th century, western Europe began to change in several fundamental ways. Most apparent, a new economic and technological system took shape in Britain that would ultimately replace agriculture as the basis for economic activity. British industrialization spread to other parts of western Europe early in the 19th century and also to the new United States. New political doctrines and institutions also began to emerge in western Europe and the United States, with fundamental beliefs about how the state should operate and what kinds of laws and social structures were appropriate. Previous changes in Western culture, plus the successful position Europe had already assumed in the world economy, now combined to generate even more sweeping transformations.

Although these developments initially were concentrated in Europe and North America, they had major implications for the rest of the world. Western Europe's power, already on the increase, soared still further, beginning in the late 18th century and extending until 1914. Until 1850, western Europe even maintained its edge in population growth rates (see Table V.1). Here was a source of immigrants for various parts of the world. Even more obvious was the increase in Western military power. New repeating rifles and, later, machine guns, mass-produced in Western factories, allowed the West a dominance in land wars similar to what it already had on the seas. By 1850, Europe could defeat almost any rival, anywhere. Never before had a single civilization wielded such worldwide influence.

The world economy, already well defined, gained new importance as well. More parts of the world were drawn into production for export markets that Europeans dominated, whereas Western manufacturing expanded its output and its impact on sales to other societies. Two changes were particularly important. First, areas such as Latin America and India, already producing raw materials, accelerated their manufacturing but fell farther behind in living standards because of the need for cheap labor. Western industrialization heightened the consequences of economic dependency for key regions, partly because it displaced even more local manufacturing. Second, areas once barely affected by the Western-dominated world economy, or even benefiting from it, like east Asia and the Middle East, were now forced to deal with the West's manufacturing advantage.

Growing dependency could be stark. During the early 19th century, the African production of vegetable oil for export reached 40,000 tons. Then the use of petroleum (first in Pennsylvania, in 1860), Indian production of nut oil, and Australian and Russian production of fats cut into the price. Africans had to increase production still further, but at steadily falling prices, and to lower wages, just to maintain meager export earnings.

Overall, two of the key trends of the early modern period—economic and military—thus intensified. European influence escalated in a new imperialism that brought many additional areas under Western control. Variants of Western civilization spread to parts of the world particularly open to European immigrants, notably the United States, Canada, Australia, and New Zealand.

Europe's industrialization did more, however, than enhance preexisting trends. As the West came to rely more on wage labor supplemented by machines, and as new humanitarian ideals gained ground, Western leaders attacked the institution of slavery worldwide. The Western-dominated Atlantic slave trade ended, and slave systems within the Americas came to an end through the first three-quarters of the 19th century. Pressure on African and Middle Eastern slavery also reduced the institution in these areas. The labor systems of many

Table V.1
ESTIMATED POPULATION OF THE WORLD AND THE CONTINENTS, 1650–1850 (IN MILLIONS)

Continent	1650	1750	1800	1850
Africa	100	95	90	95
Asia (excluding Russia)	327	475	597	741
Latin America	12	11	19	33
North America	1	1	6	26
Europe plus Asiatic Russia	103	144	192	274
Oceania	2	2	2	2
World total	545	728	906	1171

Source: Adapted from Dennis Wrong, *Population and Society* (New York: Random House, 1969), 13.

parts of the world, in other words, were dramatically challenged by new Western standards, backed by growing imperialist muscle. Africa had to redefine its world economic role as a result.

To be sure, the end of slavery did not end all negative forces in the work world. Low wages had coercive power, particularly when backed up by loans or required company stores that tied workers to a firm. Indentured contracts revived, particularly for Asian workers brought to southeast Asia, the Caribbean, and Hawaii. Over a million people from China and India were transported as indentured labor between 1850 and 1914. Still, the widespread elimination of formal, lifelong slavery was a historic change, as part of the dynamic economy and population movement of the long 19th century.

The Industrial Revolution and the intensification of the world economy also ushered in a new chapter in the world's environmental history. There were two main developments. First, in industrial centers themselves, environmental quality often deteriorated massively. Factories spewed smoke in the air. Many factories dumped chemical products in rivers and lakes, where they joined the raw sewage produced by rapidly growing cities. Water quality suffered dramatically. Coal mines generated huge slag heaps that were both ugly and useless. By the mid to late 19th century, industrial societies began to modify these effects, but challenges remained. From the 1830s onward, a growing number of Western cities installed underground sewage systems, and by the 1870s regulations increasingly modified the dumping of raw sewage. Other regulations sought to regulate factory activities, as well as to protect certain forest areas from commercial exploitation.

The second environmental impact occurred in many of the dependent economies. Eager to increase output of export commodities, many planters began to expand the process of introducing new crops to areas in which they were not native. Forests were rapidly reduced, both for timber export and to create new agricultural lands. The forested parts of west Africa, for example, began to decline rapidly by the late 19th century, in favor of production of coffee, cotton, and the like. The result was a reduction in soil fertility, since forest products were no longer available to re-enrich the soil, and also increased erosion. By the 20th century, developments of this sort could limit agricultural productivity, creating new or expanded deserts. The growth of colonial cities also had environmental effects, particularly because of increased concentrations of human waste. Environmental change in dependent economies was not given much attention before 1914, and it would intensify during the 20th century with some global as well as regional results.

New beliefs spread on a global basis during the long 19th century. Mass nationalism first arose in Europe, as a means of expressing new secular loyalties and supporting political change. Latin American people used a budding nationalist sentiment as one of their motives in demanding independence from Spain or Portugal. By the second half of the 19th century, nationalism spread to the Middle East, India, and elsewhere. Nationalism challenged many local and religious attachments. It focused new attention on the state (or on a desire for political independence) and wider changes needed to make one's nation a viable force in the modern world.

Western Civilization	East Asia	Middle East	Indian and Southeast Asia
c. 1770 Invention of steam engine by Watt. **1775–1783** American Revolution. **1787** Constitutional Convention, Philadelphia. **1780 ff.** Industrial Revolution. **1789–1799** French Revolution. **1793–1794** Radical phase. **1799–1815** Reign of Napoleon. **1800–1850** Romanticism in literature, arts. **1815** Congress of Vienna. **1820** Revolutions in Greece, Spain. **1830 ff.** Rise of liberalism, nationalism. **1829–1837** Jacksonian period in United States; universal white male suffrage. **1830, 1848** Revolutions in several European countries. **1832** British Reform Bill. **1848 ff.** Writings of Karl Marx.	**1820s** Growing Western trade with China. **1839–1842** Opium Wars in China.	**1793** Failure of sultan's efforts at military reform. **1798** Napoleon's Egyptian expedition. **1811 ff.** Reforms in Egypt by Muhammad Ali. **1820–1829** Greek war for Independence. **1826** Dissolution of Janissaries by Sultan Mahmud II. **1828–1833** Russian-Ottoman War. **1830** Takeover of Algeria begun by France. **1830 ff.** Steamship routes established in eastern Mediterranean and Persian Gulf by Britain, France. **1839** Ottoman reform attempt.	**1825 ff.** Extension of Dutch control over interior of Indonesia. **1827–1829 ff.** Reorganization of British rule in India, development of Civil Service, new legal codes.

Russia and Eastern Europe	Latin America	Sub-Saharan Africa
		1787 ff. Sierra Leone founded as British colony for freed slaves.
	1808 Formation of governing junta in Venezuela.	**1807–1834** Abolition of Atlantic slave trade.
	1810 Leadership of Mexican revolt by Hidalgo.	
	1810 Independent government in Argentina.	**1814** Acquisition by British of Dutch South Africa.
	1811 Proclamation of independence; Bolivar leadership.	**1821** Extension of British rule in West Africa.
1812 Failure of Napoleonic invasion of Russia.	**1814** Regain of control by Spain.	**1822** Liberia founded as colony for freed American slaves.
1815 Poland acquired by Russia in Treaty of Vienna.	**1821** Independence regained in "Gran Colombia."	**1830 ff.** Formation of firmer Bantu governments in southern Africa.
1825–1855 Heightening of repression by Tsar Nicholas I; increase in secret police.	**1814 ff.** Wars of independence led by San Martin in Chile, Peru.	**1835–1837** Great Trek of Boers; clash with Zulus.
1829 Full autonomy gained by Serbia within Ottoman Empire; fuller independence achieved in 1856; complete independence granted in 1878.	**1821** Proclamation of Mexican independence by conservatives.	**1840 ff.** Increased Protestant missionary activity.
	1822 Pedro emperor of Brazil.	
1830–1831 Polish revolt put down by Nicholas.	**1823** Independence of United Provinces of Central America.	
1831 Full independence gained by Greece.	**1825–1850** Consolidation of new nations; division of Gran Colombia, Central America.	
	1829–1852 Manuel de Rosas caudillo in Argentina.	
	1833 ff. Santa Anna leader in Mexico.	
	1836 Independence of Texas.	

Western Civilization	East Asis	Middle East	India and Southeast Asia
1859 Darwin, *Origin of Species.*	**1850–1864** Tai Ping Rebellion.	**1853** Russian Ottoman War.	**1850 ff.** Development of railroad in India.
1859–1870 Italian unification.	**1853** Perry expedition to Japan.	**1854–1856** Crimean War.	**1852–1853** British war with Burma; growing influence gained by Britain.
1861–1865 U.S. Civil War.	**1857–1859** Second Opium War.	**1856** Ottoman reform attempt; new rights for Christians.	**1855** Growing British influence over Siam; trade opened by treaty.
1864–1871 German unification.	**1867** Mutsuhito emperor of Japan.	**1869** Completion of Suez Canal.	
1867 Unification, dominion status for Canada.	**1868–1912** Meiji period in Japan.	**1876** Promulgation of Ottoman constitution, guaranteeing individual freedoms, establishing parliament.	**1857–1858** Sepoy mutiny, India.
1870 ff. Spread of compulsory education laws.	**1872** Universal service in Japan.		**1858 ff.** British reform of government in India.
1870–1879 Institutions of French Third Republic.	**1890** New constitution, legal code in Japan.	**1877** Lapse of constitution.	**1858 ff.** Takeover of Indochina begun by France.
1871–1914 Highpoint of Western imperialism.	**1894–1895** Sino-Japanese War.	**1877–1878** Russo-Turkish War; independence gained by new Balkan nations.	**1861** Establishment of advisory councils, with Indian representation.
1871 ff. Rise of socialist movement.	**1896 ff.** Chinese students abroad.	**1870s** Growing Western control over Egypt.	**1864** Indians allowed in upper Civil Sevice.
1879–1907 Alliance system: Germany-Austria (1879); Germany-Austria-Russia (1881); Germany-Italy-Austria (1882); France-Russia (1891); Britain-France (1904); Britain-Russia (1907).	**1897–1899** Chinese port concessions gained by Western nations and Russia.	**1881** Occupation of Tunisia by France.	**1885** Formation of Indian National Congress.
	1899–1901 Boxer Rebellion in China.	**1882** British protectorate over Egypt.	**1885–1886** British takeover of much of Burma.
		1888 Construction begun on Berlin-Baghdad railway.	**1886** Modern steel industry begun in India.
1881–1889 German social insurance laws enacted.		**1896 ff.** Rise of Young Turk movement.	**1896 ff.** More formal British control of Malaya (completed 1914).

Russia and Eastern Europe	Latin America	Sub-Saharan Africa
1854–1856 Crimean War. **1856** Gain of virtual independence by Romania. **1861** Russian emancipation of serfs. **1864** Abolition of serfdom by Romania; little land obtained by peasants. **1860s–1870s** Additional reforms by Alexander II in judiciary, local zemstov government. **1865–1876** Russian conquests in central Asia. **1867** Alaska sold to United States by Russia. **1875–1878** War with Ottoman Empire, gain of new territory. **1878** Independent Bulgaria created. **1881** Anarchist assassination of Alexander II. **1881 ff.** Growing repression in Russia; attacks on minorities. **1884–1887** New gains in central Asia. **1884 ff.** Beginnings of Russian industrialization; Sergei Witte the leading minister; completion of trans-Siberian railway. **1898** Formation of Marxist Social Democratic party.	**1844–1846** Mexican-American War; occupation of Mexico by United States; upper California, New Mexico acquired by United States. **1858** First Benito Juarez government in Mexico. **1861–1867** French intervention in Mexico. **1876–1911** Porfirio Diaz caudillo in Mexico. **1880 ff.** Growing commercialization of Latin American economy. **1870–1888** Guzmán Blanco caudillo in Venezuela. **1889** Republic of Brazil; abolition of slavery. **1898** Spanish-American War; acquisition of Puerto Rico by United States; protectorate over Cuba.	**1854 ff.** Expansion of French from Senegal. **1857–1863** French exploration in Congo basin. **1960** German trade station established in Cameroons. **1861** Beginning of British expansion in Nigeria. **1867** Discovery of South African diamonds; increase in import of Indian laborers. **1875 ff.** Explosion of European imperialism in Africa. **1876** Congo claimed by Belgian king. **1878 ff.** New Catholic missions set up. **1878 ff.** Expansion of British, French interior expeditions in West Africa. **1899** Nigeria a full British colony. **1877–1879 ff.** New missionary efforts in east Africa; curtailment of East African slave trade. **1879** Defeat of Zulus by British. **1880** Acquisition by French of separate Congo colony. **1884** Organization of German treaties by Karl Peters to gain Tanganyika.

TIMELINE: The World in the First Industrial Century

Western Civilization	East Asia	Middle East	India and Southeast Asia
			1896–1899 Revolt against Spain in Philippines.
			1898 U.S. capture of Manila. Defeat of Philippine independence movement by United States.
	1904–1905 Russo-Japanese War.		
	1910 Annexation of Korea by Japan.		
	1911 Chinese revolution.	**1911** Occupation of Morocco by France; takeover of Tripoli (present-day Libya) by Italy.	
	1912 Fall of last (Qing) dynasty.		
		1918 Collapse of Ottoman Empire.	
1914 Beginning of World War I.			

Russia and Eastern Europe	Latin America	Sub-Saharan Africa
		1886 Discovery of South African gold; development of railway. **1892 ff.** Expansion of East Africa Company into Uganda. **1890s–1905** Uprisings in West Africa (Ashanti); in Sudan, Tanganyika (Muslims and animists). **1899–1902** Boer War. **1901 ff.** Development of railway in East Africa. **1904** Great insurrection in German Tanganyika, defeated with 20,000 troops.
1904–1905 Loss by Russia of war with Japan. **1905** Revolution in Russia; peasant reforms and Duma. **1912–1913** Two Balkan wars. **1917** Russian Revolution; abolition of tsarist regime; Bolshevik victory.	**1903** U.S.-backed revolt in Panama; independence from Colombia. **1904–1914** Construction of Panama Canal by United States. **1905 ff.** Growing U.S. political and military intervention in Central America, Haiti, and Dominican Republic. **1911** Beginning of Mexican Revolution.	

Because of growing Western power and the challenge of industrialization, a wider set of global forces influenced individual societies during the 19th century than had characterized the early modern period. Every society faced the necessity of coming to terms with the expanding world economy and Western imperialism—the impossibility of isolation, the worldwide growth of market labor instead of slavery or other traditional work systems, and the growing spread of nationalism all signaled the presence of these new international forces. Every society now had to ask questions about what changes must be contemplated in order to gain or maintain independence and to adapt to an industrially driven world economy.

New global forces, however, did not produce uniformity from one society to the next. Traditional beliefs and institutions continued to shape different responses. One of the reasons for nationalism's success lay in its ability to combine new political impulses and loyalties with devotion to older, distinctive values. Forces within the 19th century impacted different societies in different ways. Some places became new colonies; others freed themselves from colonialism; still others faced growing Western intrusion without the indignity but also without the protections of colonial control. As

before in world history, tracking the different responses to the growing array of international contacts constitutes a major analytical challenge. On the surface, the extended 19th century seems perhaps the simplest of all world history periods, because it did not break fully with the trends of the early modern period. Its basics included the expanding world economy, Western imperialism, spreading nationalism, and other efforts to adapt to Western-dominated change. Nonetheless, the ways individual societies combined these factors and reacted to them involved considerable complexity. Careful comparison remains essential. The world by 1914 was much different from what it had been in 1750, but it was hardly more uniform.

This section deals first with changes in the West itself, including industrialization. It then turns to the surge of imperialism, with particular attention to Africa and southern Asia. It then deals with the Americas and a few other societies in which imperialism and European influence took different forms, in two chapters on Latin America and the settler societies. Two chapters then return to Asia and to eastern Europe, where again distinctive responses to imperialism and Western industrialization developed. Finally, a brief chapter deals with the end of the era and World War I.

The First Industrial Revolution: Western Society, 1780–1914

The Industrial Revolution was the predominant development in western Europe during the 19th century. Along with industrialization came a host of new political movements associated in particular with the great French Revolution of 1789. New approaches in science and art constituted a third area of innovation. Developments in all three areas significantly altered western Europe. They had major implications for the rest of the world as well.

The Industrial Revolution transformed agricultural society much as the Neolithic revolution had once transformed hunting-and-gathering cultures. Associated with this economic and technological upheaval in western Europe and North America was the development of new political forms, ushered in by a variety of revolutions in many countries. Industrialization and political change also introduced major shifts in cultural life and basic social relationships, including class structure, family roles, and the locations of people's homes and work. The West did not lose all touch with its traditions in this sweeping process, but it was forced to reshape those traditions it retained.

This chapter deals with the transformation of the West itself, including the causes of change that evolved from previous developments in Western society, before proceeding to its global impact. With industrialization, the West traded in the social and intellectual currents of the early modern period and the capital amassed from its control of world trade, in order to produce a society the likes of which had never been seen before in world history.

KEY QUESTIONS *How did the main changes in the West relate to each other? Did new political ideas such as liberalism and democracy fit easily with industrialization? Did new trends in art mesh or conflict with a machine age? How were daily lives, including family lives, affected by the key changes?*

PATTERNS OF INDUSTRIALIZATION

Typically, when we examine major historical periods within a civilization, political or cultural developments hold center stage. Thus, there are centuries during which new political organizations seem to dominate other activities, and other centuries in which new religions, scientific innovations, or shifts in popular beliefs are the primary focus. In 19th-century Europe, however, economic and technological change must be studied in advance of other features; economic change meant, above all else, industrialization.

In its essence, the Industrial Revolution consisted of a fundamental shift in technology and power sources. Instead of relying on human and animal power for virtually all production, the Industrial Revolution substituted fossil fuel power, first by means of coal to drive steam engines and later with electric and internal combustion engines. Along with the revolutionary power sources came new production equipment that could apply power to manufacturing (and later to other activities), with less dependence on human effort. Spinning jennies wound fiber into thread,

applying steam or, in the early days, waterpower through gear transmissions. The flying shuttle was adapted to steam engines for weaving. Hammering and rolling devices allowed the application of power machinery to metallurgy. Although, in early industrialization, textile manufacturing and metallurgy, along with coal mining, received the greatest attention, engines were also used in sugar refining, printing, and other processes. The industry of machine building arose to construct engines, looms, and presses—the new tools of production. Machine building was greatly aided by the American invention of interchangeable parts, initially introduced for the manufacture of rifles.

The technological breakthrough spread quickly to communication and transportation. The development of the telegraph, steam shipping, and the railway, all early in the 19th century, provided new speed in the transport of information and goods. These inventions were vital in facilitating Western domination in world affairs.

Innovations were applied to agriculture, particularly after 1850, with new harvesting and planting equipment and gasoline-powered tractors. Scientific farming methods also produced artificial fertilizers and new strains of seeds and

Power loom weaving in a cotton textile mill, 1834.

livestock. Technology also reached offices, through typewriters and cash registers, and homes, with sewing machines and refrigerators, although again, the major changes surfaced in the later 19th century onward. By this point, virtually all kinds of work had been altered by new equipment and power sources.

Furthermore, technological change was a recurrent process once the Industrial Revolution was launched. New generations of equipment displaced earlier machines. By the late 19th century, when the United States assumed the lead in technological advances, many power looms were sufficiently automated for one weaver to operate 16 or more looms, in contrast to the one or two looms per worker in earlier decades. Metallurgy was transformed, beginning in the 1850s, by new blast furnaces that increased the capacity for refining iron ore and allowed the automatic reintroduction of minerals to convert iron into steel. Coal mining, although less open to modernization, saw the introduction of engines to move ore and then cutting devices to use in the pits. Clearly, the Industrial Revolution may be linked to no single change in methods, but to successive waves of innovation.

Along with revolutionary inventions came major changes in economic organization. Manufacturing was becoming concentrated in factories, rather than in small shops. With steam equipment, it was necessary for workers to cluster around the engines. Even apart from technological requirements, there were advantages to be gained from grouping larger numbers of workers: both discipline and specialization increased. Finance, too, became more sophisticated. New equipment and factories required growing investments. Banks began to play a greater role in funding industry. Corporations grew, particularly after 1850, to sell shares to large numbers of investors. In industrial economies, big firms assumed a dominant position. Even in sales, small shops increasingly faced the competition of department stores and mail-order houses. Thus, the fundamental characteristics of economic organization were concentration, bureaucracy, and impersonality.

CAUSES OF INDUSTRIALIZATION

The Industrial Revolution first took shape in Great Britain, where key inventions, including the steam engine, had been introduced by 1780. British developments were quickly copied and other inventions added so that, by the 1820s, most of western Europe and the new United States were actively engaged in the early stages of the Industrial Revolution as well. Indeed, during the 19th century, the United States and Germany caught up with Britain, particularly in their emphasis on coal and iron production. The first Industrial Revolution was thus a Western-wide phenomenon, despite some interesting regional variations within the West.

The position the West had acquired in the world economy provided an active framework for the Industrial Revolution. European nations gained large amounts of capital from their colonial trading activities, including the slave trade. Businessmen also learned that there were markets for processed goods, which helped motivate them to devise new and cheaper ways to produce such goods. The privileged position of the West in world trade unquestionably explains why it was this society that first introduced industrialization and why it long maintained an industrial lead over other areas.

The internal causes of the Industrial Revolution were exceedingly complex, a fact that helps explain why many societies continue to find it difficult to complete the process the West first introduced. The factors that went into the West's Industrial Revolution range from a massive population increase, which forced many workers to accept factory jobs simply because they had no alternative, to new ideas and a business mentality that made some industrial entrepreneurs positively eager to introduce risky changes. Material resources and capital constituted other Western advantages in pioneering the industrial spirit.

Industrialization built on many of the trends in Western society prior to the 1780s. The new

Westward the Course of Empire Takes Its Way: railroad across the North American continent.
(Currier and Ives lithograph)

technologies were related to the rise of science. James Watt, the inventor of the first manufacturing steam engine, worked closely with scientists at the University of Glasgow. During the 19th century, the link between the economy and science grew closer, as university chemists worked on developing new dyes, fertilizers, and explosives. More widely, the outlook accompanying the rise of science promoted beliefs in change and control over nature that guided many manufacturing innovators even without specific exposure to formal science.

Industrialization required capital and a willingness to take risks. Western experience in colonial trade had encouraged a daring merchant spirit that was now applied to manufacturing. The colonial trade and earlier improvements in agriculture and domestic manufacturing had resulted in considerable capital, available for investment in the new equipment. Industrialization also required favorable natural resources, particularly coal and iron ore; parts of Europe and North America had these in abundance, along with rivers and canals that facilitated transport even before the rise of the railroads.

Along with science, an openness to risk and change, the availability of capital, and a massive increase in population growth spurred the Industrial Revolution in western Europe. Beginning early in the 18th century, the population began to soar, rising between 50 to 100 percent in all Western nations before 1800. The population revolution was itself caused by relatively peaceful conditions, a temporary decline in epidemic disease, and above all, the introduction of new foodstuffs brought from the Americas. Europeans had initially hesitated to try new foods, but by 1700 they began to convert rapidly, particularly in their adoption of the potato into their diets. The use of new foods caused agricultural production to rise

History Debate

CONSUMERISM AND INDUSTRIALIZATION

Until about 15 years ago, historians thought they completely understood the relationship between Western industrialization, which was a major new production system, and the advent of a society in which the consumption of goods played a transforming role in defining the economy and personal goals. Industrialization came first, and only later did output reach levels at which people gained both the time and money needed for mass consumption.

Major discoveries in recent years, however, demonstrate that the first stage of a consumer society arose in places such as England during the 18th century. New shops opened, advertising and sales gimmicks gained ground, and ordinary people began to place new meaning on acquiring goods, particularly clothing and furniture. New levels of consumption helped cause industrialization, which then accelerated consumerism to yet another stage. What historians still debate, however, is why consumerism arose in advance of major new production levels. Enjoyment of products from the world economy—sugar, for example—played a role. So did prior changes in social structure, which created more fluid boundaries in which people sought to establish identities by wearing stylish clothes. So did a decline in religious fervor. But the precise causes remain to be established through fresh historical inquiry.

and the death rate to drop, which in turn allowed more offspring to live to adulthood and have children of their own. Hence, the population booms in a civilization that, unlike Asia's, had not been particularly crowded previously. Population pressure rose rapidly, forcing many people off the land and creating a labor force for the new cities and factories. It also spurred merchants to take new risks in order to provide for their own growing families. The population revolution thus helps explain the timing of the West's Industrial Revolution as it combined with other factors.

Adding to population pressure was a new spirit of consumerism. Many people, in countries such as Britain, sought new forms of pleasure and identity in buying fashionable clothes and furnishings. Shopkeepers learned new methods of advertising and sales gimmicks to fuel this process. The acknowledgment of early consumerism was a major advance in historical knowledge, and it explains the existence of new markets that could

convince manufacturers to innovate in the interests of increasing production.

In several Western countries, full industrialization also depended on political change. In general, industrialization relied heavily on private capitalists, who built the new factories and offices. But governments played a role as well. In the United States, government provision of free land was vital to the development of the railroad network; in France and Germany, governments built rail systems outright. At the same time, governments had to abandon certain traditional practices in order for industrialization to occur. They could no longer, for example, defend the guild system, which tended to restrict technological innovation and the free movement of labor. Nor could they continue to defend slavery. Political revolutions in France and its neighbors, and the Civil War in the United States, served a vital function in establishing governmental systems favorable to industrialization and promoting a sense among government officials that industrialization was a good thing. Although a host of factors, such as the bitter moral debate over slavery, entered into U.S. political conflicts, a key ingredient was the clash over how the economy should be organized, with the North urging mobile wage laborers tied to rapid technological change. In the 1861–1865 Civil War, Northern industrial strength provided a vital edge, and in turn, after the war, U.S. encouragement of rapid industrialization increased.

Industrialization was no simple development, even in its first, Western home. Many people resisted the changes in habits and the new, materialistic values it promoted. A complex set of causes, ranging from population growth to the dissemination of modern ideas, was needed to generate wide adoption of the new inventions and forms of organization.

EFFECTS OF INDUSTRIALIZATION

The economic effects of industrialization did not end with the rise of the factory system and the new equipment. Industrialization produced new wealth. With machines, productivity per worker rose rapidly. Even with the equipment available by 1800, a single worker using steam-driven spindles, for example, could produce as much thread as 100 manual spinners. Not all improvements in productivity were this vast, and the resulting new wealth was not evenly distributed. The West, already a wealthy society by world standards, became richer. Expanding wealth brought major changes in living standards and a desire for further improvements. By the later 19th century, the apparatus of a consumer society expanded further, as factories turned out growing quantities of goods. Advertising also developed, promoting a new mass press. Shopping gained public attention; even a new disorder, kleptomania, reflected the obsession with consumer goods.

Industrialization, which had depended on greater agricultural output through new crops, transformed farming in turn. Growing factories and cities required major improvements in the output of food. The average farmer had to produce more, so that an increasing percentage of society could live and work off the farms. New equipment, fertilizers, and scientific techniques promoted the spread of market agriculture. More and more European peasants tried to increase their landholdings and employ landless laborers, to take advantage of market opportunities. This kind of peasant was still tied to village traditions but more open than before to production growth and moneymaking. Some peasants specialized in dairy farming or vegetable production for the cities, buying more processed goods as a result. Finally, particularly after the rise of steam shipping, canning, and refrigeration in the later 19th century, western Europe looked to other parts of the world for some of its food. Grain imports from eastern Europe were surpassed by the highly productive commercial farms of the United States, Canada, Australia, and Argentina—where technological change far outstripped peasant levels—and meat was imported as well. Industrialization reduced the size of the agricultural population in the Western world while transforming economic life for those who remained on the farms.

Industrialization also created new needs for management skills and the handling of information. Early factories were small, often run by a single family. But with growth came larger and more complex hierarchies, with supervisors directing the workers, a sales staff, secretaries, and file clerks. Along with the spread of large department stores, the rise of management created an expanding white-collar workforce, which by 1870 had growth rates even more rapid than those of factory labor. Like factory workers, white-collar employees were highly specialized and closely supervised according to rules designed to encourage maximum productivity.

Another effect of industrialization was the development of cities, and particularly big cities

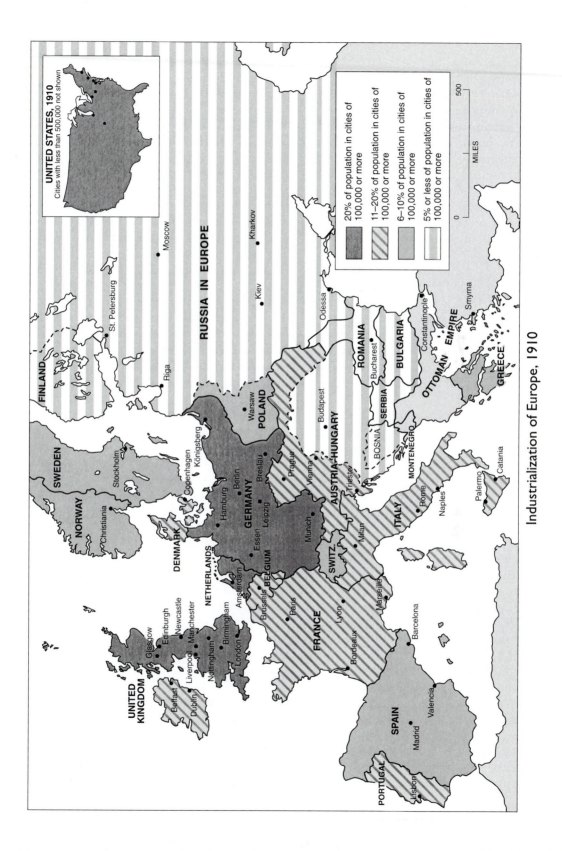

UNITED STATES, 1910
Cities with less than 500,000 not shown

Legend

- 20% of population in cities of 100,000 or more
- 11–20% of population in cities of 100,000 or more
- 6–10% of population in cities of 100,000 or more
- 5% or less of population in cities of 100,000 or more

MILES
0 — 500

Industrialization of Europe, 1910

Place labels

FINLAND
SWEDEN
NORWAY
Christiania
Stockholm
Copenhagen
Königsberg
DENMARK
NETHERLANDS
Amsterdam
UNITED KINGDOM
Belfast
Dublin
Glasgow
Edinburgh
Newcastle
Manchester
Liverpool
Nottingham
Birmingham
London
Brussels
BELGIUM
Paris
FRANCE
Lyon
Bordeaux
Marseilles
SPAIN
Madrid
Valencia
Barcelona
PORTUGAL
Lisbon
SWITZ.
Milan
ITALY
Rome
Naples
Palermo
Catania
GERMANY
Hamburg
Berlin
Breslau
Essen
Leipzig
Munich
Prague
Vienna
Budapest
AUSTRIA-HUNGARY
Trieste
BOSNIA
SERBIA
MONTENEGRO
POLAND
Warsaw
Riga
St. Petersburg
Moscow
RUSSIA IN EUROPE
Kiev
Kharkov
Odessa
ROMANIA
Bucharest
BULGARIA
Constantinople
OTTOMAN EMPIRE
GREECE
Smyrna

located at transportation hubs, near coal fields, or as banking and political centers. During the Industrial Revolution, hundreds of thousands of people, mostly young, migrated from country to city, prodded by population pressure and the prospect of new, better-paying jobs. By 1850, for the first time in history, half of Britain's population lived in cities. By around 1900, the same was true of Germany, France, and the United States. The rapid growth of cities placed tremendous stress on existing urban structures and governments. Many early industrial cities suffered appalling conditions in housing and sanitation. Gradually, however, aided by industrial wealth, cities improved; by 1850, the worst was over in the West, as cities began to process sewage, pave streets, inspect the quality of food and housing, and provide parks and various other amenities. Adjusting to urbanization—or failing to adjust— was an important aspect of the whole industrialization process.

Closely related to urbanization were changes in health conditions. In agricultural societies, urbanization on the scale now introduced by the West would have been impossible, not only because of insufficient food supplies but also because cities had long bred disease. Indeed, during the first two-thirds of the 19th century, urban health was a serious problem in the West, as poverty and inadequate sanitation caused continuing high death rates. However, more efficient urban organization, particularly in the provision of better treatment of sewage and purer water supplies, plus related gains in medical knowledge through the development of the germ theory of disease, caused significant health improvements after 1880. Child death rates, especially, began to drop rapidly. Instead of a third of all children dying before adulthood, by 1900 the figure was down to less than 20 percent and falling fast. Here was another important use of the wealth, technical knowledge, and organizational skills that resulted from the Industrial Revolution.

The Industrial Revolution, itself primarily a transformation in technology and economic organization, had wide-reaching effects on where people lived, how healthy and well off they were, and what jobs they had. The transformations engendered by industrialization were not sudden, nor were they uniform. Early factories were small, and the large factory run by a hierarchy of supervisors and managers was only a development of the later 19th century. Many groups continued to work along rather traditional lines, well into the Industrial Revolution. Artisans still produced luxury products and even some necessities such as housing; most women employed in the cities worked as domestic servants, with their jobs remaining largely traditional. But change, if sometimes gradual and uneven, was the primary characteristic of the West's industrial century. Even artisans faced pressures to become less creative and more efficiency-minded in their work, while rising factories eclipsed their overall importance. By 1900, most people in the West were not working at the same jobs their great-grandparents had performed in 1780; they were not living in the same place; they did not engage in the same recreational activities. In 1780, most people had worked in or near the home; by 1900, most work was separate from the home. In 1780, most people had used traditional herbal remedies when ill, viewing hospitals as places where the desperately poor went to die; by 1900, many people in the West were beginning to rely on hospitals and doctors regularly and to believe that many age-old health problems could and should be eliminated. Here were some human measures of the change that the Industrial Revolution had produced.

THE PERIOD OF REVOLUTION, 1789–1848

Industrialization was a large, subterranean, often faceless process that altered the shape of Western society between 1780 and 1914. Particularly in its early phases, Western people were not always aware of exactly how their lives were changing. The concept of an industrial revolution itself arose only late in the 19th century, after the most basic changes had already taken place in the West. Along with industrialization, and more noticeable to most articulate observers, came a compelling number of political and intellectual innovations that produced a seemingly endless series of dramatic events.

The period began with a series of political revolutions, starting with the Revolutionary War in North America in the 1770s, which led to the formation of the United States. Americans, stirred by the liberal political values of the Enlightenment and pressed by new British restrictions on trade and political autonomy, engaged in the first modern struggle for national independence. They established a republican form of government, with a decentralized federal system and wide male suffrage. U.S. ties to Europe remained close, which enabled Americans to pick up quickly on European industrialization; European investment in the United States also supported economic change and expansion, while growing waves of European immigrants provided much of the necessary labor.

The American Revolution helped inspire a more sweeping revolution in France, starting in 1789. This great event resulted from an absolute monarchy grown inefficient, the power of Enlightenment ideas, and the discontent and confusion brought about by population growth and rising commerce in advance of outright industrialization. The French Revolution was the first of many struggles in various parts of the world that would stem from pressures to change that could not be contained within traditional political and social structures. Moreover, the French Revolution, although not fully successful, did alter the political and legal framework of French society and, through conquest and imitation, that of much of the rest of western Europe.

The French had grown restless under an absolute monarchy that was ineffective and unable to produce meaningful reforms. Many French people resented the powers of the church and the aristocracy. Population pressure added to the discontent, as did the growing popularity of Enlightenment ideas. Although France was not yet industrializing, groups of peasants and artisans were already hostile toward the increasingly commercial spirit of many merchants and farmers; they saw revolution not as a blow for new political forms so much as a way to regain older values. This complex mix came to a head in 1789 when the king, Louis XVI, strapped for funds, had to call a meeting of the Estates-General, the former medieval parliament that had not met for 175 years. Business and professional people, inspired by the Enlightenment, were unwilling to meet as a separate estate, giving greater power to the aristocracy and clergy as the first two estates. Peasants in many parts of France also rose against the remnants of manorial obligations. The great political revolution of modern Western history was underway.

The revolution went through several stages. For two years, relatively moderate leaders tried to set up a constitutional monarchy, which would protect the freedoms of the press, religion, and assembly. The idea was to scale down the power of the church, while abolishing serfdom and the guilds, thus abolishing the underpinnings of traditional social structure. The government divided up many of the estates of the aristocrats, making France a country of peasant owners. The Constitution of 1791 proclaimed the legal equality of all French people, as opposed to the traditional idea that different social groups had different rights of heredity. A parliament was established, with the vote confined to the relatively wealthy—a strong suggestion that middle-class rule, based on the power of money, was replacing aristocratic rule, based on legal privilege by birth. But, partly because of opposition inside France and attacks by foreign monarchies, the revolution turned steadily more radical. Many aristocrats and other opponents were killed in what was called, somewhat grandiosely, the Reign of Terror (1793–1794); radicals executed the king and proclaimed a republic. The power of the central government increased over traditional local bodies;

Romantic nostalgia: Painting of the harbor at La Rochelle, 19th century.

every man was allowed a vote. The most important result of the revolution's radical phase was the organization of a new, mass conscript army—now that citizens were equal, they had equal obligations to serve—which helped the revolutionaries gain new territories in western Germany, the Low Countries, and elsewhere. This successful war spread many of the revolutionary principles to larger parts of western Europe.

The radical phase of the revolution was soon overturned, and in 1799 a military dictator, Napoleon Bonaparte, took charge of France. There followed 15 years of recurrent fighting as Napoleon sought to carve out a European empire. Within France, Napoleon confirmed revolutionary law and promoted new secondary schools to recruit talented bureaucrats. Napoleon's conquests outside France weakened the manor system and advanced the idea of equality under the law throughout much of western Europe. Wars during the revolution and under Napoleon also encouraged considerable popular nationalism. The French, armed with their new political rights, became enthusiastic about being citizens of France; Germans and Spaniards, angered by Napoleon's invasions, grew more

nationalistic in opposition. Nationalism supplemented the efforts of Europe's monarchies to put down the dangerous revolutionary upstart. Britain was a consistent enemy of France, with Austria and Prussia frequent opponents of Napoleon. The tsar of Russia, now intervening more in Western affairs than ever before, also played an important role in the final alliance that vanquished Napoleon. An attempt by Napoleon to invade Russia, in 1812, ended in disaster. As Russian forces retreated, the French armies followed and were subsequently caught in the frozen hold of a Russian winter; here was a sign of how much Russian military organization and size had changed since the days of the Mongols. The allies finally conquered France and exiled Napoleon in 1814–1815. A glittering diplomatic gathering, the Congress of Vienna, then tried to reassemble Europe's pieces.

For the next 30 years, Europe seemed dominated by conservative attempts to contain the forces that the revolution had unleashed. The monarchy was restored in France, and some, although not all, of the revolutionary legislation undone. The Catholic church, vigorously allied with the antirevolutionary cause, gained new rights in France and elsewhere—however, it never recovered the vast property lost during the revolutionary period. Conservatism was buttressed by a new intellectual current called *romanticism*, which opposed Enlightenment values. Romantic writers and artists wished above all to express emotion; they disdained the cold rationalism of the 18th century. They adored gothic styles and medieval adventures. Some romantic theorists went further, opposing Enlightenment political values in the name of religion or the mystical collective power of the state, which, they felt, should not be constrained by constitutions or individual rights.

Although conservatism gained new ground, the old order that had existed before the French Revolution and the Napoleonic Wars could not be recaptured. The Congress of Vienna, for example, did not restore the small states into which Italy and Germany had been divided; it thus encouraged Italian and German nationalists to hope that their respective countries could be unified outright. At the same time, liberals in France and elsewhere wanted to regain revolutionary achievements such as constitutions, parliaments, wider voting rights, and full religious freedom. And a new, small group of socialists began to encourage protest in the name of economic equality. Thus, western Europe was besieged by periodic efforts at agitation. Conservative leaders, headed by the tsar and the Habsburg monarchy, with its able minister Prince Metternich, tried in vain to keep the lid on popular unrest. Revolutions broke out in Spain, parts of Italy, and then Greece after 1820, with the Greeks winning independence from the Ottoman Empire. Again in 1830, further revolutions developed, leading to a new monarchy in France with a more liberal air, independence and a liberal monarchy for Belgium, and upheaval elsewhere. A final series of revolutions, in 1848, swept over much of western Europe. It destroyed manorialism in Germany and Austria, encouraged Italian and German nationalists without, however, winning unity, and unseated the monarchy in France, this time for good.

A few Western countries were exempt from the tide of revolution. Britain, although strongly conservative in its opposition to the French Revolution, already had a parliamentary system. Popular protests in Britain sought political and social liberalization. In 1832, a reform bill gave most middle-class people the right to vote, and other reforms extended fuller religious tolerance, even to Catholics and Jews; regulated women and child workers in the factories; and granted new powers to city governments in improving material conditions. British politics became increasingly liberal, without revolution. Scandinavian governments also granted new powers to their parliaments and widened suffrage. In the United States, where revolution had already produced a constitutional republic and protection for individual liberty through the Bill of Rights, further pressures for political change were met, in the Jacksonian era of the 1830s, by reforms such as the secret ballot and extension of voting rights.

The revolutionary era in the West ended with the uprisings of 1848. There has been no major political revolution in this civilization since that time. The assurance of food supplies, prevention of famine, and stronger police forces contributed to the end of Western revolution, as did various political changes. On the surface, the revolutions of 1848 were political failures. Liberal leaders, eager for new rights and parliaments, grew afraid of the demands of the growing urban masses. Urban workers, pressed by the crowding and upheaval of early industrialization, sought economic reform, and a few fought for socialism as a means of creating economic equality. Socialists argued for group control over property and production, often urging governmental attacks on capitalist ownership and capitalist values. Revolutionaries were divided still further in many countries by their nationalist interests. German nationalists, for example, often wanted unity more than liberal political reforms. Amid these divisions, the forces of the traditional monarchs reasserted themselves, chasing revolutionaries from Hungary to Italy. In France, a nephew of the great

Napoleon won popular election as president and soon established a new empire. The new or restored regimes proceeded to create police forces that helped stamp out political agitation.

THE POSTREVOLUTIONARY ERA AND NATIONALISM, 1848–1871

Political repression was not the whole story after 1848. The revolutions had won new freedoms for the peasantry, in their complete abolition of the manor system. Most of western Europe now became a region of small peasant farmers; the aristocracy, although still powerful, was weakened. Furthermore, government leaders began to realize that concessions were necessary in the political arena, if a new round of revolution was not to begin. So they granted constitutions and new powers to parliaments, plus a widened suffrage; these changes contented many liberals. Conservatism, in other words, became more adaptable. Two particularly flexible conservatives also worked to meet nationalist demands. In Italy, Count Cavour, the leader of a regional state in the north, engineered a series of wars beginning in 1859 that freed Italy from Austrian control and unified the entire peninsula. Otto von Bismarck, a Prussian politician, followed by orchestrating three regional wars, from 1864–1870, that unified the states of Germany. His final war, against France, also led to the downfall of Louis Napoleon's empire and the establishment of a new republic.

By 1870–1871, then, with the unification of Italy and Germany, political and diplomatic changes in western Europe had delighted most moderate nationalists. The new nations, and also Habsburg Austria–Hungary, had constitutions with some real protection for personal liberties, including religious freedom; they had parliaments with some real power over the budget. Germany even offered universal male suffrage, although the measure was qualified by a complex voting sys-

tem. France, newly republican, also confirmed universal male suffrage. These developments, along with continued reforms in other states—as in Britain, where suffrage was extended in 1867 and 1884 so that a majority of men could vote—seemed to satisfy most Westerners sufficiently that basic issues of political structure no longer dominated the scene.

The United States also addressed a fundamental issue of political structure in the same period, through the Civil War. The preservation of the Union and the abolition of slavery did not end important political divisions in the United States or the continuing problems faced by the black minority. As in much of Europe, political change was qualified by conservative principles. Thus, while Germany granted parliamentary rights but kept basic sovereignty in the hands of the monarch, who appointed the state's chief ministers, the United States abolished slavery but then allowed new kinds of legal discriminations against black citizens after the Reconstruction period. However, such changes reduced internal friction, another of the adjustments that brought revolution to an end throughout the West and resolved some long-standing issues related to political and legal structures.

Western society had thus gone through several political phases by 1871: outright revolution and upheaval, dominated by the French Revolution and Napoleon (1789–1815); conservative–liberal contest (1815–1848); and consolidation, under the auspices often of flexible conservatives (1849–1871). This last period had produced several sharp conflicts and the bloody American Civil War, which was the first war to signal the importance and destructive power of armies backed by industrial arsenals. The era of romanticism had ended in the West, and with it some of the more visionary political efforts; politicians now preferred hard facts and cold steel to enthusiasms either revolutionary or conservative. Bismarck, in fact, talked of having created the new, united Germany through "blood and iron."

"THE SOCIAL QUESTION," 1871–1914

Between 1871 and 1914, most Western governments were concerned with protecting the gains and compromises of earlier times. There was no major war within the Western world, although rivalries spilled over into struggles for colonial empires elsewhere. Germany's unification and the consolidation of the United States brought these powers increasingly to the fore, which automatically generated new tensions by altering the balance of forces in the West. One result was a new system of diplomatic alliances, as Germany sought to protect itself by linking with Austria and Italy, whereas France, eager to regain territories lost to Germany in 1871, gradually constructed its own alliance with Russia and then Britain. Diplomatic maneuvering among the leading Western powers won growing attention by the end of the century; it would ultimately, in 1914, help lead to unprecedented world war.

The final decades of the century saw two major developments in the internal politics of Western nations. Governments began to react more clearly to the pressures and problems of industrial society, taking on new functions. Many countries followed Germany's example and maintained mass conscript armies even in peacetime. Most countries extended a national system of compulsory education. National—or, in the United States, state—governments also took on new functions in inspecting factory conditions, setting housing standards, and the like; many began to provide health services to the poor. A number of governments, finally, led by Bismarck's Germany in the 1880s, passed social insurance laws, granting some state-sponsored protection against financial problems caused by illness, accident, or old age.

The expanded functions of governments were prompted in part by new political pressures, the second important domestic political development. Socialist parties arose everywhere after 1871. Many were inspired by the doctrines of Karl Marx, who had worked out his theories between 1847 and 1870. Socialist parties urged major reforms to protect working people; their goal was an alternative to capitalism that would provide economic equality. Some advocated revolution to reach this goal, but in fact most Western socialists worked within the political system, seeking to obtain power by a majority vote. Careful political organization and wide appeal made socialist parties the strongest single political force in Germany and an important third force, along with liberals and conservatives, in Britain, France, and (until after World War I) the United States.

The rise of socialism and the new functions of governments made what was called "the social question"—what to do about poverty and working-class demands—the leading domestic political issue in the last decades of the 19th century. Political alignments around this issue overshadowed the year-to-year shifts in parliamentary votes or presidential elections, as this level of politics became relatively routine. Thus, after a series of earlier periods in which the *form* of government had been the leading issue, Western politics settled increasingly into debates about the *functions* of government, the role of government in the reshaping (or preventing the reshaping) of society; and, with growing urgency, about the role of government in international affairs, as the armies and arsenals of the Western nations were mobilized around a tense network of diplomatic rivalries. Some observers believed that divisions over the social question encouraged Western governments to think in terms of diplomatic initiatives that could unite their nations, thus distracting them from new signs of unrest.

Another key shift occurred in the final decades of the 19th century: the growth of military rivalries. As Western nations built or expanded overseas empires, they increased military spending, forming huge peacetime armies and navies. Soon after 1900, for example, Britain and Germany competed to see who could build the biggest battleships, providing new links between the state and the industrial economy in the process. The sense of national competition expanded, particularly with the rise of a powerful Germany. Government leaders spent much of their time on diplomatic and military issues, amid recurrent crises. The popular press also played up rivalries, creating a sense of tension and excitement that could push leaders to new adventures, particularly in the imperial field. Between the 1870s and the 1890s, two alliance systems took shape, one linking Germany, the Habsburg Monarchy, and Italy, the other France, Britain, and Russia. The systems were defensive, but there was great potential for new conflicts. Both sides engaged in active planning for war. The West had long defined the state in part for its role in war and expansion, but with modern military technology, these functions took on new implications.

WESTERN POLITICAL INSTITUTIONS IN THE INDUSTRIAL REVOLUTION

The age of revolution in Western society recalled earlier political traditions in this civilization by calling for new balance against the power of the monarchy. However, this traditional impulse was reshaped by new political ideologies and the demands of an industrializing society. The result was a new kind of government, neither medieval nor absolutist in structure. Liberals leaders pressed for new protections for individual rights and for elected parliaments, and this led to new rights for newspapers, religious groups, even trade unions. Popular pressure and more radical leaders gradually persuaded some liberals to demand a democratic voting system.

Nationalism constituted another new force, fed by revolutionary beliefs in popular government and reactions to French invasions. Nationalists argued that the state should be linked to a single basic culture—a "national" culture, which should override minority differences within the society and should clearly delineate each nation

in relation to others. Nation-states were partly invented—national cultures were not, in fact, so clear-cut—but the association of a state with a dominant language, literature, and history proved to be a powerful mix, first in Europe, then elsewhere in the world. Nationalists could either call for allegiance to existing territorial states, as in revolutionary France, or, as in Germany, they could claim ethnic cultural unity and urge its political expression. In Europe, nationalism fed the long-standing military and economic competition among states and ultimately encouraged a growth in the power of the state.

The result of liberal and popular pressure, through the decades of revolution and reform, was a new structure for most Western states. By the 1870s, the Western political framework involved parliaments, based on wide voting rights, which served as the source of most legislation and acted as a check on executive authority. Monarchies had either been abolished, as in France, or greatly reduced in power. The political activities of the Catholic and Protestant churches had been radically scaled down, and most governments no longer believed that they should perform significant religious functions. It is important to realize that Western governments varied in the extent to which they had embraced liberal goals; the new German state, for instance, was notably less liberal in structure and intent than the governments of France, Britain, and the United States. And there were important political movements in many countries that opposed liberal values in the name of the older principles of monarchy and aristocracy. Nevertheless, despite variety and opposition, liberal values had significantly reshaped Western politics during the 19th century, among other things creating more similar political forms among the major Western states than had existed during the 17th and 18th centuries.

One key result of the development of liberal institutions was the rise of modern political parties, designed to organize members of parliament and to campaign for popular votes. In the United States, both major political parties espoused broadly liberal goals, although they differed significantly at important points of American history—for example, on the issue of slavery. In most European countries, liberal political parties competed with more conservative groups. By the 1870s, most conservative parties had added nationalist appeals to their political agenda, using this new force to advocate a strong state and military. Nationalism also gained force from the disruptions caused by industrialization. As people moved to the cities from their local villages, they were open to new loyalties, and a fascination with national achievements often served this purpose well. Finally, particularly after 1870, socialist parties began to grow, adding a new element to the political spectrum of most Western countries. Socialists were wary of nationalism and found liberalism too limited, although they largely accepted the importance of parliamentary institutions. Socialists pressed for major legislation on behalf of working people, and their revolutionary rhetoric often frightened liberals and conservatives. Nowhere, by 1914, had socialists won major positions in government, but their growing power helped generate new legislation to address important social questions.

Western politics, then, involved not only new political institutions, but also a multiparty system embracing a wide variety of political opinions. These views, expressed through a host of new "isms"—liberalism, socialism, nationalism, and formal conservatism—coexisted uneasily, and some politicians questioned the ability of the parliamentary system to manage all the forces it had unleashed. But most groups accepted at least tentatively the possibility of working within the system, seeking to win enough votes to enact the government measures they sought. Continuing changes in voting rights opened the way to additional issues. A rising feminist movement in many countries by 1900 pressed for women's right to vote; this was mainly an issue for the future, but several American states did grant women's suffrage, and Scandinavian governments did so shortly after 1900. Here was an important exten-

sion of the idea that basic political power should rest with the people themselves, expressed through equal voting rights.

Along with new constitutional structures and parties, the modern Western state assumed important new responsibilities and created the bureaucracy to carry them out. Some old functions were, of course, dropped or reduced, including the support of a single official religion and of aristocratic privilege. Governments after 1848 had also stopped defending the rights of groups such as guilds to establish work rules. But the new tasks of government were more extensive than those that were abandoned; one sign of this was that government staffs and budgets grew steadily, with rare exceptions, throughout the 19th century.

Western nations now clearly recognized their duty to encourage economic growth. Some used tariffs to protect particular industries. All supported the spread of railroad and canal networks. Governments also took on the function of mass education. All Western governments by the 1870s not only operated primary and secondary schools but also required attendance to at least age 12. Schools had as their role the teaching of useful economic skills to promote agricultural and manufacturing productivity. They also vigorously preached national loyalty, hoping the national literatures and histories would instill a new consensus among its citizens. Mass education was a new phenomenon, and levels of literacy, reaching 80 to 90 percent in Western society by 1900, had no precedent. The idea of the state, rather than the churches, serving as main educator was also novel. In addition, governments gained new contact with citizens through the practice of universal military conscription. The draft was used only in wartime by the United States and Britain, but even so, military forces grew larger than ever before. Since most male citizens spent a period in military service, as in France and Germany, they experienced firsthand the new power of the modern state—and, of course, had yet another occasion to learn national loyalties. Finally, as we have seen, governments began to take on responsibility for providing some

World Profiles

MARY WOLLSTONECRAFT (1759–1797)

Mary Wollstonecraft was one of the world's first explicit feminists. Her book *A Vindication of the Rights of Woman* (1792) applied the doctrines of the ongoing French Revolution to women's issues and effectively launched the modern women's movement, not only in her native Britain but throughout the Western world.

Wollstonecraft was the daughter of a tradesman who abused her mother and squandered his own inheritance. She early rebelled against some of the conventional practices applied to women, and her first writings addressed the lack of occupations open to them. She frequented radical circles in London and followed a deliberately unconventional lifestyle, bearing two children out of wedlock. (She died after the birth of her second child, Mary Shelley, the author of *Frankenstein*.) Wollstonecraft's sometimes shocking behavior caused subsequent feminists to shy away from citing her literary examples until a full century later. What combination of personal characteristics and more general social forces would prompt such a radical life and outlook at this time?

This portrait, by John Opie, shows Wollstonecraft as a powerful woman with a trace of sadness. She may have been pregnant with her second child at the time.

protection for the health and well-being of all citizens. Laws regulating working conditions and consumer rights, efforts to build sewers and other public-health facilities, and social insurance measures were important signs of the new welfare functions of the Western state.

To meet the new demands, the Western state not only expanded its bureaucracies but also began to recruit according to talent. Secondary schools in many countries served particularly to train future bureaucrats. All Western governments introduced civil service examinations by the 1870s—imitating practices long ago developed in China. Although most upper bureaucrats still came from the aristocracy and wealthy business and professional groups, there was a new chance for ordinary people to rise on the basis of academic achievement and test results.

The Western state, as it had emerged by 1914, embodied some interesting tensions. Liberal structures implied controls on government power, through bills of rights and parliamentary limits. However, government functions and bureaucracies had grown, often with the blessing of liberals themselves. This tension was, in important ways, a restatement of older Western ambiguities about the state. It also reflected the fact that different political groups disagreed about the state's proper role. The tension over the state and its limits would continue to color Western history into the 20th century.

WESTERN CULTURE IN THE INDUSTRIAL CENTURY

The 19th century produced a bewildering variety of intellectual movements. Major novelists abounded: Dickens, Austen, and many others in Britain; Hawthorne, Melville, and others in the United States; Balzac, Zola, and others in France. Poetry was slightly less important, as was drama, but here too literary production soared, and with it a host of new styles. In the arts, romantic painters focused on pastoral scenes, and then, in the last decades of the century, impressionists challenged old traditions of literal representation in their attempt to use the canvas to convey the essence, rather than the surface reality, of what the eye beholds. Interestingly, the 19th century did not produce a distinctive architectural style; revived gothic buildings predominated, but there was also classical and even byzantine imitation. Science continued its advance, with major strides in biology, notably Darwin's theory of evolution; in electricity and magnetism as well as other aspects of physics; discovery of the germ theory in medicine; and important innovations in applied chemistry.

Industrializing society, as it generated growing wealth, almost naturally produced a growing array of cultural expressions. New money built new churches, new public buildings, new

art galleries, and new laboratories. Industrial technology directly aided science, in promoting devices such as the X-ray machine or more powerful telescopes. New wealth also supported growing numbers of artists, even if many of them struggled lifelong with poverty. Inventions such as the camera and discoveries in optics also powerfully influenced artistic styles—impressionism rebelled against the camera's literalness, at the same time using new knowledge of how the eye perceives color. Rising literacy along with growing wealth supported new legions of writers; authors such as Dickens directly serialized their novels in middle-class newspapers, where payment by the word encouraged a rather long-winded writing style.

The role of religion in determining the intellectual agenda continued to decline. Christian faith remained important in the 19th century, even as the political role of organized churches waned. Many new churches were built, and Western society funded a vast missionary effort. In the United States, religion retained a particularly lively function, as revivals and immigrant churches powerfully shaped American culture. Religion faded more definitively as a popular force in Europe, where nationalism and socialism provided competing loyalties; here, however, Christianity continued to sustain many people. But as a formal intellectual force, religion was less vigorous even than in the age of Enlightenment. Few leading writers cared greatly about the nature of God or the fine points of theology.

Western society continued to reshape its intellectual heritage. This effort involved two major elements: first, ongoing work within the rational, scientific tradition of the Enlightenment, and second, a vigorous artistic statement that new styles were essential to capture the meaning of life and provide an alternative to scientific modes of thought.

The Enlightenment heritage persisted, as we have seen, in political theory. Liberal writers modified Enlightenment beliefs. They no longer argued in terms of natural right, preferring instead to talk in terms of what was useful. However, they maintained the traditional beliefs that individuals were rational, education was worthwhile, and scientific and industrial progress was desirable. Most socialists also clung to Enlightenment beliefs. Karl Marx (1818–1883), the leading theorist of the entire century, used a historical rather than a strictly rationalist basis for his grand scheme. To Marx, history changed on the basis of who controlled the existing technology, or means of production. Class struggle resulted, with those in control fighting those below. In modern society, the middle class had wrested power from the aristocracy but had created a new class enemy, the property-less proletariat, or working class. This class would grow until revolution became inevitable. But once the proletarian revolution had occurred, an Enlightenment-style utopia would result. The state would wither away, as each individual would be able rationally to determine his or her own interests; goods would be distributed according to need; class struggle would vanish once the vestiges of the middle class had been eliminated. More prosaically, most socialist theorists agreed with liberals about the basic goodness and rationality of humankind and the importance of material progress, education, and science.

In addition to liberal and socialist theory, the rationalist tradition was also kept alive through scientific inquiry. Indeed, as scientists learned about new fertilizers and health measures, science became more firmly linked than ever before with the idea of progress on this earth. On the more theoretical level, science advanced on every front. The great contribution was Darwin's evolutionary theory. On the basis of careful observation, Darwin argued that all living creatures had evolved into their present form through the ability to adapt in a struggle for survival. Biological development could be scientifically understood as a process taking place over time, with some animal and plant species disappearing and others evolving from earlier forms. Darwin's ideas clashed with traditional Christian beliefs

that God had created humankind directly, and the resulting popular debate, on the whole, weakened the intellectual hold of religion. The picture of nature that Darwin suggested was far more complex than the simple natural laws of Newton. Nature worked through random struggle. However, Darwin confirmed the idea that scientists could advance knowledge, and his theory was compatible with the idea that natural laws encouraged progress.

The social sciences also continued to advance, on the basis of observation, experiment, and rationalist theorizing. Great efforts went into compilations of statistical data concerning populations, economic developments, and health problems. Sheer empirical knowledge about the human condition had never been more extensive. At the level of theory, leading economists tried to explain business cycles and the causes of poverty; social psychologists studied the behavior of crowds. Toward the end of the century, the Viennese physician Sigmund Freud began to develop his theories of the workings of the human unconscious, arguing that much behavior is determined by impulses but psychological problems can be relieved by rational understanding. Like many other scientists, social scientists complicated the traditional Enlightenment view of nature and human nature by studying the animal impulses and unconscious urges of human beings. However, they continued to rely on standard scientific methods in their work, believing that human behavior can be rationally categorized, and most of them asserted that ultimately human reason would prevail, as manifested in appropriate economic, political, or personal behavior.

The artistic vision developed by the 19th century was rather different. To be sure, many novelists realistically portrayed human problems, believing that their efforts could contribute to reform. Artists, as we have seen, were aware of scientific discoveries. Beginning with romanticism, however, many artists looked to emotion, rather than reason, as the key to the mystery of life. They sought to portray longings and even

Bucolic romanticism: landscape by the British painter Constable, early 19th century.

madness, not calm reflection. They also deliberately endeavored to violate traditional Western artistic standards. They proclaimed their freedom from the traditional rules characterizing drama or poetry. This impulse was taken up, after romanticism declined around 1850, by new artists who attempted to defy literal representation. Leading poets shunned conventional rhymes and meters, writing abstract, highly personalized statements. Artists and sculptors sought suggestive images, while later 19th-century composers began to work with atonal scales that defied long-established conventions in music. Some artists talked of an "art for art's sake"—that is, art that had it own purposes, regardless of the larger society. Other artists and philosophers rejected rationalism outright, stressing the power of impulses or the human will.

The new split in Western culture, between rationalists and nonrationalists, had institutional overtones. By the late 19th century, most scientists and social scientists worked in or around universities. Western universities, in a virtual eclipse since the end of the Middle Ages, now revived as great research centers that also trained society's elite. This model of the university developed first in Germany and spread quickly to France, the United States, and to a lesser extent Britain. Many artists, in contrast, worked outside any institution. Artistic communities, called "bohemian" by respectable middle-class observers who distrusted the artistic lifestyle, developed in most major cities, with the community in Paris the most glittering. Most artistic patrons preferred older styles, particularly in painting and music. But modern art continued to grow, its lack of clear standards and its defiance of ordinary taste and tradition clearly expressing an important aspect of Western culture in the modern age. It was revealing that in an age of great economic change, Western culture did not rely simply on existing artistic traditions as an anchor. The same individualism and secularism that helped spur business competition spilled over into culture, prompting many artists to seek alternatives to ordinary values, scientific modes of inquiry, and the sheer ugliness of the industrial environment itself.

INDUSTRIAL SOCIETY

Industrialization left a decisive mark on the shape of society in Western nations. In combination with the legal changes ushered in by the decades of revolution, it produced a new social structure. Property and earnings, plus the level of education one had achieved, increasingly determined position in society. Former measures, such as birth, legal privilege, and purely landed estate, declined. In this new social structure, wealthy business executives and professional people gained growing prestige, at the expense of aristocrats and old merchant families. In the United States, where an aristocracy had never seriously existed and the Civil War decimated the landowning class in the South, the middle class reigned supreme. In most European countries, aristocrats continued to wield cultural and political influence, but they no longer dominated the social pyramid. Middle-class culture, evincing a broadly liberal faith in science and education and a passion for respectable, restrained behavior, increasingly set the social tone. The ranks of the middle class grew, with the expansion of business and the rise of professions such as engineering, law, and medicine, in which individuals could claim unique expertise on the basis of special knowledge, training, and licensing.

The second leading social class of modern Western society consisted of urban workers, particularly in the factories. This group, far larger than the middle class, had scant property and much lower earnings. It did not accept all middle-class values but was nonetheless influenced by their powerful expression in the popular media, notably books and newspapers, and the school system.

Not everyone fit into the basic middle-class/working-class division of industrial society, even aside from the important remnants of an aristocracy at the top. Artisans clung to older values, in some countries even hoping for a restoration of the guild system; they merged only gradually and incompletely with the new working class. The rural population, still massive, continued to reflect the distinctive features of a peasant tradition and agricultural life. Even here, however, the division increased between peasants or farmers who owned their land and employed others, on the one hand, and a growing number of landless laborers, on the other.

The rise of white-collar workers added another, newer complexity to the modern Western social structure. White-collar workers such as secretaries and telephone operators owned little property. Although they needed some education to perform their jobs, they could not claim professional status. But white-collar workers did share styles of dress and values with middle-class people. They liked to think—usually incorrectly—that they or their children could rise into the managerial or professional ranks.

Family life was powerfully affected by industrialization. Family responsibilities changed, although gradually. The family ceased being the main center of production, as work moved outside the home. But the family gained or enhanced some other functions. It served as a consumer unit; most major purchases were affected within the family, and a new division of labor freed some family members—mainly housewives—for the important and time-consuming tasks of shopping, now that families did not make most of their own goods. Much leisure time was spent with the family. Holidays more and more became family occasions rather than community affairs. The idea of family vacations spread, first in the middle class and then, in the form of daylong excursions, to workers. The family also became the center of emotional gratification. Family members were supposed to love each other. The middle-class belief that the family should be a haven against the

History Debate

WOMEN IN INDUSTRIAL SOCIETY

Historians continue to disagree on what happened to women in Western industrial society. There are disputes of interpretation. Initially, for example, historians saw laws that limited women's hours of work as humanitarian gains. But feminist historians note that these laws made it less attractive to employ women and formed part of a new emphasis on the importance of the male breadwinner. Women were now supposed to maintain sexual respectability, but this power had a downside, for respectable women were not supposed to be sexually eager.

There are disputes of emphasis. Women were pushed out of the urban labor force, particularly after marriage. However, they were given greater moral esteem and power within the home. Women provided the "essential elements of moral government," and it was assumed that their purity would overcome men's baser impulses. Educational gains for women did not result in equality, but they increasingly eliminated gender gaps in literacy.

Even feminism, rising in the second half of the 19th century, becomes controversial in this discussion. Did it result merely from new and old inequalities, or did it reflect women's new cultural status and other gains such as a reduction in family size? Is the 19th century to be seen as the triumph of a new form of patriarchy, or as a crucial, albeit complex stage of women's liberation?

stress of the outside world was also reflected in some working-class sentiments. Courtship became increasingly romantic; at least in the working class, the importance of sexual pleasure deepened. Ironically, this emphasis on emotional satisfaction produced a noticeable growth in the divorce rate, with the United States taking the lead. As families declined as units of economic activity, it became more possible and perhaps more necessary to dissolve marriages that were not providing personal gratification.

Changes in family functions had vital implications for the roles of family members. The man was increasingly seen as the breadwinner, with his earnings from work his main responsibility. Married women were largely kept out of the formal labor force; in the middle class, even most girls did not work. According to middle-class family ideals, women were to serve as the exponents of culture and the moral center within the family. This gave

them a new significance, as women in fact came to dominate child rearing and the household more fully than before, but it also removed them from many public activities, since women lagged far behind men in political rights. Industrialization raised important questions about women's roles. Women were given new esteem, and their educational gains were more rapid than those of men although women started from a lower position on this scale. In the working class, moreover, women were vital to the labor force; girls worked in factories, as domestic servants, and later as clerks and public school teachers. However, in day-to-day activities, married women were increasingly separate from men. The rise of feminist movements, seeking expanded rights and opportunities for women, reflected the anomalies of this aspect of the Western family.

Attitudes toward children changed as well. Most middle-class children were expected to learn, not earn. Working-class children, on the other hand, were essential to the operation of early factories, maintaining the traditional assumptions that children should contribute to the family economy. But many people from all classes objected to the factory conditions to which children were exposed, particularly the frequency of accidents; in fact, as machines became more complex, children's usefulness declined. Moreover, the advent of compulsory education took most young children out of the labor force. Most adolescents still worked in 1914, although in the United States a high school education became more commonplace, even among working-class youth. Parents grew concerned with fostering their children's learning ability. Their emotional expectations of children also increased, their hope being that such attention and the resulting affection would compensate for the fact that offspring had become a greater economic burden. At the same time, parents' roles in children's lives decreased, and interaction among young people in schools heralded the development of separate generational cultures by the end of the 19th century. Being a child in the industrial West was different from being a child in a traditional agricultural society, but it was not necessarily easier.

The final impact of industrialization on the family involved population structure. In what is called the *demographic transition*, Western families quickly reacted to the population boom of the 18th century by reducing their birth rates. Birth rates began to fall gradually in the United States and France as early as 1790. The middle class led the way in this demographic transition. Middle-class culture emphasized the importance of sexual restraint, and most middle-class people married fairly late. Gradually, a birth-rate limit spread to the working class and peasantry, although under the new demographic regime, poorer families, on average, had larger families than the middle class—the reverse of traditional patterns. With children now an expense and parents expected to provide careful supervision and

training to children, large families began to decline. By 1914, the average Western family included only three to four children. By this point, the medical advances that would almost eliminate deaths in childhood were underway, making birth control even more imperative. Most families relied mainly on sexual restraint for this purpose, although new contraceptive devices became more common, particularly after the vulcanization of rubber in the 1830s; the incidence of abortion also increased. Thus, by 1914, the industrial, demographic regime was clearly in place in the West, with lower birth rates than ever before in human history, combined with low mortality rates for children as life expectancy steadily rose. This new demography produced important changes in family life and the roles of women, now that mothering required less effort than before; it also produced considerable tension, given the need for sexual restraint. The new demography had wider consequences, too, as the population of the West began to decline in relation to that of other parts of the world.

Despite all these changes, the family thrived in Western society, adapting new purposes and roles as old ones dwindled but also maintaining some traditional functions. Change itself was often concealed. As new household equipment made women's work easier, standards of household cleanliness increased, so the effort involved in housekeeping, in fact, remained the same. Mothers were praised despite the decline in the birth rate—the U.S. Congress, for example, enacted Mother's Day soon after 1900. Of all the traditional institutions from agricultural society—the village, the guild, even the church—the family survived the best. However, it did change, and Westerners worried out loud about the stability of this basic institution, as they continue to in the present day.

Along with social structure and family, popular culture altered its shape under the effects of industrialization. Growing literacy, exposure to political campaigns, and increasing wealth—at least, for most by 1914, slightly above subsistence—all had an impact. Ideas about the value of education, science, and technology spread more widely, and the gap between popular and elitist values narrowed by 1914.

However, industrialization imposed a general strain on society, as do ongoing changes in technology and business organization. The nature of work shifted, and probably its quality deteriorated. Before the Industrial Revolution, work for most people had been a social act, punctuated by gossip and naps, accomplished within a family context. With the rise of factories and offices, not only was work taken out of the home, but it also became increasingly regimented. Shop rules forbade workers from singing, chatting, or wandering about. The pace of work quickened, as a clock routinely timed workers' efforts. Strangers supervised more people than ever before, and workers performed specialized tasks, rather than creating whole products.

These changes were hard to integrate, and many would argue that they have not been fully assimilated even now. In the early stages of the Industrial Revolution, particularly before 1850, the impact of new work forms was intensified by the rapid decline of popular leisure traditions. Festivals virtually vanished. As communities dissolved through migration to the cities, these highly local events were hard to maintain. Furthermore, the middle class disapproved of festivals as a threat to public order and sheer waste of time; the newly created police forces actively discouraged such public gatherings. Middle-class leisure consisted chiefly of useful activities such as family reading or piano playing that would showcase cultural achievement and train the young. Many workers did not accept this utilitarian definition of leisure, but they had few alternatives. Tavern drinking became one of their major pastimes (one that middle-class temperance reformers fought in vain) because it provided a glimmer of former sociability.

Many workers protested the changes in their lives. The decades of revolution depended heavily on working-class protest in the name of older work values, with artisans taking the lead. Workers also sought to cushion the impact of industrialization on their lives, by taking time off from their jobs or changing employment with great frequency, to the fury of middle-class managers. Gradually, however, workers found some solace in the concept of instrumentalism; they recognized that they could not necessarily control the quality or conditions of their work, but they would accept their job's constraints for the sake of rising earnings. In other words, work became an instrument to other things. After 1850, working-class protest, although it increased as workers became better organized, largely changed from attempts to control the job itself, to demands for shorter hours and higher pay. The worker looked forward to new economic benefits, rather than backward to older values.

At the same time, new recreational outlets arose. Popular reading, vaudeville theaters, and professional and amateur sports proliferated in Western society after 1870, for various social groups. The new leisure was highly commercialized, signaling the growth of a consumer society. Sports also served to discipline people for the workplace, as they learned team cooperation and obedience to the rules imposed on every modern sport; sports also served to condition possible future soldiers. Some critics at the time and even today have blasted the new sports culture, its emphasis on pleasure seeking and physical release, and wondered if leisure was as satisfying and expressive as it should be, given the limits of industrial work. Whatever its quality, mass leisure was a uniquely modern creation and a vital part of the new culture spawned by industrialization. Some games, such as soccer football, first developed in industrial England, would spread around the world much faster than industrialization itself.

GAIN AND STRAIN IN INDUSTRIALIZATION

In 1900, heralding the advent of a new century, many Western newspapers looked back on the past century and found it satisfactory. Improved health conditions, new wealth, greater political freedom, more education—all suggested an improved quality of life, one that was getting better. Great change had unquestionably occurred, but by 1900 many people were becoming accustomed to it, bolstered by their belief in progress. Only a few groups in Western society, such as the new immigrants to the United States, were confronting urban, industrial life for the first time.

However, change had brought strain as well as apparent progress, and it continued to do so. An aristocratic German general, a Catholic bishop, and an old-fashioned New England intellectual would all take issue with the idea of progress, seeing the values that were lost as more important than the material gains. From other vantage points, many workers, particularly those who could find no meaning at all in their work, and many feminists would also quarrel with the idea of progress, hoping that their satisfaction or ideals would some day come to fruition.

The strains within Western society spilled over into the West's world role. Industrialization brought new power to Western society, which it used to gain more complete control over more areas of the world than ever before. Imperialist expansion reflected not only business success but also the desire of aristocratic officers and Christian missionaries to find new arenas for their values, even as conditions at home became more challenging.

In turn, groups from China to Latin America, although proud of their own cultures, recognized that they had to copy some features of industrial society if they wanted to prevent total Western domination. A key question was which aspects of the Western industrial process had to be, and could be, imitated. Was it just the military technology and organization, or the wider economic revolution, or did Western-style politics, or art, or changes in women's roles also inextricably enter the process? Western history between 1789 and 1914 had brought profound transformations to one of the world's major civilizations; it also established a complex model for others to ponder.

ISSUES AND CONNECTIONS

The biggest challenge in dealing with western Europe in the long 19th century is simply that so much happened. Not only the Industrial Revolution, but also the French Revolution, Darwinism, modern art, and Marxism were fundamental developments, significantly changing the fields involved. It helps to recognize that not all of this fits together tidily. Political developments on the whole implied growing freedom and participation. But in the factories, people lost much of their voice over conditions, and much personal freedom as well. What other major tensions built up during this period of Western history?

Another problem involves the gap between several common trends and growing nationalist rivalry within Europe. Industrialization, the rise of modern parliaments, scientific discovery, and artistic innovations involved all parts of western Europe, despite some regional variants. But nationalism and the growth of military power created new internal rivalries. Italian and German unifications added to the number of competitors.

The trends that were shaped by the French Revolution, the new science, and an industrial economy and society, all fruits of the long 19th century in the West, continue to operate in Western society today. Westerners build on the scientific, technological, and political capacities developing 200 years ago. The same applies to more specific developments such as agitation for women's rights, consumerism, and the fascination with professional sports. Westerners still worry about issues such as the tension between working outside the home and family life, created in this period. In many of these developments—for example, consumerism and parliamentary democracy—the West was adding to the definition of the civilization in ways that have proved durable.

SUGGESTED WEB SITES

On industrial workers, see http://applebutter. freeservers.com/worker/index.html; on working women, see http://www.womeninworldhistory. com/lesson7.html. On Marxist ideas and the great Marxist anthem, go to http://www.anu.edu.au/ polsci/marx/marx.html (which includes a very clear RealAudio file of the "Internationale" sung by an Irish folksinger accompanied on the guitar). For a Web site on the British working class, see http://www.history.rochester.edu/pennymag. A rich site on the French Revolution is http://chnm.gmu.edu/revolution. On James Watt, see http://homepages.westminster.org.uk/hooke/ issue10/watt.htm.

SUGGESTED READINGS

Recent work includes Brenda Stalcup, ed., *The Industrial Revolution* (2002); Robert Marks, *The Origins of the Modern World: A Global and Ecological Narrative* (2002); Joel Mokyr, *The British Industrial Revolution* (1999); Carolyn Tuttle, *Hard at Work in Factories and Mines: The Economics of Child Labor During the British Industrial Revolution* (1999).

Fine studies of the early industrial period include Phyllis Deane, *The First Industrial Revolu-tion* (1980) (on Britain), and E. J. Hobsbawm, *The Age of Revolution: Europe 1789–1848* (1962) (on Europe generally). See also Peter N. Stearns, *The Industrial Revolution in World History* (1998). An excellent recent study highlights Europe by comparison: R. Bin Wong, *China Transformed: Historical Change and the Limits of European Experience* (1997). A more general survey of the social history of the period is Peter N. Stearns and Herrick Chapman, *European Society in Upheaval: Social History Since 1750*, 3rd ed. (1992); a more interpretive study is Barrington Moore, *Social Origins of Dictatorship and Democracy* (1966). For more specialized aspects of industrial change, see L. Tilly and J. Scott, *Women, Work and Family* (1978); E. A. Wrigley, *Population and History* (1969); F. D. Scott, *Emigration and Immigration* (1963); and E. P. Thompson, *The Making of the English Working Class* (1963). On leading developments in political history, a useful volume is R. R. Palmer's *The Age of Democratic Revolution: A Political History of Europe and America, 1760–1800* (1964); a good text survey is John Merriman, *Modern European Civilization*, Vol. 2 (1996). See also Harvey Graff, ed., *Literacy and Social Development in the West* (1982); Albert Lindemann, *History of European Socialism* (1983); and David Kaiser, *Politics and War: European Conflict from Philip II to Hitler* (1990).

22

World Economy and Western Imperialism: Africa and South Asia

European industrialization, supplemented by the growing industrial power of the United States, inevitably transformed the world economy. Merchants ventured forth from the industrialized nations, seeking markets and raw materials all over the world. Pressure to participate in world commerce increased everywhere. Previously isolated economies, like Japan, now had to interact with the West. Economies already selling to the West now had to increase those levels of export; this was the case in Latin America.

The links in the world economy expanded steadily. New and speedier shipping played a vital role, making the crossing of the oceans a matter of a week or two rather than months. At the same time, railroads reached into continental interiors. More rapid communication, provided by the telegraph and later the telephone and the wireless, transmitted an unprecedented amount of information about business conditions around the globe. Levels of international trade rose as a result. By the 1830s, many industrial concerns were opening branch offices in major cities in various parts of the world.

Along with the great increase in volume came some alterations in the nature of the world economy. The Industrial Revolution gave the West new quantities of manufactured products to sell, including factory equipment, locomotives, and steamships. The West had already sold manufactured goods to other societies, but its capacity was now literally revolutionized, as was its intense need to find available markets for its soaring output. Europe and North America also had capital to export, particularly after 1850. Earnings from early industrialization begged for profitable investment outlets; although domestic economies provided some of these, there was an avid search for opportunities, at higher interest rates, in less industrialized areas. The development of the U.S. West, including the rapid expansion of a railroad network, owed much to British and French investment, but significant capital also went to Latin America, Africa, and Asia—at a price. Western investment in Russia also increased rapidly.

New Western opportunities to export industrial products and capital were matched by growing needs for imports. There was one huge change: slaves were no longer necessary. The transatlantic slave trade was abolished between 1807 and 1834, mainly on British initiative; as of the latter date, slavery was ended in the British colonies. In succeeding decades, slavery was abolished in the Americas and elsewhere.

Cheap labor, however, continued to be essential. Nonindustrial societies intensified their commitment to food exports, as Europe's urbanization and growing wealth increased the market for both staples, such as wheat and beef, and specialty products, such as coffee and sugar. The need for raw materials became even more intense. Western transportation and recreational requirements opened a wide market for rubber, for example, which could be produced only in tropical areas. Growing production of steel made certain rare alloys vital, whereas other metals (such as copper) and chemicals were sought outside the West as well.

In brief, with the important exception of the end to massive international slave trading, the world economy proceeded along the lines previously established: The West supplied more expensive manufactured products, while most of the rest of the world exchanged food and raw materials. The earlier result—a fundamental economic advantage to the West—persisted as well, particularly because until 1900, most of the world's trade was handled by Western ships and merchant firms. However, the new volume of economic exchange made the disparity between the West and most other civilizations far more significant than it had previously been. Spurred by Western merchants and capital, producers in other regions found themselves more deeply affected by the world economy than ever before. Huge numbers of Latin American peasants, for example, were now drawn into the production of

coffee, or hemp for rope making, and away from their traditional village agriculture. The influx of Western capital into mining, transportation facilities, and market agriculture literally around the world also increased the direct involvement of millions of people in the international economy. There was another significant change: no part of the world could now isolate itself from Western commercial pressure.

The solidification of the world economy was recognized and furthered by new European-sponsored economic arrangements, from the 1850s onward. International regulations facilitated telegraphic links; the new Postal Union systematized worldwide deliveries of mail.

The expansion of the global economic structure under Western control was a basic force in world history throughout the 19th century, affecting all other civilizations. Its impact was enhanced by the new surge of outright imperialism, based on growing European appetites and new military technology such as the repeating rifle. Western European nations and the United States claimed huge chunks of territory, from the islands of the Pacific to the interior of Africa. Land previously acquired, particularly in India and southeast Asia, was now more closely controlled, as Europeans had both the military and organizational means and the economic need to go beyond port cities and loose alliances with regional governments in the interior. The expansion of a Western empire and the subsequent changes in its nature bore most heavily on three non–Western regions: sub-Saharan Africa, India, and southeast Asia. But the threat of imperialist control, along with the expansion of the West's world economic role, affected all civilizations by 1900, accentuating the problem of what to do about the power and example of the West.

This chapter examines the new imperialism and the areas it most directly touched; the following chapters consider the varying reactions of other civilizations to what became, by 1900, a set of common themes in modern world history.

KEY QUESTIONS   *What caused Europe's imperialist surge? This is the first question, addressed in the following section. But more subtle questions are equally important. How did different parts of the world react to European pressure, and what caused the differences? What were the main differences among major colonial regions—comparing, for instance, Africa and India? What kinds of resistance and cooperation developed?*

THE REASONS FOR IMPERIALISM: MOTIVES AND MEANS

At the end of the 18th century, Western imperialism extended to North and South America, save for the newly independent United States; India, although the process of British control had yet to be completed; the islands of Indonesia; and scattered port holdings, particularly in parts of sub-Saharan Africa. The bulk of the Latin American empire was lost soon after 1800, through wars of independence; this civilization nevertheless remained closely tied to the Western economy.

By 1900, Western empires included all the 1800 holdings outside Latin America; most of the mainland of southeast Asia, as the French conquered Indochina (present-day Vietnam, Laos, and Cambodia), while Britain seized Malaya and effectively controlled Thailand and Burma; the entire continent of Africa with minor exceptions, the most important of which was the proudly independent kingdom of Ethiopia; Australia and New Zealand; and the various Pacific islands, including Hawaii, Samoa, and Tahiti, which were divided mainly among Britain, France, Germany, and the United States. Western nations also had colonies along the coast of China, holdings on the eastern coast of the Arabian Peninsula, and a growing influence in Persia, Afghanistan, and parts of the Ottoman Empire. North African regions were colonies or about to become so. Britain proudly claimed that the sun never set on its empire, because of its worldwide span, and to many other Westerners the world seemed, for all intents and purposes, a Western holding. Never before had so much territory been acquired in so little time.

During the 19th century, moreover, the Western concept of empire changed. Earlier colonies had been regarded primarily as market outposts. Catholic powers, notably Spain and Portugal, had thought also in terms of Christian conversion, which extended European control in Latin America and the Philippines. The British colonization of the eastern coast of North America had also been an important exception to the common pattern. Outside the New World, limited control for trading purposes described the Western approach. After about 1800, this guiding viewpoint began to change rapidly. Trade alone was not enough when new market agriculture, transportation networks, and investment outlets had to be established. The redefinition of the world economy suggested more extensive penetration. Furthermore, Europeans and North Americans began to develop a greater sense of cultural superiority. Protestant groups now joined Catholics in seeking missionary contacts. More generally, Westerners began to claim a clearer mission to bring civilization to the peoples of the world—civilization, of course, being as the West defined it. The English poet Rudyard Kipling described a widely held sentiment in arguing that the West had such superior moral and political values that it had a responsibility—the "white man's burden"—to reshape the rest of the world. Missionaries brought not only Christianity but also Western styles of dress and approaches to education and medical care. Business managers, convinced of the inferiority of "native" ways, tried to tell non-Westerners how to work and organize their businesses. Imperial governments sought to redefine marriage customs, caste systems, and tribal politics. In both old colonies and new, European imperialism now meant an effort to establish effective government and supervision over wide areas.

History Debate

CAUSES OF THE ABOLITION OF SLAVERY

In 1833, arguing for the abolition of slavery in all British colonies, the British colonial secretary explained the need in terms of the "liberal and humane spirit of the age." For over a century, historians echoed this explanation. It was new, humanitarian ideas that led to the abolition of slavery in Britain, France, and the northern United States after centuries of acceptance.

Then, in 1944, a West Indian historian, Eric Williams, took a radically different approach. He claimed that it was not humanitarianism but, rather, economic self-interest that explained the shifting viewpoint. British and other industrial capitalists were now in a position of power where the world economy was concerned. Slave economies were fading within this context. It was not idealism but simple materialism that now put slave owners on the defensive.

More recent work, by historians such as David B. Davis and Seymour Drescher, has complicated this picture even further. Drescher has shown that the slave economies were still very profitable apart from slavery, so it was not simple materialism that prompted the institution's abolition. Davis argues, however, that industrial capitalists now needed to defend wage labor, being imposed (amid great hardship) on European workers themselves. To do this and distract workers from their own plight, they attacked slavery. Again, material self-interest rather than humanitarianism ruled the day, but such an analysis is complex. Drescher defends humanitarianism a bit more but contends that it was popularized among artisans and other people frightened by the industrial economy, who used abolitionism to bolster their own sense of morality. The current effort, then, is to combine a recognition that there were new humanitarian arguments involved in this historic change, with a belief that key changes in the capitalist economy were involved as well.

Can you think of other debates about the extent of idealism vs. material self-interest in explaining historical change?

Two other points are worth mentioning. First, during the 18th century as a whole, as abolitionism spread in the nations of the Americas, rapid world population growth made it relatively easy to replace the slave trade with imported workers from Asia and Europe. Second, although slavery was increasingly abolished, it was often replaced with systems that were still coercive to some extent. For example, immigrant workers might be tied by indenture contracts. Company stores might place workers in debt, so they could not legally leave or change jobs. Practices of this sort continue into our own time.

How do these points affect the idealism vs. materialism debate?

Why did Western imperialism change and advance into so many new parts of the world? The West's growing technological sophistication assumed a major role, although colonialists also played on ethnic and other divisions in the societies they conquered. European imperialism in Africa can be explained in large part by the ability of Western ships, steam-propelled, to navigate up the previously impenetrable African rivers. This allowed contacts with the interior that no people, including Africans themselves, had ever before achieved. Steam-driven iron boats were also basic to the European penetration of China. Western facility in weaponry continued to increase, even as Africans and Asians gained access to old-fashioned rifles. By the late 19th century,

Fight between the German army and native troops in Tanzania: early 20th-century African art.

Western soldiers were armed with repeating rifles, which did not require separate reloading and thus represented a huge advantage. The introduction of the machine gun was another fundamental step. Winston Churchill, later the British prime minister, described an 1898 battle near the Upper Nile, pitting a small British force armed with 20 early machine guns against 40,000 Muslim troops:

> The infantry fired steadily and stolidly, without hurry or excitement, for the enemy were far away and the officers careful. Besides, the soldiers were interested in the work and took great pains. . . . And all the time out on the plain on the other side bullets were shearing through flesh, smashing and splintering bone . . . valiant men were struggling on through a hell of whistling metal, exploding shell, and spurting dust—suffering, despairing, dying.

When the battle ended, 11,000 Muslims and 48 British soldiers were dead, and the British had conquered the territory now known as the Sudan.

If technology, backed by medical advances that allowed Westerners to avoid contracting many tropical diseases, accounts for a key part of the Western advantage, particularly in Africa but to an extent elsewhere, it does not explain the motives for the new imperialism. Gains resulting from the Industrial Revolution, including technology but also improved organization, better health care, and expanded literacy, fed the growing belief that the West was superior to the rest of the world, with a right and duty to rule. This attitude now combined with Christian beliefs in religious superiority, a current that had been evidenced in earlier Western expansion attempts from the Crusades onward. Economic motives played a prominent role as well. Not only were Europeans eager for markets and raw materials, but they were also anxious about the stability of their own changing economy. Even confident U.S. business leaders sought secure markets and supplies through colonies or, in Central America, semi-colonies. Many people believed that domestic sales and supplies were insufficient for an economy that depended on growth. They also saw imperialism as a way to excite and divert ordinary people who might otherwise join in social protest—and indeed imperial conquest did arouse popular passions in Europe and the United States, aided by the stirring headlines of the new mass press.

Certain groups in the West, left behind in the rush to industrialize, found solace in their empires. Aristocrats, increasingly displaced at home, could win prestige as imperial bureaucrats, living the good life while ruling the natives. Christian missionaries sometimes experienced greater satisfaction in preaching to the heathen than in facing the gradual decline of religion in their own lands. Individual adventurers, tired of the increasingly bureaucratic life of industrial corporations, found excitement in seeking fame and fortune in distant places. In various ways, then, imperialism expressed social tensions generated by industrialization, as well as the power that the Industrial Revolution provided.

The most direct factors in the imperialist scramble, however, were the claims and rivalries of various states in the West. Nationalist loyalty motivated many explorers and adventurers, like the German Karl Peters, who staked Germany's claims to Tanganyika in eastern Africa, because of his desire to see his country assume its rightful place among the great powers—and who operated at first without official state backing. Patriotic assertions prompted European governments to intervene on behalf of individual missionaries or business entrepreneurs, who could not be tampered with lest national honor be impugned. Above all, chauvinist rivalries spurred new states to claim a share in imperial glory and old states to protect their existing holdings through expansion. Britain acquired many new colonies—such as Egypt, which guarded the quickest route to India after the building of the Suez Canal—to defend old ones against possible rivals. France sought additional territory in north Africa to protect its first north African colony, Algeria. Newly imperialist countries included Italy, which won important territory in north Africa; Belgium, which acquired the vast Congo region; and Germany, which displayed its greatness by taking possession of two major African colonies plus areas in China and the Pacific. To this list may be added the United States, which tended to oppose imperialism in principle, in part because of a long pre-

occupation with overland expansion to the west and in part because of its own national experience as a colony, but which in fact acquired extensive Pacific holdings, including the Philippines, won from Spain in the Spanish-American War in 1898, and several West Indian islands, most notably Puerto Rico. The appearance of new imperialist nations heightened a growing French desire, after 1871, to gain colonies to compensate for defeat at Germany's hands back home in the Franco-Prussian War. The various pressures for conquest, which developed particularly after 1870, added to the belief that every available territory should be claimed as quickly as possible, for the sake of national security and national glory. Ironically, this same spirit of heedless rivalry would later intensify conflict in Europe, when, after 1900, all available lands were taken and attention returned to competition nearer home.

IMPERIALISM IN INDIA AND SOUTHEAST ASIA

The new European imperialism focused particularly on conquering relatively populous territories that had important traditions of their own. It involved, in other words, ruling millions of other people and encountering considerable resistance in the name of established values. Most of the new colonies received European administrators and some business entrepreneurs, missionaries, doctors, and teachers, but few ordinary settlers. Important Italian immigration occurred in parts of north Africa, and some Europeans established themselves in the rich agricultural lands of east Africa as a new and privileged minority, but these were exceptional patterns.

European imperialism in Asia was completed—with the British conquest of India and extension of influence to Thailand and Burma and the French takeover of Indochina—without in any sense drawing these regions into the orbit of Western civilization. Revealingly,

British colonial officials at Delhi: a herald reads a proclamation that declares Queen Victoria empress of India. (Granger Collection)

Christian missionary efforts in India and southeast Asia had little success, winning only small minorities of converts—a clear sign of the continued validity of traditional cultures. The new imperialism had a vital impact nevertheless. In India, Britain's rule had far more sweeping consequences than most previous periods of foreign control, including the recent Mughal Empire. Indeed, India and Dutch Indonesia became showcases for the kind of penetration that 19th-century imperialists sought. With such colonization, in turn, came important resistance, which itself established new patterns while confirming some older cultural values. One important result was that British rule lasted a considerably shorter time than had previous foreign occupations. This fact suggests some interesting features about the British commitment, which never evolved into a fully Indian regime, while also revealing important changes in the Indian political tradition itself, which became less tolerant of foreign rule.

India

As Britain completed its conquest of India during the first half of the 19th century, it began also to take a more active hand in Indian affairs. Control by the British government substantially replaced that of the East India Company, and at the same time the respect British officials had for Indian culture declined. India became a place to change, to westernize. Thus, laws (not totally unlike those of the early Mughals) sought to limit child marriage and religious sacrifices; Hindu converts to Christianity were rewarded with government jobs.

British rule during most of the 19th century had a significant impact on Indian politics. The very fact of unification of the entire subcontinent was a major development. British rule permitted considerable autonomy for individual areas, with regional princes allowed to maintain governments under British advisors, but a uniform code of laws, derived from British precedent, was imposed over the entire country. Administration became steadily larger and more efficient. Direct taxation, based on land values, replaced earlier regional collection. Britain established tax levels it regarded as equitable; however, the fact that it gathered taxes directly, rather than using regional lords and village headmen, who in earlier times determined taxes based on how much their clients were able to pay, meant that taxes tended to rise—a source of considerable discontent among Indians who were unaccustomed to dealing with government without intermediary patrons. Britain also established a civil service, based on an examination system. Top officials were always British until 1864, and mainly so thereafter, but lower-level officials were drawn from high-caste Hindus, who were thus exposed to Western administrative ideas.

British rule had considerable cultural impact as well. Although relatively few Indians converted to Christianity, new missionary pressures prompted Hindu leaders to reexamine their own practices. They tended to downplay the worship of lesser gods, although this custom continued at popular levels, and to emphasize the monotheistic elements of Hinduism. This reaction was similar to that which had greeted earlier Muslim influence. It involved an attempt to adapt traditions to the standards of India's new leadership.

Still more important for Indian culture was a British-sponsored school system, seen as vital to reversing the decline of Indian education that had occurred under the later Mughals. British-sponsored secondary schools and universities were bent on teaching Western values. As one British liberal put it: "The great end should not have been to teach Hindu learning, but useful learning." This meant increased emphasis on science and technology, not totally foreign to Indian traditions in any event, and modern (mainly European) history. Many schools taught their subjects in English, which meant that English became a second language among many upper-caste Hindus and Muslim leaders.

Economic development was another British target. During the 1850s, the British began to construct railroad and telegraph systems. The new facilities aided the administration and military control of the vast country, but they also brought some prosperity. The governor general stated, in 1853:

> A system of railways . . . would surely and rapidly give rise to the same encouragement of enterprise . . . and some similar progress in social improvement that have marked the introduction of improved and extended communication in various kingdoms of the western world.

By 1900, India had over 26,500 miles of rails, plus a number of new roads and canals. Britain also encouraged better agricultural methods, again along Western lines, and some industrial development. The subcontinent was no longer seen as a colony simply to exploit, but as a place where substantial economic activity could be pursued.

Railroads in India: change in an established civilization. This is a railroad station near Calcutta, 1867.

Socially, the British sought to change the caste system. Britain allowed different castes to mix in prisons and on trains, and lower-caste members could sue upper-caste people in British courts. The British also tried, although cautiously, to alter conditions for women. The biggest short-term impact of such attempts actually was an increase in women's economic difficulties, by reducing traditional manufacturing jobs. However, this ramification was not clearly understood, as respectable women were, according to the Western viewpoint, no longer supposed to work. Disdain for Hindu customs led to more explicit changes, as British observers claimed that, "Nothing can exceed the habitual contempt which the Hindus entertain for their women." British officials attacked female infanticide and the practice of sati, and some Indian reformers soon joined the call for change. Colonial administrators also sought to modify marriage laws, by allowing widows to remarry. Here too was a theme that

would continue to inspire Indian reformers, including later nationalists.

The British presence had mixed results. Many measures did not reach the Indian masses, who remained largely illiterate and wedded to traditional family and religious practices. The caste system persisted for the most part. On the other hand, some Indians, particularly those educated in the upper schools, welcomed aspects of the Western occupation. Rammohun Roy blasted traditional education and praised the British for promoting "a more liberal and enlightened system of instruction, embracing mathematics, natural philosophy, chemistry, anatomy, with other useful sciences."

Important resistance developed as well. Many Indians detested the more efficient tax collection, looking back fondly on the days when they could count on the informal patronage of local elites. Upper-caste Indians resented attacks on the caste system, and many lower-caste people also preferred traditional demarcations, disliking what they perceived as the demeaning treatment of the upper castes. Hindus and Muslims alike were suspicious of Christian missionary efforts and certain aspects of the new schools. Muslims also resented British preference for Hindus in government posts; they increasingly saw themselves as a beleaguered religious minority rather than, as in many past centuries, a ruling group. Rumors abounded, amid fears and resentments about British influence. For example, many Indians spread the word that colonial officials not only would allow widows to remarry, against Hindu custom, but would force them to. From various sources, then, tradition encouraged hostility to the new Western administration.

This antagonism led to one of the great 19th-century uprisings against Western imperialism. The Sepoy Rebellion of 1857 pitted Indian soldiers in the imperial army, numbering about 200,000, against 16,000 British troops stationed on the subcontinent. Many sepoys were of high caste and resented British officers. They also were disgusted by European customs such as eating beef; they insisted on traditional religious practices, for which the British refused to provide facilities. The incident that touched off the revolt was the greasing of bullets to fit in a newly introduced rifle. Animal fat was used for grease, and rumors spread among Hindu troops that the grease was from cows, among Muslims that it was from pork—in both cases, a highly offensive practice. Mutiny resulted, and for a time the rebels held the city of Delhi and much of north-central India, massacring many English families. British reinforcements broke the mutiny in 1858, aided by the fact that most Indian civilians had not joined the protest.

Britain responded to this challenge by introducing limited political representation for Indians, through local governments; they also established an advisory legislative council. Thus, some Indians gained new experience in parliamentary matters. Britain also ruled that no native of India should be barred from any job or office

because of skin color or religion, and while Indians advanced only slowly into the upper reaches of bureaucracy, there were some gradual improvements. The number of Indians with civil service experience grew steadily. Britain also increased centralized supervision of the Indian regions, encouraged English-language education, and attempted new social reforms, including the abolition of slavery (never a very extensive institution in India since the classical age). In other words, pressures to westernize intensified, as Britain stepped up its efforts to alter the colony without undue repression.

During the later 19th century, moreover, the Indian economy began to develop in new directions. Many estate owners and peasants were encouraged to grow crops for a world market. During the American Civil War, for example, the production of cotton in India increased to compensate for the decreased availability of cotton in the American South. Some factories also were opened, in textiles and metallurgy, and directed by Indian entrepreneurs using equipment imported from Britain. In 1886, Jamshedi Tata, an Indian from a wealthy Bombay family, established a large steel plant in western Bengal, near India's richest coal and iron deposits. Although still dependent on imported machinery, the Indian steel industry began to export some of its products soon after 1900. Industrial development remained rather localized, and no full industrial revolution was underway, but change was taking place.

Economic transformation was a double-edged sword in India, however. British efforts to encourage higher agricultural production, including the sponsorship of large irrigation projects to reduce traditional problems with periodic droughts, stimulated rapid population growth in an already crowded country. Government attempts to introduce some Western medical procedures, through inoculations and sanitary reforms, worked to the same end. India's high birth rate, linked to the traditional desire to have enough sons to protect parents into their old age, rose further, and the death rate, although still high by Western standards, declined. Population growth seriously limited the effects of economic development, as did continued competition from British factories that displaced hundreds of thousands of traditional manufacturing workers; the prosperity of the average Indian did not increase.

Many Indian traditionalists continued to resent British practices. At the same time, a new opposition force emerged among educated Indians concerned about their own national identity but also influenced by key Western political and educational values that, in their view, argued against undemocratic foreign rule. Several Indian newspapers sprang up, resulting in lively political discourse. The first Indian National Congress, with Hindu and Muslim delegates drawn mainly from the ranks of civil servants, met in 1885. Its initial demands were modest, focusing on greater opportunities for Indians in the imperial bureaucracy. From this base, a nationalist sentiment spread among educated groups, particularly Hindus. This represented a new loyalty in Indian history, cutting across caste, regional, and to some extent religious lines. Nationalism encouraged Indians to think in terms of growing political freedom as well as a culture independent of Western influence. Successive National Congresses became increasingly vigorous in requesting reforms. They focused not only on civil service jobs, but also on British economic control, seeking the creation of an India that could advance to the ranks of industrial nations on its own. As one 1910 speaker stated: "India has come to be regarded as a plantation of England, giving raw products to be shipped by British moguls in British ships, to be worked into fabrics . . . to be re-exported to India by British merchants." Here was a resentment of the Western-dominated world economy that would echo through the 20th century in many civilizations.

Indian nationalism imitated European, and particularly British, political beliefs, while insisting on India's special qualities. Nationalist leaders opted for an inclusive definition of nationalism—including various religious, racial, and social groups—unlike the narrower ethnic nationalism that had developed in Germany. Key questions of precise definition, however, were overshadowed by the obvious need to reduce British control.

Before 1900, Indian nationalism did not pose a major threat to British rule. Periodic riots by peasant groups, against taxes or census taking (seen as a government plot to raise taxes), or in the name of traditional religion, were a greater problem, resulting in the assassination of several British officials.

India by 1900 was by no means westernized, but it had altered substantially because of both British initiatives and the new interests of Indian leaders themselves, particularly in education, nationalist politics, and industrial management. Indian cultural vitality had in many ways increased, spurred by the revival of Hinduism and active use of traditional artistic and literary styles. At the same time, gaps had opened between Indian leaders, mostly upper caste in any event and now exposed to Western ideas and Indian nationalism, and the masses of Indians who revered traditional forms and viewed changes largely as impositions—new taxes, new and often poorly paid wage labor—by British or Indian masters.

Southeast Asia

Many developments in southeast Asia resembled trends in India—as had long been the case. The regional politics of this area continued, as different European powers controlled different countries. There was no substantial redrawing of the religious map, although a minority of southeast Asians, particularly in French Indochina, converted to Christianity. In Dutch Indonesia, the government built railroads and created a Dutch-language education system for the elite, along with a growing bureaucracy and new tax structure. New laws attempted to regulate the planters' use of native labor on the large estates devoted to export production. Essentially manorial controls, involving significant rights over peasant labor, were converted after 1870 to a wage labor system.

Particularly during the second half of the 19th century, increasing numbers of southeast Asian peasants were drawn into a market economy, employed as workers producing goods ranging from spices and tea to rubber, for sale on the world market. Many of these goods commanded relatively low prices; as a result, the system depended on low wages.

Imperial governments, as in India, began to introduce Western-style administrative measures. Bureaucrats busily collected census data. The independence of local leaders, including village headmen, was reduced. New police forces attempted to regulate crime and local unrest. As in India, more efficient administration and some agricultural improvements led to population increases, putting new pressure on available land.

Nevertheless, although traditionalists bitterly resented many European impositions, there was little systematic protest against imperialism before 1900. Nationalism was slow to surface, although soon after 1900, Indonesian civil servants sought greater equality with Dutch officials. Some local peasant uprisings occurred, expressing the need for land and resentment against tax collection, and in Indonesia a movement to renew Islamic fervor took shape. But the main wave of protest against European control, as in India, still awaited the future.

IMPERIALISM IN AFRICA

New Western penetration of sub-Saharan Africa became a dominant force only after the 1860s. During much of the 19th century, African history essentially followed an established path, with scattered innovations, although economic changes were significant. In the northern region, below the Sahara desert, Islam continued to spread through the popular missionary and holy war movement that had evolved in the later 18th century. A literature began to develop in Swahili, east Africa's written language linked to Islam. Later in the 19th century, the dissemination of

Islam was furthered by Western imperialism, for Islam was seen as a vital, well-organized religion that had the merit of not being Western. Even before this, in the regions it touched, Islam attacked many African cultural traditions as superstitions, much as Western and Middle Eastern popular beliefs had been challenged by monotheism some centuries before. This process, in turn, helped launch a painful but exciting redefinition of African civilization to which Western imperialism would ultimately contribute as well.

Africans did face a clear economic challenge. With the end of the Atlantic slave trade, the balance of trade shifted sharply. It became harder to acquire goods such as guns manufactured abroad. Many African leaders and merchants worked hard to develop alternative exports, such as vegetable oils made from peanuts or coconuts. In the process, they increased internal slavery as a means of providing cheap labor. Conditions for women often deteriorated, as their use as slaves expanded. Some of this foreshadowed the economic impact of imperialism on labor conditions, even when outright slavery was abolished.

The same developments helped draw new European interest in Africa. Some European intervention was justified by the new desire to stamp out slavery. Probably more important was the incentive to push farther into Africa in search of profits, now that the slave trade no longer provided easy pickings.

In west Africa, before imperialism took firm hold, Britain and France gradually acquired new port territories. Britain, for example, took over the key city of Lagos, in what is now Nigeria; France, the city of Dakar, in Senegal. In European-controlled port cities, a small number of Africans converted to Christianity and had other contact with Western values. Some began to think in terms of developing African states along liberal political lines, although this remained as yet a dream. Finally, two small states were formed, Liberia and Sierra Leone, by freed slaves from the United States and British West Indian colonies,

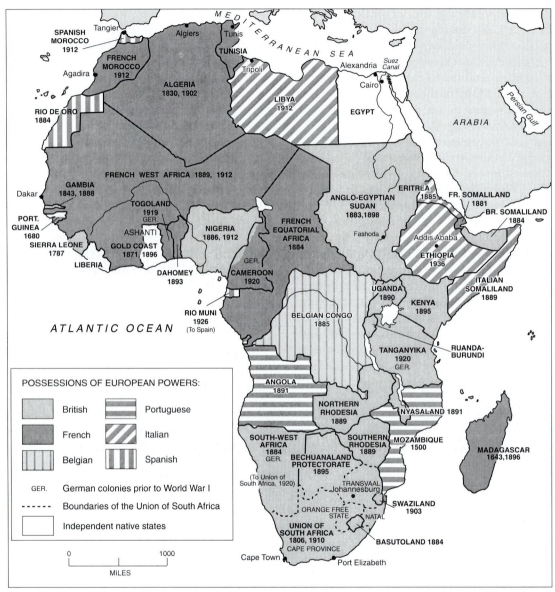

POSSESSIONS OF EUROPEAN POWERS:

British	Portuguese
French	Italian
Belgian	Spanish

GER.   German colonies prior to World War I

- - - -   Boundaries of the Union of South Africa

Independent native states

Imperialism in Africa

respectively. The freed slaves formed an elite governing group, which was heavily influenced by American and British governments, over the African majority in these states; here was another source of new Western influence in this region.

Greater change occurred in southern Africa. The migration of Boer settlers from the Cape province increased when Britain acquired control of this colony from Holland during the Napoleonic Wars. Boer farmers conducted many battles with

World Profiles

JOHN MENSAH SARBAH (1865–1910)

European imperialism created complex pressures for new African leaders. John Mensah Sarbah chose a path of utilizing Western standards in defense of African rights. A member of the Fante tribe on the Gold Coast, in the area now known as Ghana, Mensah Sarbah was a scholarly man who trained in English law and was the first African from his region to be admitted to the English bar. Mensah Sarbah used English constitutional arguments to claim that the British had no right to rule the Gold Coast and were consistently violating established African laws. He actively urged expanded responsibilities for educated Africans who could preserve Africa's traditional communal virtues. His multivolume *Fante National Constitution* (1906) followed from his elaborate research on customary law. He also founded several organizations designed to protect traditional African rights to land ownership, and his arguments did secure African land titles in British legislation of 1898. Mensah Sarbah thus worked in two worlds, an early example of a leader striving to unite Western methods and African goals. Was this a more effective approach than outright violent opposition to imperialism?

John Mensah Sarbah

African forces through the 1830s, gradually enlarging their own zone of settlement. At the same time, Bantu groups north of this zone faced crowded conditions because of their own population growth. The result was the formation of a number of tightly knit regional monarchies, organized along the traditional lines of a divine monarchy with highly ceremonial rule. Some of these kingdoms, such as the Zulus in Natal (now a state in South Africa), developed well-organized military forces,

able to hold their own against not only other Bantu states but also the Boers until the late 1880s.

In sum, most of sub-Saharan Africa continued patterns of regional government, mainly under a divine kingship, and traditional religion well into the later 19th century. Scattered European gains, more export-oriented farming, and the growth of Islam constituted new forces in some regions. On the other hand, there was no sweeping technological or political transformation.

Then came the new imperialism, bursting into this civilization with full force after 1870. To many European leaders, as well as many Africans, its force seemed bewildering. The British foreign minister lamented in 1891, "I do not know the cause of this sudden revolution, but there it is." And there it was, indeed. By conquest and negotiation, by 1900, Britain had developed an extensive empire in west Africa, including Nigeria, and a north–south axis running from southern Africa toward Egypt and embracing the modern nations of the Sudan, Kenya, Uganda, Zambia, and Zimbabwe. The British also conquered the Boer states north of its Cape Colony through the bloody Boer War of 1899–1902, forming a united South African state with a large European minority. France concentrated on east–west expansion from its holdings in Senegal, winning control over most of the territory just south of the Sahara. Belgium had the Congo, Germany possessed Tanganyika and southwest Africa, and Portugal increased its control over Angola and Mozambique.

These new empires were not won without hard fighting. France and Britain both faced bitter resistance from Muslim forces below the Sahara, leading to battles such as the one Winston Churchill described. Full subjugation of this region occurred only in the late 1890s, because Muslim armies were well organized, if poorly armed, and consumed with a spirit of jihad, or holy war, against the intruders. In both their colonies, Germans met with vigorous African resistance, which they vanquished only by brutal massacres in which tens of thousands of Africans were killed. European intervention was compounded by frequent insensitivity toward local customs, as the imperialists tried to export or destroy religious symbols and some of the ceremonial apparatus of the divine kingship. In west Africa, for example, a British governor provoked a war when he tried to seize the traditional Golden Stool of the Ashanti king, to send back to Queen Victoria.

The consequences of new European rule in Africa were dramatic, although colonialism by no means overturned all African customs. As in India, Western institutions were only one among many forces at work. Furthermore, by 1914, the European regimes were barely in place, and much of the impact of the West would become clear only later. Different imperialist countries followed somewhat different policies in their colonies. France, for example, was eager to educate an African elite in Western ways, whereas Britain concentrated more on basic education and medical care for a larger number of people while discouraging the formation of a new elite. However, some main lines of development were emerging by 1914, across the new political divisions of the continent.

The first consequence was the new political units themselves. Africa had always been divided, but now it was broken up into states artificially created by accidents of European competition and timing. None of the colonial states had any clear precedent. Many mixed different tribal, language, and religious groups that had long been rivals. A few regional kingdoms persisted under British supervision in southern Africa, and Ethiopia remained independent, defeating Italy in an 1896 war. Otherwise, however, the map of the civilization was entirely, and from an African standpoint arbitrarily, redrawn. European administrations tried to impose Western concepts of property law, sanitary regulation, and police on their new domains. Few Africans by 1914 were included in the new imperial bureaucracies.

The cultural impact of the Europeans was initially limited. Intense missionary activity created an important Christian minority in many parts of Africa, which added to the culture's religious diversity. But most Africans remained polytheist or, in the north, Muslim. Some combined Christianity with traditional beliefs, like the witch doctors who converted but still prayed to other spirits for protection, relying on Christianity for favor in the afterlife. Knowledge of a European language spread among an educated minority, along with growing familiarity with Western science and some Western political ideas.

The economic impact of the Europeans was far greater than their cultural influence. The new rulers were eager to make the most profit from their colonies. Small numbers of white settlers claimed the most fertile land, a process already established in southern Africa and now applied to east Africa as well. Colonial administrations imposed new taxes, which forced many Africans to seek paying work on European-owned plantations and mines simply to obtain money in an economy that had previously relied heavily on barter. Colonial officials in some cases requisitioned labor directly, enforcing their demands by brutal physical punishments, including dismemberment. In general, Africans working the mines and the estates suffered harsh conditions—including frequent brutal physical punishments—and of course low pay. Europeans did improve port facilities and other aspects of the communication and transportation system, although there was much less railroad construction in the difficult African terrain than in India or southeast Asia. New medical facilities to combat traditional tropical diseases were also of some benefit, and the African population began to increase. Still, by 1900 and even beyond, the main economic results of European control were largely exploitative, as Africa supplied food and minerals—copper from the Congo, gold and diamonds from South Africa—to the Western market from the sweat of miserably paid laborers.

Most Africans, however, were not directly caught up in the institutions of imperialist rule. Village agriculture changed slowly, and other village institutions persisted; European ability to reach most Africans directly was quite limited in a vast and diverse continent where, even with European technology, communication remained difficult. At the same time, the relatively recent nature of European conquest hampered ongoing African reaction. Nationalist movements and other forms of resistance would come, but by 1914, the bloody defeat of initial opposition efforts was a setback to further response.

COMPARING COLONIES

Colonialism brought many similar experiences to otherwise different societies. Foreign rule raised some common issues, as did the subjection to an economic system dominated by industrial Europe. However, colonies often differed in their responses, depending on prior culture and institutions and variations in European policy.

India, with a major religion of its own and extensive experience of outside control in the past, adjusted its culture more selectively than did Africa; there were fewer Indian religious conversions, for instance. Indian civilization also had a longer time to come to terms with Western control, in comparison with the more sudden domination of Africa and the ensuing shock among local populations. Sub-Saharan Africa, by 1900, was beginning to experience the more systematic loss of traditional values, particularly in some areas where Christian missionaries had made advances. The rawest economic exploitation of India occurred around 1800. But in Africa, the European exploitation of resources and labor only increased from the 1890s onward. Competition among European states also affected conditions in Africa, in contrast to India by this point. Although European beliefs in their racial superiority affected policies everywhere, the impact was sharper in Africa than India. Such differences impacted the colonial experience during the 19th century, and also native reactions later on, when independence became a viable possibility.

European imperialism had a worldwide impact, as a threat if not always fact. The balance of power among the civilizations of the world was dramatically shifted not only by European control of major civilizations—India, southeast Asia, and Africa—but also by the extension of essentially Western societies to north America, including the U.S. Western frontier as well as Canada, and to Australia and New Zealand.

In India and southeast Asia, and ultimately in Africa, the fact of European control shaped vital questions of change and adaptation. New

Western rule, efficiently administered, brought major innovations, including new political boundaries and new levels of commercialization. It was clear that the colonized societies were not going to become Western. Their traditional cultures were too deep rooted, their populations and territories too vast; European ambivalence about reforming the natives and seeing them as inherent racial inferiors, as children to be disciplined by wiser Western parents, also limited the process of westernization. However, European occupation did provide direct tutelage in Western ways, allowing leaders in southern Asia, and later in Africa, to decide what concepts they wished to borrow, which ones they wanted to reject. One idea that was assimilated, if only to give shape to what may have been an inherent desire for independence, was nationalism, as was already evident in India. Through nationalism, leaders attracted to some Western patterns, and others eager simply to restore preimperialist traditions, could at least briefly join together in a fervent demand for independence. Imperialism clearly generated its own resistance, and this interplay would dominate much of the history of the 20th century.

Nevertheless, imperialism also uprooted a host of traditional economic, social, and cultural patterns. An independent India or Africa would not go back to preimperialist ways of life. Imperialism also resulted in new political problems in uniting or dividing earlier units. It brought economic benefits, in the form of improved transportation and agricultural methods, along with the often harsh use of local labor and integration of colonies into a Western-dominated world market. Population growth posed its own new challenge to the economies of Africa and southern Asia. Limited medical advances, such as inoculations, swamp-draining, and other disease-control measures, had a tremendous impact just as Western population growth was ebbing. In 1914, the major question for Indian or Nigerian or Indonesian leaders was clear: how should we respond to Western rule? But imperialism raised wider political, economic, and cultural concerns also, which would outlast the struggle for independence in setting an agenda for world history well into the 20th century and beyond.

Many similar issues would also affect those parts of the world not subject to full imperialist control, such as China and the Ottoman Empire, or newly freed from it—Latin America, for example. Would outright imperialist rule help or hinder a civilization in addressing problems of population growth, imbalance in the world economy, and new political tensions? Was India, to use the clearest example, better off for having experienced an intense if relatively brief period of Western rule than China, which faced Western depredations without the possible benefits of Western influence? Imperialism provided a shock to the civilizations that came under its full sway in the 19th century; its impact and the reactions it provoked conditioned the history of these areas even after independence was won.

ISSUES AND CONNECTIONS

Three obvious issues emerge regarding the century of imperialism. The first has been tackled directly: colonial experiences were not the same, which means active comparison among colonies is essential. The second relates to the first. While the history of European imperialism used to be written in terms of white men bringing progress to backward peoples, this story has long since stopped ringing true. Imperialism brought many cruelties and disadvantages. It promoted change, but not unilaterally; colonial peoples played their own role by resisting or partly cooperating. Some changes may, intentionally or not, have been beneficial. So imperialism must be interpreted as a mixture: a mixture of plusses and minuses, and a mixture of European initiatives, local responses and initiatives, and local continuities. The third issue involves comparing the outright colonies to other parts of the world where European intervention occurred with less colonial apparatus; this comparison becomes possible in the following chapters.

The empires that formed or intensified in the long 19th century are gone, or nearly so. But their memory is recent, which is an active factor in world affairs. Furthermore, many economic arrangements and cultural influences established in the period outlasted imperialism and are still in operation. Most parts of Africa, particularly, are finding a difficult time escaping economic dependence in the world economy, into which they were further driven through imperialism. Africa and India are also still involved in dealing with the heritage of Western-instituted reforms (for example, the attack on the caste system in India) and with the nationalism that formed in response to imperialism. This is an active heritage.

SUGGESTED WEB SITES

On the causes of imperialism, see http://www.fordham.edu/halsall/mod/modsbook34.html. For an African nationalist perspective, go to http://www.anc.org.za/ancdocs/history/misc/isandhlwanaa.html. On American imperialism in Asia, see http://smplanet.com/imperialism/toc.html.

SUGGESTED READINGS

Recent work includes Timothy Parsons, *The British Imperial Century, 1815–1914: A World History Perspective* (1999), and Lester Alan, *Imperial Networks: Creating Identities in the 19th Century South Africa and Britain* (2001).

Excellent general surveys of 19th-century imperialism and its causes include Winifried Baumgart, *Imperialism* (1982); D. K. Fieldhouse, *The Colonial Empires* (1968); and Bernard Porter, *The Lion's Share: Short History of British Imperialism, 1850–1970* (1975). See also C. H. Peake, *European Colonial Expansion since 1871* (1941), and the imaginative study by Michael Adas, *Machines as the Measure of Men* (1989). On specific areas and imperialist powers, W. Baumgart, *Imperialism: The Idea and Reality of British and French Colonial Expansion* (1982), is an excellent discussion. On Africa, worthwhile sources include Colin Turnbull, *The Lonely African* (1971); A. Moorehead, *The White Nile* (1971); Woodruff D. Smith, *The German Colonial Empire* (1978); Walter Rodney, *How Europe Underdeveloped Africa* (1982)—a vital study; R. P. Masani, *Britain in India* (1961); and M. D. Lewis, ed., *The British in India: Imperialism or Trusteeship?* (1962). See also C. A. Bayley, *Indian Society and the Making of the British Empire* (1988). On peasant resistance, refer to J. Scott, *The Moral Economy of the Peasant: Rebellion and Subsistence in Southeast Asia* (1976). On women's conditions, see Clare Midgley, ed., *Gender and Imperialism* (1998).

23

The Settler Societies: The West on Frontiers

The rise of the West, including its dynamic industrial growth and steady rise in population through much of the 19th century, had particular impact on several overseas regions, which in turn received the majority of their populations and much of their political and cultural inspiration from Europe. The new United States, Canada, Australia, and New Zealand built on Western traditions, but they had to combine them with the values of more diverse peoples—native inhabitants, plus, in the case of the United States, African slaves and a small but important stream of Asian immigrants. These countries also faced frontier conditions long since eradicated from Europe, and in this respect they more closely resembled contemporary Russia and Latin America. These evolving centers became increasingly important in world history from about 1870 onward, when their economic growth generated growing agricultural (and, in the case of the United States, industrial) exports.

The settler societies differed from Europe in several key respects. They did not have an established aristocracy or a peasant class. Innovative, profit-minded farmers increasingly dominated the agricultural market. Abundant land, plus opportunities to export to Europe, encouraged commercial farming. The societies were not initially as wealthy as their European counterparts, although their standards of living were high; they depended greatly on capital investments from Europe. These people were not as culturally creative as Europeans, looking to them for most basic styles, although a regional art and literature took shape during the 19th century (particularly in the United States). The settler societies escaped some of Europe's political tensions, establishing democracy relatively early, but they faced specific political problems of their own—as, for example, in the American Civil War between the antislavery North and the slaveholding South.

The settler societies also followed many of the same trends Western Europe did during the 19th century, being affected by liberalism, nationalism, and (to a lesser degree in the United States) socialism. They underwent a demographic transition that cut their birth rates. Family patterns and women's roles were redefined in a similar fashion. Western-style science held a firm place, along with currents of thought derived from romanticism. Industrial technologies spread quickly. Canada, New Zealand, and Australia relied heavily on mineral or agricultural exports, but they were well rewarded because of their rich resources and use of advanced technology. Canada, as its vast territory was linked by a rail network in the later 19th century, also began an industrial revolution of its own, and Australia and New Zealand had important regional factory centers. The United States, importing its first equipment from England before 1820, began industrializing rapidly, particularly as it participated in railroad and heavy industrial development. On the basis of its economic power and political independence, the United States even began joining in European-style imperialism by the 1890s, taking over islands in the Caribbean and assuming rule over the Philippines and other Pacific island territory.

Residents of the settler societies—aside from the native peoples whose numbers and power declined rapidly—had something of a love-hate relationship with western Europe. They recognized their affinity and dependence and in many ways felt part of Western civilization, although the connection was not yet acknowledged, but they were also proud of their differences and realized that their tasks of settlement and state-building differed from those of the mother countries. In addition, the United States maintained a tradition of isolation from Europe's diplomatic squabbles, while it tried (not always successfully) to discourage European intervention in the Western Hemisphere from the Monroe Doctrine (1823) onward.

KEY QUESTIONS *The overriding question is whether the settler societies were part of a single Western civilization or a major variant because of frontier conditions and different population mixes.*

Another comparative question involves the societies themselves: how similar were the main settler societies? Were Canada and New Zealand more "European" than Australia and the United States (as some observers believe), and if so, why? Finally, what were the main results of Western interaction with Polynesian peoples?

THE UNITED STATES

After the American Revolution, the constitutional structure of the new United States was established in 1789. The republic launched a period of consolidation—interrupted by the War of 1812 with England—and westward expansion, as the new nation acquired the Louisiana Purchase from France in 1803. Democratic voting systems, with rights for free males, were widely completed by the 1820s. The nation's federal system led to a fairly weak central government, and many major developments were the result of state action or business initiatives. Thus, the Erie Canal, which helped link the Midwest with the East coast, was sponsored by New York State. However, the federal government was heavily involved in further westward expansion and warred with Mexico to acquire Texas in the 1840s. Within the federal government, there was also a growing tension between the Northern states and the slaveholding South, which culminated in the Civil War.

American culture began to take shape before the Civil War, personified by many New England writers and thinkers and a smaller group of painters and musicians. Also before the Civil War, new waves of European immigrants, particularly from Ireland and Germany, added to the size and mix of the American population.

The North's victory in the Civil War led to a new period of consolidation. Efforts to reform the South, beyond the abolition of slavery, were largely abandoned by 1877, as the United States settled into a succession of undistinguished presidencies and relatively modest basic divisions between the two major political parties. Settlement of the western

History Debate

EXCEPTIONALISM

For over a century, most approaches to U.S. history have emphasized the distinctiveness of American society—its "exceptions" to the norms of European history (or, presumably, any other history). American exceptionalism features arguments that the United States was unusually democratic, or unusually open to social mobility, or unusually free from political division. An exceptionalist argument can also be used in a less benign fashion: the nation as unusually racially divided or harsh to factory workers. Exceptionalism is, of course, a comparative statement, although many historians have not bothered to compare their observations. Should the United States be regarded as a separate civilization? If so, how can one account for similar dates and patterns of industrialization, demographic transition, and feminism? Should the United States be viewed as a somewhat unusual but definite part of Western civilization? If so, how can one account for the unusual per capita rates of American violence (well above European levels from the late 18th century to the present), the unusual hostility to the state as an active force in society? The comparative problems run deep, and they have not yet been resolved.

In terms of world history, the ongoing debate over American exceptionalism raises additional issues. If the United States differs from Europe, how much does it resemble other frontier societies, such as Australia or Latin America? As the United States gained a growing world role (particularly in the 20th century) did it behave differently from previous European great powers such as Britain, and if so, how? Finally, did the United States grow more or less different from west European nations as it became more industrial and a great power, and as Europe became more fully democratic?

territories continued, amid recurrent American Indian wars. The pace of industrialization increased, and labor agitation led to new unions, strikes, and occasional political assassinations. Waves of immigration from southern and eastern Europe brought much-needed labor to the nation's growing industries, and by 1914, the growing migration of African Americans from the South increased urban populations as well.

U.S. entry into the world economy, as more than a source of cotton or an investment opportunity, began in the 1870s. Massive agricultural exports combined with significant industrial ventures abroad. Several American companies, such as the Singer Sewing Machine Company and International Harvester, established subsidiaries in Europe and Russia. American arms manufacturers sold weapons abroad after the Civil War's end, including among their clients a newly opened Japan. Although still importing technologies from Europe in such industries as the manufacture of chemicals, the United States contributed a number of inventions, including major developments in the uses of electricity. Even more significant were American innovations in the management of labor, where the democratic system sponsored new ways of regimenting large groups of workers. American initiatives in time and motion studies, designed by industrial engineers to speed the work process, and then the assembly line, spread widely to other industrial societies after 1900.

America's diplomatic expansion showed in not only imperialism but also its growing involvement in other international issues; President Theodore Roosevelt, for example, sponsored the conference ending the 1904–1905 war between Russia and Japan. American cultural influence was more modest outside its borders, although the introduction of the skyscraper in Chicago soon after 1900 suggested the new union and power of art and technology. Individual American artists and scientists went to Europe to learn and sometimes made their mark as creators or thinkers, but in most cultural arenas the United States remained largely a borrower.

HAWAII

The 1890s saw the United States join the imperialist scramble, essentially adding to the list of Western powers involved. Territory was added in the Caribbean, including Puerto Rico, seized from Spain. The Philippines essentially became a colony. New interventions occurred in Cuba and Central America, including sponsorship of a new nation, Panama, taken from Colombia to facilitate American control of the new canal.

One new territory became a distinctive kind of settler society. Hawaii had been opened to the West by the voyages of British Captain James Cook, 1777–1779. Hawaiian rulers, headed by King Kamehameha, introduced Western-style reforms. American missionaries and planters began to move to the islands, causing major cultural and economic change. Western-brought diseases reduced a Hawaiian population of half a million to 80,000 by 1850. New workers were imported from Japan, China, and later the Philippines. Urged on by pineapple and sugar planters, the United States annexed Hawaii in 1898. The islands increasingly reflected American and (at a lower social level) Asian settlers. But there was little outside racism against native Hawaiians, and there was some respect for their culture even as a new, settler-dominated colony took shape.

NEWER EUROPEAN SETTLEMENTS

At the same time that the United States expanded, Canada, Australia, and New Zealand also filled with immigrants from Europe and established parliamentary legislatures and vigorous commercial economies that placed them effectively in the general orbit of Western civilization. Like the United States, these new nations looked primarily to Europe for cultural styles and intellectual leadership. They also followed common Western patterns in such areas as family life, the role of women, and the extension of mass education and culture. Unlike the United States, however, these nations remained part of the British Empire, although with growing autonomy.

Canada, won by Britain in its wars with France during the 18th century, had been preserved from the uprisings of the American Revolution. Religious differences between French Catholic settlers and British rulers and settlers troubled the area recurrently, and a number of revolts occurred early in the 19th century. Determined not to lose this colony in addition to the United States, the British began to grant increasing self-rule after 1839. Canada was permitted to establish its own parliament and laws, while remaining under the umbrella of the larger empire. Initially, this system applied primarily to the province of Ontario, but other provinces were gradually included, creating a federal system that describes Canada to this day. French hostilities were eased somewhat by the creation of Quebec, a separate province, where the majority of French settlers remained. Massive railroad building, beginning in the 1850s, brought settlement to western territories and a great expansion of mining and commercial agriculture in the vast plains. As in the United States to the south, new immigrants from southern and particularly eastern Europe poured in during the last decades of the century, attracted by Canada's growing commercial development and spurring even further gains.

This depiction of sheep-washing in the Australian outback shows one of the export staples of the Australian economy and the nation's frontier expansion, from the 19th century onward.

Britain's Australian colonies originated in 1788 when a ship deposited convicts to establish a penal settlement at Sydney. Australia's only previous inhabitants had been the aborigines, a hunting-and-gathering people who were in no position to resist European settlement and exploration. Unfamiliar European diseases and guns took a predictable toll. By 1840, Australia had 140,000 European inhabitants, based mainly on a prosperous sheep-growing agriculture that provided needed wool for British industries. The exportation of convicts ceased in 1853, by which time most settlers were free immigrants. The discovery of gold in 1851 led to further pioneering, which resulted in a population of over one million by 1861. As in Canada, major provinces were granted self-government with a multiparty parliamentary system. A unified federal nation was proclaimed on the first day of the 20th century. By this time, con-

siderable industrialization, a growing socialist party, and significant welfare legislation had developed.

New Zealand, discovered by the Dutch in the 17th century and explored by the English in 1770, began to receive British attention after 1814. Here the Polynesian hunting-and-gathering people, the Maoris, were well organized politically. Missionary efforts converted many of them to Christianity between 1814 and the 1840s. The British government, fearful of French interest in the area, moved to take official control in 1840, and considerable European immigration followed. New Zealand settlers relied heavily on agriculture (including sheep growing), selling initially to Australia's booming gold-rush population and then to Britain. As in Canada and Australia, a parliamentary system was created that allowed the new nation to rule itself as a dominion of the British Empire, without interference from the mother country.

World Profiles

HONGI HIKA

Hongi Hika is probably the most famous of all New Zealand's Maori warriors. Estimated to have been born around 1772, Hongi was from the Ngupuhi tribe and uncle of Hone Heke, chief of the Ngapuhi tribe in the north. Interestingly enough, *Hongi* not only means "smell" but is also a derivative of the word that represents the Maori greeting of pressing noses together. Nevertheless, Hongi Hika helped to single-handedly transform the nature of Maori warfare.

During Hongi's formative years, Thomas Kendell, a British missionary, formed a close and long-lasting friendship with him. Kendell believed that Hongi had converted to Christianity, and he invited Hongi to England. Kendell hoped to get Hongi's assistance in translating the Bible in the Maori language. Hongi, however, had his own agenda. He hoped a trip to Europe would enable him to obtain weapons for his intertribal wars. Thus, in 1820, Hongi embarked upon the long journey to Great Britain. Not surprisingly, Hongi's tattooed appearance caused quite a stir in England. Instead of the weapons he was hoping for, King George IV gave him many ceremonial gifts. However, thanks to innovative trading and a stop in Sydney, Australia, on the way to New Zealand, Hongi was able to obtain the muskets and ammunition he was seeking.

After he returned to New Zealand, Hongi was able to use the weapons he had secured, leading a series of successful raids against rival tribes. Suddenly, other tribes needed the modern weaponry

Hongi Hika

that Hongi's tribe had. Consequently, his journey to England began a Maori trend of obtaining European weapons. Lacking the ceremonial gifts that Hongi had been able to exchange, other tribes began to trade preserved human heads for modern weapons. Hongi died in 1828 due to a bullet wound received in a battle.

New Zealand was something of a special case among settler societies because of the continuing importance of the native peoples, the Polynesian Maoris. Initial British settlements on the coasts in the 1790s brought disruption, with increasing prostitution and alcoholism among the Maoris. Use of guns made traditional Maori warfare more dangerous. More important was the impact of disease, cutting an initial population of 130,000 by about 70 percent on the north island by the 1840s. But Maoris survived and began to use new Western tools for farming and cattle-raising (with animals purchased from Europeans). An influx of British farmers in the 1850s led to new disputes over land and a series of wars. The Maoris also developed frenzied new religious movements in the 1860s and 1870s that promised to drive the invaders out. But despite predictions of Maori collapse, the Maoris learned to use British laws to defend much of their land; they also adapted to Western education. The result was a settler society within the British Empire but with a distinctly multiracial flavor.

Like the United States, Canada, New Zealand, and Australia each had distinct national characteristics and national issues. These new countries were far more dependent on the European, particularly the British, economy than was the United States. Industrialization did not overshadow commercial agriculture and mining, even in Australia, so that exchanges with Europe remained unusually important. Nevertheless, these countries followed the basic patterns of Western civilization from this point onward, from political forms to key leisure activities. Currents of liberalism, socialism, modern art, and scientific education, which described Western civilization to 1900 and beyond, thus largely characterized these important new countries.

It was these areas, finally, along with the United States and parts of Latin America, particularly Brazil and Argentina, that received new waves of European emigrants during the 19th century. Although Europe's population growth rate slowed after 1800, it still advanced rapidly on the basis of previous gains—that is, as more children reached adulthood and had children of their own. Europe's expansion was, in fact, greater than Asia's in percentage terms until the 20th century, and Europe's export of people helped explain how Western societies could take shape in such distant areas.

SPECIAL FEATURES OF SETTLER SOCIETIES

The extension of Western society through most of North America as well as Australia and New Zealand depended on the fortuitous absence of large previous populations, compounded by the continued ravages of Western-imported diseases on the indigenous people in these locations. Other parts of the world, more thickly inhabited, had quite different experiences under the impact of Western influence and some outright settlement. The spread of the settler societies also reflected the new power of Western industrialization. Huge areas could now be populated quickly, thanks to steamships and rails, while remaining in close contact with the Western home base in Europe. The expansion of the West revealed the power of Western values and institutions, as colonists deliberately introduced most of the patterns that had prevailed in Europe, from parliaments to Western-defined standards for women and children.

ISSUES AND CONNECTIONS

The emergence of settler societies was a key development in the long 19th century. Each of the societies participated actively in the world economy, contributing foods and raw materials (and in the United States' case, industrial products) of vital importance. The societies were able to do this without developing low-wage, dependent economies. Two key issues accompany this new development. The first involves defining civilization, with the relationship to west European civilization the question to be resolved. The second involves some internal comparison, and this can affect the response to the issue of definition. Were all these societies sufficiently alike that they can be accurately lumped in a single category? Or is Canada different enough from the United States—a bit more European, a bit less industrial, certainly less an independent great power by 1900—that greater complexity is required? Is New Zealand (a bit more English-like, less boisterous, and with the multiracial quality) different enough from Australia for a distinct category?

The effects of the rapid growth of the settler societies, their additions to the world economy, and the additional support they provided to many Western institutions and values were all clearly established by 1914, and they all continue in the present day. Here was one of the big changes, for world history as a whole, of the long 19th century.

SUGGESTED WEB SITES

On the revolutionary war in America, see http://www.revwar.com. On Eli Whitney, the controversial American inventor, see http://www.eliwhitney.org/ew.htm.

SUGGESTED READINGS

On U.S. history, in addition to several excellent textbooks with good reading lists (e.g., Gary Nash and Julie R. Jeffrey, *The American People: Creating a Nation and a Society* [1990], and James Kirby Martin et al., *America and Its People*, 2nd ed.

[2001]), see Eugene D. Genovese, *Roll, Jordan, Roll: The World the Slaves Made* (1974); Thomas Cochran, *Frontiers of Change: Early Industrialization in America* (1981); Steven Mintz and Susan Kellog, *Domestic Revolutions: A Social History of American Family Life* (1988); and Albert W. Niemi, *United States Economic History* (1987).

On Canada, Australia, and New Zealand, see J. M. Bumstead, *A History of Canada* (1992); Alastair Davidson, *The Formation of the Australian State* (1991); Charles Wilson, *Australia, 1788–1988: The Creation of a Nation* (1988); and Miles Fairburn, *The Ideal Society and Its Enemies: Foundations of Modern New Zealand Society, 1850–1900* (1990).

For additional recent work, see Jonathan Glickstein, *American Exceptionalism, American Anxiety: Wages, Competition and Degraded Labor in the Antebellum United States* (2002); William Barney, *A Companion to 19th Century America* (2001); Alyson Greiner, *Anglo-Celtic Australia: Colonial Immigration and Cultural Regionalism* (2002); and Patricia Jalland, *Australian Ways of Life: A Social and Cultural History 1840–1914* (2002).

24

The Development of Latin American Civilization

Latin American civilization had been a settler, frontier society of a sort in the early modern period. But the results of slavery and a plantation economy, plus the long period of Spanish or Portuguese political control, plus the dependent position of Latin America in the world economy made the Latin American experience distinctive. The long 19th century was a crucial period in Latin American development. Patterns should be compared with those of the settler societies, as well as with those of the more obvious targets of European imperialism such as Africa or India.

During the century of imperialism, Latin American nations won independence, and the civilization as a whole further defined its identity. Latin America was seriously affected by the currents of imperialism, despite newly achieved independence, and it was even more severely constrained by the West's domination of the world economy. Ironically, Latin America's failure to free itself from dependence on Western-controlled economic patterns was one of the key signs that the civilization differed from that of the West. In politics and culture, Latin American leaders combined a deep devotion to many Western styles and values with some distinctive features that resulted from the civilization's racial diversity, its own colonial past, and the social structure that stemmed from a semicolonial economy. Thus, Latin America emerged as a civilization unusually tied to the West, not only through imperialism and economic dependency but also through shared religious and political ideas—but one that forged its own character by blending Western influence with other currents. The result was a distinctive combination, in the 19th century and after.

Latin American history through the 19th century established much of the basic framework for this newest of the world's major civilizations. One of the primary challenges to 19th-century Latin America was the formation of new nations where no clear precedent served to guide. These new nations were inevitably concerned with the establishment of territorial boundaries and with generating a leadership that could function despite the lack of prior political tradition. Hereditary rule, for example, made little sense in this context because there were no indigenous ruling families. Previous American Indian regimes had long since been destroyed, and rule from Spain and Portugal was now ended as well. Along with new leadership, the nations had to set up legal structures and work to establish some kind of national loyalty. These were difficult tasks, yet for all their undoubted political problems, the new countries of Latin America achieved some success in addressing them during the 19th century. Other emerging nations in the 20th century would face similar challenges and would adopt solutions like those pioneered in Latin America.

KEY QUESTIONS   *The most obvious question involves interpreting the combination of new political independence with Latin America's dependent position in the world economy. A second question involves culture: what were the key features of Latin American culture as it was further defined in the long 19th century, and did it provide a distinctive identity?*

THE WARS OF INDEPENDENCE

The 19th century began with the wars of independence from Spanish rule. Conflict broke out at several points in 1810, and the drive for independence was essentially completed by the mid-1820s. There followed another 30 years of consolidation, when the boundaries of the new nations were largely set, amid considerable strife, and the broad outlines of internal politics established. This was a period of economic hardship throughout most of Latin America, as the wars of independence disrupted earlier trade patterns and consumed substantial tax resources. It is important to realize that the countries of Latin America were formed in a harsh economic context, when material distress heightened the possibili-

ties of discontent and disorder. After 1850, economic conditions tended to improve, as the civilization underwent extensive commercial development—although such development brought new hardship to important segments of the lower classes. Further imbalance divided a wealthy minority of landowners and merchants from the low-paid masses, even though slavery was abolished. Political instability did not end in this final 19th-century period, but it did follow some clearly established lines. The late 19th century also saw new pressures from the outside world, in the form of the imperialist actions of Western nations, particularly the United States, and a massive wave of immigration from southern Europe.

The wars of independence—unquestionably the most dramatic events in Latin America's 19th-century history—had several causes. Example was one. The revolution that had produced the United States showed that European colonial authority could be defeated. The French Revolution of 1789 also provided an example of the principles of political liberty and nationalist loyalty. Latin American leaders, particularly those drawn from the Creole class, racially European but native to Latin America and often of considerable education and wealth, were keenly aware of what was happening in the Western world, and the new examples became inspirations.

The French Revolution and its Napoleonic aftermath, indeed, provided an opportunity for Latin American leaders. Spain, with a somewhat inefficient government already, became distracted by the new danger on its northern borders, as the Spanish monarch sought to prevent revolutionary uprisings in his own land. Then Napoleon's armies invaded Spain, briefly establishing a regime that controlled most of the country. Neither this regime nor the beleaguered Spanish king Ferdinand had much time or resources to keep Latin American colonies in line. Ferdinand regained his throne in 1815, but by this point the drive for independence was well established. A later Spanish revolution, in 1820, led in fact by

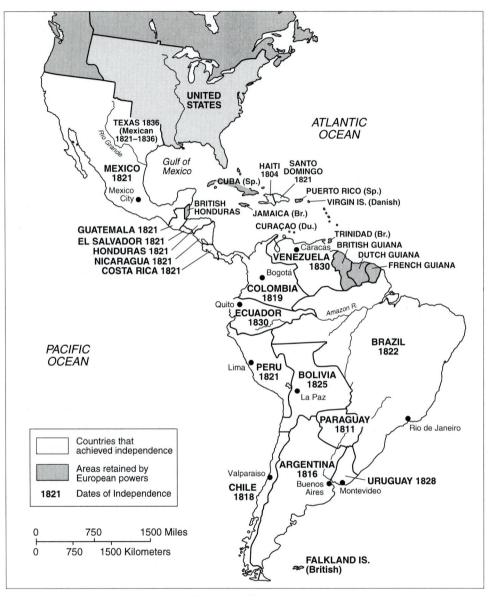

Latin American Independence

discontented troops about to be sent to put down colonial unrest, provided an additional diversion that allowed independence to be won.

Example and opportunity were fueled by serious grievances. In many regions, the colonial economy had depended on extensive slaveholding, and the slave population grew restless during the later 18th century. Material conditions and discipline were harsh. Many slaves expressed their discontent by fleeing; by 1800, over a quarter of all black slaves in Venezuela were fugitives, hiding out in self-governing communities in the jungles and mountains. Slave revolts also peppered 18th-century history in Latin America. In 1796, Toussaint L'Ouverture, a black leader in the French West Indian colony of Haiti, proclaimed outright independence. L'Ouverture, inspired by French revolutionary doctrines and eager to capitalize on France's own distraction by the war and revolution at home, not only ended Haitian slavery but also established the first black republic in the New World. Because most West Indian islands remained under Spanish, French, British, or Dutch control throughout the 19th century and beyond—although slavery was abolished during the middle decades of the century—Haitian independence did not have widespread repercussions. But pressure from discontented slaves was a more serious factor in the Caribbean and Latin America around 1800 than it was in the United States.

American Indians and mestizos also had grievances. Many were bound to labor on haciendas run by Creoles, Spanish officials, or the church; others worked in the silver mines. Discipline was harsh, and there was little legal freedom. Most workers were forced to buy goods from estate stores and so suffered from a lack of economic options besides material misery. Revolts by American Indian and mestizo estate workers had broken out in the 1770s, centered at first in Peru and spreading to Colombia. The insurrections attacked both the estates system and the high taxes levied by Spanish administrators. These uprisings, although they led to initial success, were ultimately defeated by a combination of military force and trickery. However, they did greatly contribute to the desire for greater freedom from Spanish rule.

At the top of Latin American society, another set of grievances existed. Creoles, often aware of Enlightenment ideals, resented their lack of political opportunity. Although Creoles had been part of colonial administration early in the 18th century, after 1750 Spain largely eliminated this role, returning to a policy of appointing only Spanish-born officials. These officials often disdained Creoles, which only added to this group's resentment. Creole merchants and professionals, moreover, disliked Spanish taxes and economic restrictions, which prevented legal trade with the more prosperous nations of western Europe. As in the United States, revolt was fueled by regulations that seemed excessive and also arbitrary, since they were set without consultation, for the benefit of the mother country. It was Creole leadership that largely sparked the drive for independence. American Indian, slave, and mestizo dissatisfaction did not play a direct role, save in Haiti, in part because popular revolts had been recently vanquished. The Latin American wars of independence were not, then, truly popular uprisings, calling social as well as political institutions into question. And while the resulting regimes changed some economic conditions, abolishing slavery in a few cases, such as in Mexico, and weakening the estates system for a time, the social system of colonial Latin America, with its pronounced divisions between Creole owners and mestizo, American Indian, and black workers, remained largely intact.

The first blow in the war for independence occurred in Venezuela in 1810, when the Caracas city council debated whether it owed loyalty to the new Napoleonic regime in Spain. The council decided on disobedience and urged other city councils to do likewise. King Ferdinand's government in flight from Napoleon was greatly displeased by these actions, even though they were technically directed at his French enemy; he declared the new regimes in revolt and ordered the death of its leaders—an order he was powerless to enforce. The new administration in Venezuela promptly established its own army and proclaimed its independence, drawing up a constitution modeled on that of the United States and the French Declaration of the Rights of Man. Spanish forces were able to put down this regime in 1812, but their harsh retaliation against early leaders engendered further opposition. Simón Bolívar, a wealthy Creole trained in

World Profiles

SIMÓN BOLÍVAR (1783–1830)

Simón Bolívar was perhaps the most well-known and revered leader for independence in Latin America, often compared to George Washington. Like Washington, Bolívar was born into the upper classes. A wealthy Creole officer with close intellectual ties to Europe, he developed a passion for national freedom and republicanism, and his fervor plus real military skill catapulted him to leadership of the Caracas-based independence movement in 1810. He was able to mobilize diverse support and won a series of victories against the Spanish in Venezuela, Colombia, and Ecuador between 1817 and 1822. Running the new country, Gran Colombia, was more difficult, however, and as it broke up into smaller nations, Bolívar became bitterly disillusioned. "America is ungovernable," he said, and "those who have served the revolution have plowed the sea." His principles remained firm, nevertheless, and he (again like Washington) refused popular efforts to crown him as king. Why is it often easier for individuals such as Bolívar to mobilize forces for national independence than to govern the new nation after victory?

Simón Bolívar (1783–1830), the great liberator.

the Spanish army and deeply influenced by Enlightenment ideas, now took leadership of the northern independence movement, rather like George Washington in North America, with whom he was often compared. Several years of fighting ensued, in which Bolívar assembled an army composed of many former British, Irish, and German soldiers, along with Creole nationalists and some American Indian troops. By 1819, Bolívar was strong enough to defeat the Spanish army; he proclaimed a new republic, called Gran Colombia, which united Venezuela and Colombia. Spanish attempts to recapture

this nation, hampered by its own 1820 revolution, ultimately failed. Bolívar's armies invaded Ecuador, adding this province to his country.

In 1810, independence movements sprang up in the south as well. In Buenos Aires, a provisional regime was formed with a strong liberal element. An army was organized, ultimately under the leadership of another able Creole general, José de San Martín. This army established a full-fledged government in Argentina and also aided the independence movement in Chile. Again, Spanish attempts to recapture these territories after 1815 were defeated, and the rebel armies also invaded Peru.

The final center of the independence movement took place in Mexico and Central America. Two priests, Miguel Hidalgo and José Morelos, led a lower-class rebellion of Spanish-speaking American Indians and mestizos against the constraints of the hacienda system in 1810. Some Indians even talked of an Aztec government. The violence of the lower-class rebellion persuaded Mexico's Creoles to remain loyal to Spain until 1820. At this point, however, Spain's own weakness convinced the Creole elite that they should take matters in their own hands, so they would not end up powerless against further social upheaval. Hence, they supported an independent Mexico, hoping to create a monarchy that would attract a European prince. Finding no takers, a conservative Mexican emperor was crowned in 1822. Here was a clear case of decisive action as Creole landlords, in defending their own elite position, severely limited the social impact of freedom movements. Mexico's choice also foreshadowed political patterns in other Latin American areas, when strongman rule would be seen as essential support for the elite against possible lower-class radicalism.

Independence for the Central American areas south of Mexico initially assumed more liberal lines. Centered in Guatemala, the movement proclaimed a United Provinces of Central America in 1823, with a constitution closely modeled on that of the United States.

No war was needed to bring independence to the final major nation of Latin America, Brazil. Threatened by Napoleon, the Portuguese ruler had fled to Brazil; when he was able to return to Portugal in 1815, his son, Pedro, remained as regent. Portugal then tried to reimpose colonial controls over Brazil, but Brazilian leaders, now accustomed to a government based in Rio de Janeiro, resisted. Pedro joined this movement, proclaiming Brazilian independence in 1822, with himself as emperor.

By 1825, then, virtually all of Latin America was free from colonial rule. Small European holdings persisted on the northeast coast of South America and in one part of Central America. And, of course, the bulk of the West Indies remained in European hands. Nonetheless, the spirit of freedom prevailed elsewhere.

THE PERIOD OF CONSOLIDATION

Following the intense activity of the liberation movement, a period of consolidation set in. Between 1825 and 1850, a number of the original nine new nations of Latin America split apart. Bolívar had cherished some hope of a political union among all the regimes, but this was clearly impossible because of disagreements among independence leaders, some of whom wanted to establish monarchies while others sought liberal republics. Similar kinds of disputes, plus personal rivalries, then divided even the original states. Gran Colombia fell apart by 1830, splitting into Colombia, Venezuela, and Ecuador. A brief union between Bolivia and Peru failed, in part because the stronger states of Argentina and Chile sought to avoid a powerful neighbor. The United Provinces of Central America had dissolved into five small states by 1840. Finally, a number of border clashes between some of the new nations marked this early period.

The period of consolidation also saw considerable instability in internal politics. Liberals dominated most governments, advocating free trade and a federal government system, but their policies were too idealistic. Debates soon surfaced between advocates of a central government and federalists. Mexico, for example, seesawed between the two systems, with one leader, the colorful general Santa Anna, taking contradictory positions at different points. Liberal rulers sought parliamentary institutions and religious freedom, whereas conservatives wanted to protect the church and upper classes; the latter controlled most regimes between 1830 and 1870. Many new governments were hampered by the lack of extensive political experience of the Creole group. Because Spanish administrators had so systematically excluded the Creoles, save at the

Mexican *hacienda* owner with overseer, 1830. (Granger Collection)

level of city councils, few leaders could be found who knew how to operate a government. In this situation, military leaders, drawn from the independence armies, often played an unusually large role. They had a power base and organizational skills. They also characteristically enjoyed the support of landlords, who were eager for forceful military action against peasant unrest. But factional fighting plagued the military as well, leading to frequent coups and revolts. During the 19th century, for example, Bolivia experienced 60 revolts and coups, Venezuela 52. Lack of previous political activity, the important role in internal politics taken by the military, and the obvious lack of agreement on political principles ensured considerable instability for most Latin American nations. Even Brazil, under the steady rule of the Emperor Pedro and then his son until 1889, ultimately followed this pattern, as a republic was proclaimed that soon generated battles among liberals, conservatives, and army leaders.

By 1850, however, despite instability and dispute, many new governments managed to establish some key institutions. New legal codes were written, based largely on Spanish precedent. A number of countries opened school systems and assumed the task of developing port facilities and other public works. Few regimes set up particularly effective bureaucracies, and personal corruption played a frequent role in Latin American affairs. However, the military hierarchy helped compensate for weakly developed civil administrations, and the promotion of military and police functions was obviously vital to the preservation of public order, in turn a cherished goal of the Creole landlords and also church officials.

Although political instability by no means ended after 1850, it is possible to recognize some changes by this point, as initial consolidation was completed. A number of individual nations emerged from early disputes with a forceful government ready to pursue vigorous policies. By

1840, for example, Chile had settled several key issues of political structure, and during a series of administrations under capable presidents, it was able to expand the education system, offer wider voting rights for parliament, and open new lands in the south through the defeat of American Indian groups. A number of governments had also abolished slavery, although the institution would survive in Brazil until 1888.

More impressive than internal political consolidation was the achievement of relative stability in foreign affairs. Many Latin American states remained rivals, sometimes contesting border areas. Britain prompted the creation of Uruguay in the 1820s as a buffer between Argentina and Brazil. However, the Latin American map remained quite fixed after 1850. The only major changes, all provoked by the United States, involved the massive loss of territory by Mexico (Texas, the U.S. Southwest, and California). Later, a semi-independent Cuba was established, after the Spanish-American War in 1898, and then an independent Panama, also under U.S. influence, was carved from Colombia to promote U.S. control of the canal constructed through the isthmus there. A few wars dotted Latin American history in the later 19th century. Paraguay took on Argentina and Brazil in the 1860s, provoking great devastation, and Chile warred with its Andes neighbors in the 1870s, taking Bolivian and Peruvian territories. But for the most part, Latin America was free from major strife between nations—far more free, certainly, than western Europe at the same time. The concentration of military leaders on their often repressive internal political role distracted Latin American countries from foreign exploits.

LATE-CENTURY TRENDS: DICTATORSHIP, IMMIGRATION, AND WESTERN INTERVENTION

No single political pattern describes Latin American developments during the late 19th century, but one significant trend was the tendency toward

strongman rule. Venezuela, for example, went through three constitutions after 1870, but in fact was ruled mainly by a series of dictators, of whom the most successful was Antonio Guzmán Blanco. Mexico experienced a dizzying succession of changes before also settling into dictatorial rule. The final defeat of General Santa Anna had ushered in a period of liberal government under the American Indian leader Benito Juárez. Juárez sought to reduce the power of the church in Mexican affairs and to extend a secular system of education; he also wanted to decrease landlord influence, although he pressed less vigorously in this regard than he had initially promised his American Indian supporters he would. Even so, his efforts aroused the opposition of conservatives, who looked to France for help. During the 1860s, when France was eager to establish a new empire and the United States was divided by the Civil War, Mexico was ruled by an Austrian duke backed by French armies. However, these armies retreated and liberal insurgents captured and executed the hapless duke. Juárez returned, and with him another series of important liberal reforms. But on Juárez's death, a strongman regime was installed, under Porfirio Díaz, which lasted from 1876 to 1911. Díaz radically curtailed political rights, arranging for the assassination of major opponents. Even in Colombia, where a parliamentary regime had usually prevailed, a brief series of strongman governments assumed power after 1900.

The tendency to adopt strongman rule, amid the considerable shifting of regimes, was only one of the major trends in Latin American history during the second half of the 19th century. Liberals returned to power in most countries, after decades of conservative rule. They were eager for economic development and better, less constrained trade, but their policies were more authoritarian than before. Hence, a number of strongmen, such as Porfirio Díaz in Mexico, were actually liberal in orientation. Many regimes held regular elections but with very restricted voting rights, creating what some historians have called *oligarchic democracies*.

World Profiles

BENITO JUÁREZ (1806–1872)

Benito Juárez was one of those rare but particularly significant individuals in world history who rose from humble origins to gain an important role in society and then helped shape events. Juárez was a Mexican Indian who acquired an education in law and became a state governor. He was an avid liberal, eager to reduce the privileges of church and army and to promote economic change. After a liberal revolt in the 1850s, Juárez became president of Mexico and undertook a sweeping reform program including the sale of church property. He also backed a land reform act that restricted traditional communal landholdings among Indians in favor of private property; his hope was to spur modern, independent farming, but in fact, the lands were often purchased by speculators, lead-

ing to increased landlessness. Conservatives in reaction removed Juárez from power and installed a French-backed emperor whom Juárez opposed in the name of Mexican independence. Juárez returned to office but became increasingly autocratic in reaction to the previous period of instability. Juárez's personality and goals had made him a national symbol by the time of his death in 1872. His legacy, however, was more mixed than he would have wished. A period of strong government and economic growth followed Juárez, but social reform for the groups from which Juárez had risen proved more elusive. Why do leaders such as Juárez sometimes fail to help their own people, despite a sincere desire to do so?

Mural showing Benito Juárez, by Diego Rivera, circa 1920.

A third theme, steadily accelerating after 1870, was the surge of commercial development. Estate agriculture spread, as Latin American leaders sought to take advantage of new European markets for beef and coffee. Extensive mining resumed: A silver boom arose in Mexico, while the extraction of copper and other products took hold along the Andes. This economic expansion was encouraged by increased foreign investment in Latin America. It was also supported by the interest of a number of Latin American governments, including dictatorships such as that of Guzmán Blanco in Venezuela, in extending roads and rail networks to the interior.

In several regions, a massive new wave of immigration provided the backbone for the commercial upswing. Many governments promoted immigration, often inspired by a belief that American Indian and black labor could never be suitably trained in the ways of a modern society. The Argentine constitution even included a provision that "the Federal government will encourage European immigration," and by 1895, with three-fourths of all adults foreign born, it had a far higher percentage of immigrants than the United States. The end of slavery in Argentina and Brazil, by the 1880s, created a new need for labor. Freed slaves encountered far less complete discrimination in Latin America than in the United States. More intermarriage occurred, as blacks added to the mestizo population, and light-skinned mestizos were not considered "colored" or black. However, considerable prejudice continued against dark-skinned former slaves and American Indians. This created a favorable climate for the use of immigrant labor, which in fact decreased the number of job opportunities for former slaves in many regions. Latin American interest in immigration peaked just as population pressure in southern Europe crested. Hence, although some immigrants came from Britain and Germany, often bringing capital and organizational skills, the majority came from Italy, Spain, and Portugal. A small number of Asians, from China

and Japan, also arrived. Immigrants provided labor for the expanding economies and rapidly growing cities. They also represented new markets for the foods produced by estate agriculture. Many settlers adapted readily to Latin American life, often intermarrying with American Indians and mestizos. While immigrants promoted some European ideas, such as socialism, for the most part they accepted local beliefs, aided by the fact that many shared the Catholic religion with their new compatriots. Immigration thus brought important changes to Latin America, but it did not overturn established political or cultural patterns.

New problems with Western powers constituted the final major factor in late-19th-century Latin American history. Western nations had not left Latin America alone during the consolidation period; their businesses had a major impact on economic life. Britain, which ruled the seas, also blocked the slave trade. France and occasionally Britain interfered militarily, and both Britain and the United States also officially discouraged outside intervention, although the United States consumed approximately half the territory of Mexico between 1830 and 1860, through the annexation of Texas and other lands won by war.

From the 1870s onward, however, foreign intervention increased. Heavy Western investment brought government action to enforce debt payments. British and French ships frequently threatened Latin American ports to compel fiscal reforms. U.S. ventures were still more significant. In addition to strong U.S. nationalist and imperialist sentiment, North American corporations acquired extensive estate and mining holdings and often called for military and diplomatic support against local reform movements. U.S. influence bore particularly heavily on governments in Mexico and Central America, although there were also important conflicts with Chile and other states. Through the war with Spain, the United States acquired the island of Puerto Rico directly and established a protectorate over Cuba. The building of the Panama Canal resulted in new pressure, leading to Panamanian independence from Colombia, under U.S. auspices. And shortly after 1900, the United States began a policy of frequent military intervention in unstable countries in Central America and the West Indies, out of concern for its business interests in these regions. The problem of dealing with Western nations, especially the United States, began to rank high on the agendas of all Latin American states.

Events during the 19th century, and particularly after 1850, had established a number of distinctive regions within Latin American civilization. The great states of the south—Argentina, Uruguay, Chile, and Brazil—took the lead in the new prosperity of the late 19th century. They were most active in commercial development, and they also encouraged the highest levels of immigration. Several states, led by Argentina, prided themselves on their European airs. Buenos Aires became almost Parisian in its elegant boulevards, with stylish French and English shops serving the wealthy classes. Although Brazil had large black and American Indian populations, the southern states were overall more European racially than was Latin America as a whole.

A second group of countries covered the Andes region—Bolivia, Peru, and Ecuador. Here, the percentage of American Indian population was highest and the poverty greatest. Political instability and military rule were also somewhat more pervasive in this region than in Latin America generally.

Mexico, Central America, Colombia, and Venezuela all had sizable American Indian populations, although the majority was mestizo. This region enjoyed some commercial expansion in the late 19th century. It was also the region most vulnerable to imperialist pressures, a major factor in the development of both foreign and economic policy.

Latin American regionalism, although significant, took shape amid a number of roughly common developments, from independence onward, and amid some widely shared patterns of politics and cultural life.

POLITICAL INSTITUTIONS AND VALUES

The instability of Latin American politics became notorious in foreign eyes, particularly in the United States. Frequent violence and the collapse of one regime after another encouraged people in the United States to look down on the Latin American political style, because stability and a consensus on basic values seemed the hallmark of U.S. political life, at least after the devastating Civil War. Latin American politics were certainly distinctive, responding to factors rather different from those that described Western politics during the same period.

Politically active groups in Latin America tended to divide, from independence onward, between liberals and conservatives. A small, mainly intellectual socialist movement arose in some places toward 1900, but it had yet to win political significance. Liberals, strongly influenced by their Western counterparts, stood for genuine parliamentary governments, constitutions, and civil rights, and a reduction in the power of the Catholic church. They welcomed economic development and sometimes considered limited social or land reforms; they were eager to extend education. On the other hand, they had little commitment to social reform, often scorning or repressing peasant and American Indian values, and they supported elitist economic interests. After 1870, they increasingly supported the notion of strong governments that could back economic development but also regulate aspects of popular behavior that the liberals found distasteful.

Conservatives, often attracted in the early days to the ideals of a monarchy, distrusted parliaments. They directly backed the power of the dominant landlord class and were less interested in commercial or industrial development than liberals. They also stood in firm defense of the rights of the Catholic church, which maintained a powerful role in education and possessed considerable wealth and land.

Disputes between conservatives and liberals helped account for political instability. When they were not clearly resolved, as in Colombia and Venezuela in the late 19th century, changes in regime were particularly frequent. Generally, however, liberal victory in the 1870s ushered in a period of greater political calm—it has been compared to the general triumph of democratic regimes in Latin America in the late 20th century. Liberals rarely gained a popular following, but they did ally with business interests and a growing urban middle class in promoting not only commercial expansion but also European-style urban renewal projects and efforts to improve public health and eliminate prostitution and other forms of crime.

Accompanying liberal and conservative conflicts was the frequency of strongman rule. *Caudillismo*, derived from the Spanish word for "leader," described this governmental form. Caudillos usually favored the conservative bastions of church and landlord but sometimes represented the liberal camp. Their tactics often cut through some of the conservative–liberal debate, if only by force. At times, some even worked for reform, scaling back church prerogatives and seeking economic development. By reducing liberal attacks on American Indian or mestizo traditions and offering public works, some conservative caudillos garnered ardent mass support. But all caudillos relied on force. They outlawed political opposition, regulated schools and newspapers, and used jails, police, and firing squads with abandon. Some, without question, were simply corrupt, lining their pockets and those of their cronies. Porfirio Díaz, the last Mexican caudillo, in addition to brutalizing his political opponents, encouraged landlords and U.S. investors to take over vast stretches of Mexican land, receiving extensive kickbacks in return. His government, indeed, sold off literally 20 percent of all the land in Mexico, much of it previously held by American Indians and mestizo villagers.

In the 19th century, Latin American politics had little contact with the masses; except for the times it exploited them. Few liberals were ardent democrats; they shared a distrust of American Indians and blacks. Liberal constitutions gradually increased the suffrage, but few liberals favored democracy; hence, mass political action was not an important feature of Latin America during this period. Liberals, indeed, were in some ways less sympathetic to mass interests than conservatives, which helps explain their limited popularity. Liberals stood for individualized property rights; they promoted rationality and different, typically grueling, work habits; they attacked tradition, including, of course, popular religious customs. Liberal caudillos such as Porfirio Díaz brutally suppressed incipient trade union movements among urban workers. Other caudillos at times developed political symbols and public works projects that did have mass appeal. Even before 1850, for example, an early Argentine caudillo, Manuel de Rosas, won considerable popular support by requiring church prayers for his regime, and by the widespread use of his image and his political symbol, a red rose, in public places. De Rosas and many other caudillos, particularly during the decades of consolidation, often helped build a national consciousness among elite groups and the masses, even when they were by Western standards unusually repressive. The tensions between the articulate political forces in Latin America and the somewhat separate masses were one of many traditions established in the 19th century that would affect Latin American politics into our own time.

Most Latin American governments remained weak in the 19th century, even when caudillos officially claimed great power. The ability to regulate landlord or foreign business interests, or even, in some cases, roving bands of criminals, was limited (as was true to some extent in the United States). This was the context in which, after 1870, liberals often advocated greater state powers in the interests of economic development, government-sponsored education, or regulating Indians.

History Debate

IS LATIN AMERICA WESTERN?

In 1997, a large number of Latin American historians, mostly but not exclusively from the United States, debated on the Internet whether Latin America should be judged a "non-Western" civilization. A few argued that Latin America should be viewed as part of the West because it shared a Western language and active participation in a common literary and artistic culture. Latin America is also the only society outside western Europe, North America, Australia, and New Zealand where political liberalism gained widespread support in the 19th century.

Other historians of Latin America, however, objected. Some argued that parts of Latin America—a city such as Buenos Aires, for example, or a group such as the middle class—were Western, but other key parts—the poor, or a city such as Tucuman—were not. Costa Ricans may view themselves as Western, but the Quechua speakers in the Andean highlands would not. The majority of the debaters argued that the solution to the question was not to decide whether Latin America was Western or not, but to avoid the use of the term *Western*. For these historians, the term implied a certain superiority, and in their view such an interpretation did not reflect an accurate picture of any society. They further attacked the related tendency of many historians to lump together many civilizations in a "non-Western" category, as if a culture's not being Western was a coherent feature. Finally, they argued that Latin America should be seen as a syncretic civilization, combining many influences—but that other civilizations, including western Europe, were also syncretic. Interestingly, broad discussions of social and economic features did not loom large. The debate focused on culture and whether one was sympathetic or not to the viewpoint of Latin America as a Western civilization.

CULTURE AND THE ARTS

The Catholic church continued to provide one of the key cultural bonds throughout Latin American civilization. The institution operated schools and charitable facilities for the poor, in addition to maintaining its political role. Church ceremonies and buildings provided aesthetic as well as spiritual experiences for Latin Americans from almost all social classes and racial groups. Latin America thus remained largely separate from the assaults on religion as an intellectual and cultural force that arose in Western civilization during the same period, although liberals generated fierce attacks on the church as an institution. Debates such as that over Darwin's theory of evolution, in its implications for Christian belief, had little echo in Latin America. Indeed, Latin American culture, even at elitist levels, remained relatively disinterested in science. Although in most countries universities were established by 1850 that gradually developed some scientific and medical training, science remained less prestigious in this civilization than in the West, with its contribution to the general culture less significant.

Latin American culture was framed not only by religion but also by class structure. A considerable gap divided educated Latin Americans from the largely illiterate masses. A few governments, particularly in the southern region or under regimes such as that of Juárez in Mexico, made strides in promoting literacy. Argentina's literacy

The European look: section of Buenos Aires in the late 19th century.

rate, 22 percent in 1876, jumped to 50 percent by 1895—the highest of any Latin American nation. These developments, along with a growing prosperity, help explain why cultural activity increased in Latin America during the later 19th century. Nonetheless, most formal intellectual activity still played to what was, by Western standards, a limited audience.

Culture was also shaped, again especially in the southern region, by the immense popularity of Western trends. Latin America developed no architectural style of its own during this period, in part because those who could afford major building projects thought in terms of replicating what they had seen in Paris or Madrid. Many artists and writers patiently reproduced European-style portraits and novels for an eager,

wealthy audience. Even intellectuals who cultivated originality did not think in terms of an entirely independent Latin American culture, as they kept careful tabs on European, and particularly French, styles.

However, formal culture in Latin America, especially in literature, did achieve a distinctive tone. Poetry played an important role. Many poets were retained on university faculties, and in general, poetic expression became more vigorous in Latin America, in comparison with other literary output, than in the West. A number of women writers contributed to the impressive body of work in poetry. Using romantic styles, a number of poets and novelists also tried to convey the popular themes and concerns within their own civilization. They wrote of the frontier,

American Indians, and slave life. Many were politically radical, using literature to spur social reform. They were joined by many historians and folklorists, who strove to describe the special features of the Latin American experience and its racial diversities. Finally, a number of writers, both conservative and radical, sought to convey something of the spirituality of life, and particularly Latin American life. In the 1890s, one Uruguayan novelist, Enrique Rodo, who achieved wide popularity in Spanish-speaking countries, highlighted what he perceived to be the special virtues of his civilization over the materialism and mediocrity of Western culture, most notably in the United States.

Along with formal culture, a vigorous popular art continued to flourish. Many American Indian weavers and potterers used traditional themes, designs, and vivid colors in their work. Festivals, even when organized around Christian celebrations, provided American Indians and former Africans with an opportunity to participate in lively folk dances. Popular dance music, using Spanish instruments such as the guitar but traditional American Indian or African melodies and rhythms, included the fast-paced tango and samba—styles that would later have an influence in Western popular culture as well.

Overall, despite the limitations of poverty, illiteracy, and frequent political repression, a vibrant cultural life emerged at various levels of Latin American society. As in politics, Latin Americans worked toward a distinctive amalgam of Western styles and their own customs and values. Artistic expression became a vital facet of the maturing civilization.

ECONOMY AND SOCIETY

Economic and social patterns in Latin America most clearly separated this civilization from that of western Europe and the United States, and indeed accounted for many of the distinctions visible in politics and culture. For the most part, dynamic sectors of the Latin American economies arose as suppliers to the West; manufacturing was weakly developed throughout most of the 19th century, except for the peasant production of cloth and other simple items for local use. Since colonial times, Latin America's great export facilities had been geared for the sale of goods in the Western-dominated world economy; this orientation endured after independence, which helps account for the long hold of slavery in a few states such as Brazil. As many regions became commercially active in the second half of the century, Latin American dependence on Western markets and a low-paid labor force actually increased.

The first half of the century produced bleak economic news for much of Latin America. The wars of independence disrupted previous economic activities. Because few of the new regimes attempted significant land reform, most commercial production remained in the hands of great estate owners; nonetheless, there was a good deal of confusion because of unrest and the disruption of trade with Spain. The abolition of slavery in places like Mexico and Venezuela led to the erosion of a prime source of cheap labor that was not quickly replaced, with taxes rising to support growing armies. Furthermore, boundaries in several countries were drawn without regard to earlier economic patterns. Thus, Bolivia and Peru, centers of the great silver mines, were cut off from the rich agricultural plains of Argentina. More serious still was the decline in the production of precious metals, particularly in the Andes region, which reduced the availability of one of Latin America's chief exports. At the same time, independence opened Latin American markets to industrially produced cloth and tools from the West, especially Great Britain, which overwhelmed many local suppliers. Poverty among urban workers increased, and rural manufacturing was nearly eliminated.

By 1850, as we have seen, conditions often improved. There were exceptions, however—poverty increased in Mexico under Porfirio Díaz even as economic development advanced. Large estate owners, some of them foreign, tightened their grip on the American Indian and mestizo labor force. But many Latin American countries developed a key cash crop or mineral specialty that allowed them to capture a growing export market. In Cuba and part of Central America, the production of sugar was a primary focus. Brazil concentrated on coffee, and in 1889, the country produced 56 percent of the world's coffee; by 1904, the figure had risen to 76 percent. Argentina exported beef and wheat from vast ranches; Chile focused on copper and nitrates, Bolivia on tin. Mexico became a leading petroleum producer after 1900, spurred by U.S. investments and much foreign ownership. These concentrations on food and raw materials were highly vulnerable, however. Latin American production increased rapidly, but this risked flooding the market and thus lowering prices and total earnings. Brazil, for example, faced a devastating slump in coffee prices around 1900. The environment in many countries was also affected by deforestation and the promotion of crops such as coffee that were not native to the region.

At the same time, demand for products manufactured in the West tended to grow rapidly. Upper-class Latin Americans, often possessing new revenue from trade, mines, or estates, wanted European luxury items. They quite consciously backed the growth of export sectors as the basis for their style of life. Further, the railroads and ports that governments sought to promote required imports of equipment from the United States and Europe. Latin American nations accumulated rising foreign debts when their exports did not match their imports. Government indebtedness led to frequent Western intervention, which often averted bankruptcy but never addressed the problem of a basic economic imbalance.

Outright foreign economic control compounded the problem. Britain led in investments to Latin America during this period, but the United States and other Western nations were also heavily involved. Foreigners owned many of the most lucrative estates and industries. In Díaz's Mexico, they purchased a great deal of land; in Colombia and Chile, they owned most railroads, banks, and mines. Western investments brought frequent pressures on Latin American governments to protect Western property. They deprived Latin America's struggling business class of a full range of opportunities, for top management remained in foreign hands. And they removed much-needed profits from the region altogether.

Further, the economic development that did take place in the later 19th century, whether foreign based or not, created intense pressures on the lower classes. While Latin American dependence on the world economy was not new, it had previously coexisted with village agriculture. Into the 1880s, many American Indians and mestizos operated village farms adequate for local subsistence needs. They were able to work according to traditional rhythms and organize frequent festivals, replete with dance, song, and drink. This pattern yielded quickly to the growing commercialization of the Latin American economy during the last decades of the 19th century. In virtually every region, more land than ever before was consumed by large estates. American Indians, accustomed to community ownership, were forced to sell out to individual owners. In Mexico, for example, a law of 1894 ruled that land could be declared vacant and open to purchase if legal title to it could not be produced, but few American Indians had such title, relying on traditional terms of use rather than modern notions of property. In Colombia and elsewhere, governments, often in liberal hands and eager to promote economic growth, opened new territories to bidding, which in fact displaced many traditional villages not regarded as having property rights. Other peasant owners were simply defrauded by shrewd speculators, or encouraged to go into debt. Some of the new estates embraced thousands, even millions of acres; one Mexican estate was as large as West Virginia.

The peasants, once displaced, encountered still further indignities. They had little choice but

Mexican rebels on the march toward Xochamilcu, August 15, 1914.

to work on the large estates, where they were paid low wages or, even more commonly, paid in kind and kept permanently in debt. Virtual serfdom spread, as workers were not allowed to leave the land until they had paid their debts, and not allowed to earn enough money to have any hope of making these payments. Furthermore, hard-driving commercial estate owners tried to spur greater zeal on the part of workers. They clamped down on traditional festivals, regarded as a sheer waste of time. This was a pattern not entirely different from the pressures earlier placed on European or U.S. industrial workers, for a real commercial revolution was underway. But Latin American peasants suffered far less freedom and far more poverty than most Western workers, for the economy, because of its weak position in the world markets, depended on exploited labor. Investment in new equipment, which might have provided an alternative to cheap labor, lagged. And, although many estate and mine owners worked conscientiously to expand production, as opposed to the stereotype of idle drones living in luxury with no attention to management, the gap

between the wealthy, mainly Creole or foreign, landowning classes and the impoverished masses grew ever wider.

Finally, many former peasants, forced off the land, sought refuge in the growing cities, where they faced competition for jobs from new immigrants from Europe. A large, often miserable property-less class spread in the cities, pitting sprawling slums on the outskirts against the impressive upper-class districts nearer the center of town. Because industrialization was slow, there were relatively few factory jobs to absorb the newcomers. Aided by foreign capital and European immigrants, countries such as Brazil did develop some industries in food processing, textile, and metallurgy. However, the numbers of workers these industries employed were small, as Western competition continued to cut into the available markets for manufactured goods. Hard-pressed governments had few resources to devote to welfare programs, so urban poverty and shantytowns grew unchecked.

The Latin American masses were not quiet under this new assault. The organization of urban trade unions was difficult, because of widespread misery and sheer confusion; government oppression also complicated any protest efforts. However, peasant uprisings to seize land and escape the commercially driven work routines became common from the 1880s onward; indeed, they persist in many areas even today. Peasant rebellions were not regular occurrences, for peasants were usually repressed and could not be supported by legal organizations. But they also proved impossible to put down permanently. Mexico, Bolivia, and Colombia faced major revolts every 10 or 20 years. Rural banditry also increased in many regions, recruiting displaced peasants and winning the quiet support of even larger numbers, who saw the bandits as expressing their discontent and hatred of landlords. Finally, rates of individual violence were high in many countries. Essentially frontier conditions existed in many places, as the formal presence of a central government was sporadic at best. Hence, many peasants took vengence into their own hands. High levels of violence also reflected the deep grievances of landless peasants whose cheap labor sustained Latin America's production for trade.

The expansion of exports to the world economy placed new strains on the environment in many parts of Latin America. Mining or sugar growing had already reduced the forested areas in places like Bolivia and Brazil. The spread of coffee growing in southeastern Brazil, introduced from Africa in the later 18th century, created additional pressure. During the 19th century over 30,000 square kilometers of forest were cleared to allow coffee growing, and the extension of railroads and urban growth reduced forests still further. Soil erosion, particularly on mountain slopes where coffee is grown, was the principal environmental result. Many species of animals and plants also suffered as their habitat was destroyed. No attention was paid to these developments, however, until the 1930s, and few controls have proved successful even by the early 21st century.

Latin America during the late 19th century thus generated a paradox of rapid change and continued vulnerability in the world markets. Many sectors of the economy were out of Latin American hands. Emphasis on agriculture and mining continued, with only halting industrial development. Cities grew, but without a vigorous manufacturing base. Social structure remained oddly traditional, with great estate owners at the top of the heap, masses of peasants and property-less workers at the bottom, and a small middle class in between. Slavery had been abolished, but poverty and near-serfdom replaced it not only for many blacks but also for American Indians, mestizos, and many immigrants as well. Family structure remained rather traditional, with a strong emphasis on the inferiority of women. Many lower-class women, in fact, entered the labor force, both on estates and in the cities, but officially and legally their place remained subordinate to men at virtually all social levels.

TENSION AND CREATIVITY

The tensions of Latin American society help explain the importance of strongman governments and the diverse roles of religion, through the late 19th century and beyond. One country, Mexico, was on the verge of revolution in 1900, driven by the unusually heavy hand of Porfirio Díaz and the extensive exploitation of American Indian and mestizo labor. However, most of Latin America would long avoid outright revolution, although not recurrent protest, as army, church, and sometimes foreign intervention combined to keep the lid on unrest. Efforts by artists and intellectuals to voice the yearnings of the masses or to provide a spiritual identity distinct from Western values gained growing significance. Latin American civilization was formed under many unusual difficulties and under the strong tutelage of the more powerful West, yet it managed to generate not simply an array of problems but also a unique flavor that blended diverse traditions with the creation of new countries and rapid economic change.

ISSUES AND CONNECTIONS

Latin America was not a powerful force in world history during the long 19th century: it acted less than it was acted upon. But its role in spurring the world economy, in contributing to major changes in the history of labor systems, and in receiving new population groups from Europe and Asia must be recognized. Further, this was a formative period for Latin America itself. It is both possible and important to build Latin America into the understanding of world history during this period, and to use it as a focus for some key comparisons.

Without question, current features of Latin American history, while different from those of 1900, derive from the 19th-century heritage. The struggle against economic dependency continues, precisely because that dependency became so well established through the intensifications of the late 1800s. The effort toward political definition continues as well, against the 19th-century backdrop of quarrels over legitimacy, considerable instability, recurrent authoritarianism, but also significant impulses toward liberalism. A distinctive culture, though linked to the West, persists as well. Many Latin American authors in the late 20th century worried about new challenges to Latin American identity, from global consumerism for example, but their ideas assumed that an identity had been forged.

SUGGESTED WEB SITE

The life of José San Martín is examined at http://www.pachami.com/English/ressanmE.htm.

SUGGESTED READINGS

Recent work includes Eric Van Young, *The Other Rebellion* (2001); Ivan Jaksic, *Andres Bello: Scholarship and Nation-Building in 19th Century Latin America* (2001); Carlos Forment, *Democracy in Latin America, 1760–1900* (2003); and Douglass Sullivan-Gonzalez, *Piety, Power and Politics: Religion and Nation Formation in Guatemala, 1821–1871* (1998).

A useful collection of sources is B. Keen's *Readings in Latin American Civilization* (1955). For discussions reflecting recent scholarship, see T. Skidmore and P. Smith, *Modern Latin America* (1984); the book's only drawback is its concentration on single national or regional cases. See also David Bushnell and Neil Macauley, *The Emergence of Latin America in the Nineteenth Century* (1994), and Fernando Henrique Cardoso and Enzo Faletto, *Dependency and Development in Latin America* (1979), which disagree on the issue of dependency. On political patterns, see Tulio Halperin Donhi, *The Aftermath of Revolution in Latin America* (1973), and Claudio Veliz, *The Centralist Tradition in Latin America* (1980). On key topics, see E. Bradford Burns, *Poverty or Progress: Latin America in the Nineteenth Century* (1973); Herbert Klein, *Bolivia* (1982); June Nash and Helen Safa, eds., *Sex and Class in Latin America* (1980); and Charles Berquist, *Labor in Latin America* (1986).

The Middle East and China in the Imperialist Century

25

China and the Ottoman Empire, like Latin America, were largely independent in the 19th century, though under great pressures from the West. The pressures were newer than in the Latin American case. This newness, combined with the proud traditions of both societies, complicated response. In some ways, the two societies resembled the West's outright colonies, but being technically independent did count for something.

The Islamic Middle East and China, although quite different as civilizations, displayed some similar reactions to the heightened pace of the world economy and the threat of Western imperialism during the 19th century. Neither the Middle East nor China came fully under Western control, in part because of the continuing strength of their governments and in part because Western rivalries canceled each other out, so that no one imperialist power could win predominance. Their patterns thus differed from those of southern Asia and sub-Saharan Africa. But both areas lost territory and increasingly felt the threat of further takeovers. Nonetheless, the Middle East and, particularly, China responded sluggishly to the transformations in the wider world during most of the 19th century, and both lost additional ground as a result. Change came, but haltingly. Traditionalist leadership and a long habit of looking down on foreigners, in the Chinese case, or Westerners, in the Muslim case, delayed vigorous reactions. Late in the 19th century, however, new forces arose in both societies ardently seeking fundamental reforms that would make their societies more competitive with the West and more like the West in certain ways. This outlook set the stage for a much more active period of development during the 20th century.

China and the Middle East, then, followed a 19th-century pattern somewhat in between the societies under outright imperialist control, such as India, and those that were stimulated during the century itself to radically new kinds of responses. Ironically, it was

China's east Asian cousin, Japan, that provided the most successful example of the latter type of approach. This means that China and Japan diverged increasingly despite shared traditions.

KEY QUESTIONS   *What were the new forms of pressure from the West and the world economy, on both China and the Ottoman Empire? Beyond this are issues of causation and differentiation. Why were both these societies somewhat slow to develop effective responses? But also why, and in what ways, were reform efforts in the Ottoman Empire more effective? Finally, there are additional comparisons, for example toward explaining why Chinese responses differed from Japanese. Compare both these cases also to colonial situations in India: some historians have argued that India, as a colony, was less seriously exploited than China was, precisely because no Western power took real responsibility for China. Is this a plausible comparison, and how can degrees of damage or constructive impact best be assessed?*

THE ATTEMPT TO MODERNIZE EGYPT

The Middle East began the 19th century with a fascinating initiative, although one that ultimately failed. The Ottoman Empire had been rocked, in 1798, by Napoleon's successful invasion of Egypt. When Napoleon was forced out, by British pressure plus Napoleon's own ambition, an Ottoman military officer named Muhammad Ali took over Egypt as a virtually independent ruler, and indeed the Ottomans never did fully regain control of this vital province. At points, Muhammad Ali also conquered areas of the Arabian Peninsula adjacent to Egypt, although he was blocked by not only Ottoman resistance but also British fear of any strong power in this region so close to key routes to India.

As ruler of Egypt, Muhammad Ali represented one of the first non-Western leaders, and certainly the first in the Middle East, to adopt a self-conscious mission to modernize his society in Western terms. Unlike Peter the Great, Muhammad Ali never visited the West, but he greatly admired Western achievements and also realized that he must try to match some of them if he was to preserve the independence of Egypt. Under his sponsorship, Western, and particularly French, advisors flooded the country to aid in education, technology, and science as well as military affairs.

Muhammad Ali saw the need to alter traditional economic patterns. Although unable to spur outright industrialization, he introduced agricultural improvements and, in particular, developed an active export market for Egyptian cotton. The hold of landlords, traditionally uninterested in innovation, was weakened. Muhammad Ali also established a printing press and sponsored the translation of many Western books on science and technology into Arabic. In addition to using Western teachers, he sent a number of Arabs to study abroad. French became a second language to educated Egyptians. Despite these many developments, Muhammad Ali was unable to break through either the hold of tradition on much of Egyptian society or the limitations imposed by Western dominance of the world economy. Egypt became increasingly dependent, for export earnings, on the Western market for cotton; it thus had to compete with other producers of cotton, including the southern United States and India, and its cotton did not always command favorable prices. Its export earnings were frequently insufficient to pay for the machines and military equipment that Muhammad Ali sought, so his regime was increasingly forced to go into debt to Western banks. Here was a tragic irony, repeated many times in many countries, in the Middle East and elsewhere, throughout the 19th and 20th centuries. Governments seek to modernize, adopting new armaments, industrial machinery, and often an array of public buildings and urban amenities. But these innovations, designed to spur independence, cost money at a time when the economy remains sluggish. Hence, nations must face the temptation to borrow, which gives foreign banks new powers to supervise policy in the interest of protecting their loans. Muhammad Ali, in sum, managed to change Egypt, but he saw Western control steadily increase; by 1849, when he died, he was bitterly disappointed in his limited achievements. His efforts stand more as an early example of an attempt to adapt in response to Western standards than as a successful revitalizing regime.

DECLINE OF THE OTTOMAN EMPIRE

The bulk of the Middle East remained largely immune to Muhammad Ali's influence. The Ottoman Empire reacted to growing Western pressure and the de facto loss of Egypt in much more limited terms. The sultans established somewhat more centralized controls over great estates, in the interests of ensuring higher tax revenues. The sultan Mahmud II (1808–1839) dismantled the corrupt janissary corps. This group had long since lost its military skills and morale and had turned to political intrigues while living well from state revenues. Mahmud II created a separate, modern artillery corps armed with a European cannon; on this basis, he was able to eliminate the janissaries and develop a new officer group eager to rival Western military organization and technology.

These reforms, focusing on military structure primarily, were not sufficient to revive the decaying Ottoman Empire or to limit growing Western strength in the region. Important provinces of the empire were lost during the first half of the 19th century. Not only Egypt (although it technically remained a province until 1914) but also the north African states of Algeria, Tunisia, and Libya (Tripoli) became independent; these last regions had never been fully integrated into the empire in any event. Piracy from the north African shores provoked a military response from Europe and also the United States, which attacked the "shores of Tripoli." In 1830, France began its outright conquest of Algeria, the first of many European takeovers in this area. On the Arab peninsula new, religiously inspired rebellions against the Ottoman Empire broke out, although with the help of Muhammad Ali, they were defeated. Finally, the European provinces of the empire became increasingly restless, inspired by the example of liberalism and nationalism in the French Revolution. In 1820, a major war for independence erupted in Greece, which after a decade, and with wide if informal support from western Europe, won its independence. Nationalist agitation also stirred in Romania and Serbia, putting new pressure on the Ottoman regime.

West European economic influence in the Middle East intensified during the first part of the 19th century. Outside the boundaries of the Ottoman Empire, on the east coast of the Arabian Peninsula, Britain established a number of protectorates to limit piracy. London established steamship routes between India and eastern Arabia; by the 1830s, Britain and France operated steamship routes across the Mediterranean to Egypt and the Ottoman Empire itself. Thus, Middle Eastern shipping and foreign trade lay increasingly in Western hands. British companies even operated some river shipping within the Ottoman Empire. Western economic power severely limited the revenue capacity of the empire, which was barred from taxing foreign enterprise. World economic position, in other words, greatly constrained the Ottoman political response.

Finally, pressure on the Ottoman Empire continued from yet another traditional source—the surging Russian empire. Several regional wars occurred between Russia and the Ottomans during the first half of the 19th century, resulting in a loss of territory. Russia could have gained still more save for the intervention of France and Britain, who now had their own stake in this region and feared Russian dominance. The Crimean War of 1854–1856 resulted from

The opening of the Suez Canal: the French Empress Eugénie on her way to the ceremonies.

British–French opposition to further Russian expansion in the Mediterranean, and indeed the Russians were defeated. Another Russo-Turkish war occurred in 1877–1878, and again only Western intervention prevented Russian dismemberment of the empire, which lost new territory even so.

By this point, the Ottoman Empire risked becoming the puppet of forces beyond its control. The empire was not fully carved up only because the Europeans and Russians could not agree on the spoils; each power feared that the others would gain too much. The Middle East was too close to Europe to allow the kind of free-for-all that ultimately occurred in Africa; the danger of all-out war was too great. So the empire survived until 1918. Various sultans continued to experiment with reforms. Occasionally, they granted constitutions, in an effort to follow Western practices, but in fact the rule of the sultan and the bureaucracy remained unchecked. Slavery was abolished in 1908—quite late, of course, by

some standards. Substantial military reforms concentrated much of the impetus for change within the ranks of the armed forces. Many Ottoman officers were trained in Europe, and European—particularly German—advisors were brought in to improve technology and modernize military administration. However, the Ottoman army remained weak and relatively backward, in part because military reforms were unable to transcend the loose political organization and largely agricultural economy. Tax revenues and morale were both inadequate to provide new vigor to the Ottoman state as a whole.

Nevertheless, there was some real change. Particularly important was the Tanzimat reform movement between 1839 and the 1870s. The reforms aimed at a partial westernization of the Ottoman state and society, through greater centralization and partial secularization of law and education. All subjects, regardless of religion, gained equality under the law. Penal codes and commercial law were revised according to French models. But Islamic law was also embraced in new codes. A constitution was issued in 1876, providing for a parliament, but the experiment did not last long. Outside the government proper, the rise of modern journalism and other developments added to the reform current.

But the overall results were limited. Efforts at land reform actually strengthened the hold of large landowners over peasants. Periodic revolts, for example in the Balkans, were usually put down, but this helped create an atmosphere of repression as well as provoking European hostility. After 1876, the regime became more autocratic and religious, and the reform current dwindled.

Hence, the empire continued to lose territory on its fringes and suffer growing Western economic penetration. Nationalist uprisings in the Balkan area, supported by Russia and some of the Western powers, produced a network of small, independent states by the end of the 1870s: Serbia, Romania, and a few still smaller states joined Greece. As a result of further Balkan agitation, which led to an independent Bulgaria, the Ottoman Empire had, by 1914, lost almost all hold in Europe, save for a patch of territory including Constantinople.

Direct imperialist conquest in north Africa also continued, although this region, of course, had already been lost to the Ottomans. In 1869, a French company completed construction of a canal through the Isthmus of Suez, the narrow strip of land that had connected north Africa and the Middle East. By using the new Suez Canal, European ships could save immense time in reaching the Indian Ocean, by sailing from the Mediterranean to the Red Sea rather than around Africa. Egypt's importance increased because of its new strategic position. Britain, anxious as always to safeguard its interests in India, began to interfere more and more in Egyptian affairs, mainly to preempt French influence. Heavy Egyptian debts to British banks provided an obvious opening. Britain was able to buy controlling shares in the Suez Canal and then, in the 1880s, established a protectorate over the Egyptian gov-

ernment; the Egyptian ruler became a virtual figurehead. In response, France took over outright control of Tunisia. Soon after 1900, Italy gained Libya; France captured Morocco. All of Muslim north Africa lay in European hands.

To the east of the Ottoman Empire, British and Russian representatives divided influence over the kingdom of Persia, while direct British hold over the small states of the eastern Arab coast continued. Within the empire itself, European interests gained increasing economic power. German businesses, backed by the government, constructed a major railroad linking Berlin to Baghdad. French and English merchants bought quantities of luxury items. In Turkey proper, a number of rug factories were established, utilizing machines imported from the West and displacing many traditional handworkers, to fill the growing markets of western Europe and the United States, where Turkish carpets and other furnishings became the rage in middle-class homes in the later 19th century. Although some Turks and Arabs gained experience and wealth as factory owners or agents for Western companies, the new industry rested heavily on low-paid labor, and its basic directions were determined by Western merchants, not those in the Middle East. The Ottoman Empire, bounded by Western colonies, new and aggressive Balkan nations, and the ambitious Russian state, was no longer master in its own house.

THE RISE OF NATIONALISM

Although the Ottoman government proved unable to respond successfully to these new developments, several important events occurred that would shape Middle Eastern history in the 20th century. A strong current of Arab nationalism began to emerge, directed against both European imperialists and the hold of the Ottoman state. In Turkey, a modernizing movement arose among younger army officers. Finally, some efforts were made to rouse new Islamic fervor.

In contrast to India, a large Middle Eastern nationalism did not take clear shape, although there were efforts to encourage patriotic loyalty to the Ottomans. Nationalism increasingly meant particularism, associated with a smaller region, such as Egypt, or an ethnic-linguistic group, such as the Turks.

Arab nationalism developed most vigorously in Egypt, where Muhammad Ali had first opened the way to growing European influence and example. There nationalism, in fact, emphasized Egypt more than Arabs in general, and a full nationalist statement would not emerge until the early 20th century. Many educated Egyptians followed Muhammad Ali's goal in wanting to create a modern state and economy, along something like Western lines, but they also desired a proudly independent Egypt, inspired by the same nationalism they saw in western Europe. Nationalism was a new force in the Middle East (as in India), in its quest for loyalty to secular states and specific peoples instead of Arabs or Muslims in general. Nationalism's newness for a time limited its appeal, particularly to peasant masses, but it did focus attention on the important twin goals of independence and political change. As the Egyptian government grew weaker and more indebted toward the middle of the 19th century, nationalist opposition increased. It was inflamed still further by a British takeover. Britain regularized Egyptian finances and helped sponsor some railroad construction and a massive dam on the Nile at Aswan, which increased the amount of water available for irrigation in agriculture. London also abolished slavery in Egypt and expanded the school system. However, these reforms did not daunt the new nationalism. Egyptian nationalists resented economic controls that, in their view, prevented full industrialization. They also resented the lack of political rights and the arrogance of many British colonial administrators. As mostly educated city dwellers, the nationalists were able to easily see firsthand the privileged position and luxury of foreigners in their own country.

Arab nationalism also sprang up elsewhere in north Africa, in response to new imperialist regimes. In Tunisia, for example, the French built port facilities, rails, and a telegraph and telephone system; they also introduced new schools and hospitals. However, they did not encourage much industry and were careful to retain control of most export trade. A handful of French settlers took over some of the most fertile land in the country. These developments, as well as the gap between French and Tunisian culture, were more than enough to stimulate nationalist concerns. As in Egypt, north African nationalism before 1900 mainly took the form of political rallies and newspaper diatribes—themselves new political experiences for the Arabs involved. Little nationalist rioting occurred. But there was no question that a new political force was rising in this ancient region.

Some Arab nationalism also spilled over to the Ottoman Empire. A number of governors of Arab provinces, including the one that contained Mecca, flirted with nationalism; their loyalty to the sultan was questionable by 1900. In 1913, Arab nationalists were able to meet in Persia to discuss independence for Iraq.

Other kinds of nationalism also entered the field. A movement among European Jews, called *Zionism*, arose in the later 19th century in response to European patriotic claims and new kinds of intolerance against the Jews. The Zionists argued that Jews should reestablish their homeland in Palestine, and by 1914, a number of Jewish settlers were entering the area. This current had no great political consequences as yet, but it would prove vital in the region's future.

Further north, in the Ottoman heartland, more serious reform currents from the early 19th century set the basis for Turkish nationalism. Even though the Ottomans lost the ability to rule their empire vigorously, they did introduce changes affecting Turkey proper. The strengthening of the military, following the courageous dissolution of the janissaries, brought many Turkish officers into contact with Western training. University education was reorganized along

World Profiles

LALLA ZAINAB

Between 1897 and her death in 1904, Lalla Zainab directed a major Islamic religious center in southern Algeria. Her role was shaped by the continuing power of Islamic belief in north Africa and the Middle East, by hostilities roused by French conquest of Algeria (from 1829 onward), and by her own convictions and personality. Zainab's father, who claimed descent from the prophet Muhammad, had established the religious center. He provided an extensive religious education for his daughter, who was raised in a large harem. Zainab decided not to marry, and her celibacy, as well as her simple style of life, enhanced her reputation for spirituality. Clearly impressed with her abilities, Zainab's father gave her an inheritance equal to that of his sons. When her father died, Zainab successfully resisted the efforts of a male cousin to take over the community, as well as interference by the French colonial administration. To carve out considerable autonomy, Zainab was able to use a French lawyer and the French governor's new interest in establishing better relations with Islamic religious groups. Zainab used her power, including superb understanding of how the French administration operated, to provide assistance to many Muslim refugees, women, and the poor throughout the region. Her life demonstrates the role unusual individuals could gain even under imperialism, and the place an exceptional woman, with a clear record of piety, could obtain under Islam.

An Algerian mosque around 1900.

Western lines, and the government launched new postal and railway services in Turkey. These changes were important, but they whetted appetites for more. Muslim leaders clashed with the westernizing elite, and Sultan Abdul Hamid reestablished authoritarian rule after 1878. This was the context, around 1900, in which a number of younger army officers began to push for reform of the sultan's government and modernization of the empire. This movement of *Young Turks*, as they were called, sought political rights similar to those promised in a constitution of 1876 that the sultan had quickly withdrawn; they wanted an end to political corruption and a more vigorous foreign policy. They demanded new limits on European economic activities in their land. As one Young Turk put it, "We follow the path traced by Europe . . . even in our refusal to accept foreign intervention." Young Turks participated in a number of violent attempts to overthrow the sultan's government, although without initial success.

The Young Turk movement was long unclear as to whether it wanted to revive the Ottoman Empire or form a modern nation-state in Turkey. It talked mainly of the empire, but the movement relied so heavily on Turkish pride and the imposition of Turkish force that it was, in fact, more narrowly nationalistic. Nonetheless, the movement proved to be the basis for the modern Turkish nation that emerged after the larger Ottoman Empire collapsed.

In 1914, the Middle East was caught between the pressures of imperialism and the structures of the Ottoman state on the one hand, and the forces of a modernizing nationalism on the other. These latter forces, including the Young Turks, constituted an important new ingredient in the region, a sign of Europe's great influence but a symbol also of a vigorous desire for independence. Nationalism was not a native Middle Eastern development. The idea of breaking up the region into separate states, which even most Arab nationalists suggested in their concentration on Iraq, or Egypt, or Tunisia, had some precedent in earlier periods of regionalism in the Middle East, but it ran against the Islamic as well as the Ottoman tradition. The nationalists were not worried about precedent, however. They wanted not only independence but also a new society, no matter how vague their definitions. They often embraced a reformist version of Islam, but they were positively hostile to the traditional social structure and educational system of their region. They wanted new political regimes, not only independence but also parliaments and voting rights. For them, as many admitted, the West was both the example and the enemy.

Most people in the Middle East were still peasants and only vaguely affected by the new currents. They remained faithful to Islam, educated in the laws and ceremonies of the Qur'an. Some were drawn into new economic endeavors, such as the rug factories or cotton estates, but most continued to work by traditional methods and to rely heavily on village institutions. No serious change occurred in the lives of Middle Eastern women, still largely isolated in extended family households according to Islamic law. Even in the upper classes, few women came into contact with Western ideas, as even imperialist regimes did not try to alter this basic feature of Islamic life. A few Muslim leaders talked of trying to adapt the religion to modern life, and to use Islam as a unifying force for the whole civilization against Western pressure and nationalism alike. Islam was not an unchanging force, although it embraced strong traditionalist elements. Several religiously inspired revolts broke out against Europeans in north Africa, and Islamic belief in the superiority of their religion continued unabated, easily sufficient to doom Christian missionary movements in the region. In this context, Islam conveyed anger and anxiety, a role that was to continue into the 21st century.

CHINA FACES IMPERIALISM

China by the end of the 18th century had been able, proudly if not entirely realistically, to maintain its empire's isolation, which remained far more complete than in the days of Mongol rule, when Western travelers like Marco Polo had roamed widely through the vast country. The Chinese economy remained at this point largely self-sufficient, despite modest exports in return for gold. The Qing dynasty, although past its prime, was still functioning fairly smoothly in the hands of the fabled bureaucracy.

A mere 40 years later, China was forced to open its borders to new Western trading and cultural activities as a result of one of those imperialist wars barely noticed in Europe, involving handfuls of Western troops, which dramatically revealed the new balance of power between a declining imperial China and the industrial West.

British East India boats destroy Chinese junks during the Opium Wars period, 1841, in this 19th-century line engraving. (Granger Collection)

From the 1820s onward, Western traders became increasingly insistent on gaining access to the vast Chinese markets and the products of Chinese artisans. As they became better established in other parts of Asia, such as India, they gained new knowledge of the profit potential of greater Chinese trade. Growing wealth at home spurred new demand for Chinese vases, porcelain, and other artifacts. At the same time, the Qing dynasty lost vigor rapidly, in a process familiar in Chinese history but now fatefully juxtaposed against the new Western strength. Local rebellions began to increase early in the 19th century. A major uprising, the Taiping Rebellion, arose in the 1850s. Led by a man who claimed to be the younger brother of Jesus Christ, the rebels sought traditional peasant goals: lower taxes and more land. Peasants were pressed by a rapidly rising population; simultaneously, the efficiency of the central government declined. The bureaucracy could no longer collect taxes effectively, and the quality of the imperial army deteriorated. This made unrest harder to put down and more difficult to prevent. The government struggled for years with the Taiping rebels, finally requiring Western military support to conquer them. Increasingly, the government was forced to rely on locally trained militias, but these forces, newly

armed, often turned against the emperor as well, stepping up rebellion and banditry. The costs were staggering. Overall, the rebellion resulted in the loss of over 20 million lives, disrupting China even after the fighting ended.

The first clash between a waning empire and the greedy West occurred in the Opium War of 1839–1842. British merchants in India had been exporting opium for sale in China. Ironically, they still had trouble finding goods that would appeal to the Chinese market. Because of the adequacy of traditional Chinese manufacturing, factory-made textiles, for example, had little appeal. So opium was seen as an important item of exchange that would allow the West to pay for Chinese goods without offering valuable gold. However, the Chinese empire objected to the opium trade. Opium use was not traditional in China, and there was widespread knowledge of its harmful effects. Furthermore, the government continued to treat British representatives as annoying inferiors. A government effort to seize all opium in the harbor of Canton (Guangzhou) led to a fight with British sailors and an attempt to prohibit all British trade in the area. War followed, as the British blockaded the entire coast; the Chinese were powerless to resist because they had no effective navy. The Chinese finally yielded, paying for all British property they had destroyed, opening several ports including Canton and Shanghai to British merchants, and giving Britain the island of Hong Kong.

The defeat in the Opium War was a bitter blow to Chinese leaders, who would long remember not only the loss but also the fact that Britain was willing to fight for the right to export a substance that resulted in the addiction, albeit enslavement, of many Chinese people. But bitter memories did nothing to stop further Western penetration. On the heels of British gains came France and the United States, demanding new trading rights. By 1850, foreign colonies existed in a number of ports. A second war, in 1857, led to the opening of still more ports and additional

An English church in Shanghai, late 19th century: transporting Europe to China as literally as possible. Compare this style to the Jesuit approach in China, illustrated in chapter 20.

rights that allowed Westerners to trade and conduct missionary activity even in the interior. An Anglo-French army pushed to Beijing, driving the emperor from the city, in order to enforce these concessions.

These early imperialist advances did not alter the basic direction of Chinese policy. The Chinese leadership still believed that traditional ways were best, seeing Western gains as temporary setbacks like other brief invasions that had occurred earlier in Chinese history. No new measures were taken to either imitate or counter Western developments. For their part, Western nations, led by Britain and France, were learning that China was a weak empire, not all that different from the Ottomans in basic strength, and hence an easy victim for any modern state with a good navy. Ironically, by the middle of the 19th century, the Chinese government was not particularly interested in copying Western military technology—in contrast even to the Ottoman regime. Chinese officers regarded technology as uninteresting, treating engineers with contempt as social inferiors. The reverence for tra-

dition and for cultural as opposed to military or business concerns in the Confucian value system, plus the real weakness of the imperial administration at this point, combined to make innovation seem both undesirable and impossible.

Nonetheless, beneath the level of imperial administration, China was changing. Population growth continued, creating a great demand on the part of many peasants for land. A relatively small number of peasants even sought relief in emigration—an unusual development in Chinese history—as they were recruited by railroad or estate bosses in the United States and some parts of Latin America. This movement, however, had no real impact on continued unrest at home. At the same time, Western influence affected some Chinese as well. Missionary efforts converted small groups of Chinese to Christianity and promoted some wider interest in Western ways. More importantly, Western business activity in the open, or treaty, ports helped sponsor wider economic development on a regional basis. The ports grew rapidly in population and wealth; they stimulated market agriculture and some manufacturing, even a few mechanized factories, in the surrounding countryside; and they gave some individual Chinese business executives experience with Western commercial methods, often resulting in profit-making zeal. A few entrepreneurs and Christian converts began to gain experience abroad, some attending foreign universities, although this was for the time being the merest trickle against the backdrop of centuries of isolation.

Western imperialists remained uninterested in trying to take over China directly, which would have been a difficult task and was unnecessary, given their new access to Chinese trade. They even aided the Qing dynasty in putting down the Taiping uprising during the 1850s; Western regimes preferred a weak imperial administration to outright disorder. Given growing unrest over land, taxation, and corruption among many officials, the Qing dynasty became increasingly dependent on European—particularly British—assistance during the second half of

History Debate

CHINA'S 19TH-CENTURY SLUGGISHNESS

A key task in exploring culture is to understand its role in causing historical or current developments. But cultural causation, although real, is difficult to measure. China in the 19th century provides an important case in point. Historians debate the balance among three factors: the nature of Chinese culture, and particularly Confucianism, long a strength but now perhaps a weakness in response to unprecedented change; the deterioration of Chinese government and society—in other words, internal problems that were not however primarily cultural; and the nature and destructive force of outside intervention, including of course the pressure to expand the use of opium.

There is no question that China was slow to respond to Western intervention, despite a proud tradition of strength. The Confucian tradition—a core component of Chinese culture—is often blamed, not only by historians but also by subsequent Chinese leaders. Confucianism did engender two weaknesses in China's responses to modern Western pressure. It encouraged traditionalism, as opposed to praising innovation, and it tended to downplay science in favor of more literary cultural emphases. Chinese bureaucrats, in resisting Western models, reflected these Confucian principles.

Nevertheless, other Confucian societies, notably Japan, found it possible to modify but use the Confucian legacy as part of a commitment to change. Reduce the traditionalism and aversion to science, but keep the emphasis on group loyalty, obedience, and education, and a society could emerge with a strong basis for successful change. The basis would be perhaps different from that of the West, but no less effective.

Too much emphasis on culture, in China's case, may therefore be misplaced. Of course, there are other cultural components to consider, such as the long-standing aversion to foreigners (Japan shared this perspective to a degree, although earlier it had successfully and very deliberately imitated China). But in addition to culture, maybe as important, was the abusive manner of Western intervention, with its stress on opium trade, which hardly encouraged imitation. And there was a period of ineffective government as the Qing dynasty declined, plus massive population pressure. Cultural causation, and particularly Confucianism, needs to be understood in a more complex context in contemplating China's 19th-century dilemmas.

the 19th century. Western advisors were employed to improve the army and also increase efficiency in tax collection—a real paradox for an empire with the greatest bureaucratic tradition in the world. The use of Western advisors signaled a new awareness of the need to change. Some Chinese officials grew more interested in Western weaponry—as one writer put it, "Learn the technology of the Barbarians in order to control them." However, there still was no commitment to significant reform. Indeed, after the Taiping Rebellion was finally crushed in 1864, the government directed most of its efforts to restoring the prestige of the emperor and traditional Confucian principles. The government even tore up a rail line built by private interests in the 1870s, in the hopes of maintaining traditional ways. Such actions showed a firm desire to avoid westernization—indeed, some clashes with Christian missionaries occurred—but no grasp of what measures might be necessary to keep the Westerners out. Furthermore, the revival of traditional culture did not effectively deal with internal problems, as bureaucratic corruption increased

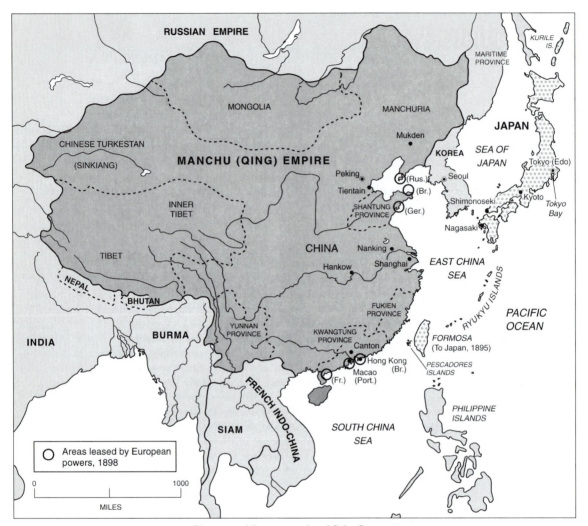

China and Japan in the 19th Century

and regional officials became harder to control. Some economic change occurred, in part because of Western influence in the port cities, but most Chinese manufacturing continued with traditional, hand-labor methods. The Chinese imported machine-made thread from Europe and the United States but continued to weave cloth manually. A handful of Chinese bankers and merchants built prosperous enterprises in the port cities, but most economic patterns stagnated.

Products exported to the West, such as tea and craft goods, were generated by small-scale operations, not the big estates characteristic of India or southeast Asia. China was moving only slowly toward the new principles of world commerce.

China, in fact, was faced with a situation that had no precedent. With the lone exception of Buddhism, foreign influence had never been seen as a source of inspiration—only as a nuisance to be outlasted through superior Chinese traditions. Most other cultures, including Japan, India, and even the Ottoman Empire, had more experience with selective borrowing. Chinese politics had long stressed not only tradition but also the prevention of conflict; it was not well suited for promoting change. Bureaucrats saw no particular reason for new, Western-style efficiency, since they defined bureaucratic talent more in terms of cultural interests and the promotion of harmony. The expansionist, profit-seeking values of Western-dominated trade were also at serious odds with Chinese tradition, despite the vigor of many Chinese business executives even in the past. An old Confucian adage held: "Acknowledgment of limits leads to happiness." This was hardly the capitalist spirit. Added to these cultural impediments were the growing weakness of the reigning dynasty and the stark pressure of rapid population growth, which diverted resources and political attention from other issues. Thus during most of the 19th century, China changed less rapidly than not only the West or Japan but also colonial India or Turkey.

This lack of change, in the context of 19th-century world history, meant an invitation to imperialism. France's conquest of Indochina from the 1850s onward was a blow to Chinese prestige, as Vietnam had long been an imperial protectorate. Russia, again on the advance, took over some territory in northern China in 1860.

The huge blow, however, came in 1894–1895, in a war with Japan. The Sino-Japanese War was triggered by a rebellion in Korea. Both Japan and China intervened to suppress this revolt. China had long treated Korea as a vassal state, whereas Japan, now rapidly industrializing, sought new spheres of influence. Both China and Japan also wished to prevent Russian action in Korea. But the two nations attacked each other as well, and Japan, with a modern navy, easily won—to the astonishment of literally the whole world outside of Japan. China was forced to yield not only Korea but also the island of Taiwan to the Japanese, plus the Liaotung peninsula. This region was regained only by the intervention of Western powers, who wanted no Japanese influ-

Western troops in the Boxer Rebellion raise the American flag on the Great Wall.

ence in China proper. China was shown to be a hollow power, unable to fend off its much smaller Japanese rival. This fact, plus concern about Japanese gains and the intense rivalry among the European states, which had by now consumed most of Africa and was searching for new pastures, produced a scramble for Chinese holdings.

The result, by 1900, was a series of new treaties giving France, Germany, Britain, and Russia long-term leases on a number of key ports and surrounding territories. This was not outright imperialist annexation, but it amounted to much the same thing as the imperial governments established their own local administrations. Russia also seized some additional northern territory outright. Western nations proceeded to expand their business influence from their new centers, building rail networks and setting up river shipping toward the Chinese interior.

At last, China started to decisively react. A new young emperor, Kuang-hsu, ordered military reforms, railroad building, and the extension of education. But Tzu-hsi, the widow of the previous emperor, seized power in 1898 and canceled these reforms, executing several of the leaders of the westernization movement. Tzu-hsi believed that China could still go its own way despite the presence of foreigners. She gave secret support to a society called the Righteous Harmony Fists, or

Boxers, who began killing Europeans and Christian Chinese in 1899. The Boxer Rebellion was suppressed fairly easily by a combined European-American military force, and China was required to grant additional legal privileges to foreigners, making them virtually immune from Chinese jurisdiction throughout the country. Tzu-hsi herself established a Western-style military structure and updated the education of imperial bureaucrats.

But by this point, shortly after 1900, it was clear that the waning Qing dynasty could not master the three forces bedeviling China: internal problems of decline and population growth; imperialist pressure; and a new force among Chinese who were aware of Western ways and eager to "modernize" their country along partially Western lines. From 1896 onward, a flood of Chinese students began to attend schools in Japan, Europe, and the United States, to gain access to the knowledge that their country so painfully lacked. They wanted to learn new technology, new science, and to an extent new organizational methods. In the process, they also learned about new political ideas, including nationalism but also liberalism, democracy, and socialism. There was no full agreement on what the new China should look like. Some reformers wanted only a limited imitation of the West, in purely practical matters; others desired a full parliamentary regime, new roles for women, an attack on Confucian tradition. However, there was agreement that change was essential and, increasingly, a sense that the existing regime had to go. Students returning from experiences abroad were joined by other students influenced by missionary schools or simply impressed by the growing translations of Western science and literature. Forced finally by defeat to open the gates to change, China's old regime could not contain the resulting flood.

THE NEED FOR FURTHER CHANGE

Even more clearly than the Ottoman Empire, China was poised on the brink of revolution by 1900. Population pressure caused more internal unrest in China than the Middle East, whereas the intellectual minority, newly aroused by Western ideas, was more excited in China than the Middle East, where Islam continued to exercise cultural control. Both areas, of course, suffered from weak imperial administrations and infuriating levels of interference from the Western powers and Russia. The resulting mixture was too unstable to last, and it did not survive. Revolution was to break out in China in 1911, ending the Qing dynasty the following year and installing a republic in its stead—ending the world's oldest imperial government. The Ottoman Empire crumbled in the aftermath of World War I, and the political cohesion of the Middle East was shattered as well. Both these developments highlighted the tensions that had developed as a result of internal change and external pressure, particularly during the last decades of the 19th century.

ISSUES AND CONNECTIONS

One way to understand the new kinds of Western pressure on China and the Ottomans is to compare their different responses. How and why did reform efforts diverge? At the same time, both regimes ultimately failed to meet the new Western challenge. Was this failure inevitable, given the nature of Western interference, or could different approaches and more forceful leadership have turned the tide?

The legacy of the long 19th century for the Middle East and China is twofold. In the first place, the leaders of these regions in the 20th and 21st centuries would deeply remember the failures and indignities of this period. They would vow to do things differently—though this did not mean that they would easily agree on what "differently" meant. Most dramatically, the 19th century set the stage for an unprecedented revolution in China, precisely to repudiate this past.

The second aspect of the legacy involves the forces that were developing by the later 19th century, often outside the regimes themselves. New student groups and foreign contacts in China, the rise of Arab and Turkish nationalism, the reassertion of Islamic values—these were elements that continue to play a role in both regions today.

SUGGESTED WEB SITE

On Ottoman reform, see http://landow.stg.brown.edu/victorian/history/dora/dora9.html.

SUGGESTED READINGS

On the Middle East, see W. R. Polk and R. L. Chambers, eds., *Beginnings of Modernization in the Middle East: The Nineteenth Century* (1968); H. A. R. Gibb, *Modern Trends in Islam* (1947); Alan Palmer, *The Decline and Fall of the Ottoman Empire* (1992); and M. G. S. Hodgson, *The Venture of Islam* (1971). See also David Kusher, *The Rise of Turkish Nationalism* (1977), and P. J. Vatikiotis, *The History of Egypt* (1985). On China, an excellent short survey is M. Gasster's *China Struggles to Modernize* (1983); for a related study, see Gilbert Rozman, *The Modernization of China* (1981), and Jonathan Spence, *The Search for Modern China* (1990). See also Immanuel C. Y. Hsu, *The Rise of Modern China* (1970); Mary Wright, ed., *China in Revolution: The First Phase* (1968); and Li Chien-nung, *The Political History of China, 1840–1928* (1956). A useful source collection is Ssu-yu Teng and J. K. Fairbank, *China's Response to the West: A Documentary Survey, 1839–1923* (1954).

For additional recent work, see Fatma Gocek, ed., *Social Constructions of Nationalism in the Middle East* (2002); Joseph Tse-Hei Lee, *The Bible and the Gun: Christianity and South China, 1860–1900* (2003); and R. K. Schoppa, *Revolution and Its Past; Identities and Change in Modern Chinese History* (2002).

26

Russia and Japan: Industrialization Outside the West

Among societies outside the West or the settler societies, Japan and Russia alone launched industrial revolutions by the late 19th century in response to the Western challenge. They escaped full Western economic dominance. Russia remained backward by Western standards, and its leaders grew painfully conscious of this fact. Even after 1900, its economy depended heavily on Western trade, technology, and capital; only revolution, in 1917, would seriously alter this situation. However, Russia had displayed dynamism in previous centuries despite an economic lag, and this pattern persisted during the 19th century. Russia continued to expand, although it met Western and, at the end of the century, Japanese resistance at key points. The nation gained territory in central Asia and the Far East, and it achieved important influence over new, small states in southeastern Europe. Finally, the Russians began to sketch their reaction to the Western example of industrialization. Without becoming Western, Russia tried to alter its social pattern to conform to the requirements of an industrial society, and by 1890, it had launched the early phases of a real industrial revolution.

The response of Japan was even more striking. Continuing its policy of isolation until the 1850s, when Western pressure forced new contacts, the Japanese then rapidly transformed their basic political and social institutions, generating initial industrialization and a military reform that soon made Japan Asia's leading power. These events more clearly than ever before divided Japan from its Chinese neighbor, although in fact they still shared many cultural and artistic customs. For a time, indeed, the Japanese seemed bent on imitating everything Western, as the tradition of isolation made it difficult to sort out which Western habits were essential to economic and military strength and which were optional. But no more than Russia did Japan become Western: a key aspect of both Japanese and Russian development was an ability to industrialize without sacrificing all the distinctive features of their societies.

Japanese and Russian efforts form the first examples of what can be called "latecomer" industrial revolutions, in that they began after the West had established a pronounced lead in the process. Latecomer industrialization involved certain factors that had not been necessary in the West. Capital was hard to come by for essential investment; neither Japan nor Russia had the West's advantage of prior colonial and merchant wealth. Unfamiliar technology must be mastered. There may be an inevitable tendency for the government to assume a greater role in latecomer industrializations than was true in the West, to amass scarce resources through taxation and to guide manufacturers in the adoption of foreign techniques. At least this was clearly the case in both Russia and Japan, where, in any event, previous political structures made a strong government seem logical. Latecomer industrialization may also impose greater strain on the population involved, because change is even more abrupt than it was in the West, where innovation caused enough tension even without these additional factors.

Although sharing both the ability to respond strongly to Western example and some common features of the latecomer pattern, Russian and Japanese initiatives differed in crucial respects. Russian efforts to change, and failures to change rapidly enough, produced a revolutionary climate by 1905, when the first Russian revolution broke out. Japan avoided revolution in a literal sense, although in some ways revolutionary transformation was imposed from the top down after an intense internal struggle in the 1860s. At the same time, Japan shifted its traditional policies more radically than Russia, in not only industrializing so rapidly but also adopting an aggressive diplomatic stance quite foreign to its own precedents.

Neither Russia nor Japan was fully industrialized by 1914; both would continue to lag behind the West for some decades still. Nevertheless, the 19th-century breakthroughs were crucial in both countries. They ultimately had an influence even beyond national borders, in showing people in other parts of the world that Western economic tutelage was not the only way to produce change, and that a strong response could keep Western imperialism at bay.

KEY QUESTIONS *Causes head the list here: why were Russia and Japan able to respond relatively successfully to the Western/world economy challenge? What factors did they share? Then of course, there were dissimilarities: how did the two reform processes differ, and why by 1914 was Russia, but not Japan, headed for revolution?*

RUSSIAN CONSERVATISM: AN ALTERNATIVE TO THE WEST

The first half of the 19th century saw relatively little change in Russian culture and society. Russian leaders were indeed proud of their seeming immunity to the revolts and tensions that plagued western Europe during the same period. After the defeat of Napoleon's armies, the Russian state viewed itself as one of the guardians of conservative order in Europe. Its acquisition of new territory in Poland at the Congress of Vienna, in 1815, furthered its long-standing interest in expansion. The Russian tsar Alexander I flirted with liberal ideas, and a few reforms were introduced, notably to improve the training of Russian bureaucrats. But neither the authoritarian state nor the tight system of Russian serfdom was seriously altered.

In December 1825, a minor revolt broke out, led by Western-minded army officers who wanted to see their country change. The Decembrist revolt was easily vanquished, but it inspired the new tsar, Nicholas I, to embrace more outright conservatism. The repression of political opponents increased, as the secret police expanded. The press and schools were tightly supervised. What political criticism survived did so mainly in exile, in places such as Paris and London, and with little impact on Russia itself.

In 1830–1831, Nicholas I brutally put down a nationalist uprising in Poland led by Catholics and liberal aristocrats who chafed under foreign rule. He also intervened in the revolutions of 1848, sending troops to Hungary in 1849 to help the Habsburg monarchy restore their government. Russia itself remained untouched by the revolt and agitation that spread virtually throughout western Europe.

Although the situation in Russia seemed calm, the country was, in fact, falling farther behind the technological and economic levels of the West. Russia responded to Western industrialization initially by a further tightening of labor obligations of the serfs, so that the great grain-growing estates would have more to export. Individual factories did sometimes use Western equipment, but there was no significant change in overall manufacturing or transportation methods. Russia remained a profoundly agricultural society based on essentially unfree labor. Russian aristocrats, conscious of the West's greater dynamism, attempted to conceal the differences by their enthusiastic embrace of European cultural styles, remaining up-to-date on the latest fashions in dress, dance, or painting, but this important cultural current did not close the economic and social gap between the two societies.

This gap was dramatically highlighted by an apparently minor though bloody war in the Crimea in the mid-1850s. Russian leaders had continued to peck away at Ottoman holdings in central Asia, maintaining what was by now a traditional foreign-policy interest. However, British and French power in the Middle East constituted a new force of opposition. When Nicholas provoked war with the Ottomans in 1853, the Western countries came to the sultan's aid. Essentially because of industrialization, which provided superior equipment and relatively rapid transport, the Western forces, far from home, prevailed over the Russian army in its own backyard. Both sides, however, suffered huge loss of life. The war's result was a particularly severe blow for a Russian regime that prided itself on military dynamism.

The Crimean War contributed to the greatest event of 19th-century Russian history, the emancipation of the serfs. Some aristocratic landlords were no longer sure that serfdom provided the most profitable system of labor. Many Russian leaders were also concerned with the periodic peasant uprisings, against their lack of land and freedom, that continued to punctuate Russian history even after the collapse of the great Pugachev Rebellion. Some upper-class Russians were swayed by ideals of liberty and humanitarianism, finding serfdom wrong in principle. Above all, Russian leaders, including the new tsar Alexander II, wanted to rid Russia of a social system that seemed to be holding it back in relation to the West. If Russia were to develop a more dynamic economy, it needed workers that were free to move to cities and factories. It needed to encourage better methods even in agriculture, which the easy reliance on servile labor prevented. It needed, in sum, a partial revolution from above.

THE BEGINNINGS OF RUSSIAN INDUSTRIALIZATION

The decision to emancipate the serfs came at roughly the same time as, in the United States and, shortly before, in Brazil, the decision to free slaves. Some of the motives, including humanitarianism and a desire to convert more fully to a free labor market, were also similar. No more than slavery did rigorous serfdom suit the economic needs of a society that could hold its own in modern world trade.

In some ways, the emancipation of the serfs in 1861 was more generous than the liberation of slaves in the Americas. Although aristocrats retained part of the land, including the most fertile holdings, the serfs got most of it—in contrast to slaves who received their freedom but nothing else. But Russian emancipation was careful to preserve essential aristocratic power and above all the tight grip of the tsarist state. The serfs obtained no new political rights at a national level. They were still tied to their villages until they could pay for the land they were given—the money from such a redemption going to the aristocrats. Many peasants, as a result, could still not travel freely or even sell their land, although some became more mobile. High redemption payments, in addition to state taxes, kept most Russian peasants miserably poor. Emancipation did bring change; it helped create a larger urban labor force. However, it did not spur a revolution in agricultural productivity, as most peasants continued to use traditional methods on their small plots. And it did not bring contentment; indeed, peasant uprisings became more rather than less common, as hopes for a brighter future now seemed dashed by the limits of change.

Alexander did, to be sure, introduce further reforms during the 1860s and 1870s. He created local political councils, the *zemstvos*, that had a voice in regulating roads, schools, and other conditions. The zemstvos gave some Russians, particularly middle-class people such as doctors and lawyers, new political experience, but they had no influence on national policy, where the tsar resolutely maintained his own power and that of the extensive bureaucracy. Alexander liberalized legal codes and created new courts. Reformers modernized the army, by encouraging promotion by merit and other organizational changes. Recruitment was extended, and many peasants learned new skills, including literacy, through their military service.

These adjustments, like emancipation itself, were important. They imitated some Western principles; the new law codes, for example, provided milder punishment for crimes and enforced equality before the law. However, they were not designed to create a Western society: they did not attack the fundamental power of the aristocracy and modify political authoritarianism. The reforms were sufficient to spur the beginnings of Russian industrialization. They were not sufficient to provide a stable social base for economic upheaval. Political as well as peasant unrest increased and provoked a return to more repressive measures.

From the 1870s onward, Russia began to construct an extensive railway network. It served as a vital link in the giant country—the establishment of the Trans-Siberian Railroad, connecting European Russia with the Pacific, was the crowning achievement of this drive, largely completed in the 1880s. Railroad facilities were also necessary to integrate Russia's wealth in coal and iron and to bring these resources, in turn, to markets—Russia's river system, running south to north, was not particularly useful in this regard. Moreover, rails aided Russia's drive to export grain, essential for earning capital to purchase Western machinery. The rail system, finally, helped spur a modern coal and metallurgical industry, for although some key equipment had to be purchased from the West, the government stimulated native industry as much as possible. By the 1880s, when Russia's railroad network had almost quintupled compared to 1860, modern factories had sprung up in Moscow, St. Petersburg, and several Polish cities, and an urban working class was growing at the same pace.

Russian industrialization was not unopposed, however. Quite apart from impoverished factory workers, who soon proved susceptible to revolutionary doctrines, some Russian leaders worried about the unsettling impact of this Western force. But industrialization appealed to the widespread desire to catch up with the West. It allowed further Russian territorial expansion in central Asia and northern China, for rails enabled Russia's massive armies to be moved more quickly and established technological superiority over many Asian states. Furthermore, Russian industrialization flowed in part from the authoritarian position of the state. Railroad development was a state-run operation. Many factories were also state-run, and the government oversaw some of the industrialization effort.

Under Count Witte, minister of finance from 1892 to 1903 and an ardent economic modernizer, the government enacted high tariffs to protect new Russian industry, improved its banking system, and encouraged Western investors to build great factories with advanced technology. As Witte put it, "The inflow of foreign capital is . . . the only way by which our industry will be able to supply our country quickly with abundant and cheap products." By 1900, approximately half of Russian industry was foreign owned and much of it foreign operated, with British, German, and French industrialists taking the lead. Witte and others were confident that government controls could keep the foreigners in line, rather than converting Russia into a new imperialist playground, and for the most part, they seemed correct. By 1900, Russia had surged to fourth rank in the world in steel production and was second to the United States in petroleum production and refining. Russian textile manufacture was also impressive. Long-standing Russian economic backwardness was beginning to yield.

This was still, however, an industrial revolution in its early stages. Russia's world position was a function more of its great size and population, along with rich natural resources, than of really thorough mechanization. Agriculture remained backward, as peasants had neither the means nor the motive to change their ways. Literacy was gaining and peasant habits did begin to change—for example, thanks to urban contacts, the rules of courtship relaxed, with more sexual overtones permitted—but agricultural methods lagged. This, in turn, retarded the growth of cities and made periodic famine a recurrent threat. Many Russian factories were vast—the largest, on average, in the world—and urban artisans also gained ground in fields such as printing. But the urban labor force, although expanding rapidly, was still a minority, and many workers had yet to convert to new work values. Nor did a powerful business class arise in Russia. Government controls and foreign investment produced industrialization without a surging middle class. Some Russian entrepreneurs showed impressive dynamism, and the number of businessmen and professionals increased, but Russian industrialization did not engender the kind of assertive, self-confident middle class that had arisen in the West. Industrialization was, in sum, still tentative, and it was definitely proceeding along distinctive lines in Russia.

THE FOUNDATIONS OF REVOLUTION IN RUSSIA

The nation's early industrialization increased the already fearsome tensions within the society. Peasant discontent, although not a constant force, continued to rise. Famines regularly provoked uprisings. Peasants, who deeply resented aristocratic estates and the redemption payments and taxes that burdened them, were also pressed by rapidly growing population levels, which augmented land hunger. Along with the peasantry, many educated Russians, including some aristocrats, clamored for revolutionary change. Their goals and motives varied, but in general they wanted political freedoms while maintaining a Russian culture different from that of the West, which they saw as hopelessly plutocratic and materialist. Upper-class radicals claimed that a spirit of community lay deep in the Russian soul, which could serve as the basis for an egalitarian society free from the injustice of the capitalist West. Many Russian radicals were anarchists who sought the abolition of all formal government. Although anarchism was not unknown in the West, it took on particular force in Russia in opposition to unyielding tsarist autocracy. Many anarchists turned to extremely violent methods, forming the first large terrorist movement in the modern world. Terrorism, in the form of assassinations and bombings, seemed an essential approach, given the lack of other political outlets. It appeared that anarchist terrorist tactics often focused more on destruction than on coherent political goals for the future. As the anarchist leader Bakunin put it:

Shooting of strikers in St. Petersburg, January 1905. This sort of bloodshed helped launch the revolution of 1905.

We have only one plan—general destruction. We want a national revolution of the peasants. We refuse to take any part in the working out of schemes to better the conditions of life; we regard as fruitless solely theoretical work. We consider destruction to be such an enormous and difficult task that we must devote all our powers to it, and we do not wish to deceive ourselves with the dream that we will have enough strength and knowledge for creation.

Not surprisingly, the recurrent waves of terrorism merely reinforced the tsarist regime's resolve to avoid further political change, in what became a vicious circle in late-19th-century Russian politics.

By the late 1870s, Alexander II pulled back from his reform interest, fearing that change was escalating out of control. Censorship of newspapers and political meetings tightened; many dissidents were arrested and sent to Siberia. Alexander himself was assassinated by a terrorist bomb in 1881, and his successors, while escalating the effort to industrialize, continued to oppose further political reform. New measures of repression were also directed against minority nationalities, as a conservative nationalism, hostile to internal minorities and Western influence alike, swelled in praise of Russian values. The Poles and other groups were carefully supervised, and persecution of the large Jewish minority increased, resulting in many executions and seizures of property; as a consequence, many Russian Jews emigrated. In general, moreover, the late-19th-century tsars sponsored a vigorous drive to impose Russian culture and language on the minority peoples. They thus tried to Christianize many Jewish children by force, while forbidding Poles and other

Searching passersby in Riga during the Revolution of 1905.

minorities from using their own language for public purposes. In response, many minority nationalist movements spread on an underground basis, joining the anarchists in their energetic, if illegal, resistance to the tsarist regime.

One final political current arose by the 1890s. A number of radical leaders, drawn from the same educated circles as the anarchists, were attracted to the Marxist doctrines that were being disseminated in the West. Largely underground or in exile, Marxist groups formed, committed to a tightly organized proletarian revolution. Although the Marxist movement remained small, its ideas took hold among some urban industrial workers, who chafed under the harsh conditions of the early factories and the illegality of ordinary trade union activity.

By 1900, the contradictory currents in Russian society may have made revolution inevitable. Although the forces demanding change were not united, and although extensive police work and

military repression kept most uprisings in hand, the combination of pressures may have been too powerful to resist. Peasants had little concern for the more formal political ideas; indeed, anarchist efforts to reach out to the people in previous decades had been largely ignored. Marxists and anarchists, in fact, often disliked each other, for indeed both their methods and goals were different. The small middle class, interested in some political voice but not eager for full-scale social upheaval, was yet another piece on the complex Russian chessboard. Revolution did come in 1905, after Russia had suffered another disastrous and surprising military defeat, this time at the hands of Japan, who opposed further Russian expansion in northern China and Korea. Defeat unleashed massive general strikes by urban workers and a tumultuous series of peasant insurrections. In response, the tsarist regime relaxed the constraints of the post emancipation rural system, allowing peasants greater freedom to buy and sell land and operate

Understanding Cultures

PERSISTENCE AND CHANGE IN RUSSIA

Even before the 19th century, Russia had a very westernized high culture. Its participation in Western music and literature increased during the long 19th century, though with some special Russian flavors. Reform efforts increased exposure to Western culture. There was more emphasis on science education and more contact with Western visitors, at least in the cities. By the 1850s, even before the reform currents began, Western-style department stores spread to Moscow and other cities, offering the upper class new opportunities at consumerism. By the 1890s, thanks to more urban contacts and looser community controls, sexual behavior among ordinary Russians became freer, suggesting parallels with patterns in the West.

Yet Russian culture did not become fully Western. There are three points here. In the first place, precisely because of new influences, a number of conservative critics specifically attacked the West in favor of what they saw as Russian values. They emphasized Russian spirituality against Western materialism, Russian community spirit against corrosive Western individualism and industrial exploitation, and Russian loyalty against Western political radicalism. Some of this approach can be found in Russia today, in efforts to define and maintain a separate identity.

Second, even as it changed, Russian popular culture remained distinctive. The importance of the Orthodox religion obviously differed from trends in the West. As Russian literacy spread, a new market for popular adventure stories opened—as in the West. But whereas Western stories often sided with outlaws, Russian stories almost always ended with the triumph of order and the state.

Third, even when they borrowed from the West, Russians were selective. While Western liberalism had some Russian audience, Western socialism turned out to have a larger one—ultimately, larger than in the West itself. This obviously reflected different social conditions in early industrial Russia, but it might reflect different values as well. It would certainly help cause different values.

The challenge, obviously, is to note real cultural change in Russia, but to note as well that it was not complete change and not change simply in Western directions.

independently of redemption payments and village controls. However, a halting pledge to appease middle-class sentiment by creating a national parliament, the Duma, was soon dashed by renewed political repression; the Duma became a hollow institution, satisfying no one. And no gains were offered to the Marxists at all. The prospect of further revolution loomed large and then became reality when Russia plunged into yet another conflict—World War I—hoping that battle would bring new territory and distraction from internal stress. The gamble failed and, in 1917, one of the great revolutions in world history took place.

THE CULTURE OF EASTERN EUROPE

Many smaller east European countries followed patterns similar to those of Russia during the later 19th century. New nations such as Romania, Bulgaria, and Serbia, free from Ottoman control, liberated the serfs, but amid restrictions that retained the bulk of the land for the aristocracy. Parliaments were established on superficially Western lines, but they had little power and were based on very limited voting rights. Most of the smaller east European nations industrialized less extensively than Russia and remained even more dependent, as agricultural producers, on Western markets.

Despite economic problems and political tensions, however, eastern Europe, including Russia, enjoyed an impressive cultural surge, a final ingredient in the complex developments that accompanied reactions to Western industrialization. Many Western artistic styles were appropriated. Russian and other east European novelists and essayists wrote in the romantic vein, glorifying national ways; the Russian novel enjoyed unprecedented popularity in the hands of writers such as Tolstoy, Turgenev, and Dostoyevsky. Composers such as Tchaikovsky brought romanticism to music. Modern art currents in the West also found an echo, as abstract painting and atonal music took shape in the hands of Russian practitioners soon after 1900. East European intellectuals also participated in the scientific developments of the later 19th century. The important experiments on conditioned reflexes conducted by a Russian physiologist, Ivan Pavlov, advanced the understanding of unconscious responses in human beings.

In many ways, then, eastern Europe seemed to be drawing closer to the West in cultural activity, continuing a pattern visible since the time of Peter the Great. With growing industrialization and some political impulses borrowed from the West, including Marxism, it seemed possible that, despite its political peculiarities, Russia might produce a version of Western civilization, just as it had moved into the Western diplomatic orbit in many respects.

However, east European culture remained ambivalent about the West. Although some intellectuals were ardent admirers of Western culture, others used only partially Western styles to comment on the distinctiveness of the Russian or Slavic spirit. Many novelists joined political conservatives in finding a unique soul in their people, which they believed should be exalted and protected against Western influence. Romanticism, in its east European manifestation, encour-

aged a vigorous set of cultural and political nationalisms, designed to capture the glories of Russian, or Ukrainian, or Serbian peoples. A Pan-Slavic movement arose also—particularly in Russia, which claimed leadership of Slavic Europe—that argued for Slavic unity against the more materialistic and individualistic West.

Furthermore, the masses in eastern Europe, mainly peasant, remained firmly attached to older traditions, including the Orthodox religion, different from those of the West and the partially westernized upper classes. Popular culture changed through the impact of growing literacy, rising urbanization, and military service, but it did not merge with the popular culture of the West. Indeed, popular resentment against growing Western influence, including the power of foreign capitalists, would be yet another revolutionary rallying cry during and after World War I.

By 1900, then, Russia and much of the rest of eastern Europe represented a distinctive amalgam of tradition and change. Principles of authoritarian rule remained virtually unaltered, but they now joined with diverse political opposition concentrated for the most part on sweeping revolution rather than purely liberal reforms. The tradition of territorial expansionism, although checked by resistance from the West and Japan, still ran strong. Pan-Slavic sentiments indeed encouraged new Russian influence in southeastern Europe. Massive social change had resulted from emancipation and early industrialization, but east European society continued to be more agricultural and in many ways more traditionalist than its Western counterpart. Finally, a larger ambivalence toward Western values persisted. East European intellectuals contributed creatively to general European artistic and scientific work, but a desire to define distinctive features, to resist full westernization, remained all-important in many quarters, both elitist and popular. Eastern Europe was, in sum, developing its own pattern of change as it entered the industrial age. This pattern would soon embrace a distinctive kind of revolution as well.

THE OPENING OF TRADE IN JAPAN

Even more than Russia, Japan faced new pressure from the West during the 1850s, although it took the form of a demand for more open trade rather than outright war. After a tense debate during the 1850s and 1860s, Japan's response was more direct than Russia's and, on the whole, more immediately successful. Despite the long history of isolation, Japanese society was better adapted than Russia's to the challenge of industrial change. Market forms were more extensive, reaching into peasant agriculture; levels of literacy were higher. Japan, nevertheless, had to rework many of its institutions during the final decades of the 19th century, and the process produced significant strain. The result, by 1900, was different from both purely Western patterns and the more obvious tensions of Russian society.

On the surface, Japan experienced little change during the first half of the 19th century. The Tokugawa shogunate remained intact, although there were signs that it was becoming less effective. The shogunate ran the country through a combination of central bureaucracy and alliances with the regional daimyos. It also encouraged some business interests and provided a central banking system. Japanese culture still relied heavily on Confucianism, and participation in Confucian schools grew rapidly. Traditional artistic and dramatic styles remained lively. The interest in Western science that had developed among a small number of scholars continued, through 18th-century contacts with the Dutch trading outpost in the port of Nagasaki, but no technological breakthroughs occurred. The Japanese boasted a productive agriculture and considerable rural manufacturing, but there were signs of economic stagnation, particularly in a growing number of peasant riots against poor conditions. Nevertheless, there is no reason to believe that Japan was on the verge of significant change before change was thrust upon it.

Commodore Perry's "Black Ship" as seen by the Japanese, 1854.

In 1853, the American commodore Matthew Perry arrived with a fleet in Edo Bay, near Tokyo, insisting through threats of bombardment that Americans be allowed to trade. In 1854, he returned and won the right to station an American consul in Japan; two ports were opened to commerce. Britain, Russia, and Holland quickly won similar rights. As in China, this meant that Westerners living in Japan would be governed by their own representatives, not by Japanese law. Other privileges soon followed, along with a few military skirmishes. Leading Western nations simply insisted on their need and right to trade, as part of the expanding world economy, while also seeking fishing rights in Japanese waters. For several decades, they limited Japan's ability to decide on its own tariffs. Russian pressure was a problem as well, as the nation's eastward expansion had already produced a few small clashes over control of islands in the North Pacific.

Some Japanese had already grown impatient with strict isolation. More important was the now obvious fact that Japan could not compete with Western navies and so had to defer to their interests. But many Japanese leaders, including conservatives who feared Western influence, wanted to strengthen their government in order to control their nation's future. Their interest caused them to bypass the shogun and appeal directly to the emperor for support. Long secluded as a religious figure, the emperor now began to gain power.

In the 1860s, a political crisis came into the spotlight, involving a clash between many samurai and the shogunate. The crisis was marked by attacks on foreigners, including one murder of a British official, matched by the Western naval bombardments of feudal forts. Virtual civil war broke out in 1866 as the samurai eagerly armed themselves with surplus weapons from the American Civil War, causing Japan's aristocrats to finally come to terms with the sheer power of Western armaments. When the samurai defeated a shogunate force, a number of Japanese finally were shocked out of their traditional reliance on their own superiority, with one author arguing that the nation was, compared to the West with its technology, science, and humane laws, only half-civilized.

This multifaceted crisis came to an end in 1868, with the proclamation of rule by a new emperor named Mutsuhito, whose regime was soon called *Meiji*, or "enlightened rule." Backed by some samurai leaders, the new emperor managed to put down the troops of the shogunate and gradually built up support, establishing his capital in Edo, now named Tokyo. The crisis period had been shocking enough to allow further changes in Japan's basic political structure—changes that went much deeper at the political level than those introduced by Russia from 1861 onward. With the chief ministers actually taking the major initiative, the imperial government sponsored three decades of rapid change, designed to make Japan competitive with the West and thus save national independence in what was, for Japan, a radically new and perilous environment.

The key to the Japanese response was heightened governmental centralization. Meiji leaders abolished feudalism, as the regional lords surrendered their land rights to the government. Ministries in the central government now directed national policy in a surprisingly quick political adjustment. The ministers in the Meiji period were committed to further reform, as a govern-ment-sponsored reshaping of Japanese society was underway. Such reshaping, however, did not call into question the Japanese belief in their independence and basic superiority of their culture. An early Japanese visitor to the White House wrote a self-satisfied poem that captured part of the national mood:

> We suffered the barbarians to look upon the glory of our Eastern Empire of Japan.

JAPANESE INDUSTRIALIZATION IN RESPONSE TO THE WEST

The Japanese combination of rapid adaptation and firm belief in the validity of their own values and institutions may explain the distinctive Japanese response in matching Western pressure without outright revolution and full-scale westernization. Japanese leaders carefully blended economic political change with existing institutions and values.

Reform interests, in the Meiji period, focused on several targets. A new army was established, modeled on the German system. It was based on the universal conscription of young males. The training of officers improved, as new men replaced older feudal generals. Military armament was brought up to Western standards, and a navy was formed, initially with the aid of Western advisors. The government also quickly introduced Western public-health measures, which promoted population growth.

Mass education spread rapidly from 1872 onward, for women as well as for men. Elite students at the university level often emphasized science, many of them studying technical subjects abroad. The rapid assimilation of a scientific outlook was a major new component of Japanese culture. Other cultural changes ranged farther afield. Fearful of embarrassment in Western eyes—a factor of growing importance in world history—the Japanese government even tried to outlaw homo-

The first Japanese parliament meets, 1890.

sexuality around 1900 and to increase differences in dress between boys and girls.

Reform also meant further political change. A new constitution took effect in 1890, again based on the German model. A two-house parliament, elected by men of property, served under the supreme emperor. The parliament did not develop extensive powers, as the emperor named his own ministers and controlled basic policy. But several political parties competed for votes. The Japanese political style now combined centralized imperial rule with limited representative institutions; the combination gave great power to a new oligarchy of wealthy businessmen and aristocrats, who influenced the emperor and also pulled strings within parliament. This rule by an elite echoed earlier Japanese reliance on cooperation rather than competition in politics, as well as a tradition of considerable deference to the authority of the upper classes. Here was a clear case of blending Japanese values with Western-style institutions.

Above all, reform meant industrialization, with the government taking a far more active role than its Russian counterpart. New banks were created by the government to fund growing trade and to provide capital for industry. State-built railroads spread across the country, and rapid steamers connected the islands. Although Japan still relied heavily on home or small-shop production, particularly of goods such as silk cloth that were widely exported, factory industry expanded steadily. Finally, the market emphasis on agriculture increased, as new methods were introduced to raise output to feed the growing cities.

Japanese state initiative not only built transportation and banking systems but also led to the government operation of mines, shipyards, and metallurgical plants. Scarce capital and the unfamiliarity of new technology seemed to compel state direction, which also served to supervise the many foreign advisors the Japanese required. Japan established a ministry of industry in 1870, and it quickly became one of the key government agencies, setting overall economic policy as well as operating specific sectors. However, private initiative played a role as well. In textiles, private businessmen, many of them from older merchant families, ran the leading companies. In other industries, government concerns, tax-financed, were later sold to private interests, to the profit of the latter. Close collaboration between government agencies and private firms, especially big business concerns, early formed a hallmark of the new Japanese economy.

History Debate

DIFFERENT CONFUCIAN PATHS

Japan and China were both societies strongly shaped by Confucian beliefs, yet Japan proved much more quickly capable of adaptation to change. Why? Some clues lie in prior cultural experience. China had been Confucian longer, and more people had a stake in preserving the emphasis on tradition and a nontechnical education. Japan already had imitated other cultures, as when it had turned to China during an earlier period, and had learned that one could engage in imitation without destroying all vestiges of one's own distinct culture. Its feudal traditions also encouraged a more prompt response to the West's military challenge. Its interpretation of Confucianism was different; hence, it had a more extensive educational system prior to Western influences. (Consider as another example of its intellectual open-mindedness the earlier "Dutch school" interest in Western science.) Scorn for merchants was less intense in Japan than in China, and Confucianism had not led to as complete a subjugation of women.

Cultural factors may not provide the primary explanation for the new differentiation between China and Japan. Japan had the good fortune of a stronger government when interaction with the West occurred. It also faced much less population pressure at that point.

Both China and Japan ultimately had to modify Confucianism. Both preserved elements of the Confucian heritage, but in very different 20th-century political and economic systems. At the beginning of the 21st century, however, some observers wondered whether the same heritage might draw the societies of east Asia, all now dynamic, into a renewal of more commonly shared patterns.

Although Japanese big business developed rapidly, early industrialization also depended on the massive exploitation of workers, particularly women workers. Tens of thousands of women were sold for labor service by fathers or husbands in the overpopulated Japanese countryside. They worked particularly in the silk industry, developed by the state on a labor-intensive basis to capture vital export earnings as Japan surpassed China in producing this luxury commodity.

CULTURAL AND ECONOMIC EFFECTS OF JAPANESE INDUSTRIALIZATION

As had earlier occurred in the West, industrialization altered the existing social structure. Only a

handful of aristocrats and people from the samurai warrior class entered the ranks of successful businessmen. A new elite was formed that embraced leading entrepreneurs for the first time, and while old merchant families contributed to this group, talented people from diverse backgrounds, including former peasants, now rose to the top. Among the masses, the rise of a huge, property-less class of urban workers was a new development. Both peasants and workers endured low wages and high taxes, as Japanese leaders used cheap labor to compete with Western enterprise and to amass the capital needed for further investment. And while the new elite did not cultivate the luxurious life style of Western business magnates, being content with lower profit rates, it did insist on retaining power. Unions and lower-class political parties, although they began to emerge by 1900, made only slow

Women of Fashion Sewing, Japanese woodblock print, 1887.

headway, and a militant socialist movement was outlawed without difficulty.

Many Japanese copied Western fashions as part of the effort to become modern. Western-style haircuts replaced the samurai practice of a shaved head with a top knot—another example of the fascinating westernizing of hair throughout modern world history. Western standards of hygiene spread, and the Japanese became enthusiastic tooth brushers and consumers of patent medicines. Japan also adopted the Western calendar and the metric system. Few Japanese converted to Christianity, however, and despite fads imitating Western popular culture, the Japanese managed to preserve an emphasis on their own values. What the Japanese wanted and got from the West involved practical techniques; they planned to infuse these with a distinctively Japanese spirit.

Thus, in education, an initial surge of interest in Western schooling in the 1870s, which included the use of hundreds of European and American teachers, yielded in the 1880s to a reassertion of Japanese group loyalty and attacks on excessive individualism. New exposure to science changed culture, but the growing stress on nationalism provided a new focus for traditional beliefs in Japanese cohesion and distinctiveness.

Japanese family life retained many traditional emphases, as opposed to Western customs. To be sure, unprecedented population growth forced increasing numbers of people off the land, which disrupted families and caused the unusual reliance on women's work in industry. However, the Japanese were eager to maintain the traditional inferiority of women in the home. A new law promoted monogamy, but in practice, mistresses were still widely accepted in the upper classes. The position of Western women seemed repellent. Official Japanese visitors to the United States were appalled by what they saw as the aggressive, domineering ways of women: "The way women are treated here is like the way parents are respected in our country." Standards of Japanese courtesy also contrasted with the more open and boisterous behavior of Westerners—particularly Americans. "Obscenity is inherent in the customs of this country," noted another samurai visitor to the United States. Other basic features of Japanese life, including diet, were maintained in the face of Western influence. Japanese religious values were also distinctive. Buddhism lost some ground, although it remained important, and Confucianism was undermined through the new emphasis on science in the schools. But

Shintoism, which appealed to the rising nationalist concern with Japan's own unique mission and the religious functions of the emperor, won new interest.

By 1900, Japan's industrial success did not bring the country to Western levels, and the Japanese remained intensely fearful for their independence. Economic change, and the tensions as well as the power it generated, however, produced a shift in Japanese foreign policy. With only one previous exception, the Japanese had never before been interested in territorial expansion, but by the 1890s, they joined the ranks of imperialist powers. Partly this shift was an imitation of Western models, and at the same time it was an effort to prevent Western encroachment. Imperialism also relieved some strains within Japanese society, giving displaced samurai a chance to exercise their military talents elsewhere and providing symbols of nationalist achievement for the populace as a whole. The Japanese economy also required access to markets and raw materials. Because Japan was poor in many basic materials, including coal and oil for energy, the pressure for expansion was particularly great.

Japan's quick victory over China, in the quarrel for influence over Korea in 1894–1895, was a first step. Japan convincingly demonstrated its new superiority over all other Asian powers. Humiliated by Western insistence that it abandon the Liaotung peninsula, the Japanese planned a war with Russia as a means of striking out against the nearest European state. A 1902 alliance with Britain was an important sign of Japan's arrival as an equal player in the Western-dominated world diplomatic system. The Japanese were also eager to undermine Russia's growing strength in east Asia, after the completion of the Trans-Siberian Railroad. Disputes over Russian influence in Manchuria and Japanese influence in Korea led to the Russo-Japanese War in 1904, which Japan won handily on the basis of its superior navy. In 1910, Japan annexed Korea outright; it was now not only a modern industrial power but also a new imperialist force as well.

THE STRAIN OF MODERNIZATION

Japan's success by 1900 was amazing. Its victories over China and then Russia surprised virtually every observer outside of Japan. There is no question that Japan's rapid transformation, like its more recent success in becoming one of the most advanced industrial societies in the world, constitutes a unique achievement. Furthermore, Japan—unlike Russia or major parts of the West—prepared the groundwork for industrialization without the serious threat of popular revolution.

However, this achievement, even combined as it was with significant currents from earlier Japanese culture and political styles, had its costs. Many Japanese conservatives resented the passion that some Japanese displayed for Western fashions. Their concern helped ensure that Japanese women, initially the subject of some reform interest, would be mainly confined to family roles. Nevertheless, disputes between generations, with the old clinging to traditional standards, the young more interested in Western culture, were commonplace and very troubling in a society that stressed the importance of parental authority. Social tensions added to the strain, as expectations rose more rapidly than standards of living. Crowded conditions in the growing cities produced misery at least as great as in earlier Western slums. Rising divorce rates—Japan had the highest in the world by 1900—showed another kind of strain.

Some tension translated into politics, even with the narrow voting system. Political parties in Japan's parliament, the *Diet*, sometimes clashed with the emperor's ministers over rights to determine policy. The government frequently had to dissolve the Diet and call for new elections, seeking a more workable parliamentary majority.

Another kind of friction emerged in intellectual life. Many Japanese scholars emulated Western philosophies and literary styles. But other intellectuals retained an interest in more traditional forms and expressed a deep pessimism about the Japanese loss of identity in a changing world. Some wanted the government to become more fully Western; many were concerned about jobs, as universities tended to turn out more graduates than the economy could handle. The underlying theme was confusion about a Japan that was no longer traditional, but not Western either. What was it? Thus, some writers spoke of Japan heading for a "nervous collapse from which we will not be able to recover."

As an antidote to social and cultural insecurity, Japanese leaders urged national loyalty and devotion to the emperor, and with considerable success. The official message promoted Japanese virtues of obedience and harmony that the West lacked. School texts thus stressed:

> Our country takes as its base the family system; the nation is but a single family, the imperial family is our main house. We the people worship the unbroken imperial line with the same feeling of respect and love that a child feels towards his parents. . . . The union of loyalty and filial piety is truly the special character of our national polity.

Nationalism was a partially new force in Japan, and of course it was common in the West and other parts of the world in 1900 as well. However, Japanese nationalism built on traditions of superiority and cohesion, deference to rulers, and the new tensions generated by rapid change. It became if not a deeper force in Japan than elsewhere, at least one that played a unique role in justifying sacrifice and struggle in a national mission to preserve independence and dignity in a hostile world. Nationalism, along with the firm police repression of dissent, certainly helps explain why Japan avoided the revolutionary pressure that plagued Russia, China, and other countries after 1900, and also the kind of unrest that had characterized early Western industrialization around 1848.

Japan's traditions thus enabled it to foster rapid change from above, without the need for a literal revolution to either purge the existing system or respond to the undeniable tensions that modernization produced. The result, by 1900, was a dynamic country newly powerful on the world scene, shaping a distinctive kind of industrial society. No other country would match its achievements for over half a century.

ISSUES AND CONNECTIONS

Placed in a broader context, Russian and Japanese industrialization points in several directions. What aspects of Russian and Japanese societies explain why their trajectory differed from that of China or the Ottoman Empire, or indeed of Latin America? Another comparison: how did later industrializations compare to the earlier versions in the West, for example in the role of the state, or in the degrees of strain involved? Finally, Russia and Japan must be compared, for the reform processes and the nature of industrialization differed in the two cases, with different 20th-century results.

Connections are obvious. The surge of reform and industrialization by 1900 forms the basis for the growing importance both of Japan and of Russia in world affairs through much of the 20th century. The way Japan handled its degree of westernization, imitating but not completely, has continued to characterize Japan into the 21st century. Russia changed more, because of the massive, intervening revolution. But key aspects of its early industrialization and its evolving relationship to the West provide clues to the nation today, even so.

SUGGESTED WEB SITES

On the emancipation of the serfs and later peasant life, see http://russianculture.about.com/culture/russianculture/msub23.htm. On the formation of

Meiji industrial policy, including an early industrial fair and Japan's wars with China and Russia, see http://www.Meiji.com/index.html.

SUGGESTED READINGS

A. Gerschenkron, *Economic Backwardness in Historical Perspective: A Book of Essays* (1962), helps define the conditions of latecomer industrialization. Russian reforms and economic change are discussed in W. Blackwell, *The Industrialization of Russia*, 2nd ed. (1982), and Jerome Blum, *Lord and Peasant in Russia from the Ninth to the Nineteenth Century* (1961). On social and cultural developments, see Victoria Bonnel, ed., *The Russian Worker: Life and Labor under the Tsarist Regime* (1983); Barbara Engel, *Mothers and Daughters: Women of the Intelligentsia in Nineteenth Century Russia* (1983); and Jeffrey Brooks, *When Russia Learned to Read: Literacy and Popular Culture* (1987). On another vital area of eastern Europe, see L. Stavrianos, *The Balkans, 1815–1914* (1963).

Japan in the 19th century is viewed from the perspective of modernization in R. Dore, ed., *Aspects of Social Change in Modern Japan* (1967). For a comparative view, see Peter N. Stearns, *Starting School: The Rise of Modern Education in France, the United States, and Japan* (1997). See also W. W. Lockwood, *The Economic Development of Japan: Growth and Structural Change 1868–1938* (1954); J. C. Abegglen, *The Japanese Factory: Aspects of Its Social Organization*, rev. ed. (1985); Hugh Patrick, ed., *Japanese Industrialization and Its Social Consequences* (1973); Andrew Gordon, *The Evolution of Labor Relations in Japan* (1985); R. H. Myers and M. R. Beattie, eds., *The Japanese Colonial Empire, 1895–1945* (1984); and E. O. Reischauer, *Japan, the Story of a Nation* (1981). Recent work includes Rudra Sil, *Managing Modernity: Work, Community and Authority in Late-Industrializing Japan and Russia* (2002).

World War I and the End of an Era

One of the most devastating wars of all time broke out in Europe in 1914. World War I had international significance and international causes. It marked the beginning of the end of western Europe's world supremacy and ended a major period in the world's history. This short chapter sums up the factors that led to the massive conflict. The same factors help explain why the conflict was so decisive.

Dramatic events are involved in the end of many eras in world history, of course. The collapse of the great classical empires might be compared to World War I, although their collapse occurred over a far longer period of time. World War I had its own character, however. Although many Europeans launched the war almost eagerly, thinking it would lead to glory and power, the mood soon changed. By the war's end, many people knew that an age had ended. The causes of the war highlighted the century of imperialism, but they also led to the erosion of Europe's dominance.

KEY QUESTIONS *What major changes were accumulating by 1914? What were the causes of World War I? Did the war result from purely diplomatic issues and miscalculations among the European powers, or did it suggest wider breaks in the patterns of world history that had developed during the previous century?*

THE ONSET OF WORLD WAR I

Events soon after 1900 signaled an end to what some historians have called the "long 19th century."

Item: Women obtained the right to vote in several Scandinavian countries plus Australia, and feminist agitation heated up in other parts of Western society.

History Debate

CAUSES OF WORLD WAR I

For many decades, even after World War II, historians and others passionately discussed the causes of World War I in terms of national responsibility. The big issue was whether the Germans were solely, or almost entirely, responsible. This was the assumption in the Versailles Treaty that punished Germans so badly. The argument was that Germany was war-hungry, could and should have restrained the Habsburgs, was so anxious about the two-front war that they launched action early, and so on. Not everyone agreed. There were discussions of early Russian mobilization: Russia, less efficient and huge, took longer to mobilize its armies than did Germany, so Russia started even earlier, which helped scare the Germans. How much were the Habsburgs at fault for being so edgy about southern Slav nationalism that they wanted to punish Serbia once and for all? How about the British, who might have held back and tried harder to prevent all-out war?

Today, these discussions seem outmoded, though the issues are still interesting. More attention today goes to larger factors, such as industrial competition, or the spill-over impact of imperialist rivalry. Did World War I suggest fundamental flaws in European society? Or is the idea of national faults or even the deficiencies of individual leaders still relevant?

Item: Australia became fully independent in 1900, a symbol of the changing role of the European settler societies in world history.

Item: A Chinese revolution in 1911 toppled the imperial system for the first time since the collapse of the Han dynasty. China was in the throes of massive change.

Item: A Mexican revolution began in 1910 that called into question some of the political and social arrangements that had been common in 19th-century Latin America.

Item: Japan's victory over Russia and the Russian revolution of 1905 signaled dramatic new power alignments and the potential for turmoil in one of the world's major empires.

Item: The outbreak of World War I in 1914 launched a conflict that would have massive effects in Europe and the Middle East, with important spillover in east Asia and the Pacific, south Asia, Africa, and North America. The war pitted Britain, France, and Russia against Germany and the Habsburg monarchy—the world's most heavily armed nations came to blows through rival alliance systems. Other areas joined as colonies of the European powers or independently through hopes of territorial gains or other advantages. By the time the war ended in 1918, the 19th-century world order had been severely disrupted, although many Western leaders, eager to return to what they called *normalcy*, refused to recognize this fact.

The causes of World War I hardly sum up all the major trends that had emerged by the end of the 19th century, but they capture a fair number. The specific trigger for the war lay within the small nations of southeastern Europe, recently independent from Ottoman control. Ottoman decline had created a vacuum of power in this region that continues to this day. The new Balkan states, all highly nationalistic, frequently quarreled among themselves, conducting two regional wars before 1914. Russia and the Habsburg monarchy vied for influence in the area, hoping to distract their own peo-

Women help carry heavy rucksacks to the station during Germany's troop mobilization. The rifles are decorated with flowers.

ples from internal tensions. Russia sponsored Slavic nationalism, whereas the Habsburgs, with large and restless Slavic minorities, tried to suppress the same force. In 1914, a Serbian nationalist assassinated a member of the Habsburg royal family. Austria threatened war. Russia backed Serbia. Then the larger European alliance system came into play. Germany feared abandoning Austria lest it face Russia and France alone. France and, more reluctantly, Britain decided they had to support Russia. Rigid diplomacy and fervent nationalism among all the European great powers parlayed a regional crisis into full-scale war. Europe's alliance system, combined with growing military rivalry and massive armaments, thus trapped the major powers into decisions that led inevitably to war.

Larger issues were at play, as the causes of war revealed massive fault lines in Western society. Huge weapons industries had evolved in all the powerful European nations, partly because of imperialist rivalries, partly to ensure sales to influential industrialists. Arms races—particularly navy-building competitions and especially between Britain and Germany—enhanced public anxiety and made it more difficult for nations to compromise when disputes broke out. Russia, Germany, and France all had rigid strategic plans that encouraged prompt military action—in the hope, which proved completely illusory, of delivering quick knockout blows to the enemy. Germany, for example, hoped to knock France out quickly, to concentrate on Russia. But this plan involved moving through Belgium, which would galvanize British fear and outrage.

Imperialism had created a growing sense in Europe that aggressive expansionism was normal state policy. But by 1914, the opportunities for further colonies were essentially exhausted, and the fervor that had gone into empire building now turned back on Europe itself. Politicians had increasingly pointed to nationalist triumphs as a means of wooing voters, and the habit persisted. Russia and Austria–Hungary, keenly aware that they had fallen behind in imperialist races, hoped for triumphs that would divert public opinion.

European political and military leaders also worried about broader social tensions within their societies. Labor unrest was mounting, joined in some cases by feminist agitations and the push for independence by other repressed groups such as, in Britain's case, the Irish. Many officials worried that internal difficulties would erode national power—believing that it would be wisest to engage in war now, while strength was still high. Others argued that a successful war would unify the population, reducing the strength of socialist dissent. Ordinary people, bored or oppressed by industrial life, saw war as an exciting option—unaware of how devastating industrial warfare would actually be. Boys in various social classes had been raised on a diet of toy soldiers and aggressive sports—war seemed a glorious prospect in societies in which the importance of masculinity was asserted but not always easily expressed. The enthusiasm for war, in sum, drew on a number of tensions and anxieties created by industrial society.

Europe's decision to embark on a war also reflected its position in the world, strengths and weaknesses alike. Europeans were feeling at least vaguely threatened by the rise of societies outside their borders. Japan's industrial and military surge, plus stirrings in China, made some European nationalists talk of a new "yellow peril" that might displace Western supremacy. U.S. economic rivalry was keenly felt. British observers, greeting the new century in 1900, wondered if their days of easy empire were numbered, given new rivals and the sheer numbers of its colonial peoples. Oddly, given Britain's strength, but revealingly, they looked forward to the new century with real dread. These anxieties might, of course, have prompted a new European unity, in order to protect their general interests, but national divisions ran too deep for this.

Instead, countries concerned about their future turned to the familiar, nationalist military response. In essence, Europeans worried about their world position, but at the same time they assumed a position of assured dominance, believing it was safe to engage in internal conflict. This assurance would lead, among other things, to a rapid impulse to extend European warfare to the colonies themselves and to use colonial troops on the European front. The result was a genuine world war and one that would redefine world alignments.

But war in an industrial age, and in the changing world context, had itself changed. Although many Europeans entered this conflict optimistically, assuming a quick and glorious end, World War I resulted in unprecedented dislocation and death, and a host of unforeseen consequences. A new period in world history was baptized in blood, as the most powerful civilization tore itself apart.

A WORLD HISTORY WATERSHED

Even more than the fall of Constantinople to the Turks in 1453, World War I constituted an event that reshaped world history. Along with other developments, such as upheaval in east Asia, it furthered a realignment of power in the world. The war also promoted other shifts, such as changes in gender relations in Western society, that had been taking shape more gradually. It spawned one of the world's great revolutions, in Russia, that had its own impact on other societies. It also caused the final collapse of the Ottoman Empire, and the Middle East has never been the same. The use of troops from Africa and India energized nationalisms there. And the Far East was disrupted, particularly through new Japanese initiatives during and after the war. World War I, in other worlds, striking in its own right, was prologue to a long and lasting global drama. The Western powers would seek to return the world to its prewar condition after the great conflict ended, but their success was both fleeting and superficial. A new age was brewing.

ISSUES AND CONNECTIONS

World War I created a number of new problems and, for some groups and some parts of the world, new opportunities. There is no question about that. The chief issue is to figure out whether the war emerged from deep, if partly unseen, weaknesses in Western society and its relationship to the wider world, or whether the war can be explained more simply and then interpreted as the cause of new weaknesses. A specific example: World War I undoubtedly triggered the Russian Revolution, which then had huge consequences not only in Russia but in much of the rest of the world. Some historians think that revolution was inevitable anyway, and also the revolutionary tensions help explain why Russia was so eager to go to war. What about social hostilities in other countries, such as Germany or Britain? Socialism was rising, strike movements were increasing, and this might suggest some kind of new breakdown even aside from the war, which the war then made worse. Many statesmen who decided on war were partly motivated by their desires to distract from social problems they did not know how to solve. Even feminist demands, in Britain, added to anxieties of those in charge. Then there was the growing concern about growing strengths in other parts of the world, east Asia for example, that might challenge European control. Thus, did the war result from the end of the 19th-century framework, and then confirmed and intensified this collapse? Or was it the tragic result of more superficial European diplomacy, with a disastrous heritage?

Today, the European countries that fought in the war are mostly close friends. It took another war to achieve this, but World War I helped set in motion a reconsideration of what Europe was all about. Other aspects of the war linger still, some for better, some for worse. The war gave women in Western society new chances to work. They then were pushed back home, but ultimately the momentum returned, changing gender relations dramatically. The war led to the collapse of the Ottoman Empire, and we are still living with the results of the lack of any remotely great power in the Middle East. The war raised new questions about Western dominance from Africa to India and beyond, and that helped set the stage for the global society of today. Most importantly, the war established a new level of military horror, which still marks the world's experience of and thinking about war itself—though tactics have changed greatly in part because of the experience of 1914–1918.

The cemeteries of World War I, dotting places like northern France, are quiet, largely forgotten, though still moving when one sees them. But the war is an active presence still, for what it set in motion.

SUGGESTED WEB SITE

On World War I, see http://www.WorldWarI.com.

SUGGESTED READING

On the causes of World War I, see James Joll, *Origins of World War I* (1980), and K. Robbins, *The First World War* (1984). For a wider view, see Eric Hobsbawm, *The Age of Extremes: A History of the World, 1914–1991* (1996), and G. Barraclough, *An Introduction to Contemporary History* (1968).

Recent work includes Sean Cashman, *America Ascendant: From Theodore Roosevelt to FDR* (1998); Aviel Roshwald, *European Culture in the Great War* (1999); Robert Zieger, *America's Great War: World War I and the American Experience* (2000).

CONTACTS AND IDENTITIES

Part V The World's First Industrial Period, 1750–1914

It was impossible for any society of any significant size to avoid intense global contacts during the period 1750–1914. For most societies, the level of contact increased steadily, particularly after about 1850. By then, the impact of steam shipping, the telegraph, and other new technologies was effectively shrinking the world. So were innovations such as the Suez and, later, Panama canals. Japan, China and Korea were forced open to new global interactions.

In contrast to the early modern period, contact during the long 19th century meant substantial cultural pressure from the West, and also from those who advocated reforms along Western lines. This raised huge questions of identity. Egyptians debated the veiling of women around 1900, often in terms of Islamic identity issues: would dropping the veil help modernize Egypt, making it a more respectable civilization, or would it mean the surrender of a key symbol of identity? Older Africans worried about the newly zealous missionary religions, which obviously cut into traditional values and meanings.

Japanese leaders sought ways to maintain identity amid rapid imitation of many Western ways. The emphasis on Shintoism and on group loyalty, particularly from the 1880s onward, was designed for identity as well as stabilization of power under the imperial state.

Even Westerners were not exempt from identity concerns. Peasants, uprooted into industrial cities and the working class, might wonder what meaningful symbols they had left. The same applied to European immigrants flocking to the United States, Australia, or Argentina.

For many people, nationalism provided at least a partial new answer to the loss of older identities. Nationalists recalled traditions of the region, such as the Russian conservatives who claimed special Russian values of spirituality and community even among rapid changes. Nationalists could invent new traditions, as did the Japanese leaders who found new uses for the Shinto religion and the symbol of the emperor, pretending that these were age-old bulwarks of the nation. At the same time, nationalism was modern, approved by the West (even though Western leaders, for the sake of power politics, resisted nationalist objections to their imperialism.)

Particular areas improved their definitions of identity through a combination of nationalism and wider cultural expression. A Latin American identity had clearer focus than before; the same was true for a United States identity. However, new solutions were not always adequate to the challenge. Questions of how to define identity, through what combination of old and new values, were widespread through much of the period.

Moreover, the pace of international contact accelerated. By the last decades of the 19th century, the world was experiencing a genuine process of globalization, though the term was not yet used. The pace of global trade was matched by the long reach of industrial firms with factories and sales outlets in many countries or by Western investment bankers. The spread of key sports, headed by soccer football, showed the potential for global forms of entertainment.

490

Experiences in international policy produced agreements that allowed letters to be mailed around the world (the Universal Postal Union, 1874), or that dealt with the treatment of prisoners of war (the Geneva Convention, 1864) or humanitarian activity (the International Red Cross, 1863), or that organized sports (the modern Olympic games, 1896, or the Fédération internationale de Football Associations, to coordinate soccer). All of this was organized and dominated by the West, not "the world" as a whole. But there was every reason to believe that global organizations and values would spread further. Only the advent of an unprecedented military clash, World War I, called this prospect into question by sharpening international divisions. But even this clash, though centered in Europe, created secondary battlefields in the Middle East, Africa, east Asia, and the Pacific, drawing troops from North America and south Asia as well—another example of global forces, though this time in bitter conflict.

PART VI

The Contemporary World

INTRODUCTION: KEY CHANGES IN THE 20TH CENTURY

With the dramatic, often violent events that unfolded between 1900 and 1918, headed by World War I itself, the 20th century marked a new phase in world history. The transition was bathed in blood. Several even larger themes, apart from the war, also distinguished the 20th century from the previous period.

The virtually unchallenged rise of the West, which along with the related development of a genuine world economy formed the central theme of world history from 1450 to around 1900, ended in the 20th century. The change was not immediately clear. Much of the first half of the century marked the end of the old order rather than the visible shaping of the new. Nonetheless, three trends came together to end the West's continued dominance. First, various regions gained ground in the West in military terms. Second, parts of eastern Asia, particularly Japan, became industrial equals to the West, undergoing much more rapid economic transformation than the West itself experienced after 1900. Finally, the age of Western imperialism ended with a wave of decolonization that established independent nations throughout the Middle East, southern Asia, Africa, and the islands of the Pacific and the Caribbean.

Quite simply, developments in the 20th century reversed several basic trends in world history, most of which had existed since the 15th century:

493

- The West's clear military supremacy, initially established through naval gunnery and then increased by industrial armaments, began to fade. The West, increasingly headed by the United States in the military sphere, remained stronger than any other civilization, but its advantage narrowed. Not only the military strength of powers such as the Soviet Union and, for a time, Japan, but also new methods of warfare, particularly guerrilla tactics developed in places such as Vietnam and Algeria, made military operations more difficult for Western armies. New wealth allowed many nations to acquire modern armaments sufficient to deter easy Western invasions.

- The West's near monopoly on world trade dissipated. Several areas generated more rapid economic growth rates, allowing them to catch up with the West. Even many poorer regions developed dynamic industrial sectors that made them competitive and also reduced their dependence on the West for manufactured goods.

- Decolonization obviously reversed the long period of growing territorial acquisition by the West. Growing Western weakness and a desire to concentrate on rebuilding one's own society combined with growing demands for independence that echoed around the world. Here, tensions between the world wars set the stage for the rapid establishment of new nations between 1946 and the mid-1970s. Decolonization was one of the leading developments in the century as a whole.

The diminishment of Western power was not the same, to be sure, as outright Western decline. The expanding strength of the United States

helped to qualify any notion of a complete setback in the West. So did new signs of economic and political vigor in Europe, particularly after 1945. Throughout the century, some observers claimed to see symptoms of the kind of decay in the West that had earlier toppled the Roman Empire or led to the more subtle deterioration of Arab civilization. Although such forewarnings might turn out to be justified, they remain speculative. What is demonstrable is that the balance among societies began to alter during the 20th century, and Western dominance of the world lessened.

Western culture continued to exercise worldwide influence, which further complicates an assessment of the West's relative decline. Western intellectual standards in science and modern art still define many fields, although researchers and artists from many societies now participate in these fields. In modern architecture, for example, architects from Japan, Latin America, and elsewhere now gained world-class status, but major styles still reflected their Western origins. The West, including the United States and Europe, also set international standards in popular culture, from sports through music, costume, and film. One of the key issues in 20th-century world history involved the reactions of different societies to Hollywood movies, fast foods, and Anglo-American rock music. Changes in the cultural balance around the world, in other words, lagged behind the redistribution of power, although new religious currents by the 1970s signaled attempts by several societies to counteract Western influence in this area too.

Issues of power were not the only items on the new agenda of the 20th century. It also witnessed an unprecedented increase in the world's population. By 1970, there were more people living than had ever reached adulthood in the entire previous history of the human species. World population nearly tripled in the first three-quarters of the century. Improved border controls by newly efficient governments and international organizations helped control devastating plagues. Swamp drainage, insect control, and basic sanitary measures reduced other traditional killers. Although dire hunger persisted, advances in agriculture enabled greater numbers of people to be fed adequately. Falling death rates, though at varying levels in different regions, not only increased population outright but also allowed more people to reach adulthood and have children of their own. Despite the fact that per capita birth rates did not rise, overall birth rates did. The result was a massive number of people, whose lives easily compensated for the devastation of 20th-century wars, with hundreds of millions to spare.

Massive population growth helped account for a number of other key developments across the world. Urbanization proceeded rapidly in most civilizations. Individual cities in Asia and Latin America easily outstripped the Western giants in size. The growth of Tokyo, or Shanghai, or Mexico City involved huge movements of people. New migrations also occurred across the boundaries of nation and civilization. The West began to attract millions of immigrants from other societies—particularly southern Asia and the Middle East, Africa, and Latin America. The world population explosion also helps explain the frequent unrest of urban and rural masses in many 20th-century societies.

The nature of war and diplomacy changed during the 20th century. Imperialism had already established world diplomacy, although of a one-sided sort; in the 20th century, particularly after 1945, international diplomacy became a commonplace practice. Alliances were routinely formed, and broken, across civilization boundaries. Wars intensified in scope. They involved greatly heightened powers of governments, as many states learned to mobilize entire economies and to inflame national opinion as part of the military effort. Above all, wars became more violent. New technologies facilitated the killing of more people than ever before. World War I saw the introduction of tanks, submarines, long-range artillery, aerial bombing, and poison gas; World War II brought more massive aerial and naval clashes and the dawn of nuclear and missile warfare. After both world wars, diplomats and ordinary people alike operated amid an atmosphere of fear and uncertainty engendered by steady advances in weaponry. Blood baths in many regions, involving often millions of deaths amid ethnic conflict, were another sign of new violence and the combined power of hatred and technology. Key episodes involved political attacks in the Soviet Union in the 1930s, Hitler's Holocaust against the Jews, genocide in central Africa in the later 20th century, and what was called "ethnic cleansing" in the former Yugoslavia.

The pace of many human endeavors quickened in the 20th century. Air travel shrunk the globe even further than steam shipping had. Telephones, radios, and later, satellite and computer communications allowed the more rapid transmission of greater volumes of information across greater distances than ever before. Multinational companies, operating on all inhabited continents, became capable of transporting goods and people with unprecedented swiftness. Popular culture, particularly but not exclusively in industrialized societies, adopted the theme of speed. Olympic Games promoted competition in all sorts of speed-related sports. People ate faster; by the 1980s, most Japanese schoolchildren could no longer be bothered with chopsticks because the utensils made eating too slow, while fast-food restaurants cropped up in most major cities. Although speed was a factor first and foremost in transportation and communication, it also affected the way people thought and the stresses, often job-related, they imposed on themselves.

Finally, three major trends swept across many different societies in the 20th century, creating parallelisms, although not full homogeneity, in regions otherwise as different as Germany and Korea. Political change constituted the first common theme. Almost all nations had different political systems, by 1994, from those that had been in operation in 1900. Some regions had gone through several different political systems, in fact. This widespread pattern meant that many societies had to develop new beliefs and defenses of their political legitimacy, while governments took on important new functions. Even the United States, which retained its basic system, redefined the role of the state from the 1930s onward.

The second change involved culture. Many people believed in different ideas, by the 1990s, from what their counterparts had embraced in 1900. In some areas, traditional religions were challenged, whereas in other regions, religious conversion topped the cultural agenda. As in politics, the point was not a common pattern but rather a common participation in change.

The third change was social. The landed aristocracy gave ground everywhere, because of political attacks and economic change. In many areas, a business middle class surged forward. New questions also developed about women's rights and conditions, though specific patterns varied.

The 20th century thus contained most of the standard characteristics involved in the advent of a new period of world history. The balance of power among civilizations shifted from what had prevailed in the previous centuries—hence, the relative decline of the West and the rise of new dynamism in places such as Japan. Contacts among civilizations intensified, thanks to new technologies, new cultural diffusion as in the exchange of film and television, and new international organizations such as multinational businesses. The world became even smaller than it had been during the century of Western industrialization. Finally, a number of common themes spread around the world, inducing revisions of established political and cultural forms, the impact of unprecedented population growth, and the altered nature of war and diplomacy. Not since the 15th century had so many facets of the framework of world history altered direction.

In addition to these changes, of course, were a host of developments in individual civilizations. Russia, China, and, more briefly, Germany pioneered new forms of government controls. Experimentation in modern art and sleek architectural styles spread from the West to many parts of the world. The list of innovative trends and shattered traditions is long. They add up, in the view of many observers, to what one historian has termed "a world different, in almost all its basic preconditions," from that of the late 19th century.

Identifying major breaks in world history, and not just the history of a single civilization, is a tricky business. We have emphasized long periods: the birth of agricultural society; the elaboration of key classical civilizations; the expansion of civilization and the impact of the great religions; and the rise of the West and the development of a new global economy. We cannot be absolutely sure, living in what is at best the beginning of a new period, that a definitive new era has dawned, and we certainly cannot be sure of all its major characteristics. In world history terms, a mere 100 years—even allowing for a faster rate of change—is a rather brief span of time by which to judge.

Nevertheless, if the 20th century does constitute a break in world history, as events and themes suggest, it is possible to speculate about the underlying dynamic that is evolving. The 20th century marked the start of the industrialization of the world. The 19th century had seen the first industrial revolutions, to be sure, and their results were brought to the world by Western merchants and imperialists. But the 20th century saw full industrialization achieved in some areas outside Europe and North America, particularly in eastern Europe and the "Pacific Rim," including Japan, and the beginnings of gradual industrialization elsewhere—notably in China, southeast Asia, India, and parts of Latin America. The world was by no means completely industrialized by the 1990s, of course, and in some ways economic disparities among some major civilizations increased. However, the strivings for economic modernization and the adjustments to its impact now form a theme that literally encompasses the world.

Global industrialization, understood as a common process rather than a uniform economic system, underlies the other trends that can be identified, on an international basis, as distinguishing the 20th century. It was the industrialization of Russia and Japan that most clearly ended the undisputed rise of the West in world affairs. Offshoots of mechanization, in new sanitation procedures and agricultural techniques, led to world population growth. Industry was behind the fearsome technologies of contemporary war and, of course, set the stage for the new theme of speed. Political changes resulted in part from growing industrialization, as new government functions both preceded and followed economic shifts; more traditional regimes, for the most part failing to keep pace, had to be replaced. Cultural changes, including new secular loyalties, followed from the development of more industrial economies. Traditional social structures often shifted as well, as aristocracies largely disappeared and peasantries declined, to be replaced by new kinds of managers and a growing urban working class.

Industrial growth also redefined the kind of global economy that had come to life in the early modern period and then intensified during the 19th century. The West no longer monopolized the top spot in the world economy as Japan claimed a share. And although some regions were still exploited for their raw materials and cheap labor, a larger number of nations reached a middle ground in world trade during the second half of the 20th century. Rapid industrial growth, at 5–10 percent a year by the 1970s, characterized places such as Brazil, Mexico, India, Turkey, and China. Rates of this sort could double industrial output every 10–20 years. Huge economic divisions persisted, and some areas still had only tiny industrial sectors. Nonetheless, significant industrial evolution was a genuine international trend. International trade and technological exchange became more important than ever before; societies that isolated themselves usually suffered after a decidedly short time. However, the nature of the world economy was more complex, with a wider variety of roles, than in the simpler days of the 19th century when the West led the band, and almost every other region danced to its tune.

Not all was new. Many developments, including even massive population growth, built on earlier trends. Modern war was foreshadowed by the American Civil War and by the sophisticated weaponry of the later 19th century. One can view the 20th century as the beginning of a transition to a new stage of world history without denying that earlier developments had paved the way. The revival of traditional antagonisms between Christians and Muslims in central Asia and the Balkans in the 1990s reminded the world of just how many issues have their roots in the more distant past.

Furthermore, the major civilizations responded to the challenges of the 20th century in different ways, in large part because of their distinctive traditions. Some developments, to be sure, became in fact global. It was possible to find examples of the same building styles, the same mode of dress, the same soft drinks, and the same sports in most parts of the world. But along with closer international links came varied reactions, depending on prior experience. Thus, although the monarchy lost its grip, several different political forms took its place. The desire to industrialize spread, but the economic system a given society would adopt, the kind of cultural change it would embrace, or the way it would define the roles of different family members all varied widely. The world, although growing smaller, was not necessarily becoming more homogeneous; as a result, 20th-century history must be interpreted as a combination of sweeping trends and particular reactions based on tradition. Each civilization changed, without question; even the West went through an important transformation

of its earlier industrial order. However, it is important to recognize new and old distinctions among civilizations, as well as shared problems and responses.

THEMES, SUBPERIODS, AND CIVILIZATIONS

Looking at the 20th century as the beginning of a new period in world history means asking some common questions about each major civilization. How did each area participate in cultural change, and how did it react to Western influences in popular culture? How did change in each area relate to the redefined patterns of global trade, and to what extent did the area gain greater control over its own economy? What impact did the major wars have, or the surge of world population? Did the area develop a new political style, and in response to what forces? How did responses to the common issues reflect the particular characteristics of each civilization, in relation to its own long history?

The 20th century as a whole, and the histories of most of the major civilizations, must also be divided into three major subperiods, each relating to the unfolding of the new global framework. The period from 1914 to 1945 was clearly transitional. Western Europe and, to an extent, the United States suffered the agonies of war and economic dislocation, but Japan and Russia, although ravaged by war, solidified their industrial economies. Central governments strengthened in Latin America, while the nationalist challenge to imperialism surged forward in Asia, the Middle East, and Africa. From a Western standpoint, these were dreadful decades, but from other vantage points, they were decades full of new promise. Also in these decades, however, globalization retreated. Many key societies tried to reduce or eliminate international exposure.

From 1945 onward, new political structures arose, as imperialism dissipated. New nations were built, while Japan and its neighbors in the Pacific Rim advanced economically. The "industrialization of the world," although very uneven, clearly moved ahead. But these developments occurred under the shadow of the great cold war between the United States and the Soviet Union. Political and economic systems varied greatly depending on cold war alignments.

Finally, beginning in the 1970s, the cold war became less of a threat, coming to an end with the collapse of the Soviet system in 1989–1991. New diplomatic issues came to the fore, including a host of regional trouble spots. Four other major trends shaped world developments at this point. First, industrial growth in virtually every society heightened the levels of global competition, while multinational companies established operations wherever they could find suitably trained but cheap labor (and, often, relaxed environmental regulations). New economic problems and new areas of growth resulted. Second, almost all societies decided to reduce the economic role of government in the interests of faster economic growth. The results varied, in part because the roles of government already differed, but on the whole the policy shift seemed to spur production while creating new gaps between the rich and poor within most societies. And the decision itself constituted unprecedented, if not necessarily permanent, international agreement on basic economic goals and means. Third, a new enthusiasm for democratic political forms spread almost everywhere—although there were a few revealing exceptions. Never before had this political structure spread so widely, as many societies tried to replace authoritarianism or communism. Finally, religions revived in many areas, often in quite novel forms, resulting in new cultural tensions between secular and religious styles and commitments. These trends have continued boldly into the 21st century.

Chapters in this section return to each of the major areas of civilization. Each region experienced its own set of changes. Each had its own reaction to global forces. Here is an opportunity to see how patterns from earlier civilizations interacted within the framework of the new period of world history. Some areas, to be sure, were divided in new ways. China and Japan followed different patterns in east Asia. The Middle East split between secular and religious states. Amid great change, each civilization sought to accommodate innovation with past traditions. All experienced the new international pressures of growing trade, migration, and cultural influence. The tension between regional traditions and globalism was obvious everywhere. The contemporary world continues to be shaped by the dynamic interplay between past and present.

TIMELINE: Patterns of 20th-Century History

World Events	Western Civilization	Soviet Union and Eastern Europe	East Asia
	1905 Einstein's theory of relativity formulated.	**1905** Revolution in Russia.	
			1911 Revolution led by Sun Yat-sen.
1914–1918 World War I.	**1910** First use of assembly line production.		**1912** Fall of Chinese empire.
1917 Russian Revolution.	**1918–1919** End of German empire, Habsburg Empire.	**1917** Revolution in Russia. Bolshevik takeover in October.	**1916** Yuan Shi-h'ai named China's president.
1919 Formation of Communist International.	**1919–1939** Period of U.S. isolationism.		**1919** Former German islands in Pacific taken by Japan.
1919 Paris Peace Conference (Versailles); founding of League of Nations.			**1919 ff.** Growing regional warlord power in China.
	1920s Rise of fascism.	**1921** Lenin's New Economic Policy promulgated.	**1921** Formation of Chinese communist movement.
	1923 Fascist regime in Italy.	**1923** New constitution.	
	1920–1923 Rapid inflation.	**1927** Stalin in full power.	
		1928 Beginning of collectivization of agriculture, five-year plans.	**1927** Communists expelled by Kuomintang.
1929–1939 Worldwide economic depression.	**1929** Depression.		
			1934 "Long March" led by Mao Zedong.

India and Southeast Asia	Middle East	Latin America	Sub-Saharan Africa
		1910–1917 Mexican revolution.	
1914–1918 Participation of Indian troops with Britain in World War I.	**1915 ff.** Rise of Arab nationalism, encouraged during World War I.	**1917** New constitution; nationalization of mineral rights.	**1914–1918** Use of African troops in World War I; British takeover of German colonies.
1919 British colonial reforms; limited representative government.	**1917** Promulgation of Balfour declaration, promising Jewish homeland in Palestine.		**1919** First meeting of Pan-African Congress; rise of African nationalism.
1920 Beginning of Gandhi's nonviolent movement.	**1920** Treaty of Sèvres, ending Ottoman Empire.	**1920** Obregón president; rise of National Revolutionary Party.	**1921 ff.** Sporadic religious and nationalist riots against European rule.
	1920 ff. Growth of Jewish settlement in Palestine.	**1929 ff.** Depression; rise of economic nationalism.	**1924** Color bar bill backed by Afrikaner Nationalist Party in South Africa, limiting black–white social contacts.
	1922 Partial independence granted to Egypt by Britain.		
	1923 ff. Independent Turkey created by Atatürk; beginning of modernization drive.		
	1923 ff. Rise of independent Persia under Shah Riza Khan.		
	1935 Name changed from Persia to Iran.		

TIMELINE: Patterns of 20th-Century History

World Events	Western Civilization	Soviet Union and Eastern Europe	East Asia
	1933–1939 U.S. New Deal.	**1937–1938** Great Purge conducted by Stalin.	**1931** Japanese invasion of Manchuria.
	1933–1944 Nazi regime in Germany.	**1939** Signing of Soviet-German pact.	**1932** End of political party government in Japan; rise of military rule.
1939–1945 World War II.	**1938** Munich agreement; effort at British, French compromise with Hitler.	**1941** German invasion of Russia.	
1945 Atomic bomb dropped on Japan.	**1939** German-Soviet alliance.	**1943** Red Army pushes west.	**1937** New Japanese attack on China.
1945 United Nations established.	**1940–1944** Holocaust, slaughter of 6 million Jews.	**1945–1948** Soviet takeover of Eastern Europe.	**1941** Pearl Harbor attacked.
1947 ff. Cold war begun between United States and Soviet Union.	**1940 ff.** Rise of women in labor force.		**1942–1945** Momentum against Japan gained by United States.
1947 ff. Decolonization; rise of new nations.	**1945–1948** Postwar reconstruction; new democratic regimes in France, Italy, West Germany; rise of welfare state.		**1945** Atom bomb dropped on Nagasaki and Hiroshima by United States; surrender of Japan; beginning of U.S. occupation.
	1948–1949 Berlin airlift.		**1945 ff.** Communist-Kuomintang war in China.
	1949 Formation of NATO.		**1949** Communist victory.
			1949 Start of Chiang Kai-shek's regime in Taiwan
			1950 Korean War; U.S. intervention.
			1950 Chinese intervention in Korea.

India and Southeast Asia	Middle East	Latin America	Sub-Saharan Africa
1930–1931 Rioting in Indochina; rise of communist movement under Ho Chi Minh.		**1930** Military coup in Brazil; Vargas caudillo to 1945.	
1934 Philippine self-government increased by United States.		**1933** Power in Cuba seized by caudillo.	
1935 New British constitution for India.		**1934 ff.** U.S. "good neighbor" policies begun.	
1935 Nationalist victory in Siam; nation renamed Thailand.	**1936** Syria promised independence by France.	**1934–1940** Cardenas president of Mexico; formation of Pemex.	**1936** Exclusion of blacks from South African voting.
1937 Nationalist petition in Indonesia.	**1945** Syria and Lebanon fully independent.		
1940 ff. Japanese invasion of Southeast Asia.	**1948** State of Israel declared.	**1945** Juan Péron president of Argentina.	
1946 Hindu-Muslim clash in India.			
1946 Philippines independent.			
1947 India and Pakistan independent.			
1948 Sri Lanka and Burma independent.			**1948** Full control of South African government gained by Afrikaners' independence from Britain and extension of apartheid.
1949 Indonesia independent.			**1953** Strikes by black workers barred by law.
			1959 Enactment of Bantu self-government law, setting up 10 homelands as the only legal black residences.

World Events	Western Civilization	Soviet Union and Eastern Europe	East Asia
	1950–1973 Growing economic prosperity.	**1951** Atom bomb developed by Soviets.	**1950 ff.** Rapid economic advance in Japan.
	1958 Establishment of French Fifth Republic.	**1953** Death of Stalin.	
1955 First meeting of non-aligned nations.		**1955** Formation of Warsaw pact.	
1957 Sputnik, first artificial satellite, launched by Soviet Union, beginning the "space age."		**1956** Stalinism attacked by Khrushchev.	
	1958 Founding of European Economic Community (Common Market).	**1956** Hungarian revolution and its suppression.	
		1961 Berlin wall erected.	**1960s** Mao's Cultural Revolution.
		1962 Cuban missile crisis.	**1969** Russian–Chinese border fighting.
	1968 Student protests, in United States and Western Europe.	**1968** Revolt in Czechoslovakia and its repression.	

India and Southeast Asia	Middle East	Latin America	Sub-Saharan Africa
	1950–1962 Complete independence of Arab states.		**1952–1959** Mau Mau terrorism against white landowners, Kenya.
1954 End of French war against Vietnamese nationalists and communists; independence and division of Vietnam.	**1952** Egyptian revolution, fall of monarchy.	**1953** Reformist regime in Guatemala unseated by United States.	
	1956 Egyptian seizure of Suez Canal.	**1955** Péron overthrown by military coup.	
1955 First meeting of non-aligned nations, under India's leadership.	**1956, 1967, 1973** Israeli–Arab wars.	**1966, 1976** Other Argentine military coups.	
		1959–1960 Castro's revolution in Cuba.	
		1960 ff. Independence achieved by most West Indies territories.	**1957–1980** Independence granted to most of black Africa.
			1957 Ghana independent.
		1960 ff. Rise of liberation theology in Latin American church.	**1958** French colonies semi-independent, soon fully so.
	1962 Algeria independent.	**1961** Failure of U.S. "Bay of Pigs" invasion.	**1959** Riots leading to Congo independence (Zaire).
		1964 Military coup in Brazil.	**1965** Southern Rhodesia declared independent under white rule.
			1974–1975 Angola and Mozambique independent from Portugal.
			1980 Rhodesia renamed Zimbabwe under black government.
1963 Beginning of authoritarian rule under Marcos in Philippines; military coup in Indonesia.			**1960–1963** Civil war in Zaire.
1964 ff. Growing U.S. participation in North–South Vietnam war.			**1967–1970** Nigerian civil war.

World Events	*Western Civilization*	*Soviet Union and Eastern Europe*	*East Asia*
1973–1979 Increase in world energy prices promoted by OPEC.	**1970s** Introduction of microchip computer.	**1979** Uprisings in Poland and their suppression.	**1971** Partial Chinese–U.S. reconciliation.
1978 ff. Widespread trend to more market economies, reduction of state role.	**1979 ff.** New economic tensions.	**1985** Gorbachev assumes power in Soviet Union; reform follows.	**1976** Death of Mao; more pragmatic regime in China.
1989 End of cold war.	**1981** Reagan president in United States.	**1988–1989** Liberalization sweeps throughout Eastern Europe; new constitutions, economic reforms; nationalist agitation in Soviet Union.	**1978** More market economy in China.
1989 ff. Growing U.N. role in intervention in regional conflicts.	**1990** German unification.	**1988** New Soviet constitution; establishment of the Congress of People's Deputies.	**1980** End of U.S.–Taiwan treaty alliance; economic rise of Pacific Rim.
1988–1993 Widespread economic recession, rising unemployment: United States, Europe, Japan.	**1992** End of economic restrictions within common markets.	**1989–1991** Collapse of Soviet empire; new elections throughout much of Eastern Europe; Gorbachev selected as President.	**1984** British–Chinese agreement to return Hong Kong to China in 1997.
1990 ff. Increased U.N. peace-keeping and relief efforts in Africa, Eastern Europe, Southeast Asia, Middle East.	**1992–1993** Negotiations in extending Common Market toward single currency, etc.	**1991** Collapse of Soviet Union, replaced by Russia and numerous European and central Asian republics; Yeltsin replaces Gorbachev.	**1988–1989** Growing student agitation for liberal political reform in South Korea; elected civilian government installed.
1994 North American Free Trade Association.	**1993** Full unification of European Economic Community (now known as the European Union). Maestricht treaty urges more coordination.	**1991–1996** Civil war in parts of former Yugoslavia.	**1989** Suppression of democratic protests in China.
1998 International environmental agreements in Kyoto.	**1994 ff.** Entry of Finland, Austria, Sweden to European Union.	**1997** NATO invites Poland, Hungary, Czech Republic as members.	**1993** Split of factions within Japan's Liberal Democratic Party; Liberal Democrats fall from power in Japan.
2000-2001 Protests against globalization.	**1999** Single European Union currency, the euro, begins.	**1999** Russia wars with Muslim region, Chechnya.	**1997** Hong Kong is returned to China.
2001-2002 Terrorist attacks on U.S.; U.S. war in Afghanistan.	**2003** Expansion of European Union to much of east-central Europe.	**2000** Putin wins election as Russian president.	**1998** Asian economic crisis.
			2003 SARS epidemic.

India and Southeast Asia	Middle East	Sub-Saharan Africa
1971 Revolt in Pakistan; creation of independent Bangladesh.	**1970s** Rise of Muslim fundamentalism.	**1980s** Growing problems of hunger in parts of Africa.
1973 End of Vietnam War.	**1977** Egypt–Israeli peace.	**1989** DeKlerck charts a path of peaceful reform in South Africa.
1975 Control by North Vietnamese of all of Vietnam; movement into Laos and Cambodia.	**1978–1979** Iranian revolution. **1980–1988** Iran–Iraq war.	**1984 ff.** New wave of black protest against South African apartheid.
1975–1977 Suspension of civil liberties in India; sterilization campaign.	**1981** Assassination of President Sadat of Egypt.	**1990** Nelson Mandela released from prison.
1984 Assassination of Indira Gandhi by Sikh extremists; smooth transition of leadership to her son Rajiv.	**1982** Invasion of Lebanon by Israel.	**1990 ff.** Dismantling of apartheid.
1986 Fall of Marcos regime in the Philippines.	**1985** Withdrawal of Israel from Lebanon; Lebanon in chaos.	**1990** Several democratic elections in Kenya, other nations.
	1990 Iraqi invasion of Kuwait.	**1992** U.N. intervention in Somalia famine.
	1991 Gulf war against Iraq.	**1993** Agreement on democratic elections in South Africa.
1990 Economic reforms in India.	**1993–1994** New peace movement. Palestinian autonomy in Israel. Israel–Jordan treaty.	**1994** Election of Nelson Mandela as South Africa's president.
1998 Testing of nuclear weapons tests in India and Pakistan.	**1997** More moderate regime in Iran.	**1994 ff.** Democratic regimes in several African states.
	1998 International environmental agreements in Kyoto.	**1997** Insurgent army establishes new regime in Congo (Zaire).
		1999 Democratic regime in Nigeria.
2002 India and Pakistan mobilize armies over Kashmir dispute, but no war.	**2002** Israeli armies re-occupy Palestine; growing violence. **2003** U.S. led war against Iraq.	**2002-2003** Civil war in Congo.

28

The West in the 20th Century

Although one of the themes of 20th-century world history is the relative decline of the West, particularly for Europe, Western civilization remained a standard-bearer in many ways. By the late 1980s, it still was the wealthiest society in the world. The artistic and popular cultural forms it generated had far more influence on other civilizations than those of any other single society. Western nations continue to set much of the tone for world diplomacy. One sign of the West's continued importance has been its role as a target for people in many parts of the world who dislike not only Western power but also the threat it poses to traditional values.

KEY QUESTIONS *The West encountered unusual troubles during the world war decades. What significant changes resulted? Do they still affect the West? What is the best definition of the principal features of Western civilization by the early 21st century, in light of 20th-century developments? Finally, are the United States and western Europe part of the same civilization, or have they parted ways?*

PATTERNS OF WESTERN HISTORY: 1914–1945

World War I, the explosive event that effectively opened the new century, had international repercussions. Britain and France used many troops from their colonies. Some fighting occurred against German holdings in Africa. The Ottoman Empire's alliance with Germany produced conflict in the Middle East, which, among other things, encouraged Arab nationalism while further weakening the Ottoman state; many nations, including Italy, hoped for big colonial gains in the Middle East after the hostilities ended. Finally, Japan entered the war on the side of Britain and France and seized a number of German territories in the Pacific.

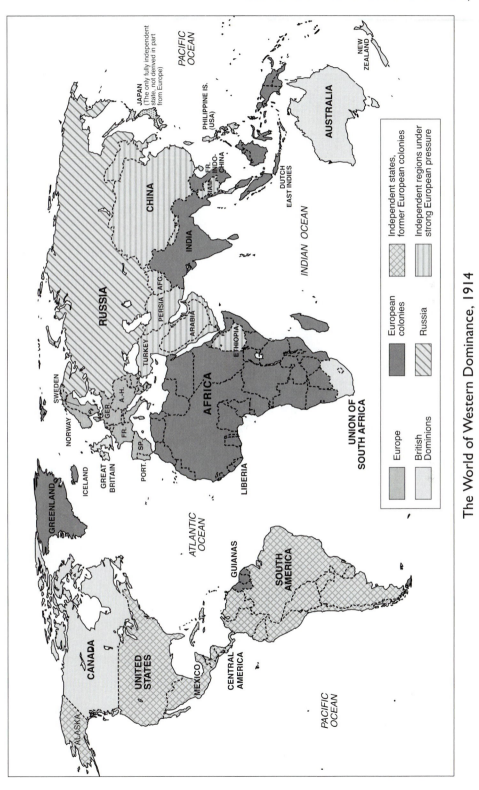

The World of Western Dominance, 1914

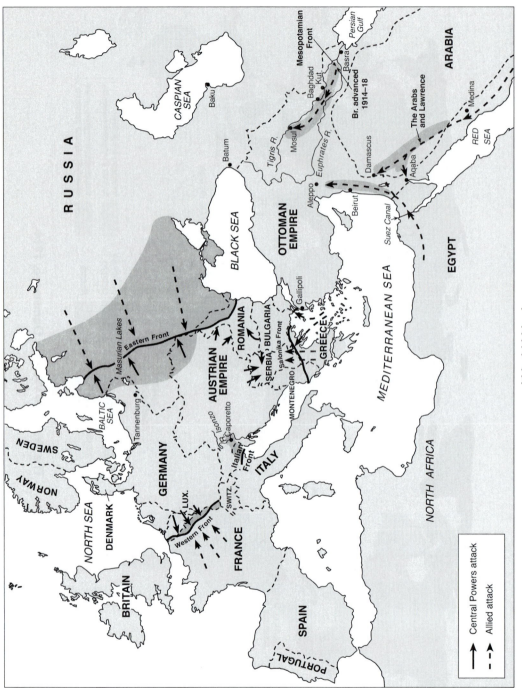

World War I

RUSSIA

CASPIAN SEA

Baku

Batum

BLACK SEA

OTTOMAN EMPIRE

Tigris R.

Mosul

Euphrates R.

Baghdad

Kut.

Basra

Persian Gulf

Mesopotamian Front

Br. advanced 1914–18

ARABIA

Medina

RED SEA

The Arabs and Lawrence

Damascus

Aqaba

Aleppo

Beirut

Suez Canal

EGYPT

MEDITERRANEAN SEA

NORTH AFRICA

Masurian Lakes

Eastern Front

Gallipoli

GREECE

Salonika Front

ROMANIA

BULGARIA

SERBIA

MONTENEGRO

AUSTRIAN EMPIRE

Tannenburg.

BALTIC SEA

SWEDEN

NORWAY

NORTH SEA

DENMARK

GERMANY

LUX.

Western Front

FRANCE

SWITZ.

Isonzo

Caporetto

Italian Front

ITALY

SPAIN

PORTUGAL

BRITAIN

Central Powers attack

Allied attack

Nevertheless, the bulk of the fighting occurred within Europe, including European Russia. Germany invaded large parts of Russia, fueling the growing discontent that finally brought the 1917 revolution, which took Russia out of the war. Combat on the Western Front, located mainly in France, was still more bitter. New weapons, including more effective artillery and tanks, led to the construction of defensive trenches, from which neither side could advance without huge casualties. Occasional offensive efforts cost tens of thousands of lives each day. The sheer loss of life and the frustration of nearly four years of virtual stalemate had a devastating material and psychological impact on the European combatants. Finally, in 1918, the exhausted allies managed to invade a still more exhausted Germany. The German emperor abdicated (as did the Habsburg ruler), and the war was over.

Picking up the pieces after World War I was extremely difficult, however. More than 10 million people had been killed in Europe. Vast amounts of property had been destroyed, and the European economy suffered a shattering blow through the loss of investments abroad and huge debts accumulated internally to fund the wasteful war effort. A peace conference was held at Versailles, its work divided between desires for revenge against Germany and the idealism represented by President Woodrow Wilson of the United States. Idealism led to the establishment of the League of Nations, designed to promote international harmony in the future, and the creation of a series of new states in central and eastern Europe, from the territory of Russia, the Habsburg monarchy, and Germany. Poland resurfaced, along with other new Slavic states and an independent Hungary. The new states were weak, however, and this created a source of tensions in European diplomacy for the foreseeable future. The League of Nations, although not insignificant in world affairs during the next 15 years, proved largely ineffective as well. At the same time, motives of revenge resulted in huge reparation payments and a loss of territory for

Germany, generating further resentments. Even the victorious allies were unsatisfied: France still feared its German neighbor, the United States pulled back from European entanglements into an unrealistic isolationism—not even joining the League of Nations—and Italy bemoaned its lack of success in acquiring vast new territory.

World War I and Versailles set the stage for the next two difficult decades of Western history. Diplomatic tensions eased somewhat during the 1920s, as Germany made some efforts to adjust to its reduced position, but fears and resentments still ran high. European and U.S. internal politics were largely ineffectual as a series of mediocre leaders gained power. Germany, now a republic, suffered at the hands of a number of groups who opposed democracy. Communist movements, linked to the Soviet regime that now ruled Russia, emerged to the left of socialist parties in many countries, serving as small but frightening revolutionary forces. The liberal middle sector of Western politics weakened, as many erstwhile liberals became more conservative in their desire to prevent major social reform. The absence of a strong center made effective government difficult, even in Britain, where the parliamentary tradition was particularly strong.

New political tensions might have been manageable had postwar economic trends not proved so disastrous. Many nations suffered from massive inflation during much of the 1920s, the result of wartime debts and postwar dislocations. Prosperity returned toward the middle of the decade and the United States, in particular, enjoyed an industrial boom. But in 1929, a major economic depression occurred, as banks failed first in the United States and then throughout the Western world. The Great Depression resulted from a number of factors. Purchasing power was too low among many peasants and workers to sustain increased industrial production. Many peasants and American farmers faced a rapid decline in agricultural prices, due to overproduction; mechanized agriculture outstripped the demand for food in the Western world, and this limited farmers' ability to buy. Nonindustrial countries in eastern Europe and many other parts of the world also saw prices for their raw materials tumble as their production increased faster than Western demand; this crisis also weakened markets for Western goods. High tariffs, imposed by many nations to protect their own economies, added to the difficulties of trade. In essence, Western productive capacity outran available markets. As a result, speculative investments finally proved hollow, causing the stock market crash and bank failures of 1929.

The ensuing economic depression was the worst in modern memory. Millions of workers lost their jobs. Wages plummeted, and insecurity spread even among those who were employed. Levels of production collapsed, as up to a third of the economic capacity of countries such as Germany and the United States was idled by 1932. Although the worst of the Depression was over by the mid-1930s, its traces remained strong throughout the rest of the decade.

Only a few Western governments responded constructively to this economic crisis. Scandinavian states increased government spending, providing new levels of social insurance against illness and unemployment and foreshadowing the modern welfare state. In the United States, Franklin Roosevelt's New Deal, from 1933 onward, enacted a number of social insurance measures and used government spending to stimulate the economy. The New Deal did not cure the American Depression, but it alleviated the worst effects and provided new hope that forestalled major political pressure against the established order. Britain and France, however, reacted weakly to the economic catastrophe. Both countries continued to be plagued by inept leadership. They were also torn between socialist and conservative forces, and their allies on the political extremes; effective action seemed impossible.

The Depression led directly to a fascist regime in Germany in 1933. Fascism was a product of World War I; the movement's advocates, many of them former veterans, attacked the weakness of parliamentary democracy and the corruption and

Nazi Party Congress in Nuremberg, Germany. The Führer is saluted by his "storm troopers," in a demonstration of the effective Nazi use of mass orchestrations.

class conflict of Western capitalism. They proposed a strong state ruled by a powerful leader, who would revive the nation's forces through vigorous foreign and military policy. Fascists vaguely promised social reforms to alleviate class antagonism, and their attacks on trade unions and socialist parties pleased landlords and business groups alike. The first fascist regime arose in Italy in 1923, and fascist parties complicated the political process in a number of other nations during the 1920s. However, it was the advent of the National Socialist, or Nazi, regime in Germany, under Adolf Hitler, that made this new political movement a major force in world history.

Hitler appealed to a country bitter about its defeat in war and unusually hard hit by economic disorder. He promised many groups a return to more traditional ways; thus, many artisans voted for Hitler in the belief that pre-industrial economic institutions such as the guilds would be revived. The middle class, including the leaders of big business, were attracted to Hitler's commitment to a firm stance against socialism and communism. Although Hitler never won a majority popular vote in a free election, his party did attain the largest single vote total by 1932. By this time, the effects of the Depression were compounded by the weak, divided response of Germany's parliamentary leadership, in a country that had never fully accepted the validity of liberal political forms.

Once in power, Hitler quickly set about constructing a totalitarian state—that is, a new kind of government that would exercise massive, direct control over virtually all the activities of its subjects. Hitler eliminated all opposition parties; he purged the bureaucracy and military, installing loyal Nazis in many posts. His secret police, the Gestapo, arrested hundreds of thousands of political opponents. Trade unions were replaced by government-sponsored bodies that tried to appease workers with low pay by offering full employment and various welfare benefits. Economic planning on the part of government helped restore production levels, with a particular emphasis on the manufacture of armaments. Hitler solidified the power of his regime with constant, well-crafted propaganda, strident nationalism, and an incessant attack on Germany's Jewish minority. Hitler's hatred of Jews ran deep; he blamed them for various personal misfortunes and also for movements such as socialism and excessive capitalism that in his view had weakened the German spirit. Obviously, anti-Semitism served as a catchall for a host of diverse dissatisfactions. Anti-Semitism also benefited Hitler's cause by providing a scapegoat that could rouse national passions and distract the population from other problems. Measures against Jews became more and more severe, as Jews were forced to wear a letter on their clothing identifying them as Jews, their property was attacked and seized, and increasing numbers were sent to concentration camps. After 1940, Hitler's policy took an extreme turn, focusing on the total elimination of European Jewry. In this Holocaust, 6 million Jews were killed in the concentration camps of Germany and conquered territories; other groups, such as gypsies and homosexuals, were targeted as well.

Hitler's policies were based on preparation for war. He wanted not only to recoup Germany's World War I losses but also to create a land empire that would extend across much of Europe, particularly toward the east into the territory of allegedly inferior Slavic peoples. Progressively Hitler violated the provisions of the Treaty of Versailles that had limited German rearmament. In 1936, he intervened in a civil war in Spain, on the side of fascist forces. Within two years, he had annexed Austria and seized part, then all, of Czechoslovakia. To all these steps, the other European powers responded only weakly. France and Britain were too divided to pursue a resolute foreign policy. They negotiated with Hitler at Munich in 1938, offering him part of Czechoslovakia in the hopes that this concession would satisfy his appetite, but their feeble attempt at appeasement merely inspired Hitler to further demands. The United States remained isolationist; the Soviet Union was worried but too isolated from potential Western allies, who feared its communism, to pose an effective counterbalance.

With nothing standing in his way, Hitler moved forward, forming an alliance with the Soviet Union in 1939 that allowed both powers to attack Poland. This act finally convinced Britain and France that they could no longer sit idly by, and war was declared in September 1939. Hitler was far better prepared for conflict than were his opponents, and during the first three years of the war, his forces, in alliance with Italy, swept over much of western Europe. By 1942, Germany held France, Norway, the Low Countries, and the small Balkan states. However, an invasion of Russia in 1941, following the collapse of the brief alliance between Russia and Germany, resulted in Germany's armies being bogged down much as Napoleon's had been 130 years before. Furthermore, the United States, goaded by the Japanese attack on Pearl Harbor, entered the war in December 1941 on Britain's side. Three years of bitter fighting in Europe, the Pacific, and elsewhere followed. The Russian armies gradually recovered, with some assistance in the form of armaments from the United States, and pressed inexorably toward Germany's eastern borders. American and British forces, aided by

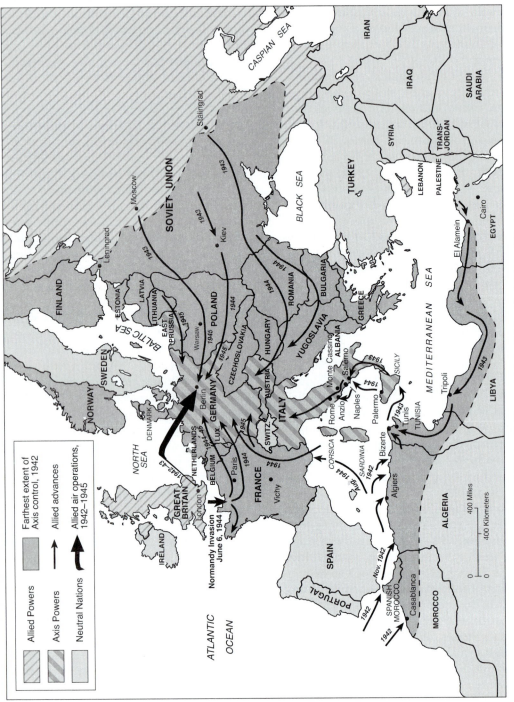

World War II: European and North African Theaters

Legend:

Farthest extent of
Axis control, 1942

Allied advances

Allied air operations,
1942–1945

Normandy Invasion
June 6, 1944

Allied Powers

Axis Powers

Neutral Nations

ATLANTIC OCEAN

IRELAND

GREAT BRITAIN

London

NORTH SEA

NETHERLANDS

BELGIUM

Lux.

FRANCE

Paris

Vichy

SWITZ.

SPAIN

PORTUGAL

SPANISH MOROCCO

Casablanca

MOROCCO

ALGERIA

Algiers

Nov. 1942

NORWAY

SWEDEN

DENMARK

BALTIC SEA

FINLAND

Leningrad

Moscow

SOVIET UNION

Stalingrad

CASPIAN SEA

ESTONIA

LATVIA

LITHUANIA

EAST PRUSSIA

Warsaw

POLAND

GERMANY

Berlin

CZECHOSLOVAKIA

AUSTRIA

HUNGARY

ITALY

Rome

Anzio

Naples

Monte Cassino

Salerno

Palermo

SICILY

SARDINIA

CORSICA

Aug. 1944

Bizerte

Tunis

TUNISIA

Tripoli

LIBYA

MEDITERRANEAN SEA

YUGOSLAVIA

ROMANIA

BULGARIA

ALBANIA

GREECE

BLACK SEA

TURKEY

SYRIA

LEBANON

PALESTINE

TRANS-JORDAN

IRAN

IRAQ

SAUDI ARABIA

EGYPT

Cairo

El Alamein

1943

1944

1945

400 Miles

400 Kilometers

resistance movements against Nazi occupation, drove Germany first from north Africa, then gradually from Italy. In 1944, a massive invasion force moved across the English Channel into France, and within a year the allies entered Germany from the west. Hitler committed suicide, and the European war drew to a close.

Like its predecessor, World War II resulted in a massive loss of life. Russia and Germany were hardest hit, along with the Jewish population of central and eastern Europe. Economic devastation was even greater than before. Hitler had drained the occupied countries of labor and productive goods, as part of his frenzied war effort. Massive bombing had destroyed many cities and factories, as well as transportation networks. For several years after the war, western Europe was the scene of grinding poverty, massive movements of dislocated people, and seeming hopelessness.

The war also redesigned the European map more fundamentally than World War I. Russian dominance extended through virtually all of eastern Europe. Only two countries in eastern Europe preserved any real independence: Greece, which was aided by Britain and the United States in maintaining a noncommunist government, and Yugoslavia, which established a communist regime independent of Soviet control. Germany was divided. Initially, the Soviet Union, France, Britain, and the United States each occupied a zone of Germany. But the three Western powers gradually allowed their zones to be united in an independent Federal Republic, whereas the Soviet zone converted into a communist state heavily dependent on Russian military support.

The new boundaries of Europe initiated a prolonged struggle between the Soviet Union and the United States, each with a network of European allies and dependencies. A "cold war" started in 1947, pitting the two postwar giants against each other. Russia, with its virtual empire extending into central Europe, saw the United States construct an alliance system among the leading Western states and retain a substantial military presence of its own to guard against possible

Soviet attack. Here, within Europe's own boundaries, was the cruel result of half a century of disarray and violent internal struggle.

PATTERNS OF WESTERN HISTORY: 1950 TO THE PRESENT

To many observers, by 1950, the future of the Western world, or at least its traditional European base, seemed unbelievably bleak. If World War I had caused two decades of virtually unqualified confusion, could the consequences of a second conflict be anything but worse? In fact, the West seemed to recover both economic and political vigor in the decades after 1950; although the results were far from problem-free, they were certainly more constructive than the record of the years between both world wars.

Postwar Europe did not regain its previous diplomatic position. The dominance of the superpowers, the Soviet Union and the United States, continued. The United States formed the North Atlantic Treaty Organization (NATO) with most other Western governments in 1949, to oppose the Soviet threat; creation of the alliance ensured American influence over western Europe in dealing with the Soviet Union. At the same time, weakened by world war and pressed by surging nationalist movements throughout the world, western Europe lost most of its colonies, sometimes as a result of bitter struggle. India, southeast Asia, and then Africa all gained independence. Although many Europeans resented this sign of decline, attempts to reassert some shadow of earlier authority largely failed. In 1956, for example, Britain and France tried to seize control of the Suez Canal from a newly independent Egypt, only to be forced into retreat as a result of Egyptian resistance and U.S. and Soviet pressure. Even aside from the great power of the United States as a representative of generally Western values, the West did not suffer perpetual diplomatic decline. Decolonization was largely accepted by the people of western Europe, who did not attempt to hold out at the expense of political stability and economic growth at home. West European cultural and economic influence in many former colonies remained considerable. With time, leading European powers also gained a more independent voice vis-à-vis the United States. Although not military equals, individual states such as France were able to oppose American policies at key points.

Make no mistake: after World War II, the world's diplomatic framework decisively changed, and in many ways this transformation worked to the West's disadvantage. The balance of power within the West shifted to the United States. When the age of imperialism ended, the West's direct voice in Asia and Africa was dramatically lessened. The cold war between the United States and the Soviet Union meant that even the West's leading power could not set the tone for world affairs, instead facing a roughly equal rival. By 1951, when the Soviet Union developed the atomic bomb, it became clear that centuries of Western military superiority over all other civilizations had ended, and that eastern Europe now shared this claim of strength. The fearsome power of modern weapons and the intense East–West rivalry left many Westerners concerned that a new war could destroy their own civilization and that of most other parts of the world. At times, diplomatic processes seemed to have escaped human control.

Nonetheless, the Western world itself remained free from war after 1945. Early cold war tensions, particularly over the new divisions of Germany, brought war scares. In 1948–1949, the Soviet Union blocked off the city of West Berlin, a western enclave within East Germany, and only a massive American airlift relieved the pressure on supplies. Colonial wars also involved the West. France lost a bitter war to retain its possessions in and around Vietnam and then faced a long, ultimately unsuccessful struggle to keep Algeria. Finally, in 1949, the United States, with wider world interests now than western Europe, became involved in a war in Korea and then, in

the 1960s, in a long and disheartening struggle in Vietnam, both against communist forces. These regional wars were important, of course, but the fact remains that even major threats of war within the West now receded, as at least for a time the West became one of the world's more internally peaceful civilizations.

A key ingredient of the West's new diplomatic environment involved explicit initiatives by western Europe to set its own diplomatic house in order after 1945, with some American encouragement. Eager to prevent further nationalist wars and also anxious to promote economic development, leading west European nations joined hands in economic cooperation. Initial moves to coordinate industrial policies led in 1958 to the formation of the European Economic Community, which promoted full-scale exchange across national boundaries. Although the Common Market, as it is called, ultimately broadened to include Britain, Ireland, Denmark, Greece, Spain, and Portugal, in addition to its initial members, West Germany, France, Italy, and the Low Countries, it did not become a single government. However, the organization did develop common policies and a common bureaucracy to oversee economic relations and, to an extent, coordinate other policies. Nationalist tensions receded to a lower point than ever before in modern European history. In 1993, the organization—now known as the European Union, or EU—created full tariff unity and planned further integration, possibly involving a single currency and exchangeable rights of citizenship. The new currency unit, the euro, was launched in 1999, even as additional countries moved closer to membership in the European Union. In 2004, a number of east-central European countries joined the EU.

More striking still were new economic and political trends. Particularly during the 1950s and 1960s, the doldrums of the interwar decades were reversed. Political tensions declined, while economic growth soared. Western society avoided major economic depressions, although there were years of slackening prosperity; most Western nations enjoyed a 2–8 percent growth rate per year. The West easily retained its lead over most other civilizations in terms of per capita prosperity, and indeed the gap between its wealth and that of many agricultural societies widened. Only Japan caught up in this regard. Within the West, mass affluence, now exhibited by widespread ownership of cars, refrigerators, and the now ubiquitous television set, reached unprecedented levels. The United States, whose population had achieved affluence earlier, found its prosperity rivaled by dynamic European countries such as West Germany and France.

Western economic development was spurred by the widespread transformation of leadership after World War II. In western Europe, men and women who had fought in resistance movements against Nazism vowed to avoid the errors of the past and to create a new society. The influence of the older aristocracy was further reduced. Training for west Europe's elite now broadened to recruit more talented people from worker and peasant families, as support for higher education and the availability of scholarships increased. University education itself was revamped to focus on more technical subjects. A new generation of managers, with a redefined mission and educational background, brought new dynamism to the West in various fields.

During the crucial years immediately after 1945, Western society also forged new political institutions. Carefully wrought democratic constitutions were developed in West Germany and Italy, providing more stable parliamentary institutions than ever before. France revived its parliamentary system after the years of Nazi occupation; in 1958, government instability in the face of the paralyzing colonial war in Algeria prompted the nationalist leader Charles de Gaulle to engineer a new constitution, providing for a strong but democratically elected presidency overseeing parliament. Spain, Portugal, and Greece installed new democratic systems in the 1970s. Democracy and relative political stability were encouraged by the virtual destruction of the radical right in politics, discred-

ited by Nazi excesses and defeat in war. Most Western countries had a strong conservative party fully committed to the democratic system. On the left, although significant communist movements remained in a few countries, reformist socialist parties, also committed to the democratic process and extensive personal liberties, won wide support outside North America. The communist minority itself declined by the 1980s. The new political spectrum thus provided a multiparty system, with leadership characteristically alternating between major parties, depending on the performance of the economy, but the spectrum was bounded by the commitment of most groups to the basic political process. Even communist parties in western Europe relied mainly on election efforts, abandoning attempts at revolutionary agitation.

The political system was altered, finally, by the construction of more extensive welfare institutions. In France and Italy, coalition governments combining conservatives, socialists, and communists enacted new welfare programs between 1945 and 1948. These programs provided state-sponsored medical insurance, payments to large families, and greater regulation of working conditions. France and other countries also created more formal state economic planning, to guide in postwar recovery and then further industrial development. Between 1945 and 1951, Great Britain extended its welfare state under the leadership of the Labor Party. The British welfare state featured an unusually elaborate program of socialized medicine, with the government paying most medical bills from tax revenues; it also entailed government housing programs and other social measures. Most other Western nations extended their welfare and economic planning activities; Canada, for example, enacted a state-funded medical insurance program. Even the United States, which had a more restricted array of welfare programs than most other Western countries, initiated the Great Society measures of the 1960s, providing medical insurance for the indigent and elderly, expanding the Social Security system, and passing a number of laws to protect the rights of minorities and women.

Youth antiwar protest: Washington, D.C., 1967.

The pattern of economic growth and political stability that took shape in the postwar West was disrupted in the late 1960s by a series of student protests, compounded in the United States by civil rights demonstrations and rioting among urban blacks. Campus unrest at major American universities focused on the war in Vietnam, which many students regarded as futile and immoral. Young people in Europe and the United States also targeted the materialism of their societies, seeking the embrace of more idealistic goals and greater justice. Student uprisings in France in 1968 created a near revolution. By the early 1970s, new rights for students and other reforms, combined with police repression, ended the most intense student protests. But some ongoing political concerns, including feminism and environmental protection, entered the arena during the 1970s partly as an aftermath of the student protests; in some western European countries, a terrorist movement, focused on the kidnapping of political and business leaders, and sometimes their assassination, caused anxiety as well. Economic growth also slowed during the 1970s, partly because of rising energy costs; in the late 1970s and early 1980s, the Western world faced its greatest economic recession since the postwar recovery. New leadership sprang up within the British Conservative Party and the U.S. Republican Party, seeking to reduce the costs and size of the welfare state to spur new economic growth. Additional political currents arose in other Western countries, including new rightist parties and "Green" environmentalist movements.

Key problems intensified in the 1990s and early 2000s. Global economic competition hit the West hard. In Europe, the result was substantial unemployment, up to 12 percent or more, as goods requiring less skilled labor now came from elsewhere. The United States faced similar pressures but created a larger number of low-paying jobs; here, the new trend involved growing inequalities in income, greater than in any other industrial society. All Western nations, amid economic pressure, had to reconsider welfare state expenditures, and most cut back; again, the United States, with a smaller welfare system than most others, reduced protections for the poor most systematically. Various political changes accompanied these developments. More zealous conservatism surfaced particularly in the United States. Liberal and socialist movements in western Europe as well as in North America developed a more moderate stance, less wedded to welfare traditions. A few new currents of protest developed: a racist, neo-fascist movement in France called the National Front, a surge of paramilitary groups in the United States on the far right.

Terrorist activity was another problem. This activity involved usually random attacks, with guns or explosives, to dramatize a cause. Some terrorist activity within Europe lingered from the protests of the 1960s, with radical gangs in Italy, for example, periodically attacking businessmen. Some activity resulted from nationalist agitation, as in violence by people advocating independence for the Basque ethnic group in Spain. Irish nationalist battles with British control over Northern Ireland also resulted in terrorism. A right-wing zealot in the United States bombed a federal building in Oklahoma City. By the 1990s, tensions with some elements in Islam generated terrorism. Countries such as France, with a growing Islamic minority, saw small groups generate some incidents, designed to protest Western activities in the Middle East or to attack Jews. Czechen rebels in Russia used bombs in Moscow. On September 11, 2001, individuals associated with the militant Al Qaeda movement flew jetliners into the World Trade Center, in New York, and the Pentagon. This produced growing international police and military activity against terrorism.

Despite these important issues, Western society after 1950 has been relatively free from traumatic events, compared to the frenzy of the 1920s and 1930s. Decolonization created tension; U.S. involvement in world diplomacy produced a number of new concerns; the student movement of the late 1960s was an indication that all was not well in the affluent society. Cushioned by the rapid rise in wealth, however, the Western world remained considerably freer from major upheavals than most other civilizations in the postwar decades. Indeed, boredom itself became an issue, as observers worried that the welfare state created too much security, and political apathy was so pervasive that many people no longer bothered to vote. In western Europe, periodic terrorism reflected the discontent of a small minority against the calm of the existing system, whereas in the United States, declining voter participation raised questions about the vigor of the political process. Had Western society achieved a new harmony, or were the postwar decades a period of deceptive tranquility before a new storm?

WESTERN POLITICAL INSTITUTIONS IN THE 20TH CENTURY

Two somewhat contradictory themes ran through the political development of Western society after 1900. On the one hand, the power of the state increased; on the other hand, a commitment to democratic and liberal values remained strong and, after 1945, gained ground.

The rising power of the state showed in both world wars. Governments in democratic nations such as Britain and the United States increased their regulation of economic activities, introducing rationing and the allocation of labor. Governments mounted massive propaganda campaigns to win the passionate loyalty of citizens to the military effort; enemies were pictured as the epitome of evil; newspapers were censored and the new media of radio and motion pictures were used to further intensify patriotism. The powers of wartime government helped inspire the totalitarian dictatorships of Nazi Germany (and also communist Russia). Nazism demonstrated that under stress, a major Western society could abandon liberal values in favor of a government dedicated to the destruction of all competing sources of power and the manipulation of individual citizens through mass education and propaganda. Authoritarian governments in some other states, such as fascist Italy and, after 1936, a semi-fascist Spain, also used new police and propaganda powers to repress opposition.

More generally, the rise of the welfare state throughout most of the West after 1945 represented a major extension of government power. Government expansion under the New Deal greatly increased the importance of the American state, which was then extended by the growth of military spending from World War II until the end of the cold war. Throughout the West, governments assumed the responsibility for providing some coverage of health-care costs, adequate working conditions, and protection against dire poverty. The United States,

History Debate

CONVERGENCE

The Western world split apart during the 1930s, between fascist and democratic systems. After 1945, however, European nations became more similar than ever (although not identical)—a phenomenon called *convergence*. Industrial growth reached countries such as Italy. The results of World War II eliminated some German peculiarities, such as a rabidly conservative aristocracy. The spread of democracy was obviously a convergent development. So were key social trends, such as an aging population and new roles for women. Nationalism declined. Growing west European unity both reflected and furthered the convergence phenomenon.

Convergence also reduced some key differences between Europe and the United States. On the west European side, the elimination of the traditional peasantry and the final demise of the aristocracy, along with rapid economic growth, made social and economic structures more similar on both sides of the North Atlantic. A prosperous Europe also opened the door to the consumer culture of the United States, providing a growing (if occasionally critical) market for American TV shows, fast foods, even a Euro-Disney. Because of new immigration, Europe also developed some racial tensions similar to those in the United States, although usually less severe. On the American side, the New Deal and World War II had created a stronger government, more like its European counterparts, but the United States did not develop as extensive a welfare state. Although American popular culture predominated, European contributions such as the miniskirt and the Beatles moved easily across the Atlantic in the other direction.

Differences remained. The United States participated with Europe in more open sexuality, but the nation was more prudish; topless beaches, the norm in Europe, were not popular in the United States. American moralism also showed in an unusually intense antismoking crusade. The largest new distinction involved obvious differences in military policy. The United States, the world's greatest power, rapidly increased its peacetime army and armaments expenditures—spending rose 300 percent in the 1950s alone. American foreign policy, as a result, was more influenced by military pressures than was true in Europe, which often boasted of pioneering in a civilian society. Correspondingly, Europe depended on American military protection while its own global military capacity steadily diminished.

Different reactions to the economic pressures of the 1990s also seemed to contradict transatlantic convergence. Western Europe was more reluctant to dismantle the welfare state or to accept growing gaps between the rich and poor, although it was affected by both trends. Convergence might not be permanent.

more fully committed to older liberal values that relied on individual initiative, stood slightly apart in this movement. But even here, by the 1970s, 21 percent of total tax income was applied to social welfare payments. Expanding welfare functions and growing involvement in economic planning obviously broadened the role of the state in individual lives. Taxes increased, and so did the regulation of how employers could hire and fire, what crops farmers could plant, where poor people could live. Government bureaucracies expanded steadily.

The rise of the state has been balanced, however, outside the period of fascist regimes, by the West's continued devotion to a multiparty democracy and substantial freedoms of speech, press, religion, and assembly. The West has developed a mixed system, in which important governmental authority is combined with private enterprise. In the economy, for example, state planning has left the operation of most businesses in private hands. West European countries did nationalize some economic sectors, such as railroads and mines. The nationalization movement took place primarily during the period of recovery after World War II, but a French socialist regime extended nationalization again in the early 1980s. Even here, however, most businesses have operated through private decision making within frameworks partly established by government.

The extension of liberal, democratic systems after 1945 showed the continuing strength of parliamentary institutions in Western political culture. West Germany established a far more solid democracy than it had managed in the 1920s. Political debate has centered on significant disagreements between conservatives and socialists about the extent of the welfare state or diplomatic policy, but it has not called the system into question. Although conservatives dominated German politics through most of the 1950s and 1960s, and again in the 1980s and early 1990s, socialist leadership took power peacefully at a number of points. The 1989 collapse of the Soviet empire brought about German unification in 1991, partly because of extensive East German demands for democracy. By the mid-1980s, the Western world was more fully characterized by a single political system—liberal democracy—than at any time since the decline of feudalism. From Australia and New Zealand through North America to western Europe, a tension between multiparty rivalry and personal freedom on the one hand, and powerful state planning, taxation, and welfare systems on the other, has constituted the core of modern politics. Alternative political ideologies such as fascism and even Marxism have declined.

The rise of a strong state democracy was accompanied by the decline of classic diplomatic and military issues in Europe. Old antagonisms between France and Germany or Britain and the continent declined. So did commitments to imperialism. Although west European governments participated in the cold war, military issues and expenditures receded. U.S. military concerns, however, increased, as did American diplomatic influence in European affairs—even after the cold war had ended, the United States continued to take a lead in new issues such as the strife in the former Yugoslavia. Tensions between the United States and western Europe occurred at times, particularly during surges of French nationalism or when American policy became high-handed, but they were rarely acute—never reaching the pitch of the former nationalist rivalries within the West.

CONTEMPORARY WESTERN CULTURE

Western culture continued to display great vitality during the 20th century, although at times it seemed to lack coherence. Artists and composers stressed stylistic innovation, against older traditions and even the efforts of the previous generation. Scientific work flourished, as the West remained the center of most fundamental inquiry in the theoretical sciences. However, complex discoveries, such as the principle of relativity in physics, qualified older ideas that nature can be explained in a few sweeping scientific laws. And the sheer specialization of scientific research removed much of it from ready public understanding. Because no unifying assumptions represent the essence of formal intellectual activity in the contemporary West, neutral terms such as "modern" or "postmodern" are used even in the artistic field. Disciplines that once provided an intellectual overview, such as philosophy, declined in the 20th century or were transformed into specialized research fields; many philosophers, for example, turned to the scientific study of language, rather than writing basic statements about the nature of life and the universe. Although work in theology continued between both Catholic and Protestant thinkers, it no longer commanded center stage in intellectual life. No emphasis was placed on an integrated approach;

no agreement was reached on what constitutes an essential understanding of human endeavor.

The dynamism of scientific research formed the clearest central thread in Western culture after 1900. Growing science faculties commanded the greatest prestige in expanding universities; individual scientists made striking discoveries, while a veritable army of researchers cranked out more specific findings than scientists had ever before produced. In addition, the wider public continued to maintain a faith that science held the keys to understanding nature and society and to improving technology and human life. Finally, although scientific discoveries have varied widely, a belief in a central scientific method persists: form a rational hypothesis, test through experiment or observation, and emerge with a generalization that will show regularities in physical behaviors and thus provide human reason with a means of systematizing and even predicting such behaviors. No other approach to understanding in Western culture has had such power or widespread adherence.

The first scientific breakthrough of the 20th century took shape with the discovery of the behavior of atomic particles. Experiments with X-rays and uranium produced the knowledge of electrons and the nucleus of the atom. At about the same time, by 1905, the work of Albert Einstein in Berlin transformed the former idea, central to Newtonian physics, of physical matter as a solid essence that behaved in absolutely uniform ways. According to Einstein's theory of relativity, space and time are not absolutes but are always relative to the observer measuring them. Einstein used time as a fourth dimension to explain behaviors of light and planetary motion that had been misstated in Newtonian physics. Radiation and other electronic activity are not regular but occur in discontinuous waves. Increasingly complex mathematics, involving the abstract language of differential equations, was essential in understanding the actual behavior of both planetary bodies and particles within the atom. By the 1930s, physicists began to experiment with bombarding basic matter with neutrons, particles that carry no electric charge; this work was to culminate during World War II in the development of the atomic bomb. Research in physics continued after World War II with a combination of increasingly sophisticated observation, made possible by improved telescopes and then lasers and space satellites, and the complex mathematical theories facilitated by the theory of relativity. Astronomers made substantial progress in identifying additional galaxies and other phenomena in space; the debate about the nature of matter also continued.

Breakthroughs in biology have primarily involved genetics. The identification, in the 1860s, of inheritance characteristics received wide attention only after 1900. By the 1920s, researchers experimenting with the increasingly familiar fruit fly determined exact rules for genetic transmission. In the 1940s, the discovery of the structure of the basic genetic unit by British and American scientists, the famous "double helix" pattern of deoxyribonucleic acid (DNA), advanced the understanding of how genetic information is transmitted and can be altered.

Biologists were also responsible for major improvements in health care. New drugs, beginning with penicillin in 1928, revolutionized the treatment of common diseases, whereas immunization virtually eliminated scourges such as diphtheria. Findings on hormones and their connection to certain behaviors, leading in the 1920s to the science of endocrinology, also had widespread medical applicability. Genetics itself, by the 1970s, gave rise to a host of industries that utilized scientific principles to produce new medicines, seeds, and pesticides.

Nevertheless, the new science has also had some troubling features, even apart from its use in weapons of destruction and its sheer complexity. The physical world is no longer considered neatly regulated, as it had been by Newtonian physics. Genetics made it clear that evolution proceeded by a series of random accidents, not through any consistent pattern. The use of the rational, scientific method thus has not produced the kind of simple worldview that it had resulted in a century or so before, and the ensuing uncertainties have influenced some artists in their attempts to convey an irrational, relativist universe. However, for most people in the West, the belief in progress, defined in terms of both better technology and a rational understanding of nature, largely persists.

The rational method, broadly conceived, also advanced in the social sciences from 1900 onward. The German sociologist Max Weber worked to characterize general features of institutions such as bureaucracies, for analysis and comparison. Many sociologists' promulgated theories of human society, or aspects of it such as the behavior of elites, on the assumption that rationally conceived models captured the essential reality of human affairs. In economics, quantitative models of economic cycles or business behavior have increasingly gained ground. Work by the British economist John Keynes, stressing the importance of government spending to compensate for loss of purchasing power during an economic depression, played a great role in the policies of the American New Deal and efforts by European planners to control the economic cycles after World War II.

Like the sciences, the social sciences became increasingly diverse and specialized. As in the sciences, many social scientists sought practical applications for their work. Psychologists became involved, for example, in not only defining and treating mental illness but also trying to promote greater work efficiency. Governments called on economic forecasting. Social science thus added to the impression of an explosion of rationally generated and useful knowledge, even when research pointed to deterministic or irrational aspects of human affairs. Most leading social scientists continued to emphasize the quest for consistency in human and social behavior. After World War II, the increasing use of mathematical models and laboratory experiments in the social sciences enhanced this emphasis.

Most 20th-century artists, concerned with capturing the world through impressions rather than through reason or the confinements of literal reality, worked against the grain of science and social science. Painting became increasingly nonrepresentational. The cubist movement, headed by Pablo Picasso, rendered familiar objects as geometrical shapes; after cubism, modern art moved even further away from the tenets of normal perception, stressing purely geometrical design or other expressionistic techniques. The focus was on mood, the individual reaction of viewers to the individual reality of the artist. Musical composition involved the use of dissonance and experimentation with new scales; after World War II, a growing interest in electronic instrumentation added to this diversity. Because writers are, in fact, constrained by words, their stylistic innovation was generally less extensive. However in poetry, the use of unfamiliar forms, ungrammatical constructions, and sweeping imagery continued the movement of the later 19th century. Playwrights experimented with new types of staging and unconventional dramatic norms, often seeking to involve the audience in direct participation. In literature, the novel remained dominant, but it turned toward the exploration of moods and personalities, rather than the portrayal of objective events or clear story lines. A vast gulf grew between the scientific approach and the artistic framework as to how reality can be captured and, to an extent, what constitutes reality.

Many people ignored the leading modern artists and writers, in favor of more commercial artistic productions and popular stories. The gap that had evolved earlier, between avant-garde art and public taste, generally continued. Some politicians, including Adolf Hitler, campaigned against what they saw as the decadence and immorality of modern art, urging a return to more traditional styles. Certainly art did not hold its own against the growing prestige of science.

However, artistic vision was not simply a preoccupation of artists. Designs and sculptures based

This example of the cubist style is by Pablo Picasso, a leading figure in 20th-century modern art, who was born in Spain but worked primarily in France. *Céret et Sorgues* (*Violin and Grapes*), spring–summer 1912. Picasso, Pablo, *Violin and Grapes. Céret et Sorgues* (spring-summer 1912). Oil on canvas, 20 x 24" (50.6 x 61 cm). The Museum of Modern Art, New York. Mrs. David M. Levy Bequest. Photograph © 2004 The Museum of Modern Art, New York © 2004 Estate of Pablo Picasso/Artists Rights Society (ARS), New York

on abstract art began to grace public places from the 1920s onward; furnishings and films also reflected modernist themes. Most revealing of a blend between art, modern technology, and public taste was the development of a characteristic 20th-century architectural style, the "modern" or "international" style. The use of new materials, such as reinforced concrete and massive sheets of glass, allowed the abandonment of much that was traditional in architecture. The need for new kinds of buildings, particularly for office use, and the growing cost of urban space also encouraged the introduction of new forms such as the skyscraper, pioneered in the United States. In general, the modern style of architecture sought to develop individually distinct buildings—sharing the goal of modern art to defy conventional taste and cultivate the unique—while conveying a sense of space and freedom from natural constraints. Soaring structures, free-floating columns, and new combinations of angles and curves were features that described leading Western buildings from 1900 onward. Following World War II, when reconstruction in Europe and the growth of the U.S. West and Southwest provided massive opportunities for building, the face of urban space in Western society was greatly transformed.

There were a few unifying themes between the artistic and scientific approaches. A constant quest for the new was one feature: as artists sought new styles, scientists sought new discoveries. Furthermore, Western culture in the 20th century, in both art and science, became increasingly secular. Individual artists, writers, and scientists might proclaim religious faith, but church institutions had long since lost control over basic style or content. In western Europe, despite an important reform movement within the Catholic church that abandoned traditional ceremonies in favor of more direct contact between priest and worshippers, religion played a minor role in both formal and popular culture. Regular church attendance tended to be of interest only to a minority—5 percent of the British population, for example, by the 1970s. In the United States, religion maintained a greater hold, and both church attendance and popular belief remained at much higher levels than elsewhere in Western society. The United States also witnessed, both in the 1920s and again after World War II, a greater variety of popular revival movements and attempts to use religion to maintain or restore traditional values. Here was a clear indication that, for some individuals, neither the artistic nor the scientific approach to understanding was fully satisfactory—and this became yet another ingredient in the cultural diversity and tension of Western society.

Western culture was not a monopoly of European civilization in the 20th century. Western art forms, particularly in architecture, spread widely. The achievements of Western science, at least those related to technology and medicine, often had to be taken into account by societies seeking their own industrial development. Western arts and sciences were, by the same token, greatly enriched by many practitioners from other cultures—by Japanese artists, for example, or Indian medical researchers and computer scientists. Elements of Western culture thus became international, and in tracing their roots, we must link most accomplishments to a number of other civilizations. Yet no other culture, not even the Japanese, created quite the same balance between an overwhelming interest in science and an all-

important concern for stylistic innovation and individual expression in the arts.

ECONOMY AND SOCIETY

During the 20th century, rapid transformation characterized the economy and social organization of Western civilization. By the latter part of the century, some of the changes seemed almost as fundamental as those that had ushered in the Industrial Revolution two centuries before. The recurrent shifts in technology, economic organization, and social structure in Western industrial society had significant effects on the rest of the world as well, making it hard for industrializing nations to "catch up" to Western levels.

To begin with, economic change involved new products. During the first decades of the century, synthetic textile fibers, such as rayon and nylon, introduced variety into the clothing industry. Radios and, by the 1950s, early television brought instant entertainment and news into homes across the land (see Table 28.1). The automobile, although invented before 1900, increasingly became a consumer staple, first in the United States and then, after World War II, in western Europe.

Economic change involved, in addition, new forms of organization. The growing role of the state in formal planning was one aspect of this. In the private sector, corporate business became increasingly common, furnishing giant companies

Table 28.1
TELEVISION OWNERSHIP IN 1957 AND 1965

Country	1957	1965
France	683,000	6,489,000
Germany	798,586	11,379,000
Italy	367,000	6,044,542
The Netherlands	239,000	2,113,000
Sweden	75,817	2,110,584

Sources: The Europa Year Book 1959 (London, 1959) and The Europa Year Book 1967, vol. 1 (London, 1967).

with extensive funds for widespread investment. Older family enterprises declined further. By the 1920s and again after World War II, many corporations established an international base of operations. U.S. firms took the lead here, for the extensive American market provided both capital and experience in dealing with large markets. However, a number of European-based firms became multinational as well. They had marketing and supply offices, and production subsidiaries, on several continents. In domestic markets and to an extent internationally, the concentration of ownership among a small number of corporations was the rule. A multitude of aspiring automobile producers before World War I thus settled into a handful of big producers in most Western countries between the wars, and further concentration, including international operations, occurred after World War II. As one result, the Ford Motor Company manufactured cars in Britain and Germany, whereas German and French automakers stepped up operations in the United States, Mexico, and Brazil.

Agriculture experienced an organizational revolution of its own, particularly after World War II. In western Europe, peasant farming gave way to cooperatives for purchases and sales; most small landholders acquired new market skills as well as modern equipment, making them more like rural business executives than peasants. In the United States, Canada, and Australia, great concentrations of land operation, called *agribusiness*, arose after 1950, as purely family farms became increasingly marginal. Organizational change plus improved machinery, seeds, and fertilizers steadily raised agricultural productivity in the Western world, although some worried about a decline in the actual quality of foods and also growing environmental damage from the chemical spraying and other measures designed to maximize production.

Refinements in organization also affected the structure of work. Early in the 20th century, U.S. firms took the lead in developing ways to increase the pace of manufacturing by defining jobs and supervising workers more closely. By 1910, early

forms of the assembly-line system were in effect, pioneered at Henry Ford's automobile plant. Such operations had workers performing repetitious tasks with a minimum of motion and thought, becoming as much like the machines they worked with as was humanly possible. After World War II, assembly-line procedures were modified by the use of more automated equipment, with machines themselves—including, by the early 1980s, robots—performing some of the most routine functions.

As it had since industrialization began, economic change meant new technologies. The growing use of the internal combustion engine in manufacturing and transport, and growing use of petroleum instead of coal for fuel, marked important steps early in the century. Coal mining, long a staple of Western industrialization, declined, and some regions, particularly western Europe, became dependent on fuel imports since their own oil holdings were small. Faster and more mechanized equipment steadily increased manufacturing productivity. Early in the century, the production of machines was revolutionized by the use of automatic riveters, drills, and other equipment that provided the technological basis for an assembly-line operation in what had been a craft industry. The production of chemicals and ubiquitous plastics required automated procedures for transporting, mixing, and molding ingredients. After World War II, a technological revolution took shape in communications and information storage as well, with the introduction of computers; in the 1970s, the development of the microchip made computers smaller and more flexible, and increased the speed and volume of information flow, while displacing conventional storage operations such as manual filing.

The economic advance of Western society was not, of course, without its setbacks. During the decade of the Depression, many wondered if the economy could ever recover its former vitality. The two world wars resulted in immense loss and dislocation. The economic slowdowns of the late 1970s and early 1980s, with rising rates of unemployment and fierce foreign competition, particularly from east Asia, raised anxieties anew. In the 1990s, global competition produced high unemployment in western Europe, while inequality in income increased in the United States. Furthermore, not all Western nations fared equally well in the economic development process; previous leaders such as Great Britain fell behind. Australia and Canada produced large quantities of foods and minerals for export, which made them unusually dependent on the prosperity of more fully industrial centers such as Japan or the United States, although they maintained considerable industries of their own.

Nevertheless, for the century as a whole, the theme of continued economic vitality and change remains valid. Western society was quick to recover from wartime destruction, for example, bouncing back rapidly from the bombings of World War II, a sign that basic industrial capacity and know-how accounted for considerable resilience once they were firmly established.

Yet another area in which economic change had an impact was the class structure of Western society. A basic division between the middle class and working class continued. But the middle class was defined increasingly by its managerial skills and education, rather than property ownership; the working class became less distinctive as its affluence increased. In the United States, indeed, the majority of workers identified themselves as middle class, on the basis of earnings. Furthermore, increased mobility, particularly in the decades after World War II, blurred class lines somewhat. Making the most of new educational opportunities, a number of people from working-class backgrounds entered corporate upper management and the top levels of government service, although they still formed a minority. Interestingly, social mobility in western Europe soon matched that of the newer nations of the Western world, such as the United States, despite a more explicit class structure.

The greatest change in social structure, however, was the rise of workers in the service sector of the economy. The percentage of farmers, already small, dropped further. But by the 1920s, the number of factory workers began to stabilize as well, as production increased mainly through continuing mechanization. By the 1950s, it was clear that service work—that is, jobs involving steady interaction with people and the processing of paperwork rather than producing goods—was the wave of the future. Restaurant workers, health-care workers from hospital janitors to doctors, teachers, recreation workers—all rapidly expanded in number, as did the secretaries and salespeople needed in a bureaucratized, consumer-oriented economy. By the 1970s, over half of all workers in Western society were employed in the service sector.

Finally, again particularly after 1945, a new wave of unskilled workers entered the labor force, many of them immigrants. Western Europe drew hundreds of thousands of workers from the Middle East, north Africa, the West Indies, and Asia; immigration to the United States reached higher levels than ever before, drawing mainly from east Asia and Latin America. Not all the newcomers were unskilled, but many filled the ranks of agricultural laborers, maintenance workers, fast-food personnel, and other slots where pay was low and rates of unemployment often high. Many urban blacks in the United States also fit into this growing category, which often seemed tragically isolated from the prosperity and security of most sectors of Western society.

Racial antagonisms flared periodically, for example in attacks on Turkish workers in Germany. A number of political groups worked to limit immigration. The United States worked hard, though with limited effect, to control illegal immigration from Latin America. The new mixture of peoples, both in western Europe and the United States, produced important changes—opportunities as well as tensions.

Like social structure, family life changed considerably during the 20th century without being totally transformed. Birth rates remained relatively low. Western society experienced an increase in

World Profiles

SIMONE DE BEAUVOIR

Simone de Beauvoir was a vigorous French intellectual, particularly known for her feminism. Born in Paris in 1908, she received a Catholic upbringing but went on to a career of philosophical radicalism. She wrote widely, not only in philosophy but also in literature. She advocated greater protection for workers, better treatment of the elderly, abortion rights, but above all equality for women. Her book *The Second Sex*, published in 1949, provided the intellectual foundations for later 20th-century feminism. The American feminist leader Betty Friedan, for example, helped popularize de Beauvoir's ideas and apply them to contemporary American women.

De Beauvoir graduated from university in 1929 and spent about 15 years teaching in secondary school. During these early years, she formulated not only her basic philosophy, associated with the movement called *existentialism*, but also her passionate social voice. She also formed a close friendship with Jean-Paul Sartre, another leading philosopher. De Beauvoir's final active decades saw her become increasingly involved in political activism, including feminism. Sartre's death in 1981 hastened her own physical and mental decline, and she died in 1986. She is buried next to Sartre.

Simone de Beauvoir

birth rates from the late 1940s until the early 1960s—the famous baby boom. The boom was caused by growing prosperity, after many families had delayed births during the Depression, and in some cases in response to government aid to families. But even the baby boom, while it severely pressed schools, day-care facilities, and so on, produced relatively modest birth rates. After 1963, the baby boom ended, with birth rates again dropping rapidly. Further decreases in death rates for most age groups, due to improved medicine and a new interest in exercise and fitness, have maintained the basic population pattern of the later 19th century: low birth rates and low death rates adding up to a stable or slightly rising population and a growing number of elderly people. The increase in the elderly population, while a significant burden on social security systems, has had only limited impact on families, as older people in the Western world now live apart from younger relatives—a major change in residential patterns that began in the 1920s.

Modern leisure: bathers at Coney Island beach and amusement park, New York, 1952.

Western family life continued to emphasize the importance of close emotional ties, between spouses and between parents and children, along with a new emphasis on sexual satisfaction before and during marriage. The role of the family in recreational activities increased. The annual family vacation became a standard experience as time at work was shortened. After 1945, the advent of television made the home an attractive place to spend leisure hours.

Although family functions and family demography displayed striking continuities with the past, but with some interesting new twists, the roles of family members were revolutionized by new patterns of women's work. During World War I, with many men away in battle, women entered the labor force in vast numbers. This movement was largely cut off in the 1920s. But in World War II, women returned to the factories and offices, and after the war they tended to remain there. Increasing numbers of women in western Europe and North America, now as well educated as men, with relatively few children to care for, and in a society where earnings bring self-fulfillment and power, sought an identity and income through work. At the same time, the rise of service occupations deemed suitable for women facilitated the movement of women into the labor force, while increased expectations—a desire for better housing, travel, or education—encouraged women to work.

In all Western countries, women's participation in the labor force rose steadily, reaching roughly 45 percent of the total by the late 1970s. Women of all social classes were now working, and they were doing so after marriage and even during active motherhood. Their earnings lagged behind those of men, and in response to this, an active feminist movement seeking fuller equality sprang up by the 1960s. Nonetheless, the change in work patterns easily reversed the earlier trends of Western industrial society, in which women had been encouraged to concentrate on family life.

Women's work fostered greater equality in family decision making. However, although the authoritarian position of husbands declined, new roles for women brought great confusion as well, for all parties concerned. Men did not always equally share household work, even when women found their time at home with the family decreased. Child care was another key issue. Increasing numbers of children, particularly in western Europe, were raised, in part, in day-care centers, one of the new functions of the welfare state. But worry persisted about the quality of children's upbringing, as older values of maternal nurturing changed less rapidly than mothers' activities did. Many thus professed that mothers, at least those of young children, should not work.

Tensions of this sort easily fed concern about the family itself, a theme already raised during the Industrial Revolution. Many people complained about changes in family roles, claiming that children were receiving too little adult supervision and spending too much time in front of television sets. Certainly, the Western family became unstable. Divorce rates rose during most decades of the 20th century, with the United States leading the way. By the 1970s, one marriage in two in the United States, and one in three in Great Britain, ended in divorce. The fact that changing laws made divorce easier to obtain was merely a symptom of a growing tension between individual fulfillment and continued interest in family ties. The family has survived in the West and in many ways adapted to new functions. One of the reasons for rising divorce rates has indeed been the high expectations Western people have about the family, as they seek love, sexual pleasure, and freedom from dispute. However, there is no question that the concept of the family often failed in practice, and the resulting strains on and conflicts for family members occasioned great anxiety in the 20th-century West.

Along with social structure and family, pleasure seeking became an important theme of Western society in the 20th century, most obviously during the 1920s and again in the affluent era following World War II. With growing prosperity and shorter working hours—by the 1940s, most people worked an eight-hour day—interests in leisure exploded. Mass media, including popular novels as well as movies, radio, and television, brought escapist entertainment to millions. Professional sports commanded growing attention, particularly soccer in western Europe and football and baseball in the United States. Sex also garnered more open public interest than was the case during the 19th century. Birth control remained an essential consideration, but it was provided increasingly by artificial devices, not abstinence. A society concerned with pleasure and the consumption of goods found sex an important consideration. More revealing fashions, particularly those for women; the more open use of sexual themes in films and on television; and manuals devoted to teaching methods of greater sexual pleasure all marked this new chapter in Western history. Whether people actually experienced greater sexual pleasure than before is open to question, but there was no doubt of great public interest in the subject. Sex or sexual allure became a vital part of having fun and of selling products. To some observers, indeed, sports and sex seem to have taken the place that religion once held in popular Western culture.

The changes in Western society during the 20th century—including technological advances as well as setbacks such as the Depression—caused considerable social tension. Burgeoning unionization and rising rates of strikes into the early

1950s expressed class conflict, as workers reacted to automation and the power of their middle-class bosses. However, with growing affluence and the rise of the service sector, where unionizing came harder, strikes and unions receded somewhat. Other protest movements, including the student risings in the 1960s and feminism, reflected social change, including discontent within the family. Overall, though, collective protest did not surge in the West. But there were also more individualized signs of distress. Rates of violent crime increased in Western society after World War II, initially because of the dislocation of war itself but then as a result of new conflicts among youth and also racial minorities. For the most part, the United States had the highest per capita crime rates, but western Europe faced an upward trend as well. The growing use of drugs was also interpreted as a reaction to boredom and the lack of meaning in Western life.

Western society, like Western politics and art, seemed enmeshed in a fundamental contradiction of the 20th century. On the one hand, the society encouraged individualism. Children were raised to think of themselves as individuals, to rise above their parents' achievements if possible, to embrace new educational and employment opportunities. Leisure interests appealed to individual pleasure seeking. But individualism was severely curtailed by the growing bureaucratization of society. Most jobs involved routine activities, controlled by an elaborate supervisory structure; individual initiative counted for little, in not only factories but also the offices of giant corporations. Leisure, appealing to individual self-expression in one sense, generally meant mass, commercially manipulated outlets for all but a handful of venturesome souls. By the 1950s, television watching had become far and away the leading interest of Western peoples, and most television fare was deliberately standardized. Individualism also came into conflict with the continued devotion to family bonds, as we have seen. Ironically, individualism and its manifestations often made collective protest against bureaucratization and routine extremely difficult.

To critics, inside Western society and without, late-20th-century Western society seemed confused, in constant conflict. Poverty and job boredom coexisted with affluence and continued appeals about the essential value of work. Youthful protest—as expressed in defiant styles of dress and jarring forms of music—family instability, and crime might be signs of a fatally flawed society. Rising rates of suicide and an increasing incidence of mental illness were other troubling symptoms. At the least, Western society continued to display the strains of change. People displaced by change or troubled by the rejection of former values, as well as people caught up in new styles but disappointed by their results, showed the tensions of adjusting to a society still in rapid flux.

A POSTINDUSTRIAL AGE?

Many people in Western society came to believe that they were facing greater changes than ever before, whether for better or for worse. By the late 1960s, a new concept of a "postindustrial" society took shape in both western Europe and North America. It held that Western society was the leader in a transformation as fundamental as the Industrial Revolution had been. The rise of a service economy, according to this worldview, promised as many shifts and changes as the rise of an industrial economy had precipitated. Control of knowledge, rather than control of goods, would be the key to the postindustrial social structure. Technology would allow the expansion of factory production with a shrinking labor force, and attention would shift to the generation and control of information. The advent of new technology, particularly the computer, supported the postindustrial concept, by applying to knowledge transmission the same potential technological revolution that the steam engine had brought to manufacturing.

Changes in the role of women paralleled the postindustrial concept, and some observers began to talk of a postindustrial family in which two equal spouses would pool their earnings for a high-consumption lifestyle. Postindustrial cities would increasingly become entertainment centers, as most work could now be decentralized in the suburbs, linked by the omnipresent computer. Postindustrial politics were less clearly defined, although some noted that the old party structure might loosen as new, service-sector voters sought issues more appropriate to their interests. The rise of environmental and feminist concerns that cut across former political alignments might thus prove an opening wedge to an unpredictable political future for the West.

The postindustrial society was not an established fact, of course, even by the late 1990s. Important continuities with earlier social forms, including political values and cultural directions, suggest that new technologies might modify rather than revolutionize Western industrial society. It is clear, however, that Western society has taken on important new characteristics, ranging from age brackets to occupational structure, that differentiate it from the initial industrial patterns generated during the 19th century. And this fact, even if more modest than the visions of some of the postindustrial forecasters, raises an important question for the West and the world: how would a rapidly changing, advanced industrial society fit into a world that has yet to fully industrialize? How could the concerns of an affluent, urban, fad-conscious Westerner coexist with the values of the world's peasant majority?

ern history, and the relationship among the phases, is an important challenge. The other issue involves the position of the United States (and, to a degree, other former settler societies) in the West. It is important not to assume that everything that happened in the United States now became typical of the West. But there are overlaps, in some cases increasing with shared consumerism and more frequent contacts.

Defining Western civilization in relation to its own past was complicated both because of the twists and turns of the 20th century and because many other societies now shared Western features at least in part. Still, by the early 21st century, Western society remained linked to various stages of its past in several ways. The commitment to parliamentary democracy was no longer unique. It had faltered in key Western countries in the interwar decades but had emerged as a strong commitment. Distinctive conditions for women, and attention to women's issues, was another point that in some ways could be traced back to the European-style family several centuries back. Many societies shared a devotion to science, but this remained a key part of Western culture. The same applied to a commitment to consumerism. The same applied, certainly, to a sense of superiority in world affairs, however modified by the loss of colonies. What else should be put on a "Western" list, as key features coming from earlier periods in Western history but continuing to evolve in the 20th and 21st centuries?

ISSUES AND CONNECTIONS

The two big issues for the study of 20th-century Western history involve change and geography. How could the West collapse so badly in the interwar decades, and then recover and innovate after World War II? Figuring out the causes of different phases of contemporary West-

SUGGESTED WEB SITES

On personal experiences in the Great Depression, see http://www.sos.state.mi.us/history/museum/techstuf/depressn/teacup.html. On the Holocaust, see http://www.remember.org. On the feminist leader Simone de Beauvoir, see http://members.aol.com/CazadoraKE/private/Philo/Beau/USimone.html. For efforts at European union, see http://www.eurunion.org.

SUGGESTED READINGS

Important overviews of recent European history are Walter Laqueur, *Europe Since Hitler* (1982); D. A. Low, *Eclipse of Empire* (1991); Helen Wallace et al., *Policy-Making in the European Community* (1983); Alfred Grosser, *The Western Alliance* (1982); and R. Paxton, *Europe in the 20th Century*, 2nd ed. (1985). On the Holocaust, see R. Hilberg, *Perpetrators, Victims, Bystanders: The Jewish Catastrophe* (1992). Some excellent national interpretations provide important coverage of events since 1945 in key areas of Europe. See A. F. Havighurst, *Twentieth-Century Britain* (1982), and John Ardagh, *France in the 1980s* (1982). Volker Berghahn, *Modern Germany: Society, Economy and Politics in the 20th Century* (1983), is also useful. On post–World War II social and economic trends, see C. Kindleberger, *Europe's Postwar Growth* (1967); V. Bogdanor and R. Skidelsky, eds., *The Age of Affluence* (1970); R. Dahrendorf, ed., *Europe's Economy in Crisis* (1982); and Peter Stearns and Herrick Chapman, *European Society in Upheaval*, 3rd ed. (1991). On the welfare state, see Stephen Cohen, *Modern Capitalist Planning: The French Model* (1977), and E. S. Einhorn and J. Logue, *Welfare States in Hard Times* (1982).

On the relevant Commonwealth nations, see Charles Doran, *Forgotten Partnership: U.S.–Canada Relations Today* (1983); S. M. Lipset, *American Exceptionalism: A Double Edged Sword* (1995), which compares Canada and the United States; Edward McWhinney, *Canada and the Constitution, 1979–1982* (1982); and Stephen Graubard, ed., *Australia: Terra Incognita?* (1985). On the United States in the cold war decades, see Walter LaFeber, *America, Russia and the Cold War, 1945–1980*, 4th ed. (1980); Thomas Patterson, *On Every Front: The Making of the Cold War* (1979); David Oshinsky, *A Conspiracy So Immense: The World of Joe McCarthy* (1983); Richard Polenberg, *One Nation Divisible: Class, Race and Ethnicity in the United States Since 1938* (1980); Harvard Sitkoff, *The Struggle for Black Equality, 1954–1980* (1981); and William Chafe, *The American Woman: Her Changing Social, Economic and Political Roles* (1972).

29 Eastern European Civilization

The Russian Revolution and its aftermath dominated eastern European history in the 20th century. Russia experienced many of the events that also rocked the West during these decades, but it also developed a distinctive kind of industrial society under a communist system. This society reflected earlier Russian traditions and the massive innovations produced by the revolution of 1917. Until the 1940s, the smaller nations of eastern Europe stood apart from this system, but as the Soviet Union extended its military influence, they too were brought under a communist economic and political framework. The result was considerable unity, but also significant tensions in east European civilization as a whole. Then, in the late 1980s, the whole communist system split apart, within Russia as well as its empire.

The fundamental transformation in Russian society during the 20th century resulted from industrialization and the creation of a new social structure, freed from traditional aristocratic control and supported by mass education. The communist regime installed in 1917 was an instrument of change. Revolution itself resulted from the conflicts of a society in which population pressure, new political aspirations, and the early stages of Russian industrialization challenged older social and political forms without reforming them. As in France in the later 18th century and China and other countries in the 20th century, massive revolution was essential in responding to the initial forces of change and in opening the way for further shifts. However, the Russian Revolution did not alter every facet of society—no revolution does. The new Soviet political system, although vastly different from tsarist times, preserved the authoritarian tradition in Russian life, including many specific institutions such as the secret police. An expansionist foreign policy continued as well, but it was one shaped by the results of two world wars. Russia's expansionism, combined with its new industrial strength, catapulted the country into superpower position, along with the United States, after 1945. Russia also preserved its long-standing ambivalence regarding Western culture, at once seeking to imitate features of the West but then trying to avoid its influence in the name of distinctive east European values. Thus, although science and a secular outlook gained ground in Russia, bringing it closer to modern Western culture in many respects, deliberate efforts to avoid Western artistic and popular cultural styles created divisions between the two civilizations. The events of 1989–1991 reopened the relationship to the West, redefining yet again the question of Russia's identity.

KEY QUESTIONS *What were the main changes the 1917 revolution brought to Russia and, later, eastern Europe more widely? What caused the collapse of east European communism in the 1980s? What were the principal changes and continuities in Russia's relationship with the West from 1917 into the 21st century?*

THE RUSSIAN REVOLUTION

The impetus behind Russia's 1917 revolution was its suffering during World War I. Russian forces encountered many defeats, particularly at the hands of the better-equipped German armies, and civilian conditions deteriorated dreadfully as the country sought to sustain the war effort. Food shortages and high prices spurred massive discontent. However, the underlying problems ran deeper. The government had refused to provide meaningful political rights, as the parliament (Duma) remained a shallow exercise. The tsar Nicholas II was both impervious to the legitimate grievances of the masses and stubborn; he surrounded himself with corrupt advisors who weakened the regime's reputation. Urban workers formed the clearest revolutionary class, as they were subjected to harsh conditions in the early industrial factories that only intensified the resentments they had harbored from their peas-

ant background. But middle-class liberals and the peasantry had grievances of their own, and a variety of revolutionary movements and factions, mostly operating illegally, were eager to channel any and all discontent. In essence, Russia constituted a traditional rural society being hurried into the industrial age at a dizzying pace, with an unresponsive political system—the formula for 20th-century revolution.

In March 1917, strikes and food riots broke out in Russia's capital, and they quickly assumed revolutionary proportions, calling for not just material aid but a new political regime. A council of workers, called a *soviet*, took over the city government and arrested the tsar's ministers. The tsar abdicated, thus ending the long period of imperial control. For eight months, a liberal provisional government struggled to rule the country. But liberalism was not deeply rooted in Russia, if only because of the small middle class, and the regime also made the mistake of trying to continue the war effort. Nor were liberals ready to grant massive land reforms, for they respected existing private property and thus disappointed the peasantry. So a second revolution took place in November (October, by the Russian calendar) that soon brought the radical wing of the Communist party—the Bolsheviks—and their dynamic leader—Vladimir Ilyich Ulyanov, known as Lenin—to power.

The Bolsheviks formed one of the smaller revolutionary forces in Russia, but they had the advantage of tight organization and a coherent plan of action. They also had, in Lenin, one of the great revolutionary organizers of all time. Although in exile during most of the early years of the 20th century, Lenin had hammered out a distinctive version of Marxist theory, arguing that a country such as Russia, even though not fully industrialized, could have a working-class revolution on the basis of a well-organized vanguard of the proletariat. This vanguard would operate in the proletariat's name, initially as a dictatorial force. Revolution was further possible, according to Lenin, because international capitalism had

Parade of the Red Army, Moscow, soon after the revolution.

extended so widely in the world. Here was a powerful statement in the age of imperialism, facilitating Marxist movements not just against native capitalism but against Western domination as well. Lenin built a cadre of trained, professional revolutionaries under his leadership. He dominated other Marxists, many of whom believed that Russia must first pass through a middle-class phase; he outmaneuvered other radical groups as well. His organization became known as the Bolsheviks, or "majority," even though they were, in fact, outnumbered. His most formidable opponent was the Social Revolutionary party, which had anarchist roots and won wide appeal among the peasantry by arguing for the primary importance of land reform. During the early months of the revolution, Lenin also worked for peasant support, pressing for state control of all the land, and he gained growing influence among urban workers by backing their spontaneous revolutionary councils, the soviets. Above all, Lenin surpassed his rivals by calling for radical revolution

immediately, rather than taking the cautious approach that most others advocated. As popular discontent persisted, with urban strikes and rural riots, Lenin's firm position won growing prestige. By October, Lenin had a majority in the leading urban soviets. On November 7, Bolshevik leaders seized power throughout the capital city, and a national Congress of Soviets established a Council of People's Commissars, headed by Lenin, to govern the state.

Bitter struggles remained after the Bolshevik seizure of power, however. Popular elections produced a majority for the Social Revolutionary group, but Lenin forced this party to dissolve, concluding that "the people voted for a party which no longer existed." The assembly was shut down, and the Bolshevik-dominated Congress of Soviets took its place; Russia was to have no Western-style, multiparty system. A greater problem was posed by massive resistance in various parts of the country. The Bolsheviks had only a vague notion of what to do after power was

History Debate

WOMEN AND THE RUSSIAN REVOLUTION

Following the revolution, Russia's new communist leadership proudly claimed major advances for women. The Marxist assumption was that destruction of capitalism would cure social ills for women, eliminating sexual exploitation and prostitution for example. Women were carefully included on key government committees, though rarely in a leadership role. Russian industrialization had already emphasized women's work, and this continued. Leaders proudly noted women's economic roles in contrast to Western patterns of housewifery.

But Western critics often attacked this vision, often as part of cold war debates. They argued that while women worked, they received low pay and status. Most doctors were women, for example, but their wages were quite low. Furthermore, women often had to combine full-time jobs with full responsibility for housework, for in this respect the attitudes of Russian men changed little. The long lines associated with shopping added to women's burdens here.

Recent work by historians paints a more subtle picture. During the early phase of the construction of communist society, in the 1920s, women's groups had considerable freedom. All sorts of innovations were discussed, including alternatives to the traditional family. It was also in this context that the birth rate began to drop and educational opportunities for women to expand. These changes continued, but under Stalin's government, family policy turned far more conservative, emphasizing the dominance of husband and father. Some problems, such as prostitution, were swept under the rug in an effort to emphasize communist achievement. Women's conditions had changed, but not as far as official rhetoric suggested.

Questions continued after the fall of communism in 1991. Rising consumerism meant, for some women, new opportunities to be fashionable; but other women could find the need to dress stylishly a constraint. New levels of unemployment were another challenge. Sexual exploitation and more open levels of prostitution were one consequence throughout the former Soviet realm.

obtained. They ended the war effort, signing a humiliating peace treaty with Germany that cost considerable territory. And they redistributed land to the peasantry. Gradually, they also nationalized basic industry under the Council of People's Commissars. But tsarist generals fought the new regime in many regions, backed at points by troops from Japan, France, Britain, and the United States, all appalled at the radical regime that ruled Russia. Civil war raged for three years, until the communists managed to construct a powerful Red Army of their own and win widespread popular support against foreign interven-

tion. Internal opposition, including competing revolutionary leaders, was gradually crushed, with numerous executions. Lenin also found it necessary to curry popular favor by issuing a New Economic Policy in 1921, which promised greater freedom for small businesses and peasant agriculture than the Bolsheviks had intended. Under this temporary policy, food production began to recover after years of widespread famine, and the regime had time to formulate the more permanent policies of the communist system.

By 1923, the Bolshevik revolution was an accomplished fact. A new constitution established a federal system of socialist republics, which gave minority nationalities some sense of freedom while preserving the dominance of ethnic Russians. The new nation was known as the Union of Soviet Socialist Republics, but firm Communist party control over the state governments, and centralization of all basic decisions in the new capital of Moscow (moved from St. Petersburg, now named Leningrad, to provide a more Russian, less Western tone to the revolutionary state), formed the basis of an authoritarian rule more effective than the tsarist regime had ever been. The revolutionaries also began to concentrate more exclusively on Russian affairs, after a brief period in which great hopes had been pinned on promoting a communist revolution in other European states. The Bolsheviks maintained a Communist International Office (Comintern) to support and guide communist parties elsewhere, but their main focus was on building their own state.

The Russian Revolution was one of the most important transformations in human history. Building on widespread if diverse popular discontent and a firm belief in centralized leadership, the Bolsheviks beat back foreign intervention and avoided even a partial restoration of the "old regime," as had occurred in France after Napoleon. Although the Bolsheviks utilized features of the tsarist system, including its authoritarian principles, they managed to create a new political, economic, and cultural structure without serious internal challenge after the initial years of chaos.

PATTERNS OF SOVIET HISTORY AFTER 1923

Lenin died in 1924, and after a few years of jockeying, Joseph Stalin succeeded him as undisputed leader of the Soviet state. Stalin, with his base in the Communist party, which now clearly dominated the new government, was a man of working-class background, with limited education and scant interest in theoretical Marxism, but he had a relentless obsession with power. Under his rule, Russia was to develop its own version of a socialist society—"socialism in one country," as Stalin put it, as opposed to the vision of worldwide revolution that had inspired many earlier leaders. By the time Stalin had fully eliminated potential rivals in 1927, Russia had advanced only slightly toward a socialist system, although its revolutionary momentum had not ended. Much of the land was in the hands of wealthy peasants, or kulaks, who seemed attuned to a profit-based market agriculture; even in industry, state-run enterprises and planning had only limited effect. Stalin devoted himself to a double task: to make the Soviet Union a fully industrial society, and to do so under the full control of the state, rather than private initiative. In essence, Stalin wanted modernization, but with a revolutionary, noncapitalist twist.

A massive program for collective agriculture began in 1928. Collectivization meant large, state-run farms, rather than individual holdings as in the West. Communist party agitators pressured peasants to join the collectives. The vast majority of kulaks refused, but through threats and mass executions and deportations to Siberia, they were forced to submit. Agricultural production fell drastically as a result, and although it gradually recovered during the later 1930s, the Soviet Union was saddled with the persistent problem of lack of peasant motivation. Although collective farms allowed peasants small plots of their own and job security, they created an atmosphere of factory-like discipline and rigid planning from above that left many peasants reluctant participants.

The collective farm system did, however, facilitate control of the peasantry so that rural profits could be reduced, in favor of providing capital for industrialization, and excess workers could be forced into the ranks of urban labor. If Stalin's handling of agriculture had serious flaws, his approach to industry was in many ways miraculously successful. A system of five-year plans under the state planning commission began to construct massive state-run factories in metallurgy, mining, and electric power, to make Russia an industrial country without foreign capital or more than very limited foreign advice. The focus was on heavy industry, which built on Russia's great natural resources and also served to prepare for possible war with Hitler's Germany. This unbalanced allocation, which slighted consumer goods, was to remain characteristic of the Soviet version of an industrial society. Further, Stalin's ambitious hope to replace market forces with government choices led to many allocation bottlenecks plus a wasteful use of resources and labor, as production and supply quotas for individual factories were set in Moscow. However, there was no question that rapid industrial growth had occurred. During the first two five-year plans, to 1937—the period when the West was mired in the Depression—Russian output of machinery and metal products grew 14-fold. Russia had become the world's third industrial power, behind only Germany and the United States. Russia's long history of backwardness seemed to have ended.

Along with forced industrialization, Stalin continued to maintain the police powers of the state. Opponents and even imagined opponents were executed. During the great purge of high party leaders in 1937–1938, hundreds of people were intimidated into confessing imaginary crimes against the state, and most of them were executed. Party congresses and meetings of the executive committee, or Politburo, became mere rubber stamps, and a zealous internal police, renamed the MVD in 1934, perpetuated an atmosphere of terror in Russian society.

Ironically, Stalin's purges had weakened the nation's ability to respond to the rising threat of Hitler, the self-proclaimed leader of anticommunism. Along with an understandable suspicion of the motives of the Western powers, this internal weakness encouraged Stalin to sign his pact with Hitler in 1939. The alliance bought some time for greater war preparation and also enabled Russian troops to attack eastern Poland and Finland in an effort to regain territories lost in World War I. Here was the first sign of a revival of Russia's long interest in conquest, which would be born out by the results of World War II.

The war itself was devastating for the Soviet Union. German invasions, although ultimately unsuccessful, brought massive death and hardship. Russia's new industrial base, hastily relocated to the Ural Mountains and beyond, proved vital in providing the material needed for war, along with some U.S. and British aid, but the effort was extremely costly. Great cities such as Leningrad and Stalingrad were besieged by the Germans for months, with a huge loss of life. The war heightened Russia's age-old fear of invasion and foreign interference, already enhanced by World War I and Western intervention during the revolution. However, as the Red Army pressed westward after 1943, finally penetrating to the Elbe River in Germany, there was new opportunity for aggrandizement as well. Russia was able to regain its former western boundaries, at the expense of nations such as Poland; some small states, established by the Treaty of Versailles, were swallowed up entirely. Larger east European states were allowed to remain intact, but their regimes were quickly brought under the control of communist parties backed by the Soviet occupation forces.

Most of the small nations of eastern Europe had encountered serious problems between the world wars. They were mostly new, the product of particular nationalisms honored by the Versailles treaty and carved from the western parts of the Russian empire plus the now defunct Habsburg realm. Only in Czechoslovakia did a democratic, parliamentary regime achieve durable success. Most states, after a brief democratic experience, had turned to authoritarian rule under a monarch or army general. Land reform had been ignored in favor of continued aristocratic dominance. Bickering over boundaries had added to severe economic distress; industrialization lagged, and agricultural productivity actually declined. Then came the Nazi attack that easily overwhelmed the smaller, more backward armies of states such as Poland. This was followed, between 1944 and 1948, by effective Russian control. Through a

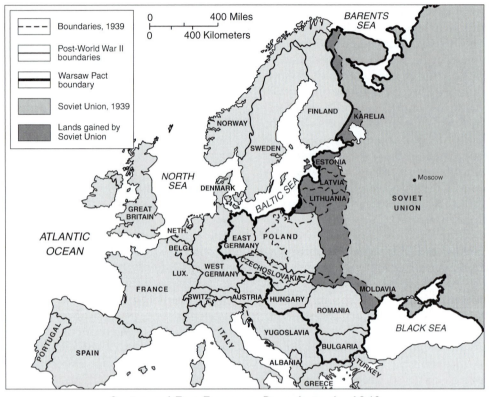

Soviet and East European Boundaries by 1948

combination of sheer military might and collaboration with local communist movements, opposition parties were crushed and an essentially Soviet political system installed in Poland, Hungary, Romania, Bulgaria, Czechoslovakia, and East Germany, in an unprecedented westward extension of Russian power. Only Yugoslavia and Albania, with separate communist regimes, plus Western-oriented Greece escaped the new Soviet empire. Elsewhere, Russian-style agricultural collectivization and state-run industrialization began to take shape along with a single-party communist government. Ultimately, the Soviet Union forged the Warsaw Pact alliance of military cooperation, to confront NATO in the West.

Although the extension of Soviet control to the rest of eastern Europe was the most dramatic diplomatic result of World War II, there were other significant developments as well. Russian participation in the late phases of the war against Japan presented the Soviets with an opportunity to seize some islands in the northern Pacific. Russia established a protectorate over the communist regime of North Korea, to match the American protectorate in South Korea. Russian aid to the victorious Communist party in China resulted in new influence in that country for a time. In the 1970s, Russia gained a new ally in communist Vietnam, which among other things provided naval bases for the Russian fleet. Russia's growing military and economic strength gave the postwar Soviet Union new leverage in the Middle East, Africa, and even parts of Latin America. Communist ideology, attacking Western domination and capitalist exploitation, won wide followings in

Uprising in Budapest, 1956. At this stage of a temporary victory, the citizens control a tank.

many parts of the world. The Soviet Union's superpower status was confirmed by its development of the atomic and hydrogen bombs and deployment of missiles and naval forces to match the rapid expansion of U.S. arsenals. Russia had become a world power.

Internally, the Stalinist system remained intact during the first postwar years. The regime was supported by the growing cold war with the United States, which convinced many Russians that firm authority was essential to counter the new foreign threat. But Stalin died in 1953, and from that time onward no single leader gained comparable power. Choice of single leaders by ruling committees balanced various interest groups in the Soviet hierarchy—the army, the secret police, the bureaucracy of the Communist party. The Soviet government had rigidified, with entrenched bureaucratic interests ready to

defend their prerogatives, and no ruler could produce sweeping change. But in 1956, a new Russian leader, Nikita Khrushchev, attacked Stalin's dictatorial policies, blasting the late dictator's crimes against opponents. The de-Stalinization current roused great interest in the satellite states of eastern Europe, chafing under Russian control. More liberal communist leaders arose in Hungary and Poland, seeking to create states that, while communist, would permit greater diversity and certainly more freedom from Soviet domination. In Poland, the Russians accepted a new leader more popular with the Polish people; among other results, Poland was allowed to halt agricultural collectivization. However, a new regime in Hungary was brutally crushed by the Russian army—de-Stalinization clearly had limits. Within the Soviet Union itself, de-Stalinization produced a reduction in the number of political trials and the most overt forms of police repression. But the apparatus of the state, including the one-party system and centralized economic planning and control, remained intact.

After the furor of de-Stalinization, patterns in Russia remained unusually stable until the 1980s. Economic growth continued, but with no dramatic breakthroughs and with recurrent worries over sluggish productivity and especially over periodically inadequate harvests, resulting in expensive grain purchases from Western nations including the United States. A number of leadership changes occurred, as party chieftains aged and died, but such transitions occurred smoothly. Russian military development continued, including substantial troop deployment throughout eastern Europe; the Soviets' world position was dramatized by leadership in many space probes and space flights, and by growing success in international athletic competitions, including the Olympic Games. The Soviet hold over eastern Europe loosened slightly after the trauma of 1956, for heavy-handed repression cost considerable prestige. East European governments were given a freer hand in economic policy and allowed to experiment with greater cultural freedom in a limited sense. As a result, Hungary emerged as a state with considerable intellectual diversity and extensive consumer-goods industries. However, severe limits remained, as Soviet leaders insisted on basic political and military control of the border states. An attempt to create a more liberal regime in Czechoslovakia, in 1968, brought Russian army repression, while renewed agitation in Poland during the late 1970s, although controlled by the Polish army, was carefully monitored by Soviet leaders. Finally, in the one direct military thrust outside the postwar orbit, Russian troops entered Afghanistan in the late 1970s, to protect a regime friendly to Soviet interests against Muslim opposition. Russian foreign policy, in other words, while not literally imperialist, remained opportunistic and particularly bent on buffering Soviet borders against a potential threat, although Russia's only actual war after 1945 was in Afghanistan.

SOVIET POLITICAL INSTITUTIONS

The political system that the Soviet leaders built after the revolution, and then extended to the smaller states of eastern Europe, maintained the authoritarian traditions of the tsar in many ways. Stalin's brutal treatment of opponents and his paranoid suspicion of potential rivals were accurately compared to the actions of tsarist predecessors such as Ivan the Terrible. Even forced industrialization, although it represented a dramatic shift in Russia's economic structure, bore the marks of Peter the Great's state-sponsored westernization. Finally, the parliamentary system that evolved under Stalin, creating impressive-sounding institutions that were elected under Communist party supervision, with no opposition tolerated, bore more than a small resemblance to the essentially powerless Duma that the last tsar had created to try to pacify liberal opposition. By Western standards, the Soviet Union had no more parliamentary power than the tsars had allowed, despite carefully worded constitutions and a universal suffrage system that, in fact, compelled most Russians to vote but offered no choice save the officially sponsored candidates and policies.

Nonetheless, the Soviet system was far more efficient and sweeping than tsarist authoritarianism had been. It utilized modern technologies, including rapid communications, and the experience of Western governments in mobilizing their societies during World War I. The Soviet system, like Hitler's Germany, was sometimes called a totalitarian government in that it sought to reach citizens directly, to shape their thoughts and actions and command their loyalties. Thus, it developed far more extensive functions than the tsarist regime had attempted. Under Stalin, control of virtually all agriculture and industry, under state planning ministries, meant that the economy and the state were fully intertwined. Peasant garden plots, a few small shops, and an often extensive black-market system were the only economic forces that escaped state direction. The state was also responsible for cultural policies, and although this had been foreshadowed by the church-state links under the tsars, it had no full precedent. The communist regime tried to shape a secular population that would believe in the political doctrines of Marxism and embrace a scientific outlook on the world, monitoring artistic and literary styles as well as purely political writing. The educational system was greatly extended, yielding rapid gains in literacy and considerable access to higher education for talented students; this system, too, was designed to promote the state's vision of a loyal and productive citizenry.

Soviet leaders also constructed an elaborate state-sponsored welfare system. Able-bodied citizens, men and women alike, were required to work; the Soviets permitted no unemployment, although extensive underemployment often existed. But the state operated medical facilities, day-care centers, and youth organizations, and provided payments to the disabled and elderly. Many of these programs were administered by Communist party organizations, including the loyal trade unions that were not permitted to strike but did mobilize many group recreational activities. Athletic clubs and beach resorts in southern Russia were among the state-run operations that cemented the welfare system. Far more literally than the welfare system developed in the West, the Soviet version embraced its citizens from cradle to grave.

Networks of political police and police informers attempted to ensure loyalty to the state, continuing and extending the tsarist tradition. Communist party members monitored all major operations, from youth groups to collective farms. Foreigners visiting Russia and Russian groups traveling abroad were carefully supervised. Groups and individuals suspected of dissidence were intimidated, often arrested. In the Stalinist era, in addition to the widely publicized purge trials and executions, millions of suspected opponents were sent to forced labor camps in Siberia. Under de-Stalinization, intimidation was moder-

In Memoriam to Y. Gagarin, a painting of Yuri Gagarin, a leading early cosmonaut, by A. Shmarinov, member of the USSR Academy of Arts, 1971.

ated somewhat. Some opponents of the regime were allowed to go into exile; others were sent to psychiatric clinics. Outright political executions became rare, but an atmosphere of considerable fear remained.

Along with policing came extensive positive efforts at persuasion and propaganda. The press and other media were strictly state-controlled, offering carefully filtered versions of the news. Massive banners, pictures of leaders, and patriotic parades stimulated devotion and a sense of identification with the regime. The Soviets introduced a new set of holidays, commemorating the

Parade of athletes and workers: Red Square, Moscow, May 1, 1981. May Day was a major civic celebration in the USSR and for workers' movements in many other countries.

revolution and other anniversaries, including the international workers' day, May 1. Under Stalin, efforts to instill Marxist loyalty to the cause of the proletariat were blended with more traditional nationalism against foreign enemies, a powerful brew that unquestionably created a high level of commitment among many Russian people.

The construction of the Soviet state was in many ways a remarkable achievement. The tsarist precedent helped, but tsarist officials and church leaders were cast aside during the revolution, while a host of new functions were undertaken. The Soviets tapped vast reservoirs of popular talent and enthusiasm to construct their new

bureaucracy. At the same time, this very creation became increasingly unwieldy. After important new access to political power for able workers and peasants in the 1920s, recruitment to the party and the bureaucracy increasingly came within the ranks of bureaucratic families, which favored their own. The Communist party itself was effectively run by a top committee, the Political Bureau, or Politburo, consisting of 20 people who were the real rulers of the country. Decisions were made at the top tier, often in secret, and then transmitted to lower levels for execution; little reverse initiative, with proposals coming from lower bureaucratic agencies, was encouraged. Just as the

In a Designing Office, an example of socialist realism. Notice bust of Stalin at left of painting.

new bureaucracy replaced the tsarist aristocracy in ruling the country, so it raised some of the same problems as a power elite often more concerned with self-perpetuation than innovation.

SOVIET CULTURE

As in politics, Russian culture in the 20th century exhibited a fascinating blend of new elements, products of the revolution and industrialization, and more traditional themes. Soviet leaders from the beginning viewed key features of traditional Russian culture as forces to be attacked and undermined. Religion headed the list. Although the new regime did not attempt to abolish the Orthodox church outright, it greatly limited the church's outreach. Thus, the church could not give religious instruction to anyone under 18, and state schools vigorously preached that religion is mere superstition. The Soviet regime also limited freedom of religion for the Jewish minor-

ity, often characterizing Jews as enemies of the state in what was, in fact, a manipulation of traditional Russian anti-Semitism. The larger Muslim minority was given greater latitude, on the condition of firm loyalty to the regime.

The Soviet state also opposed the strong Western orientation of the 19th-century tsarist elite, although it should be pointed out that this preference had never widely touched the masses. Modern Western styles of art and literature were attacked as decadent. Earlier styles, appropriated as Russian, were maintained. Thus, Russian orchestras performed a wide variety of classical music, and the Russian ballet, although rigid and conservative by 20th-century Western norms, commanded wide attention. Soviet culture emphasized a style of "socialist realism" in the arts, intent on glorifying heroic workers, soldiers, and peasants. A vigorous strand of modern art in prerevolutionary Russia was repressed under Stalin, in favor of grandiose, neoclassical paintings and sculpture. Russian architecture emphasized functional, classical lines, with a pronounced taste

Understanding Cultures

THE IMPACT OF REVOLUTION

Many major revolutions try to change culture, as part of creating the conditions for a better, or at least different, world. English Puritan revolutionaries, in the 17th century, passed laws to limit what they saw as immorality and a lack of religious zeal. Revolutionaries during the radical phase of the French Revolution hoped to create a new, civic religion to replace what they viewed as older superstitions.

Communist revolutionaries during the 20th century often sought even more systematic cultural change. Their Marxist doctrine stressed that old cultures are tainted by an outdated and unjust economic structure and must be attacked. Religion, particularly, was in disfavor; Marx had called it the "opiate of the masses." At the same time, new cultural values had to be created, as part of building a perfect communist society in which people could govern themselves and contribute freely to the common good.

In addition to the vigorous attack on traditional popular culture, new beliefs had to be constructed that were different from those of the contemporary—capitalist—West. This was one of the reasons for an emphasis on the new socialist-realist artistic style, to replace not only older styles but also to provide a clear alternative to "decadent" Western art. Education emphasized science and communism, in the hope of creating the desired new cultural values. Russian leaders even aspired to provide an alternative to the consumer culture of the West, which was seen as shallow as well as unjust because of the continued inequality within Western society.

The revolutionary approach to culture was extremely ambitious. It did generate some change, but its goals were impossible to pull off entirely. Thus, many artistic traditions, such as the ballet, coexisted within the new cultural effort; the past was only attacked selectively. In the name of protecting revolutionary culture, many intellectuals were jailed, or worse, because they would not toe the party line. It was also impossible to prevent the influence of outside values, and by the 1960s, an awareness of Western consumer and popular culture caused increasing unrest, particularly among Russian youth. Finally, when the communist effort failed by 1989, Russian culture was severely impacted. The past was gone, although there was some effort to revive it. The culture of the future had failed. What new beliefs would fill this vacuum?

for the monumental, although various sorts of historical buildings were carefully preserved.

Russian literature remained diverse and vibrant, despite official controls sponsored by the communist-dominated Writers' Union. Leading Russian authors wrote movingly of the travails of the civil war and World War II, maintaining the earlier tradition of sympathy with the Russian people, great patriotism, and a concern for the eternal Russian soul.

The most creative Soviet artists, particularly writers, often tread a fine line between conveying some of the sufferings of the Russian people in the 20th century and courting official disapproval. Their freedom also varied depending on the mood of Russia's leaders; thus, censorship eased after Stalin and then tightened again, although not to previous levels. Nonetheless, even authors critical of aspects of the Soviet regime maintained distinctive Russian values. Aleksandr Solzhenitsyn, for example, was exiled to the West after the publication of his history of Siberian prison camps, *The Gulag Archipelago*, but found the West too materialistic and individualistic for his taste. Although barred from his homeland until 1993, he continued to seek some alternative to both communist policy and westernization, clinging to his belief in the durable solidarity and faith of Russia's common people.

Along with an interest in the arts, Soviet culture placed great emphasis on science and social science. Social scientific work, heavily colored by Marxist theory, nevertheless produced important analyses of current trends and history. Scientific research was even more heavily funded, and Soviet scientists generated a number of fundamental discoveries in physics, chemistry, and mathematics. At times, scientists also experienced the heavy hand of official disapproval. Biologists and psychiatrists, particularly, were urged to reject Western theories that called human rationality and social progress into question. Thus, Freudianism was banned, and biologists who overemphasized the uncontrollability of genetic evolution were jailed. But Russian scientists overall enjoyed considerable freedom as well as great prestige. As in the West, their work was linked with advances in technology and weaponry.

Shaped by substantial state control, 20th-century Soviet culture was neither traditional nor Western. Considerable ambivalence about the West remained, as Russian leaders shared Western enthusiasm for science while trying to redefine artistic styles and popular beliefs.

ECONOMY AND SOCIETY

The Soviet Union became a fully industrial society between the 1920s and 1950s. The rapid growth of manufacturing and rise in city populations to over 50 percent of the nation's total were measures of this development. Most of the rest of eastern Europe was also fully industrialized by the 1950s. East European modernization, however, had a number of distinctive features. State control of virtually all economic sectors was one key element: No other industrialized society gave so little leeway to private initiative. The unusual

imbalance between heavy industrial goods and consumer items was another distinctive aspect. Because of the low priorities it placed on consumer goods, the Soviet Union lagged behind in not only Western staples such as automobiles but also housing construction and simple items such as bathtub stoppers. Consumer-goods industries were poorly funded and did not achieve the advanced technological level that characterized the heavy manufacturing sector. The Soviet need to amass capital for development, in a traditionally poor society, contributed to this inattention to consumer goods; so did the need to create a massive armaments industry to rival that of the United States, in a society still poorer overall. Living standards improved greatly, and extensive welfare services provided security for some groups that was lacking in the West, but complaints about poor consumer products and long waiting lines to purchase desired goods remained a feature of Soviet life.

East European industrialization also paid little regard to the environment. Chemical pollution and the exhaustion of waterways endangered large stretches of the region; some estimates held that as much as 40 percent of Russian agricultural land became endangered, whereas over 20 percent of Soviet citizens lived in areas of "ecological disaster." Damage in parts of eastern Germany and other centers was also extensive. The effort to force-feed industrial and military growth was costly, and some environmental problems may prove irreversible.

The communist system throughout eastern Europe also failed to resolve problems with agriculture. Capital that might have gone into farming equipment was often diverted to armaments and heavy industry. The arduous climate of northern Europe and Asia was a factor as well, dooming a number of attempts to spread grain production to Siberia, for example. But it seemed clear that the east European peasantry continued to find the constraints and lack of individual incentive in collective agriculture a deterrent to maximum effort. Thus, eastern Europe had to retain a larger percentage of its labor force in agriculture than was true of the industrial West and still encountered problems with food supply and quality.

Despite the importance of distinctive political and economic characteristics, eastern European society echoed a number of the themes of contemporary Western social history—simply because of the shared fact of industrial life. Work rhythms, for example, became roughly similar. Industrialization in Russia brought massive efforts to speed the pace of work and introduce regularized supervision. Incentive systems designed to encourage able workers resembled those used in Western factories. In the 1930s, the Soviets adopted a practice of rewarding the heroes of labor—workers who exceeded production quotas—with extra benefits and prestige. Along with similar work habits came similar leisure activities. For decades, sports provided excitement for the peoples of eastern Europe, as did mass media such as film and television. Family vacations to the beaches of the Black Sea were cherished.

Russian social structure also grew closer to that of the West, despite the continued importance of the rural population and the impact of Marxist theory. The aristocracy ended. Particularly interesting was an increasing division of urban society along class lines, between workers and a better-educated, managerial middle class. Wealth divisions were not as great as in the West, to be sure, but the perquisites of managers and professional people—particularly if they were Communist party members—set them off from the masses and their lower standard of living.

Finally, the Russian family had to cope with some of the same pressures of industrialization that the Western family experienced. Massive movement of people to the cities and crowded housing helped to undermine the nuclear family unit, as ties to a wider network of relatives loosened. The birth rate dropped. Official Soviet policy on birth rates varied for a time, but the basic directives became similar to those in the West. Falling infant death rates, with improved diets and medical care, plus growing periods of schooling and some increase in consumer expectations, made large families less desirable than before. Wartime dislocations contributed to a decline in the birth rate at various points as well. By the 1970s, the Russian growth rate was about the same as that of the West. Also as in the West, some minority groups—particularly Muslims in southern Russia—maintained higher birth rates than the Russian majority.

Patterns of child rearing showed some similarities to those in the West, as parents, especially in the managerial middle class, devoted more attention to their children's education and ensuring good jobs for them in the future. At the same time, children were more strictly disciplined than in the West, both at home and in school, with an emphasis on authority that might have political implications as well. Russian families were never afforded the domestic idealization of women that had prevailed in the West during industrialization. Most married women worked, an essential feature of an economy struggling to industrialize and offering relatively low wages to individual workers. As in the peasant past, women performed many heavy physical tasks. They also dominated some professions, such as medicine, although they were far lower in status than their male-dominated counterparts in the West. Russian propagandists took some pride in the constructive role of women and their official equality, but there were signs that many women suffered the psychological burdens of demanding jobs with little help from their husbands at home.

By the 1970s, many Russians seemed satisfied with their political and social system. Police repression remained, but Stalinist excesses had been reduced. Pride in Russian space and athletic achievements were coupled with a realization of the improvements in living standards and opportunity that had grown with the Soviet system. Many Russians also noted weaknesses in the West that enhanced their faith in their own institutions. Family instability, greed, and crime seemed lesser problems in the Soviet context, and only partly because the regime concealed accurate statistics.

Except for the unpopular war in Afghanistan, Russian foreign policy had remained fairly prudent; American diplomacy could be construed as more unpredictable and warlike. In 1962, for example, the Soviets pulled back their missiles from Cuba, rather than risk outright conflict with the United States. Furthermore, of course, the Soviet system had partially isolated much of eastern Europe, allowing only limited trade outside the communist system and only carefully regulated cultural contacts. The imagery of an "iron curtain" enclosing this civilization was not entirely an exaggeration.

THE EXPLOSION OF THE 1980s

Despite its many achievements, Soviet society began to come unglued by the early 1980s, opening a dramatic new chapter in east European and central Asian history. The initial cause of this extraordinary upheaval lay in deteriorating economic conditions, intensified by the costs of a military rivalry with the United States. The Soviet economic system, after a strong growth rate in the 1950s and 1960s, stopped functioning well by the late 1970s. Industrial production began to stagnate and even drop, as a result of rigid central planning, health problems, and poor worker morale. Growing inadequacy of housing and common goods resulted, further worsening motivation. As economic growth stopped, yet cold war military competition continued, the percentage of resources allocated to military production escalated toward a third of all national income. This reduced the funds available for other investments or for consumer needs. Disease rates, infant mortality, and alcoholism all increased. Younger leaders began to recognize, at first only privately, that the system was near collapse.

Nevertheless, the Soviet system was not incapable of change, despite its complex bureaucracy. In 1985, after a succession of leaders whose age or health precluded major initiatives, a new, younger official rose to the fore. Mikhail Gorbachev

quickly renewed many of the earlier attacks on Stalinist rigidity and replaced some of the old-line party bureaucrats. He conveyed a new and more Western style, dressing in fashionable clothes (his wife, Raisa, publicly did the same), holding relatively open press conferences, and even allowing the Soviet media to engage in active debate and reporting on problems as well as successes. Gorbachev also urged a reduction in nuclear armament, and in 1987, he negotiated a new agreement with the United States that limited medium-range missiles in Europe. He ended the war in Afghanistan and brought home Soviet troops.

Gorbachev proclaimed a policy of *glasnost*, or "openness," which implied new freedom to comment and criticize. He pressed particularly for a reduction in bureaucratic inefficiency and unproductive labor in the Soviet economy, emphasizing more decentralized decision making and the use of some market incentives to stimulate greater output. In many ways, Gorbachev's policies constituted a return to a characteristic Russian ambivalence about the West as he reduced Soviet isolation while continuing to criticize particular aspects of Western political and social structure. Gorbachev clearly hoped to use some Western management techniques and was open to certain Western cultural styles, without, however, intending to abandon the basic controls of the communist state. Western analysts wondered if the Soviet economy could improve worker motivations without embracing a Western-style consumerism or whether computers could be more widely introduced without allowing the free exchange of information.

Gorbachev also sought to open the Soviet Union to fuller participation in the world economy, recognizing that isolation in a separate empire had restricted access to new technology and limited the motivation to change. Although the new leadership did not rush to make foreign trade or investment too easy—considerable suspicion did persist—the economic initiatives resulted in symbolic changes, such as the opening of a McDonald's restaurant in Moscow, and a whole array of new contacts with foreigners. Participation in cultural as well as economic globalization increased.

The keynote of the reform program was *perestroika*, or economic restructuring, which Gorbachev translated into more leeway for private ownership and decentralized control in industry and agriculture. Farmers, for example, were given the chance to lease land for 50 years, with rights of inheritance, whereas industrial concerns were authorized to buy from either private or state operations. Foreign investment was newly encouraged. Gorbachev urged more self-help among Russians, including a reduction in the consumption of alcohol, arguing that he wanted to "rid public opinion of . . . faith in a 'good Tsar,' the all powerful center, the notion that someone can bring about order and organize perestroika from on high." Politically, he encouraged a new constitution in 1988, giving considerable power to a new parliament, the Congress of People's Deputies, and abolishing the communist monopoly of elections. Important opposition groups developed both inside and outside the party, wedging Gorbachev between opposing factions—liberals pressing for faster reforms versus conservative hard-liners. Gorbachev himself was elected to a new and powerful position as president of the Soviet Union in 1990.

DISMANTLING THE SOVIET EMPIRE

Gorbachev's new approach, including his desire for better relations with Western powers, prompted more definitive results outside the Soviet Union than within, as the smaller states of eastern Europe uniformly demanded greater independence and internal reforms. Bulgaria moved for economic liberalization in 1987 but was held back by the Soviets; pressure resumed in 1989 as the party leader was ousted and free elections were arranged. Hungary changed leadership in 1988 and installed a noncommunist president.

A new constitution and free elections were planned, as the Communist party renamed itself "Socialist," and Hungary moved rapidly toward a free-market economy. Poland installed a noncommunist government in 1988 and again acted quickly to dismantle the state-run economy; prices rose rapidly as government subsidies were withdrawn. The Solidarity movement, born a decade before through the merger of noncommunist labor leaders and Catholic intellectuals, became a dominant political force. East Germany displaced its communist government in 1989, expelling key leaders and moving rapidly toward unification with West Germany, which occurred in 1990—a dramatic sign of the collapse of postwar Soviet foreign policy. Czechoslovakia installed a new government in 1989, headed by a playwright, and again sought to introduce free elections and a more market-driven economy.

Although mass demonstrations played a key role in several of these political upheavals, only in Romania was there outright violence as an exceptionally authoritarian communist leader was swept out by force. As in Bulgaria, the Communist party retained considerable power, although under new leadership, and reforms moved less rapidly than in countries such as Hungary and Czechoslovakia. The same held true for Albania, where the unreconstructed Stalinist regime was dislodged and a more flexible communist leadership installed.

New divergences in the nature and extent of reform in eastern Europe were exacerbated by clashes among nationalities—as in the Soviet Union itself, where both Baltic nationalists and Asian Muslims raised new demands. Change and uncertainty brought older traditions to the fore. Romanians and ethnic Hungarians clashed, while Bulgarians attacked a Turkish minority remaining from the Ottoman period. In 1991, Yugoslavia, where an existing communist regime—although not Soviet-dominated—also came under attack, a bloody civil war developed from nationalistic disputes as Slovenia, Croatia, and Bosnia-Herzegovina proclaimed independence and then Bosnia divided among warring Serb, Croat, and Muslim factions. Czechoslovakia was peacefully broken up into a Czech republic and Slovakia.

Amid many conflicts and uncertainties, the Soviet empire was dismantled. Gorbachev reversed postwar imperialism completely, stating: "Any nation has the right to decide its fate by itself." In several cases, notably Hungary, Soviet troops were rapidly withdrawn, and generally it seemed unlikely that a change of heart, toward an attempt to reestablish a repressive empire, would be possible.

RENEWED TURMOIL AFTER 1991

The uncertainties of the situation within the Soviet Union were confirmed in the summer of 1991, when an attempted coup was mounted by military and police elements. Massive popular demonstrations, however, asserted the strong democratic beliefs that had developed in the Soviet Union since 1986. The contrast with earlier Soviet history and with China's suppression of democracy two years earlier was striking. But Gorbachev's authority ironically weakened. The three Baltic states gained full independence, although economic links with the Soviet Union remained. Other minority republics proclaimed independence as well, but Gorbachev struggled to win agreement on a continued economic union and some form of political coordination. By the end of 1991, leaders of the major republics, including Russia's Boris Yeltsin, proclaimed the end of the Soviet Union and a commonwealth of the leading republics in its stead, including the economically crucial Ukraine.

Amid the disputes, Gorbachev fell from power, doomed by his attempts to salvage a presidency that depended on the survival of a greater Soviet Union. His leadership role was assumed by Boris Yeltsin, president of Russia and an early critic of communism, who now emerged as the leading, although quickly beleaguered, political figure in Russia.

Most of the now independent republics tentatively agreed to the resulting Commonwealth of Independent States. But tensions immediately surfaced about economic coordination amid the rapid dismantling of state controls; about control of the military, where Russia—still by far the largest state—sought predominance, including nuclear control, amid challenges from the Ukraine and Kazakhstan (the two other republics that could claim nuclear weaponry); and about relationships between the European-dominated republics, including Russia, and the cluster of central Asian states. Unity within the former Soviet Union had largely ended, although Russia retained economic influence in central Asia and close ties with some new Slavic states such as Belarus.

The fate of economic reform was also uncertain, as Russian leaders hesitated to convert to a full market system lest transitional disruption further antagonize the population. Here again, more radical plans emerged at the end of 1991, calling for the removal of most government price controls. Economic conditions improved by the late 1990s; food supplies, for example, were plentiful. A growing middle class, called "New Russians," eagerly engaged in consumer delights. However, inefficient state-run factories persisted. Government revenues dropped. New gaps between rich business groups and workers and retirees resulted in important tensions.

Political directions also became complicated. Russian leaders outlawed the Communist party, in retaliation for its leadership of the failed coup, but an alternative party system emerged only slowly. Soviet citizens took delight in tearing down the old emblems of the revolution, including massive socialist-realist statues of Lenin. Even old tsarist flags and uniforms were trotted out for display. But effective new emblems had yet to be generated. Nonetheless, in some republics, including in central Asia, party leadership retained considerable vigor, and political strife in several now independent republics allowed the Russian army to regain some role. In Russia itself, Yeltsin quarreled bitterly with the parliament dominated by former communists, dissolving it by force in 1993. Communist politicians retained a strong following, whereas an equally vigorous, militaristic nationalist movement

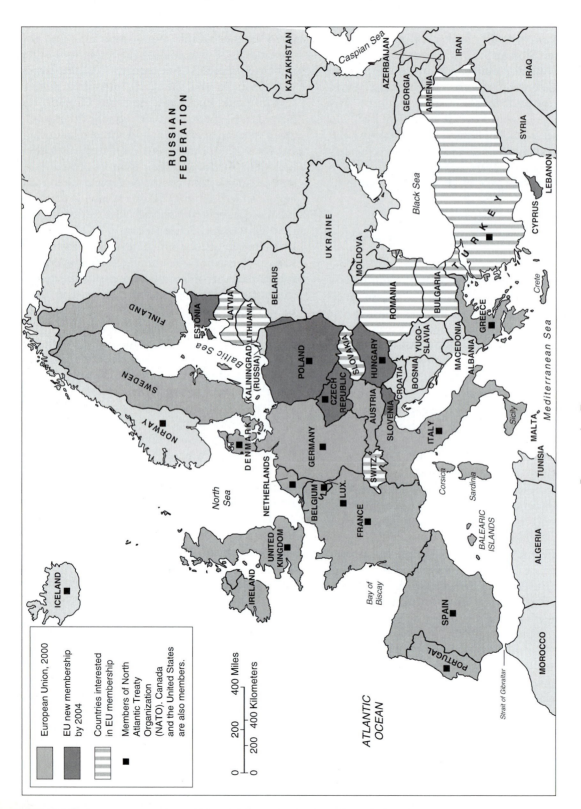

Present-day Europe

European Union, 2000

EU new membership by 2004

Countries interested in EU membership

Members of North Atlantic Treaty Organization (NATO). Canada and the United States are also members.

0	200	400 Miles
0	200	400 Kilometers

won some support. Yeltsin himself, struggling with personal problems, displayed inconsistent attitudes toward economic reforms and politics. Finally, regional conflict in Muslim areas within Russia, particularly the region of Chechnya, resulted in bitter fighting in the late 1990s and early 2000s.

Russian politics seemed to stabilize somewhat, particularly when Vladimir Putin replaced Yeltsin as president in 1999. Putin won a general election handily in the following year. Putin maintained a foreign policy favorable to the West. He talked of democratic commitment but introduced new controls over the media and took other steps to tighten central authority. Elections in 2002 showed a decline of democratic liberal parties in favor of supporters of presidential authority. Economically, Russia's fortunes improved in the early 21st century, particularly with an increase in oil exports.

UNCERTAIN FUTURES IN EASTERN EUROPE

Inevitably, Soviet and east European history in the late 1990s was dominated by the surprising events of the most recent period and by huge uncertainties about their futures. Certain stirring events made clear that much less had changed in this region during the 20th century than had been recognized—even by Soviet citizens themselves. Soviet law had long trumpeted women's equality and, indeed, Soviet women played an important role in the labor force. However, inequality within the household continued, while the unavailability of reliable birth-control devices—a result of shoddy consumer goods production—resulted in a high rate of abortions. Soviet constitutions had featured a system of federated republics, but in fact, central government control and Russian ethnic dominance spurred minority nationalism, causing new nationalist hostilities to develop. Indeed, nationalism in Russia and among newly independent east European nations threatened to profoundly divide the region. Religion also remained a vital force despite decades of secularization.

Catholicism within the smaller nations and western republics of the former Soviet Union, and Judaism and Islam in central Asia, made for important loyalties that could now be acknowledged.

Revolution and a totalitarian state had exerted only a limited impact despite theories of absolute control and undeniable police terror during key periods. The same system had done less to diminish a traditional attraction to Western values and standards than might have been imagined. Several east European states indeed rushed to proclaim a Western-style devotion to individual liberty as well as a market economy. In 1997, NATO granted membership to Poland, the Czech Republic, and Hungary, pulling them further into a Western orbit as the former border lands embraced the institutions and culture of the West. In 2003, these and several other nations joined the European Union. In Russia itself, although nationalist loyalties and economic lags might ultimately limit the country's openness to westernization, in the long run it seemed unlikely that isolation could be resumed—a sign of both long-standing east European interest in the West and the new intensity of international contacts.

Amid a host of questions about the future, once the Soviet mantle of protection had been withdrawn, several key issues dominated any analysis of the new eastern Europe and central Asia. The first involved sheer stability. Conversion to a market economy and a democratic political system was bound to be difficult. Many experts thought Poland, Hungary, and the Czech Republic stood an excellent chance to succeed, because of their relatively advanced industrial structure and unusually great contacts with Western cultural and political values. Prospects for southeastern Europe and Russia itself were less clear, and efforts to move toward market structures and abandon former communist leadership were characteristically less rapid in these areas. Ethnic and religious battles seemed to promise more instability in the former Yugoslavia, central Asia, and possibly other parts of the Balkans.

The second key issue involved traditionalist revivals. As communism fell in this region of the world, many people reembraced former loyalties, such as religion or ethnic nationalism, because they had no other beliefs to follow. Would these more traditionalist impulses persist, or would a more Western-style, semisecular mentality develop? Although predictions are inherently best guesses, history did offer some guidelines. It was important to realize that the revolution of 1917, extended to the rest of eastern Europe after 1945, would not be entirely undone. No one seriously called for a return to peasantry or the aristocracy, or an end to industrialization or mass literacy. Despite dramatic changes, there was no revolutionary dismantlement of the prior system; most of the new leaders in politics and business came from the communist bureaucracy and cautiously renounced their past. Specific features of the revolution connected to the communist system came under bitter attack, but not the more fundamental restructuring. This might facilitate democracy, compared to its fate in places such as Poland between the wars. At the same time, history also warned against facile assumptions that this region would easily assimilate with Western society after some period of adjustment. Russians, for example, maintained their commitment to a more extensive welfare system, while attacking unattractive features of Western individualism such as high crime rates and unrest among youth. Many resented profiteering, on the grounds of more egalitarian beliefs than were common in the West. Many disdained, for instance, the new influx of American "junk food," sold for high prices.

Finally, Russia's relationship to not just the West but also the wider world focused new attention on important questions. The Soviet empire, although somewhat closed to outside contact, had organized politics and economics in a huge part of Europe and Asia, building on the previous expansion of the tsars. Much of this was now undone. The empire had also played a vigorous role in world affairs, providing political guidance and economic and military aid to every continent. Economic failure eclipsed this role, at least for the moment. But what world role would Russia and its neighbors

now play? In the immediate aftermath of collapse, particularly after 1991, Russian leaders carefully supported most Western diplomatic initiatives. This included many aspects of the United States–led campaign against terrorism, with particular attention to rebellious forces in Islam. Was this likely to persist, given different traditions and interests? Would Russia, still industrial and still a territorial giant, renew contact with its long-standing, if variously defined, sense of mission? These are questions not yet answered. Russia's new role continues to unfold as we move further into the 21st century.

ISSUES AND CONNECTIONS

The most important issue in dealing with Russia and eastern Europe during the 20th century involves not becoming blinded by very recent developments alone. It is vital to take the communist revolution seriously. Most Americans opposed communism, and during the cold war there were barriers to studying it carefully. Communism now seems to have failed, at least outside of Asia. But it was a serious and, to many, attractive movement that helped organize significant changes in Russia and elsewhere. The 20th century was not simply a holding pattern waiting for the 1990s to happen. Many east Europeans—particularly but not exclusively the elderly—look back on the days of communism with nostalgia, and communist parties still have substantial followings in several countries. Even in east-central Europe, which resented Russian domination, developments between the wars remind us not to assume that full westernization will be easy, though it is now clearly widely desired.

Several connections tie Russia and eastern Europe to their past, despite the huge changes of revolution and more recent democratization. Three stand out. The first involves the importance attributed to the state and state-sponsored order, which continued under communism. Since the fall of communism, this emphasis has diminished a bit, but the Russian state still assumes powers over newspapers and television, for example, that differ from the policies of Western societies. And many Russians approve of measures that will reduce protests and signs of disorder. This pattern reflects centuries of Russian political tradition, including the communist decades.

Many Russians also remain committed to a focus on community ties, over rampant individualism. They welcome consumerism, when their incomes permit, but many also resent signs of pronounced income inequalities. Group loyalty can show up in schools. A parent, told that her children helped others cheat on a test, approves of this sign of solidarity with other children. Again, patterns of this sort echo not only communism but also older peasant values.

Finally, there is the ambiguity about the West itself, particularly in Russia, echoing three centuries of debate. Majorities in east-central Europe are less hesitant. But Russians, after a burst of enthusiasm following 1991, are now more cautious about whether the West as a whole provides the model they wish to follow.

SUGGESTED WEB SITES

For Web sites on Lenin, see http://soften. ktu.lt/~kaleck/Lenin/. On leaders of the Soviet Union and Russia from Stalin to Yeltsin, see http://home.mira.net/~andy/bs/index.htm. On changes in the former Soviet Union since 1991, see http://www.learner.org/exhibits/russia.

SUGGESTED READINGS

Recent work includes Ronald Powaski, *The Cold War* (1998); Jeffrey Brooks, *Thank You, Comrade Stalin! Soviet Public Culture from the Revolution to the Cold War* (2000); Joseph Rothschild, *Return to Diversity: A Political History of East Central Europe since World War II* (2000); Sabrina Ramat, ed., *Eastern Europe: Politics, Culture and Society since 1939* (1998); Rex Wade, *The Bolshevik Revolution and the Russian Civil War* (2001) and *The Russian Revolution, 1917* (2000); Terry Martin, *The Affirmative Action Empire: Nations and Nationalism in the Soviet Union* (2001); Lee Edward, *The Collapse of Communism* (2000); Stephen Kotkin, *Armageddon Averted: The Soviet Collapse, 1970–2000* (2001); Terry Martin, ed., *A State of Nations: Empire and Nation-Making in the Age of Lenin and Stalin* (2001); and Wendy Goldman, *Women at the Gates: Gender and Industry in Stalin's Russia* (2002).

Recent Soviet history is examined in Martin McCauley, *The Soviet Union, 1917–1991* (1993); Richard Barnet, *The Giants: Russia and America* (1977); A. Rubinstein, *Soviet Foreign Policy Since World War II* (1981); Alec Nove, *The Soviet Economic System* (1980); Stephen Cohen et al., eds., *The Soviet Union Since Stalin* (1980); and Ben Eklof, *Gorbachev and the Reform Period* (1988). On the Russian Revolution, see B. Wolfe, *Three Who Made a Revolution* (1955); D. Footman, *Civil War in Russia* (1962); and T. Skocpol, *States and Social Revolutions* (1979), a major interpretive effort.

Other areas of eastern Europe are explored in Joseph Held, *The Columbia History of Eastern Europe in the 20th Century* (1992); F. Fetjo, *History of the People's Democracies: Eastern Europe Since Stalin* (1971); J. Tampke, *The People's Republics of Eastern Europe* (1983); Timothy Ash, *The Polish Revolution: Solidarity* (1984); H. G. Skilling, *Czechoslovakia: Interrupted Revolution* (1976), on the 1968 uprising; and B. Kovrig, *Communism in Hungary from Kun to Kadar* (1979).

On the early signs of explosion in eastern Europe, see K. Dawisha, *Eastern Europe, Gorbachev and Reform: The Great Challenge* (1988). Bohdan Nahaylo and Victor Swoboda, *Soviet Disunion: A History of the Nationalities Problem in the USSR* (1990), provides important background information. An excellent recent study is Ron Brady, *Kapitalism: Russia's Struggles to Free Its Economy* (1999). On women's experiences, see Barbara Engel and Christine Worobec, eds., *Russia's Women: Accommodation, Resistance, Transformation* (1990).

30 ◆

East Asia in the 20th Century

In the 19th century, east Asia had been divided by the differing responses of Japan and China to Western pressures. These divisions continued into the 20th century. Japan maintained an aggressive foreign policy that helped launch World War II and then developed one of the most successful economies in the world. China, in contrast, continued to struggle in order to industrialize. The giant nation was wracked by two revolutions, the second initiating a communist regime that resembled Soviet Russia in important ways.

Nevertheless, east Asia has maintained something of its own character. Japan, although an advanced industrial nation and a democracy, continued to differ from the West in many ways. China, although ultimately a communist society, showed marked variations from the Soviet model. It borrowed selectively from the Soviet example, somewhat as Japan had earlier picked and chosen from the West. There were some signs, also, that the unique characteristics of east Asia would propel much of the region, and not just Japan, into the ranks of fully industrialized nations by the early 21st century. Certainly, the rapid economic growth of South Korea, Hong Kong, and Taiwan, and the possibility that China itself might make the turn to full industrialization, has raised new discussion of east Asian "advantages" in the process of latecomer modernization. Finally, even amid great diversity, east Asian nations continue to interact. Japan's invasion of China in the 1930s colored the development of both nations. New economic exchanges by the 1970s again focused some attention on the links within this historic region.

East Asia in the 20th century thus split between the Chinese communist pattern, shared to an extent by Vietnam, and Japan's rapid industrialization, joined after the 1950s by other parts of the Pacific Rim, including parts of southeast Asia. Both sections of east Asia continued to utilize former traditions of strong government and

Confucian values, blending them with new ingredients—in China's case, outright revolution—to gain increasing impact in the world at large.

KEY QUESTIONS *Both China and the combined area of Japan and the Pacific Rim were unusual centers of 20th-century activity and change. Can you think of reasons for this, compared to other areas? What were the major changes that communism brought to China? What did Japan westernize, and not westernize, during the century? (This question has two parts, one for the war period and one for after 1945.) In what ways have China and the Pacific Rim been drawing closer together since 1978? What are the key remaining differences?*

A CLASH OF CULTURES: REVOLUTION AND WAR

During the first two decades of the 20th century, Japan continued its policies of rapid industrialization and imperialist expansion. The exploitation of Korea developed rapidly from 1910 onward. Japan's participation in World War I involved little major fighting, but it provided Japan with a chance to acquire former German colonies in the Pacific islands. At the same time, Japan was not granted high status at the Versailles Peace Conference, which Japanese leaders found humiliating. Internal pressure mounted for a more aggressive foreign policy that would compel the Western powers to recognize Japan's greatness. Internal stresses were also accumulating within Japanese society. A growing radical-socialist movement attempted to address working-class grievances, although it was successfully outlawed. Intellectuals continued the discussion of Japan's identity.

But as important tensions swirled in Japan, China faced more dramatic events in the century's first decades. Growing Western penetration of the empire, combined with the government's sluggish response and the wave of students eager

to see major reform, produced a revolutionary climate. A new republican movement sought to replace the age-old empire. Headed by Dr. Sun Yat-sen, the educated son of a poor family who had spent time in both British-controlled Hong Kong and Hawaii, the republicans believed that China should imitate Western principles of nationalism and democracy while introducing socialist policies to protect the people's welfare. Sun Yat-sen was no blind admirer of Western values; his emphasis on socialism was designed to guard against the excesses of capitalism and individualism. Nonetheless, he and his student followers advocated a radical departure from Chinese political traditions.

In 1908, the death of the dowager empress brought government promises of a written constitution and an examination of other aspects of Western government. But these vague assurances were not enough to prevent widespread student rioting, which led to outright revolution in 1911. Sun Yat-sen hurried back from a trip abroad to head the provisional government, as the empire was ended in 1912.

The revolution demonstrated the weakness of the imperial regime, victim of the long decline characteristic of earlier Chinese dynasties but heightened by its inability to counter growing Western imperialism. However, although the old regime was easily displaced, the issue of what to do next was far less quickly resolved, for China was not ready to spring into a modern, Western lifestyle. Sun Yat-sen's movement had attracted student support because of its optimistic belief that China could regain its full independence and become politically like the West with no difficulty. However, the Chinese had never had direct experience with voting or representative bodies. The decline of the imperial institutions made it difficult simply to govern the country, much less reform it. The revolutionaries appointed a military general, Yaun Shi-h'ai, as president of the new republic, to conciliate the army and prevent foreign, particularly Japanese, intervention. The choice also reflected the fact that Sun Yat-sen and

World Profiles

SUN YAT-SEN (1867–1925)

Dr. Sun Yat-sen was an important figure in 20th-century Chinese history; he helped solidify the revolution that toppled the traditional imperial government. Sun failed, however, to create a fully successful alternative, becoming one of those world leaders whose reach exceeds their grasp. Sun Yat-sen was born into a poor family near Canton (present-day Guangzhou), but he acquired an education at that point in history when students experienced new influences from the West and became resistant to Chinese traditions. Because of his opposition to the conservative imperial regime, Sun was forced to spend much time abroad, particularly in the United States, and he was thoroughly familiar with Western political thought. His writings proclaimed goals of nationalism, democracy, and ultimately socialism for a China that would be new, but not necessarily a victim of some of the social ills that plagued the West. These writings made him the hero of Chinese students educated overseas.

When a revolution broke out in China in 1911, Sun rushed back to China from the United States and became its provisional president. At his insistence, no compromise was struck with the imperial regime, and China's boy-emperor resigned in 1912. Sun Yat-sen could not control the presidency, however, which passed to a military general. Sun formed the Guomindang (Nationalist party) to join forces with the military as part of an effort to organize a parliamentary state. However, these efforts to unite communists and conservatives in one

China's first great modern revolutionary, Sun Yat-sen.

movement failed with his death in 1925. China remained deeply divided for another two decades. Was Sun Yat-sen the best kind of leader to create a new state in China? What were the main barriers he faced in fulfilling his self-proclaimed tasks?

his colleagues had no government experience, and they proved to be indifferent administrators. But the new president was no reformer; although he briefly tolerated an elected parliament, he worked to consolidate his own power as a possible future emperor. He was not capable of improving government efficiency, as tax revenues dwindled and Western influence expanded. In fact, China by 1916 was collapsing into a series of regional governments, headed by competing warlords, each with his own local army. Sun Yat-sen and his associates tried to counter the growing chaos by forming a political party of their own, the Guomindang, but they gained influence only in part of China, mainly around the city of Canton (present-day Guangzhou). Thus, the 1911 revolution had destroyed key traditional institutions, but it had not created adequate substitutes for them. For this reason, revolution simmered in China throughout the next few decades, producing one deficient new regime after another until after World War II.

There was, briefly, a more hopeful interlude. During the later 1920s, the Guomindang armies were able to subdue a number of the warlords. The regime also induced the major Western powers to renounce their claims on Chinese territories; the Western-controlled treaty ports thus returned to Chinese hands, with the exception of Portuguese Macao and British Hong Kong. Revolutionary leaders became more skeptical of Western political models and capitalist economics, and the values behind them, and the idea of a Chinese version of modern society gained ground. The new leader of the Guomindang, Jiang Jieshi (Chiang Kai-shek), formulated a constitution that established authoritarian rule but was designed to lead the country to democracy. New laws also attacked traditional constraints on women in Chinese society, including the practice of footbinding; growing numbers of students attended modernized universities, some run by Christian missionaries, where Western-style science and social science were taught. Nonetheless, this period of renewal was short-lived. Jiang Jieshi did not effectively rule the whole country, and the warlords soon resurfaced. Jiang's own government became increasingly opportunistic, making deals with warlords and business leaders rather than focusing on political reform, and the hope for a complete democracy increasingly dwindled. Furthermore, the Guomindang faced another internal opponent in a strong communist movement, inspired by Marxism and the Russian Revolution. Driven out of the Guomindang itself, the communists staged the heroic Long March to the distant Shensi province in the northwest, where they held out under the leadership of Mao Zedong.

It was in this confusion that Japan's path fatefully crossed China's once again, as Japan's industrial strength continued to grow. As in the Soviet Union, the 1920s and 1930s constituted an important second stage in the Japanese process of industrialization. Heavy industry expanded rapidly; the Japanese developed their own machinery production, and the use of electrical systems spread widely. With a growing and skilled labor force, mostly male, the Japanese also reconsidered earlier industrial policies. Many workers were given security of employment in return for hard work and loyalty to the firm, whereas the government itself increasingly combined worship of the emperor with nationalism in order to prevent social unrest. Political stability, however, proved elusive.

After a period of moderate politics during the 1920s, in which Japan seemed to accept a multiparty political system, even allowing nonaristocrats to serve as prime ministers for the first time, Japan abandoned liberalism after 1930. The nation suffered severely from the early stages of the economic depression, as international trade plummeted. Dependent on exports for food and fuel, Japan saw unemployment rise steadily when the depression in the West reduced its available markets. The silk industry, long an export staple, suffered when Western synthetics like nylon cut into sales—a sign of Japan's continuing industrial vulnerability. Furthermore, population growth contributed to the pressure, as 65 million inhabitants were crowded into territory about half the size of the state of Texas. A million people a year were added through the combination of high birth rates and falling death rates.

Economic chaos, although short-lived, allowed Japan's military leaders, allied with conservative business and agricultural interests, to regain the upper hand in politics. This group rebelled against the cautious liberalism of the reigning politicians, using assassination and the threat of mass unrest as weapons. Japan's powerful but fearful oligarchy turned to an essentially

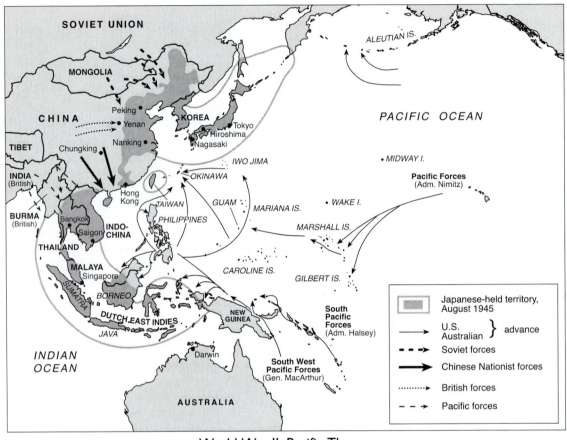

World War II: Pacific Theater

fascist approach that was foreign, in its violence and methods of intimidation, to Japan's political tradition. This transformation reflected not only the crisis of the economic depression but also the strains that rapid industrialization had placed on Japanese society—strains that did not produce outright revolution but did lead the ruling oligarchy to its militaristic lines of defense. Parliamentary rule became increasingly shallow, as military leaders manipulated the politicians or, like General Hideki Tojo, held office directly. With this authoritarianism came renewed interest in foreign expansion; the Japanese sought a sphere of influence in eastern Asia to deal with the nation's overproduction and overpopulation.

The more aggressive foreign policy aided, and was aided by, Japan's quick rebound to renewed industrial growth.

In 1931, the Japanese launched an undeclared war on China, seizing the province of Manchuria and turning it into a satellite state. This was the first act of aggression in the interwar period that led toward World War II; Chinese leaders were unable to gain Western support, beyond moral condemnations of Japan, and this failure helped teach other rulers, such as Hitler, that aggression reaped worthwhile dividends. Jiang Jieshi hoped to satisfy the Japanese by agreeing to the loss of Manchuria, but in fact the Japanese soon resumed their advance, extending control over additional

Hiroshima, 1945, after the first atomic bomb was dropped.

provinces in 1935, and in 1937 mounting a new war against China, which effectively continued until Japan's World War II defeat in 1945. Thus, China, already internally divided, faced 15 years of invasion and occupation. Vast stretches of the country were seized, many resources diverted to Japanese war industries, and millions of people killed or uprooted. Jiang Jieshi's regime was driven from the great cities, but he was able to maintain control of many rural provinces. Both the warlords and communists now joined in opposition to the Japanese, the communists gaining prestige and important military experience through their role in the resistance.

Stalemated in China, Japan used the outbreak of war in Europe as an occasion to turn its attention to other parts of Asia. It seized Indochina from France's troops and then allied with Germany and Italy in a pledge of mutual military assistance. This alliance, along with continued expansion in southeast Asia as the Japanese attacked Malaya and Burma, put the Japanese on a collision course with the United States, which as a Pacific power itself was unwilling to allow Japan to become a predominant force in the Far East. U.S. holdings in Hawaii and the Philippines, the fruit of earlier imperialism, convinced Japanese leaders that a clash was inevitable. Negotiations with the United States broke down with the American insistence that Japan renounce all lands acquired since 1931. It was within this climate that the Japanese attacked Pearl Harbor on December 7, 1941, and then in the following months seized American possessions in the eastern Pacific, including the Philippine islands. Only toward the end of 1942 did the United States begin to turn the tide, making the most of its superior level of industrialization. Scattered islands were reconquered, followed in 1944 by the Philippines, while massive air raids began an onslaught on Japan itself. Meanwhile American, British, and Chinese forces continued to bog down a considerable Japanese army on the Asian mainland. Finally, in 1945, the United States dropped atomic bombs on the cities of Nagasaki and Hiroshima, forcing the full surrender of Japan and a period of American occupation.

RETURN TO STABILITY IN JAPAN

The end of World War II separated the paths of Japan and China once again. Japan's imperialist surge ended, seemingly for good. It had been an anomaly in Japanese history in any event, and American-imposed changes in government personnel and limitations on military activity further reduced the potential for military adventurism. Victims of the only actual use of atomic weapons, many Japanese advocated an antimilitarist stance, whereas official Japanese policy accepted American protection against possible Soviet aggression rather than mounting a significant defense capacity directly.

Internal politics were restructured as well, as American occupation forces helped produce a more liberal constitution, which enhanced the power of parliament, reduced the emperor from a religious figure to a national figurehead, and provided important safeguards for freedom of speech and press. Universal suffrage, first granted during the moderate period of the 1920s, was restored, and a number of political parties contested the major elections. In fact, a single party, the Liberal Democrats, held the reins of government throughout most of the postwar decades, but extensive political criticism and continued potential opposition affected its policies. Japan produced a new era

of political stability, in which major concentration turned to economic development, and the Japanese soon entered the ranks of the world's most technologically sophisticated nations.

UPHEAVAL AND ONGOING REVOLUTION IN CHINA

With Japan's defeat, China emerged as the leading power in the Far East. Jiang Jieshi was welcomed as a postwar leader, particularly by his U.S. allies; the Chinese were treated as a great power, along with Britain, France, the United States, and the Soviet Union, in forming the new United Nations. This was the first time an Asian nation had been accorded such status in Western-dominated diplomacy. However, the honeymoon was short-lived. Jiang Jieshi was unable to assert a firm hold on China, for communist opposition began to mount.

The communist struggle with the Guomindang dated back to the aftermath of China's first modern revolution. Inspired by the revolutionary atmosphere and also the example of Russia's Bolshevik success, a communist movement formed among students in Beijing between 1919 and 1921; the movement quickly came under the leadership of Mao Zedong, a librarian who was from a wealthy peasant family. Communists and Guomindang collaborated for a time, both interested in establishing a revolutionary regime and opposing the warlords. But the goals of the two groups were quite different, and Jiang Jieshi expelled the communists in 1927, summarily executing anyone who wore the emblematic communist red scarf. Recurrent battles continued, for although the communists were weakened, they were not eliminated. Then a renewed military effort in 1934 culminated in the historic Long March, in which Mao led his followers to a remote northwestern province, where they built a strong reform movement among the peasantry and an independent power base. World War II gave the communists a chance to display their solid organization and guerrilla fighting techniques, and they also gained important new territory in their resistance effort against Japan.

By the war's end, the communists claimed to control over 70 million Chinese, with an army of almost a million. The Guomindang, in contrast, had been exhausted in its war effort, as the Japanese had taken over the coastal cities where the movement had its power base. Economic problems and internal divisions and corruption further weakened the Guomindang, which could not prevent communist guerrilla attacks and sabotage that undermined support for the existing regime. The communists offered not only successful military strategies but also a much clearer program of land reform to China's peasant majority than the Guomindang, which increasingly seemed little more than a Western-dominated militarist group, its heritage from Sun Yat-sen mere rhetoric. Soviet aid to the communists also helped, whereas American support for the Guomindang actually enhanced the government's organizational confusion. While Stalin had no love for the Chinese communists and Mao had long since diverged from the Russian model in peasant issues, a temporary union between the two was a critical factor in communist success.

Civil war between the communists and Jiang Jieshi's armies broke out in 1945, and the Guomindang lost ground steadily. Indeed, the speed of communist success surprised everyone, including the communists themselves. By 1949, the communists were in full control of mainland China. By 1950, Jiang Jieshi had been driven to the island of Taiwan, which the communists could not capture because they had no navy. There, Jiang and his army imposed an authoritarian regime, while still plotting an eventual return to the mainland. But, in fact, the mainland now squarely belonged to Mao and the communists.

Communist victory, in turn, meant a second revolution in modern Chinese history—or a culmination of almost half a century of revolutionary agitation. The new rulers executed at least 800,000 political opponents and arrested many more. Their goal was to destroy all traces of China's forming rul-

Mao Zedong poster helps inspire election workers as they count the vote during elections to the National People's Congress.

ing class—educated bureaucrats, landlords, and capitalists alike. In their place, the communists constructed a strong centralized state dedicated to economic modernization and social change. Five-year plans were issued, based on the Soviet model, to encourage heavy industry. Agriculture was collectivized, with peasant communes replacing traditional villages. With property seized from landlords, the revolution in the countryside reached major proportions. The government strictly controlled education and information, mounting a major attack on the various religions of China.

In its early years, Mao's regime maintained its close alliance with Soviet Russia. This alliance, plus a desire to assert China's traditional power in Asia, prompted the communist regime to resist U.S. advances in the Korean War. Divided between a communist north and noncommunist south after World War II, Korea had become a battleground in 1950 when the communists invaded South Korea. The United States came to the aid of its southern protectorate and then crossed into North Korea. This move resulted in massive Chinese intervention, which ultimately forced American retreat and a restoration of the previous Korean regimes and boundaries. China thus served notice that no outside power could claim east Asian dominance, in contrast to the humiliating decades of Western and Japanese imperialism. However, this same new strength soon caused a rift between Chinese and Russian communists. Mao began to attack post-Stalinist Soviet policy as a violation of true Marxism. Russian aid and advisors to the new Chinese regime were withdrawn, and tensions along the Soviet–Chinese border increased. Although ideological differences colored the new disagreement, it became clear that territorial disputes were an important consideration as well: the Chinese had not forgotten the earlier Russian seizure of some northern lands, whereas Russian rulers were keenly aware of the potential pressure of China's massive population on their sparsely peopled Asian republics. By the 1960s, the two giants of the communist world had become virtual enemies.

The rift with Russia prompted Chairman Mao to experiment with a different path to communism during the 1960s. Instead of five-year plans for heavy industry, Mao began to emphasize small-scale workshops in which intensive labor would substitute for advanced technology. Peasant communes stressed the need for a new Chinese personality, with common dining halls and large-scale propaganda attacking the evils of traditional family ties and Confucian hierarchical values. Finally, schools were transformed into pure agencies of Maoist propaganda, and technical and scientific study was abandoned. Many teachers and other intellectuals were ordered to the countryside to perform agricultural work. During the 1960s,

Peasants thrashing rice on an agricultural commune near Beijing.

China seemed engulfed by this new revolutionary fervor, as Mao sought to solidify his power, to defy the Soviet model, and, above all, to attack many of the traditions of Chinese society, in order to produce a modern nation that was also free from the trappings of Western modernization or the bureaucratic conservatism of the Soviet Union. During this period of the Cultural Revolution, bands of youths were organized to attack any vestige of traditional hierarchy in schools, family, and even the army. As one manifesto proclaimed, "We are bent on striking down not only the reactionaries in our school, but the reactionaries all over the world. Revolutionaries take it as their task to transform the world."

The Cultural Revolution in China began to yield, however, by the late 1960s. Disruption of the schools and the attempt at backyard industry had worsened the Chinese economy. Pressure from the Soviet Union, including outright border fighting in 1969, prompted Mao to seek a partial reconciliation with the United States, which occurred in 1971. More moderate communist leaders also regained influence, and on Mao's death, in 1976, they assumed control. Under the leadership of Deng Xiaoping, the communist regime, although maintaining tight political authority, began to devote itself to intensive but rather conventional modernization efforts, stressing technical education and industrial development. In fact, an important student movement for democracy in 1989 was vanquished in favor of continued authoritarianism.

EAST ASIA TOWARD THE END OF THE CENTURY

The major events of east Asian history in the 20th century may seem bewildering in their complexity. Japan moved from imperialism to modernization, from authoritarianism to democracy and a concentration on economic advance. China endured two revolutionary periods punctuated by Japanese invasion and then, under the communists, three distinct periods: Russian-style consolidation, radical experimentation during the Cultural Revolution, and more pragmatic modernization since the late 1970s. Clearly, east Asian nations struggled for appropriate political forms during much of the 20th century. Stability in Japan since World War II, and considerable stability in China since the end of the Cultural Revolution, suggest that such a goal has finally been achieved.

East Asia was also adjusting to new power alignments. Along with the period of conflict between Japan and China, the region was engaged in limiting Western influence and preventing major new Soviet gains. China's expulsion of special Western treaty rights, Japan's attack on Western-held territories, and China's Korean intervention all worked to this end, albeit in different ways. Although Soviet and American influence in east Asia remained considerable, there was little question by the 1970s that the region had regained substantial freedom of action. Internal conflicts subsided as well, so that since

the end of the Korean War, a period of effective peace took hold within the region. Tensions continued, to be sure: the regimes of North and South Korea faced each other across a precarious border, the Chinese People's Republic officially claimed sovereignty over a now separate regime on Taiwan, and China encountered tensions with Vietnam to the south. But compared to many other parts of the contemporary world, the region became fairly trouble-free—as it had so often been in earlier periods of history. Relative stability and a reduction in the turmoil that had marked the earlier decades of the century have given the major regimes of east Asia a chance to define their own characters.

JAPAN, INCORPORATED

Japan in the 20th century, for all its transformations in political regime and foreign policy, displayed two consistent traits: an ability to combine adaptation to selected Western imports and technologies with a distinctive cultural identity, and a dynamism that brought the nation to world prominence first as a military force and then as one of the economic giants of the final decades of the 20th century. The two traits were interrelated. Japan's skill in borrowing without a loss of identity, and its ability to utilize traditional characteristics such as strong group cohesion, had much to do with military and economic success. Such was Japan's impact that by the 1970s, along with continued Japanese interest in Western ways, came an almost obsessive Western eagerness to learn Japanese secrets, including traditional social traits that seemed so strikingly useful in an advanced industrial age. Western business and labor leaders began to make pilgrimages to Japan with some of the same zeal that Japanese students had displayed in their visits to Western nations during the previous century.

Japanese politics certainly blended modern democratic forms with traditional elitist ties. As in the Meiji era and to an extent during the

History Debate

JAPAN AND WESTERNIZATION

Japan had copied the West extensively in the late 19th century. Imitation proceeded even farther under American occupation after World War II. Japan's industrial success, its democratic political system, its increasingly ardent embrace of consumerism all suggested a society that was increasingly Western, despite its history and geography. Conservative critics who attacked modern Japan because of loss of tradition implied the same judgment.

Yet many observers insisted that Japan remained different from the West in crucial ways. They used the country, in fact, as an illustration of how a society could become successfully modern without westernizing entirely. Personal and family values formed one distinctive area. Respect for the elderly, though challenged by the costs of an aging society by the early 21st century, seemed different from the West. So, in subtle ways, did the status of women. Advertisers rated Japan one of the industrial societies in which commercials slanted toward strong masculinity had the greatest success. Business forms and the close links between business and the state were another area in which Japan was not just like the West. Many interpreters, in Japan and outside, pointed to the ongoing impact of modified Confucian values in instilling respect for group loyalty and respect for hierarchy. By the 1990s, when Japan's economy slowed, some Americans argued that the Japanese government was too cozy with business, tolerating inefficiency and subsidizing bad decisions. But it was not clear if this judgment was correct, or that Japan would choose to change its distinctive habits even if it was.

authoritarian period of the 1930s, postwar politics were dominated by civil servants and business leaders. Although democratic suffrage prevailed and a number of political parties showed strength, the fact was that postwar Japan experienced no shifts in party leadership. Opposition groups were less important than factional jockeying within the Liberal Democratic party. Few major policy shifts occurred after World War II. Only in 1993, amid growing evidence of business payoffs, did the Liberal Democrats split and lose their parliamentary majority, opening the possibility of more innovative politics. Up to this point, unusual stability in party dominance made Japan less similar to the Western political system than the constitutional structure would suggest. The other distinctive feature of the contemporary Japanese state was

an unusual alliance with business interests toward the promotion of economic development and the expansion of exports. Government economic planning remained extensive, and business leaders willingly acquiesced to government production guidelines and other regulations; there was no sense of a division of interests between public and private spheres, as still prevailed to an extent in the West. Small wonder that the coordination of economic policies produced the half-admiring, half-derisory Western label of "Japan, Incorporated."

Close business and political interaction resulted, in part, from the needs of a wartime economy and then postwar reconstruction. It was supported by Japan's precarious position in terms of resources, as the nation needed to import petroleum and most other vital raw materials, and so

Contemporary Tokyo.

depended on active exports, which, in turn, the government helped promote. However, the inter-action also followed from a long cultural tradition in which group cohesion was seen as the logical basis of society's functioning, a cohesion that easily blurred what Westerners saw as the lines between private enterprise and the role of the state. Government initiative also played a key role in ending Japan's rapid population increase. Once imperialist expansion ended, Japanese leaders realized that population must stabilize, and they used government, in the late 1940s and 1950s, to organize an active campaign promoting birth control and legalized abortion, which indeed reversed a century-long trend of demographic expansion. Unlike the West, where government policy had little to do with population trends and sometimes ran counter

to such trends, Japan's more integrated political-social system allowed concrete action in a vital area of human behavior, which, in turn, encouraged more orderly economic growth and an improvement in living standards.

Important segments of Japanese culture were also oriented toward the goal of economic development. The extensive school system established during the Meiji period was further expanded. Japanese children were encouraged to achieve academic success, with demanding examinations for entry into the university becoming the primary goal of ambitious young men and women. Higher education, in turn, placed a major emphasis on technical and scientific subjects, although general research and teaching in the social sciences gained ground as well. Growing university enrollments, based on examination performance, thus recruited students on the basis of educational merit, creating one of the most open social systems in the world.

Japanese culture also preserved important traditional elements, however, providing aesthetic and spiritual satisfaction amid rapid economic change. Japanese films and novels recalled earlier history, including the age of the samurai warriors; they also stressed group loyalties, as opposed to individuality or strong assertions of personal will. An interest in rituals, including tea ceremonies and traditional costumes for recreation, remained an important theme as well. Japanese artists participated actively in the "international style" developed in the West, but they typically infused it with earlier Japanese motifs such as stylized nature painting. Japanese architects, also working in the modern style, incorporated traditional themes as well. Finally, both Buddhism and Shintoism, despite a largely secular culture, sustained religious forces in Japanese life. Overall, Japan during the 20th century produced a blend of new cultural interests, many of which originated in the West, and older approaches, which allowed Japan, in turn, to make distinctive contributions to international artistic and scientific movements.

Particularly after World War II, however, it was through rapid economic growth that Japan made its clearest mark. Industrial development had continued at a steady pace through the 1920s, and again in the late 1930s, as Japan built upon its efforts during the Meiji era and produced a fully industrialized society. Then from the 1950s onward, the Japanese moved into the orbit of advanced industrial nations, easily surpassing the level of technological development current in eastern Europe and challenging Western nations for world leadership. Beginning in the middle of the century, economic growth rates were among the highest in the world. By the 1970s, Japan became the world's chief producer and exporter of automobiles and many kinds of electronic equipment.

Japan's economic success rested on several factors. Wages remained lower than those common in the West, although living standards improved

rapidly, particularly by the 1960s. The collaboration of business and government was supplemented by the large corporate combines, called *zaibatsu*, that emerged by the 1920s as a means of reducing competition within Japan itself. Business concentration took place in the West as well, but the mutual arrangements among large Japanese concerns, backed by government planning, went further still. The Japanese also cultivated an unusual degree of worker loyalty and diligence. Although some labor unrest occurred both in the 1920s and after World War II, strike rates were low by Western standards and Japanese workers were noted for their careful workmanship and productivity. In the large companies, workers were assured of job security; they could not be fired. They were often consulted on possible technical improvements. At the same time, businesses sponsored group exercises and other collective activities that increased worker morale. Japanese managers also showed less interest than their Western counterparts in high profits, while emphasizing group decision making and loyalty over individual ambition within a corporate hierarchy.

The Japanese approach to labor relations had some serious political and social costs, however. Many workers were forced to join company unions, as Japan's ruling oligarchy continued to find ways to undermine protest. Pressure to maintain high productivity was intense, and some workers who would not toe the line were forced to retire. Workers were divided between those with job security and a large number, about 60 percent of the manufacturing labor force, including most working women, who faced more unstable market pressures. The *zaibatsu* system, effective in economic coordination, also helped suppress political competition, although less completely and arbitrarily than in the 1930s. But at least into the early 1990s, the Japanese way, in the eyes of a significant number of Westerners and many Japanese themselves, was a powerful economic instrument, creating unprecedented productivity and economic growth and a rising margin of exports over imports that steadily increased Japan's role in the world economy. Economic growth slowed in the 1990s, partly because of new global competition, but the nation remained a world powerhouse.

An additional element in Japan's economic success was the application of distinctive social relations to an advanced industrial technology. By Western standards, the Japanese seemed extremely nonindividualistic, loyal to group endeavors and not very concerned with personal reward or private expressions of discontent. Continued elaborate expressions of politeness, plus a heavy emphasis in the schools on the importance of patriotism, helped explain this unique national psychology. So did Japanese methods of child rearing. Children were encouraged to conform to group standards, among other things by the use of shame as a punishment for nonconformity— an approach in child rearing that the West had largely abandoned by the early 19th century. Japanese social solidarity showed even in the nation's legal practices. Lawyers were uncommon in 20th-century Japan, for it was assumed that people could resolve certain issues on the basis of mutual agreement and that individuals had no reason to use the courts to protest the activities of neighbors or business leaders, or the government.

Not surprisingly, Japanese family customs and important aspects of personal behavior continued in ways that were significantly different from those of the contemporary West. Male authority remained preeminent in 20th-century Japan. Relatively few women worked after marriage, and women's wages lagged well behind male levels— about 40 percent compared to the 70 percent that was common in the West. Women's role in the family, particularly in rearing young children, was heavily stressed. Japanese family structure stabilized after the high incidence of divorce around 1900, but it emphasized more than ever the domestic functions of women. Although a few Japanese feminists emerged, there was no movement comparable to that in Western society demanding new rights for women. However, Western influence showed, for example, in growing tolerance toward expressions of romantic love. In intimate life as in culture, Japan blended diverse ingredients. In the area of personal behavior, Japanese psychiatrists reported a distinctive pattern of mental illness. Problems of loneliness and alienation were far less significant than in the West, as the Japanese remained highly dependent, emotionally, on group activities. Conversely, in situations where individuals encountered competition alone, as in university entrance tests, stress levels were much higher than in analogous Western experiences. The Japanese also had their particular ways to relieve tension. Bouts of drunkenness were more readily tolerated than in the West, as a time when normal codes of conduct could be suspended. Businessmen had recourse to traditional geisha houses as a normal and approved activity.

Japanese popular culture was not static. Western influences permeated this area too. During the 1920s, Western styles of dress, sports, and music gained acceptance in the cities. Fashionable residents of Tokyo were even called *maden boi* and *modan garu* (modern boy or girl). The U.S. presence after World War II resulted in a growing fascination with the sport of baseball, and a number of professional teams were established. In the early 1980s, a new passion for television game shows, adapted from their American progenitors, took hold, although the Japanese typically altered the characteristic format of such shows to engender more elaborate humiliation (or shame) for losers. Romantic soap operas hit Japan with *Tokyo Love Story*, in 1989, quickly the most watched TV show in the nation's history. In popular as well as formal culture, Western domination caused some concern among conservatives, who worried that important traditions—such as the use of chopsticks—might be lost for good. But to Western eyes, the Japanese ability to assimilate imported culture within a distinctive context seemed far more striking.

In terms of the global economy and culture, Japan was no mere imitator but an active contributor. Japanese firms were among the most powerful multinational organizations, gathering resources, locating production sites, and selling products literally around the world. Japan played a lead role in global consumer culture. Japanese animated films had wide audiences in regions such as the Middle East. Japanese toys gained large markets in the West and other parts of the world. The Japanese doll series "Hello Kitty" won a large following by combining Japanese styles with growing Western beliefs in children's cuteness. The Pokemon toys (derived from traditonal Japanese games and figures) also sold massively. Japanese rock music groups toured widely. By 2003, Japan had become a model for "cool," at least to many parts of the world, and exports of popular culture constituted a leading economic sector for the nation.

As noted, Japan was not without its problems amid economic success. Many nations both in the West and Asia resented Japanese competition, often seen as unfair because the Japanese were slow to open their own markets to outside goods. Japanese dependence on imported oil and other products made the nation vulnerable to events in distant areas, such as the oil-producing Middle East. Pollution became an increasing problem with industrial growth and the rapid expansion of cities; traffic police, for example, often had to wear protective masks simply to breathe. New regulations after the 1970s did reduce pollution problems and helped generate growing environmental industries. Competition from other parts of Asia increased. Some Japanese experts, worried that the nation's economic vigor would prove fragile, wrote articles with such titles as "The Short, Happy Life of Japan as a Superpower," and growing unemployment plus sluggish production rates caused new concern by 1995. Economic stagnation continued into the first years of the 21st century, with higher-than-average unemployment and slow overall growth. This situation prompted other kinds of change, including an increase in the percentage of wives seeking jobs.

THE PACIFIC RIM

A number of other east Asian nations developed an extensive industrial economy from the 1950s onward, although none could rival the advanced methods and accomplishments of Japan. South Korea, Taiwan, the British colony in Hong Kong, and, farther to the south, the city-state of Singapore (whose population is largely Chinese) produced rapid economic growth. By the 1980s, Malaysia, Thailand, and Indonesia joined in. Most of these nations were long ruled by authoritarian regimes; political opposition was suppressed. Governments and business leaders collaborated to develop new factory industries, with an emphasis on both consumer goods and metallurgy. Growing exports earned revenues needed for the import of raw materials and advanced Western or Japanese technology.

As in Japan, the Pacific Rim states—the coastal countries of east and southeast Asia—stressed national and group loyalties and limited what they saw as excessive individualism, including undue consumerism, which they considered to be wasteful and a threat to economic growth. Korean leaders emphasized traditional Confucian morality as part of this effort. The intent, as in Japan, was to change traditional values and social structures sufficiently to modernize the economy but to preserve enough of these same values to avoid westernization. The success of these nations suggested that east Asia, led by but not confined to Japan, was becoming the world's second industrial civilization, along with the West, as the region easily outstripped eastern Europe. The prospect was made all the more probable by the region's ability to maintain the world's highest rates of economic growth during the 1970s and early 1980s. Greater openness to democracy was an important additional development in much of the Pacific Rim by the 1990s. A near revolution generated a more democratic regime in Indonesia by 1999, whereas greater political diversity in Taiwan contrasted that country with communist China. The Pacific Rim weathered a major financial crisis in 1998, but growth trends soon resumed.

CHINA UNDER COMMUNISM

China, the mother country of east Asian civilization, did not participate fully in the initial east Asian economic boom. The political system remained resolutely authoritarian. Once again, east Asia was a divided region, in politics and economic patterns, as the fits and starts of the communist regime in China abundantly demonstrated.

Communism took hold in China for a number of reasons. Historical accident played a role: the Japanese invasion distracted the Guomindang and thus prevented a concerted attack on the communist forces and allowed the latter to consolidate their provincial power base. The inspired leadership of Mao Zedong was another important ingredient; as in Lenin's Russia, the communist revolution depended heavily on individual talent. Mao converted to communism during his student years, in 1918, seeing it as a means of challenging Western economic dominance while also facilitating fundamental changes within China. The all-encompassing belief system that Marxism provided played a role here as in the West and Soviet Russia. But Mao adapted Marxism to Chinese circumstances early on, particularly in his emphasis on the power of the Chinese peasantry. He argued in 1927 that "the force of the peasantry is like that of the raging winds and driving rain. . . . The peasantry will tear apart all nets which bind it and hasten along the road to liberation." By promising land reform and conciliating peasants during the revolutionary struggle, Mao's forces gained crucial support in their war against the better-armed Guomindang.

Although communism was a new force in Chinese history, with the goal of genuine revolution and not simply the seizure of power, it coincided with traditional features of Chinese society—as had been the case in the Soviet Union. The Chinese legacy of a strong state, with an elaborate bureaucracy, lent itself readily to a communist system, in which state power was further extended and in which government bureaucrats, although recruited from new sources and held to a new political faith, regulated large sectors of the economy and even family life. Mao's success, after the earlier failure of more liberal politics during the 1920s, was in this sense no accident. From the late 1940s onward, communist officials prevented political opposi-

tion, monopolized the main sources of information and propaganda, and abandoned all pretense of establishing a Western-style parliamentary regime. The Communist party ruled the new People's Republic of China, and Mao dominated the party. Although the communist state was more efficient in its use of police and active promotion of political loyalty than the empire had been, there were some strong similarities between the two. Indeed, Communist leaders themselves soon found that they had recreated a complex bureaucracy that posed some of the same barriers to change that the old Confucian bureaucracy had. By the 1970s, appeals to bureaucrats to recognize the importance of new technologies and management methods became standard, as the Chinese continued to seek a reconciliation between a strong state authority and revitalized economic growth.

Mao's state and that of his more pragmatic successors was bent on transformation outside the political arena. China had been changing even before the communist revolution. During the 1920s, the port cities continued to expand, and factory industry took root. Modernized patterns of work and education gave a new voice to young people, weakening the Confucian tradition of ancestor worship. The importance of student groups expressed this shift. The position of women also began to change, as women in the cities acquired formal education and practices such as footbinding declined. More and more marriages were based on mutual affection rather than economic arrangements alone. Educational reforms brought even greater shifts in outlook, as science began to play a more significant role; many educated Chinese, at home and abroad, contributed actively to scientific and technological research.

Mao sought to extend and formalize the pattern of cultural and social change. He attacked Confucian values head-on. Harmony, ceremony, and ancestor worship were impediments to the liberation of China's masses, in his view. He encouraged the new importance of youth, the validity of attacks on established hierarchies and even on the authority of parents within the family. Officially, at

The first-anniversary celebration of the founding of the People's Republic of China, October 1950. Workers carry hundreds of portraits of Mao in the parade.

least, revolutionary China mounted a far more sweeping attack on the traditions of its civilization than did the other societies of east Asia, including Japan. Plays, operas, and art embraced the revolutionary regime, abandoning older themes in favor of praise for the heroic peasant and worker and attacks on China's enemies, among them the United States. The commune system in the countryside, which placed children under the charge of nurseries long before formal schooling began, and limited young people's contact with parents, was designed to eliminate traditional values at their root. Here, Mao's regime went further than Russian revolutionaries had ever attempted.

Chinese habits, however, were not easily undone. The Communist regime dislodged the former landlord class, putting the land directly in the hands of the peasantry, who were then organized into state-directed communes. Agricultural production proceeded more smoothly than had

been the case in Soviet Russia during collectivization. Foreign business interests and native capitalism were unseated in favor of state-directed enterprise. However, more subtle traditions, including family values and a tendency to venerate the elderly, seemed to persist. The Communist party itself was soon dominated by older men, as Mao's group aged. After the furor of the Cultural Revolution, it was not clear that youth would become the new heroes in China. Women gained greater equality and participated actively in the labor force, as had long been the case, but particularly in the countryside, older traditions such as arranged marriages persisted. Other customs, such as extreme politeness and the careful control of emotions, proved durable as well.

Furthermore, Communist leaders were eager to utilize some traditional practices as an alternative to a simple imitation of the West. In health care, for example, teams of "barefoot doctors"—hygiene officials rather than formally trained medical specialists in the Western sense—were dispatched to numerous rural villages, where they were responsible for raising health standards without fully imposing the concepts of modern medicine. Traditional remedies, including acupuncture, were maintained along with Western-style hospitals.

The Communist regime had a mixed impact on the Chinese economy, particularly in the area of industrialization. State control furthered the accumulation of resources for mechanization but resulted in some of the same problems of inflexible planning that plagued the Soviet Union. The sheer chaos of decades of Japanese invasion and then civil war, and the renewed turmoil of the Cultural Revolution, retarded economic advance. Furthermore, Chinese population growth continued at high levels. Mao wavered in his approach to this issue, at times believing that China's great resource, militarily as well as economically, lay in increasing numbers. However, as before, population growth consumed immense resources and produced widespread poverty. By 1979, China's population stood at 23 percent of the world's total, but the nation accounted for only 3 percent of the world's industrial product. Clearly, a full industrial revolution had yet to occur, although most observers agreed that the country was farther along the path than most other agricultural nations.

Chinese leaders after Mao's death, especially under Deng Xiaoping, worked more single-mindedly toward the goal of industrialization. High-level technical and scientific training returned to the universities, after the disruption of the Cultural Revolution. In 1978, the government began to favor more competition and also wider outside contacts, to spur economic expansion. Many groups and individuals were sent abroad to study. The regime adopted an unprecedented rigorous policy toward the population problem, aiming at zero growth almost immediately. Marriage before the age of 25 was forbidden, and couples having more than one child were punished. Here, not only the policing apparatus of the communist state

but also earlier traditions of state control over society combined to produce a startling reversal in social customs. Again, official policy and reality, particularly rural reality, may differ. There were reports that the new rigor produced a wave of female infanticides, as couples were more interested in producing male heirs. However, the regime claimed, with apparent justification, that the birth rate had radically slowed. Finally, the regime collaborated with Western and Japanese enterprises, seeking more advanced technology. Individual managers and also rural producers were given greater authority and some profit incentives to obtain higher output, as the communists sought a new balance between state control and individual initiative. Industrial development was given clear priority over military concerns, as China returned, more clearly than under Mao, to a position of largely defensive foreign policy. China's new leaders projected an essentially completed process of industrialization by the year 2000. Improvements in living standards, most notably in the cities, were an early and popular result of the new policies, and economic growth rates stood at 10 percent a year by the 1990s. A rising pollution problem resulted as well, as Chinese cities filled with industrial gases referred to as the "yellow dragon."

China (and, in its wake, Vietnam and North Korea) firmly resisted the democratizing trends of the 1980s that so altered eastern Europe. Even as more democratic systems were installed in South Korea, Taiwan, and the Philippines, and in the face of their own massive student rebellion of 1989, Chinese leaders maintained an authoritarian regime. Russia's troubles in combining political and economic reform further convinced them that the toleration of dissent would be a significant mistake. The regime eagerly moved forward toward a more market-based economy, with profit incentives and private initiative along with state planning. Chinese exports soared in order to pay for new equipment and expertise from abroad. However, China insisted—as it had so often done in the past—on its own political formula. Assimilation of the former British colony of Hong Kong, from 1997 onward, exposed China to another dose of ardent capitalism but also another set of issues concerning freedom of expression.

Rapid change continued into the early 21st century. Chinese industrial growth maintained 10 percent annual rates, and the nation became a leading exporter of goods to places such as the United States. Cities like Shanghai mushroomed with growth. Some state-run enterprises stagnated, and there was growing unemployment. Foreign companies often exploited low-wage labor, as did export-minded Chinese firms—the downside of globalization for China as for other areas. Political tensions surfaced as well. Hong Kong was promised its own political system, but the national government imposed a somewhat authoritarian leader. Significant protests resulted in 2003. Another challenge was the Falun Gong, a new, widely popular religious movement in a strongly secular society. The government viewed the movement as subversive and arrested many proponents. The challenge of running an authoritarian state in a global environment was not simple.

EAST ASIA AND THE WORLD

As the communist revolution spread across China, while Japan adapted to a more democratic political structure after World War II, the differences among east Asian societies seemed overwhelming. Even by the 1990s, the variations in levels of economic development and political forms constituted major distinctions not only between Japan and China, but also among the smaller nations as well. Japan, along with the leading Western industrial states, was a key participant in annual "free world" economic conferences, because of shared political concerns as well as world market interests. Countries such as South Korea and Taiwan were less industrialized, although growing rapidly; they also faced periodic protest against their authoritarian political structures, which liberalized somewhat toward the end of the 1980s. On the other hand, China and Vietnam, still partially isolated,

attempted economic reforms while maintaining their communist systems.

Over time, some enduring common features among east Asian societies have reemerged. An emphasis on strong social cohesion is one such element. China's communist regime seeks tight social solidarity, whereas Japanese values stress group ties from the family through the nation. From a common Confucian past, admittedly one much altered by recent events, east Asian nations also preserve an interest in ceremony and emotional restraint. They share a desire to develop or maintain industrial dynamism without necessarily becoming a carbon copy of either Western or Russian society.

Both China and Japan, although open to more international influences than ever before in their history, have continued to stand somewhat apart from other civilizations. Visitors to Japan report a polite but somewhat detached welcome, as the Japanese continue to honor the distinctiveness and superiority of their own culture, to which foreigners are rarely, if ever, fully admitted. China, although embarking on renewed contacts with the West after the vigorous attack on all foreign influences during the Cultural Revolution, continues to monitor outsiders closely, making it clear that selective imitation should not make the Chinese people fully tolerant of foreign ways. East Asia, more influential in the wider world by the early 21st century than at any previous point in history, has maintained its traditional ability to see the world through its own lens.

ISSUES AND CONNECTIONS

To what extent do the Pacific Rim (including Japan) and China share remnants of a Confucian tradition in the 20th century? Or, given the huge differences in politics and economic development, should east Asia be seen as two quite separate civilizations? These issues are much debated, because they involve connections with past history and also anticipations about what east Asia may become in future. If China industrializes successfully, east Asia may once again appear as a single civilization area, China-dominated but sharing other cultural features, with some modest regional distinctions.

But it is also important, for both China and Japan, not to rush to the present too rapidly. Both countries had challenging experiences during the world war decades, in part because of Japan's invasion. Do significant traces of the earlier 20th-century experience remain today?

Connections with the past are central to discussions about the qualities of east Asian civilization. Japan's emphasis on group loyalty, not only in business but in early schooling, represents active links with earlier traditions of feudalism and Confucianism. The devotion to education is partly modern, but partly traces back 300 years. China's stress on order under communism is partly a reaction to the chaos of the early 20th century, but it recalls older commitments as well. When the communist regime battled the Falun Gong, the Buddhist-derived religious movement that won a wide following by the 1990s, it mirrored uncannily the attacks on Buddhism of the later Tang dynasty. Many of the same arguments, about distractions from proper loyalty to state and society, were actively invoked. An industrializing, communist China, with no landlord class, was surely not the China of the dynasties, but it maintained an active presence from the past even so.

SUGGESTED WEB SITES

On leaders in Japanese industrialization, see http://www.historynet.com/WorldWarII/articles/11963_cover.htm. On the Korean War, see http://socrates.berkeley.edu/~korea/koreanwar.html. On Japan's economic boom after World War II, see http://www.iss.u-tokyo.ac.jp/Newsletter/SSJ1/gluck.html. On leaders of the communist revolution in China, see http://cnd-f.org/fairbank/prc.html.

SUGGESTED READINGS

For an overview on China, see I. Hsu, *The Rise of Modern China*, 2nd ed. (1975). For an excellent interpretive study, using a modernization model, see G. Rozman, ed., *The Modernization of China* (1981); see also Wolfgang Franke, *A Century of Chinese Revolution* (1970). On the Chinese revolutions, J. Spence, *The Gate of Heavenly Peace: The Chinese and Their Revolution, 1895–1980* (1982), is invaluable; on the communist revolution specifically, Edward Snow, *Red Star Over China* (1968), is quite readable. See Margery Wolf, *Revolution Postponed: Women in Contemporary China* (1988). Consult also, as a source, A. Freemantle, ed., *Mao-Tse Tung: An Anthology of His Writings* (1962). On developments after Mao, I. Hsu, *China Without Mao: The Search for a New Order* (1983), is worthwhile.

On Japan, an excellent cultural interpretation is E. O. Reischauer, *The Japanese* (1988). See also P. Duus, *The Rise of Modern Japan* (1976), and M. Howe, *Modern Japan: A Historical Survey* (1986), as well as H. Patrick and H. Rosovsky, *Asia's New Giant: How the Japanese Economy Works* (1976). An important specific topic is covered in R. Story, *The Double Patriots: A Story of Japanese Nationalism* (1973). Japanese economic success and its significance are addressed in Ezra Vogel, *Japan as Number One: Lessons for Americans* (1980). On the Pacific Rim, see Philip West et al., eds., *Pacific Rim and the Western World: Strategic, Economic and Cultural Perspectives* (1987); see also G. Rozman, ed., *East Asian Region: Confucian Heritage and Its Modern Adaptation* (1991), and Bruce Cuming, *Korea's Place in the Sun: A Modern History* (1997).

Recent work includes Merle Goldman, *Historical Perspectives on Contemporary East Asia* (2000); Alexander Pantsov, *The Bolsheviks and the Chinese Revolution, 1919–1927* (2000); Ian Cook, *China's Third Revolution: Tensions in the Transition towards a Post-Communist China* (2001); Edward Beauchamp, ed., *Women and Women's Issues in Post-World War II Japan* (1998); Vera Simons, *The Asian Pacific: Political and Economic Development in a Global Context* (1995); and S. Ichimore, *The Political Economy of Japanese and Asian Development* (1998).

31

India and Southeast Asia: World War I to Independence

During the first half of the 20th century, nationalist pressures built steadily on the Indian subcontinent and in southeast Asia. Dislocations produced by World War II prompted the end of European controls. In a few cases—most notably Vietnam—the struggle to achieve independence continued well after World War II, but in most instances, including India, decolonization occurred quickly and without much further conflict with the former imperialist powers. Thus, the history of India and southeast Asia since the late 1940s is characterized by the formation of newly independent nations and the establishment of their distinct political styles. India became the world's largest democracy, building on older political traditions as well as the legacy of British rule and nationalist struggle. Other nations on the Indian subcontinent and in southeast Asia were more authoritarian in political structure, whereas Vietnam became communist. The earlier pattern of political division thus persisted in southeast Asia, although in new forms. Problems of economic development also loomed large. Again, there was great diversity; a few new nations, such as Bangladesh, proved to be among the world's poorest. But in India itself, significant economic change took place, while parts of southeast Asia were pulled into the dynamic orbit of the Pacific Rim. India also experienced rapid population growth, heading toward becoming the world's most populous country early in the 21st century.

KEY QUESTIONS *The Indian subcontinent was part of the larger process of decolonization. But results were distinctive. Why, compared to most other new nations, was India able to maintain a democracy? What was the balance between tradition and change in newly independent India?*

THE RISE OF NATIONALISM

India provided a key example of the growing struggle for independence after 1914, just as it would help lead the movement of new nations after World War II. Rising nationalism in much of southeast Asia proved somewhat similar to patterns in India. Throughout southern Asia, indeed, the issue of national freedom moved to the top of the agenda during the years between the world wars. Problems in Europe weakened the hold of the imperialist nations, although they remained militarily dominant until the 1940s. Many Europeans became increasingly open to the idea that their colonies should work toward ultimate freedom. New currents in India and southeast Asia provided an even greater impetus to nationalism. The example of the Russian Revolution and the Leninist concept that a massive social revolution was possible as part of the struggle against an empire also converted some Indian and southeast Asian leaders. Outside Vietnam, where nationalism and Marxism were closely linked, Marxism had less impact in southern Asia than in China, but it was a significant element nonetheless.

More important still was a new wave of peasant unrest in various parts of southern Asia. Peasant agitation resulted from growing population pressure combined with the more efficient tax collection and commercial agriculture that were part of imperialist rule. Peasants had their own idea of social justice, which included the more tolerant leadership of village headmen and greater access to land; they were rarely directly concerned with national independence, but their goals were compatible with liberation movements in that they resented the economic and administrative measures induced by outside rule.

Nonetheless, it was nationalism itself, gaining new vigor and popularity, that characterized the political history of southern Asia during the first half of the 20th century. Copied from Europe initially, nationalism took on, if anything, greater importance in India and southeast Asia. Here, it meant freedom from foreign domination and a chance to come to terms with the modern world while preserving important features of traditional civilization. In India, nationalism promised a kind of unity that the country had almost never known and a self-expression that had not been possible for many centuries. The Indian patriot Chittaranjan Das, writing early in the century, advanced the nationalist cause as follows:

> What is the ideal, which we must set before us? The first and foremost is the ideal of nationalism. Now what is nationalism? It is, I conceive, a process through which a nation expresses itself and finds itself, not in isolation from other nations, not in opposition to other nations, but as part of a great scheme by which, in seeking its own expression and therefore its own identity, it materially assists the self-expression and self-realization of other nations as well: Diversity is as real as unity. . . . I contend that each nationality constitutes a particular stream of the great unity, but no nation can fulfill itself unless and until it becomes itself and at the same time realizes its identity with Humanity.

The idealistic fervor of southern Asian nationalism, and especially the form of nationalism that took root in India, was a real force on its own, quite apart from specific issues and grievances.

Indian nationalism was given direct impetus by the events of World War I. Three million Indian soldiers fought in British armies during the war. At the same time, taxes and food shortages at home created discontent, bringing new strength to the Indian National Congress and an alliance between the Hindu leadership of the Congress party and the nation's Muslim League. This united front called for self-government within the British Empire. Britain did indeed establish new provincial legislative councils as a result, providing voting rights for 6 million of the nation's 250 million people; the councils had jurisdiction over such areas as education and public health. But this 1919 measure was obviously half-hearted, indicating London's continued suspicion of India's ability to rule itself. The central government remained firmly in British hands, with advisory councils elected by only a million Indian voters. The British followed a classic pattern of offering enough reform to encourage new expectations—along with the excitement caused by World War I and the principles of national self-determination discussed at Versailles—but not enough to satisfy all. At the same time, the British tightened police measures against those they viewed as troublemakers. The new repression resulted in a wave of rioting across the subcontinent. Police anxiety even prompted clashes at Hindu religious festivals; in one such confrontation, 379 celebrants, all unarmed, were killed by British-led troops. Police brutality here, and in major labor strikes, heightened Indian nationalism and helped unite upper-caste leaders with large numbers of workers and peasants.

Popular agitation continued in the 1920s. An influenza epidemic and crop failures that killed 5 million people led to a wave of rural uprisings against landlords and moneylenders. Some urban protest developed as well, with strikes among textile and railroad workers; Marxist doctrines made some headway. This diverse discontent was grist for the nationalists' mill, as it served to pressure the British. Middle-class nationalists even discussed a boycott of British goods, to protest India's economic dependence.

THE NONVIOLENT STRATEGIES OF GANDHI

In this context of growing agitation, the emergence in 1920 of Mohandas Gandhi as the leader and master tactician of the nationalist forces was a key development. Gandhi became an almost universally respected symbol of India's political awakening, the most important political figure in Indian history since the Mauryan and Gupta dynasties of the classical period. Gandhi had been born into a merchant family that also wielded great political influence in a small princely state north of Bombay, under British rule but shielded from the most direct Western pressure. His family had been devout Hindus, keenly persuaded of the importance of group loyalties. Gandhi himself studied law in Britain and practiced it for a time in South Africa, where he became keenly aware of the desperate plight of many Indians whom the British had imported as indentured laborers and who, like Gandhi himself, were often victims of brutal discrimination in public. Gandhi's reaction was not just one of indignation, but a deep search for a strategy by which the weak could overcome imperialist strength. His conclusion, drawn from his version of Hindu tradition plus other religious reading, was collective nonviolence in resistance to injustice. He organized a campaign of peaceful marches to protest discrimination in South Africa, including nonviolent resistance to police attacks and arrest, which was successful in removing some of the most overt forms of discrimination against Indians in that colony.

Then, in 1915, Gandhi returned to India, and after a few years of reflection and experimentation with different tactics, he seized the opportunity provided by growing popular and nationalist unrest to mount a campaign of nonviolent resistance. Gandhi's great gift was to unite educated nationalist leaders with the rural masses, who saw in Gandhi an incarnation of deep spiritual values and whose own Hinduism was in accord with his emphasis on nonviolence. Gandhi told the Indian masses, who had long left the fighting to the warrior castes, that they too could be courageous:

> Wherein is courage required—in blowing others to pieces from behind a cannon, or with a smiling face to approach a cannon and be blown to pieces? Who is the true warrior—he who keeps death always as a bosom-friend, or he who controls the death of others? Believe me that a man devoid of courage and manhood can never be a passive resister.

World Profiles

MOHANDAS GANDHI (1889–1948)

Mohandas Gandhi was unquestionably the leading figure in India's independence movement and one of the most important individuals in 20th-century world history. Trained in part in England, Gandhi later turned to modifications of Hindu tradition in his nonviolent mass protests against British rule. In particular, he attacked traditions of caste and the subjugation of women. He also projected an Indian alternative to modern society as it had developed in the West. He urged a craft-based, rather than factory- and common-based, economy. Gandhi's protest tactics worked, although his goals were less completely realized. Tragically, he was killed by a narrow nationalist group hostile to tolerance for Muslims. How much did Gandhi shape and reflect a distinctive Indian experience, and would India's independence have occurred differently without his guidance?

Mohandas Gandhi

Under Gandhi's leadership, the Congress movement became a mass political force for the first time, giving Indians a far greater taste of political participation than Britain's timid legislative experiments had allowed. Gandhi served also as a significant figure in a revived and revised Hinduism, in which ethical principles were stressed over both ceremonialism and the caste system.

Gandhi was also a master of tactics. His simple, holy style of life, which included a renunciation of sex, brought him the title *Mahatma*, or "saintly one." He could attack castes, and so please the masses and Muslims, while also wooing Brahmin religious leaders by praising tradition. He could converse with both striking workers and moderate reformers. He appealed to new public interests for women, urging women to abandon domestic isolation for the sake of national freedom. However, he did not renounce Hindu family ideals. Above all, his stress on nonviolence confounded British authorities, who found it difficult to respond with all-out repression. Gandhi was frequently arrested, but his sentences aroused so much mass furor—heightened by well-publicized refusals to eat during imprisonment—that he ultimately was released. Although Gandhi was not able to prevent periodic violence against British officials, he did direct most attention to peaceful mass disruption, refusals to pay taxes, and other tactics that were hard to counter. "We must voluntarily put up with the losses and inconveniences that arise from having to withdraw our support from a government that is ruling against our will." In this spirit, Gandhi and his followers boycotted elections, blocked trains by lying down on the tracks, and surrounded government buildings with thousands of quiet demonstrators so that officials had to walk over bodies in order to get to work.

By the 1930s, the British realized that they had to offer further reforms. However, a series of conferences with Indian leaders convinced the British that there was no way to please Hindus and Muslims, radicals and princes. Indeed, many Muslim leaders were increasingly antagonized, despite Gandhi's efforts at reconciliation, by the development of an Indian nationalism based largely on Hindu symbols and customs. They began talking of the need for their own nation, a *Pakistan*, or "land of the pure," instead of a unified India. Britain also played its own role in encouraging Hindu-Muslim divisions, in spite of considerable Muslim support of Congress party goals. In this context, the British issued a new constitution, in 1935, that provided for a federal system of 11 provinces, each with an elected assembly and ministers responsible to it, with a British-appointed governor to oversee. At the center, a two-house parliament would have some real power, although British officials remained in charge of defense and foreign affairs. The vote was extended to 35 million people.

Although disappointed at the lack of full self-government, the Congress party ran in the new elections and won majorities in most states. Gandhi himself advocated service in the new governments as long as the British did not unduly interfere, whereas more radical leaders, including Jawaharlal Nehru, preached continued resistance. But all leaders agreed on the need for ultimate independence, and when Britain became unresponsive on this point after 1940, they refused to cooperate in the government's World War II effort. Gandhi, Nehru, and other leaders were arrested as a Japanese attack threatened, and Britain ruled India through military control until the war's end. Throughout this period, the British also played Hindu and Islamic leaders against each other, in ways that affected the later development of the subcontinent.

NATIONALISM IN SOUTHEAST ASIA

A similar national awakening developed in southeast Asia during the 1920s and 1930s, although without such a compelling figure as Gandhi. In French-ruled Indochina, an advisory council was permitted, but as in India, such halfway reforms proved insufficient. Rioting broke out in major cities in 1930–1931. Although it was suppressed by force, nationalist agitation continued. Serious peasant outbreaks occurred as well, caused more by economic hunger than by nationalism, as the market for agricultural exports collapsed during the economic depression. A significant Marxist movement also took shape under the leadership of Ho Chi Minh, who became an enthusiastic convert to Marxism while working as a waiter in Paris, finding it a faith that could sustain him in his country's long battle for national freedom. But amid the new unrest, the French were determined to preserve their power. A similar pattern prevailed in Indonesia. Dutch rulers granted local leaders half the seats in a national assembly, but when nationalist and socialist unrest spread against the limited reforms, the government responded by jailing the leaders—which only stimulated further agitation. In 1937, the nationalists petitioned the Dutch crown for dominion status within 10 years.

Nationalism and peasant unrest against lack of land and high taxes created new ferment in Burma and Siam, where British influence predominated. In Siam, nationalist sentiment prompted a successful attack on Western control of tariff policy and special legal rights for foreigners. The nationalists celebrated their achievement by renaming their nation *Thailand*, or "land of the free." Finally, nationalists attacked U.S. control over the Philippines, where a popularly elected legislature already had real powers. Although Americans talked of ultimate independence for this land, they also discriminated against native Filipinos, whom they tended to treat with the same racism that they expressed toward blacks at home. Thus, Filipino nationalism persisted, and it also was enhanced by the economic problems brought about by the Great Depression, as U.S. resistance to Filipino exports grew amid that crisis. In 1934, the U.S. Congress increased Philippine rights to self-government and promised outright independence in 1944.

Southeast Asian nationalism generally was stimulated by the results of World War II. Japanese control of the Philippines, Indochina, and other areas was often harsher than Western imperialism, but it demonstrated that the West was vulnerable and to this extent spurred hopes for ultimate freedom. When Tokyo surrendered in 1945 to the Allies, many Westerners prepared to return to the southeast Asian plantations and social clubs as if nothing had happened, but in fact, a new era had begun in the whole region. Imperialism, difficult in the 1930s, had now become impossible.

DECOLONIZATION AFTER THE WAR

It was not surprising that the current of decolonization, which would soon sweep the world, bore its first postwar fruit in southern Asia. With nationalist resistance already well established in places such as India, most European powers, now exhausted, were unwilling to experience the trouble and risks of hanging on any further—even assuming that they could have done so successfully. The new Labor party in Britain was positively eager to leave India after 1945, for the costs of operating a government there had become too great to bear. A crucial issue remained the split between Hindu and Muslim, which, to the sorrow of leaders such as Gandhi, occasioned bitter rioting as independence neared. The deepest conflict was resolved in 1947 by the creation of two states, a Muslim Pakistan and a predominantly Hindu India. Religion-based nationalism triumphed over the larger territorial nationalism in the Congress tradition, although this tradition persisted in India along with frequent religious and ethnic challenges.

Britain extended its decolonization policy by granting freedom to Ceylon (present-day Sri Lanka) and Burma (present-day Myanmar) in 1948. Malaysia also won independence after the British successfully suppressed a communist guerrilla movement. The United States made good on its earlier pledge by freeing the Philippines in

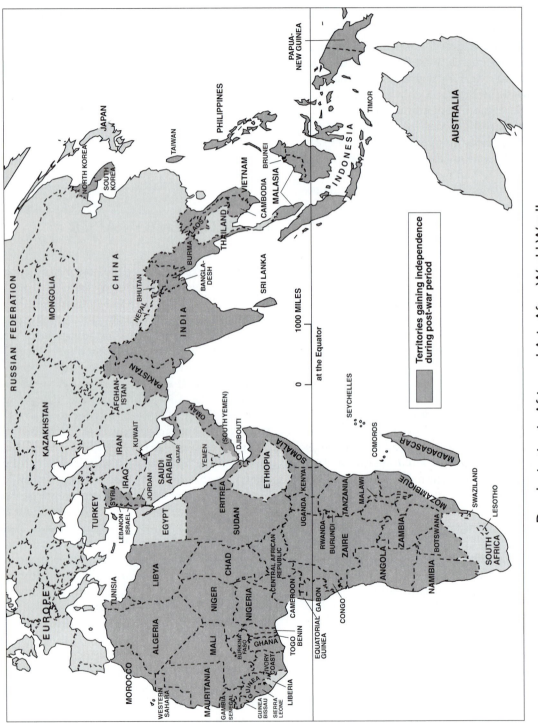

Decolonization in Africa and Asia After World War II

Territories gaining independence during post-war period

1946, while retaining substantial military bases on lease. The Dutch retreat from Indonesia was somewhat less graceful, as there was an attempt to reconquer the territory after the end of World War II. However, this effort failed, and an independent Indonesia was recognized in 1949.

Only in Indochina was national independence seriously delayed after World War II. The French, particularly eager to reassert their military strength after their disastrous loss to Hitler's armies in 1940, were unwilling to recognize the strength or validity of the nationalist movement. They were aided by the United States, which was hostile to communism, especially after the success of the Chinese revolution, and eager not to "lose" another Asian region to their cold war enemy. Ho Chi Minh, however, proved to be a stubborn opponent, successfully organizing a guerrilla warfare that depended on widespread peasant support and was impossible to suppress by conventional tactics. A series of defeats suffered by French troops led to a peace settlement in 1954, which brought division between a communist North Vietnam and a noncommunist South Vietnam. The French also withdrew from Laos and Cambodia. North Vietnam soon began to press its southern neighbor, with aid from the Soviet Union and China. As South Vietnam faced guerrilla attacks, it turned to the United States for aid. American participation in the conflict escalated in 1964, after North Vietnamese ships allegedly attacked American vessels, and over the next 10 years, more than 2 million U.S. soldiers were sent to fight in Vietnam. Despite massive American bombing raids, however, communist guerrilla forces gained ground, and the fighting also spread to Laos and Cambodia. Opposition to the war effort within the United States helped prompt peace talks, begun in 1969, which finally resulted in an end to the war in 1973. With U.S. forces withdrawn, and amid accusations from both sides about treaty violations, North Vietnam increased its troop levels in South Vietnam, and by 1975 it had gained full control of this region. A united, communist

Vietnam then proceeded to impose military control over Laos and Cambodia, although these nations later regained a shaky independence.

The rise of a communist regional state in southeast Asia was an extremely important development. The bitter warfare that had led to this state played a significant role first in French and then U.S. politics. More importantly, the same warfare resulted in massive devastation and loss of life within the region itself, creating long-lasting scars and severe problems of economic reconstruction. Military experience and a communist regime distinguished this part of southeast Asia from the majority of the new nations, where independence had come earlier and with far less trauma.

SOUTHEAST ASIA AFTER INDEPENDENCE

The rise of nationalism during the first half of the 20th century had provided most of southern Asia with such a compelling cause that the problems which independence itself would bring were often obscured. The focus was on freedom from outside control. Leaders were less clear about what would be constructed when and if the Westerners left. Most nationalists assumed a democratic, parliamentary structure—to this extent, they copied Western values. However, there was profound division among religious groups, as in India, and between educated leaders and the peasant masses. This could make democracy difficult. Nationalists were also typically vague about economic and social issues. Gandhi, for example, had little interest in economic development in the sense of industrialization. He was not opposed to factory production but insisted on preventing its dehumanizing effects on workers; at times, he seemed to prefer enhancing peasant agriculture and home-based manufacturing. But other Indian leaders called for an aggressive drive toward economic modernization. Peasants, although often drawn to the nationalist cause, were far more interested in land

and protection from world market fluctuations than in purely political reforms or economic modernization. Urban workers, poorly paid and badly housed amid the conditions of early factories, also pressed for greater social justice. Dealing with these various pressures, while also establishing the institutions of government, was an arduous task after the excitement of attaining national freedom.

The new or revived nations of southeast Asia illustrated the range of possibilities and problems that followed from decolonization. Southeast Asian civilization had always been diverse. Traditional variations continued to be important, as differing religious and ethnic backgrounds determined distinctive policies. However, new distinctions now arose as well, as in the split between communist Vietnam and the noncommunist—sometimes anticommunist—policies of the other states of the region. With encouragement from the United States, a number of southeast Asian governments formed a loose alliance to coordinate resistance to Chinese and Vietnamese communist influence and to discuss common economic interests. Nonetheless, this grouping was not a significant unifying force amid the region's fascinating cultural and political diversity.

Most southeast Asian nations attempted to establish democratic parliamentary institutions after attaining independence, but most found these institutions impossible to maintain. Lack of political experience among the peasant masses, divisions within the population that prompted frequent rioting, and, often, the ambition of individual nationalist leaders tended to turn governments toward more authoritarian policies. In the Philippines, for example, a parliamentary system modeled on that of the United States lasted until 1963, when President Ferdinand Marcos seized full power, which he would retain, amid considerable corruption and political violence, for over two decades. The Philippine government faced attacks from communist guerrillas, which were mostly controlled. It largely avoided any effort at land reform; a wealthy elite dominated the coun-

try, sharing power with the military. The gap between rich and poor was significant, and there was little progress toward economic development. The government nevertheless received substantial U.S. aid and support, from postwar reconstruction onward, in part because of American concern for maintaining its military bases on the islands. Only in 1986 was the Marcos regime toppled, after trying to rig a new election, and replaced by a reformist regime that initiated more genuine democracy.

In Malaysia and the monarchy of Thailand, parliamentary institutions functioned somewhat more effectively than in the Philippines, and the repression of political opposition was less complete. By the 1970s, Thailand faced considerable pressure from the powerful Vietnamese armies on its northern border. Malaysia had earlier suppressed a communist guerrilla movement run mainly by the ethnic Chinese minority on the peninsula. Tension between native Malays and the Chinese minority continued to produce friction, however. It also made impossible a brief union with the city-state of Singapore, dominated by the Chinese; Singapore split off under a strong-willed leader bent on rapid economic growth and tight control of the city's population.

Burma, like Thailand a largely Buddhist nation still, opted for considerable isolation soon after independence, hoping to avoid the influence of both the West and communist nations. A series of generals ran the country, whose culture remained highly traditional, one of the only nations in the world that isolated so fully from broader international currents. Only a few indications of greater openness occurred by the early 2000s, as the country adopted the new name Myanmar.

Indonesia gained independence under the leadership of Achmed Sukarno, who soon established authoritarian rule, in part, as a means of unifying a diverse population. A strong communist movement influenced Sukarno, but an outright communist uprising in 1963 was defeated and the army seized power, killing at least half a million communists and radicals. The military also attacked the ethnic Chinese minority, who were resented for their hold over merchant activity in the cities. Sukarno was forced out of power, and the army generals ruled with no pretense of democracy. Firmly Muslim, the new government supported Islamic law and customs, although without the rigor of some other nations in the Islamic orbit. The authoritarian regime did, however, attack several minority nationalities as it retained its hold against the currents of democracy into the late 1990s.

In Vietnam—first the North, after 1954, and then the larger nation after 1975—a political and social system developed with many similarities to that of China under Mao Zedong. Private businesses were seized, and land was taken from the large landowners and turned over to government-controlled communes. Vietnamese society was colored by the heavy toll of prolonged war, including the military outlays needed for the conquest of Cambodia against considerable resistance. The Vietnamese regime relied heavily on Soviet support, as relations with China soured. China had never welcomed a strong Vietnam and objected strenuously to the attack on Cambodia. Border tensions, including one brief war, further encouraged the strong militaristic tone of the Vietnamese version of communism. Economic development remained meager into the later 1980s, because of wartime dislocations and continuing military costs. By the 1990s, Vietnam followed China's policy of greater openness to the outside world and a more market-oriented economy, still combined with a strong communist state. Ties with the outside world increased, and many foreign firms located factories in Vietnam to take advantage of cheap labor.

Except for Vietnam, and the Philippines until 1986, most southeast Asian governments tried to combine an interest in social reform, including aid to the peasantry, with considerable private enterprise. A number of nations experienced noteworthy economic growth. More productive crops were developed in the 1960s as part of the Green Revolution, which brought the aid of Western science to bear on the food problems of agricultural countries, thus allowing most southeast Asian nations to feed themselves. Particularly important were new strains of rice, which grew faster and had higher yields than those grown formerly. The Green Revolution favored wealthy farmers who could afford expensive seeds and fertilizers, but it nevertheless helped many nations regain self-sufficiency in food production. Even so, economic advance was modified by considerable population growth. Most southeast Asian nations continued to depend heavily on raw materials and cash crop exports to the industrialized nations of the West or Japan, and this dependence brought the usual problems of low and uncertain incomes on the world market. Except in dynamic Singapore, full industrialization had yet to come.

INDIA AND PAKISTAN

India presented an unusual mixture of strengths and weaknesses as it attained independence in 1947. It lacked a consistently successful political tradition, having far more often been divided and ruled through outside conquest than by self-government. It embraced a wide array of regions, religions, and languages. Despite important pockets of modern industry, it had a largely agricultural economy pressed by a rapidly growing population. On the other hand, India had an unusually well-established nationalist movement, which had a recognized and experienced leadership. Because of roughly two centuries of British rule, it also had been exposed to Western political ideas and institutions, including an effective civil service system.

The birth pains of the new nation were a severe disappointment to Gandhi and other nationalist leaders. Growing Muslim insistence on a separate nation met vigorous Hindu opposition, as Congress-style nationalism ultimately failed to override religious divisions, but massive violence during 1946 convinced both sides that unity was

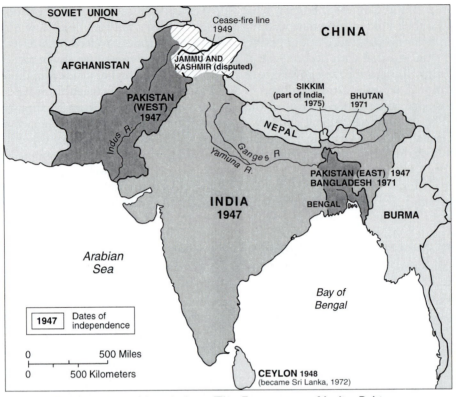

The Partition of South Asia: The Formation of India, Pakistan, Bangladesh, and Sri Lanka

indeed out of the question. The new nation of Pakistan comprised two regions: the heartland was West Pakistan, to the northwest of India, in the portion of the subcontinent nearest the Middle East, where Islam had the strongest roots; the second area was East Pakistan, to India's northeast. Even partition was insufficient to prevent further religious antagonisms. In the weeks after independence, Hindus and Muslims battled each other, causing at least 100,000 deaths and forcing 3 million people to flee their homes to seek sanctuary with coreligionists in one of the two new nations. Gandhi and the Congress party were powerless to stop the bitter hatred. Gandhi, who started a fast to protest Hindu persecution of Muslims and to restore the "best friendship"

between the two peoples, was shot by a Hindu fanatic. Tensions with a Muslim minority continued to affect India. Furthermore, relations between the nations of India and Pakistan were hostile, each eyeing the other warily and devoting hard-won tax revenues to military expenditures designed to keep the other at bay.

Pakistan followed a political pattern rather similar to that of the southeast Asian nations. It adopted an authoritarian form of government in 1958, under military leadership. Even under these conditions, the nation proved unable to maintain unity between its two main provinces, as East Pakistan constantly complained of neglect. In 1971, a revolt in the east produced the new nation of Bangladesh, the eighth most populous

Rioting in India against Muslim shrine.

country in the world and one of the poorest. Pakistan itself, although less crowded, faced serious problems of economic development. Land reform was slighted in favor of supporting the regional elite. In the 1970s, in an appeal to religious tradition, Pakistan's military government adopted increasingly rigorous Islamic laws. The nation also faced tensions with the Soviet Union as a result of the invasion of Afghanistan, and this too became a burden despite U.S. aid. More democratic elections occurred in the 1990s, but political stability was fragile and the army kept a watchful eye. A military regime returned in 1999, just after Pakistan tested its first nuclear bomb and as tension with India mounted. Pakistan cooper-

ated with the United States in attacks on terrorists in neighboring Afghanistan from late 2001 onward. Islamic political agitation within Pakistan continued, however. Tensions with India, particularly over control of the disputed region of Kashmir (whose population was largely Muslim), continued to simmer as well.

India, which controlled the majority of the territory and population on the subcontinent despite the 1947 partition, developed a distinctive political and cultural pattern that combined tradition and change. Most striking was its ability to maintain democracy; indeed, India has been one of the few newly independent nations to preserve this political form with any consistency since World War II. Equally important was India's resolve to combine serious social reform with economic development and esteem for many aspects of Hindu culture.

Politically, India retained a federal system, which reflected the nation's regional diversity and the pattern set under British rule. Individual states had considerable power, although there were disputes with the central government at various points. The nation was ruled by the nationalist Congress party with only two exceptions—in the late 1970s, when a coalition of conservative groups assumed office briefly, and again through the 1990s and early 2000s in what was a significant political change. However, multiparty competition was free and fierce, and freedoms of the press and association were not normally limited. Control of many state governments, indeed, passed to parties other than the Congress group, including the Communist party. Congress party leaders, although mainly drawn from the political elite, learned to campaign effectively among the masses, combining the prestige of high status with genuine popular appeal.

There were some questions about Indian democracy, to be sure. Congress party dominance prevented a great deal of experience with partisan shifts at the central government level. As in the Japanese Liberal Democratic party, more political maneuvering took place among factions

History Debate

WOMEN'S CONDITIONS IN INDIA

For many Indian women, conditions changed during the 20th century. Early in the century, a number of Western feminists encouraged new schools; Christian missionaries also worked for schooling. Gandhi actively combated traditions of domestic isolation, or purdah. This was one of the changes he had to promote in order to form an effective mass political movement, and women played a prominent part in many of his demonstrations. There was no hesitation about granting the vote to women when independence came.

But patterns were complex, and scholars debate how to sort out the complexity. Two issues predominate. First, there were huge variations by region and social class. Rural women, still usually uneducated, saw only gradual change. Their family lives were heavily defined by patriarchal traditions. Birth rates gradually dropped, but they remained high enough to condition women's lives.

The second complication, affecting urban women aware of Western models, involved some degree of backlash against change. Many women found Western models irrelevant or harmful. A woman's magazine argued that Indian traditions were much better for women than the styles of the modern West. With arranged marriages, women did not have to think constantly about finding a man or sacrificing everything to beautification. Many urban women worked for their own combination of tradition and change. They enjoyed many global consumer forms, often spoke English, but also tried to live up to the expectations of being a good Hindu wife and mother. Would this kind of approach prove temporary, as more pressure for westernization set in, or was it a potentially durable mixture?

within the dominant group than among different parties. India also experienced few leadership changes at the top. The first prime minister, the nationalist Jawaharlal Nehru, held power for 17 years. He was succeeded by his daughter, Indira Gandhi (no relation to Mohandas Gandhi). Although Indira Gandhi was initially selected by Congress party stalwarts for her presumed susceptibility to manipulation, she proved to be a tough-minded leader who was very conscious of her power. Indeed, it was under her rule that liberal rights were suspended, from 1975 to 1977, as she tried to clamp down on a number of opposition groups and arrested many political critics. These policies led, however, to the Congress party's defeat in 1977, which suggested that the curtailment of democracy within India was costly. New elections in 1980 restored Indira Gandhi to power, but there was no attempt to revive authoritarian rule. Regional disunity, however, remained a serious problem. Gandhi faced growing opposition from the minority Sikh religion, which demanded greater autonomy for the Sikh-dominated state of Punjab. This led in the early 1980s to renewed religious rioting, this time between Hindu and Sikh, and Indira Gandhi's assassination by Sikh militants. Her successor was her son Rajiv, which raised concern about a new dynasty ruling India; again, the formal institutions of a liberal democracy continued to function, doubtless solidified by some popular faith in the ruling family. Rajiv's assassination by southern Tamil separatists ended his family's reign. The Congress party also yielded its control, but a new political coalition assumed power smoothly. India had produced four decades of strong political performance, suggesting that its democratic forms responded to traditions and needs alike and had become part of the nation's political heritage.

India also took the lead in establishing a distinctive diplomatic policy. The new nation remained friendly with its former British rulers and participated actively in Commonwealth meetings to discuss mutual concerns with Britain, Canada, Australia, New Zealand, and the growing number of other former British colonies. At the same time, Nehru and his successors were firmly resolved to avoid entrapment in alliances that were irrelevant to India's needs. The government thus assumed the initiative in organizing interested non-Western nations in a nonaligned, or "third force," bloc that would seek to deal with both the West and Soviet Union while shunning military pacts with either side. The first meeting of this neutral group took place in 1955, and although the cohesion of the group oscillated, India persevered in establishing good relations with both the United States and Soviet Union, often lecturing the great powers on the evils of their competition. India itself faced diplomatic problems, particularly with Pakistan and, at times in the 1960s, with China as well. However, the nation avoided extensive involvement in issues outside its regional concerns, except perhaps for a sometimes moralizing rhetoric.

Congress party leaders from Nehru onward were eager to remake their nation without losing its identity; independence and political power were not enough. Their vision differed somewhat from that of Mohandas Gandhi's in that they were more concerned with economic modernization and less disdainful of factories and sophisticated commerce. Nevertheless, Gandhi, too, had sought some changes in India's old order. Key targets in early legislation were the caste system and traditional gender relations, as India sought to institute equality under the law. The nation's constitution granted equality to women, including the right to vote, and allowed women to seek divorce and marry outside their caste. The caste system itself was outlawed. The government tried

to encourage former untouchables to participate more fully in Indian society, by establishing quotas for "ex-untouchables" in the universities and government jobs. But India's attack on these ancient social traditions was of necessity less forceful than China's war on ancestor worship and other family practices, for outright coercion or the formation of radical new institutions such as communes would have been incompatible with democratic forms. India had no revolution. Therefore, in fact, strong remnants of the caste system remained in India, although not enforced by law. Most government leaders were drawn from the traditionally higher castes, as were most of the growing numbers of university-trained professionals and managers. At the family level, the authority of men continued to be strong, particularly among the rural majority. Practices such as arranged marriages, often with the partners pledged during their teens and not even necessarily meeting before their wedding, continued to be widespread at all social levels.

In economic policy, India's leadership professed a nondoctrinaire socialism. This meant, in practice, considerable economic planning toward the allocation of scarce resources; it also meant government operation of key services such as airlines and railroads. But substantial private enterprise remained as well. Government welfare services focused mainly on basic hygiene, as the nation's poverty prevented a more elaborate social security system. The government also encouraged widespread peasant landownership, dismantling some former estates and helping to clear new land toward this end. This policy, along with progressive taxation, reduced the economic power of the old princely aristocracy.

A key concern, even in the heady early days of independence, was economic development. Congress party leaders had long wanted fuller economic equality for India, as a weapon against Western dominance. Furthermore, steady population growth virtually compelled attention to the issue of economic growth. Government planning and private enterprise, plus some foreign economic aid, promoted substantial growth during the 1950s; the national income expanded by 42 percent. However, the nation's population grew from 360 to 439 million during the same decade, which eliminated half the economic gain. During the 1960s, per capita income stagnated, and India was forced to import food to prevent starvation. This prompted greater concern for improved agricultural production. The government helped sponsor Green Revolution research on better seeds; it also promoted the widespread use of fertilizers and pesticides. These measures yielded impressive results; despite continued population growth, the nation remained self-sufficient in agriculture from 1970 onward.

The government also attacked the population problem directly. Under Nehru, official measures were half-hearted, but with a growth rate of 2.4 percent per year, it became increasingly clear that no serious improvement in living standards for the impoverished masses could occur without birth control. Indira Gandhi's government stepped up propaganda efforts, with slogans such as "A Happy Family Is a Small Family," and medical personnel provided free birth-control devices and procedures, including vasectomies for men. But the campaign met massive popular resistance. Men and women alike feared to tamper with God's ways. Men worried that an operation such as a vasectomy would destroy their "male power," making them as docile as castrated animals. They also continued to value a large family as a sign of good fortune, seeking particularly a sufficient number of sons to ensure their own care in old age. Popular resistance to birth control helped prompt Indira Gandhi's suspension of liberties in 1975 as the government launched an effort to force poor men with large families to undergo vasectomies. This campaign stopped, however, in 1977, as the government returned instead to a policy of intense propaganda and widespread medical services. India's birth rate did begin to slow in the later 1970s, as people became more aware of family planning as an alternative to grinding poverty, but birth rates remained high.

Despite population pressure, which diverted extensive resources to increasing agricultural production and was unquestionably responsible for massive poverty in the countryside and crowded cities alike, India managed to resume its pattern of economic growth in the 1970s. Modern industrial technologies were applied to metallurgy and chemical production, creating pockets of advanced factory industry in a still agricultural nation. India produced cars and tried to limit imports. With ready technological interchange with the West as well as Soviet Russia, India for a time in the early 1980s surpassed the technological level of China. Modern factories as well as rising agricultural productivity accounted for a 4 percent annual growth rate in the years after 1975. By the 1990s, a significant software industry had emerged as well. India has remained vulnerable in the world economy, and its export performance has lagged despite important industrial sales in the Indian Ocean region. The nation's growth record fell well behind that of the Pacific Rim, particularly after the mid-1980s. But despite widely publicized problems, it has engaged in serious economic change. Efforts to reduce state controls to spur growth occurred in the 1990s, while training in computer science expanded.

Indian cultural life showed a predictable balance between new themes and old, but with a bias here toward the more traditional. India's leaders encouraged a rapid expansion of education, which gradually cut into widespread illiteracy. By the 1970s, literacy rates had doubled over the 1947 figure to 30 percent. At the elitist level, scientific training spread widely, and Indian researchers participated actively, in both India and foreign laboratories, to advances in physics, biology, medicine, and computer science. The Indian government even mounted its own space program. Cultural change was also encouraged, although particularly among the elite, by the continued reliance on the English language, which helped maintain India's openness to developments in Western culture. Congress party leaders had

Movie poster in Bombay, featuring the actor Shashi Kapoor in the film *Deewangee*.

hoped to promote Hindi as a new national language, but regional resistance was so great that English remained the only language with countrywide currency in government, the universities, and the press. A number of leading writers also relied primarily on English. Because Indian universities produced more trained professionals than the society required, a large number of doctors and lawyers emigrated to Britain or North America, giving India further ties to the West, although at some economic cost.

At the popular level, however, traditional cultural forms predominated, albeit sometimes in new guises. An active film industry produced innumerable stories of adventure and romance, couched in the terms of traditional popular literature. Few foreign movies penetrated beyond elitist levels, while at the same time Indian films almost never reached beyond the country's borders. Along with films, literature in the various traditional languages remained active, as did traditional artistic styles. Indian painters and sculptors did not participate widely in modern or "international" artistic developments, preferring to continue working mainly in older modes. Artistic imagery, both old and new, remained a vital part of Indian popular life, as did religion. Devotion to Hindu ritual and belief was widespread among the majority, and reverence for holy men continued to be a high priority.

Part of India's distinctiveness rested in the ongoing divisions between the elite and popular culture. The elite, drawn mainly from higher castes, were responsive to new educational opportunities as well as to the new outlets for political and managerial leadership. In this group, both men and women played a meaningful role, for here India's attack on gender divisions had a significant result. Women graduated from universities in growing numbers and held important government and professional positions. The elite did not become Western. Traditional patterns such as arranged marriages continued among this group, as did distinctive religious and cultural interests. However, there was significant change in elitist values, including significant contact with Western (particularly English-language) cultural and scientific developments. Popular culture was quite a different matter, which helps explain the widespread resistance to government-sponsored measures such as birth control in the name of religion and family. India's masses did change, as a minority entered jobs in modern factories and a larger number altered some of their agricultural methods. But change here definitely took place amid vigorous devotion to a number of earlier values. Distinctive religious and cultural interests showed even in basic outlook, as Indians preserved a greater place for imagination in their child-rearing practices, putting less stock than Westerners (or east Asians) on careful lessons in the distinction between pretend and "reality."

India's divisions were regional and religious as well as social. Lacking a highly centralized culture, India had long experienced religious diversity. Despite Mohandas Gandhi's hopes to use nationalism to transcend these differences and a long tradition of considerable tolerance, relations among Hindus, Muslims, and Sikhs grew tenser by the 1990s and early 2000s. Cultural change, including the partial secularism of the elite, helped explain new concerns among religious leaders; so did the older tensions with Muslims. The result was recurrent clashes that threatened the stability of the government. A Hindu fundamentalist movement arose, calling on the government to promote Hinduism at the expense of other religions—a fascinating, perhaps ominous development, all the more interesting in that the use of the state was not, in fact, a Hindu tradition. Fundamentalist political power increased in the 1990s and early 2000s, and Hindu nationalists assumed control of the government, increasing military spending and nuclear development and occasionally talking tough in confrontations with Pakistan. While the Hindu government largely avoided extreme intolerance, it was under pressure from its supporters to attack the Muslim minority within India and to limit foreign influence.

Change and continuity remained complex. The boom in high-technology sectors helped expand a middle class, estimated at as many as 80 million people. Along with the new vigor of Hinduism, a secular popular culture emerged. Indian moviemakers increasingly combined traditional themes with Hollywood techniques, operating from a center in Bombay called *Bollywood*. Film stars enjoyed great prestige. Some practitioners also combined traditional musical forms with rap and other Western styles, drawing attention outside India as well as within.

INDIA AND CHINA

Because India established an independent democracy just as China underwent its communist revolution, comparisons between the two Asian giants became commonplace. Which path would produce greater political success? Which path would prove most compatible with economic development? American observers initially pinned their faith on India, convinced that democracy and real modernization would ultimately go hand in hand. But just as India's democracy proved incapable of stemming population growth—and as India insisted on neutrality rather than an alliance with the West, to the annoyance of many Americans—opinion veered, and China often seemed the better bet. Indian traditions, including religious beliefs and a certain idealism coupled with the country's phenomenal population growth, now seemed less suited than forceful Chinese methods to the necessary reforms. As China became friendlier with the United States in a number of well-publicized moves, enthusiasm for China's development prospects increased.

By the late 1990s, neither China nor India had managed to achieve a full industrial revolution in the style of Japan. At the same time, both have experienced significant economic change. Both have health rates and per capita income rates significantly above those in the poorest agricultural nations, with China, however, now in the lead. Both have seemingly vigorous governments, albeit with quite different institutions, styles, and problems. A comparison is complicated, to be sure, given our ignorance of some Chinese developments, as official control of information remains extensive. Nonetheless, it seems certain that, building on government tradition and communist zeal, China has become more effective than India in reducing its rates of population growth. Most experts assume that India will indeed surpass China as the world's most populous country soon after the year 2000. On the other hand, India has advanced more consistently in technological development and higher education, and it has also had more regular contacts with the outside world. Each nation, then, uses both distinctive traditions and distinctive current political forms to produce its own balanced mix of strengths and weaknesses. Ongoing differences between India and China recall different traditions established in the classical period, particularly in terms of political values and institutions but also attitudes toward the outside world. Later developments are also compelling examples of other important distinguishing factors: India's complex experience as a colony compared to the Western treatment of China, the fact that China had a revolution and India did not, perhaps even the different creative styles of Gandhi and Mao as seminal 20th-century leaders. If China has ultimately gained the edge in economic growth, it may have suffered more in terms of cultural instability and dislocation.

ISSUES AND CONNECTIONS

India offers a fascinating combination of tradition and change, and this is the most compelling analytical focus. There is also the comparative question, about why India's democracy succeeded in contrast to most of the political efforts in south and southeast Asia until quite recently. This occurred despite the great poverty of large numbers of Indians, amid relatively slow

economic growth plus massive population pressure. It is helpful to think of Indian traditions, colonial experience, and individual leadership in dealing with the comparative issues.

Jawaharlal Nehru once lamented the huge weight of tradition on modern India, though he took pride in this identity as well. Certainly, in a society that did not experience revolution, the hold of prior social forms was noteworthy. Castes were abolished, which was a huge change, but caste identity and discrimination continued. Hinduism was another link, though it too changed, particularly with the rise of greater intolerance. Among rural Indians, a host of other traditions, including family relationships, persisted as well. There were even isolated cases in which specific practices such as sati were revived, though they were illegal. Even in urban groups, including people quite comfortable with many Western styles, commitments to older patterns such as arranged marriages showed the contact with India's past.

SUGGESTED WEB SITES

On Gandhi, see http://dwardmac.pitzer.edu/anarchist_archives/bright/gandhi/Gandhi.html. On the life of Mohammad Ali Jinnah, the early leader of Pakistan, see http://www.rediff.com/news/1998/sep/10jinnah.htm.

SUGGESTED READINGS

Recent work includes Gianni Sofri, *Gandhi and India* (1999); Susan Bayly, *Caste, Society and Politics in India from the 18th Century to the Modern Age* (1999); Nicholas Dirks, *Castes of Mind: Colonialism and the Making of Modern India* (2001); and Vikrameditya Pradash, *Chandigarh'd Le Corbusier: The Struggle for Modernity in Postcolonial India* (2002).

India's recent political history is covered in J. Brown, *Modern India: The Origins of an Asian Democracy* (1985), and S. Wolpert, *New Oxford History of India* (1983). On specific topics, see J. Brown, *Gandhi's Rise to Power: Indian Politics,*

1915–1922 (1978); F. Frankel, *India's Political Economy, 1947–1977* (1981); V. B. Singh, ed., *Economic History of India, 1857–1956* (1965); K. M. Panikkar, *The Foundation of New India* (1963); V. P. Menon, *The Transfer of Power in India* (1957); and A. de Souza, *Women in Contemporary India and South Asia* (1980).

A provocative general study of Asian politics, with particular reference to southern Asia, is L. W. Pye, *Asian Power and Politics: The Cultural Dimensions of Authority* (1985), which argues for the difficulty of using Western concepts to understand the Asian state. Eric Wolf, in *Peasants* (1966) and *Peasant Wars of the Twentieth Century* (1970), offers considerable coverage of this general subject within a south Asian context.

On southeast Asia, D. G. E. Hall, *A History of South-East Asia* (1981), is a good survey; see also R. N. Kearney, *Politics and Modernization in South and Southeast Asia* (1974). Useful works on the Vietnam conflict are E. J. Hammer, *Struggle for Indochina* (1954); C. Cooper, *The Lost Crusade: America in Vietnam* (1972); and J. Zasloff and M. Brown, *Communist Indochina and U.S. Foreign Policy: Forging New Relations* (1978). An important study on recent southeast Asian history, with larger theoretical implications, is James Scott, *The Moral Economy of the Peasant: Rebellion and Subsistence in Southeast Asia* (1976).

Excellent source reading on 20th-century India is provided by various English-language novelists, who write directly of Indian life, although using Western languages as well as literary conventions. A well-known example is Rabindranath Tagore. More strictly contemporary authors are Kamale Markhndaya, Shanta Ramarao (on women), T. Shizasankara Pillai (on the south), and R. K. Narayan (on peasants). Also relevant is the work of novelist and essayist V. S. Naipaul, who is of Indian extraction but, because he was raised in the West Indies, writes as an outsider.

Middle Eastern Civilization in the 20th Century

Several major themes weave together in the most recent historical patterns of the oldest area of civilization in the world. Political unity in the Middle East, already tenuous during the 19th century, ended completely after World War I. A few subsequent efforts to revive larger segments, usually under the banners of Arab nationalism or Muslim brotherhood, failed. As new nations were carved out of the former territory of the Ottoman Empire, semi-imperialist controls by various European states coexisted with the independence of several regional states between the wars. After World War II, the entire region gained independence. Divisions among Middle Eastern nations were compounded by a diversity of political forms. Monarchies arose in a few cases—virtually the only recent instances in which monarchy remained a serious political force in the 20th century. Strongman regimes were even more characteristic. Some Middle Eastern states worked vigorously to modify age-old traditions, including the force of Islam, in the name of more secular goals. Others sought to preserve older values above all else.

Partly because of political divisions, the Middle East became the world's leading trouble spot after World War II. This status was not entirely new; already in the 19th century, the weakness and instability of the Ottoman Empire had resulted in conflict. The oil wealth discovered in the Middle East during the 20th century gave the region new importance in the world economy, but it also attracted greed; this intensified the potential for outside interference in Middle Eastern affairs. Further, the creation of a new Jewish state after World War II produced a seemingly irresolvable tension that provoked internal warfare within the region and a series of interventions from the leading powers in the cold war.

Finally, the Middle East generated an unusually complex pattern of reform efforts and counter reactions. A new regime in Turkey (Tûrkiye), installed in the wake of the collapse of the

Ottoman Empire, provided the first of many sec-ularization attempts that would succeed in pro-ducing some industrialization and agricultural development, as well as new systems of education and relationships both in society at large and within the family. Nonetheless, change came painfully in the Middle East, and a number of Islamic leaders, in the name of traditional ideals, helped mobilize reactions against the new trends. A current of Islamic fundamentalism arose, par-ticularly from the 1970s onward; by the 1990s, acts of terrorism against apparent enemies of Islam increased as well. Thus, the Middle East produced a more bitter and overt clash between reformist and conservative forces than any other civilization in the contemporary world. Friction was often heightened by disputes over political form and rivalries among the new nations, adding greatly to the intricacy, and often the tragedy, of recent Middle Eastern history.

KEY QUESTIONS   *The Middle East is in the daily news. Because we know the region is troubled, and because we know that some Middle Easterners dislike the United States, it is sometimes tempting to generalize about the region only in terms of religious fervor and political violence. What were the main patterns in the region during the 20th century, in addition to the persistence of Islam? What features has the region shared with other civilizations in the 20th century, for example in terms of the impact of anti-colonialism or of globalization?*

REPLACING THE OTTOMAN EMPIRE

The Ottoman Empire's alliance with Germany during World War I opened the most recent chap-ter of Middle Eastern history. Britain and France worked to undermine Ottoman rule as part of their own war effort; they encouraged Arab nationalism, against Turkish control, and the British also vaguely promised Jewish leaders a new homeland in Palestine. Wartime pledges plus the ringing ideals of President Wilson at the Versailles Peace Conference prompted many Arab leaders to hope for outright freedom. Instead, they encoun-tered victorious Western allies bent on extending imperialism to their region; not only Britain and France but also Italy and Greece were eager for new territory as the spoils of war. Thus, Middle Eastern nationalism was at once stimulated and frustrated, a dangerous combination.

One point was clear, however: the Ottoman Empire could no longer be supported. Arab lead-ers, united in their hatred of the Turks, agreed on this point with European imperialists, who hoped to carve up the region for their own purposes. Arab uprisings were led by the chief magistrate of Mecca, Hussein Ibn Ali. Then at the war's end, French and British forces moved into the Middle East, the French taking over Syria and Lebanon, the British occupying Palestine, Jordan, and Iraq. The 1920s treaty of Sèvres proclaimed the end of the Ottoman Empire. Efforts to conquer Turkey itself failed, however. A Young Turk military leader, Mustafa Kemal, organized a Turkish resistance movement, defeating both Greek and Western invasion forces. Kemal's success resulted in new negotiations with the European powers and produced a 1923 treaty that created Turkey as a new, separate nation. This treaty not only ensured Turkish independence but also guaranteed the nation's continued strategic importance in European and Russian diplomacy because of its important geographic location.

Buoyed by his military and diplomatic suc-cess, Kemal unseated the sultan and proclaimed a secular republic in the new Turkey. Like Muham-mad Ali in Egypt a century before, Kemal intended to lead the modernization of an Islamic nation, to achieve parity with the European states on their own terms. He carefully fostered a new Turkish nationalism separate from religious faith. He moved the country's capital from Istanbul to Ankara, in the Turkish heartland. Profoundly influenced by Western political ideas, Kemal introduced parliamentary institutions and a new

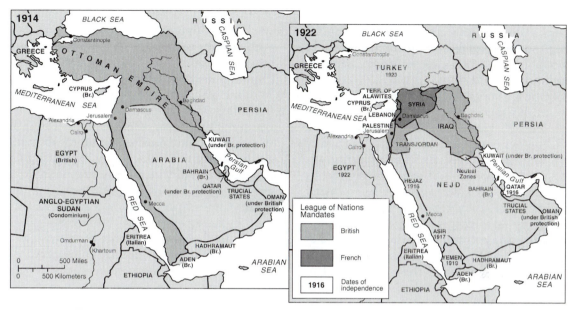

The Middle East Before and After World War I Settlements, 1914–1922

voting system. But his version of democracy was tightly controlled, with a single party—the People's party—preventing any legal opposition. Like other notable westernizers—including Peter the Great—Kemal believed that authoritarianism was an essential precondition of change, for the people had to be forced to accept reforms. Kemal, who took the name *Atatürk*, or "father of the Turks," vigorously attacked the hold of Islam. He abolished the religious caliphate and made the state secular. Civil marriage was required, and a secular school system was established. The regime outlawed many Muslim customs and symbols, including polygamy and traditional clothing—Western dress was mandatory. Sunday rather than Friday was proclaimed the national day of rest, and Muslim law was superseded by the laws of the state, which were modeled after Western codes. Arabic script was replaced with a Latin alphabet for the Turkish language, judged easier to learn and thus more appropriate for modern education. Against Islamic tradition also, Atatürk granted women the right to vote and to receive

an education. A concerted effort to extend primary schools reduced illiteracy from 85 percent in 1914 to 42 percent in 1932.

Atatürk's reforms, like those in Peter the Great's Russia or Meiji Japan, included stirring attacks on traditional clothing. It is important to recognize, and to explain, the passions involved. Here is how Atatürk framed his views on the fez, a traditional cap for upper-class Ottoman men: "It was necessary to abolish the fez, which sat on our heads as a sign of ignorance, of fanaticism, of hatred to progress and civilization, and to adopt in its place the hat, the customary head-dress of the whole civilized world, thus showing that . . . no difference existed between the Turkish nation and the whole family of civilized mankind."

Atatürk's regime also promoted industrialization. A number of factories were established under state guidance. Cities grew. Turkey vigorously pursued the training of engineers and other technical personnel, to make foreign experts unnecessary. At the same time, unions were forbidden to strike, in order to prevent any barriers to economic growth. By 1939, a year after Atatürk's death, the economy had advanced enough so that foreign railroad companies could be bought out—a major blow against lingering economic imperialism.

Atatürk's hopes were not entirely fulfilled, however. His power base was secure; nationalism unquestionably gained ground; traditional culture yielded to new interests in science and economic development. However, the rural majority was not entirely supportive of the new regime, as Muslim objections to secularism persisted. Many crusading schoolteachers reported persistent traditionalism—in their view, superstitious belief—among their students and village leaders. Atatürk's successors had to allow for this deeply rooted religious faith, as they slowed the pace of reform. Furthermore, although Turkey became a new nation and successfully maintained its independence, bolstered by the largest, best-disciplined army in the region, it did not fully industrialize. Economic growth was slow, poverty widespread. Despite the genuine revolution in Turkish politics and culture, this was no Japanese-style leap forward in terms of economic change.

Turkey was the most dramatic case of new Middle Eastern politics after World War I, but it was not the only one. Persia, dominated before the war by British and Russian influence, proclaimed new independence as well, shaking off British efforts to maintain control. Persian nationalists selected an army officer, Riza Khan, soon known as the shah, or king, as their new leader. The new ruler worked for economic change as well as independence, building rail lines and schools and creating a banking system. The government encouraged enough factory industry to provide for national needs in clothing and metals, reducing dependence on Western imports. The regime benefited from important oil revenues, developed by a British company under Persian license. In 1935, to signal the beginning of an era, the kingdom's name was changed to Iran. But the shah was deposed during World War II, in favor of his son, in part because of

efforts to gain advantages from both sides in the war. Islamic opposition to modern trends, along with hostility to the luxurious lifestyle and dictatorial methods of the shah himself, created far more tension than persisted in Turkey.

One policy that Iran explicitly introduced from the 1920s onward deserves particular note, because countries in other regions would soon move in the same direction: import substitution. At the end of the 19th century, Russia and Japan had moved toward full industrialization, hoping to catch up with the West. This approach required active exports, particularly in Japan; it was motivated by military as well as economic goals. Import substitution suggested a more modest approach: build enough factory industry to reduce dependence on Western goods in areas such as textiles and basic machinery (later, automobiles would be added to this list). Success here would give the nation more economic independence, although it might not become a world economic power. Turkey followed this policy to a degree, as did India after 1947; Latin American nations did the same from the 1930s onward. Successful import substitution would have its own impact on the world economy, and of course it did not preclude a more active export stance later on.

ASSERTIONS OF ARAB NATIONALISM

Although important new regimes arose in the northern Middle East, marked by commitment to reform and authoritarian rule, the bulk of the Middle East lay under European control during the 1920s and 1930s. North Africa, of course, was held as colonies by France, Britain, and Italy. The major areas of the Middle East proper, now taken over by France and Britain, were governed as League of Nations mandates, rather than as outright possessions, which implied some commitment to ultimate independence. Nevertheless, Arab indignation at this new foreign rule was a further impetus to nationalism. Riots and demonstrations forced Britain to recognize the technical independence of Egypt in 1922, and Iraq and Jordan soon followed, although in all these cases, Britain continued to regulate economic and military affairs. France made fewer early concessions to nationalism in its territories. It split Lebanon off from Syria, encouraging division between Christians and Muslims in Lebanon as well. And while Lebanon achieved independence under French protection, and Syria won promise of the same in 1936, European influence remained strong. Indeed, in oil-rich territories such as Iraq, European and U.S. companies quickly acquired ownership rights, which actually increased the Western stake in the region even as formal imperialism was declining.

Another key issue for Arab nationalists during the 1920s and 1930s was the growing Jewish presence in Palestine. Although Jews constituted a mere 11 percent of the total population of the region in 1914, Jewish emigration from Europe, encouraged by Zionist organizations and also by Hitler's anti-Semitic onslaught, increased the number of Jewish residents rapidly, to half a million by 1940. The Jewish population was still outnumbered by Palestinian Muslims and Christians, but Arab nationalists were alert to this threat to what they regarded as their land. They pressed Britain, as the mandate power in Palestine, to restrict immigration, but British policy in fact vacillated, failing to satisfy either Muslims or Jews. In the meantime, Jewish organization of agriculture and industry in Palestine, around communal farms known as kibbutzim, gained ground steadily, greatly increasing traditional productivity and developing new export crops such as citrus fruits.

Arab nationalism thus had a number of targets. Although nationalism became more intense, it was also a divisive force in the Middle East. Not only were nationalists distracted by the boundaries drawn among mandate territories, such as Lebanon and Syria, but they also disagreed about the future of the Middle East. Some, as in the new kingdom of Saudi Arabia, advocated tradi-tional Muslim ways, whereas others talked of Western-style parliamentary democracy; still others, like the Iraqi Kamil Chadrichi, preached an Arab form of socialism. Few groups in the Middle East were outright Marxists, for Marxist hostility to nationalism and religion, demonstrated by attacks on Islamic groups in the Soviet Union, was too severe even for most secular reformers. However, no single non-Marxist formula for a Middle Eastern future emerged.

Then came World War II, which further weakened Western Europe's tenuous hold on the region. Turkey remained carefully independent during the conflict, bent on developing its own state without distraction. But much of the rest of the area was drawn into the hostilities, as German forces invaded north Africa and then faced defeat at the hands of the British-American alliance in 1942. More important was the sheer weakness of Britain and France after the war, which gave new hope to Arab leaders. France yielded to riots in 1945, abandoning all government powers in Syria and Lebanon. Britain followed suit, although this was delayed by its attempts to find a solution to Arab-Jewish conflicts in Palestine. Riots and terrorist attacks by the two groups and even against the British marked the period of 1945–1948. When the British finally pulled out of the area, the Jews simply declared a new state of Israel (May 1948), beating off an attack by the surrounding Arab countries and conquering more territory. Almost a million Muslim refugees were expelled from Palestine, creating a legacy of great hostility between the Arabs and Israel and its political allies, including the United States.

Defeat at Jewish hands triggered a revolution in Egypt, where the army colonel Gamal Abdel Nasser drove out the corrupt, pro-Western king in 1952. The goal was a secular, reformist state under one-party leadership. Nasser, who for a time spearheaded Arab nationalism generally, seized the Suez Canal in 1956, provoking a British-French-Israeli attack that managed to invade Egypt but was forced back by U.S. and Russian pressure, as the two superpowers were

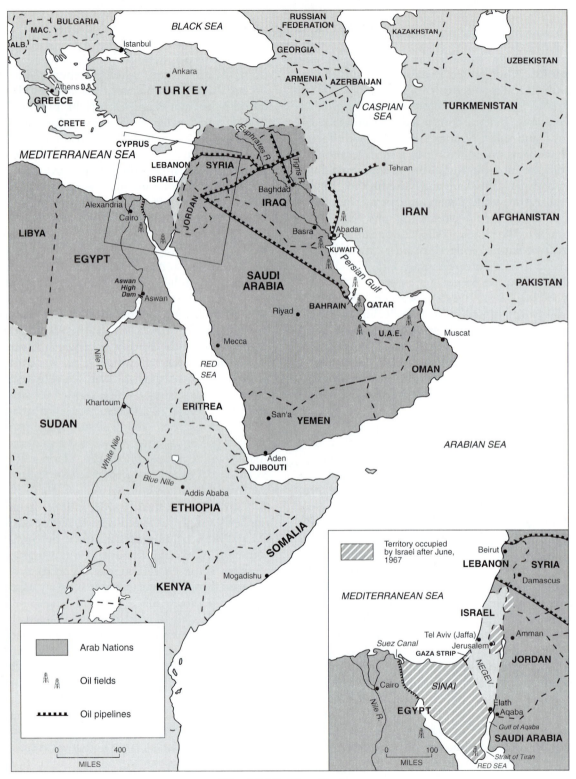

The Middle East Today

bent on courting Arab favor. A fully independent Egypt, which proved its technical competence by running the Suez Canal efficiently, was a major new player in the Middle East from this point onward. Nasser quickly demonstrated his reformist inclination internally by dividing the great estates along the Nile and awarding land to the peasants, thus ending the long-standing manorial system.

Arab independence was completely achieved between 1956 and 1962; the final north African colonies won their freedom as the states of Libya, Tunisia, Morocco, and Algeria. The key battle here focused on Algeria, a French holding since the mid-19th century and symbolic, to many French leaders, of France's battered claims to greatness in the world of power politics. Nationalist agitation led to outright civil war for almost a decade, as the minority of European settlers supported the French army against a pattern of guerrilla attacks and terrorism that proved impossible to suppress. Finally, the French, rightly worried about the effects of the long, brutal struggle on their own internal political stability and national morality, pulled back, agreeing in 1962 to Algerian independence.

With independence achieved, through an assortment of individual states, the most coherent thread in Middle Eastern affairs remained the dispute between the Arab states and Israel. Israel's immediate neighbors were most directly involved, but other Arab leaders found Israel a convenient target to generate popular enthusiasms at home, and a genuine affront to Arab and Islamic authority in the region. For its part, Israel created a strong military force, with far more modern armaments than the Arab states could boast and an aggressive outlook designed to avoid any further scapegoating of the Jewish people. Wars broke out between Israel and its neighbors in 1967 and 1973. The first war led to substantial new Israeli-controlled territory, including the entire city of Jerusalem, regarded as a religious center by Muslims and Christians as well as Jews. Even apart from outright war, guerrilla attacks and terrorism were widely employed by

The Palestinian issue, 1979: Israeli soldier patrolling Arab village during a Palestinian general strike against Israeli-ordered expulsion of a mayor sympathetic to Palestinian independence.

Palestinian groups hostile to Israel, whereas Israel frequently retaliated with bombing missions against refugee camps suspected of harboring terrorists. In 1982, Israel invaded Lebanon in order to unseat Palestinian terrorists, producing literal anarchy in this nation, as no group seemed capable of ensuring order. There were few bright spots in the seemingly unresolvable conflict over Israel. In 1977, the Egyptian president, Anwar Sadat, made a stunning gesture by visiting Israel in the hopes of negotiating a peace. Although this initiative reduced tension, it led to no overall settlement, since Israel refused to surrender most of the territories it had gained in 1967 and many Arab nationalists refused to recognize Israel's right to exist. In 1993, Israeli agreements with the Palestinians in some autonomous regions, followed by a 1994 peace treaty with Jordan, renewed optimism for settling a number of wider disputes. Tensions again increased after 1996 with the victory of a more right-wing party in Israel. The peace effort resumed in 1999 but then seemed to collapse in new violence beginning in 2000.

In addition to the issue of Israel, questions of alignment with the world's superpowers were the focus of many nations in the Middle East. Israel was a firm Western ally, receiving significant financial and military aid from the United States. Turkey, anxious about its Soviet neighbor to the north, was also in the Western camp as a member of NATO. Most other Middle Eastern nations, however, oscillated in their alignments. Egypt's Nasser helped organize "neutral" nations in the world, along with India during the 1950s, as an alternative to an alliance with either side during the cold war. Most Middle Eastern leaders would probably have preferred an essentially neutral course, so they could concentrate on foreign and domestic objectives of their own. However, Western influence continued to loom large. Western nations were often the target of attacks as allies of Israel, remembered imperialists, or capitalist exploiters. They were also valuable sources of arms, purchasers along with Japan of most of the oil produced in the region, and usefully hostile to Marxism. Most of the more conservative Arab states thus tended to develop relatively close ties with the West, whereas more secular regimes either alternated between the cold war superpowers—as did Egypt, which used Russian aid after the Suez war and later renounced it in favor of American support—or leaned toward heavy reliance on Russia—as did Syria during the 1970s. Or they tried to win support from both sides. In any event, competition between the cold war camps continued to weigh heavily on the Middle East, which could not resist substantial

outside influence because of internal divisions and military and economic weakness. At the same time, superpower rivalry gave many states a chance to play off the two sides and thus gain room for independent maneuvers.

Two other factors played a considerable role in Middle Eastern events after the end of outright imperialism: local rivalries and efforts at economic coordination. A number of newly independent states clashed over territory or policy. Egypt and Libya developed a rivalry; Morocco and Algeria disputed territory; in the early 1980s, a particularly brutal and protracted war broke out between Iraq and Iran, over territory and also a fundamental policy dispute between a secular state in Iraq and the fervent religious revolutionaries who had seized power in Iran in 1978. Hundreds of thousands of people, from both sides, died in this war, which ended inconclusively. Iraq's own expansionism led to the invasion of Kuwait in 1990. This was followed by the 1991 Persian Gulf War, in which an alliance among Saudi Arabia, Egypt, Syria, and the major Western powers beat back the Iraqis while trying unsuccessfully to replace their strongman leader, Saddam Hussein.

Against this backdrop of frequent fighting, a few institutions of greater scope provided partial balance. The Arab League existed to help reconcile quarrels in the name of the larger ideal of renewed Arab unity. Periodic efforts to unite different nations surfaced; Syria thus briefly merged with Egypt. Although these attempts seldom had much substance, they served as a reminder that a higher political dream for the region persisted and might someday have greater impact. Finally, and more pragmatically, oil-producing Arab states, headed by Iran, Iraq, and Saudi Arabia, took the lead in forming OPEC (Organization of Petroleum Exporting Countries) in 1961, although there were important non-Middle Eastern participants as well. The formation of OPEC resulted from successful Arab and Iranian efforts to reduce the independence of Western oil companies operating in their region, as either nationalization or at least significant government supervision took hold. OPEC nations also attempted to coordinate production levels and pricing policies, and during the 1970s, they had considerable success in raising the price of oil and therefore the earnings of member nations. Here, at least briefly, was an important change in the customary dependency of raw material suppliers in the world market. By the end of the 1970s, however, competition from other regions and even among OPEC members, plus Western conservation efforts, reduced OPEC's effectiveness in maintaining revenues. Nevertheless, OPEC, along with individual efforts by wealthy Arab states such as Saudi Arabia to provide economic support to petroleum-poor states such as Jordan and Egypt, again demonstrated that narrow nationalist rivalries did not alone capture the complexities of Middle Eastern politics. By 2000, coordination again improved, producing higher oil prices and revenues.

THE NEW ROLE OF THE STATE

With growing nationalism and then independence, the states of the Middle East developed a number of similar functions. Most assumed new responsibility for providing systems of education; an economic infrastructure including roads, ports, and airlines; and some limited welfare programs. Most regulated foreign companies to some extent, and the region gained leverage against the West. Universities were created, teaching secular subjects along with or instead of the basic principals of Islamic faith. Even conservative regimes such as the Saudi Arabian monarchy spurred technical training. The new functions of government demonstrated the novelty of many of the forces impinging on this region during the 20th century. What was happening in the Middle East, as elsewhere in the world, was a common pattern of political modernization, defined simply as the extension of government functions to new areas, such as mass education and economic planning, and the attempt to focus new loyalty on the state.

This effort may be viewed as an obvious development, but it was profoundly unsettling to some. Nationalism itself was a new loyalty, not an inevitable outgrowth of Middle Eastern tradition. Many Muslims believed that nationalism was irrelevant so long as pious Muslims controlled the government; thus, for example, it was unimportant that an Arab government rule Arabs. By the same token, Middle Eastern nationalists had to tread very carefully in the area of religious devotion, insisting that nationalism did not contradict true belief and emphasizing a common interest in the glorious Muslim past, while urging some reforms in Islam itself. Definitions of nationalism also varied and clashed. Was a nation a region with boundaries established by Europeans after World War I? Should it embrace all Arabs? Should it be secular or Islamic?

Changes in government functions and the rise of nationalism did not mean Western-style political forms in the typical Middle Eastern states. Liberal democracy did not take hold in this region; here was another common denominator in the Middle Eastern political style. Along with China, the Middle East indeed proved most resistant to the spread of democracy in the 1980s and 1990s. The one consistent exception was Israel, where a parliament achieved great power and a multiparty system flourished. Even here, Israel's focus on military development and repression of its Palestinian minority at times clouded the nation's liberal vision, as did the power of extremist religious groups in winning government support for Orthodox Jewish practices.

Most Middle Eastern states either did not establish parliaments or, as in the more secular states, limited their effectiveness by preventing multiparty competition. Even Turkey, which periodically experimented with opposition parties and a fairly free press after World War II, sometimes retreated into military regimes. A multiparty system did gain ground, producing the first woman prime minister in the 1990s. Then victory by a pro-Muslim party caused the military to intervene in 1997 and install secular politicians, although on the basis of a party coalition in parliament. Elsewhere, monarchy or strongman rule normally prevailed. Islamic political tradition provided scant basis for liberal political values, whereas the tensions within Middle Eastern society convinced many leaders that their power could not be preserved within a framework of political competition. Most countries, then, imposed restrictions on the press, used political police extensively, and relied heavily on military support in an essentially authoritarian approach.

Nevertheless, there was no single vision of how the state should operate. A key division erupted between the monarchies—Morocco, Jordan, Saudi Arabia, Iran before 1978, and some smaller states on the Persian Gulf—and the secular republics, where individual strongmen typically wielded power, often backed by a single political party. Most of the monarchs, while working for economic development, not only discouraged political opposition but also tended to support the existing social hierarchy and conservative Islamic social values. Saudi Arabia was the most extreme example, in part because the country emphasized the Wahabi version of Islam, which was quite puritanical. The country sought to use oil revenues to develop a wider industrial base as well as new cities and extensive education. But it also enforced traditional Arab dress and social segregation of women, as well as significant penalties for sexual misconduct or other violations of Islamic law. The government forbade women to drive cars, even though many had learned to drive during visits to the West. It promoted active Islamic education combined with intolerance for other beliefs.

Most republics, on the other hand, although just as hostile to political opposition as the monarchies, sought to encourage not only industrial development and agricultural reform but also a more secular outlook. They worked for new educational and job opportunities for women, while discouraging traditional dress. Like Atatürk's regime, they tried to limit Islamic habits—such as fasting during the day for the month of Ramadan—that would affect economic productivity. A number of the republics worked toward a policy of what was called *Arab socialism*, designed to produce a society different from the West and the communist nations alike. Arab socialism meant regulations for business—particularly foreign-owned business—but not state control of the entire economy. It involved attempts to limit inequality, through heavier taxation on the rich and land reforms to benefit the peasantry. Arab socialism did not, however, represent a full-scale attack on religion or devotion to elaborate political doctrine; it was an impulse more than a well-defined movement.

Many regimes developed extensive police powers, including arrests of political opponents and frequent torture or even assassination. In no sense did they express popular support, though some people benefited from stability and from favors from the government. Opinion polls in the early 2000s made it clear that most people in the Middle East would prefer democracy. In one opinion poll, 92 to 99 percent of all Middle Easterners favored democracy (in contrast to 89 percent in the United States). This was a huge change from the 1930s and 1940s, when many had preferred some kind of fascism. But it was hard for these opinions to win through, because of the police powers of the state. One reaction was an increase in Islamic fervor as a means of expressing political frustration as well as sincere belief. Amid internal political divisions and a host of essentially new nations, it was clear that the Middle East had not yet settled on a durable political form.

THE RISE OF FUNDAMENTALISM

Political and economic change produced an important backlash in Middle Eastern political and cultural life, which became increasingly dominant from the 1970s onward. Furthermore, failures of reform—in the continuation of massive poverty—created pressure to use religion for protest. The spiritual power and pervasive legal framework of Islam explain why many people, ordinary peasants as well as religious leaders, were tempted to use their Islamic faith as a rallying point against change or for different kinds of reform, and especially against any signs of Western cultural influence. Thus, the Ayatollah Khomeini, ultimately the leader of Iran's 1978 revolution, reacted to educational change:

> Our universities must become Islamic. . . . They have served to impede the progress of the sons and daughters of this land; they have become propaganda arenas. Our young people may have succeeded in acquiring some knowledge, but they have not received an education, an Islamic education. . . . The universities do not impart an education that corresponds to the needs of the people and the country; instead they squander the energies of whole generations of our beloved youth, or oblige them to serve the foreigners.

Thus, a new Islamic fundamentalism took shape, after 1970, that in essence sought a return to original Islamic political ideals of a state committed to religious values and the enforcement of these values as its first priority. This was not pure traditionalism; fundamentalists used novel methods and often displayed an intolerance that was not characteristic of Islam in the past. Most leaders were urban educated. But there was a protest against change. Many Islamic scholars and other religious leaders, including the ulema scholars, raised important objections to trends in the Middle East (and also in neighboring Islamic societies such as Sudan, Afghanistan, and Pakistan). They viewed concentration on economic advance as evidence of improper priorities: adherence to religious duties should come first. Westernized clothing—particularly for women and especially in recreational areas and on beaches—and other imports, including films, were attacked as scandalous and immoral. The tendencies of more secular states to promote education without a firm

An Iranian revolutionary trains women in military skills.

basis in religion and to cooperate with Christian Westerners were condemned, while Islamic purists also insisted on a more concentrated attack on the problem of Israel. In short, Islamic fundamentalists called for a restoration of many traditional values, including a reorientation of political actions.

Appeals for a return to traditional values have been a standard part of modern history in societies exposed to rapid change: they occurred in Christian societies during the 19th century, and they still occasionally surface in some parts of the West, including the United States. They also occurred, although on different terms, in Japan. Hindu fundamentalism echoed similar themes in India. However, the Islamic fundamentalist movement seems to have struck a deeper chord in the Middle East than analogous movements in other civilizations. Deeply committed Muslim groups emerged in most Middle Eastern states by the 1970s. Even in conservative Saudi Arabia, they exerted pressure on the regime to follow Muslim laws more faithfully. Thus, as the result of some court trials intended to set an example, adulterers were stoned or beheaded. A group of fundamentalists was responsible for the assassination of President Anwar Sadat in 1981, although Egyptian policy was not greatly affected by the conservative current. Fundamentalist pressure in Pakistan prompted the military regime to introduce a new code of law more in line with Muslim tradition, providing, among other things, harsher punishments for such crimes as sexual immorality. In the 1990s, fundamentalist pressure increased in Turkey, although the military tried to curtail it. Algerian military rulers faced an even tougher battle with a larger fundamentalist faction, and a great deal of violence ensued between both groups. In general, Islamic fundamentalism added an important ingredient to the Middle Eastern mix, even when states largely resisted the pressure.

The greatest victory of the Islamic militants occurred in Iran. It was revealing that the most dramatic revolution in the 20th-century Middle East was religious in spirit, unlike all other contemporary revolutions in the world. The Iranian revolution has been called, in fact, the first real "third-world revolution," in that it sought not a special national path to modernization using ideas such as Marxism first created in the West, but a commitment to the ideals of Islamic law. The revolutionaries were zealous Shi'a, a majority in Iran although a minority in Islam overall. Shi'a had long been bent on creating a purer religious state, against what they saw as the errors of the Sunni, the majority group of Muslims. This aspect of the Iranian struggle renewed a conflict that had existed for centuries within Islam.

The specific framework for the Iranian revolution involved a rapid reform program that had taken place in Iran, building on the efforts of the

The Iranian Revolution, 1979: anti-American demonstration, with posters of the Ayatollah Khomeini.

1920s and 1930s, combined with brutal political repression. The shah's government, which with U.S. help had defeated a 1953 protest, had launched a crash program of modernization rather like that of Atatürk earlier in Turkey, but with the added development of substantial oil revenues and greater contact with the West. The regime supported education, including the training of many Iranians abroad, plus industrial and military development. These changes caused much discontent. The rural majority was neglected. Inflation ran high, for even with significant oil earnings, the country's many new projects were expensive. The shah's brutal repression of political opposition, through a powerful secret police, antagonized additional, liberal segments of Iranian opinion, as did extensive corruption. Other grievances rested with the Muslim faithful. Islamic leaders were appalled at the new surge of Western influence, visible in the 100,000 foreigners who helped run the economy. They protested the resort areas developed for foreigners' use, where the use of liquor and skimpy bathing attire openly clashed with Muslim law.

Revolt broke out in 1978, forcing the exile of the shah early the following year. The new leader was the aged holy man, the Ayatollah Khomeini, who had long campaigned against the "godless and materialistic" regime of the shah. The revolutionary government quickly suppressed other discontented groups, including liberals and communists. It banned Western music, bathing suits, and liquor, and set out to create a holy Shi'a state. Traditional dress, including a veil or *chadur*, was required of women. During the long war Iraq launched against Iran, leaders hoped to export its political principles to other Islamic states; the ayatollah talked of a new jihad, or holy war, that would unite the whole Middle East in a literal version of the Islamic state. A high level of religious and revolutionary excitement continued in Iran through the mid-1980s. Fundamentalists, mainly Shi'a, were also active in the troubled nation of Lebanon, after the 1982 Israeli invasion, and they stirred elsewhere; in Syria, for example, a fundamentalist insurgency was vanquished, but only after considerable brutality. By the late 1990s, however, more moderate policies gained ground in Iran. Democratic elections produced a reformist government. Controls by Islamic clerics, however, prevented the government from changing policies too dramatically. The situation remained volatile.

Fundamentalist reaction to change in the Middle East generally formed an important current in the late 20th century. There was no way to determine its durability; certainly key states such as Iraq and Syria, as well as most north African regimes, managed to maintain their secular policies that were, in any event, not in full opposition to Islam. But fundamentalists put massive pressure on governments, as in Algeria, along with being respon-

sible for frequent acts of terrorism. Even the Soviet Union worried about a potential fundamentalism current among its own Islamic minority; this was one reason for the invasion of Afghanistan, to guard against a fundamentalist regime in this neighboring state. Debates over Islamic policy resumed in the new central Asian republics that followed the Soviet collapse. Finally, the incompleteness of industrialization and divisions of outlook, even in well-established secular states such as Turkey, suggested that Islam and some aspects of a conventional reform program were not easily compatible. Again, Islam's spiritual hold, its emphasis on obedience to Allah, and its tradition of regulating social life in some detail gave it an unusual role among world religions in the 20th century.

By the early 2000s, it was not clear how important Islamic resistance and innovation would prove to be. Certainly, the continued strength of the Muslim faith added to the diversity of Middle Eastern politics in the later 20th century. It also suggests the ongoing complexity of the process of change in this vital region, for Islamic fundamentalism has by no means been uniformly triumphant. Its surge reflects the fact that significant political and social change has already touched Middle Eastern civilization—for example, the steady urbanization, bringing over 65 percent of the population of major countries such as Egypt into the cities, away from rural roots and a different kind of economy. Even in the early 2000s, Islamic fundamentalism was not the only force for cultural change in the region. Global consumerism exerted its own pressure. A Japanese animated cartoon character became an important emblem of independence for many women in Iran. In leading Turkish cities, Christmas shopping took hold, even though the holiday was religiously irrelevant to Muslims. Many Muslims also began exchanging gifts and cards during Ramadan, a remarkable development in a holiday traditionally devoted to self-denial. If westernization obviously cannot capture the patterns of the contemporary Middle East, in politics and culture alike, no more so does an image of unaltered religious traditionalism.

History Debate

TERRORISM

Americans developed a new awareness of terrorism on September 11, 2001, and many thought the world would never be the same. Understanding brutal attacks that could kill 3000 people, totally at random, is no easy exercise. Some people simply refer to terrorists as evil, and assume that the dark side of human nature is all one needs to know.

There are, however, historical perspectives on terrorism that may be illuminating. The first recognizes that terrorism, in anything like a modern sense, began in the later 1880s. It reflected the frustration of groups confronting powerful established forces—for example, Russian protesters attacking the tsar's regime—and it reflected the new technology of guns and explosives. It was a terrorist act, the assassination of the Austrian archduke by a Serbian nationalist, that precipitated World War I. As today, terrorists were powerfully motivated, organized in secret, and willing to die for a cause. Then, as now, many terrorists believed they were responding to terrorism by governments—the attacks or torture sponsored by political police, for example.

However, two aspects of terrorism changed by around 2000. First, terrorist activities became increasingly associated with religious extremism, and not only from Islam. (It was a Buddhist-derived extremist sect that unleashed poison gas in a Japanese subway, for example.) Second, terrorist acts were increasingly directed not at government officials so much as civilian targets. Changes in terrorist weapons, including miniaturized bombs, contributed to this second change. Terrorists obviously believe that they have no alternative in expressing the need to destabilize governments and the economic and cultural influences they find repellent.

Two final points about terrorism are frustratingly inconclusive. In the first place, modern terrorism has rarely produced the results terrorists desire. Usually, terrorist acts galvanize resistance and counterattack. But in the second place, no one has yet figured out how to end terrorism, either by force or by providing other channels for effective expression of deep grievance.

MIDDLE EASTERN CULTURE AND SOCIETY

One fully industrial country emerged in the Middle East after World War II: the state of Israel. The new nation, although severely pressed to defend its existence, benefited from extensive foreign aid, a deeply felt nationalism on the part of many of its citizens, and its experience in developing an industrial economy. Most initial Israeli leaders were immigrants. Hundreds of thousands of European Jews migrated to the new nation after the Nazi Holocaust of World War II. Substantial immigration from the cities of the Middle East developed as well, as hostilities between Arabs and Jews disrupted earlier patterns of tolerance and the new Israeli state served as a beacon for the Jewish faithful. With immigration came population growth and the infusion of a multitude of skills in business and manufacturing. Israeli commitment to industrial output and market agriculture, including extensive projects of desert reclamation, produced a dynamic economy that easily placed Israel among the most

Understanding Cultures

FUNDAMENTALISM

Many Western experts on the Middle East caution great care in interpreting fundamentalism. They note that fundamentalist hostility to the West, particularly the United States, makes a sympathetic interpretation difficult. They especially urge that fundamentalism not be seen as a single movement. Not all fundamentalists oppose all change. Muslim tradition is perfectly compatible with commercial advance, for instance. Most fundamentalists accept certain kinds of change, including new technologies and the importance of mass education (although they seek a strong religious element in this education and the careful regulation of female dress). Even the effort to implement the laws of the Sharia is new, for such an attempt has never been initiated before. Further, fundamentalism addresses both traditionalist beliefs and discontent amid modern problems such as massive urban poverty.

Another important question involves the relationship between this strong, growing current in Islam and religious change elsewhere. Related Hindu movements became more vigorous in the 1980s and 1990s, as we have seen. The collapse of the Soviet system resulted in the renewed vitality of Orthodox Christianity in eastern Europe, while Protestant fundamentalists also worked for converts. In addition, religious pressures increased in Israel in the 1990s, particularly in the Orthodox Jewish stronghold of Jerusalem. Protestant fundamentalism, advanced by missionaries mainly from the United States, was the most rapidly growing new belief system in Latin America in the 1980s and 1990s. Islamic fundamentalism, in other words, played a special role in the Middle East and north Africa, plus adjacent territory in Pakistan and central Asia. However, it may be viewed as part of a wider international current in the late 20th century, which means that its explanation goes beyond strictly Islamic bounds.

Other observers, however, stress some specifically Islamic ingredients. They note the relevance of the longtime Sunni–Shi'a rift and also Islam's extensive legalism, its host of rules and regulations, that make it harder for the faithful to accept certain kinds of social and cultural change than is true for other religions. Islamic law, Sharia, applies to so many aspects of life, from the position of women to one's daily schedule, that its mandates can clash with any modern reform drive. This provides a special basis for the more general temptation to defend tradition in the contemporary world. Interpreting fundamentalism, or any specific manifestation such as Islamic fundamentalism, clearly raises important questions and challenges.

technologically advanced nations of the world. Although the new country faced economic problems, particularly because of heavy military expenditure, it had easily jumped the basic hurdles of 20th-century economic development. The country turned increasingly to consumerism by the 1990s, which caused concern among religious groups and secular nationalists alike.

In contrast, manufacturing, market agriculture, and levels of technology lagged in most other parts of the Middle East. Indeed, the gap in technological sophistication between Israel and its rivals was one of the bases of Israeli survival, as Israeli production of up-to-date armaments became a major industry. Variety among the Islamic states in economic conditions increased. The region embraces about 60 percent of the world's known petroleum reserves, but they are not evenly distributed. Nations with substantial oil production and small populations—among them some of the traditionally poorest desert states—suddenly surged to immense per capita wealth. The Persian Gulf state of Kuwait thus ranked in 1980 as the richest in the world in terms of average income. Saudi Arabia also rose to great wealth. Lavish new urban construction and extensive medical and educational services followed from oil revenues in these nations, particularly during the heyday of OPEC price manipulation. Regional manufacturing did gain ground, generating additional import substitution and a new minority of factory workers. However, although the oil-rich states struggled to invest their earnings in industries that could sustain a better-balanced economy and provide wealth even when oil production declined, they encountered serious difficulties. Many, indeed, invested substantial funds abroad, especially in the West, because there simply were insufficient productive opportunities at home. Lack of other resources, continued limitations in technical training and interest, a pronounced gap between rich and poor that restricts consumer demand—these were some general factors that inhibited the translation of oil wealth into industrialization. Heavy military expenditures also played a role, for these investments involved purchases from abroad rather than a stimulus to domestic production. When military expenditure turned into war, as in the Iran-Iraq conflict, the impact on economic conditions could be devastating.

Nations without oil wealth faced even more severe economic problems. Here, too, military expenditures and, in some cases, political instability limited economic development. Many countries were also burdened by significant population growth. Lack of available land haunted many rural people, whereas opportunities in the cities did not keep pace with need, even as urbanization accelerated. Muslim beliefs slowed conversion to new birth-control methods. A number of governments attempted massive projects to expand production. Egypt's President Nasser, for example, with substantial Soviet aid, orchestrated the construction of a huge dam at Aswan, on the Nile, designed to increase agricultural land through irrigation while providing low-cost electrical power for industry. The dam was also meant to symbolize Arab greatness and recall the glory days of ancient Egypt; thus, Nasser described the dam as "more magnificent and seventeen times greater than the Pyramids." Unfortunately, the Aswan project, although successful, did not keep pace with Egypt's population growth. Both the urban masses and peasant population of this key nation remained desperately poor.

New oil revenues, land reform, and some real growth in urban manufacturing did bring economic change to the Middle East, particularly after World War II. City populations outstripped rural populations in most countries as Middle Eastern urbanization levels exceeded those of India and China. However, outside of Israel, a breakthrough to a fully industrial economy has yet to occur, and standards of living in the larger countries tend to stagnate. One result was considerable emigration in search of jobs, as many Turks and north Africans sought work in western Europe, whereas other Arab peasants took unskilled jobs, often at low pay, in the oil-rich states. Masses of Egyptians and Palestinians (and also Indians and Pakistanis) worked in Saudi Arabia and the United Arab Emirates.

Middle Eastern culture, like the economy, also straddled the fence between tradition and change. Outside of Israel, few Middle Eastern artists participated in international styles. Most Muslim art continued to use traditional styles and themes, although "modern" architecture did find a place in the urban development of countries such as Saudi Arabia and pre-Revolutionary Iran. Although some Western films were shown in the more secular nations, Islamic filmmaking remained largely separate from patterns developed in the West, partly of course for religious reasons. The Muslim world retained an active allegiance to traditional musical styles, relying, even for most popular music, on instruments and singing techniques different from those in the West. Although important work has been done in art and literature—an Egyptian novelist won the Nobel Prize for literature in 1994, for instance—and also in

Islamic theology and law, there was little sense of a revival of creativity that would recall the brightest periods of Middle Eastern culture.

Most Middle Eastern governments encouraged a growing interest in science. Nasser established a Supreme Science Council in Egypt, arguing that

> we have to keep up with the new world and new discoveries. We suffered so much in the past because we were left behind by the ages of steam and electricity. What suffering awaits those who fail to keep up with the new dawn will certainly be much greater than whatever we have experienced in the past. . . . In this world of breathtaking discoveries, to be left behind is to forfeit one's right to existence.

Although improved scientific training added an important dimension to Middle Eastern culture, it did not propel the region into the top ranks of scientific creativity; the Middle East remained heavily dependent on the West for basic scientific research. The dissemination of a scientific outlook to a larger population through the expanding school systems, along with growing literacy, established a basis for further change in the future, although at times this viewpoint clashed with Islamic fundamentalism.

Society in the Middle East reflected the growth of cities and the policies of reform-minded governments. It also reflected population pressure and, in places, the impact of war. But there were important continuities with the past as well. Many Middle Eastern villages have changed only slowly. Some new agricultural equipment was introduced, and contacts with urban markets expanded. However, the pace of life and work remained recognizable in traditional terms. Although landlord dominance was reduced throughout most of the region, the gap between peasant masses and local notables was an important fact of life.

A key tension in Middle Eastern society involved the position of women. In a major break

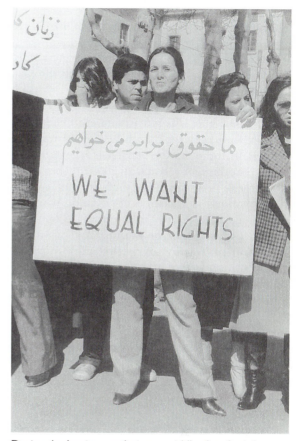

During the Iranian revolution, a middle-class feminist demonstration.

with the past, increasing numbers of women gained access to formal education. In the more secular states, such as Turkey, Egypt, Algeria, or Syria, many women also cast aside traditional clothing, abandoning the veil and adopting Western dress. Many governments tried to encourage new work patterns among women, seeing them as a vital resource for fledgling industrial economies. Thus, some women entered the ranks of factory and office workers. But the economic and social segregation of women remained severe. Work outside the home, and especially a commitment to professional jobs as doctors or lawyers, was widely disapproved of, and few women could hope to support themselves without family resources. The gap between male and female school attendance remained greater than in any other civilization. Male dominance within the household was still pronounced, and the relatively high birth rate both caused and reflected the domestic emphasis of women's lives. Conservative states such as Saudi Arabia enforced even more pronounced separation between men and women, including severe penalties for sexual infidelity. The Iranian revolution showed that even reformist regimes such as the shah's could yield to more traditional practices concerning women.

Again, the result was not uniform. Countries such as Turkey had large numbers of "westernized" women, wearing cosmetics and European-style clothes, active in urban jobs, including politics, and possessed of a secular education. They shared the streets with women in traditional dress, those enmeshed in a more traditional Islamic culture and family life. In a few cases, they also faced attack from the fundamentalist movement.

NEW TENSIONS IN THE EARLY 2000s

The early 2000s saw an escalation of violence in parts of the Middle East and neighboring countries. After some successful peace discussions led to the establishment of a semi-autonomous Palestinian state in parts of Israel, warfare resumed. Palestinian militants declared a new war on Israel, and terrorist attacks, including use of suicide bombers, increased. Israel responded with violent reprisals. This conflict, along with larger grievances about authoritarian regimes and economic frustrations, helped engender wider efforts by Islamic terrorists. Attacks occurred in other countries and also in east Africa and western Europe.

The presence of United States forces in countries such as Saudi Arabia, a result of the 1991 Persian Gulf War, fanned resentment as well. Terrorist preparations were particularly widespread in Afghanistan. Terrorist attacks on Russian forces had

flourished during the 1980s, often encouraged by the United States. The organizations remained intact after the Russians left, and they were supported by an extreme Islamic government, the Taliban. Then, on September 11, 2001, agents of the al Qaeda organization managed to seize commercial airliners to crash into the World Trade Center and the Pentagon, in the United States, causing about 3000 deaths. This massive assault prompted a successful American invasion of Afghanistan, where the Taliban regime was removed. Concern about armaments and potential terrorist support from the authoritarian regime of Saddam Hussein, in Iraq, motivated a U.S.-led invasion in 2003, which occupied the country relatively easily. The aggressive U.S. policies raised the question of whether a new American empire was being formed in the region. More modest questions, about whether the Americans would be able to bring order to their new, if temporary, territories in Afghanistan and Iraq, much less build prosperous, democratic societies, were hard to answer. Nor did the terrorist threat seem to be definitively resolved.

A TROUBLED REGION

Many more question marks dot the appraisal of trends and prospects in the Middle East than is the case for other major Asian civilizations. The region has produced no unity in political forms. The existence of divisions and diversity is no novelty in Middle Eastern tradition, of course, as periods of chaos often punctuated efforts at unification in the past. However, there is certainly no clear end in sight to some of the fundamental conflicts that describe political and military life in the region. Disputes between secular reformers and Islamic fundamentalists continue to constrain many national governments and divide behaviors among women. The precise blend of tradition and change that will continue to define a Middle Eastern civilization has yet to be found. The civilization remains unique and faces a number of problems of sig-

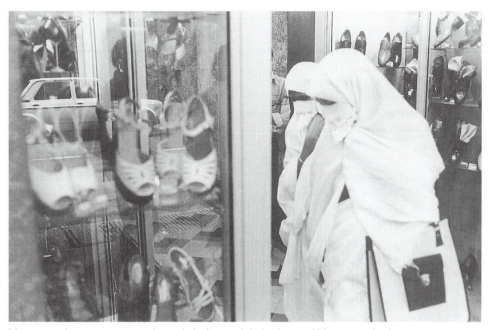

Moroccan shoppers wear traditional clothing, while looking at Western-style shoes.

nificance to other parts of the world as regional wars spill over into wider tensions.

Perhaps the troubles of the Middle East will prove transitory. Once before, when the Arab caliphate declined but before the full hold of the Turks was secure, the region passed through many decades of disarray. Regional political units refused to coordinate their policies. An outside force—the kingdom of Jerusalem established by European crusaders—seized a holy territory but could not easily be dislodged. Out of frustration, terrorist groups, called the *Assassins*, arose. However, this chaos eventually subsided, as a new wave of Turkish invasions, under the Ottomans, engendered political unity and military strength, while preserving many distinct features of Islamic civilization, including considerable tolerance and regional diversity. History may, in some basic ways, repeat itself; certainly, this particular analogy is interesting. Nonetheless, analogies are never certain—Israel is no mere crusader state; economic development issues and basic disputes

over politics complicate any earlier pattern—and this one, in any event, would take several more generations to work out. In the meantime, the Middle East, unquestionably dynamic in many ways, remains one of the world's trouble spots.

Adding to the complications facing Middle East politics was the collapse of the Soviet Union and the emergence of the new Muslim nations in nearby central Asia. These nations had their own problems: what kind of political system to establish, how to treat minorities such as Armenian Christians in their region, and how to plan economic development in an area long used by Russia as a raw-materials center. They also had a new opportunity to reach out to their Muslim brethren. Iranian fundamentalists hoped to guide them back to their version of Islam. Diplomats from more secular Turkey tried to persuade them of the virtues of top-down reform. Questions about the eventual fate of Islam became no easier to answer but gained even greater importance.

ISSUES AND CONNECTIONS

The connections to the past may seem deceptively simple for the Middle East. Obviously the Islamic heritage looms large in contemporary Middle Eastern history. It relates to other continuities, such as beliefs about women's roles and their styles of dress. Less obvious but important continuities include the region's strong commercial tradition, which can adapt to new opportunities such as oil exports. The extent of political continuity is debated. Some see traditions of authoritarianism, for example from the Ottoman Empire, maintaining a hold and helping to explain the region's distinctive political experience in recent times. Another component involves the Middle East's long suspicion of the Christian West (which the West has often returned in kind). In 2002, a group of Islamic intellectuals noted how few Western books were translated into Arabic (80 per year, the same number as in much smaller Greece), suggesting that the region maintains some earlier patterns of cultural isolation.

But it is vital not to oversimplify. Even references to the Islamic heritage are complicated, for there is no single legacy. Divisions among Islamic groups—both old ones, such as that between the Sunni and Shi'a, and new ones about fundamentalism or violence—are extremely important. In 2002, Turkey chose an Islamic party for its government, but the party was at pains to show its commitment to individual and religious freedoms and its willingness to tolerate a heavily secular society.

There are two ways to guard against oversimplification in studying the contemporary Middle East. The first is to recognize the divisions that have opened in recent decades. These include the different emphases within Islam. They include strong secular currents, including consumerism. They include the new gap between democratic aspirations among the Middle Eastern majority and the continued authoritarianism of many states. Even in U.S.-controlled Iraq in 2003, it was not clear how democracy and government interests would play out. Change, in the 20th century, has not just involved the persistence and revival of Islam.

The second vantage point involves comparison. Obviously, the Middle Eastern experience is distinctive in many ways. But the region has participated in some of the same tensions and excitements of new nationhood as south Asia or Africa—including the difficulty of forming durable regimes in countries that were somewhat artificially created by European imperialists. It has participated in some partially successful adjustments to the world economy, including not only taking greater control of the oil industry but also sponsoring import substitution and some modern domestic industry. It has participated in some changes in gender relations, though these have sparked debate. It has participated, again with debate, in global consumerism or the spread of scientific training. Seeing where the Middle East fits wider patterns and varies from them is a vital part of world historical analysis for the contemporary period.

SUGGESTED WEB SITES

On Nasser and Egypt during the cold war, see http://www.arab.net/egypt/history/et_nasser. html. On Islamic religious reactions and the works of Hasan al-Banna of the Muslim Brotherhood, see http://www.prelude.co.uk/mb/banna/message. htm. On fundamentalism, see http://abcnew.go. com/sections/world/islam/islam.html.

SUGGESTED READINGS

Recent work includes Gerges Fawaz, *America and Political Islam: Clash of Cultures or Clash of Interests?* (1999); Beverley Milton-Edwards, *Contemporary Politics in the Middle East* (2000); Elizabeth Thompson, *Colonial Citizens: Republican Rights, Paternal Privilege and Gender in French Syria and Lebanon* (2000). Several valuable sources are available on the Middle East in this period. See David Ben-Gurion, *Israel: Years of Challenge* (1963), and I. Khomeini, *Practical Laws of Islam* (1983) and *Islam and Revolution: Writings and Declarations of Iman Khomeini,* trans. Hamid Alger (1981). Mahmud Makal, *Village in Anatolia* (1951), is an exceptionally interesting account of the tension between a modernizing Turkish schoolteacher and the environment and response in his village.

A useful overall survey is G. Lenczowski, *The Middle East and World Affairs,* 4th ed. (1980); see also Hain Faris, *Arab Nationalism* (1986), and Juan Coley, ed., *Comparing Muslim Societies* (1992). On specific national and diplomatic topics, useful works are J. C. Hurewitz, *A Diplomatic History of the Near and Middle East* (1956); W. Lacqueur, *Communism and Nationalism in the Middle East* (1956); N. Safran, *The United States and Israel* (1963); W. Lacqueur, *A History of Zionism* (1972); R. Cottam, *Nationalism in Iran,* rev. ed. (1979); K. Wheelock, *Nasser's New Egypt* (1960); E. B. Childers, *The Road to Suez* (1963); and Z. N. Zeine, *The Struggle for Arab Independence* (1960). See also E. Boserup, *Women's Role in Economic Development* (1974), which covers a vital aspect of Middle Eastern development (and also the patterns in other non-Western areas), although with a controversial theoretical framework, and Nikki Keddie and Bill Baron, eds., *Women in Middle Eastern History* (1991). For information on the individual Muslim states, see Ira M. Lapidus, *A History of Islamic Societies* (1988).

33

Latin America in the 20th Century

Many Americans regard Latin America as a highly traditional area. In fact, the 20th century resulted in a number of rapid economic and political changes worldwide, although Latin America retained a great deal of its distinctive cultural identity. This society did not have to contend with the problems of new nationhood that preoccupied so many other parts of the world. Superpower intervention remained a concern, particularly because of the economic and military outreach of the United States in the Caribbean and Central America. Responding to North American influence was not a novel issue, however, although it took on some new twists, especially after World War II. Latin America also remained free from major warfare except for the 1932–1935 Chaco War between Bolivia and Paraguay. Nationalist rivalries existed and led to some conflict, but the region was far more peaceful, in terms of formal diplomacy, than most of its counterparts elsewhere in the world. There were no regional arms races, and military arsenals, although they expanded after World War II, were modest for the most part. Major internal violence was generally directed against peasant protesters and American Indian minorities, as landowners and caudillos, or military dictators, sought to maintain their power.

Nonetheless, after 1900 there were new themes and strains in Latin American society. The revolution in Mexico, early in the 20th century, reflected some of the same tensions that plagued China and Russia during the same period, although the revolution yielded a distinctive result. Latin American politics were redefined by the growing role of central states, beginning in the 1930s. Popular unrest in Latin America rivaled that of other peasant societies, although it did not always lead to significant political reform until the early 1980s, when a new democratic trend gained ground. The 20th century, in sum, saw important new political contests and governmental forms.

A second area of change focused on economic problems. Issues of economic development inevitably assumed a new urgency, as growing numbers of Latin American governments, both democracies and caudillo-led authoritarian regimes, sought a more active economic role. Moreover, rising levels of population brought Latin America new social problems, as the region became one of the most rapidly growing areas of the world. A number of societies further developed significant industrial sectors, undoing the economic weakness that had long characterized Latin America's place in the international economy in the past. Economic inequality, between a growing middle class and impoverished urban and rural groups, was considerable by world standards. New problems, but also new approaches, thus described economic patterns during this period.

Finally, the Latin nations continued to develop their distinctive cultural amalgam, blending styles generated in the West with a variety of local patterns. Indeed, the 20th century proved to be a rich period in Latin American culture, with major innovations in painting, architecture, and literature. Even as economic and political tensions garnered attention, the cultural and religious creativity of the region suggests a civilization still actively expanding its range.

KEY QUESTIONS   *How can significant economic change in Latin America be described, given the fact that the society remained quite poor by Western or Japanese standards? What were the most important new political currents? Amid growing consumerism and outside influence, was there a definable Latin American culture?*

LATIN AMERICA IN 20TH-CENTURY WORLD HISTORY

Latin America may sometimes seem a society apart. It did not participate significantly in the world wars, although the cold war had significant impact in the region. Nevertheless, international themes were vital. Industrial development coexisted alongside the older tradition of economic dependency. Most countries continued to depend, at least in part, on cheap exports produced by low-paid workers. Even the drug trade fits into the patterns of Latin American dependency in certain key respects.

Older racial issues had left their own particular legacy. Slavery was gone and explicit racism was less pervasive than in the United States. African-inspired cultural and religious movements gained wide audiences. But the color of one's skin nonetheless counted. In societies such as Brazil, with large black minorities, economic inequalities increased on racial lines.

Population movement was another important theme. Latin America and the Caribbean sent growing numbers of emigrants to the United States and western Europe.

Cultural influences, finally, interacted in two ways. Latin America continued to import cultural forms, including different versions of Christianity. However, popular music, dances, and costumes from the area also became part of international culture, providing important variety. Latin American interaction with the wider world was thus vitally important.

THE MEXICAN REVOLUTION, 1910–1920s

Revolution in Mexico, from 1910 to 1917, was the great event of the early 20th century in Latin America, although it directly affected only one major nation. The Mexican conflict articulated some of the same peasant grievances that simultaneously surfaced in Russia, as the peasantry was caught in the pressures of an expanding market agriculture while still lacking full access to the land. Discontented intellectuals also played a role, attacking a political regime seen as corrupt and inefficient—although in the Mexican case, the regime lacked the deep historical roots of the Russian or Chinese empires. Resentment against

CANADA

UNITED STATES
OF AMERICA

ATLANTIC
OCEAN

Gulf of Mexico

MEXICO

Mexico
City

Havana

Nassau

BAHAMAS

HAITI (1804)

CUBA (1898)

DOMINICAN REP. (1844)

Santo Domingo

JAMAICA
(1962)

Port-au-
Prince

San PUERTO RICO (U.S.)
Juan

BARBADOS (1967)

CARIBBEAN SEA

TRINIDAD & TOBAGO (1962)

Port of Spain

GUYANA (1966)

Caracas

Georgetown

Paramaribo

PACIFIC
OCEAN

VENEZUELA
(1811)

Cayenne

FRENCH GUIANA

Bogotá

CENTRAL AMERICA
See Inset Below

COLOMBIA
(1821)

SURINAM
(1975)

Equator

Quito

ECUADOR (1822)

Amazon R.

GALÁPAGOS IS.
(Ecuador)

PERU
(1821)

BRAZIL
(1822)

Lima

Brasilia

0   1000   2000

MILES

BOLIVIA
(1825)

La Paz

Sucre

PARAGUAY
(1811)

Rio de Janeiro

CENTRAL AMERICA

Asunción

JAMAICA
(1962)

GUATEMALA
(1821)

Belmopan

BELIZE (1981)

CHILE
(1818)

Kingston

Guatemala

HONDURAS (1821)

Tegucigalpa

Santiago

Buenos Aires

URUGUAY (1828)

Montevideo

Salvador

CARIBBEAN SEA

La Plata R.

EL SALVADOR
(1821)

NICARAGUA
(1821)

ARGENTINA
(1816)

Managua

Panama
Canal

San Jose

Panama

COSTA RICA
(1821)

PACIFIC
OCEAN

FALKLAND IS.
(Br.)

PANAMA
(1903)

Dates indicate year of independence

CAPE HORN

Latin America Today

foreign economic influence, visible in China and Russia, played an even more obvious part in Mexico. Although the Mexican Revolution produced no single leader of the stature of Lenin or Sun Yat-sen, it had its share of dramatic figures and, at least in a strictly political sense, proved more successful than its Chinese counterpart during the same period of time.

The specific roots of the Mexican Revolution dated back to 1900, when a small group of intellectuals began to agitate against the authoritarian and corrupt regime of General Porfirio Díaz. The agitators sought democracy, a more liberal economic policy, and new restrictions on the church; the movement soon broadened to include social issues of concern to urban workers and the peasantry. Landless rural laborers, receiving low wages for work on land that had once been theirs but under Díaz had been seized by a small landlord class, were particularly restless. Their resentment focused on foreign owners; economic nationalism, or a desire to return control of economic life to Mexican hands against outsiders, especially U.S. investors, formed an important part of the revolutionary movement. Peasant leaders included Emiliano Zapata, whose motto was "Land and Liberty" and who saw revolution as the uprising of rural and urban workers against capitalist owners of all sorts. Bandit leaders were also active in some rural regions. Pancho Villa established something of a Robin Hood reputation, robbing the rich and befriending the poor. Revolution, in sum, drew on diverse groups with varied goals—as successful revolutions must always do.

Fighting broke out late in 1910. At first a moderate leader, Francisco Madero, came to the fore, arranging for a new presidential election after Díaz escaped the country. Madero thought too strictly in terms of political reform to satisfy the working class and peasant leaders, however, and the revolution soon escaped his control. Zapata, in particular, organized new revolts, which in turn terrified business interests, including many Americans; with U.S. backing, a military leader replaced Madero, executing him and many other rebel lead-

ers. Revolutionary forces continued to operate, however, and in the south Zapata established a regional government of his own. In 1916, a change in U.S. policy lent support to a more moderate leader, Venustiano Carranza, who seized power in that same year. Carranza began to solidify key revolutionary gains. A new constitution, in 1917, proclaimed Mexican ownership of all mineral rights, thus reducing the role of foreign investment; landownership was reserved for Mexicans, and many large estates were broken up, to the benefit of mestizo and Indian peasants. The power of the Catholic church, which had supported Díaz and then the repressive regime that attacked Madero, was also restricted.

Carranza's reform goals were limited in practice, however. He showed little interest in a liberal political government, preferring to hold power directly; he did not, in fact, carry land reform too far. In 1920, revolutionaries pressed for new leadership; under the presidency of Álvaro Obregón, the long period of disorder drew to a close, and the results of revolution took clearer shape. Obregón continued the land redistribution in the south that Zapata had initiated; Pancho Villa and his bandit forces were bought off by the gift of a cattle ranch. Obregón moved slowly with further changes, however, lest conservative opposition overturn the new regime. Fearing U.S. hostility, he even allowed existing foreign owners to retain their holdings. Instead of a full attack on the social system, comparable to that in the new Soviet Union, Obregón preferred to concentrate on selective reforms that would encourage economic development. He advanced a widespread system of primary education that taught Spanish, and Mexican nationalism, to many American Indians for the first time. The government worked actively on public-health measures and also expanded cultivable lands through irrigation. However, the regime did not try to seize control of the urban economy from business groups, nor did it unseat the entire landlord class. And although the Catholic church found its political influence reduced, there was no effort to uproot it. Revolution in Mexico, in social terms, meant change but not upheaval.

Politically, the revolution during the 1920s ended the nation's long history of instability, creating a system that differed from both liberal democracy and caudillismo. A single political party, the PNR (National Revolutionary party), dominated political life, co-opting opposition leaders and vigorously repressing dissent. Presidents, who were selected from within the party and thus faced election with an assurance of victory, wielded huge power; some grew rich on public funds, much as old-style caudillos had done. Nonetheless, the new system prevented any one person from ruling the country permanently, for the presidency had to change hands every six years, and so the worst excesses of caudillismo were avoided. Furthermore, the PNR withstood the process of regular elections and thus remained responsive to many wider concerns. At times, its rhetoric and slogans, which boasted of worker and peasant rights, outstripped its achievements. But there was no question that the power of the traditional ruling classes was now limited by the PNR's desire to retain popular loyalty, or that foreign influence in Mexican affairs had been dramatically reduced. The regime's successful balance between forces old and new was reflected in its durability, amid only occasional, usually minor, political attacks. Into the mid-1990s, as the former PNR, now renamed the PRI, began to allow freer elections, Mexico experienced considerably more political stability and considerably more independence in policy than many other Latin American nations—particularly those close to the orbit of the United States.

Unlike many revolutions, Mexico's had little spillover to other areas. For one thing, its sometimes chaotic course reduced its appeal. Nor did the revolution produce a single doctrine, like Marxism, capable of rousing support elsewhere. U.S. opposition to political radicalism also helped limit the revolution's impact in Central America. Furthermore, although the revolution generated important reforms and encouraged a vigorous cultural movement, it did not propel Mexican economic development to new heights, nor did it lead to a full industrial revolution, again in contrast to the Soviet regime in Russia. Its social achievements were not great enough to draw discontented peasants elsewhere. For this reason also, the Mexican Revolution failed to usher in a new period in Latin American history as a whole.

EFFECTS OF THE DEPRESSION, 1930s–1950s

The worldwide economic depression of the 1930s had widespread, catastrophic effects on Latin America, which in turn triggered a new round of political turmoil. The value of Latin American exports decreased by a full two-thirds; the economy had depended on selling agricultural goods and minerals to the industrial nations of the West, which now simply could not afford to buy them. As unsold goods piled up in warehouses, poverty increased. No sweeping revolutionary movement resulted, although popular rioting broke out in many areas. But the results of the Great Depression encouraged the nation to press for fuller economic independence and to use government power to gain greater economic control. Various kinds of political regimes evinced this new, nationalistic concern.

The despair caused by the Depression did encourage Marxist movements in several countries, including Chile and Brazil, but these were generally kept in check by firm military rule. A revolutionary movement in Peru produced a doctrine combining socialism, fierce anti-Americanism, and a stress on American Indian cultural values; although it promoted agitation, it did not seize power.

The tide of economic nationalism proved more successful. Unequal land distribution, illiteracy, and poor production methods spurred a number of governments to take remedial action. Many of the regimes proved willing to run some industries directly, and most saw the need to regulate foreign investment and require foreign firms to employ Latin American managers. Most impor-

Mass demonstration for Perón in Buenos Aires, with a heroic statue.

tantly, state-sponsored programs of import substitution increased the size of the industrial sector.

A series of populist leaders came to the fore in
many countries, building multiclass alliances,
including urban workers (whose importance was
obviously growing). In Mexico, a spirit of reform
was rekindled by the election of Lazaro Cardenas
as president in 1934. Cardenas seized foreign oil
companies, establishing a state corporation,
Pemex, to manage the industry. A series of land
reforms broke up additional estates. Education
spread and with it an effort to integrate Indian cul-

ture more fully into national life. A state bank was
organized to encourage industry; as a result, Mexican production increased more rapidly than that
of any other Latin American country from 1940
to 1960, although immense poverty persisted.

In Brazil, weak political leadership and deteriorating economic conditions led to a military
revolt, headed by Getulio Vargas, which produced
a reasonably mild caudillo-style dictatorship that
lasted from 1930 to 1945. Vargas abolished elections
and parliament, while regulating the press and
operating a secret police that kept the opposition

divided. Deeply committed to economic modernization, Vargas hoped to free Brazil from its dependence on coffee exports. Under his administration, the state constructed important steel mills, and the nation began to produce most of the industrial goods it required. The Amazon basin was opened to agricultural development. Cities expanded, their centers graced by modern office buildings and apartment houses. Brazil remained a largely agricultural nation, but one capable of considerable economic growth.

The government of Chile responded to the effects of the Depression without dismantling its liberal, parliamentary system. A state-run development corporation was established during the 1930s to provide funds and planning for industrial projects.

Other parts of Latin America reacted less forcefully to the economic and political stress of the 1930s. Poverty and static social and economic conditions were particularly apparent in the Andes nations of Peru, Bolivia, and Ecuador, with their large American Indian populations. Here, as in a number of other countries, army-backed caudillos often ruled without great vision beyond the maintenance of power, amid recurrent rural unrest and frequent changes of regime.

A military and landholding elite governed Argentina during the 1930s. Only in 1943 did real change take place under the populist authoritarian Juan Perón (elected president in 1946). Even more than Brazil's Vargas, Perón appealed to the masses with a policy of benefit programs. His government crushed free trade unions and opposition parties, while directing the main branches of the economy. Foreign-owned companies were bought out, and the power of former landholders was diminished by state controls over the price of their goods. Perón promoted the general thrust of economic nationalism, but with a populist twist—an effort at frenzied mass appeal that was suggestive of European fascism. The expense of Perón's massive welfare programs limited Argentina's real economic growth, even as popular loyalty to

Perón remained high. A military coup in 1955 displaced the Argentine strongman, with an attempt to restore parliamentary democracy. But worried by the continued strength of Perón, and eager to ensure stability, the military took political control in 1966 and again in 1976, each time with vigorous police repression of opposition political forces.

REVOLUTION AND RESPONSE, 1950s–1990s

Despite important variations in political forms and economic development, by the late 1950s, there was considerable optimism about Latin America's prospects. Leading countries, including Mexico, post-Vargas Brazil, and post-Perón Argentina, were firmly bent on economic development, some social reform, and some degree of political freedom, if not usually through a full-fledged, multiparty system. Despite Marxist currents, radical political efforts had little appeal. U.S. opposition to anything that smacked of communism combined with the strength of conservative forces. A reform-minded regime in the Central American nation of Guatemala was unseated with U.S. aid in 1954, as the giant to the north briefly resumed the tradition of intervention of a half-century before. Nevertheless, the United States did not consistently oppose the nationalist policies that had emerged since the 1930s. A major social revolution in Bolivia in 1952–1953 produced significant agrarian reform. Although U.S. business interests exercised great power in many countries, Washington also welcomed the economic growth of nations such as Brazil and Mexico despite the fact that considerable planning and investment on their part were involved. "Good neighbor" policies initiated during the 1930s, during Franklin Roosevelt's administration, took some of the rougher edges off U.S.–Latin American relations, although a profound disparity in power remained, and much of the good neighbor rhetoric was purely cosmetic.

Hopes for a new level of stability were challenged by the revolution in Cuba. Long a U.S. protectorate, Cuba had suffered from weak political institutions. A strongman leader, Fulgencio Batista, had ruled since 1933, despite the great corruption of his regime. A pronounced gulf divided a rich minority from the impoverished masses, as in many Latin American nations, and although the Cuban economy was relatively prosperous, it depended dangerously on sugar exports to the United States. During the 1950s, a guerrilla rebellion arose against the Batista regime, headed by a magnetic leader, Fidel Castro. Castro's long-term political goals were unclear, but his attack on corruption and foreign influence, and his plea for land reform, constituted an important new revolutionary current, blending peasant grievances with explicit political concerns. Military victory came in 1959–1960. The new regime frightened away or expelled wealthy Cubans, while deteriorating relations with the United States followed from, and also encouraged, the increasingly communist orientation of the Castro government. The Cuban Communist party, initially hesitant to do so, soon came to embrace Castro fully. A U.S. effort in 1961 to topple Castro failed miserably, leaving the new regime free to build a society along modified Soviet lines. State ownership combined with worker committees in factories, while the great sugar estates were confiscated and turned into collective farms. The new regime promoted greater racial equality. The result was, in many ways, a more complete revolution than had occurred in Mexico—and it also led, thanks to Castro's policies and rhetoric but also to U.S. response, to the development of cold war tensions within Latin American politics. Revolution in Cuba came to mean a close alliance with the Soviet Union, and a leadership cult evolved around the strong and persuasive personality of Castro.

The Cuban revolution did not have the unsettling effects on the rest of Latin America that its supporters had hoped for or its opponents had feared. Many Latin American governments maintained good relations with the new regime, rather pleased at Cuba's success in defying the North American giant but not eager to install a communist system in their own nations. U.S. policy shifted, in reaction to its failure to dislodge Castro, toward more significant economic aid to other Latin American countries, although momentum in this effort dwindled by the 1970s. A radical regime arose in Peru in 1968, but the reform results were meager, and military coups soon killed off most of the civilian revolutionaries. Much later, in 1979, a radical uprising in Nicaragua, with assistance from Cuba, unseated a U.S.-backed dictator. The new regime promoted land reform, seizing great estates (many of them owned by U.S. concerns), and enacted education and public-health measures. It also encouraged guerrilla movements in other Central American nations, notably El Salvador. During the early 1980s, the United States provided military aid and encouraged its own guerrilla activity in defense of more conservative regimes in the region. By the 1990s, peace had been largely restored as the regime sponsored, and lost, a democratic election.

The establishment of a communist system in Cuba encouraged a new round of authoritarianism in some other countries, as military and civilian leaders sought the fullest possible protection against any new subversion. Populist regimes also seemed to have failed by the 1960s in places such as Argentina, whereas economic development increased internal disputes, often pitting workers against the middle class and elite. The resulting series of military regimes, although they did not affect every country in the 1960s, became increasingly common. Fear of communism encouraged the military regimes of Argentina, beginning in 1966. In 1970 in Chile, a Marxist-led coalition of communists, socialists, and radicals won a free election. No carbon copy of Castro's, the new regime proceeded to enact a number of key reforms, including nationalization of U.S.-owned copper mines and division of the great landed estates. This, in turn, provoked reaction from the middle and upper classes, and the conservative resurgence won U.S. support. A military coup toppled the reformist government, amid considerable bloodshed, and a strongly authoritarian dictatorship was installed that lasted into the late 1980s.

The spread of democratic systems began to overtake the surge of conservative military dictatorships in the 1980s, starting with the new Argentine regime of 1982. At first, the trend seemed merely a renewal of the oscillations long characteristic of Latin American politics. Free elections occurred in Brazil in 1984. A newly elected leader in Uruguay noted that "there are winds that blow in favor, winds that blow against. It is evident in this era the winds are favorable to democracy." Chile's authoritarian ruler yielded to democracy. Mexico retained one-party dominance, but contested elections became more common and opposition groups controlled some state governments; elections in 1997 were freer than at any point since the revolution. Paraguay, one of the classic authoritarian states, adopted democracy in 1993. At least for the moment, Latin American leaders decided that democracy spared societies the painful costs of repression and encouraged economic development. The surge resembled the rise of liberalism in the late 19th century, but it was not only democratic but less authoritarian. Amid changes in regimes and oscillations in the form of governments, Latin American political values unquestionably changed during the 20th century, even before the democratic surge. More groups gained political consciousness. In Mexico and many of the Andes nations, American Indians obtained new rights and political involvement. Women were given the right to vote for the first time in many countries—in Mexico, this occurred in 1954. By the 1990s, a significant minority of women served as elected officials in that country. The extension of education and the vote to property-less males was another important, although not necessarily continuous, tide in countries such as Brazil.

Still more significant was the growing commitment of Latin American governments to programs of economic development, although there had been some precedents for this trend in the 19th century. By the 1950s, few caudillos remained who sought only personal power and riches for themselves and their followers. Cuba's Batista was one such leader; so was the Nicaraguan head of state deposed by a revolution in 1979. Most authoritarian leaders, such as Perón or Vargas, now adopted a new stance, extending the functions of government in important new directions, whereas the same held true for the Mexican regime and expanding democratic systems at the end of the 20th century.

The new-style authoritarian leaders might be just as brutal toward political opponents as their more traditional predecessors had been, but they were increasingly likely to sponsor economic planning, to encourage new technologies, and to regulate foreign investment in order to achieve greater economic nationalism. In most cases, their interest in development led to some concern for social reform, as authoritarian as well as liberal leaders moved to dismantle at least some of the vast landed estates and to provide some welfare protection for urban workers. Except for Cuba, no government sponsored revolutionary social reform during the 20th century. However, with rare exceptions, governments did assume new functions, including the extension of education and public-health measures and the development of certain economic sectors. Here was a significant, evolutionary transformation of the Latin American political style under various constitutional arrangements. Authoritarian rulers might now appeal directly to popular support and engage in vigorous reforms unsettling to conservative interests.

The democratic current in the 1980s and 1990s emphasized greater free enterprise. Governments sold off many state-run businesses, as the international emphasis on freer trade and capitalism strongly affected Latin America. Mexico, for example, reduced the government's role in the

Urbanization: Belo Horizante, Brazil, 1967. Then only 70 years old, the city had over a million inhabitants.

economy as part of its participation in the North American Free Trade Agreement (NAFTA) with the United States and Canada. Government activities remained extensive, and in some areas, such as environmental regulation, they increased somewhat. Latin America did not return to the weak government structures that had predated the 1930s.

Partly because of more vigorous efforts on the part of government, leading Latin American nations also managed to become increasingly independent from outside influence during the 20th century. The Mexican Revolution did not

eliminate foreign economic activity, but it unquestionably reduced U.S. ability to determine key political or diplomatic policies. The nationalization of some crucial foreign enterprises, inaugurated by Mexico's control of its oil industry, was embraced by diverse governments in several Latin American countries. In the Caribbean islands, many former colonies gained political freedom after the 1950s, leading to a number of new island nations formed from previously British and Dutch holdings. In 2000, the United States finally surrendered control of the Panama Canal to the nation of Panama—another sign of the waning of the imperialism that had surged around 1900.

At the same time, Latin American independence was far from complete—again, a sign of continuity amid change. Cuba exchanged U.S. domination for Soviet influence in its economy and diplomacy. France, the Netherlands, and the United States still maintained some outright colonies, although they upgraded their status, as in the case of the Commonwealth of Puerto Rico. Britain maintained control of the Falkland Islands claimed by Argentina and rather easily vanquished a military uprising there in 1982. The ability of the United States to intervene in Central America, reasserted in the 1980s, remained an important factor, although it was not clear that such intervention could be as straightforward, or as successful, as in the past. Most importantly, the continued economic power of the United States and western Europe, in the still dependent economies of Latin America, seriously qualified the general tendency toward greater national freedom and self-assertion.

Several factors raised new questions about Latin American democracy by the early 21st century. A more authoritarian leader emerged in Venezuela. Argentina faced near economic collapse in 2002, raising real questions about whether a free market economy and globalization were doing any good. Similar issues arose elsewhere. There was as yet no decisive change. Argentina, after several short-term governments, elected a new president through democratic elections.

LATIN AMERICAN CULTURE

In culture, even more clearly than in politics, the close interaction with the West left a definite mark, as Latin Americans participated vigorously in Western-initiated artistic developments of the 20th century. However, this was no simple extension of Western culture either, for a new artistic and literary vigor resulted in a growing emphasis on distinctive styles and themes.

Most wealthy Latin Americans shared Western tastes in fashion, furnishings, and art. Throughout the 20th century, a considerable market existed for Western imports of this sort, and some Latin American artists produced for this market as well. A number of Latin American composers made a mark in symphonic music after 1920, and major cities boasted orchestras performing a wide repertoire of Western-style music. Still more impressive was the region's contribution to modern architecture. Economic and political development encouraged new building in most Latin American cities, as hotels and office complexes sprang up in the sleek styles familiar in the West. Particularly breathtaking was the erection of an entire city, Brasília, constructed in the 1960s as Brazil's new capital. Although criticized for its costliness, Brasília became a powerful symbol of modern architectural and urban-planning concepts.

Latin American initiatives in science lagged somewhat, as in the past. Major universities trained their students in science and technology, but the expense of elevating research to a more prominent position, and traditions in a civilization that still placed greater emphasis on the artistic and spiritual aspects of culture, limited the overall importance of science in intellectual life, compared to other contemporary civilizations.

In art and literature, Latin America contributed vigorous 20th-century styles, although with an ongoing link to Western influences. The Mexican Revolution spurred innovative developments in painting. Two great muralists, Clemente Orozco and Diego Rivera, created numerous and powerful epics depicting the struggle of the Mexican lower classes from colonial days to the 20th century. Their forceful human figures and stark colors emphasized the suffering and courage of agricultural and factory workers, women as well as men. Their decision to paint wall murals, rather than conventional canvases, was a result of their social commitment to the public good, for their art decorated many public buildings and was not confined to museums or private collections. Both

Mural by Diego Rivera. The subject is Mexico's Aztec past.

painters achieved international reputations. A number of other artists, from several countries, moved toward less representational styles after World War II, but an interest in the forms and coloration derived from Latin America's Indian and black heritage remained.

Contributions to Latin American literature, although at times constrained by political repression, involved both poetry and the novel. Major writers emerged in Chile, Mexico, Brazil, and Argentina. The Mexican Revolution inspired realistic novels that dramatized the plight of American Indians and other labor groups. Masterpieces of the Mexican revolutionary period include Mariano Azuela's *Los de abajo* (1916) and Martin Luis Guzmán's *El Aquila y la serpiente* (1928). The award of three Nobel prizes for literature to Latin American writers symbolized the rise of Latin American fiction after World War II. Major writers embraced many themes—history

and anthropology, foreign domination including U.S. imperialism, and a strong current of fantasy that built on earlier poetic traditions. Both fantasy and stark realism, sometimes combined in the same novel, were intended to convey the special features of the Latin American experience; they represented a balance of subject matter different from 20th-century European fiction. In addition to the use of American Indian themes and a strong social awareness, Latin American literature often addressed problems of identity—the attempt to define this part of the world's culture amid strong European and North American influences. At the same time, Latin American and Western writers worked in similar styles as well as languages, and they shared the same body of literature and criticism.

A final feature of Latin American culture, both formal and popular, was its dynamic Christianity. Although the political power and

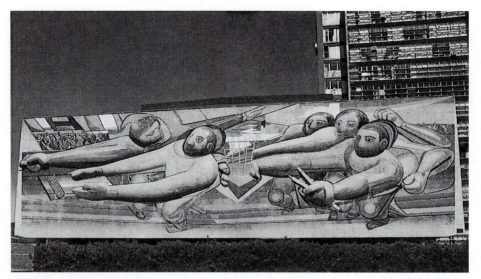

Mural to Students, by Siqueiros, University of Mexico, Mexico City. (Stuart Cohen/© Estate of David Alfaro Siqueiros/Licensed by VAGA, New York, NY)

wealth of the Catholic church declined in some countries, such as Mexico, religion remained a much more pervasive force in Latin America than in Europe and North America. In terms of sheer numbers and pious devotion, Latin America indeed became the most significant Christian civilization by the mid-20th century, with 233 million people listed as Catholics—not all, to be sure, fervent believers—by 1985. Nonetheless, Latin American Catholicism was not simply a traditional force. From the 1960s onward, a new generation of priests and theologians was responsible for increasing social commentary, urging Catholic involvement in the cause of social and political reform. Some Catholic leaders aided peasant guerrilla movements, whereas sympathetic bishops pressured governments for improved welfare programs, land reform, and popular political rights. Statements about the church's social responsibility became known as "liberation theology." The new currents within Latin American Catholicism resulted in clashes with some authoritarian governments and also criticism from the papacy, which by the 1980s was not enthusias-

tic about political activism. Catholic debate formed another important channel for Latin American culture and additional evidence of a new level of intellectual vigor. Catholicism was itself challenged, however, by popular religions that mixed Christian and African elements—particularly in Brazil—and by a surprising current of conversion to fundamentalist Protestantism, creating a vibrant new religious minority spurred by missionary activity. The advance of Protestantism, particularly among poorer groups seeking cultural outlets, was truly striking: by the late 1990s, 30 percent of the Guatemalan population was Protestant, and similar changes had occurred in Brazil. These developments complicated the society's cultural map but confirmed the unusual importance of religion in 20th-century Latin America.

ECONOMY AND SOCIETY

Latin America experienced rapid social and economic change, particularly after 1950, although important traditions continued from the past. In

History Debate

LATIN AMERICA AND THE THIRD WORLD

During the cold war, the idea of a "third world," siding with neither the West nor the communist bloc, emerged. India was a leading example. Since most of these neutral nations were also poor, the term *third world* came to imply poverty and lack of industrial development, and this is its key meaning today.

Latin American countries are often described as third world countries. Certainly they are far less wealthy and industrial than societies such as Japan and western Europe; standards of living and technologies lag. Many foreign companies set up branch operations in countries such as Mexico to take advantage of cheap labor and weak environmental regulations.

But the third world idea can be misleading. Many Latin American countries have fairly high rates of literacy (over 70 percent), and life expectancy has gained. They have large middle classes, with high consumer standards including routine ownership of items such as televisions and refrigerators. Significant industrial sectors have emerged in Mexico and Brazil, while commercial export agriculture has promoted greater prosperity in Chile. Many analysts argue that *third world*, as a term, does not capture the variation among the countries and regions to which it is applied, and that it also does not capture significant change. Ironically, some of the same foreign companies that located in Mexico have since moved to China and southeast Asia, because Mexican wages have risen somewhat—while remaining far below Western standards. What kind of terminology makes most sense for Latin American countries? Should the terminology used for countries in Africa or southern Asia be used for Latin American countries?

most countries, the social division between rich and poor remained great. The wealthy minority controlled landed estates in many countries—in some cases, only 4 percent of the population owned 80 percent of the land—and also operated the leading commercial and manufacturing concerns. In many cities, luxurious mansions and lifestyles juxtaposed with mass squalor. The widespread employment of female domestic servants remained a standard prerogative of upper-class households. Social reform efforts, even in revolutionary Mexico, rarely did more than scratch the surface of such a basic division, although some changes occurred. Regional disparities remained considerable as well. The Andes nations were particularly impoverished. Argentina maintained its position as a significant exporter of grains and meats, but the Argentine economy was

often hampered by political problems and a level of government spending that encouraged paralyzing inflation.

Another troubling continuity involved Latin America's inability to free itself from reliance on vulnerable export items. Despite concerted policy attention and some diversification, the civilization continued to depend on imported Western technology, and exports consisted disproportionately of agricultural goods such as coffee, sugar, raw materials, and oil, all vulnerable to low and fluctuating prices. Furthermore, most Latin American nations, because of their poor earnings position in the world economy, remained heavily indebted to Western banks. Ambitious development programs often merely increased the debt, which by the 1980s severely burdened both richer and poorer economies

Understanding Cultures

ADAPTING CONSUMER VALUES

The pressure of foreign (mainly west European and U.S.) consumer forms and other societies' responses to them was one of the great cultural issues of the 20th century and promises to remain one in 21st-century world history. Western consumerism stands for the importance of acquisition, secular values, and new products as a measure of personal and national success and modernity. Some groups deeply resist this kind of pressure—Islamic fundamentalists, for example, who promote a religious alternative to consumer culture. Other groups gleefully join in, such as the many Japanese who made McDonald's and the Disney theme park near Tokyo instant successes.

Nevertheless, a common response involves embracing a consumer trend while adding a distinctive regional twist. This is, in fact, a common pattern in cultural contact, involving the blending, or syncretism, of an outside model with local elements. But it is particularly important to grasp this in terms of contemporary consumerism, because otherwise it becomes easy to mistakenly assume that the whole world, except for pockets of resistance, is largely becoming American.

The history of comic books in Mexico provides a specific example of such a pattern. Comic books were imported from the United States to Mexico as early as the 1930s, and they caught on quickly thanks to the prestige of U.S. products and the low levels of average literacy. However, comics were soon modified to meet Mexican standards of beauty and political values. Thus, one series noted: "He was no vulgar bandit, he shared with the poor who live under the lash of vile capitalism"—this was hardly a common theme in the United States at the same time. Macho exploits were touted, but there was also great emphasis on kinship and community ties. In contrast to American warriors, Mexican heroes were not loners. Indeed, they were often pitted against American villains, such as the "Invincible Jack Superman of Indianapolis," and in these imagined conflicts, the gringos lost almost every time. By the late 20th century, comic books were read far more regularly in Mexico than in the United States, precisely because Mexico had changed the medium to make it part of a national culture. Important local ingredients thus blended with the influence of American styles.

within the civilization. Even Cuba, which defied tradition in many ways, proved unable to escape economic dependency, as it relied for its export earnings on sales of sugar to eastern Europe and million-dollar-a-day Russian aid. The Soviet collapse brought new problems to the island that highlighted its failure to industrialize.

Nonetheless, many areas of Latin America gained new economic strength. Agricultural production improved in many countries, as new techniques, including the innovations of the 1960s, the Green Revolution, were adopted.

Tourism expanded, resulting in foreign earnings and influences. Chile dramatically expanded its exports in commercial agriculture, gaining growing prosperity by the 1990s. Manufacturing output advanced, too, and the wealthier Latin American nations began to produce most of the industrial goods they required for normal consumption. Textile and metallurgical industries spread widely, and a few countries, headed by Brazil, began to export basic manufactured goods to other parts of the world, including the United States. Brazil also developed the world's fourth largest computer industry, specializing in less sophisticated computers than those from Japan or the United States, but ones deemed reliable in other less developed, less technologically advanced nations.

To be sure, advancing mechanization still fell short of a full industrial revolution. It did not bring Latin America to the levels of economic development being achieved in the Pacific Rim. The high birth rate, averaging between 2 and 3 percent annually after World War II, limited gains in the standard of living. Catholic hostility toward birth-control measures and the strong traditionalism of many Latin American families contributed to this growth in population, which in many countries literally consumed the gains in food and manufacturing production. One result of population pressure was the extraordinary rate of emigration, both legal and illegal, to the United States. Another result was a low-wage economy that induced many U.S. and some European and Japanese firms to establish factories in Latin America for inexpensive exports to industrialized areas of the world.

Many Latin American countries, however, did make a turn to greater population control. Mexico, for example, underwent a demographic transition in the 1960s, resulting in markedly smaller families even though population expansion continued on the basis of earlier growth. Furthermore, the manufacturing gains—the evolution toward a more industrial society—engendered measurable improvements in living standards for many people. Brazil's economic growth, at 6 percent per year during some decades, increased both the middle class and urban working class. Many began to participate in new consumerism. By 1990, 22 percent of all Brazilians owned cars, 56 percent had televisions, and 63 percent had refrigerators. These gains, which were echoed in Mexico and elsewhere, surpassed levels in eastern Europe or the Pacific Rim (apart from Japan). Not yet industrialized, Latin American economies were nevertheless carving out a distinctive position among the major societies of the world.

Urban slums in Caracas, Venezuela. Migrants to the city stake out their unauthorized living spaces.

Both population pressure and industrial gains furthered the rapid urbanization of Latin America from the 1930s onward. Here too, the society held an unusual place, becoming more urban than most of Asia and Africa although less so than the industrialized societies. City growth was itself distinctive, combining new manufacturing with huge enclaves of dire poverty. The rural populations simply could not be accommodated in the countryside, particularly when the land was held in large estates. Cities provided some factory jobs to a privileged segment of the masses; to even more people, they offered some hope of occasional work plus charity or welfare.

In 1925, only 25 percent of Latin America's population was urbanized; by 1975, 60 percent lived in cities—in contrast to a mere 30 percent in China or India. Massive shantytowns arose in Mexico, Brazil, and elsewhere, as a largely unemployed population constructed houses out of cans and boxes. The world's largest city took shape in the Mexican capital, which had 3 million people in 1950 but an overwhelming 9 million by 1970, and 16 million by 1995, with projections of over 20 million by 2001. Excruciating problems of pollution as well as dire poverty resulted from this extraordinary urban development.

Population pressure and urban problems inevitably added to earlier social grievances, notably the unequal distribution of land and the gap between rich and poor, to produce recurrent popular protest. Rural rioting occurred in many countries in the 20th century, even aside from the major revolutions. Peasant attacks on landlords paralyzed much of Colombia in 1947. Indian peasants formed guerrilla bands that controlled stretches of Bolivia and Peru in the 1970s and 1980s. A rural rebellion erupted in southern Mexico in 1994. Urban strikes and riots dotted the 20th-century landscape as well. Violence spilled over into other areas. Mass sports events often featured fights between partisan crowds. In Mexico and Venezuela, murder rates were among the highest in the world.

Nevertheless, there were strengths in Latin American society as well as fearsome tensions. Family structure remained tight, characteristically under male domination. Yet women made some gains, through new voting rights, education, and legal protections. The number of women in parliaments increased. It was often women, acting even against the wishes of priests and husbands, who made the decisions that limited population growth. Popular festivals and religious celebrations featured traditional dances and music and provided joyful release to many groups. The ability of Latin Americans to preserve family institutions and cultural forms in the face of rapid population movement to the cities set some lim-

its on the worst confusions of social transformation, although the same traditionalism enforced limitations on the conditions of women under the sway of *machismo* traditions and a strong emphasis on sexuality. Amid problems common to many parts of the world—such as underemployment—Latin American popular culture retained a distinctive flavor.

TOWARD A GREATER WORLD ROLE?

Latin America has long occupied a somewhat ambiguous place in world history. The civilization first developed as one dependent on the West, a status still not fully shaken off. Although Latin Americans participate fully, if not always influentially, in the world economy, they have generated neither dramatic cultural forms nor catastrophic military upheavals of international impact. Nationalism and literary preoccupation with issues of Latin American identity follow from a sense of being ignored or misunderstood in the wider world. The United States, which continues to play a powerful role in Latin American affairs, stands particularly accused of ignorance and neglect.

However, the trends of Latin American history in the later 20th century suggest an increase in the civilization's visibility. Latin America constitutes a growing share of the world's population. Its economic advance, although often troubled, places it in the middle rank of developing nations. Its importance in world religious life is on the increase. Some observers would add that the civilization's potential for social upheaval remains unusually great, although the 20th-century experience has suggested a balance between unrest and conservative continuities. The directions of Latin America's future are at least as unclear as those of other major civilizations. Brazil and a few other leaders may soon make the turn to a self-sustaining industrialization—but hopes of this sort have been dashed before in the past century. Democracy may solidify Latin America, but the civilization's history reminds us that it also may not. In 2000, a new strongman leader in Venezuela and growing guerrilla warfare in Colombia highlighted democracy's fragility. But the likelihood of growing international impact in the future seems high, as the 20th century brought new self-consciousness and millions of new people to a civilization increasingly proud of its achievement, if still resentful of its economic dependency.

ISSUES AND CONNECTIONS

Many Latin American nations failed to achieve what their leaders hoped for during the 20th century. Mexico did not break its levels of poverty as a result of revolution. Cuba did not lead the way for communism in the hemisphere. Many hopes for rapid economic development were dashed. But there was significant change, and the challenge is to capture this change despite some partial failures in goals. Latin American politics were different from those of the 19th century, even before the wave of democracy around the century's end. For many regions, economic dependence declined, even though huge weaknesses remained.

Leading Mexican writers worried, by the late 20th century, that Mexicans were losing their identity to imported mass culture and consumerism. They argued that an earlier identity had been achieved by fusing Spanish and American Indian styles, but now it was challenged. Changes in the status of women, disruptions of traditional Catholicism, and other developments clearly challenged traditions as well. But, partly because of economic differences, Latin America did not simply mimic global styles. Religion changed, but a high level of religious interest continued to characterize the culture. Complex

mixing of different races was another heritage from the past. Artists, helping to set modern styles, nevertheless used many traditional forms and themes. There were many links to the past.

SUGGESTED WEB SITES

On the art of Diego Rivera, see http://www.arts-history.mx/museomural.html. On the Cuban revolution, see http://www.neravt.com/left/allende.htm. On revolutionary leaders, see http://flag.blackened.net/revolt/mexico.html; on Che Guevara, see http://pbs.org/newshour/forum/november97/che.html.

SUGGESTED READINGS

Recent work includes Peter Winn, *Americas: The Changing Face of Latin America and the Caribbean* (1999); David Craven, *Art and Revolution in Latin America* (2002); John Peeler, *Building Democracy in Latin America* (1998); Carlos Alonso, *The Burden of Modernity: The Rhetoric of Cultural Discourse in Spanish America* (1998); John C. Chasteen, *Born in Fire and Blood* (2001), a survey of developments since 1945; Alezandro de la Fuente, *Race, Inequality and Politics in Twentieth-Century Cuba* (2001); Gilbert Joseph et al., eds., *Close Encounters of Empire* (1998), on United States impacts on Latin America; and Greg Grandin, *Blood of Guatemala* (2000), on social tensions and reform.

General coverage of 20th-century Latin America is provided by Tulio Halperin-Donghi, *The Aftermath of Revolution in Latin America* (1973), and R. A. Humphreys, *Tradition and Revolt in Latin America* (1969); see also T. Skidmore and P. Smith, *Modern Latin America* (1984). On economic dependency, see E. Bradford Burns, *Latin America: A Concise Interpretative History*, 4th ed. (1986). On revolution and other developments in Mexico, helpful texts are John M. Hart, *Revolutionary Mexico* (1987); R. D. Anderson, *Outcasts in Their Own Land: Mexican*

Industrial Workers, 1906–1911 (1976); and Jan Bazant, *A Concise History of Mexico from Hidalgo to Cardenas, 1805–1940* (1975). Other key countries are covered in H. S. Ferns, *Argentina* (1969); Robert Potash, *The Army and Politics in Argentina, 1945–1962* (1980); and E. B. Burns, *A History of Brazil* (1970). On the Cuban revolution, consult Hugh Thomas, *Cuba: The Pursuit of Freedom* (1971), and Carmelo Mesa Lago, *Revolutionary Change in Cuba* (1971). For economic patterns, important works include Celso Furtado, *The Economic Development of Latin America* (1970), and N. Sanchez-Albornoz, *The Population of Latin America* (1974). On women, see June Hahner, *Women in Latin American History* (1976). On labor, see Charles Berquist, *Labor in Latin America* (1986).

Sub-Saharan Africa: From Colonies to New Nations

34

Emerging Nationalism

The Transformation to Independence

The Challenges of New Nationhood

African Political Culture

African Culture

HISTORY DEBATE
The Question of Identity

Economy and Society

Defining the New Africa

Issues and Connections

Africa south of the Sahara had been fully consumed by European imperialism only 20 years before the 20th century began. For several decades after 1900, when other areas of the world were rousing to new nationalisms, African history continued to be characterized by the operations of the colonial governments and western Europe's increasing economic impact. However, nationalism took root here as well, and after World War II it gained momentum. The result, occurring only slightly later than in most of Asia, was the independence of a number of new nations. From the 1960s onward, their efforts to establish the institutions and loyalties of nationhood represented the primary focus in the region. Problems of economic development, and in some areas recurrent famines and disease, complicated national politics. And the continued existence of a powerful, white-dominated South African nation long cast its shadow over the continent.

Even before independence was achieved, and certainly after its first results were taken into account, issues of cultural identity and social and economic transformation played a vital role in the patterns of Africa. Imperialist policies brought fuller contact with the world economy and encouraged some internal economic development along with great dislocation. One result was a marked resemblance to earlier characteristics of Latin America, the other society most fully touched by Western economic dominance and cultural and political influence. African civilization, to be sure, was not obliterated to the extent that American Indian cultures had been. Nonetheless, Africa displayed patterns of economic dependency comparable to colonial and 19th-century Latin America, including a reliance on vulnerable cash crops and mineral exports; of tensions of new nationhood, including frequent reliance on authoritarian political forms; and even of considerable cultural innovation, the result of both Muslim and Christian missionary efforts that made this civilization, again like that of Latin

African mission school run by Europeans. Probably from the Belgian Congo, 1920s.

America earlier on, the scene of great religious fervor and creativity.

Africans, on the other hand, were less closely linked to Western cultural styles than were Latin Americans, and they faced more acute problems of defining their identity amid new or outside influences. And Africa emerged from its brief colonial experience less developed—in terms of city size, literacy levels, amount of manufacturing and commercial agriculture—than any of the other major contemporary civilizations. Generating further change, particularly toward industrialization or a better-rounded economy, and adjusting to 20th-century trends such as population increase and urbanization have posed acute challenges for contemporary Africans. Efforts to combine cultural and family traditions with modernization reflect a desire to maintain a distinctive African character and to cushion the impact of new political and economic styles.

KEY QUESTIONS *The central issue in contemporary African history involves striking a balance between outside pressures, sometimes combined with internal crises, and independent initiatives. How can the new initiatives coming from Africa and Africans best be defined?*

EMERGING NATIONALISM

World War I triggered some new currents in colonial Africa. Scattered fighting took place in the German colonies in the south, which were then taken over by the British, with one possession, South West Africa, or what is now called Namibia, administered as part of South Africa. The French used large numbers of loyal African troops in their European campaigns. Discussion of national rights after World War I encouraged a rethinking of the future of the African colonies. European diplomats spoke of their holdings as "a sacred trust of civilization" to help educate peoples "not yet able to stand by themselves under the strenuous conditions of the modern world." This outlook produced new efforts to better the standard of living of the colonial peoples by building local schools, hospitals, libraries, and so on. Belgium, known for its harsh exploitation in the Congo, shifted its policies significantly. Colonial-run police forces tried to prevent tribal warfare, and attention was paid to improving agricultural techniques.

Western imperialism did not change entirely, however. Assumptions of African inferiority continued. Schools reached only a minority of Africans, and they often taught details of European history and culture that made little sense in the African context. Belgian officials in the Congo, for example, insisted that educated Africans learn Flemish as well as French, although the language had little wider applicability, simply because the civilization back home and its language were regarded as the pinnacle of culture. Many schools were run by missionaries, including large numbers from the United States, who attacked local religious traditions in the name of Christianity; a Christian minority, both Catholic and Protestant, did develop in most colonies as a result. Most colonial governments allowed Africans to enter only the lower levels of the bureaucracy and military. French policy encouraged an African elite to enroll in schools in France and assimilate into French culture, but there was little real concern for the African masses. Britain paid attention to a larger number but reserved the upper ranks of administration for British officials. Few African soldiers could rise above the rank of sergeant. Thus, 20th-century imperialism, although it involved new expenditures for the colonies—Britain may have spent more in Africa during the 1920s and 1930s than it earned there—remained very much an imposition from the outside.

Imperialism also resulted in continued pressure for economic change. In largely British-ruled eastern Africa, where population levels were low and prior political forms relatively loose, a wealthy minority of white colonists established estates on the rich agricultural lands of the plateaus, using African labor; other Africans preserved a hunting-and-gathering existence or worked as farmers on the less fertile

lands. In Portuguese Mozambique, many Africans were required to grow cotton, because Portugal thought this would feed its own industrialization. But cotton was not best suited to the soil, resulting in environmental damage, and the workers, mostly women, did not have time to grow much food for themselves. The result was increasing poverty and malnutrition. In western Africa, with more of its own commercial experience, African business entrepreneurs along with Europeans introduced cash crops, such as peanuts and cocoa, for sale on the world market. Railroads and shipping lines also opened further access to raw materials. Belgium drew rubber, copper, and vital minerals from the Congo; British Rhodesia exported copper; South Africa mined gold and diamonds. Mining operations were owned and operated by Europeans, or by white South Africans, using poorly paid gangs of African labor. Thus, the ties of Africa to the world economy became more extensive, but largely on terms that reaped profits for Europeans.

The impact of this burgeoning economic activity on Africans was mixed. Some businessmen drew substantial profits while becoming accustomed to the ways of international commerce. In the boom years of the 1920s, rich business leaders in British West Africa acquired an extravagant lifestyle: "Motor cars were purchased right and left, champagne flowed freely, and expensive cigars scented the air." This elite also participated in local elections, for governing bodies that had a limited voice over such issues as roads and public health. Larger numbers of Africans were drawn into the emerging cities and the mining centers as laborers. Many traditions and family ties were disrupted by the move to the cities, particularly because women were often left behind. A tension began to develop, between older customs and the attractions of a partially westernized urban life, that would influence African culture from this point onward. Finally, large numbers of Africans remained generally isolated from the economic transformation, in scattered agricultural or hunting settlements rarely reached by Europeans.

In South Africa, a special pattern of European-African relations continued to develop. Here, white settlers, some of English origin but primarily Afrikaners of Dutch extraction, were more numerous than in any other African region. Clashes between the English and the Boers, the name given to the Dutch settlers, intensified the friction. The Afrikaners increasingly supported the Nationalist political party, which talked of leaving the British Empire and vowed to keep black Africans, the majority, in a subordinate place. The party slogan was "South Africa: A White Man's Land." During the 1920s, the Nationalists sponsored the Color Bar bill to prevent blacks from holding skilled jobs. In 1936, blacks were excluded from voting in elections. White South Africans were gradually creating two separate societies, preventing any contact between whites and blacks save that between employer and unskilled laborer.

Nowhere, of course, did Africans have extensive political rights. What was unusual in South Africa is that representative institutions did exist but were reserved mainly for whites. In other colonies, voting rights, if any, were limited to an urban minority of Africans, and the bodies they elected had few powers and were dominated by whites.

African bitterness toward white rule broke out periodically. To promote black rights, a group ultimately named the African National Congress formed in South Africa as early as 1912. In 1921 in the Congo, a carpenter named Simon Kimbangu formed a religious movement with impressive rituals and revolutionary political doctrines, drawn in part from the Bible. His movement aroused considerable mass support until Kimbangu was arrested and executed. In Kenya a government clerk, Harry Thuku, organized the East Africa Native Association to protest a reduction in wages; his arrest in 1922, on charges of sedition, led to a wave of riots.

Outright African nationalism developed only gradually. The experiences of the African elite, some trained at European universities, brought growing awareness of nationalist ideas. The Pan-African Congress met in Paris in 1919 to press for national independence, and similar meetings occurred periodically through 1945. Pan-African nationalism, bent on not only freedom from European control but also a glorification of the strengths and traditions of Africa and the hope for a new, unprecedented African unity, received powerful stimulus from the writings and political leadership of U.S. and West Indian black leaders in the 1920s and 1930s. Figures such as the American Marcus Garvey, who sought new links with Africa as part of the black struggle for freedom in the United States, helped African nationalists, particularly in the British colonies, articulate their own strivings. However, the limits to Western-style education in Africa meant that nationalist ideas spread slowly. To many Africans, the concept of nationhood was an abstraction, compared to the known loyalties of the tribe and extended family. Even more than in the Middle East after 1918, most African colonies were arbitrary units, embracing many tribes and language groups with no precedent in Africa's earlier political history. Loyalty to these nations thus came hard. Nationalist leaders themselves debated inconclusively about whether to pursue a larger African unity, tribal units, or nation-states based essentially on colonial boundaries. This was a period of genesis for African nationalism, not, before 1945, a full flowering. Many individual leaders who would emerge after World War II developed their nationalist convictions during this period, however. For example, Jomo Kenyatta, educated at the London School of Economics and later in Moscow, began to write of the strengths of African traditions as opposed to Western materialism and corruption. Kenyatta would later lead the nationalist movement in Kenya and become its first president. Leopold Senghor, a Catholic native of Senegal who lived in Paris, learned of the cultural traditions of Africa and also admired the achievements of blacks from the United States and West Indies. He began to write of the beauties of *négritude*, or blackness, seen as a source of racial pride and confidence in black creativity, particularly within the arts.

The worldwide economic depression hit Africa hard. The region's growing dependence on the sale to the West of low-price items such as cocoa beans, and on Western companies that directly organized raw-materials production, was vividly highlighted. Loss of jobs and wages increased unrest and spurred the nationalist movement as strikes and riots attacked the power and greed of European and U.S. companies.

World War II heightened nationalism still further. A number of black leaders in French colonies supported the resistance movement against Nazi control of France. They felt real loyalty to France, but they expected growing political rights in return. The rise of anticolonial movements in other parts of the world and the retreat of once-proud empires in Asia served as an obvious inspiration in Africa. For their part, European administrations recognized the need to work harder for social and economic improvements in Africa. France thus poured more money into its African colonies between 1947 and 1957 than it had done in the whole previous half-century. British leaders began to talk of ultimate self-government, suggesting that the role of the mother country was to now train its colonies in nationhood. Nonetheless, many Europeans seemed in no hurry to admit that Africans were ready to take over their own government. Their belief in African inferiority and a desire to hold fast to this one vestige of imperialism, while the rest of the empire was crumbling, posed obvious barriers. In many colonies, particularly in British East Africa, the demands of the influential white-settler minority also slowed change: how could this group be protected if colonialism came to an end?

European hesitation was met by a new generation of nationalist leaders, most of them trained in European or North American universities; many had experience in trade unions or local governments. They thought in terms of independent nations built on the basis of existing colonies; ideas of African unity or a return to tribal organization now faded. The new leaders mounted mass rallies of urban Africans. Often arrested, they used imprisonment to dramatize their cause. Many also battled traditional African leaders, including the tribal chiefs, to whom the concept of nationalism remained foreign. Direct raids on European settlers, as in Kenya, added to the pressure from yet another source, as villagers and hunters protested the white control of the best lands.

THE TRANSFORMATION TO INDEPENDENCE

Between 1957 and the mid-1970s, the colonial era drew to a close. The country named Ghana arose first, based on Britain's western Gold Coast colony; Kwame Nkrumah was its nationalist leader. A schoolteacher, he had studied for a decade in the United States, where he was deeply influenced by both European socialism and American black nationalists who called for a rebellion against white domination. Returning to the Gold Coast in 1945, Nkrumah built a mass political movement among urban elements and commercial cocoa farmers with the slogan "Self-Government Now." Many of his followers saw independence as a key to a brighter future across the board, in which economic as well as political problems would be swept away by the searchlight of freedom. Nkrumah organized a series of riots and strikes, which landed him in jail; he dominated local elections from 1951 onward. Britain conceded the inevitable, and Ghana, drawing its name although not its boundaries from the historic kingdom, won its freedom in 1957.

Other British colonies in West Africa gained independence soon after. France sought to prevent a complete rift within its colonies, after its bitter experiences in Indochina and then Algeria, by granting commonwealth status to its 13 sub-Saharan holdings in 1958. African leaders deeply loyal to France supported this move, although Sékou Touré, a radical leader in the

Native Nigerians rehearse a traditional dance to prepare for independence celebrations, 1960.

THE CHALLENGES OF NEW NATIONHOOD

The ease with which most—although not all—former colonies had achieved their freedom was deceptive. Many Africans and Westerners alike expected great gains once imperialism ceased to be a distraction. In fact, most African states found independence a greater challenge than the battle against European control had been. Although conditions varied widely in a civilization still quite diverse, most of the new nations were poor. Independence did not transform the economy or promote new power on the world market. In a few cases, as in the former Belgian Congo, initial disorder disrupted trade patterns and caused the flight of Western managers and technicians, a situation that was only later repaired. Many new nations, such as Nigeria, adopted policies of "indigenization," or partial nationalization, which required that business and landed estates pass from European hands to majority African control within a decade or so. This approach, in seeking fuller national command over the economy, was understandable; indeed, it resembled the economic nationalist policies of Latin American countries in the earlier decades of the 20th century. But indigenization efforts had to be balanced against continued needs for Western technologies and capital. Nor could indigenization free most economies from the previous status of dependency. For many African workers, indigenization merely substituted African for European capitalists in a cash-crop or mining operation, as land was not widely redistributed and reliance on poorly paid labor remained extensive.

colony of Guinea, insisted on full independence immediately. The other nations gained national status in the early 1960s, but most retained close ties to France. Belgium lost the Congo in a series of riots in 1959—one of the only cases outside southern Africa where the granting of independence did not come peacefully. Britain's east African colonies also gained national freedom, despite the agitation of white settlers. Only in Southern Rhodesia did a major delay in independence arise, as the white minority broke away from Britain in 1965 and held out for over a decade against a guerrilla war conducted by black nationalists, and against substantial diplomatic pressure from Britain and the United States. Here too, independence triumphed, through the creation of a black-run government with assurances of white minority representation; in 1980, the new nation shook off its colonial name and took on another historic name—Zimbabwe. Finally, also in the 1970s, a change in the political regime of Portugal, along with significant guerrilla warfare and some backing from the Soviet Union and Cuba, led to independence for Angola and Mozambique. In the space of two decades, approximately 40 new nations had been born in sub-Saharan Africa.

Leadership was also a problem in the new nations, along with agonizing economic issues. Some stirring nationalists proved inept or corrupt once in power—Ghana's Nkrumah was a case in point. Filling bureaucracies with competent staff was not easy when so few Africans had prior political experience. Here was one reason for frequent reliance on authoritarian rule, after

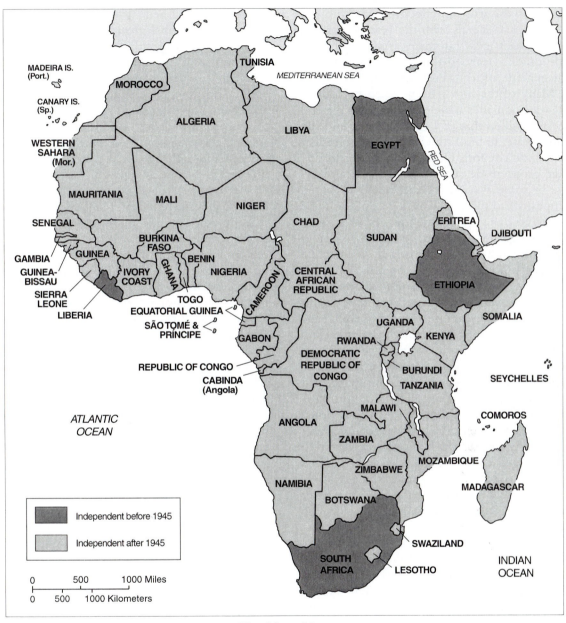

The New Africa

brief attempts at parliamentary systems, as firm lines of control might compensate for political inexperience. The fact that army leaders had more organizational training—of the modern, bureaucratic type as opposed to the personalized, tribal sort—than most and national rather than local loyalties helps account for frequent periods of military control. However, this reliance on the army for effective leadership was no panacea. Generals who the year before had been sergeants now ran many armies; although some quickly learned the lessons of complex management, others were inefficient.

Many of the new nations faced periods of civil war soon after independence. This experience resembled that of Latin America and the United States in the 19th century, but precedent was of little comfort. Divisions by tribe and language group made central administration difficult, in some ways more difficult than when Europeans had ruled. Leadership could now be ascribed to one group, which tended to antagonize other groups. The former British colony of Nigeria, in west Africa, dramatically illustrated a common problem. A large, populous nation, potentially one of Africa's wealthiest because of rich oil holdings as well as commercial farms, Nigeria was divided among three major language groups. Each group had distinctive political and cultural traditions—some emphasized military values, others business success. Nigerians in the north were Muslim; southerners were Christian or polytheist. Independent Nigeria was thus initially organized as a federation of three regional governments, but internal warfare resulted nevertheless. A group of army officers, committed to national unity, took control in 1965 and abolished these regions, but because most of the new leaders were from a single tribe, the Ibos, the result was a fierce attack by the Muslim north. The attempt by the Ibo region to form an independent state in 1967 led to three years of bloody warfare in which hundreds of thousands died of starvation. However, national unity survived; the central military leadership held on and then made peace with the defeated Ibos through economic aid and local autonomy.

Internal warfare also surfaced in Congo, whose name was changed to Zaire in 1971, although in this case regional conflicts were heightened by Western and Soviet interference. With backing from European business leaders and military forces, a pro-Western dictatorship was ultimately established. Warfare between majority and minority tribal groups also plagued Zimbabwe after independence, although outright civil war was avoided. Another bloody clash between two tribes broke out in Rwanda in 1994. Tribal conflict and also hopes for political and economic reform led to an insurgent military movement in Zaire in 1997 that displaced the aging dictator and restored the country's former name, Congo. But internal ethnic conflict, plus interference from neighboring nations, led to renewed violence in 2002–03, resulting in hundreds of thousands of deaths in Congo. Civil wars that combined tension among ethnic groups with battles for power in authoritarian states also broke out in Liberia and in northeast Africa. Huge numbers of people were killed, injured, or displaced. Armed teenage boys—"child soldiers"—filled the armies of all sides.

In general, the problems of joining nations that had no real tradition, which embodied a host of diverse, often antagonistic peoples, dominated African history after independence. Problems persisted or recurred in some areas for a distressingly long time. Former colonial powers, such as France, and also the United Nations periodically tried to intervene. But the outside world hesitated over Africa, not sure what to do and not sure that African problems were as important as issues in other areas. The end of the cold war, reducing competition for loyalties in Africa, also reduced interest to some extent.

There were also other complications. Boundary disputes led to regional warfare in a few instances. Ethiopia and Somalia engaged in a bitter territorial quarrel in the late 1970s. The Pan-African Congress met periodically to resolve disputes, often with considerable success, and the civilization was far freer from warfare than the neighboring Middle East. Cold war tensions also affected the new nations. Soviet backing for Angolan independence included the provision of Cuban troops. The Ethiopian-Somali dispute was fueled by aid from both the Soviet Union and the United States, as first Somalia and then Ethiopia

Protesting apartheid: demonstration at the funeral of a riot victim shot by South African police, 1985.

became Soviet allies. Most African nations tried with some success to stay clear of a firm alignment with either cold war side, but superpower rivalries could be an undeniable distraction.

South Africa proved to be one of the most intractable problems of the late 20th century. White minority rule continued in this powerful country, long defying the movement toward black independence. South Africa boasted the only industrialized economy on the continent, built on unusual mineral wealth and rich agriculture; it also maintained the continent's strongest military force. Afrikaner power in South Africa, which had increased gradually during the first half of the 20th century after the Boer War, culminated in outright victory in the 1948 national elections. The National party ruled the country until 1994, seceding from the British Commonwealth in 1961. The Afrikaners progressively constructed a system called *apartheid*, or separation, to keep the black majority in economic and political subjugation. In most public places, blacks were not permitted to use white facilities; intermarriage was

forbidden; blacks, even when working for white-owned firms, were required to live in segregated urban compounds; and many rural blacks were forced onto artificially created homelands, usually on the worst lands, where superficial self-government barely masked white control. Protests from a liberal white minority were silenced by police action and censorship, although moderate opposition was allowed to continue. Agitation from black groups, and also from Indian and mixed-race minorities, surfaced periodically, only to be crushed amid widespread brutality.

However, pressures from blacks for political rights and against an economic discrimination that confined them to unskilled jobs could not undo the existing system of apartheid. Unrest developed particularly among black workers in the urban compounds. Many parts of the world supported these actions, which also prompted some superficial concessions in apartheid policy during the 1970s, although in 1984–1986, a new series of bloody riots led to the reinstatement of martial law. Only at the end of the 1980s did a breakthrough begin, as a new white leader, F. W. de Klerk, negotiated with Nelson Mandela of the African National Congress. Apartheid was legally dismantled and negotiations continued toward election-based universal suffrage with some protections for the white minority. Conditions remained uncertain, and violence between whites and blacks and among black groups continued to run high, but the long era of white domination ended. Mandela was elected president in the first elections based on universal suffrage, in 1994.

For most of sub-Saharan Africa, which remained rather separate from South Africa while denouncing apartheid, three themes dominated the decades after independence was first achieved. First, national unity was successfully maintained in most cases, though there were agonizing exceptions. Administrations were extended over the new nations, school systems expanded, national loyalty preached through the government-dominated press and the ubiquitous transistor radio. In key cases, as we have seen, secessionist movements were defeated, and except in a few cases a full commitment to either side in the cold war was avoided.

Second, initial attempts to maintain democratic political structures were quickly abandoned. Despite Western expectations, in part because of the limited political experience that had been possible during the colonial period, virtually all the new nations dismantled parliamentary institutions, multiparty political systems, and guarantees of political freedom. In Ghana, Kwame Nkrumah soon jailed his political opponents and outlawed all parties save his own. His goal was a one-party state capable of arousing the kind of loyalty that would hold together the nation and maintain his personal power. Nkrumah finally failed, victim in part of poor economic management that bankrupted the new nation. Military leadership replaced him. Most other African countries converted to either military rule or one-party systems that brooked no legal opposition. One-party governments arose in Kenya and Tanzania and in most of the former French

colonies. Military rule predominated in Congo, Ethiopia, Liberia, and elsewhere. During the 1950s and 1960s, Africa experienced at least 70 attempted military takeovers (20 of which succeeded), and the pattern continued in later decades. Nigeria's military government turned power over to an elected civilian government in 1979, but another military coup soon followed.

Third, determined efforts were pursued in many nations to promote economic change. Most of the new African leaders saw economic development as a vital expression of independence, an essential component to the national unity they worked hard and successfully to preserve. Such a goal proved far more compelling than Western-style liberalism, although its achievement remained elusive amid a particularly daunting set of economic and demographic barriers.

AFRICAN POLITICAL CULTURE

The almost uniform conversion of independent African states to authoritarian political structures in the later 20th century is not surprising. Latin America and many Asian nations have shown a similar pattern in response to new nationhood. African political traditions, which so often emphasized the divine power of kings and had been shaped more recently by repressive colonial administrations, offered scant basis for a more liberal political approach in the Western or Indian sense.

African leaders, many personally ambitious and almost all eager to defend the unity of their new countries as the top political priority, found it hard to countenance opposition that seemed a personal affront and often expressed regional or tribal loyalties that threatened the nation. Success in maintaining unity—and the new African nations fared better in this regard than the initial Latin American nations had done in the first half of the 19th century—seemed to require strong police effort. Authoritarian rule also came naturally to many military leaders, who represented one of the more solid national institutions in most new nations. Many ordinary Africans, particularly in the fast-growing cities, placed great faith in the more charismatic leaders. Rural Africans might be less involved politically, but their loyalties, more traditional, corresponded to smaller segments of society such as family, village, and tribe, not to a national force of opposition. Although a number of Africans defended liberal values, the extent of support for parliamentary politics that helped forge an oscillation between liberal and authoritarian forms in the Latin American tradition did not surface, at least during the first decades of independence. The authoritarian style went largely unchallenged until the 1990s, except for attacks by rival aspirants to authoritarian power.

Although authoritarian government in Africa characteristically meant attacks on opposition leaders, monopoly of the press and radio, and an emphasis on an internally strong army, other policies of authoritarian leaders varied widely. At one extreme was the brutal corruption of a number of leaders in Uganda, where at least two dictators used their armies to attack rival tribes and kill hundreds of thousands of civilians. This kind of brutality resulted in no stability, as rival claimants to power chased each other out of office with some frequency. Another authoritarian style involved emulation of the Soviet Russian example. Ethiopian Marxists, who took power after a revolt toppled the nation's ancient monarchy, talked in terms of a totalitarian state that would represent workers and peasants. But the Soviet model was unusual in Africa. Few Africans found that doctrinaire Marxism described their political or economic conditions. Even in Ethiopia, the active power of the government, in an impoverished agricultural economy and amid great regional strife, hardly permitted the political controls of the Soviet state. A few kingdoms bordering South Africa, in yet another pattern, maintained some of the trappings of divine kingship, with rulers enjoying lavish ceremonies. The ruler of the giant state of Zaire (which after he was ousted resumed the name Congo) assumed the trappings of a divine kingship, stressing ritual demonstrations of power

and receipt of tribute, along with a strong army, but the actual administration of government under his rule was very loose.

A number of nations with one-party systems achieved impressive political stability. Kenya faced tensions between two main tribal groups, but the ruling party created considerable unity and produced able leaders who transferred power without engendering strife. Kenya's capital city of Nairobi gained stature as the headquarters for several UN agencies and a meeting place for African organizations.

Several African nations pursued non-Marxist socialist policies, hoping to combine economic advance with social reform. In Tanzania, Julius Nyerere tried to build on African community traditions to create a distinctive form of rural socialism. The government supported village cooperation. Nyerere argued that "socialist societies in different parts of the world will differ in many respects . . . reflecting both the manner of their development, and their historical traditions." An African definition of socialism appealed to nationalist sentiment and reflected an unquestionable distaste, on the part of many Africans, for the greed and competitiveness of Western capitalism. Nyerere's practical policies in Tanzania, however, were hampered by poor economic management, and the country did not develop rapidly. Zimbabwe, although late in winning its independence, was a more hopeful example. Robert Mugabe, the prime minister, although a Marxist in theory, devoted himself to a program of practical reforms, which would redistribute some land and offer a degree of protection to manufacturing workers but would not antagonize the white minority or repel foreign investors.

Several west African governments made little reference to socialist ideas. Leaders in Nigeria supported private enterprise while also using government funds and planning to encourage further economic development. Great hope existed in the 1970s that government oil revenues could be channeled into industrial investment, although the decline of oil prices in the early

1980s threatened economic advance and resulted in widespread unemployment.

Early in the 1990s, a resurgence of democracy began to emerge. Although stable political regimes collapsed in some nations, such as Somalia, Africa (including the now democratic regime in South Africa) was influenced by international trends and pressures toward more open political regimes. By 1997, 17 countries had installed freer elections with multiparty competition. Nigeria joined this list in 1999. The trend was still halting, but it suggested some interesting political potential for the future and the closeness of African ties with influences in the wider world. Tensions within the military persisted, however, partly because the end of the cold war reduced foreign aid and the weapons supply that had been used to placate the armed forces. Military coups continued. Several major states, such as Kenya, saw democratic elections set aside by authoritarian leaders, whereas the successful military movement in Congo resulted in a leader whose promises of future elections were at best tentative. The African definition of a stable political order that was not simply authoritarian proved to be no easy task.

AFRICAN CULTURE

Men and women who, as artists or writers, attempted to articulate African culture in the 20th century faced an important contradiction. On the one hand, a widespread awareness existed of traditions that should be maintained, as a bridge between the civilization's past and its future and as alternatives to Western (or Marxist) styles. In this sense, contemporary African culture served many of the same purposes as cultural traditions in the Middle East or India. On the other hand, a defense of African culture has often involved the use of alien languages and forms of expression. For example, the novel, as a work of literature, did not evolve from the African heritage. Moreover, except for those who wrote in Arabic or Swahili, most novelists turned to West-

ern languages—English, French, or Portuguese. They thus were detached from the African masses, many of whom remained illiterate, even as they tried to express and further guide public values. Here was a source of friction inherent to some extent in any formal intellectual life, in a culture that had long been largely oral. In Africa, the newness of many cultural outlets, particularly the educational system and the written word, posed a fundamental challenge to the preservation of vital traditions.

Indeed, one sign of the tension of intellectual life showed in the characteristic education of the small minority that passed beyond the primary level in the independent African nations. African secondary schools preached nationalism and taught African history; to this extent, they departed from the conventions of the former colonial schools. However, the schools taught in Western languages, of necessity. They maintained a strong interest in European history and social science, as well as some Western science. Large numbers of British, American, and French schoolteachers served the system, which was still linked to examination procedures in European countries. Zambia's standardized secondary tests, for instance, were prepared and graded in England. Despite the drawbacks, genuine progress resulted as the educated African leadership expanded. Nonetheless, the challenge to older cultural habits was far greater than in any other 20th-century civilization.

An important group of African writers emerged after 1920. Crafting essays and poetry, but particularly the novel, these writers came to terms with a number of contemporary African issues. White South African writers, many critical of the policy of apartheid but deeply loyal to their homeland, wrote of the tensions and brewing trouble within their society. Black writers typically stressed the virtues of African traditions, pointing out that their people had a rich heritage long before Europeans arrived on the scene. The Senegalese poet and political leader Leopold Senghor thus criticized Western scientific traditions that separate

History Debate

THE QUESTION OF IDENTITY

During the 20th century, intellectuals in a number of societies worried about what they called *identity*. They saw their societies changing rapidly, in part because of heavy influences from the outside world—particularly western Europe and the United States. They did not necessarily object to all the changes, only the crucial loss of what was distinctive or traditional about their societies. With this, they further argued, came a loss of cultural value. The notion of identity is abstract, and certainly many people prefer newer identities as Western-style consumers or economic modernizers. But for some, including certain leading intellectuals, the concern was very real.

Africa was one of the centers of discussion around the issue of identity. African nationalist leaders did not worry too much about identity when there was a common enemy—European colonialism—to attack. But once independence was achieved, nationalists faced several difficulties in the area of identity. First, their nations lacked traditions, for the boundaries had been defined by colonialists. Second, key tribal customs had to be opposed, for they might undermine fragile loyalty to the new nations, which were usually made up of several groups. In contrast to the Middle East or India, there was no great religion to uphold with pride, as part of a valid tradition, for the religions that were spreading most rapidly, Islam and particularly Christianity, came from the outside. Third, certain cultural imports from the West—for example, science and medicine—continued to seem attractive. Where was identity in all of this? Some leaders emphasized a common African character, one that cut across national boundaries; ideas about blackness, or *négritude*, had a similar ring. Nationalists also stressed what they saw as key African virtues, such as communal and family loyalty as opposed to excessive individualism and exploitation; reverence for nature; distinct artistic styles; and a spirituality that transcended specific religions. Were these virtues enough to provide an identity to a people experiencing rapid change?

Chinua Achebe, the Nigerian novelist, wrote directly (in English) about the issue of identity. His book *Things Fall Apart* told of how traditional religion was undermined by Christian missionaries. He bemoaned the loss, although he could not bring himself to advocate a complete return to traditional religious practices, some of which now seemed either superstitious or cruel. Another novel, *No Longer at Ease*, discussed how Western urban culture, with its emphasis on consumerism and sexuality, attacked traditional family values. Again, however, Achebe did not expressly advocate a return to the past. His work raises a question that still preoccupies many: where does African identity lie?

humankind from nature; he advocated, instead, an African tradition of intuition about nature through experience in it. The Angolan Agustinho Neto praised the power of African culture, again attacking many Western standards and describing a unique black point of view. Jomo Kenyatta, glorifying tribal culture in Kenya, elevated the position of women in African society. A West Indian poet, popular in Africa, praised the new black consciousness of superiority over Western values:

Hurrah for those who never invented anything hurrah for those who never explored anything hurrah for those who never conquered anything hurrah for joy hurrah for love hurrah for the pain of incarnate tears.

Modern African art showing traditional themes. Cameroon brass sculptures of two "juju men" wearing the costumes used at religious ceremonies. (Granger Collection)

More soberly, Nigeria's leading novelist, Chinua Achebe, stated "the fundamental theme" of the rising group of African writers:

> the African people did not hear of culture for the first time from Europeans; . . . their societies were not mindless but frequently had a philosophy of great depth and volume and beauty, . . . they had poetry and above all, they had dignity. It is this dignity that many African peoples all but lost in the colonial period, and it is this that they must now regain. The worst thing that can happen to any people is the loss of their dignity and self-respect. The writer's duty is to help them regain it by showing what happened to them, what they lost.

However, the new African novelists were not simply apostles of tradition and black pride. They also wrote of the anxieties that accompany modernization. Achebe's brilliant novels dealt with the corrosive effect of Western ideas, including Christianity, on powerful village characters. In his works, he examined the stress of city life on popular traditions and expressed the disillusionment of many African intellectuals with corrupt and power-hungry rulers, worrying that the masses "had become even more cynical than their leaders and were apathetic in the bargain." African culture, with writers such as Achebe, combined traditional values with new forms of expression to present powerful dramas of a changing society.

African artists and craftspeople preserved a thriving legacy, working in older stylistic conventions largely apart from the "modern art" styles of the West, which, ironically, had been partly inspired by African forms. Design and decoration in village houses retained their distinctive quality. Sculptors continued to create powerful figures for both religious and aesthetic purposes. African artistic productivity continued at very high levels in the early 20th century and beyond, using traditional masks and sculpture, though often incorporating objects, such as glass beads, imported from the West. French colonials, sending some of this art back home around 1900, helped inspire modern art forms such as cubism in Europe. Later in the 20th century, African dance and music remained lively art forms, both at the popular level and in formal government-sponsored troupes that toured internationally. African culture was not isolated, however, and many craftsmen and musicians interacted with the proponents of other styles. Some crafts, catering to tourism, pandered to Western ideas of what African art should be like.

The interactions that dominated 20th-century African culture showed clearly in the area of religion. Africa remained a religious society, although in the cities, secular values competed for center stage. Islam, which gained many new converts in the north and center, maintained a tra-

jectory as the most rapidly growing popular religion, claiming about 40 percent of all Africans south of the Sahara. Africa's Christian minority, almost as large, grew rapidly as well. Black Protestant leaders played a leading role in moderate resistance to apartheid in South Africa. African Catholicism assumed a growing role in the Roman church, as the first African cardinal was named and the pope visited the continent for the first time in the 1970s. Catholicism in Africa expanded more rapidly than in any other area, as the number of African Catholics more than doubled from 29 million in 1965 to 66 million in 1985. Christian and Muslim gains meant that Africa experienced the kind of growth of monotheism and new spirituality that had characterized civilizations such as western Europe after the classical age. The result, as in these earlier cases, was both exciting and unsettling. New converts often retained former beliefs in part, for syncretism was common. African Christianity characteristically combined conventional Christian doctrine with traditional values—including, in some areas, a continued belief in polygamy and a definite scorn for Catholic celibacy—and traditional rituals. At the same time, outright polytheistic beliefs retained some vitality, in both the city and countryside. Traditional remedies were often used to treat disease, following the quite logically presented principles of spirit-caused illness and its cure. Popular religious leaders, some of them women, helped arouse fervor in several regional 20th-century revolts, in which faith in divine guidance combined with worldly grievances against colonial rule or economic exploitation. A number of movements, focusing less on protest than on healing by prayer and the promise of the millennium, blended traditional animist creeds with ideas adapted from the Bible. Overall, although religious diversity—and sometimes bitter conflict—continued, a general esteem for the applicability of religion to life, society, and nature continued to dominate African culture.

The surge of literary creativity and the complex religious transformations were not the only cultural innovations in 20th-century Africa. Nationalist leaders obviously urged cultural change, away from purely traditional concepts; while attacking imperialism, they usually argued for the adaptation of some concepts from the West, including new kinds of science and medicine. However, they also tried to highlight important African qualities, such as community and family solidity. In the cities, other Western cultural influences, including consumerism, constituted yet another force, adding to changes in belief and creating complicated combinations of old and new.

ECONOMY AND SOCIETY

Changes in African culture, and particularly the spread of education and Western-language literature, raised some basic questions about the relationship between culture and social change. Even as praise for traditional styles and values resounded, there were signs of the unusually rapid disruption of many customary social forms. Writers such as Achebe wondered whether the breakup of long-held beliefs had not weakened Africans' ability to find an anchor amid so much change. Other intellectuals, however, stressed the continuing validity of basic religious orientations and family ties, contrasting African strength in this regard with what they saw as the demoralization of Western society.

Most of sub-Saharan Africa did not face, throughout the 20th century, the kinds of pressure for land redistribution that deeply affected Latin America and parts of Asia. White minorities opened large estates in east and south Africa; many of these remained, after independence, in white or African hands, although some African governments were able to introduce limited land reform. In more populous west Africa, peasant small-holding remained the norm, except for the cash-crop estates that relied on low-wage labor.

Nevertheless, the persistence of village-based agriculture raised issues of its own. During the colonial decades, Western governments pressured African peasants to convert to cash crops such as peanuts or cotton. Some farmers made profits on such crops, but others had to minimize the production of basic foods for subsistence in favor of meeting commercial quotas. Although a few village headmen made money on market sales and then bought bigger homes, bicycles, and even art reproductions, the bulk of the population suffered.

Commercial pressures often continued after independence was gained in Africa, although some areas reverted to more localized agriculture. Major gains in agricultural production came slowly, as peasants lacked both the capital and education to undertake new methods. Many governments were more concerned with creating public works and factories than with modernizing agriculture. Despite the clearance of new lands for farming, agricultural production lagged in many parts of Africa. Dependence on root crops in the drier lands meant that the gains of the Green Revolution were irrelevant. Agricultural stagnation plus population growth made key regions vulnerable to disasters of climate. In the early 1970s and again in the early 1980s and 1990s, drought conditions on the Sahara's southern rim and down the east coast caused widespread famine. Intense cultivation in some areas was exhausting the soil and expanding the desert, creating more than temporary problems in places such as Ethiopia. More generally, agricultural lag promoted inadequate nutrition and helped explain widespread poverty, even when severe weather problems did not add to the burdens. Finally, reliance on cash crops such as cocoa, cotton, or peanuts for export continued to distract from well-balanced agricultural production, leaving many nations divided between export farmers and a subsistence-minded peasantry wedded to largely traditional methods.

Development of the cash-crop system continued to tie many African countries closely to the Western-dominated world economy. This dependence did not disappear with decolonization. Despite their nationalism, many African countries remained firmly linked to the markets, shipping, and commercial know-how of their erstwhile European rulers. Despite a brief flurry of radical rebellion against Belgian business in Congo, for example, Belgian capital and expertise remained fundamental to the nation's economy, as the mineral wealth of the mines continued to be directed toward Western markets almost exclusively. No African country aside from South Africa created a large industrial base of its own. Government encouragement promoted factories for local food processing and clothing and tool production in countries such as Kenya. By the late 1990s, a few countries, including Botswana and Uganda, reported rapid manufacturing growth, leading some observers to wonder if Africa might finally begin to participate in the kind of industrial evolution that had taken root in Latin America and parts of the Middle East some decades before. Everywhere, however, reliance on the technologies and manufactured imports of the West remained significant. Many African nations ran up huge debts because of the gap between export earnings and import needs.

Despite the limits of economic change, a new class of wealthy, urban Africans took shape both under colonialism and with independence. Merchants, the cash-crop landlords, and top government officials stood apart from the African masses in their luxurious lifestyle, as Africa joined other agricultural societies in a radical division between the wealthy and the masses. In Swahili-speaking east Africa, common people called the new elite *wa Benzi*, meaning "those who ride in a Mercedes-Benz." In stark contrast, per capita annual income for the general population often stagnated; in mineral-rich Congo, for example, average income stood at $137 in 1976 and $160 in 1985.

Furthermore, substantial population growth hit sub-Saharan Africa during the 20th century. Medical and public-health measures promoted by colonial regimes and extended by independent African governments accounted for some of the gain. So did disruption of village community controls as a result of new market earnings from commercial agriculture or labor in the mines and cities. Population increase occurred despite the absence of a real agricultural revolution and the severe limits of climate and soil fertility in many regions. Indeed, population growth helped worsen agriculture in some cases. As land was overfarmed, its fertility declined—hence, there were recurrent famines in key regions that, ironically, did not halt population growth.

From the 1970s onward, the spread of AIDS in east Africa added to economic woes, as many children and young adults became afflicted—over 25 percent in some regions—thus curtailing the available active labor force. The AIDS crisis hit eastern and southern Africa particularly hard. Local governments were often slow to respond, amid some belief that this was a crisis manufactured in the West as a means of regulating African sexuality. The big problem, however, was poverty, as no African nation could afford the drug costs for the best available treatments. By 2003, a few countries, such as Uganda, were making progress in preventive campaigns, emphasizing condom use.

Rapid population growth continued despite the AIDS crisis, as Africa remained one of the regions in which new forms of birth control spread most slowly. This growth, new transportation facilities, and more modern forms of government, along with some growth in commerce, spurred the rapid expansion of African cities, particularly after World War II. Only 8 percent of the population throughout the entire African continent was concentrated in cities in 1925 and only 13 percent in 1950, but by 1973, the percentage had soared to 23 and this trend gained momentum. Most urbanization did not depend on the expansion of factories; it was based on trade, political concentration, and above all, the absence of alternatives in the countryside, as population growth and cash-crop estates increased the number of property-less poor. As in Latin America, urban populations crowded into hastily built slums, hoping for survival by means of occasional unskilled jobs, begging, or prostitution, or peddling in the omnipresent open markets of the African city.

African urbanization, unlike that in Latin America, involved considerable family disruption. Because far more men than women moved to the cities, a significant number of families, particularly in the countryside, were headed by women. Indeed, Africa resembled the West, by the 1970s, in the dissociation of a growing minority of men from their families and the problems, economic and psychological, that occurred when women had to raise children on their own. The African tradition of an extended family modified these pressures to some extent, as relatives provided moral support and more tangible assistance to female-headed households. While their husbands toiled in urban centers or mining villages, some women found their new independence challenging and exciting, as the traditions of male domination faded. Nevertheless, issues of family disruption in Africa—a civilization proud of its close and supportive family ties—seemed inescapable as part of social change in the later 20th century. Changes in social structures and personal values stood in stark contrast to more traditional expectations, in one of the several urgent dramas of 20th-century Africa.

A weekly newspaper in Zambia featured a "Dear Josephine" column that mirrored the process of change, as urban Africans developed new and more individualized patterns in a society long characterized by strong family traditions and tightly knit communities. Africans wrote to ask if they could marry despite the fact that older brothers in their families remained unwed; tradition held that the eldest should marry first, but what should the middle son do when he found the right girl? Or how was a city dweller to pay a bridal dowry in cattle, which his intended's family, back in the village, insisted on? Or how might the tribal traditions of mutual support be continued? For example,

> I am well-known, with a big family to feed. My house is by the bus-stop and every day I receive visitors from the home village. It is my duty to give my tribes folk food and money for their journey needs. But my family suffer from hunger and I go without the decent clothes my position calls for. Though I have a good job I am kept poor by home-people. I do not dislike them, but what can I do to be saved from them?

Women's activities also began to shift. The impact of larger changes—social, economic, and political—on African women provoked important debate. On the one hand, women gained new roles as men's ties to their families loosened. On the other hand, women were typically concentrated in more traditional economic sectors, including agricultural areas, in order to protect their economic status. As governments became more effective, first under colonial rule and then with independence, the informal local power of women often declined. Some observers argued that women were net losers in this process, despite certain new freedoms. In addition in some areas, such as the Muslim northeast, traditional limitations on women persisted, including practices of circumcision that were designed to limit a woman's sexual pleasure and consequently promote fidelity. Nonetheless, growing educational opportunities and even some of the social disruptions promoted new ideas among women, including a growing belief that women should stick together; here, traditional ideas of family unity combined with a desire for education and birth control to create a novel outlook. Upper-class urban women also managed to pressure some governments to improve legal rights for all women. But battles over outside influences often complicated this process. Many women won rights to property by appealing to UN declarations on women's rights. By 2000, some courts overturned these rulings in the name of African tradition.

By the late 1990s, another change entered the mix. A growing number of multinational companies, from Korea and Japan as well as the West, began to set up factories in impoverished areas such as Lesotho. The aim was to take advantage of cheap labor, including many women.

Conditions were rigorous, with long hours and strict regulations against leaving the factory because of fears of theft. As in other parts of the world, it was not clear whether these developments would bring benefits in the long run, by cutting into high rates of unemployment, or whether they would merely confirm and perpetuate economic dependence.

DEFINING THE NEW AFRICA

Disruptive transformation was no African monopoly in the 20th century. Most civilizations faced challenges to established institutions and values. Africans in various ways remained able to rely on traditions; their lifestyles were not totally disturbed or undone by surrounding change. Nonetheless, the upheaval brought about by colonial impositions, population growth, and new urban and commercial institutions was considerable, particularly when it was not matched by significant improvements in the standard of living. At the same time, change brought new hopes to many Africans. Intellectuals proud of their culture and politicians enthusiastic about national independence were joined by more humble people, such as the young woman in Kenya who noted the opportunities available for the self-sufficient and the resourceful. Describing her mother's large family and hard physical labor on a subsistence farm, she discussed how her own views had been shaped by the experience of school:

> My life is very different from my mother's. . . . Women have to get an education. Then if you get a large family and don't know how to feed it, you can find work and get some cash. That's what I will teach my children: "Get an education first."

Africa remained the poorest of the world's civilizations through the end of the 20th century, as its vulnerability to famine starkly attested. Modernization, including political independence, had not reaped all the benefits that many had hoped for and may have jeopardized some sources of cultural strength. However, change continued to generate aspirations for the future, in a culture still defining its relationship to the contemporary world.

ISSUES AND CONNECTIONS

Problems mounted in 20th-century Africa. Economic dependence increased, and globalization brought new signs of this. Africa had far more than its share of famines, disease, and poverty. Missionary activities and urban consumerism challenged cultural traditions. Yet Africans were not always powerless in the face of these larger forces. Nationalism provided new opportunities for political and cultural expression. Some countries developed impressive political stability; by the 1990s, it could be hoped that South Africa had joined this list. Many people were able to combine older traditions with new cultural currents. Massive problems are inescapable in dealing with recent African history, but they are not the whole story.

Amid rapid change, finding links to the past was not always easy. In politics, the assertion of "Big Men" touched base with older political patterns. Massive changes in religious beliefs were obvious, but some observers argued that these built on a still-traditional African spirituality. African artists and craftspeople might modify their products to suit tourist tastes, but they still worked with customary themes. African identity was challenged, but it unquestionably survived. In 2003 a new TV series, *Big Brother Africa*, took the subcontinent by storm. English-speaking Africans in virtually all the relevant countries delighted in a program produced by Africans, for Africans, dealing with issues—such as extended family pressures—that Africans could well understand. This was a civilization being redefined, but not erased.

SUGGESTED WEB SITES

For information on apartheid, see http://www-cs-students.stanford.edu/~cale/cs201/apartheid.hist.html. On the African National Congress, see http://www.anc.org.za/.

SUGGESTED READINGS

Recent work includes Cheryl Mawaria, ed., *African Visions: Literary Images, Political Change and Social Struggle in Contemporary Africa* (2000); Adebayo Adedeji, ed., *Comprehending and Mastering African Conflict* (1999); and Einar Bratthen, ed., *Ethnicity Kills? The Politics of War, Peace and Ethnicity in Sub-Saharan Africa* (2000).

Various source materials have contributed to research in recent African history. W. E. B. Du Bois, *The World and Africa* (1974), presents an American black nationalist perspective. Works by nationalist leaders include J. Kenyatta, *Facing Mount Kenya* (1953), and from South Africa, A. Luthuli, *Let My People Go* (1962). F. Fanon, *Wretched of the Earth* (1965), is a stinging indictment of Western colonialism. Novels by C. Achebe, particularly *Things Fall Apart* (1978), deal with changes in African society and culture. See also B. Fetter, *Colonial Rule in Africa: Readings from Primary Sources* (1979). The colonial period is covered by R. O. Collins, *Problems in the History of Colonial Africa, 1860–1960* (1970). See also Ali Mazrui and Michael Tidy, *Nationalism and New States in Africa* (1984); Martin Meredith, *The First Dance of Freedom: Black Africa in the Post-War Era* (1984); and S. A. Akintoye, *Emergent African States* (1976). On more recent developments, consult P. C. Lloyd, *Africa and Social Change* (1972); A. Hopkins, *An Economic History of West Africa* (1973); and C. Legum, *Congo Disaster* (1961). Competent works on South Africa include R. W. Johnson, *How Long Will South Africa Survive?* (1977), and Gail Gerhart, *Black Power in South Africa* (1978). On an important social topic, see N. H. Afkin and E. Bay, eds., *Women in Africa* (1977).

The Early 21st Century: World History and the Future

The 20th century witnessed huge changes. The relative decline of western Europe helped usher in the cold war and decolonization. Alterations in political, social, and cultural forms affected all societies, though in different ways. By the 1990s, decolonization was largely completed, the cold war was over, and a new framework was taking shape. This framework furthered the definition of the contemporary period in world history that had begun in the 1920s and 1930s.

Three components fed the new framework, and they did not neatly combine. First, the end of the cold war left the United States as the world's only superpower, the only power capable of independent global military action. But it also furthered new regional conflicts and alliances and seemed to give older conflicts new vigor. The world is still working out the implications of the cold war's demise.

Second, globalization accelerated, after a real retreat in the middle decades of the 20th century. The pace and impact of global economic and cultural contacts, fed by new technologies, had no precedent in the human experience. Some people thought a revolutionary new phase of the human experience was in the offing as a result.

Third, a revival of religion and regional religious identities, beginning in the 1970s, affected Christian missionary activity, Islam, Hinduism, and some new forms or adaptations of Buddhism such as the Falun Gong movement in China. Religious revival did not necessarily contradict globalization, but it pushed in different directions as a whole.

The combination of new forces influenced some of the other changes taking place in the contemporary world. Again, the results were not always tidy. Global standards, for example, tended to push for further changes in women's roles and toward lower birth rates, more personal freedom, and more participation in consumerism. The global economy, however, could disrupt women's work, giving them difficult factory jobs or reducing their role altogether.

Religious revival on the whole prompted a more traditional approach for women, including hostility to the implications of consumerism for women's dress and sexuality. Neither globalization nor religious revival called for a return to a landlord-based social structure. This was gone for good. But globalization tended to shape a division between a globally conscious middle class and the working poor, who were often getting poorer. Religious revival often emanated from, or particularly attracted, the working poor. Globalization and religious revival also had different implications for ongoing discussions of political forms, including definitions of individual rights.

The result, and the resulting confusions and uncertainties, moved the early 21st-century world away from some of the leading issues of the 20th century. They also shaped some of the fundamental questions about the world's future. There is another complexity. While change could seem overwhelming, there were also important continuities from the past. Previous positions in the world economy, commitments to cultural traditions and identities, continued to mark the world in the 21st century. Many groups sought new ways to defend or revive what they saw as key elements from their past. Here was another set of components to fold into an understanding of the world's present and future.

KEY QUESTIONS   *How can the diplomatic and military framework of the post-cold war world best be defined? How can globalization be defined, and why has political globalization not kept pace with culture and economics? How do new religious interests relate to the rise of science, consumerism, and other secular attachments? What are the best ways to use history to help sort out predictions about the world's future?*

AFTER THE COLD WAR

The economic collapse of the Soviet Union and the division of the Soviet empire, between 1985

and 1991, obviously limited the power of the new Russia (see Chapter 29). President Vladimir Putin largely embraced a pro-Western diplomatic policy. His firm political control plus improvements in the Russian economy permitted some gestures of independence. Russia joined France and Germany in opposing the U.S. war against Iraq in 2003. Many Russians questioned the benefit of a close relationship with the United States, and the popularity of the United States and any "American model" had declined in Russia by 2004. However, Russia no longer provided a strong military opposition to U.S. power. By 2001, Russian military spending, at $4 billion a year, was one-thirtieth that of the United States.

Other countries worried visibly about unchallenged American strength. China, particularly, alternated between seeking favorable economic arrangements with the U.S. government (China enjoyed a great balance of trade advantage with the United States) and seeking to increase military rivalry. China's claims to control Taiwan, combined with U.S. involvement in defense of the island, were a particularly fruitful source of tension. China's military buildup, however, did not threaten the United States directly. Efforts to forge alliances against U.S. power, by greater cooperation with Russia or with other countries such as Iran, roused U.S. concern, but no full-fledged partnerships emerged.

By 2001, even western European countries expressed some misgivings about U.S. strength, particularly when the United States seemed to ignore international collaboration in areas such as the environment. In 2001, in an interesting gesture of anti-Americanism, the United Nations excluded the United States from membership on its Human Rights Commission, the first time this had happened since the commission was formed.

Still, no systematic counterpoise to U.S. power emerged after the cold war's end. U.S. power was indeed enhanced, through most of the 1990s, by unusually rapid economic growth and by U.S. leadership in burgeoning new fields of information technology and bioengineering.

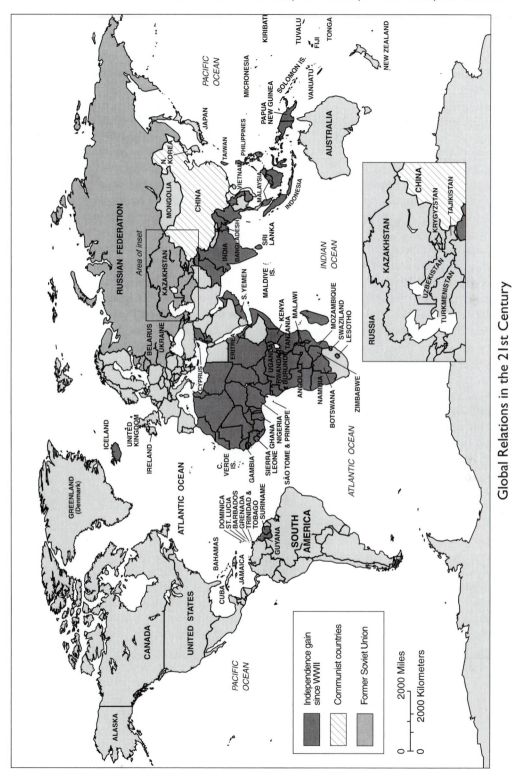

Global Relations in the 21st Century

Even Japan did not keep pace with U.S. innovations in technology and business organization, as the Pacific Rim encountered new economic difficulties at the very end of the 20th century.

Free from the cold war, the United States continued a high level of military spending, with levels above the next 13 countries combined. Not even western Europe kept pace with American military technology, especially in the air. Early in the 21st century, the United States expressed new resistance to international agreements, on the environment, the use of mines, and international prosecution of war crimes. The nation successfully appealed for extensive international cooperation after the terrorist attacks of September 11, 2001. It tried to organize international pressure against governments that were not aligned with U.S. policies and that had active weapons programs; its leaders sometimes called nations such as Iran and North Korea "rogue states" or part of an "axis of evil." But in 2002–03, the invasion of Iraq, and pronouncements about an American right to strike preemptively against nations capable of developing weapons of mass destruction, sounded a new note. Some observers saw the emergence of a new American imperialism. Even more than with Russia, the implications of the end of the cold war on American participation in world politics were not easy to evaluate.

But the most obvious results of the cold war's end were a new boost to democracy as a political form (a trend already underway before the Soviet collapse); a realignment of east-central Europe toward the West, marked by the admission of several countries into NATO and the European Union; a new band of independent states in central Asia; a new set of ethnic tensions in parts of the former communist world; an encouragement to general forces of globalization; and, ironically, a new expression of old as well as new regional conflicts. The failure of communism also contributed to revival of religious interest in several east European centers, again a part of a larger world movement that had begun before 1985.

THE SPREAD OF DEMOCRACY

The end of the cold war was clearly associated with another large trend in the world at the end of the 20th century: the spread of multiparty democracy with (reasonably) freely contested elections. This trend helped cause the cold war to end, and the end in turn gave the trend new momentum. We have seen that, through much of the century, several different government forms competed for success amid a general climate of change: communism, fascism and other authoritarianisms, and democracy itself. But from the late 1970s onward, the tide seemed to turn toward democracy in many regions that had long been inhospitable.

Economic and political success in western Europe, including the drawing power of the Common Market, helped propel Spain, Portugal, and Greece to democratic systems in the mid-1970s, after long periods of authoritarian control. Then the democratic wave hit Latin America, backed by U.S. and western European support. Beginning with new regimes in Argentina and Brazil, authoritarian controls were replaced by free elections. The process continued through the 1990s, when literally all Latin American countries except Cuba were in the democratic camp. Revolutionaries in Central America accepted the system in the late 1980s; Paraguay was the final authoritarian regime to yield a decade later. In 2000, Mexico elected its first president from a party other than the PRI, the party that had monopolized control since the revolution.

Democratic systems gained ground in South Korea and Taiwan in the 1980s. In the Philippines, an authoritarian ruler was cast aside, amid considerable popular pressure, in favor of an elected government. By this point, of course, the democratic current captured the Soviet bloc, with democratic systems winning out in most of east-central Europe, Russia, and to a degree in some former Soviet republics in central Asia.

While most of Africa remained authoritarian, democratic change spread to this region by the 1990s, headed of course with the triumph

Attack on the Russian parliament building.

of democracy over apartheid in South Africa. After new assertions of military control, Nigeria, the continent's most populous country, turned to democracy in 1999. At this point also, a near revolution toppled another authoritarian system, in Indonesia, and replaced it with competitive elections.

Never before had democracy spread so widely, among so many otherwise different societies. Only China and parts of the Middle East seemed to hold apart completely. In China, the major democratic demonstration in Beijing, in 1989, echoed the global democratic current but was brutally put down. Elsewhere, the political stability, cultural prestige, and economic success of Western democracy, supplemented by the strength of democratic systems in Japan and India,

seemed to win the day. The fall of European communism both reflected and encouraged the trend. One of democracy's main competitors was now discredited. The end of the cold war worked to the same effect: there was no superpower support for authoritarian systems in return for military alliance. The United States, in particular, became more consistent in its encouragement to democratic reforms, under Jimmy Carter and again in the 1990s.

Huge questions remained about democracy's future. The link to economic expectations—the sense that democracy was a precondition for freer markets and economic growth that supported many Latin American conversions and also Gorbachev's reforms in Russia—was an obvious vulnerability: what if

History Debate

HOW MUCH HISTORICAL CHANGE?

As the cold war drew to a close, a number of analysts, primarily in the United States, looked forward to dramatic shifts in human affairs. There were two related lines of argument. The first, summed up in the "end of history" concept, emphasized the new dominance of the democratic form of government. The contest among political and economic systems, particularly between democracy and communism, was ended; democracy, it was argued, would now sweep over the world. With this, the need for basic questioning about political institutions would also end: democracy worked best, and it was here to stay. Further, the change in political structure also had implications for power rivalries. Some analysts contended that democracies never war on each other. Once the people control affairs of state through their votes, the selfishness and power trips that lead to war will end. Ordinary people understand the horror of war. They appreciate the common humanity they share with other democratic peoples. Just as democracy resolves internal conflicts through votes, democracies resolve external conflicts through bargaining and compromise. People do not vote for wars of aggression, at most sanctioning defense against attack.

Another argument, which might be combined with the democracy approach, focused on the spread of consumer capitalism around the world. As explained by journalist Thomas Friedman in his book *The Lexus and the Olive Tree*, the consumer capitalism approach emphasized the benefits of a global economy. In this, everyone would gain access to greater material abundance and the wonders of consumerism, and they would not wish to jeopardize this prosperity through war. Shared interests, rather than traditional disputes over limited resources, would carry the day.

These kinds of arguments assumed that the world was poised to depart substantially from prior history, based on new political systems or new economic systems or both. This is a challenging kind of forecasting because it cannot be easily disproved, until the future does not correspond to the dramatic projections. The consumerism argument, particularly, had no precedent in the past. At the same time, the predictions also could not be proved, for example by pointing to some prior historical analogy. How, then, should they be assessed?

Questions: Was the world changing as rapidly and fundamentally as these predictions implied? Were new systems spreading as uniformly and consistently as the democracy and global consumerism arguments implied? Were past rivalries and cultural and institutional commitments to war and dispute so easily wiped away? These predictions were issued in the wake of the excitement surrounding the cold war's end. Developments later in the 1990s and in the first years of the 21st century did not necessarily live up to the idea of fundamental transformation. Had the predictions been wrong—and if so, why did very intelligent people find them plausible in the first place? Or was the world in the early stages of the kinds of transition the forecasters had suggested? How significant, in other words, was the cold war's end in reshaping global relationships?

the economy did not improve? New uncertainties emerged by 2000. Still, the global trend was undeniable at least for a time, and it conjoined with the hopes born of the reduction of cold war tensions.

A WORLD OF REGIONS: DISPUTES AND ALLIANCES

The end of the cold war framework highlighted certain regional rivalries. Many of them were not

Arrival of the euro.

new, but they became more acute as the controlling influence of U.S.-Soviet rivalry disappeared. At the same time, efforts to form regional cooperative arrangements also gained ground. Europe took the lead here, in building further on its Common Market structure, but there were developments also in Asia and the Americas.

The collapse of the Soviet empire raised obvious questions for the principal alliance systems in western Europe. The North Atlantic Treaty Organization (NATO) had been formed specifically to block Soviet expansionism. What was its purpose now that the Soviet threat had receded? NATO officials continued to see the alliance as a desirable stabilizing force in Europe and perhaps beyond. We will see that NATO did play a direct role in one of the greatest pockets of instability, in the

Balkans. Coordination of military planning continued. And several former Eastern bloc countries requested admission to NATO, to herald their new orientation toward the West and to insure against Russian intervention. NATO did grant admission to several east-central European countries at the end of the 1990s and again in 2002.

The economic alliance of western Europe—the European Union (EU)—was another matter, since its purposes of economic integration and stimulus to growth were unaffected by the cold war's end. Most eastern European countries, along with Turkey, sought entry into the European Union. Their economies were in the throes of conversion from communist systems to market arrangements, and their standards of living were noticeably below those of western Europe. In some cases, questions persisted also about commitments to democracy and human rights. Full integration with the European Union would clearly be a drawn-out process. But by 2003, candidacies of several countries where market reforms had been most successful, such as Poland and Hungary, resulted in agreement to enter (as of 2004). In the meantime, the European Union continued to strengthen internal integration. Amid dispute, many existing members agreed on a common currency, the euro, which went into effect in a number of EU countries in early 2002. The experiment in European unity continued.

Other areas sought benefits from economic alliances, though without moving to the level of integration Europe had achieved. During the 1990s, the North American Free Trade Agreement (NAFTA) joined the United States, Mexico, and Canada. Opponents worried about loss of jobs to cheaper Mexican labor, and about environmental damage as firms moved to more loosely regulated regions. But a considerable trade increase resulted, seeming to benefit all participants but particularly Mexico.

East and southeast Asia and the Pacific Rim formed the final center for new discussions about new levels of international economic arrangements. Several discussions explored opportunities for tariff reduction and policy coordination. Clearly, economic issues had replaced cold war rivalries as the motor for regional diplomatic experiments.

But the continued potential for regional diplomatic and military conflict was striking as well. Most of the conflicts were not new. But the end of the cold war and the decline of Russian influence at the very least highlighted regional clashes and the maturing military power of many regional players, including nuclear capacity in several cases. The United States and the United Nations sought to keep the peace in most instances, but their efforts were not always successful.

The Middle East remained a trouble spot. Even before the end of the cold war, Iraq and Iran had conducted a long, casualty-filled war, with the ambitions of Iraq's dictatorial leader, Saddam Hussein, pitted against the Islamic revolutionary regime in Iran. Iraq prevailed, and then later, in 1990, invaded the small, oil-rich state of Kuwait. This galvanized an international coalition of Western and moderate Arab states, which defeated Iraq in the 1991 Persian Gulf War but left Saddam Hussein in power. The United States maintained a large military presence in the Persian Gulf region, which drew criticism from many Arabs and Muslims. In 2003, when a predominantly U.S. and British coalition invaded Iraq and toppled Saddam Hussein, the results in terms of regional power politics were sure to be substantial.

Israeli relations with the huge Palestinian minority served as another Middle Eastern flashpoint that, on the whole, deteriorated after the cold war ended, despite some promising peace moves in the mid-1990s. Though an autonomous Palestinian government was set up over two territories within Israel, tensions continued. Bitter violence between Israelis and Palestinians revived in 2001. In 2002–03, a wave of suicide bombings by Palestinians targeted Israeli civilians, while the Israeli government attacked Palestinian cities and refugee camps in turn. Clearly, key issues in this complex region remained to be resolved.

Tensions between India and Pakistan also escalated, with various border clashes particularly around the disputed territory of Kashmir. By 2000, both countries had conducted tests of nuclear weapons. War seemed to threaten in 2002, but both sides pulled back. This was the most open case of nuclear dissemination, as the limited nuclear group of the cold war began to expand. Increased Hindu nationalism within India was matched by fiercer Muslim rhetoric in Pakistan.

No clear global pattern of activity resulted from the end of the cold war. The tensions between impulses toward integration, based primarily on economic goals, and the indulgence of rivalries, sometimes spiced by military expansion, were obvious.

ETHNIC CONFLICT

The upsurge of ethnic conflict in several areas constituted a more strikingly novel feature of the post–cold war scene. Ethnic rivalries were not new, but several components helped explain the new and troubling outbreak. Globalization provided one element. New levels of global interaction increased the potential for group identities to generate hostilities. Some groups clearly increased their investment in ethnic identity as a means of countering outside influences and global pressures. At the same time, the collapse of several key multinational states, notably the Soviet Union and Yugoslavia, opened the door to a reassertion of ethnic identity as a means of replacing discredited ideologies, such as communism, and as part of the conflict for control within new political units.

Within Europe, a number of ethnic groups developed new opportunities for expression, as the hold of the classic nation-state declined. The British government, for example, gave limited autonomy to Scottish and Welsh governments. France and Spain became more tolerant toward linguistic minorities such as the Catalans and Bretons. During the 1990s, a number of European countries saw the rise of new political movements bent on reducing immigration in favor of protecting jobs and cultural identity for the majority national group. A National Front group in France won up to 10 percent of all votes during the mid-1990s, though it then fell back a bit. Austria generated a controversial right-wing national government rhetorically hostile to immigrants. In 2001, a new government leader in Italy emphasized an anti-foreign plank. Violence against immigrant groups, such as Turks in Germany, flared recurrently as well.

More systematic violence broke out in several of the territories of the former Soviet empire. Czechoslovakia split peacefully into two ethnic segments, the Czech Republic and Slovakia, but this was not the common pattern. New or newly freed states witnessed frequent ethnic conflicts.

Hungarian minorities in Romania and Turkish minorities in Bulgaria faced new pressures during the 1990s. A bloody revolt broke out in a Muslim region of Russia, Chechnya, where a regional leader proclaimed independence in 1990. On two occasions during the ensuing decade, heavy fighting broke out between rebels, seeking an independent Muslim nation, and the Russian military. Acts of terrorism, including bombs placed in several Moscow apartment buildings and theaters, helped push Russian public opinion to greater acceptance of military action. Neither side had achieved full victory by 2004, though Russian resistance to this kind of regional and ethnic claim seemed firm.

Ethnic tension also surfaced in southeastern Europe and central Asia. Recurrent fighting occurred among ethnic groups in the newly independent nation of Georgia. More serious warfare erupted periodically between Armenian Christians and their Muslim neighbors in Azerbaijan.

Yugoslavia was the most important case where elimination of a multi-ethnic state, successfully united under communism, brought bloodshed and turmoil. Ethnic patterns were unusually complex in this region. Slavs differed linguistically from Albanians, many of whom were Muslim. Slavs were divided into groups such as Serbs and Croats, with different alphabets, religions, and historical experiences. There were also Muslim Slavs in the territory of Bosnia. Groups had been pitted against each other from the Turkish conquest to, more recently, the German occupation in World War II. After the death of the strong communist leader in Yugoslavia, Marshall Tito, ethnic divisions became more open, with rising tensions between Albanians in the region of Kosovo and the dominant Serbian group. Individual Serbian nationalist leaders, such as Slobodan Milosevic, began to gain increasing attention.

Then came the Soviet collapse, which emboldened several regions to seek independence. Slovenia and Croatia pulled away in 1991, and fierce fighting erupted between Croats and

The Implosion of Yugoslavia

Serbs before the latter reluctantly agreed to a dis-memberment of a country they believed they should dominate. The government of Bosnia and Herzegovina declared independence in 1992, but this led to bitter fighting among internal groups—Catholic Croats, Orthodox Serbs, and Muslims—aided by outside intervention particularly from Serbia. Massive killing resulted, with many atrocities against civilians under the heading of "ethnic cleansing"—which often meant killing or removing non-Serb populations to facilitate Serb control. Tremendous diplomatic pressure from western Europe and the United States, supplemented by Russia, led to tenuous cease-fires, but finally, in 1995, an international military force had to step in to impose an uneasy peace. At the end of the 1990s, warfare broke out between Serbs and Muslims in the province of Kosovo, with atrocities on both sides. Purely diplomatic efforts to stop the killing failed, and NATO forces, headed by the United States, began a bombing campaign against Yugoslavia, which finally forced an end to hostilities and the

installation of another international occupying force. By 2000, demonstrations within Yugoslavia expelled Milosevic from the presidency.

Ethnic attacks were not confined to the lands once ruled by communism. In 1990, bloody conflicts broke out in central Africa, pitting tribal groups, the Hutus and the Tutsis, against each other, particularly in the nation of Rwanda. Here, too, old rivalries blended with disputes over current power; the Tutsis had long ruled, but resentful Hutus outnumbered them. Intervention from neighboring states such as Uganda contributed to the confusion. Tremendous slaughter resulted, with hundreds of thousands killed and many more—over 2 million—driven from their homes. While outside powers, the Organization of African States, and the United Nations urged peace, there was no decisive outside intervention. Bloodshed finally ran its course, but ethnic disputes continued in central Africa, contributing to civil war in countries such as Congo. Major warfare in 2003 brought tens of thousands of deaths. Ethnic and religious disputes were also involved in a number of other African trouble spots, including Muslim attacks on Christians in Sudan, and warfare among military gangs in Sierra Leone and Liberia.

Clearly, ethnic tensions were leading not just to warfare, but to renewed acts of genocide that targeted civilians, including women and children, and the creation of massive refugee populations. Reactions from the world at large varied. In some instances, violence seemed sufficiently menacing to major powers that intervention occurred, though never without great hesitation. No policies emerged that offered great promise in abating ethnic conflict.

GLOBALIZATION

The collapse of the Soviet Union and the Warsaw Pact alliance, which effectively ended the long cold war stalemate, abruptly opened up possibilities for transglobal connections that had been limited after 1914 by successive wars and international crises. In many instances, the new linkages between states and regions that were created or greatly expanded after 1989 represented revivals of processes that had begun to flourish in the decades before World War I. But major, late-20th-century innovations in communications, banking, and computing—all of which came together in quite remarkable ways on the Internet—made possible transmissions of information, economic exchanges, and cultural collaborations at a speed and intensity beyond anything imaginable in earlier epochs. Particularly noteworthy was the rapidity with which the republics that emerged from the former Soviet Union, including Russia, and the former communist states of eastern Europe were incorporated into expanding global networks. Mainland China, which remained communist politically, also moved to adopt market capitalism and increase its trade with the United States, Japan, and the industrial nations of the European Union.

Many experts saw what they called *globalization* as the dominant theme of present and future world history. Globalization meant the increasing interconnectedness of all parts of the world, particularly in communication and commerce, but in culture and politics as well. It meant accelerating speed for global connections of various sorts. It meant openness to exchanges around the world.

The new focus on globalization in the 1990s legitimately reflected several new developments beyond the networks established from the later 19th century onwards. First, the end of the cold war and the absence of systematic patterns of international conflict meant new opportunities for, and new attention to, global connections. China, as well as the former Soviet Union, became much more fully open to international trade and many, if not all, other facets of globalization. More broadly, the growing commitment around the world to more free market arrangements, and less state intervention, opened up opportunities for foreign investment and the extension of manufacturing operations to additional areas. Latin America, India, and other places participated in this movement, along with the communist and former communist world. By the 1990s, only a handful of spots—Myanmar, North Korea, the former Yugoslavia—were largely outside the network of globalization.

Second, the late 20th century saw a new round of technical developments, associated particularly with the computer, that greatly accelerated the speed and amount of global communication. The new technology particularly facilitated international commerce, but there were global cultural and political implications as well.

Finally, though more tentatively, more people around the world became accustomed to global connections. At least in some areas, intensive nationalism declined in favor of a more cosmopolitan interest in wider influences and contacts. The spread of English as a world language, though incomplete and often resented, was part of this connection. English served airline travel, many sports, and the early Internet as a common language. This encouraged and reflected other facets of global change.

THE NEW TECHNOLOGY

A globalization guru tells the following story. In 1988, a U.S. government official was traveling to Chicago and was assigned a limousine with a cellular phone. He was so delighted to have this novelty that he called his wife just to brag. Nine years later, in 1997, the same official was visiting the Ivory Coast in west Africa, and went to a remote village, reachable only by dugout canoe, to inaugurate a new health facility. As he prepared to leave, climbing in the canoe, a government official handed him a cellular phone and said he had a call from Washington. Cellular phones became increasingly common, one of the key new communication devices that, by the 1990s, made almost constant contact with other parts of the world feasible, and for some people unavoidable. Western Europe and east Asia led in the cellular phone revolution, but leading groups in all parts of the world participated.

During the 1980s, steady improvements in miniaturization made computers increasingly efficient. By the 1990s, the amount of information that could be stored on microchips increased by over 60 percent annually. Linkages among computers improved as well, starting with halting efforts in the 1960s, mainly for defense purposes. E-mail was introduced in 1972. In 1990, a British software engineer working in Switzerland, Tim Berners, developed the World Wide Web, and the true age of the Internet was born. Almost instantaneous contact by computer became possible around the world, and with it the capacity to send vast amounts of text, imagery, and even music (both legally and illegally). While the Internet was not available to everyone—by 2001 only 25 percent of the world's population had any access to it—it did provide global contacts for some regions otherwise fairly remote. In eastern Russia, for example, international mail service was agonizingly slow, telephone access often interrupted—but a student could sit at an Internet café in Vladivostok and communicate easily with counterparts in the United States or Brazil.

Satellite linkages for television formed a final communications revolution, making simultaneous broadcasts possible around the world. A full quarter of the world's population now could, and sometimes did, watch the same sporting event, usually World Cup soccer or the Olympics, a phenomenon never before possible or even approachable in world history. Global technology gained new meaning.

BUSINESS ORGANIZATION AND INVESTMENT

Thanks in part to new technology, in part to more open political boundaries, international investment accelerated rapidly at the end of the 20th century. Stock exchanges featured holdings in Chinese utilities or Brazilian steel companies as well as the great corporations of the West and Japan. U.S. investments abroad multiplied rapidly, almost doubling in the first half of the 1970s. By the 1980s foreign operations were generating between 25 and 40 percent of all corporate profits in the United States. Japan's foreign investment rose fifteenfold during the 1970s. During the 1980s, Japanese car manufacturers set up factories in the United States, Europe, and other areas. German cars, French tires, German chemicals and pharmaceuticals, and Dutch petroleum all had substantial U.S. operations. At the end of the 1990s, the German Volkswagen firm introduced an imaginative new car design with production facilities entirely based in Mexico, but marketing in the United States and around the world.

Globalization in business involved rapid increases in exports and imports, the extension of business organization across political boundaries—creating the so-called *multinational corporations*—and division of labor on a worldwide basis. Cars in the United States were manufactured by assembling parts made in Japan, Korea, Mexico, and elsewhere. Japanese cars often had more American-made parts in them than Detroit products had. Such was the new structure of global manufacturing. Firms set up operations not simply to produce closer to markets in order to save transportation costs; they also looked for centers of cheap labor and relaxed environmental regulations. Computer boards were made by women in the West Indies and Africa. India developed a huge software industry, subcontracting for firms in the United States and western Europe. The linkages were dazzling.

International firms continued a long-standing interest in finding cheap raw materials. Companies in the West and Japan thus competed for access to oil and minerals in the newly independent nations of central Asia, after the collapse of the Soviet Union. International investments also followed interest rates. During the 1990s, relatively high U.S. interest rates drew extensive investment from Europe, Japan, and the oil-rich regions in the Middle East.

Multinational companies often had more power, and far more resources, than the governments of most of the countries within which they operated. They could thus determine most aspects of labor and environmental policy. They could and did pull up stakes in one region if more attractive opportunities opened elsewhere, regardless of the impact in terms of unemployment and empty facilities. Yet the spread of multinationals also promoted industrial skills in many previously agricultural regions, and they depended on improvements in communications and transportation that could bring wider changes.

American factories located in northern Mexico, designed to produce goods largely for sale back in the United States, showed the complexity of the new international economy. The factories unquestionably sought low-paying labor and lax regulations. Factories often leaked chemical waste. Wages were barely 10 percent of U.S. levels. But the foreign factories often paid better, nevertheless, than their Mexican counterparts. Many workers, including large numbers of women, found the labor policies more enlightened and the foremen better behaved in the foreign firms as well. Evaluation was tricky. A key question, not yet answerable, was what would happen next. Would wages improve, and would the industrial skills of the new factory workers allow a widening range of opportunities? Or would the dependence on poverty-level wages persist?

MIGRATION

Broad international patterns of migration had developed by the 1950s and 1960s, with the use of "guest workers" from Turkey and north Africa in Europe, for example. Here, patterns in the 1990s built clearly on previous trends. But the fact was that easier travel back and forth plus the continued gap between slowly growing populations in the industrial countries, and rapidly growing populations in Latin America, Africa, and parts of Asia, maintained high levels of exchange. A few areas, such as Italy, Greece, and Japan, had almost ceased internal population growth by the 1990s, which meant that new labor needs, particularly at the lower skill levels, had to be supplied by immigration. Japan hoped to avoid too much influx by relying on high-technology solutions, but even here, worker groups were brought in from the Philippines and southeast Asia. Migration into Europe and the United States was far more extensive, producing truly multinational populations in key urban and commercial centers. By 2000, at least 25 percent of all Americans, mostly people of color, came from households where English was not the first language. Ten percent of the French population in 2003 was Muslim. Here was an important source of tension, with local populations often fearing foreigners and worried about job competition. Here also was a new opportunity, not just for new laborers but for new cultural inspiration as well.

Muslim school children in France.

CULTURAL GLOBALIZATION

Thanks in part to global technologies and business organization, plus reduced political barriers, the pace of cultural exchange and contact around the world accelerated at the end of the 1990s. Much of this involved mass consumer goods, spread from the United States, western Europe, and Japan. But art shows, symphony exchanges, scientific conferences, and Internet contact increased as well. Music conductors and artists held posts literally around the world, sometimes juggling commitments among cities such as Tokyo, Berlin, and Chicago within a single season. Science laboratories filled with researchers from around the world, collaborating (usually in English) with little regard for national origin.

The spread of fast-food restaurants from the United States, headed by McDonald's, formed one of the most striking international cultural influences from the 1970s onward. The company began in Illinois in 1955 and started its international career in 1967 with outlets in Canada and Puerto Rico. From then on, the company entered an average of two new nations per year and accelerated the pace in the 1990s. By 1998, it was operating in 109 countries overall. The company won quick success in Japan, where it gained its largest foreign audience; "makadonaldo" first opened in Tokyo's world famous Ginza, already known for cosmopolitan department stores, in 1971. McDonald's entry into the Soviet Union in 1990 was a major sign of the ending of cold war rivalries and the growing Russian passion for international consumer goods. The restaurants won massive patronage despite (by Russian standards) very high prices. Even in gourmet-conscious France, McDonald's and other fast-food outlets were winning 26 percent of all restaurant dining by the 1990s. Not everyone who patronized McDonald's really liked the food. Many patrons in Hong Kong, for example, said they went mainly to see and be seen, and to feel part of the global world.

Cultural globalization obviously involved increasing exposure to American movies and television shows. Series such as *Baywatch* won massive foreign audiences. Movie and amusement park icons such as Mickey Mouse, and products and dolls derived from them, had international currency. Western beauty standards, based on the models and film stars, won wide exposure, expressed among other things in widely sought international beauty pageants. MTV spread Western images and sounds to youth audiences almost everywhere.

Holidays took on an international air. American-style Christmas trappings, including gift giving, lights, and Santa Claus, spread not only to countries of Christian background, such as France, but also to places such as Muslim Istanbul. Northern Mexico picked up American Halloween trick-or-treating, as it displaced the more traditional Catholic observance of All Saints' Day.

Consumer internationalization was not just American. The steady gains of Japanese popular culture have been noted. The Pokémon toy series, derived from Japanese cultural traditions, won a frenzied audience in the 1990s among American children, who for several years could not get enough. A Japanese soap opera heroine became the most admired woman in Muslim Iran. South Korea, historically hostile to Japan, proved open to popular Japanese rock groups and cartoon animation. European popular styles, including fashion and music groups, gained large followings around the world as well.

Dress was internationalized to an unprecedented extent. American-style blue jeans showed up almost everywhere. A major export item for Chinese manufacturing involved Western clothing pirated from famous brand names. A "Chinese market" in the cities of eastern Russia contained entirely Western-style items, mainly clothing and shoes.

Cultural internationalization obviously involved styles from industrial countries, wherever the products were actually made, spreading to other areas, as well as within the industrial world itself. Degrees of penetration varied—in part by wealth and urbanization, in part according to degrees of cultural tolerance. Foreign models were often adapted to local customs. Thus foods in McDonald's in India (where the chain was not very popular in any event) included vegetarian items not found elsewhere. The transformation of comic books in Mexico, from their U.S. origins, was another example, as Mexican cultural images came to predominate. Cultural internationalization was a real development, but it was complex and incomplete.

INSTITUTIONS OF GLOBALIZATION

On the whole, political institutions globalized less rapidly than technology or business, or even consumer culture. Many people worried about the gap between political supervision and control, and the larger globalization process. UN activity accelerated a bit in the 1990s. With the end of the cold war, more diplomatic hotspots invited intervention by multinational military forces. UN forces tried to calm or prevent disputes in a number of parts of Africa, the Balkans, and the Middle East. Growing refugee populations called for UN humanitarian intervention, often aided by other international groups. UN conferences broadened their scope, dealing for example with gender and population control issues. While the results of the conferences were not always clear, a number of countries did incorporate international standards into domestic law. Women in many African countries, for example, were able to appeal to UN proclamations on gender equality as a basis for seeking new property rights in the courts. By 2001, the United Nations became increasingly active as well in encouraging assistance to stem the AIDS epidemic.

Protest against the World Trade Organization in Seattle.

As more nations participated actively in international trade, the importance of organizations in this arena grew. The International Monetary Fund (IMF) and the World Bank had been founded after World War II to promote trade. Guided by the major industrial powers, these organizations offered loans and advice to developing areas and also to regions that encountered temporary economic setbacks. Loans to Mexico and to southeast Asia, during the 1990s, were intended to promote recovery from recessions that threatened to affect other areas. Loans were usually accompanied by requirements for economic reform, usually through reduced government spending and the promotion of more open competition. These guidelines were not always welcomed by the regions involved. The IMF and the World Bank were widely viewed as primary promoters of the capitalist global economy.

Annual meetings of the heads of the seven leading industrial powers—four from Europe, two from North America, plus Japan—usually with Russia as an eighth member, also promoted global trade and policies toward developing regions. Finally, the regional economic arrangements that had blossomed from the 1950s onward gained growing importance as globalization accelerated. The European Union headed the list, but the North American Free Trade Agreement and other regional consortiums in Latin America and east Asia also pushed for lower tariffs and greater economic coordination.

PROTEST AND ECONOMIC UNCERTAINTIES

Accelerating globalization attracted a vigorous new protest movement by the end of the 1990s. Meetings of the World Bank and the industrial leaders were increasingly marked by huge demonstrations and some violence. The current began with massive protests in Seattle in 1999, and they continued at key gatherings thereafter. Protesters came from various parts of the world, and they featured a number of issues. Many people believed that rapid global economic development was threatening the environment. Others blasted the use of cheap labor by international corporations, which was seen as damaging labor conditions even in industrial nations. Rampant consumerism was another target.

Many critics claimed that globalization was working to the benefit of rich nations and the wealthy generally, rather than the bulk of the world's population. They pointed to figures that suggested growing inequalities of wealth, with the top quarter of the world's population growing richer during the 1990s while the rest of the people increasingly suffered. This division operated between regions, widening the gap between affluent nations and the more populous developing areas. It also operated within regions, including the United States and parts of western Europe, where income gaps were on the rise. Bitter disagreements increasingly divided the supporters and opponents of globalization.

Quite apart from formal protest, different regions interpreted globalization variously, depending on economic results. From the mid-1990s onward, new economic problems affected areas such as southeast Asia, Russia, and Turkey, where unfavorable balances of trade drove down the values of national currency, while production declined and unemployment increased. International economic organizations such as the World Bank tried to help, but on condition of reforms that might, for example, force the closing of less effective enterprises, which would temporarily drive up unemployment. By 2001–02, major economic crises hit Argentina and to a lesser extent Brazil. These led to widespread beliefs that globalization was hurting, not helping, local prosperity. Whether global ties could survive these continuing regional problems was unclear.

NATIONALISM AND RELIGIOUS CURRENTS

Several trends ran counter to globalization as the 21st century began. Nationalism was one. While many nations were partially bypassed by globalization—within many countries much less powerful than the multinational corporations—nationalist resistance to globalization surfaced in many ways. Many countries opposed the erosion of traditions by global cultural patterns. Thus, the Japanese government subsidized training in the use of chopsticks, because so many Japanese children seemed to be relying on forks and fast foods instead of customary manners. The French government periodically resisted the incorporation of English words into the French language. Many European countries tried to regulate the number of immigrants from Africa, Asia, and the West Indies, in the interest of preserving dominance for families and workers of European background. The United States rejected a wide variety of international treaties, including a provision for regulation against war crimes, because they might interfere with national sovereignty. China and other states periodically bristled against international criticism of internal policies concerning political prisoners.

A global religious revival developed in the final decades of the 20th century. Religious movements were not necessarily opposed to globalization, but they tended to insist on their distinctiveness, against any uniform global culture, and they also bred suspicions of the consumerism and sexuality highlighted in many manifestations of globalization, including films and tourism.

As communism collapsed in eastern Europe, many people returned to previous religious beliefs, including Orthodox Christianity. Protestant fundamentalists, often from the United States, were also busy in the region. Protestant fundamentalism also spread rapidly in parts of Latin America such as Guatemala and Brazil. In India, Hindu fundamentalism surged by the 1990s, with Hindu nationalist politicians capturing the nation's presidency. Fundamentalism also gained ground in Islam, particularly in the Middle East and nearby parts of Africa and south-central Asia. Whether Christian, Hindu, or Islamic, fundamentalists tended to urge a return to the primacy of religion and religious laws. They often opposed greater freedoms for women, and they certainly criticized Western-style consumerism. Frequently, fundamentalists urged government support for religious values.

Religious fundamentalism ran counter to globalization in several ways, even though many religious leaders became adept at using new global technologies such as the Internet. It tended to appeal particularly to impoverished urban groups who seemed to be left behind in the global economy. Fundamentalism also tended to increase intolerance, even in religious traditions that had historically been reasonably open. Hindu fundamentalists thus frequently clashed with Muslims in India. While some advocates of globalization assumed that religious traditionalism would decline, the balance was in fact unclear as the 21st century opened.

GLOBAL TERRORISM

A new wave of international terrorism built on some of the nationalist, subnationalist, and religious currents in various parts of the world early in the 21st century. The new terrorism used some of the apparatus of globalization, particularly to reach across regional boundaries; it also attacked key institutions and principles of globalization in some instances.

Terrorists used secret military operations to counter the power of regular military forces, often targeting civilians. Terrorism was not new: bombing and assassination attempts had dotted the later 19th century, for example in Russia, directed against political regimes the terrorists viewed as oppressive. It was a terrorist assassination of an Austrian prince that had launched World War I. By the later 20th century, terrorism usually involved a minority nationalist movement, such as the Basque terrorists in northern Spain or an Indian separatist group in Sri Lanka, or a religious cause. Technological advances, including the miniaturization of bombs, expanded the destructive power of terrorist acts and their capacity to sow fear. As governments improved security protections for political leaders, terrorists increasingly turned to more random civilian targets, in hopes of destabilizing a society and undermining a hated political regime.

The terrorist attack on the United States on September 11, 2001, which killed about 3000 people, was an unusually brazen act by a group of Islamic terrorists. It obviously protested American power and policies in the Middle East, but it also chose a symbol of economic globalization, the World Trade Center in New York.

Terrorism normally provoked extensive retaliation by the police and military in societies under attack. This retaliation sometimes caused far more casualties, even among civilians, than the terrorist acts themselves. Terrorists seldom seemed to achieve many of their stated goals, but eliminating the threat of terrorism proved very difficult. As terrorism went global, particularly with the attacks on the United States, it threatened to complicate some of the institutions of globalization—for example, by provoking new limitations on international travel. Here was a key theme for at least the early 21st century.

GLOBAL WARMING AND A PLANET IN PERIL

Perhaps the most sobering problems with globalization were those associated with the environment. Increased access for travelers and reporters to once restricted areas of the Soviet Union and eastern Europe made it clear that the drive for industrial development in the communist nations had been even more environmentally devastating than the capitalist variant of that process, even in its colonial manifestations.

The impact of these revelations was intensified by the prospect of communist China's new "market-Leninist" path to industrialization, which stressed grafting free market capitalism onto dictatorial, highly bureaucratized political systems such as those long associated with communism. In China, a population of over a billion people is building on a resource base already severely depleted and degraded; widespread water shortages are another crucial problem. Long-term prognoses of the dire outcomes of unrestrained global "development" may prove to be understatements. Equally alarming have been reports on the ecological fallout of rapid development in southeast Asia, where multinationals based in Japan and in the newly industrialized countries of east Asia are extracting resources with abandon, and the rain forest is disappearing even more rapidly than in Brazil. Similar trends have been documented in sub-Saharan Africa, whose imminent economic collapse and environmental demise are now routinely predicted.

On a more literally global scale, most scientists now agree that the greenhouse effect caused by the buildup in the atmosphere of excessive amounts of carbon dioxide and other heat-trapping gasses has led to a substantial warming of the Earth in recent decades. Some of the chief sources of the pollutants responsible for the atmospheric buildup are industrial wastes—including those resulting from energy production through the burning of fossil fuels such as coal—and exhaust from millions of cars, trucks, and other machines run by internal combustion engines that burn petroleum. But other major sources of the greenhouse effect are both surprising and at present essential to the survival of large portions of humanity. Methane, another greenhouse gas, is introduced into the atmosphere in

Fish killed by industrial waste.

massive quantities as a by-product of the stew of fertilized soil and water in irrigated rice paddies, which feed a majority of the peoples of Asia, the world's most populous continent.

If scientific predictions are correct, global warming has already and will increasingly cause major shifts in temperatures and rainfall throughout much of the globe. Fertile and well-watered areas now highly productive in foods for humans and animals may well be overwhelmed by droughts and famine. If widely accepted computer simulations are correct, coastal areas at sea level—which from Bangladesh and the Netherlands to New Jersey are among the most densely populated in the world—are likely to be inundated. They are threatened not just by rising water levels in the world's oceans but by hurricanes and tropical storms that may in the coming decades generate winds up to 200 miles an hour. As climates are drastically altered, vegetation and wildlife in many areas will be radically altered. Temperate forests, for example, may die off in many regions and be replaced by scrub, tropical vegetation, or desert flora. Some animal species may migrate or adapt and survive, but many, unable to adjust to such rapid climatic changes, will become extinct.

The destruction of the rain forests is especially troublesome; unlike the temperate woodlands, they cannot regenerate themselves. In terms of evolution, the rain forests have been the source of most of the species of plant and animal life that now inhabit the earth. In this and other ways, human interventions now affect global climate and weather in the short term and will determine the fate of the planetary environment in the centuries, perhaps millennia, to come.

International discussions of environmental regulation increased from 1997 onward. A major conference in Kyoto, Japan, set limits on greenhouse gas emissions in order to curtail global warming. It was not clear, however, whether these limits would have any effect. Many individual nations, including the United States and Russia, opposed the limits proposed because of potential damage to national economies. Here was another area where global politics did not seem to be keeping pace with globalization.

DISEASE

Changes in global contacts have usually involved disease, and late-20th-century globalization was no exception. More rapid international travel helped spread the AIDS epidemic from the 1980s onward. Southern and eastern Africa were hit most severely, but AIDS also spread to the United States and western Europe. The epidemic took on even larger proportions in places such as Brazil. By the early 21st century, rates of increase in parts of Asia and in Russia began to accelerate. These were regions that had initially felt relatively safe but where global contact ultimately brought new levels of contagion. In 2003, another new disease, Severe Acute Respiratory Syndrome (SARS), spread rapidly from Asia.

The result, to be sure, was less severe than some of the earlier epidemics associated with global contacts, though some experts warned of even greater disease problems in the future. Environmental issues, newer on the global scale, may have replaced disease as the clearest downside of international connections.

PROJECTING FROM TRENDS

Human beings have always wanted to know what the future will hold. Various societies looked to the configurations of the stars for predictions, and astrology still has partisans in the contemporary world. Some societies generated beliefs in cycles, so that the future would repeat patterns already seen in the past; many Chinese scholars developed a cyclical approach. Still other societies assumed that the future would differ from the past; from the Enlightenment onward, Western culture developed an additional belief in progress.

History suggests the futility of many efforts at forecasting. It has been estimated that well over half of the "expert" forecasts generated in the United States since World War II have been wrong. This includes predictions that by 2000 most Americans would be riding to and from work in some kind of airship, or that families would be replaced by promiscuous communes. Yet if history debunks forecasts, it also provides the basis for thinking about the future.

The most obvious connection between history and the future involves the assessment of trends that are likely to continue at least for several decades. Thus we "know" that global population growth will slow up, because it is already slowing up. Many forecasts see stabilization, based on rapidly falling birth rates literally around the world, by 2050. We also "know" that populations will become older. This is already happening in western Europe, the United States, and Japan and will occur elsewhere as the birth rate drops. What we don't "know" of course is how societies will react to the demands of older people, or how much the environment will have deteriorated by the time global population stabilizes. Even trend-based forecasts can be thrown off by unexpected events, such as wars. Thus, in the 1930s, experts "knew" that the American birth rate would fall, because it was already falling; but then war and prosperity created a totally unexpected baby boom, and the experts were wrong for at least two decades.

Trend-based forecasting is even chancier when the trends themselves are already fragile. The late 20th century saw a genuine global spread of democracy, though admittedly not to every region. It was possible to venture predictions about the triumph of this form of government. But by 2004, it was hard to be confident that democracies were entirely secure in parts of Latin America or even in Russia. The hold of earlier, less democratic political traditions or the sheer pressure of economic stagnation might unseat the trend.

Forecasting is at least as complex when two different trends are in play. The 20th century saw a fairly steady rise in consumerism, which spread to all parts of the world. The appeal of mass media, commercialized sports, and global fashions reaches across traditional boundaries. But the last 30 years have also seen a pronounced increased in religious interest, in many if not all parts of the world. Some people participate in both trends, but overall, the priorities are different. Is one of the two trends likely to predominate? Or should we think of the future in terms of division and tension among cultural interests?

ISSUES AND CONNECTIONS

Some analysts have looked at the world's future in terms of stark departures from its past. They argue that trend analysis is inadequate because we are on the verge of a major shift in framework. In the 1960s, a "population bomb" analysis won considerable attention. The argument was that rapid population growth was about to overwhelm all other developments, leading to resource depletion, new wars over resources—a world far different from what we had previously known. In fact, this particular scenario has fallen from favor, despite continued rapid population growth. The slowing up in the rate of growth, combined with the fact that food productions has on the whole kept pace, has displaced this disturbing scenario. But other forecasts, of dramatic climate change, of resource exhaustion, provide some environmentalists with another dire picture of the world's future, in which other issues, such as the fate of particular political systems, fade in importance.

Another scenario that has enjoyed recurrent popularity is the vision of a post-industrial world. Some pundits argue that computer technology, genetic engineering, and other technological advances are undermining the conditions of industrial society. Information, not production, becomes the key to economic growth and to social structures. The functions of cities shift from production to entertainment. Work will become more individualized and less time-consuming, creating a new premium for expressive leisure. Again, the emphasis is on a dramatically different future. Here too, however, critics express doubts. Many parts of the world are not yet industrial, much less post-industrial. Work does not seem to be heading toward less routine, as computers promote repetitive activities at least as much as new creativity. As is always true with intriguing predictions of massive change, the jury is still out.

One of the reasons prediction is particularly difficult—though also compelling—is that world history has undergone so many fundamental changes during the past century. We know, for example, that the dominance of western Europe, for centuries a staple of world history, is a thing of the past, despite the continued vitality of the region. But what will replace it? Continued United States ascendancy? Or the rise of China or east Asia? Or, perhaps, no single dominant region at all? We know there is a question about the world balance that will replace Western control, but the answer is unclear.

The same applies to conditions for women. Improvements in women's education plus the decline of the birth rate add up to significant changes for women around the world. The pace of change varies with the region, to be sure. Many regions have given new legal and political rights to women. But is there a new model for women's roles that might be applicable around the world? Continued disputes about women's work roles, significant male backlash against change, and even disputes by women themselves about the relevance of a Western model for women's lives make forecasting difficult. We can assume continued change, but it is hard to pinpoint the results.

SUGGESTED WEB SITES

For debates about globalization, see http://globalization.about.com/library/weekly/aa080701a.htm and http://www.emory.edu/SOC/globalization. On recent trends in Islam, see http://wrc.lingnet.org/islamf.htm. On global warming, see http://www.climatehotmap.org.

SUGGESTED READINGS

Recent work includes William V. Spanos, *America's Shadow: An Anatomy of Empire* (2000), and Dieter Senghaas, *The Clash within Civilizations: Coming to Terms with Cultural Conflicts* (2002).

Globalization is covered, and debated, in Thomas Friedman, *The Lexus and the Olive Tree* (2000); John Gray, *False Dawn* (1999); and Thomas Frank, *One Market Under God* (2000). On cultural ramifications, see Peter N. Stearns, *Consumerism in World History* (2002); Walter LaFeber, *Michael Jordan and the New Global Capitalism* (2000); Stephen Rees, *American Films Abroad* (1997); and James Watson, ed., *Gold Arches East: McDonald's in East Asia* (1998). See also Bruce Mazlish and Ralph Buultjens, eds., *Conceptualizing Global History* (1993); Theodore von Laue, *The World Revolution of Westernization* (1997); Harold Perkin, *The Third Revolution: Professional Elites in the Modern World* (1996); and Francis Fukayama, *The End of History* (1991).

On globalization and women, see Kathryn Ward, ed., *Women Workers and Global Restructuring* (1990). On religion, see Dilip Hiro, *Holy Wars: The Rise of Islamic Fundamentalism* (1989); Richard Antoun, *Understanding Fundamentalism* (2001), emphasizing Christianity; and Gurdas Ahuja, *BJP and Indian Policies* (1994).

On environmental change, helpful texts include Ramachandra Guha, *Environmentalism: A Global History* (2000), and Judith Shapiro, *China's War Against Nature* (2001). On forecasting, see Daniel Bell, *The Coming of Post-Industrial Society* (1974), and Richard Heilbroner, *An Inquiry into the Human Prospect* (1974).

Studies of key diplomatic developments include David Halberstam, *War in a Time of Peace* (2001), on U.S. interventionism; Walter Laqueur, *War Without End: Terrorism in the 21st Century* (2003); Misha Glenny, *The Balkans: Nationalism, War and the Great Powers* (2000); Tim Judah, *Kosovo, War and Revenge* (2001); Levon Chorbajian and George Shirinian, *Studies in Comparative Genocide* (1999).

CONTACTS
AND
IDENTITIES

Part VI The Contemporary World

A key question for the future involves the fate of individual civilizations. World history has been shaped by the characteristics of key civilizations for over 5000 years, granting that not everyone has been part of a major civilization and that in some cases civilizations are not easy to define. Some observes argue that, by the 21st century, the separate characteristics of civilizations are beginning to yield to homogenizing forces. Many scientists, athletes, and businesspeople feel more commitment to their professional interests than to their region of origin—which means that global professional identities can override civilization loyalties. The downtowns of most cities around the world look very much alike. The same products, stores, and restaurants can be found in most urban areas. Globalization may be outpacing regional labels.

Yet we have also seen that globalization can falter, as it did in the middle decades of the 20th century. Even when it accelerates, as in the 1990s, it brings efforts to reassert separate identities. Even as China participates in the global economy, for example, it remains different, reflecting some of the political characteristics that were launched 3000 years ago. The Japanese easily move in global economics and culture, but with an emphasis on group identity measurably different from the personal goals emphasized in the United States. Major religions such as Hinduism and Islam continue to mark their regions, and in some ways their influence seems to be on the rise.

World history has long been defined by a tension between regional features and larger connections. The specifics change, for example with shifts in technology and organizational capacity. But it may be premature to assume that some kind of global homogeneity is going to change the equation altogether.

A crucial question involves identities. Many people enjoy aspects of globalization—such as a sense of participating in the most up-to-date trends—but they also, often, cherish a sense of their particular identity. Religious revival as well as nationalism often expresses the identity need. So do smaller, subnational, ethnic loyalties, some of which cause conflict and tensions as part of regional disputes and terrorism. Change, including globalization, has widely challenged identity in the past half-century. What the balance will be between identity and larger connections is far from clear.

Credits

Index

Note: Page numbers in *italics* indicate illustrations, maps, and tables.